# Professional
# ATL COM
# Programming

## Richard Grimes

D1401158

Wrox Press Ltd. ®

# Professional ATL COM Programming

Published by Wrox Press Ltd, 30 Lincoln Road, Olton, Birmingham B27 6PA , UK.
Printed in Canada
2 3 4 5 TRI 99 98

ISBN  1-861001-4-01

## *Credits*

**Author**
Richard Grimes

**Editors**
Jon Hill
Alex Stockton

**Index**
Nancy Humphreys

**Copy Edit**
Alex Zoro
Barnaby Zoro

**Technical Reviewers**
Richard Anderson
Bob Beauchemin
Davide Marcato
Shaun McAravey
Christian Nagel
Dean Rowe
Marc Simkin

**Cover**
Andrew Guillaume

**Design/Layout**
Frances Olesch
David Boyce

Many Thanks to:
Jon Borden for his valuable input on *IMarshalByValueImpl*◇
Richard Anderson for his UML Diagrams

# Biography

Richard started programming in the days when an 8-bit computer with 32K of memory was considered a powerful machine. His professional career started as a research scientist studying semiconductors, and then as a trainer teaching people how to program. Finally, Richard spent time writing distributed objects before deciding to write full time.

Richard's other books are *Professional DCOM Programming* and *Beginning ATL COM Programming* (co-authored with Alex Stockton, George Reilly and Julian Templeman). Richard has also written articles for *Visual Systems Journal, Visual C++ Developer, Windows95 Magazine* and *ComDeveloper.*

# Preface

I first came across ATL when I was part of a team developing a workflow system for the dealers of an automobile manufacturer in the UK. We needed to 'componentize' our objects, and COM was the only choice. The problem was to develop business objects as COM objects to a tight deadline. MFC was dismissed early on because MFC is an *application* framework and not a *component* framework.

Dismissing MFC left us with the option of designing the system using straight C++. Although this is a viable proposition when you're writing a single, simple component, it is inappropriate for an entire system. Why? Well, we needed to write reusable code for the module initialization (`WinMain()` and `DllMain()`), module and component registration. We also needed code for class factories, basic `IUnknown` and other standard interface implementations. Further, this code had to work with all the threading models that we might choose to use, and it had to have good error reporting and debugging support.

MFC started to appear attractive again – after all, if Microsoft has gone to the trouble of designing a class hierarchy and implementing and debugging code according to the COM and OLE Controls specifications, why should we duplicate this effort?

In fact, that was at about the time that ATL was first released, and the initial version solved many of these problems. However, it was provided as an add-on to Visual C++, there was no Object Wizard, very little documentation (there were few books on templates, and *no* books on ATL, barring an early attempt by Wrox Press covering ATL 1.1), and the ATL code was supplied as CPP as well as header files. Worse still, Visual C++ didn't know about ATL, and consequently ClassView would show *all* the ATL templates and classes as part of a project once an ATL header was added to a project. Imagine my shock when I saw thirty-odd templates in ClassView – I really started to wonder if it would be worth the effort.

Of course, it *was* worth it: we were able to write C++ objects and componentize them with ATL. This made the objects usable from other languages and frameworks, so unit tests were carried out using Visual Basic clients before installing them as part of an ISAPI application. The strengths of componentization became apparent later on when the custom ISAPI framework was ditched in favor of ASP scripts: a COM object is a COM object, whatever the client.

Visual C++ 5.0 came soon after, and this had ATL 2.1 and support within the IDE for ATL through AppWizard, Object Wizard and ClassView. Creating ATL classes became incredibly easy: you created a project with AppWizard, inserted the class using Object Wizard, and then added properties and methods to the class using ClassView. All that you then had to do was write the implementation code of the object, rather than having to worry about COM plumbing code. The advantage of ATL was clear: it acted as an entry to COM without the steep learning curve that was involved in 'straight' C++ COM development. Of course, you do not have to use all of the Wizard-generated code, and you are free to replace it with code of your own, but why bother if it meets your needs?

This is largely the approach that we took when we wrote *Beginning ATL COM Programming* – the intention was to show how to use ATL to write COM components without going into great detail about how ATL or COM works. ATL has many templates that do a lot of work for you, so we decided to concentrate on showing you how to use these templates to write real, useful, working code.

This spirit lives on in *Professional ATL COM Programming*; there are even more templates in ATL 3.0, and the best way of learning how they work is still to try them out. However, when writing this book, I had to make a thorough investigation and critique of ATL, and so I have taken advantage of the *Professional* prefix in the title to present those results to you. The intention is to show you, not only how to use ATL as it stands, but also to explain how ATL works, and how to extend it. Inevitably, this also involves answering why ATL is designed the way it is, and so you'll find a fair amount of COM explained here too.

ATL 3.0 and Visual C++ 6.0 have many new features, and these will be explained as you read on through the book. I have decided to take an incremental approach to the subject, so the chapter on Interfaces, for example, covers everything that you'll possibly want to know about implementing interfaces in ATL. As you progress through the book, the topics get more complex. I start by explaining the COM wrapper classes in ATL and the compiler COM support classes, then I explain the general architecture of ATL. After that, I progress through interfaces, the Object Wizard and class factories, covering the basic plumbing code that you need to implement a COM object.

There is a brief respite from component development in Chapter 6, where I explain the important topic of debugging ATL code, and after that I continue with threading, connection points, window classes, and finally, controls. At every stage, I have outlined the ATL code to use and show how it works. I have also taken the liberty of explaining the parts of ATL that I think do not work correctly and presented solutions where possible. Each topic is presented with complete, fully working code that you can either type in straight from the book or download from the Wrox web site.

Within these pages, I have endeavored to present a complete and original work. Isn't it annoying when you purchase a book and find that it is a regurgitation of something you've seen before – in the online documentation, or another book? It is equally irritating from an author's perspective when you find that your work has been paraphrased without accreditation. You won't find such behavior here; this text represents my own personal odyssey through ATL.

In that spirit, I really do need to acknowledge the other COM and ATL developers who have inspired some of the code. I am indebted to Daniel Sinclair for the original idea about coding DISPIDs that I used in Chapter 3. Thanks also go to Jonathon Borden who posted the `IMarshalByValueImpl<>` template that I have used in Chapter 7 to the DCOM mailing list. Jon developed this from a template presented by Don Box in *Microsoft Systems Journal*, and so my thanks go to Don too.

Of course, a book like this would never be published without the Herculean efforts from Wrox: Alex Stockton and Jon Hill have woven their magic to turn this book from a collection of musings and rantings into a flowing, entertaining read and the book was nurtured through its development by John Franklin. This book is a testament to their skill and professionalism.

I would also like to acknowledge the help and support of the ATL team at Microsoft, in particular Christian Beaumont and Dean Rowe, whose suggestions were gratefully received. Finally, I would like to the technical reviewers who ensure that what I have written is as complete and (hopefully!) as bug free as possible.

To the memory of Paul David Raven (1965 – 1994) whose tragic death made me rethink my career and pursue my aim to write for my living.

# Table of Contents

# Introduction

Welcome to *Professional ATL COM Programming*, your guide to version 3.0 of Microsoft's Active Template Library. This version of the template library is supplied with Microsoft Visual C++ 6.0.

I have structured this book to lead you through ATL 3.0 in the context of Visual C++ 6.0 by working through the elements of a COM project, examining the benefits and features of ATL as we go. By design, every chapter contains useful quantities of working code. As far as I'm concerned, the only way of learning to program with a particular technology is to see real examples of it in action. Once you have working code, you can adapt it for your own purposes, so that it solves your particular programming problems.

However, you won't find page after page of code listings without breaks or explanations. The Wizards generate a lot of code, but you won't see much of it in this book. My strategy is to concentrate on new code and divide it into pertinent sections; that way I can explain all the important features, as well as (hopefully) holding your attention.

Before I give you a better idea of what's to come, let me explain a couple of things you *won't* find in these pages. First, this book is about developing COM servers with ATL, but it's not a tutorial on COM. If you want to know about what COM provides and why it's's so useful, you should take a look at *Professional DCOM Programming*. Second, although it covers all the features of ATL, this book is not intended as an introductory text. If you're completely new to ATL, I recommend that you read *Beginning ATL COM Programming* before attempting this book.

# Synopsis

With the preliminaries out of the way, I'd like to take a couple of pages to explain how the book will proceed, what subjects I'm going to cover, and where I'm going to cover them. Although the book does tell a story, it's also my intention that it should be used as a reference to the inner workings of ATL, and it's with that in mind that I present this chapter-by-chapter guide.

# Chapter 1

COM is wonderful and it solves many problems, but it does impose certain rules on you. To use COM effectively, you must be disciplined and obey these rules; if you don't, you risk leaking resources, poor server performance, or crashes. Before going into the details of writing COM servers, therefore, I cover resource management with COM.

Essentially, you have three options: 'raw' C++, Visual C++'s compiler COM support classes, or the ATL wrapper classes. Which you use depends on your requirements. Raw C++ can sometimes produce the tightest, most efficient code, but it's error prone and often difficult to read. The compiler COM support classes go to the other end of the scale, using exceptions and smart pointers with high-level 'virtual data members' and wrapper methods to provide much clearer but also slower, more bloated code.

ATL takes a middle road. It is designed to balance efficiency with convenience and code safety; what you lose in eschewing exceptions, you gain in efficiency. Chapter 1 goes through all of the issues involved in managing interface pointers, BSTRs, and VARIANTs, and gives you all the information you need to determine what is best for your application.

# Chapter 2

ATL consists of many templates, classes, and macros, and it can be quite bewildering when you first see the list of classes in an inheritance list or an object map. However the architecture is really quite straightforward. The intention of this chapter is to give you a general overview of how it is arranged. The chapter is broken into five main sections that reflect the main tasks required when writing a COM server.

- ❑ Implementing IUnknown
- ❑ Implementing objects
- ❑ Implementing class factories
- ❑ Module entry points
- ❑ Registration

ATL has extensive support for all of these, and Chapter 2 explains the classes that it provides and how they help you. However, this *is* just an overview – some of the issues it raises are covered in greater depth in later chapters.

# Chapter 3

This leads on to **interface programming**. Because a COM object can have more than one interface, ATL must provide a flexible way to allow you to add interfaces to an ATL class. It does this through the COM map, using macros to specify the interfaces.

In this chapter, I explain how the COM map works, and how to use the various macros. I also explain how to use the new Wizards to implement new interfaces on your object, and how to provide support like connection points and rich error information. The chapter also covers how `IDispatch` is implemented in ATL, and how you can solve some of the problems that occur when you implement multiple `IDispatch`-based interfaces on a single object.

# Chapter 4

Of course, what you really want to do is write a COM class that supports interfaces, using the Object Wizard. This Wizard provides several 'templates' for object types that you can use, and while some are just improvements on the types that were available in Visual C++ 5.0, others are brand new in version 6.0. In Chapter 4, I go through all these Object Wizard types, explaining what each is for and how to use the generated code to write your own objects. In the second half of the chapter, I explain how to extend the Object Wizard with templates of your own.

# Chapter 5

Once you write the code for a COM class, you have to provide a mechanism for creating instances programmatically. ATL provides four main types of class factory, and gives you the tools to provide your own. The first two types use the 'standard' class factory interfaces of `IClassFactory` and `IClassFactory2`, these allow you to provide basic class factory behavior and licensing support.

ATL also provides class factory support for singletons. A singleton class factory will only ever return a reference to a single object, rather than creating a new instance of an object for every activation request. Chapter 5 gives an example of a singleton, as well as covering the issues around why you might, or might not, want to use one. The other type of class factory that ATL provides allows you to create object instances on a pool of worker threads. Because this is a threading issue, it is covered in Chapter 7.

Chapter 5 closes with an example of implementing your own custom class factory interface.

# Chapter 6

At this point in the book, you have all the tools that you need to develop COM servers. This chapter takes a break from plain coding and takes a look at an important but often neglected area in software development: debugging and error reporting.

The chapter starts by looking at how to get trace information in ATL. If you thought that those `ATLTRACE()` statements only sent strings to Visual C++'s output window, then you should take a look at this chapter! Visual C++ has extensive tracing support, and with the addition of a just few lines of code, you can get your debugging output redirected to a file.

In general, COM uses `HRESULT`s to return status codes back to the client. While this is useful, it is also restrictive: your COM objects can support rich error information through error objects. With ATL, adding support for rich error information is as simple as checking a check box in Object Wizard and then calling the appropriate methods in your code.

The final section of the chapter concerns debugging interface querying and reference counts. A perennial problem with COM occurs if a client does not manage reference counts correctly. This is partly alleviated by clients using appropriate wrapper classes as explained in Chapter 1, but there will always be occasions when this is not enough. What you need is a mechanism for getting output that shows what interfaces are being queried and how their reference counts are changed.

This is exactly what the new, revamped interface debugging code in ATL does. When you turn this feature on, the output window will show the results whenever `QueryInterface()` is called, and it will show a per-interface reference count. (Yes, normally ATL has an object-wide reference count, but the debugging code has a finer granularity.) Finally, a list of all the queried interfaces is maintained by ATL, so that when the server stops, all interface leaks are reported. This is a great boon if you find that your object is not being released and you want to know why.

# Chapter 7

Now we revert back to programming issues. Win32 is a multi-threaded environment, and COM is too. Serving COM objects with multiple threads, and accessing them across threads, presents specific problems that need to be addressed. You *could* take the easy option and say that your object should only be accessed by one thread at a time, or that your object server will only run a single thread, but this approach is not scaleable and will restrict your object to small-scale systems.

With a little more thought, you can make your objects work in multithreaded environments, and you can make your object servers multithreaded. If you decide to do this, you have to take precautions to make sure that global data and, in some cases, instance data is protected from access by multiple threads. ATL provides the necessary support to do this, but you need the discipline to use it.

Multithreaded servers are an interesting subject, and ATL gives you two options. You can make your server 'free threaded' (in other words, get COM to create the extra server threads), or you can create your own. To accomplish the second option, you need to provide a special class factory that can create objects on multiple threads – doing this allows you to provide load balancing across those threads, and improve on your server's performance. ATL provides you with support by means of the `CComClassFactoryAutoThread` class.

To illustrate these threading options, I show you how to develop a single threaded server, a 'free-threaded' server, and a server that uses `CComClassFactoryAutoThread` objects. I then perform stress tests on all three servers to show you how they perform. Hopefully, the results will move you toward multithreaded solutions.

Finally, COM is apartment sensitive – a COM object can only be accessed directly in the apartment where it is running. To use a COM object outside of this apartment, you need to marshal its interface, and that's my subject for the second half of Chapter 7. I have taken this opportunity to explain the various interface marshaling options in ATL, and how to use them. I also provide an example of marshaling by value, which is an optimization technique used on immutable objects.

# AMAZON.COM

We offer you 2.5 million titles (more than 14 times the number of books in the largest chain superstore), so we're sure to have the book you want.

## THE BEST PLACE TO FIND BOOKS YOU'LL LOVE

With our powerful features and services, discovering books that match your tastes is simple. At Amazon.com, you'll always find:

- A Gift Center full of great ideas, gift certificates, Amazon.com merchandise, and more

- A Recommendation Center with seven great ways to get book suggestions

- Thousands of subject areas–ranging from Children's Books to Computers–packed with reviews, interviews, excerpts and much more

- Award Winners, Bestseller Lists and lists of titles Reviewed in the Media

- Lightning-quick 1-Click℠ ordering

## GREAT SAVINGS

Enjoy everyday low prices on more than 400,000 titles:

### 40% Off
selected titles

### 30% Off
hardcovers

### 20% Off
paperbacks

YOUR NEXT BOOK IS ONLY A CLICK AWAY

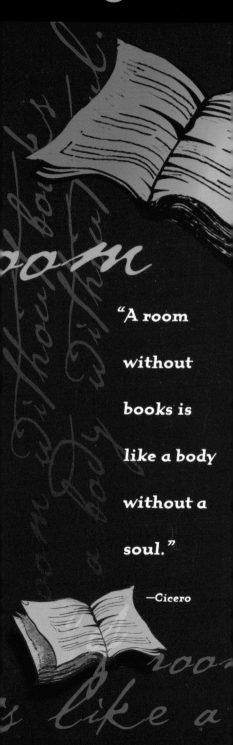

# Chapter 8

This chapter is concerned with bi-directional connections using connection points. Visual C++ 6.0 has new Wizard support to allow you to implement connection points on a server, this subsumes the proxy generator that was provided with previous versions. Connection points are useful for generating events to notify client processes. However, they are not a panacea, and before you decide to use connection points you should review all the issues involved. In this chapter, I examine the tradeoffs that you might be forced to make.

One of the biggest issues with connection points (and with callback interfaces in general) is the security aspect that comes into play when you use them with DCOM. Some of these security problems can be solved just by switching it off, but sometimes this is not possible, especially if the client end of the connection point is a control. The solution here is to use a separate 'middleman' object that gets between the client and server objects and ensures that the correct security is being used.

In this chapter I develop a 'chat' application that uses connection points to notify all connected clients when a new message is posted. The first stage of the development shows how to use this when the client and server are on a single machine, and then I go further, using a middleman object so that the client and server can be on different machines.

# Chapter 9

Most users see COM in action through ActiveX controls, because they have a user interface that the user sees! Controls must wait to be shown in their full glory, because before you can develop one, you need to understand the Windows programming issues involved.

ATL 3.0 has many new classes for Windows support, including MFC-style dialog templates and classes that allow you to host the IE4 control. In this chapter, I explain how these classes work and go into details of how to provide message handlers, how to sub- and super-class windows, and how to handle notifications from child controls. This gives you a good grounding for Chapter 10.

# Chapter 10

For a control to do anything useful, it will typically have to support many interfaces. ATL helps here by providing default implementations: you can get a fully working (but limited) control without writing any code of your own. To get the control to do something worthwhile, however, you need to know how to draw its user interface, how to make it persistent, and how to allow other code to interact with it.

Drawing is an interesting issue, because your control will have to update its image under several different situations, all of which are covered in Chapter 10. For example, you often need to redraw your control when its state changes, or if the container wants to print the control. You need different code to handle these different operations.

This brings me to control state. Controls have properties, which are used to affect their image and sometimes their behavior. A design tool like Visual Basic will allow a developer to change these properties at design time, but to make the control useful, the tool must be able to make these properties persistent, so that the control can be initialized with them at runtime.

To do this, a control must implement one of COM's persistence interfaces, and it must know what properties are to be made persistent. ATL provides default implementations of all the persistence interfaces, and the Object Wizard will add appropriate persistence interfaces when you create a new control type. ATL uses the **property map** to determine which properties are made persistent.

# Chapter 11

Finally, Chapter 11 explains the classes provided by ATL to manipulate Internet Explorer 4. It discusses the Web Browser Control, the DHTML object model, and the creation of your own controls using the new HTML control type that's provided through the Object Wizard.

# What You Need To Use This Book

In order to do *all* the samples in this book, you will need the following tools:

❑ Microsoft Visual C++ 6.0 compiler
❑ Microsoft Visual Basic 6.0
❑ The Internet Client SDK
❑ Two machines connected to a network

However, only the first of these is essential – Visual Basic is used to create a couple of simple client applications, the SDK is used in one example in Chapter 5, and COM being COM, all the code will work on a local or a remote machine. Of course, it is useful to be able to test your code in the latter scenario, but none of the examples require you to do so.

# Conventions Used

We use a number of different styles of text and layout in the book to help differentiate between the different kinds of information. Here are examples of the styles we use, and an explanation of what they mean:

> **These boxes hold important, not-to-be-forgotten, mission critical details that are directly relevant to the surrounding text.**

*Background information, asides and references to information located elsewhere appear in text like this.*

❑ **Important words** are in a bold font
❑ Words that appear on the screen, such as menu options, are in a similar font to the one used on the screen – the File menu, for example
❑ Keys that you press on the keyboard, like *Ctrl* and *Delete*, are in italics
❑ All filenames are in this style: ATL.dll
❑ Function names look like this: CoCreateInstance()
❑ Templates look like this: CComPtr<>
❑ Code that's new, important, or relevant to the current discussion will be presented like this:

```
int main()
{
    cout << "Professional ATL COM Programming";
    return 0;
}
```

❏ Code that you've seen before, or isn't directly relevant to the matter at hand, looks like this:

```
int main()
{
    cout << "Professional ATL COM Programming";
    return 0;
}
```

# The Wrox Press Web Site

Our desire to see you succeed doesn't stop once you've purchased a Wrox Press book. We believe that you've entered into a partnership with us, and as such it's our responsibility to supply you with the latest information available. To that end, the web site we maintain at http://www.wrox.com provides:

❏ Source code for this and all our other books
❏ Extensive information on our latest titles
❏ Errata sheets for current Wrox Press titles
❏ Useful tools, add-ins and tips
❏ A full book-ordering service

If you have any suggestions regarding the Wrox Press web site, please e-mail the Webmaster at webmaster@wrox.com. The web site is as much your resource as it is ours.

# Errors

While we have made every effort to make sure the information contained in this book is accurate, we're only human. If you're having difficulty with some aspect of the book, or you've found a genuine error, then please check the errata sheet for this book on our web site. If the answer to your problem isn't there, please e-mail us with your question and we'll do our best to sort it out for you.

# Tell Us What You Think

We've tried to make this book as accurate and enjoyable as possible, but what really matters is what the book actually does for you. Please let us know your views, whether positive or negative, either by returning the reply card in the back of the book or by contacting us via e-mail at feedback@wrox.com

# 1

# COM Wrapper Classes

COM solves all kinds of problems concerning code reuse and distribution. However, to take advantage of this you must follow the rules. To maintain the illusion that the object is in-process (the effect of COM's location transparency), COM will allocate buffers in the process that is receiving data, and it has stringent rules about whose responsibility it is to release these buffers. If you don't follow these rules then your applications will leak or crash. This is concerning if the application uses objects on the local machine, but it is disastrous if those objects are on a remote machine. COM resource management is therefore very important.

It is important for client applications that will use COM objects to make sure that they release resources. DCOM does provide a remote garbage collection facility that will eventually release objects that have outstanding leaked interface pointers when a client dies, but it is bad practice to rely on it. In any case, if your client creates large numbers of objects over its lifetime, garbage collection is not going to help – the problem will just get worse over time.

Resource management is also important for servers. Part of the reason is that 'servers' themselves often use COM objects and thus are 'clients'. However, even pure servers are bound by COM's rules for marshaling data from one process to another. Both processes must follow the rules of who will allocate and release resources; if they don't follow the rules, resource leaks can affect performance and eventually kill a process.

In this chapter, I will go into greater depth about how to handle this resource management by describing three ways of accessing COM objects: 'straight' C++ pointers, Visual C++ compiler COM support classes, and the ATL wrapper classes. Which of the three methods you decide to use is partly a matter of taste and partly dictated by needs like code size and performance. In addition, I will use this as an opportunity to introduce you to some of the new features of the Visual C++ and MIDL compilers.

# COM Interface Management

One of the most important principles of COM is that the reference count on an interface affects the lifetime of an object, and the lifetime of an object will affect the lifetime of a server. If you have a COM class implemented in an EXE and your client creates an instance of that class, uses it, and then omits to release an interface reference count, the object, and therefore the EXE server, will stay alive until the COM garbage collector detects that the client has died. In the meantime the client application may not need that object and the server is unnecessarily taking up resources.

This is a resource nightmare, especially if the same host machine is used to run many different object servers accessible from remote clients, or worse if your leaked object server is designed for single use – in that case, each new client will cause a separate instance of the server executable to be started.

On the other hand, if your client is over aggressive about releasing objects and releases an object before it is necessary, then when the client tries to access the object at a later time, the interface pointer is no longer valid.

The basic rules you have to adhere to are:

❑ When you make a copy of an interface pointer, you must call AddRef(). This includes actions like assigning a new interface pointer with the value of an existing one, and creating a new interface pointer and passing its value back as an [out] parameter.
❑ When you have finished with an interface pointer, you must call Release().

When you *obtain* an interface pointer via an [out] parameter (from QueryInterface() or CoCreateInstance(), for example), you can assume that the method has given you one reference count on the interface. This reference count is yours, and you must release it once you've finished with the interface. Note that if you're *writing* a method that obtains an interface pointer as an [in] parameter, you should *not* assume that a reference count has been made for you. This is because in this situation, the interface pointer has not been copied – you should act as if what you have received is the actual interface pointer from the caller of the method.

Frankly, managing interface reference counts is a pain. You can adopt a naïve strategy in which you write code to release an interface pointer immediately after you receive one and then write the rest of your code between these two lines, but this does not take into account the occasions when you may return from the function before you reach the Release(). If you're careful, you can make sure that you release any interface pointers before you call return, but this can get tedious if you use several interface pointers. If you have a large function, it becomes difficult to see all the interface pointers that you have obtained at the beginning or throughout the function, and whether they have been released. Furthermore, it becomes a particular problem if another developer comes along and tries to change your code.

## Smart Pointers and Wrapper Classes

The solution to this problem is to wrap the interface pointer in a class that will manage the interface reference count for you. Such a class can call AddRef() in its constructors and assignment operators, and Release() in the destructor. This class should enforce COM's reference counting rules, allowing you to forget all about them. Of course, interfaces have more methods than just those of IUnknown, so a wrapper class must give access to the wrapped interface pointer's methods. If you had a smart pointer class that looked like this:

```
template<class Interface>
class CSimplePtr
{
public:
    CSimplePtr() : m_ptr(NULL) {}

    CSimplePtr(Interface* ptr)
    {
        m_ptr = ptr;
        m_ptr->AddRef();
    }

    CSimplePtr(CSimplePtr& ptr)
    {
        m_ptr = ptr.m_ptr;
        m_ptr->AddRef();
    }

    ~CSimplePtr()
    {
        if (m_ptr)
            m_ptr->Release();
    }
    Interface* m_ptr;
};
```

You could write code like this:

```
int GetData(int iVal)
{
    CSimplePtr<IMyInterface> pMyItf;
    CoCreateInstance(CLSID_MyObject, NULL, CLSCTX_ALL,
                IID_IMyInterface, reinterpret_cast<void**>(&pMyItf.m_ptr));
    int iRetVal = 0;
    pMyItf.m_ptr->CalculateData(iVal, &iRetVal);
    return iRetVal;
}
```

Here, the wrapped interface pointer is initialized using CoCreateInstance() (which has already incremented the reference count for you). The interface method CalculateData() is called through the interface pointer, but note that Release() is not called explicitly. The reason, of course, is that when the variable pMyItf goes out of scope (when the function returns), the destructor of the wrapper class will be called, and this will call Release().

Because the wrapped interface pointer is accessed directly, this code is a bit clunky, but we can rectify that with the addition of an operator&() and an operator->(). So that now when the address of an instance of this class is obtained, the value returned is the address of the wrapped interface pointer. Furthermore, when the indirect member selection operator is used, the wrapped interface pointer is returned.

```
Interface** operator&() { return &m_ptr; }
Interface* operator->() { return m_ptr; }
```

The previous code can now be rewritten as:

```
int GetData(int iVal)
{
    CSimplePtr<IMyInterface> pMyItf;
    CoCreateInstance(CLSID_MyObject, NULL, CLSCTX_ALL,
                    IID_IMyInterface, reinterpret_cast<void**>(&pMyItf));
    int iRetVal = 0;
    pMyItf->CalculateData(iVal, &iRetVal);
    return iRetVal;
}
```

This function looks just like regular COM code, except that all reference counting has been omitted. Using a smart pointer class means that you can return from the method without worrying about leaked interface reference counts, like so:

```
int iRetVal = 0;
pMyItf->CalculateData(iVal, &iRetVal);
if (iRetVal == 0)
    return iRetVal;

int iNewval = 0;
CSimplePtr<IMyInterface> pMyAnother(pMyItf);
pMyAnother->CalculateMore(iRetVal, &iNewVal);
return iNewVal;
```

The first `return` here is safe, and the interface will be correctly released, because of the smart pointer destructor. The second `return` is safe too, because the copy constructor will correctly call `AddRef()`, and when the function returns, `Release()` will be called on both copies of the interface pointer. Note however that this code will only maintain a *single* reference count. Something like this *will* compile:

```
void Whoops()
{
    CSimplePtr<IMyInterface> pMyItf;
    CoCreateInstance(CLSID_MyObject, NULL, CLSCTX_ALL,
                    IID_IMyInterface, reinterpret_cast<void**>(&pMyItf));
    pMyItf->Release();
}
```

However, it will cause an exception because the `CSimplePtr` destructor will call `Release()` on an already-released pointer. Basically, when you call the reference counting methods on a smart pointer, you are absolving the smart pointer of all responsibility for maintaining the reference count. You simply should not do this, and in fact ATL has a mechanism to prevent it happening, as you'll see later on.

When you consider the benefits of using smart pointers in this way, it's hardly surprising that Visual C++ 6.0 has a smart pointer class called `_com_ptr_t<>` that provides this functionality and more. ATL also provides a smart pointer class called `CComPtr<>`, which provides a thinner but more efficient implementation. These classes will be explained later in this chapter, but before I get to them I'll go over some of the other features added to Visual C++ to support COM programming.

# Interface Names

The name of an interface is its 128-bit IID. COM does not accept any other name. MIDL generates C++ bindings for you in the form of abstract classes that have a readable name; however, this name is not the true name of the interface. This is a problem because when you call QueryInterface(), you need to supply an indirect pointer *and* the IID of the interface that you're requesting. This can be extremely error prone – the compiler can't catch mistakes like requests for incompatible interfaces:

```
ISomeInterface* pItf = NULL;
pUnk->QueryInterface(IID_IAnotherInterface, reinterpret_cast<void**>(&pItf));
```

What's needed is a way of associating the COM name of an interface (its IID), with the C++ type representing that interface. That way all the information necessary for COM and C++ can be encapsulated in a single place, reducing the chance of errors.

C++ already has the concept of run time type information (RTTI), which associates a type_info object with a class. You can use the typeid() operator to return the type_info object associated with a C++ class. Unfortunately, the type_info object doesn't hold much more than the name of the associated class, so Microsoft have extended Visual C++ with the uuid() specifier.

Because it's an extension to C++, uuid() is used with the __declspec() keyword on a class (or struct). It associates a GUID with that class so that when you create an interface pointer in C++ it has both a C++ name (which you can get through the typeid() operator) and a COM interface name (which you can get through the __uuidof() operator).

As an example take a look at the declaration of IUnknown in unknwn.h:

```
MIDL_INTERFACE("00000000-0000-0000-C000-000000000046") IUnknown
{
public:
    BEGIN_INTERFACE
    virtual HRESULT STDMETHODCALLTYPE QueryInterface(REFIID riid,
                                                     void** ppvObject) = 0;
    virtual ULONG STDMETHODCALLTYPE AddRef(void) = 0;
    virtual ULONG STDMETHODCALLTYPE Release(void) = 0;

#if(_MSC_VER >= 1200)                    // Visual C++ 6 or greater
    template <class Q>
    HRESULT STDMETHODCALLTYPE QueryInterface(Q** pp)
    {
        return QueryInterface(__uuidof(Q), (void**)pp);
    }
#endif

    END_INTERFACE
};
```

The macros you can see here are defined in objbase.h and rpcndr.h: for Intel machines BEGIN_INTERFACE and END_INTERFACE preprocess to nothing, while STDMETHODCALLTYPE becomes __stdcall. The macro MIDL_INTERFACE() is defined as:

```
#if _MSC_VER >= 1100
 #define DECLSPEC_UUID(x) __declspec(uuid(x))
 #define MIDL_INTERFACE(x) struct __declspec(uuid(x)) __declspec(novtable)
#else
 #define DECLSPEC_UUID(x)
 #define MIDL_INTERFACE(x) struct
#endif
```

This means that if you're compiling with Visual C++ 6.0, the first line of the code above becomes:

```
struct __declspec(uuid("00000000-0000-0000-c000-000000000046"))
       __declspec(novtable) IUnknown;
```

This associates the GUID for IUnknown with the struct IUnknown.

> *Since* MIDL *now declares all the C++ mapping classes it generates using the* MIDL_INTERFACE() *macro, you should not have to apply* __declspec(uuid()) *manually to any of the interfaces that you define.*

Before uuid() was introduced the COM names for the standard interfaces were held as constants in the uuid.lib library and every project that used COM had to link to this. If you created your own interfaces then the COM name for that interface was provided as a constant in a _i.c file created by MIDL. Since the COM name of an interface is now in the C++ bindings header, it means that you do not need to link your project to separate files with GUID constants.

Once you've associated a GUID with a class, you can always obtain the GUID back again with the __uuidof() operator. The definition for IUnknown in unknwn.h defines an overloaded version of QueryInterface() that uses this operator, so that you do not have to explicitly mention the IID when you want to obtain a new interface pointer.

Here's an example of using the __uuidof() operator:

```
IUnknown* ppv = NULL;
CoCreateInstance(__uuidof(MyClass), NULL, dwClsContext,
                 __uuidof(IUnknown), reinterpret_cast<void**>(&ppv));
IMyInterface* pItf;
ppv->QueryInterface(&pItf);
```

This code is creating an instance of the class described by __uuidof(MyClass), and it's requesting the IUnknown interface on that object. After that the code queries the object for the IMyInterface interface.

There are three things to note here:

- ❑ uuid() can be used to associate any type of GUID with a struct or class. That makes it useful for CLSIDs, LIBIDs, APPIDs or any other sort of GUID that you may need to refer to in code. The struct or class with which the GUID is associated doesn't need to have any role other than making the GUID available through the __uuidof() operator.
- ❑ You no longer need to provide a the IID of the interface as a separate argument to QueryInterface() because the interface pointer that you provide already has this information associated with it.
- ❑ The address of the interface pointer is not cast to void** as is the normal practice with QueryInterface(). The magic of templates allows you to pass any interface pointer type because the overloaded QueryInterface() uses the pointer type as a template parameter.

uuid() can be applied to a struct or class. The __uuidof() operator can be applied to the class name, an instance of a class, or a pointer or reference to the class, to retrieve the associated GUID.

Note that GUIDs are not inherited. If you have this:

```
struct IMyInterface : IUnknown;
```

And then you attempt to get the IID of IMyInterface, the compiler will give you an error:

```
error C2787: 'IMyInterface' : no GUID has been associated with this object
```

This makes sense, because IMyInterface is a new interface, and certainly should not 'inherit' the name of its parent.

## Example: uuid() and __uuidof()

Using __declspec(uuid()) and __uuidof(), you can write code without messing around with constants:

```
// Native1.cpp : Defines the entry point for the console application.
//

#include "stdafx.h"

struct __declspec(uuid("25c89da6-43ad-11d0-9a61-0060973044a8")) CRemoteTime;

struct __declspec(uuid("98397522-4458-11D0-9A62-0060973044A8")) IRemoteTime :
IUnknown
{
    virtual HRESULT __stdcall GetTime(DATE* date)=0;
};

int _tmain(int argc, TCHAR* argv[])
{
    CoInitialize(NULL);
```

```
    IRemoteTime* pTime = NULL;
    HRESULT hr = CoCreateInstance(__uuidof(CRemoteTime),
        NULL, CLSCTX_ALL,
        __uuidof(IRemoteTime),
        reinterpret_cast<void**>(&pTime));

    if (FAILED(hr))
    {
        _tprintf(_T("Failed to create object, ")
                 _T("did you build the TimeServer example?\n"));
        return 0;
    }


    DATE date = 0;
    hr = pTime->GetTime(&date);
    pTime->Release();

    SYSTEMTIME st = {0};
    VariantTimeToSystemTime(date, &st);

    _tprintf(_T("%04d-%02d-%02d %02d:%02d:%02d\n"),
        st.wYear,st.wMonth,st.wDay,
        st.wHour,st.wMinute,st.wSecond);

    CoUninitialize();

    return 0;
}
```

This code makes use of an object called `TimeServer.RemoteTime`, which you'll find included with the source code for this book. The object supports an `IRemoteTime` interface, which is described by the following IDL:

```
[
    object,
    uuid(98397522-4458-11D0-9A62-0060973044A8),
    oleautomation,
    pointer_default(unique)
]
interface IRemoteTime : IUnknown
{
    HRESULT GetTime([out, retval]DATE* date);
};
```

To create this console application, you can use the Win32 Console Application AppWizard type. I chose the A "Hello, World" Application option, but note that to use COM you should #include <windows.h> into stdafx.h, and remove the #define for WIN32_LEAN_AND_MEAN. I also added tchar.h so that I can have the option of Unicode compilation if I want it.

```
#include <windows.h>
#include <stdio.h>
#include <tchar.h>
```

The code needs to link to an appropriate C runtime library to use `printf()`, and it also needs to link to `ole32.lib` and `oleaut32.lib` to be able to use the COM runtime functions, but it *doesn't* need to link to `uuid.lib`, and nor does it need to include the GUID constants file `TimeServer_i.c`, or the C++ interface file `TimeServer.h` (both generated by `MIDL`).

As you can see, I've associated the CLSID of `TimeServer.RemoteTime` with the non-implemented `CRemoteTime` struct, and the IID of the `IRemoteTime` interface with the abstract `struct` `IRemoteTime`. In the call to `CoCreateInstance()`, I have used `__uuidof()` to obtain the GUIDs from the `structs`.

This is all well and good, but I still had to *find* the CLSID of `TimeServer.RemoteTime` and the IID of `IRemoteTime` to type into my source file. I also had to create the abstract `struct` `IRemoteTime` so that I could call the interface method, which means that I needed to know about all the methods in the interface. Finally, I still had to worry about the interface reference counting. It would be a lot better if Visual C++ would do this work for me.

# #import

In addition to the `__declspec(uuid())` attribute described above, Visual C++ 5.0 introduced the new preprocessor directive `#import`. This tells the preprocessor to read in type information, and generate the C++ language bindings from that. So, any `typedefs`, enums or constants in a type library are used to create the appropriate C++ equivalents, and `interfaces` are used to create abstract `structs`. In addition, the `interfaces` and `coclasses` in the type information will have their GUIDs, and the type library reader will use this to provide the information for `__declspec(uuid())`. Let's take a look at `#import` in more detail, with some code based on the previous example using `TimeServer.RemoteTime`.

```
// Native2.cpp
#include "stdafx.h"
#import "..\TimeServer\TimeServer.tlb"
using namespace TIMESERVERLib;

int _tmain(int argc, TCHAR* argv[])
{
    CoInitialize(NULL);

    DATE date = 0;

    {
        IRemoteTimePtr pTime(__uuidof(RemoteTime));
        date = pTime->GetTime();
    }

    SYSTEMTIME st = {0};
    VariantTimeToSystemTime(date, &st);
    _tprintf(_T("%04d-%02d-%02d %02d:%02d:%02d\n"),
        st.wYear, st.wMonth, st.wDay,
        st.wHour, st.wMinute, st.wSecond);

    CoUninitialize();
    return 0;
}
```

The first thing that you'll notice is the following lines:

```
#import "..\TimeServer\TimeServer.tlb"
using namespace TIMESERVERLib;
```

The first line tells the preprocessor the name of the type library to read. This will cause it to generate the code in a namespace with the same name as was used in the type library's `library` statement. The second line allows us to use the generated classes without having to explicitly specify this namespace.

> `#import` *can be followed by attributes which modify its output. You can generate the code without a namespace by using the* `no_namespace` *attribute, or you can change the namespace to another by using the* `rename_namespace()` *attribute.*

The next thing you'll notice is the rather strange extra code block. Basically, I have done this to define the scope of the `pTime` variable so that its destructor is called before `CoUninitialize()` is called. It's important to release all the interface pointers before COM is uninitialized. There are other ways of doing this, such as putting your pointers in a `try` block or another function, or even calling `Release()` explicitly, but I decided to use the extra braces to make this code more compact.

## #import Output

Under the instruction of the `#import` directive, the preprocessor generates two files that will be placed in the output directory. These have the same name as the type library, but with extensions `.tlh` and `.tli`. If you like, you can regard these as a header and an implementation file, although they are *both* `#included` like a header. You don't have to include these files in your project explicitly, as the `.tlh` file will be included automatically, and this file includes the `.tli` file.

Here is the `.tlh` file, edited a little to remove the comments it contained:

```
#pragma once
#pragma pack(push, 8)
#include <comdef.h>

namespace TIMESERVERLib {
struct RemoteTime;
struct __declspec(uuid("98397522-4458-11d0-9a62-0060973044a8"))
IRemoteTime;

_COM_SMARTPTR_TYPEDEF(IRemoteTime, __uuidof(IRemoteTime));
struct __declspec(uuid("25c89da6-43ad-11d0-9a61-0060973044a8"))
RemoteTime;

struct __declspec(uuid("98397522-4458-11d0-9a62-0060973044a8"))
IRemoteTime : IUnknown
{
    DATE GetTime();
    virtual HRESULT __stdcall raw_GetTime(DATE* date) = 0;
};

#include "TimeServer.tli"
} // namespace TIMESERVERLib
#pragma pack(pop)
```

The #include to TimeServer.tli will actually give the full path to this file.

The first #pragma ensures that the file is opened just once, while the second one saves the current packing alignment and changes it to 8-byte boundary packing. At the bottom of the code is a corresponding 'pop' that retrieves, and applies, the previous packing. This ensures that the code has 8-byte packing without affecting the packing set by files that include this file.

The next item in the file is the inclusion of the comdef.h header. I'll say more about this file and the classes it defines later on, but basically it defines a smart pointer class, an error class, and wrapper classes for BSTRs and VARIANTs.

After that, we enter the namespace where there's a forward declaration of the RemoteTime struct, followed by a line declaring the IRemoteTime interface and associating it with its IID. This struct is re-declared later in the file.

The IRemoteTime structure defines the C++ bindings of the interface by means of an abstract class, just as MIDL does in the C++ header files that it generates. The raw_GetTime() method is the interface's method (the other methods of this interface are included by deriving it from IUnknown), and you're quite free to use it, but #import has also defined a 'friendlier' high-level method, GetTime(). Since the parameter of the interface method is marked with [out, retval], #import returns this from the method and hides the HRESULT.

You can find the implementation of the GetTime() method in the .tli file:

```
#pragma once

inline DATE IRemoteTime::GetTime()
{
    DATE _result;
    HRESULT _hr = raw_GetTime(&_result);
    if (FAILED(_hr))
        _com_issue_errorex(_hr, this, __uuidof(this));
    return _result;
}
```

You can see that it just calls the raw_GetTime() method, and if the HRESULT is not successful, it throws a C++ exception by calling _com_issue_errorex(). If you choose, you can turn off the generation of high level methods by using raw_interfaces_only in the #import directive, in which case the .tli file will not be generated.

Note that you don't *have* to use smart pointers to use the classes generated by #import – you can use it to generate the C++ parts of the headers that MIDL generates. This means that rather than having to distribute a header and a constants file with your object server to developers, you can just distribute a type library. If the server has the type library bound as a resource, the only item you need to distribute is the object server.

This assumes, of course, that a type library can describe the objects in the server, and in general this means that the interface methods use Automation types. If you find that #import is creating the wrong types you can simply edit the tlh and tli files by hand.

## #import Attributes

In the discussion of the code for `Native2.cpp`, I mentioned the `no_namespace` and `rename_namespace()` attributes, but there are several others that you can apply:

| Attribute | Description |
| --- | --- |
| `exclude()` | Exclude items from the type library |
| `high_method_prefix()` | Prefix to add to generated methods |
| `high_property_prefix()` | Prefix to add to generated property access methods |
| `implementation_only` | Suppress the generation of the `.tlh` file. This option is useful for precompiled headers |
| `include()` | Override the automatic exclusion of individual items |
| `inject_statement()` | Put the parameter as a statement into the generated file, above the generated code, but within the namespace if one exists |
| `named_guids` | Declare GUIDs in the old style |
| `no_auto_exclude` | Disable the automatic exclusion of items defined in system headers or type libraries |
| `no_implementation` | Suppress the `.tli` file, used for precompiled headers |
| `no_namespace` | Generate the classes in the global namespace |
| `raw_dispinterfaces` | Generate raw wrapper functions that call `IDispatch::Invoke()` |
| `raw_interfaces_only` | Only generate the raw interface methods |
| `raw_method_prefix()` | Prefix for the raw interface methods |
| `raw_native_types` | Use BSTRs and VARIANTs |
| `raw_property_prefix()` | Prefix for the raw property methods |
| `rename()` | Give an item mentioned in the type library a new name |
| `rename_namespace()` | Define the classes in the specified namespace |

`exclude()` and `rename()` are particularly useful. If you build up a hierarchy of objects dependent on particular types – enumerations or `typedefs`, for example – and `import` these types into several IDL files, you will find that when you `#import` these files into a C++ file, there will be a clash of names. For example, imagine that you have these three IDL files:

```
// RetTypes.idl
typedef enum tagRetTypes
{
    SUCCESS, TOOLARGE, TOOSMALL
} RetTypes;
```

```
// object1.idl
[
    uuid(BADF00D2-BEEF-BEEF-BEEF-BAADF00DBEEF),
    version(1.0),
]
library LibraryOne
{
    import "rettypes.idl";
    import "oaidl.idl";

    [
      uuid(BADF00D1-BEEF-BEEF-BEEF-BAADF00DBEEF),
      pointer_default(unique)
    ]
    interface IInterface1 : IUnknown
    {
        HRESULT GetResult([out, retval]RetTypes* date);
    };

    [
        uuid(BADF00D3-BEEF-BEEF-BEEF-BAADF00DBEEF),
    ]
    coclass Object1
    {
        [default] interface IInterface1;
    };
};
```

```
// object2.idl
[
    uuid(BADF00D5-BEEF-BEEF-BEEF-BAADF00DBEEF),
    version(1.0),
]
library LibraryTwo
{
    import "rettypes.idl";
    import "oaidl.idl";
    [
        uuid(BADF00D4-BEEF-BEEF-BEEF-BAADF00DBEEF),
        pointer_default(unique)
    ]
    interface IInterface2 : IUnknown
    {
        HRESULT GetOtherResult([out, retval]RetTypes* date);
    };
    [
        uuid(BADF00D6-BEEF-BEEF-BEEF-BAADF00DBEEF),
    ]
    coclass Object2
    {
        [default] interface IInterface2;
    };
};
```

These will compile into two type libraries: `object1.tlb` and `object2.tlb`. Next, you can use `#import` to generate the smart pointer classes:

```
// MultiIDL.cpp
#import "object1.tlb" no_namespace
#import "object2.tlb" no_namespace

int _tmain(int argc, TCHAR* argv)
{
    // Use IInterface1 and IInterface2
}
```

This will not compile – you'll get an error code C2011. The reason for this is that the enumeration is included in both `object1.tlh` and `object2.tlh`, and the compiler will complain of a redefinition. One way round this is to dispense with the `no_namespace`, meaning that the enum will be defined in *both* namespaces, as `LibraryOne::tagRetTypes` and `LibraryTwo::tagRetTypes` respectively. Of course, the intention is for the *same* enumeration to be used in both interfaces, so this is hardly ideal.

A better solution is to exclude the enumeration from the second type library by amending the second `#import` directive to read:

```
#import "object2.tlb" no_namespace, exclude("tagRetTypes")
```

Now the enumeration is only defined in `object1.tlh` and not in `object2.tlh`, preventing a redefinition.

# __declspec(property())

Another attribute that Microsoft has added to be used through `__declspec()` is `property()`. This is applied to non-`static` data members in a class, and declares that the data member so declared is a 'virtual' data member. Look at this code:

```
class CCar
{
public:
    __declspec(property(get=GetSpeed, put=PutSpeed)) float Speed;
    CCar() : m_fSpeed(0) {}
    float GetSpeed() {return m_fSpeed;}
    void PutSpeed(float fVal) {m_fSpeed = fVal;}
private:
    float m_fSpeed;
};
```

Here, `Speed` is treated as a data member of the class, but the compiler does not generate any storage for it. Instead, when it is accessed, the `property()` attribute specifies that the public accessor and mutator methods `GetSpeed()` and `PutSpeed()` are called. In this case the property is read and write, but you can use this to create read-only or write-only members. In this example I have implemented the methods to use a private data member, but there is no requirement to do so.

The CCar class can be used like this:

```
int _tmain()
{
    CCar myCar;

    myCar.Speed = 10;
    _tprintf(_T("Speed is %f\n"), myCar.Speed);
    return 0;
}
```

As you can see, the result is that the Speed member is treated as if it's a 'property' of the myCar object, much like the properties you can have in languages such as Visual Basic.

When the #import directive sees the [propput] and [propget] attributes on items in type information (or properties in a dispinterface), it will create a 'virtual' data member with __declspec(property()).If the property takes a parameter (to define a property that is an array of values, for example) then #import will generate a 'virtual' array data member.

For example, if the DOptions dispinterface has an array property called Colors:

```
[
    uuid(A370206E-133B-11D2-8D06-0060973044A8),
    odl
]
dispinterface DOptions
{
properties:
methods:
    [propget, id(1)] BSTR Colors([in] LONG Index);
    [propput, id(1)] void Colors([in] LONG Index, [in] BSTR newVal);
};
```

This defines a property that is an array of BSTR values. If there is an object type (say, CarOptions) that implements this dispinterface, you could write Visual Basic client code like this:

```
Dim proposal as New CarOptions
Dim colorString as String
Dim colorIndex as Integer
colorIndex = Val(txtChosenColor)
colorString = proposal.Colors(colorIndex)
```

A C++ client using this dispinterface through #import will get the following generated class:

```
struct __declspec(uuid("a370206e-133b-11d2-8d06-0060973044a8"))
DOptions : IDispatch
{
    __declspec(property(get=GetColors, put=PutColors)) _bstr_t Colors[];
    _bstr_t GetColors(long Index);
    void PutColors(long Index, _bstr_t newVal);
};
```

The upshot is that the client can now write C++ code like this:

```
DOptionsPtr pOptions(__uuidof(CarOptions));
_bstr_t bstrChosenColor = pOptions->Colors[index];
```

This is very similar to the equivalent code in Visual Basic and I'm sure you'll agree that this is far easier to read than rather alien-looking calls to things like get_Color(index, &bstrChosenColor).

# Dispinterfaces

The previous section showed an example using a dispinterface, which, as you know isn't a *real* interface at all – it just indicates that the object supports IDispatch and has implementations for specified methods and properties. If an object has a dispinterface, then a client can access its methods and properties by calling IDispatch::Invoke().

Visual C++ provides several methods to access members of a dispinterface. These methods are implemented in comsupp.lib, and prototyped in comdef.h:

| Method | Description |
|---|---|
| _com_dispatch_propget() | Get a property value |
| _com_dispatch_propput() | Put a property value |
| _com_dispatch_method() | Call a method |
| _com_dispatch_raw_propget() | Get a property value |
| _com_dispatch_raw_propput() | Put a property value |
| _com_dispatch_raw_method() | Call a method |

The first three of these will generate C++ exceptions when a failure HRESULT is returned, while the other three will just return the HRESULT and let you deal with it as you see fit. These methods are designed to do all the messy packaging up of parameters into a DISPPARAMs structure and extracting any [out] parameters when the methods return.

The 'prop' methods accept a parameter that indicates the type of the property, for example:

```
BSTR bstr;
_com_dispatch_propget(pDisp, 0x1, VT_BSTR, static_cast<void*>(&bstr));
```

pDisp is an IDispatch pointer, while VT_BSTR is just a member of the VARENUM enumeration that indicates the type of the variable passed as the fourth parameter. Now, this is fine for single parameters, but it's not ideal for methods that could have many parameters, which is where _com_dispatch_method() and _com_dispatch_raw_method() come in. These functions can take any number of parameters (the prototypes use the ellipsis). To indicate the Automation types of the parameters passed, an extra parameter is used to hold the VT_ type. For example, if you have this ODL:

```
methods:
    [id(2)] long Add([in] long f1, [in] long f2);
```

You can call the `Add()` method with code like this:

```
long l = 1;
long r = 5;
long ret;
_com_dispatch_method(ptr, 0x2, DISPATCH_METHOD, VT_I4,
                     static_cast<void*>(&ret), L"\x0003\x0003", l, r);
```

The last two parameters are the ones to be accessed through the ellipsis, while the string immediately preceding them indicates their types as described by the VARENUM enumeration. In this case, type used for both is VT_I4, which represents a 4-byte signed integer.

Although you can use these methods to access the members of a dispinterface, it is far easier to allow the #import generator to create wrapper methods for you.

# Interface Access

The interface pointers that you use to access COM objects must be handled with great care, and in complicated code even experienced developers can neglect to Release() them when they are no longer needed, or forget to AddRef() them when they're copied. Indeed, it is tempting for a C++ programmer to do normal C++ things like casting an interface pointer to a different type. In this section, we'll take a closer look at the nature of these problems, and then examine a couple of potential solutions.

# C++ Interface Pointers

This is the 'raw' way to handle interface pointers. When you compile an interface definition file with MIDL, and that file declares interfaces outside of a library statement, MIDL will generate a header file that defines the interface using an abstract struct. The functions that return interface pointers (like CoCreateInstance() and QueryInterface()) return a pointer to an array of function pointers. When you obtain an interface pointer, you can cast it to a pointer to this abstract struct; C++ then treats it as a pointer to a vtable, and so you can call the interface's methods by calling the struct's methods through the pointer.

One of the biggest problems with this approach comes from this issue of casting interface pointers. You've already carried out one cast (from a void* to a pointer to the abstract struct), and there will always be a temptation to cast further. For example, if your interface is derived from another interface (and it always will be, because IUnknown is the top interface in the inheritance hierarchy), it is possible, though not desirable, to 'upcast' to a pointer to a base interface. When your interface inherits from another interface, the new virtual methods are added to the *end* of the function pointer array, so upcasting removes the function pointers added by the derived interface – this is the well-known problem of **interface slicing**.

Let's take a very simple example. For this IDL:

```
interface IMyInterface : IUnknown
{
    HRESULT NewMethod();
}
```

You can visualize the `IMyInterface` interface method array as:

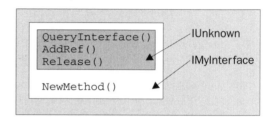

So, assuming we have an interface pointer to `IMyInterface`, we can write:

```
IMyInterface* pMyInterface;
IUnknown* pUnknown;

// Get interface pointer from somewhere
pMyInterface->NewMethod();
pMyInterface->AddRef();
pUnknown = static_cast<IUnknown*>(pMyInterface);
pUnknown->NewMethod();                  // This won't compile
pUnknown->AddRef();
```

Casting the `IMyInterface` pointer to an `IUnknown` pointer 'slices off' the `NewMethod()` function pointer in the interface. You should not do this, and especially not with `IUnknown`. The pointer that you obtain from an object when you query for `IUnknown` defines the identity of the object, and you can always check to see if two interface pointers point to the same object by querying both for `IUnknown` and comparing the pointers. The 'cast' `IUnknown` pointer shown above does not necessarily represent the identity of the object. For other interfaces it may be possible to upcast, but it is safer to use COM's own 'cast operator' (`QueryInterface()`) as explained below.

So much for upcasting, but what about 'downcasting' – that is, casting pointers of a base interface to a derived interface? Technically, it's only possible to do this *if* the object is implemented as an in-process server, and *if* the object implements the base interface by slicing off the derived interface members. However, you certainly can't assume the latter, and you don't know whether an interface pointer refers to an in-process object either. This is definitely a no-no.

If the interface *is* on an out-of-process object, a proxy will be used to remote the interface. However, proxy objects know how to remote just one interface; if you obtain an `IBase` interface pointer, the proxy for this interface will remote the `IBase` interface. If you cast the interface pointer to another type – say, `IDerived` – then even if a proxy is registered for that interface, it will not be called.

In fact, COM was designed with solutions to these casting problems in mind, and there's a method for casting from one interface to another that you already know only too well: QueryInterface(). You can imagine QueryInterface() to be like the C++ static_cast<>() operator, in that it allows you to specify the type that you want to cast the interface to. Of course, when you use QueryInterface(), you obtain a new pointer, and so there is an implicit AddRef() on the interface, thus you must treat it as being another interface, and so once you have finished with it, you have to call Release() on it in order to keep to the rules of reference counting.

I think I've made my point: using raw interface pointers to access COM objects is quite possible, and I'm sure you're quite adept at doing so. However, it makes writing COM clients prone to error, and there are now much better ways of going about the same process.

# _com_ptr_t<>

Native compiler COM support was first introduced in Visual C++ 5.0 to provide smart pointer wrapper classes for client programs. When you #import type information, smart pointer classes are generated. If you review the .tlh file generated earlier, you will find this declaration:

```
_COM_SMARTPTR_TYPEDEF(IRemoteTime, __uuidof(IRemoteTime));
```

This is much more significant than it might at first appear. In the file comdef.h, the macro is defined as:

```
#define _COM_SMARTPTR          _com_ptr_t
#define _COM_SMARTPTR_LEVEL2 _com_IIID
#define _COM_SMARTPTR_TYPEDEF(Interface, IID) \
    typedef _COM_SMARTPTR<_COM_SMARTPTR_LEVEL2<Interface, &IID> > \
        Interface ## Ptr
```

In other words, it generates a new type whose name is that of the interface passed to it, appended with Ptr. The previous application of _COM_SMARTPTR_TYPEDEF() would expand to:

```
typedef _com_ptr_t<_com_IIID<IRemoteTime,
                        &__uuidof(IRemoteTime)> > IRemoteTimePtr;
```

The template classes _com_ptr_t<> and _com_IIID<> are defined in comip.h, which is included by comdef.h. _com_ptr_t<> is the smart pointer template class, and the effect of the macro is to apply smart pointer code onto an interface class. You can apply _COM_SMARTPTR_TYPEDEF() to interfaces declared in the MIDL-generated header files, but once again it is easier to let #import do all the work for you.

_com_IIID<> is a template that encapsulates the IID and the interface in one class. This is quite interesting, because by using this template, any interface applied as a parameter is typedef'd to the generic type Interface that's used in _com_ptr_t<>:

```
template<typename _Interface, const IID* _IID>
class _com_IIID
{
public:
    typedef _Interface Interface;
```

```
        // Other methods

    static const IID& GetIID() throw()
    {
        return *_IID;
    }
};
```

The _com_ptr_t<> class is a generic smart pointer class that enforces the COM reference counting rules. In addition, the class defines a copy constructor, an assignment operator, methods to create instances of a new object, and methods to cast one interface pointer to another, all of which will be described shortly.

_com_ptr_t<> is a class of some considerable size, but here are a few of the basic constructors. As you can see, when an interface pointer is copied, AddRef() is called. Conversely, when the smart pointer object is destroyed, Release() is called:

```
template<typename _IIID> class _com_ptr_t
{
public:
    typedef typename _IIID::Interface Interface;

    _com_ptr_t(Interface* pInterface) throw() : m_pInterface(pInterface)
    {
        _AddRef();
    }

    ~_com_ptr_t() throw()
    {
        _Release();
    }
private:
    Interface* m_pInterface;
    void _Release() throw()
    {
        if (m_pInterface != NULL)
            m_pInterface->Release();
    }
    void _AddRef() throw()
    {
        if (m_pInterface != NULL)
            m_pInterface->AddRef();
    }
};
```

Under circumstances less artificial than my example code, you will normally create smart pointer objects in functions that are called by your _tmain(), or use exception blocks, as you'll see later. With that explanation given, let's now look a little closer at what the template supplies.

## Creating Object Instances

A smart pointer encapsulates an interface pointer. That interface pointer is either NULL, in which case it applies to no object, or else it is valid, and therefore a pointer to an interface on an existing object. This assumes that at some point the object has been created. There are three ways to do this.

Firstly, of course, you can create an instance of an object using `CoCreateInstance()` or one of its sister functions. You can then take the raw pointer that it returns and use either an appropriate constructor, the `Attach()` method, or the assignment operator to hook it up to a smart pointer object.

The `Attach()` method initializes the smart pointer with the raw pointer, but it does not `AddRef()` the interface. This technique is used to get the smart pointer to manage the reference count of the interface pointer, since when the smart pointer object goes out of scope, it will call `Release()`. This method has an overloaded form that takes a `bool` parameter, which if `true` *will* call `AddRef()` on the interface. Of course, both overloads will release any interface that the smart pointer may already encapsulate.

The assignment operator (`operator=()`), can be used to assign homogeneous or heterogeneous pointers – that is, the interface pointer that you're assigning can be the same as or different from the smart pointer that will contain it. If the smart pointer being assigned to already contains an interface pointer, then this is released. Next, if an homogenous assignment is made, the new interface pointer is cached and `AddRef()` is called. If the assignment is heterogeneous, the pointer being copied is queried for the interface type that is being assigned using `QueryInterface()`, and the resulting interface pointer is saved (`QueryInterface()` ensures that `AddRef()` is called).

If it helps, you can look on this as an implicit cast from one interface type to another. You can write code like this:

```
void PrintName(IStream* pStrm)
{
    // Initialize object with the data in a stream
    IPersistStreamInitPtr pInitialize;
    CoCreateInstance(__uuidof(Person), NULL, CLSCTX_INPROC_SERVER,
            __uuidof(pInitialize), reinterpret_cast<void**>(&pInitialize));
    pInitialize->Load(pStrm);
    // Get the name
    IPersonPtr pPerson;
    pPerson = pInitialize;
    BSTR bstrName;
    pPerson->GetName(&bstrName);
    _tprintf(_T("%S\n"), bstrName);
    ::SysFreeString(bstrName);
}
```

I have highlighted the line where the implicit cast occurs. Although this ability is useful, there is the problem that you don't get a visual reminder that casting is happening. If the cast fails then the smart pointer will be reset to a NULL pointer, but you will not get any other notification. If you then use the smart pointer to access an interface method an exception will be thrown indicating that the error was an invalid pointer. This is confusing because the problem was querying for an interface that the object does not support. Thus, it is prudent to check the contents of the smart pointer after doing a cast like this:

```
pPerson = pInitialize;
if (pPerson)
{
    // smart pointer is valid
}
```

If you are not happy with this, it is better to do an explicit QueryInterface() in which case you can check the returned HRESULT.

The other two ways of creating an object instance both involve getting the smart pointer class to do the work. This can be done either by calling an appropriate constructor, or by calling the CreateInstance() method (which is ultimately called by the constructors anyway). In both cases, you can indicate the COM class name in one of two ways: by providing a CLSID (in normal or string form), or a string that contains a ProgID.

```
IRemoteTimePtr pRT;
pRT.CreateInstance(CLSID_RemoteTime);
```

In the first case, CoCreateInstance() is called using the CLSID parameter and the IUnknown interface. If this is successful, then CreateInstance() calls QueryInterface() to get the required interface. If you pass a string as the parameter, then the constructor code first checks to see whether the string is a ProgID or represents a CLSID, which it does by checking for '{' as the first character. Then it obtains the actual CLSID by calling CLSIDFromProgID() or CLSIDFromString(), and passes this CLSID to CreateInstance() as before.

```
IRemoteTimePtr pRT (_T("TimeServer.RemoteTime.1"));
```

Because CoCreateInstance() is called rather than CoCreateInstanceEx(), this means that if you want to create a remote object, you will have to use DCOMCnfg to set RemoteServerName in the registry. The other alternative is to call CoCreateInstanceEx() yourself and use Attach() to attach the interface pointer to the smart pointer.

## Constructors

As mentioned above, you can wrap a smart pointer around an interface pointer to an existing object instance. The raw interface pointer passed to the constructor can have the same IID as was used as the parameter to the template, in which case AddRef() is called on the interface, or it can be a different interface, in which case QueryInterface() is called to get the interface represented by the smart pointer class. This is effectively a conversion of one interface pointer type to another.

There is another version of the constructor that takes an interface pointer of the same type as the smart pointer, and a bool parameter:

```
_com_ptr_t(Interface* pInterface, bool fAddRef) throw();
```

This is used in the case when you want to initialize a smart pointer and you *don't* want to increase its reference count. When would you want to do this? Well, consider an interface method that returns an interface pointer as an [out] parameter:

```
interface IEngine : IUnknown
{
};

interface ICar : IUnknown
{
    HRESULT GetEngine([out, retval] IEngine** ppEngine);
};
```

Objects implementing an `ICar` interface return an `IEngine` pointer when the `GetEngine()` method is called, and since it's an `[out]` parameter, the object implementation will call `AddRef()` on it, because the object has copied the interface pointer for you. (Keep that in mind: the interface pointer returned from the object will have an incremented reference count.)

When you `#import` the type library generated from this IDL, a `GetEngine()` wrapper method will be generated:

```
inline IEnginePtr ICar::GetEngine()
{
   struct IEngine* _result;
   HRESULT _hr = raw_GetEngine(&_result);
   if (FAILED(_hr))
       _com_issue_errorex(_hr, this, __uuidof(this));

   return IEnginePtr(_result, false);
}
```

This returns an instance of `IEnginePtr`, so that you can write code like this:

```
ICarPtr pLuxury(__uuidof(SilverGhost));
IEnginePtr pEngine;
pEngine = pLuxury->GetEngine();
```

The `GetEngine()` function creates a temporary `IEnginePtr` object, which is passed as a parameter to the assignment operator of `pEngine`, assigning it with the interface pointer returned from the object. However, the assignment operator will call `AddRef()` on the wrapped interface pointer, and if the constructor called `AddRef()` as well, the `IEngine` pointer reference count would be incremented by *two*. Then, when the `pEngine` object went out of scope, `Release()` would be called to reduce the reference count by one, leaving one count still outstanding: a reference count leak!

However, look again at what is actually happening here. The temporary `IEnginePtr` object is created with a call to the constructor that passes `false` as the second argument, and so *no* call to `AddRef()` is made when the temporary object is created. When execution moves to the next line of code, the temporary object is destroyed and its destructor calls `Release()` on the interface, soaking up the extra reference count from the assignment. This ensures that the call to `Release()` in the destructor of `pEngine` matches the `AddRef()` called by the assignment operator, as indeed it should.

Finally, there's yet another version of the constructor that takes a `_variant_t` parameter. This class will be described later, but it's basically a wrapper for the `VARIANT` type, and this constructor checks the `VARIANT` to see if it is holding a pointer to an interface.

Before I leave this section, I'll just give a quick mention to `_com_ptr_t<>`'s copy constructor, which enables you to copy a smart pointer safe in the knowledge that correct reference counting will be carried out on the interface.

## Other Operators

Once you have a smart pointer, you're free to copy it and pass it to methods that take interface pointers because _com_ptr_t<> has operators that expose the interface pointer and ensure that correct reference counting is maintained. The class also defines comparison operators, so there's an operator for equality (operator==()) that can compare two interfaces of the same type. If they are of different types, the operator calls QueryInterface() on both for IUnknown, and compares the resulting interface pointers. The COM specification states that the IUnknown pointer of an object defines its identity, so this tests to see whether the two interfaces are on the same object.

Of course, when you have a smart pointer, you need to be able to call the methods on the encapsulated raw interface pointer. _com_ptr_t<> defines an operator->() that returns the actual interface pointer, so when GetEngine() is called through the smart pointer in the above code, this is equivalent to (with the return value ignored for clarity):

```
(pLuxury.operator->())->GetEngine();
```

In a similar vein, you can pass the address of a smart pointer to methods that take an interface [out] pointer (like QueryInterface()), because the template defines a function operator&() that Release()s the encapsulated interface (if it is non-NULL) and returns the address of the data member for the interface pointer.

In addition to the equality operators, there are operators for >, <, >= and <=, which exist to allow you to put compiler COM support smart pointers into some of the STL containers. These work by calling the helper member _CompareUnknown() that obtains the IUnknown interface pointers from the two interfaces and does a comparison of the actual pointers. Remember that the STL containers uses these operators to order items and so this is a perfectly valid way to do this. However, you should note that you can't use *all* of the containers, because some of them need to get hold of the address of the item they are being asked to contain. When that happens, the overloaded operator&() is called, returning a pointer to the *encapsulated* interface pointer, which isn't what the container class wants at all.

This restriction means that vector<>, deque<> and map<> *can* contain compiler COM support smart pointers, while list<> and set<> cannot. A similar problem exists for the ATL smart pointer class, CComPtr<>, but as you'll see shortly, ATL solves it through the use of an adapter class, and you can use a similar solution for _com_ptr_t<> if you need to.

## Releasing Interfaces

Once you've finished with a smart pointer, you have several options. The first is to allow the smart pointer object to go out of scope. If this happens, the destructor calls the private member _Release(), which checks the encapsulated interface pointer. If it's non-NULL, Release() is called on the interface. Notice that a *single* call to Release() is made, emphasizing the fact that the smart pointer class manages only a single reference count.

A second option is to call the smart pointer Release() method. In addition to the actions carried out by _Release(), this method also sets the interface pointer to NULL. This is useful because it allows you to reuse the smart pointer object on another interface pointer.

What you should *not* do is call `Release()` on the interface through the smart pointer `operator->()`. If you do this, then you *must* have previously called `AddRef()` on the encapsulated interface pointer. As explained earlier, this means that you are effectively relieving the smart pointer of the responsibility of managing reference counts.

### Using Compiler Support Classes

Typically you will use compiler support classes in client applications. You will probably avoid using them in server code, the reason, as you'll see later, is that they require that C++ exception handling is used and this increases code size. However, the convenience of `#import` means that you cannot avoid using it for client code, and you'll notice that I will use it throughout this book for testing objects.

## CComPtr<> and CComQIPtr<>

As I mentioned in the last section `_com_ptr_t<>` smart pointers use C++ exception handling. By default, to keep the size of ATL servers as small as possible, ATL objects do not support C++ exceptions. They penalty for adding C++ exception handling is an increase in size for your executables of around 4K, so whether you choose to include it very much depends on how critical size is to your application.

ATL provides two smart pointer classes: `CComPtr<>` and `CComQIPtr<>`, defined in `atlbase.h`. These classes do not use exception handling, and although they manage reference counts like `_com_ptr_t<>`, they provide different functionality. In this section, I'll explain exactly what those differences are.

`CComPtr<>` was designed before Visual C++ had the `__declspec(uuid())` specifier. Because of this, there was no way to associate an IID with a C++ `struct`, and so you could only assign a `CComPtr<>` smart pointer using an interface of the template type. So, if you had a `IMyInterface` pointer you can use this to create a smart pointer:

```
IMyInterface* pRaw = GetMyInterfaceFromSomewhere();
CComPtr<IMyInterface> pMyItf(pRaw);
pRaw->Release();
```

but this would not compile:

```
IMyInterface* pRaw = GetMyInterfaceFromSomewhere();
CComPtr<IMyOtherInterface> pMyItf(pRaw);
pRaw->Release();
```

The compiler will complain that it cannot convert a `IMyInterface*` to a `IMyOtherInterface*` in the constructor.

For this reason, ATL also defines the `CComQIPtr<>` template, which takes two parameters: the interface `struct` (as `CComPtr<>` does), and the IID of that interface. Since the IID is not part of the smart pointer class, it can use it in calls to `QueryInterface()`. In particular, `CComQIPtr<>` has a constructor that takes an `IUnknown` pointer, and since all interfaces derive from `IUnknown`, this means that *any* interface pointer can be used as a parameter (C++ performs the necessary upcasting). This constructor then calls `QueryInterface()` to get the interface wrapped by the smart pointer.

This issue is not a problem with later versions of Visual C++ that have `__declspec(uuid())`, but for compatibility with older code, these two classes still exist. In ATL 3.0, the two classes are the same except that `CComQIPtr<>` has the aforementioned constructor and assignment operator that take an `IUnknown` pointer.

Using these smart pointer template classes is straightforward, because you don't have to generate a specialization of the templates using a macro like you do with `_com_ptr_t<>` through `#import`. Here are some examples of declaring ATL smart pointers:

```
CComPtr<IDispatch> pDisp;
CComQIPtr<IDispatch, &IID_IDispatch> pDisp2;
CComQIPtr<IDispatch> pDisp3;
```

The second of these says that if you construct a pDisp2 based on an interface pointer of another type, then the constructor will `QueryInterface()` for the `IDispatch` interface. The last example uses the default parameter of the template, which is to perform `__uuidof()` on the first parameter; this is a new feature of this class in ATL 3.0.

## Creating Object Instances

In contrast to `_com_ptr_t<>`, the constructors of these two classes do not allow you to create an instance of the object that implements the wrapped interface. Instead, you are expected to create an object instance and then use the C++ interface pointer as a constructor parameter. However, both smart pointer classes have a method called `CoCreateInstance()` that behaves much in the same way as `_com_ptr_t<>::CreateInstance()`, with one difference: the overloaded version that takes a string can only be passed a ProgID, and not a CLSID in string form.

Once again, the class methods call `::CoCreateInstance()`, so if you want to create a remote object, you'll either have to configure the registry or call `CoCreateInstanceEx()` yourself and attach the interface pointer to the smart pointer. Further, note that both classes use `__uuidof()` on the interface template parameter to get the IID of the interface to query for; this is true for `CComQIPtr<>` even though the IID is a template parameter.

`CComPtr<>` and `CComQIPtr<>` both have an assignment operator and an `Attach()` method. The former uses the global `AtlComPtrAssign()`, which `AddRef()`'s the interface pointer because a copy is being made, while the latter does not.

> Remember that `CComPtr<>` and `CComQIPtr<>` are templates, so they are used to generate code. If the functionality in `AtlComPtrAssign()` was part of the template code then if you used several different smart pointers, this code would be generated several times. Putting this code in a global function means that there is only one copy.

The classes also define operators so that you can cast the smart pointer to an interface pointer, and get the address of the wrapped interface pointer so that it can receive the results from an `[out]` parameter.

## Constructors

CComPtr<> has three constructors, while CComQIPtr<> has four. The three common ones are the default constructor, the copy constructor and a constructor that enables the smart pointer to be created from the interface it is encapsulating. The additional constructor of CComQIPtr<> takes an IUnknown pointer in order that objects may be created from *any* interface pointer – the constructor queries for the required interface.

## IUnknown Method Access

Access to the wrapped interface's methods is through the operator->(), but note that unlike _com_ptr_t<>, these smart pointer classes do not return an interface pointer. Instead, they return a pointer to _NoAddRefReleaseOnCComPtr<>:

```
_NoAddRefReleaseOnCComPtr<T>* operator->() const
{
    ATLASSERT(p != NULL);
    return (_NoAddRefReleaseOnCComPtr<T>*)p;
}
```

What's going on here? Well, earlier on I gave dire warnings about calling AddRef() and Release() through operator->(), the reason being that smart pointers can only really manage one reference count. The class below makes these methods private, and so if your code calls either, it will not compile.

```
template <class T>
class _NoAddRefReleaseOnCComPtr : public T
{
private:
    STDMETHOD_(ULONG, AddRef)() = 0;
    STDMETHOD_(ULONG, Release)() = 0;
};
```

CComPtr<> releases the interface in the destructor, and it also provides a Release() method. Both of these check that the interface pointer is non-NULL, and Release() will make the interface pointer NULL after the call. Release() is useful if you want to reuse a smart pointer object.

## QueryInterface()

In addition, the smart pointer class also defines QueryInterface():

```
template <class Q> HRESULT QueryInterface(Q** pp) const
```

This allows you to query for another interface type without needing to specify the IID of that interface. The advantage of this is that the call is type safe; it prevents the following code, the general form of which is a perennial problem with COM:

```
IUnknown* pUnk;

// Get pUnk from somewhere
IDispatch* pDisp;
pUnk->QueryInterface(IID_IOleObject, reinterpret_cast<void**>(&pDisp));
UINT count;
pDisp->GetTypeInfoCount(&count);                    // Whoops!
```

The problem here is that the call to QueryInterface() requests the IOleObject interface, but puts the result in an IDispatch pointer. This code will compile, but it will die at runtime.

> *Note that with the new overloaded version of* QueryInterface() *added to the definition of* IUnknown, CComPtr<>::QueryInterface() *is less useful than it might otherwise be. However, the asserts in the ATL implementation provide extra debugging support to validate the argument.*

## com_cast<>

ATL provides the following preprocessor definition in Atlbase.h:

```
#define com_cast CComQIPtr<>
```

This allows you to use CComQIPtr<> in much the same way as you would use dynamic_cast<>(). For example, you can write code like the following:

```
CComPtr<IOleObject> pOleObject = com_cast<IOleObject>(pUnkObj);
pOleObject->SetClientSite( com_cast<IOleClientSite>(pUnkSite) );
```

Use of com_cast<> here makes it obvious that a COM type conversion (i.e. a call to QueryInterface()) is being performed, and allows you to use a syntax that will be familiar to C++ programmers.

## Other Operators and Methods

Both ATL smart pointer classes define operators for !, <, and ==, so that they can be used in (most) STL containers (and for ease of use). The equality operator tests to see whether the wrapped interface pointers of the two smart pointers being compared are the same, and therefore it checks that the *interfaces* are the same. If you want to check whether two interface pointers point to the same *object*, then you can call IsEqualObject(). This queries both pointers for the IUnknown interface and compares the result.

I have already mentioned the assignment operators, which will assign the smart pointer with another interface pointer. In addition, these classes also define CopyTo(), which will copy the interface pointer into another variable (and correctly AddRef() the interface). If you want to get hold of the interface without calling AddRef(), you can call Detach() which will return the interface pointer and remove it from the smart pointer.

There are two more methods of interest, both of which are used to set up communications between objects. SetSite() is valid if the encapsulated interface is on an object that implements IObjectWithSite. This interface also has a method called SetSite(), which you can use to pass the IUnknown pointer of another object. Once this method is called, your object has an interface pointer on the other object, and can therefore communicate with it.

The other method is Advise(), which is used when the wrapped interface is a sink interface that's used to attach to a **connection point** on another object. Basically, this method is called with the IUnknown interface of the connectable object, the IID of the outgoing interface of the object you want to connect to, and a pointer to the DWORD that will hold the cookie that represents the connection.

*If that sounds a little woolly, don't worry: I'll be covering connection points in depth in Chapter 8.*

Unfortunately, this method doesn't take advantage of the fact that the IID of the outgoing interface is the same as the IID of the sink interface wrapped in the smart pointer, and it is therefore possible to call this method in a type-unsafe way.

### Using CComPtr<> with STL Containers

As I mentioned earlier, the list<> and set<> STL containers need to obtain the address of the items that are being inserted. If you try this with CComPtr<>, the overloaded operator&() will be called and this will return a pointer to the encapsulated interface pointer. Since this is not the same type as the smart pointer class, the compiler will complain. The solution is to use the adapter class, CAdapt<>, which is used to wrap the CComPtr<> and provides constructors and operators so that automatic conversions are made between the adapted class and the class it is adapting, for example:

```
CAdapt<CComPtr<IMyInterface> > ptr;
```

Here, ptr can be used whenever a CComPtr<IMyInterface> is needed. The advantage of using an adapter class is that it doesn't overload the address operator so the containers can get the actual address of the *adapted* object, which fulfills the requirements of the list<> and set<> containers. For example, if you wanted a set<> of CComPtr<IMyInterface>s, you should use:

```
std::set<CAdapt<CComPtr<IMyInterface> > > container;
```

### CComQIPtr<> IUnknown Specialization

As a final point in this section, take one last look at CComQIPtr<>. It has a constructor that takes an IUnknown pointer, and another that takes an interface pointer whose type is specified by the CComQIPtr<> parameter (T*). What happens if the parameter specifies IUnknown? You will have two constructors that take an IUnknown pointer, and the compiler will complain. Fear not: ATL provides a specialization of CComQIPtr<> for IUnknown that omits the T* constructor and so has only one constructor with an IUnknown pointer. This specialization is useful, because it allows you quickly to obtain the IUnknown pointer on any object:

```
IMyInterface pItf = GetMyInterfaceFromSomewhere();
// get IUnknown from this interface
CComQIPtr<IUnknown> pUnk(pItf);
// do something with these pointers
pItf->Release();
```

# Strings

In the old days, strings were represented using char arrays, which typically meant an array of 8-bit values. This is fine to represent the Latin character set used in English speaking countries, since it has space for the upper and lower case characters with room to spare for the accented characters used by other western European languages. It means that it's possible for a string originating from a machine in England to look the same on a machine in France. However, if the string was shown on a machine in Greece or Russia (where the Latin character set is not used), the string would be shown in Greek or Cyrillic characters, and would therefore be meaningless.

There have been several attempts to get round this. The MBCS (Multi Byte Character String) or the various OEM character sets used on Windows, for example, allow the Latin characters to be represented by single bytes and other characters by double bytes, enabling the construction of mixed character set strings. However, since a character can be one *or* two bytes long, it means that to get the length of a string, a function has to check each character to see if it's a single- or a double-byte character. Windows provides `CharNext()` and `CharPrev()` to allow you to iterate through all the characters in a string and interpret each correctly.

Needless to say, this is a pain, and it detracts from the simple elegance of a string as an array of characters. A better solution is to make all characters the same size, large enough to be able to hold all possible characters. Unicode does this by using a `short` for every character, making each character 16 bits. Just about every character in every alphabet used on the planet can have a representation in Unicode, but it does mean that strings take up twice the space of single-byte character sets.

Unicode is arranged so that the 224 characters from `0x0020` to `0x00ff` are the same as the ANSI character set, except that the top byte is set to zero. This means that on a little-endian machine, a string like `"Hello\0"` would appear as `"H\0e\0l\0l\0o\0\0\0"`. Passing such a thing to `strlen()` will return the length of the string as 1. The C runtime library provides Unicode functions that mirror the single byte versions; these tend to start with `wcs` instead of `str`, so the equivalent of the single-byte character set function `strlen()` is the wide character set function `wcslen()`.

In Windows NT, all the functions that use strings use Unicode. In Windows 9x, the same functions use single-byte ANSI. In fact, on NT there are two versions of each function – one with a `W` suffix and the other with an `A` suffix (e.g. `GetWindowsDirectoryW()` and `GetWindowsDirectoryA()`). The SDK headers `#define` the appropriate function to a name without a suffix according to whether the `UNICODE` symbol is defined. For example, from `WinUser.h`:

```
WINUSERAPI int WINAPIV wsprintfA(LPSTR, LPCSTR, ...);
WINUSERAPI int WINAPIV wsprintfW(LPWSTR, LPCWSTR, ...);
#ifdef UNICODE
    #define wsprintf wsprintfW
#else
    #define wsprintf wsprintfA
#endif // !UNICODE
```

If you use the 'A' (ANSI) version on NT, any `[in]` string parameters are converted to Unicode and the 'W' version is called, while any `[out]` string parameters are converted to ANSI before being returned to the caller. Therefore, it makes sense on NT to compile your projects as Unicode, and to use the 'wide' character type `wchar_t` (and the pointer types `LPWSTR` and `LPCWSTR`).

Since Windows 9x does not support Unicode, it leads to a problem: if you want your source code to generate NT object code, you need to conditionally compile so that you can use `LPSTR` on Windows 9x, and `LPWSTR` on NT. `WinNT.h` defines the following types:

```
typedef char CHAR;
typedef wchar_t WCHAR;

#ifdef UNICODE
    typedef WCHAR TCHAR, *PTCHAR;
```

```
    typedef LPWSTR PTSTR, LPTSTR;
    typedef LPCWSTR LPCTSTR;
    #define __TEXT(quote) L##quote
#else
    typedef char TCHAR, *PTCHAR;
    typedef LPSTR PTSTR, LPTSTR;
    typedef LPCSTR LPCTSTR;
    #define __TEXT(quote) quote
#endif
```

To complete the set, `ctype.h` typedef's `wchar_t` as a `short`. Thus, when you want to use strings, you should use arrays of `TCHAR`s. When you want to use a pointer to a string, use `LPTSTR` and then allow the compiler to make sure that the right type is used. If you use a string literal in your code, you should use the `_TEXT()` macro to make sure that the string contains Unicode or ANSI characters, as appropriate.

The C runtime library itself can also be conditionally compiled. To do so, you need to include `tchar.h`, which defines C runtime functions with names that start with `_t` to be the single byte or Unicode version, depending on whether the symbol `_UNICODE` is defined. (It also defines the macro `_T()` as an alternative for `_TEXT()`.)

Using all this conditional compilation and brute force preprocessor action, you can write code that will compile as ANSI or as Unicode, but the solution is still only valid within a single process and within the code that's under your control. Other code will not know whether `UNICODE` was defined when you compiled your project, and thus will not know if `LPTSTR` is a `LPWSTR` or a `LPSTR`. COM is designed to allow code reuse, and so if you create a COM object in your process, you need to know how big its characters are before you can pass strings to it. There really is only one choice here, and that is to choose a character set and stick to it. Thus, *COM uses Unicode.*

You can find the COM types defined in `wtypes.h` (search for `CHAR`). The first thing you'll notice is that `LPSTR` is defined as a `char` pointer, but forget this fact because you should not be using it – if you want to pass string parameters, use `LPWSTR`, because since you are living in a COM world you should use the COM way to pass strings. Indeed, the file defines a type called `OLECHAR` and a pointer called `LPOLESTR`, which on 32-bit systems are typedef'd to `WCHAR`s.

```
#if defined(_WIN32) && !defined(OLE2ANSI)
    typedef WCHAR OLECHAR;
    typedef OLECHAR *LPOLESTR;
    typedef const OLECHAR *LPCOLESTR;
    #define OLESTR(str) L##str
#else
    typedef char OLECHAR;
    typedef LPSTR LPOLESTR;
    typedef LPCSTR LPCOLESTR;
    #define OLESTR(str) str
#endif
```

We're not done yet; there is a further complication. As you can see above, `LPSTR` is defined as a pointer to `char` (specifically in Visual C++, `signed char`), but the default setting for `MIDL` is to treat an IDL `char` as a C++ `unsigned char`. Imagine the following two methods being compiled with `MIDL`:

```
HRESULT Method1([in, string] char* str);
HRESULT Method2([in, string] LPSTR str);
```

The result will be a C++ header that defines `Method1()` as taking an `unsigned char*`, and `Method2()` to receive an `LPSTR`, which `wtypes.h` defines as `char*`. You could make `MIDL` treat the IDL `char` as `signed char` with the `/char signed` switch, but a much better solution is to avoid the confusion completely and use wide character strings.

# LPOLESTR, wchar_t and BSTR

So: 32-bit COM uses Unicode for strings. Now, Unicode strings are arrays of `wchar_t`, but COM uses `OLECHAR` and `LPOLESTR`, and Automation uses a third type: `BSTR`. If you've ever been confused by this proliferation of different string types, I'm going to make this section a definitive comparison of all of them, describing how they are related, and how they are used.

## wchar_t and OLECHAR

The previous excerpt from `wtypes.h` showed that an `OLECHAR` is a `wchar_t` (a `short`) on 32-bit systems, and a `char` on 16-bit systems. Thus, if you define an interface that uses `LPOLESTR` parameters, you will not be able to use it between 16-bit and 32-bit applications. However, in general, making 16-bit and 32-bit COM talk to each other is not a common requirement, and so this is not a big issue. If you *do* need to do it, you can use Automation (through the Universal Marshaler), or else create your own marshaler that converts `char` strings to `wchar_t` strings. This last option is not for the faint of heart and will not be covered in this book.

The COM runtime functions that use strings use `LPOLESTR`s. For example, `StringFromCLSID()` takes a `REFCLSID` as an `[in]` parameter, and returns an `LPOLESTR*` as an `[out]` parameter. The method is used like this:

```
HRESULT hr;
LPOLESTR strClsid;
hr = StringFromCLSID(&CLSID_CMyObject, &strClsid);
// Use string
CoTaskMemFree(strClsid);
```

The last function call is important, because the memory for the string is allocated by `StringFromCLSID()` and returned to the caller. The onus is on the caller to free this memory when it is no longer needed. (Incidentally, you can convert a CLSID to a string using `StringFromGUID2()`, to which you pass a caller-allocated array and its size, but that's another story...)

The memory has been allocated by the task memory allocator, which can be accessed via the `IMalloc` interface that's obtained by calling `CoGetMalloc()`. The `CoTaskMemFree()` helper function wraps up calls to get the allocator interface, free the memory, and then free the interface. Notice that the task allocator ensures that a consistent mechanism for allocating and de-allocating memory is used throughout the process, whether it's called from the process itself or from a DLL that's loaded into it.

In a similar way, if you're *passing* a string to a runtime function, you must allocate the string and free it in your process. Most likely you will do it with a stack variable:

```
OLECHAR strClsid[] = L"{00030000-0000-0000-C000-000000000046}";
CLSID clsid;
HRESULT hr;
hr = CLSIDfromString(strClsid, &clsid);
```

Here, `strClsid` is allocated on the stack as an array of `wchar_t`s (by using the `L` in front of the quoted string).

## [string]

This brings us on to the thorny issue of marshaling strings: a proxy needs to know *exactly* how many bytes of data have to be marshaled to another process. Normally, the marshaling code knows how many bytes to transmit, because there are rules about how large data items are. A `long` is 4 bytes, for example, and this is defined by the Network Data Representation (NDR) that is used by Microsoft (and DCE) RPC.

When a method has a string parameter, you *could* specify that the string is a fixed length:

```
HRESULT PassAString([in] OLECHAR str[256]);
```

However, this is restrictive, because a 256-character string will always be marshaled. This means that strings longer than 256 cannot be passed, and if strings less than this length are sent, there is an inevitable waste because too many characters are transmitted.

Another option is to pass a pointer, and to use a separate parameter to specify how many items the pointer points to:

```
HRESULT PassAString2([in] long len, [in, size_is(len)] LPOLESTR str);
```

This might be called like so:

```
WCHAR wsz[] = L"Going in";
pObj->PassAString2(wsclen(wsz) + 1, wsz);
```

When you think about it, it's obvious that whenever you pass a string, the length of that string should be sent too. In fact, because it is so obvious, IDL has a `[string]` attribute to do just that:

```
HRESULT PassAString3([in, string] LPOLESTR str);
```

This indicates to the marshaling layer that it should call an appropriate runtime method on the `[string]` parameter to calculate the size of the buffer that it should marshal. In fact, if you look in `wtypes.idl`, you will find these lines:

```
typedef [string] CHAR *LPSTR;
typedef [string] WCHAR *LPWSTR;
typedef [string] TCHAR *LPTSTR;
```

In other words, when your IDL uses LPSTR, LPWSTR or LPTSTR, the parameter will automatically use the [string] attribute, but I do *not* advise that you do this. Consider the following:

```
HRESULT PassAString4([in, string] LPOLESTR str);
HRESULT PassAString5([in] LPWSTR str);
```

At a glance, the first method shows that the parameter is a string, and that the marshaling layer will determine how much data to marshal. The second method is not so clear, because without the [string] attribute, a wchar_t* parameter indicates to the marshaler that a single character should be marshaled. Using your inside knowledge of LPWSTR, you know that [string] is implied and so the entire string is marshaled, but there is plenty of scope for confusion, and because of this it is best to avoid using LPWSTR.

## String Allocation

When you pass a string from a client to a server (that is, an [in] parameter), the client can create the string however it likes, because the client maintains this memory. On the other hand, if the string is an [out] parameter, then the *server* must allocate memory for the buffer, and the client just has to allocate memory for a pointer to it. However, it is vital that this memory be obtained from the task allocator using CoTaskMemAlloc(). Since we're dealing with an [out] parameter, the client has the responsibility of de-allocating the memory, and must call CoTaskMemFree() once the pointer is no longer being used:

```
// HRESULT GetName([out, string] LPOLESTR* strName);
LPOLESTR strName = NULL;
pObj->GetName(&strName);
_tprintf(_T("%S\n"), strName);
CoTaskMemFree(strName);
```

We're not out of the woods yet. Since the client now allocates the buffer, and the buffer passed to the server code is allocated by the marshaling layer based on the string size, there may be problems with [in, out] parameters. The server code must ensure that it is not writing data that's bigger than the buffer it was passed. In this situation, the client will need to pass a maximum buffer length so that the server code can copy *up to* this amount:

```
HRESULT PassAString6([in] long len,
                     [in, out, string, size_is(len)] LPOLESTR str);
```

This uses the [string] to allow the marshaler to determine how many characters are actually marshaled, and it has [size_is()] to indicate to the server the maximum number of characters that it can copy into the buffer.

Another method would be to define a structure like this one:

```
typedef struct tabMyString
{
   long len;
   [size_is(len)] LPOLESTR str;
} MyString;
```

Then we can define the method as:

```
HRESULT PassAString7([in] MyString str);
```

When we use this method, the onus is on the client to fill the `struct` with a pointer to a wide character string, and also to determine the number of items (WCHARs) in the buffer:

```
WCHAR wsz[] = L"Hello";
MyString str = {wcslen(wsz) + 1, wsz};
pUnk->SendStr(str);
```

This is a pain to do, but it does mean that all strings passed between processes are automatically passed with their length, so that the marshaling layer knows how many bytes to transmit. This is a useful technique – so much so that the BSTR data type works in exactly this way.

## BSTR

BSTR are defined in `wtypes.idl` as:

```
typedef [unique] FLAGGED_WORD_BLOB* wireBSTR;
typedef [wire_marshal(wireBSTR)] OLECHAR* BSTR;
```

It doesn't look too pretty, but it's basically saying that the type the user calls BSTR is actually an OLECHAR*, but it's marshaled across the network as a wireBSTR.

The [wire_marshal()] attribute is a Microsoft extension of the DCE [transmit_as()] attribute. When BSTR is used, the marshaling layer does not marshal an LPOLESTR (that is, a string of OLECHARs), but instead uses specific BSTR marshaling code that interprets the data as a wireBSTR, which is defined as the following in `wtypes.idl`:

```
typedef struct _FLAGGED_WORD_BLOB
{
    unsigned long fFlags;
    unsigned long clSize;
    [size_is(clSize)] unsigned short asData[];
} FLAGGED_WORD_BLOB;
```

The marshaling code can use this structure to determine how much data to marshal, but what actually does the marshaling? The RPC layer looks for a series of functions called:

```
UserType_UserSize()
UserType_UserMarshal()
UserType_UserUnmarshal()
UserType_UserFree()
```

Here, `UserType` is the `typedef`'d
type. For `BSTR` (and `SAFEARRAY` and
`VARIANT`), these marshaling methods
are in `oleaut32.dll`, shown here in
a Quick View:

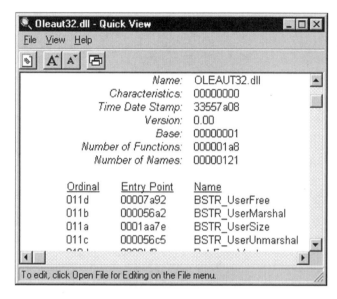

When the marshaling layer sees a `BSTR`, it calls `BSTR_UserSize()`, passing a pointer to a buffer
containing the `BSTR` that is marshaled, the actual `BSTR` within this buffer is indicated with an offset.
This function returns the total size of the data that is marshaled, including any padding. Next, the
marshaling layer calls `BSTR_UserMarshal()`, passing a pointer to the `BSTR` to marshal and a
pointer to a buffer in which the marshaled data should be written. The method writes (marshals) the
data into this buffer using the information in the `wireBSTR`, and then returns a pointer to the next
byte after the marshaled `BSTR` in the buffer. Like the others here, this method has a flag parameter
that indicates what sort of data is being marshaled and what kind of marshaling is to occur (in-
process, local or remote). The method can thus marshal the data in different ways, depending on the
context.

On the server side, `BSTR_UserUnmarshal()` is called, passing a pointer to the marshaled packet
and a pointer to a `BSTR`; the method then unmarshals the data from the packet into the `BSTR`.
Finally, when the `BSTR` is no longer used, the `BSTR_UserFree()` method is called on the server
side to free any objects that the user type may have created.

Now you can see how `BSTR`s are transmitted, but how do you use them? Your code uses the data type
as an `LPOLESTR`, but internally it's dealing with a length-prefixed string, and the code that creates a
`BSTR` must ensure that this internal structure exists. You cannot simply cast a `WCHAR` buffer to a
`BSTR`. Mercifully, the SDK provides several functions that allocate and manipulate `BSTR`s. To create
a `BSTR`, you pass a Unicode string to `SysAllocString()`; to free it, you call `SysFreeString()`.

```
BSTR bstr = SysAllocString(L"Hello");

// Use the BSTR
_tprintf(_T("%S\n"), bstr);
SysFreeString(bstr);
```

When you get a BSTR from SysAllocString(), you are returned the LPOLECHAR pointer to the string it contains, and so in this situation you can use a BSTR as a wide character string. The call to SysAllocString() reads the passed string and allocates memory for it, copying in the string. The string is NUL terminated, but since the actual length of the string buffer is also saved, it means that a BSTR can also hold NUL characters ('\0').

> *Although* BSTRs *are used almost exclusively with COM, you don't need to call* CoInitialize() *in order to use* BSTR *methods.*

However, note that SysAllocString() recognizes LPOLESTRs, which use a NUL character to indicate the end of the string. This code, for example, will create a BSTR containing only the string "Hello\0".

```
BSTR bstr = SysAllocString(L"Hello\0GoodBye");
```

Since BSTRs can have embedded NUL characters, it means that you should be careful about using CRT methods on them. For example, wcslen() will return the length up to the first NUL character, and similar warnings should be applied to other routines like wcscmp().

In most cases, you can treat a BSTR as a LPCOLESTR – that is, you can read from it as a WCHAR buffer, but you should not write to it. If you *do* want to do any manipulation on the string held by a BSTR – using wcscat() to append a string to the end of a BSTR, for example – you must first copy it into an OLECHAR buffer, and then use the runtime functions to manipulate the string. When you are finished, you can either create a new BSTR or use SysReAllocString() to reuse the previous BSTR.

The four bytes in front of a BSTR hold the number of *bytes* in the buffer (not the number of characters), and this gives the true length of the BSTR. However, you should not attempt to read these bytes. Instead, to get the length of an allocated BSTR (in characters), you should call SysStringLen().

Normally, BSTRs hold Unicode strings, but on 32-bit systems you can use a BSTR to hold a binary buffer. For convenience, the SDK provides the function SysAllocStringByteLen() that allows you to pass a binary buffer. While a call to SysStringLen() will return the number of characters in the BSTR buffer, you can get the actual number of bytes by calling SysStringByteLen(). As an aside, if you allocate a BSTR with SysAllocStringByteLen() and fill it with a wide char string then SysStringLen() * sizeof(OLECHAR) may return less than the actual number of bytes; however, SysStringByteLen() will return the actual number of bytes.

If you want to create a BSTR from a wide character string that contains embedded NULs (including other BSTRs), then you can use SysAllocStringLen() and indicate how many characters to copy. The following sample will copy all 13 characters, including those after the first NUL.

```
BSTR bstr = SysAllocStringLen(L"Hello\0Goodbye", 13);
```

Once you have finished with a BSTR, you free it with a call to SysFreeString(). It's important to do this because a call to allocate a BSTR may not actually allocate new memory for that string. COM uses a caching mechanism that when initialized will create a buffer with CoTaskMemAlloc(). Calls to SysAllocString() then return memory from this cache, and calls to SysFreeString() return memory back to it.

Even though you can use a BSTR as a binary buffer and pass ANSI strings, the convention is to use Unicode. If your client or server code is written in ANSI, you will need to convert to and from wide characters. The SDK provides two functions to do this: WideCharToMultiByte() and MultiByteToWideChar(). These functions require that you allocate buffers for the converted string that must be freed when they are no longer needed. In general, if you are developing for NT, you should be using Unicode anyway, but if your code is likely to be compiled both for Windows 9x and NT then you will have to add conditional compilation to allow strings to be converted as appropriate. You'll be pleased to know that ATL helps with conversion macros that will be described later in this chapter.

# _bstr_t

It should be clear from the previous discussion that whenever you create a BSTR to pass as an [in] parameter to an interface method, or when you receive a BSTR as an [out] parameter from an interface method, then you must free that buffer. If you do not, you will have a resource leak. Furthermore, it should also be clear that you have to be careful about allocating BSTRs and interpreting their contents.

Visual C++'s compiler COM support provides a class called _bstr_t in the header comutil.h (which is included in comdef.h). This class is used to manage BSTRs, performing the allocation and freeing of buffers, as well as conversions when needed. Using a _bstr_t is quite straightforward: there are constructors for char and wchar_t strings, as well as VARIANT (through _variant_t) and a copy constructor. You can also construct a _bstr_t from a BSTR, via a constructor that also takes a bool to determine whether a copy is to be made of the BSTR, or the existing BSTR is to be attached (indicating that the _bstr_t now manages that BSTR).

The guts of _bstr_t is a private class called Data_t. This holds a pointer to a wchar_t (which actually points to an allocated BSTR) and a reference count (it also caches a char* buffer to make conversions to char* more efficient). When a Data_t object is created, it has a reference count of 1, and the user is free to increase this reference count with a call to AddRef(), or decrease it with a call to Release(). This is not a COM object, but these two methods behave just like their IUnknown counterparts: when the reference count falls to zero, the object is deleted. Since the destructor is private, this is the only way to delete a Data_t object. (Since Data_t is a private class, the only user is _bstr_t, which holds a pointer to a heap-based Data_t object.)

Reference counting is required to handle _bstr_t assignment. Look at this:

```
_bstr_t bstrOne(_T("Hello"));
_bstr_t bstrTwo = bstrOne;
bstrOne = _T("Goodbye");
```

At the end of the second line, both variables point to the same BSTR, which has a reference count of 2 because the assignment operator copies the Data_t pointer from bstrOne to bstrTwo. However, when the assignment is carried out on the third line, you do not want the BSTR to be released completely, because bstrTwo is still using it. Instead, the reference count of the old Data_t object in bstrOne is decremented, and a new one is constructed for the new string.

_bstr_t provides methods to convert between wide characters and 'ordinary' characters: the char* operator checks to see if the cached character buffer is NULL, and calls _com_util::ConvertBSTRToString() to convert the member wide character buffer if it is. Unlike most of the COM support code, this function is not inline; instead, it is provided in the COM support library comsupp.lib that's loaded by a #pragma in comdef.h. Once the wchar_t buffer has been converted, the ANSI string is cached for any future calls to the char* operator.

You can create _bstr_t objects from char or wchar_t strings using the constructors or assignment operators. The length() method will correctly return the size of the BSTR, because it uses SysStringLen(). If you want to create a _bstr_t from data that contains embedded NULs, do not use the assignment operator or the constructors that take string pointers, because they create the underlying BSTR using SysAllocString(). Instead, use the _bstr_t constructor that takes a BSTR, or use the Assign() method:

```
BSTR bstr = SysAllocStringLen(L"Hello\0Goodbye", 13);

_bstr_t bstrOne(bstr);                  // Copies just Hello
_tprintf(_T("%s:%ld\n"), static_cast<LPTSTR>(bstrOne), bstrOne.length());

_bstr_t bstrTwo;
bstrTwo = bstr;                         // Copies just Hello
_tprintf(_T("%s:%ld\n"), static_cast<LPTSTR> (bstrTwo), bstrTwo.length());

_bstr_t bstrThree(bstr, true);         // Copies the entire BSTR
_tprintf(_T("%s:%ld\n"), static_cast<LPTSTR> (bstrThree),
    bstrThree.length());

_bstr_t bstrFour;
bstrFour.Assign(bstr);                 // Copies the entire BSTR
_tprintf(_T("%s:%ld\n"), static_cast<LPTSTR> (bstrFour), bstrFour.length());

SysFreeString(bstr);
```

This gives the following result:

```
Hello:5
Hello:5
Hello:13
Hello:13
```

In other words, the first two variables are constructed using the first part of the BSTR, and only the last two are constructed using the entire BSTR.

When you use #import to generate wrapper methods from type information, it will use _bstr_t for BSTR parameters unless you use the raw_native_types switch. If a parameter is defined as being [out, retval] BSTR*, then the wrapper methods will construct the _bstr_t using the BSTR constructor, enabling binary data to be passed. If the parameter is just [out], the wrapper methods will return the data through a BSTR* parameter. Since there is no operator&() on _bstr_t to get access to the wrapped BSTR, you have no choice but to use a BSTR to get the result. Then, if you want a _bstr_t to manage the BSTR for you, construct it bearing in mind the warnings given above.

If you want to pass a binary buffer in an [in] BSTR parameter, create the _bstr_t as explained above. The _bstr_t parameter is copied as it is passed into the method, but since the copy constructor makes a direct copy of the encapsulated BSTR, there are no special issues to consider when passing binary data.

So, what can you do with _bstr_t objects? Frankly, just about anywhere you use a BSTR, you can use a _bstr_t. Any method that takes a BSTR parameter will call the _bstr_t::operator wchar_t*(), and any method returning a BSTR can be used to construct a _bstr_t with the constructor that takes a wchar_t* parameter. Moreover, you can compare BSTRs and concatenate them, and you can also append single characters or strings of characters. All of this is done within the safety net of the native COM exception handling, as explained later in this chapter.

```
void SendName(char*);
void PassName(BSTR);
BSTR GetFirstName();

_bstr_t name;
_bstr_t surname("Grimes");
name = GetFirstName();
name += surname;
SendName(name);
PassName(name);
```

As mentioned above, there is no address operator, operator&(). This is because returning the address of the Data_t member would break the encapsulation.

# CComBSTR

The ATL class, CComBSTR, is a much thinner wrapper around BSTR than _bstr_t, the most notable differences are that _bstr_t has operators that return ANSI strings. This is not a great issue with CComBSTR because ATL provides conversion macros.

Aside from the default and copy constructor, CComBSTR provides constructors (and assignment operators) for wide character strings and ANSI strings, and you can create a CComBSTR from a CLSID or an uninitialized string of a specified size:

```
CComBSTR name(_T("Richard Grimes"));
CComBSTR guid(CLSID_MyObject);          // 'Stringified' GUID
CComBSTR uninitialized(256);            // 256 characters allocated
```

The class defines some assignment operators, but it doesn't define an operator+(). Instead, there are four overloaded versions of the Append() method (and the operator+=() defined for const CComBSTR&) that allow you to add data to existing BSTRs. Note that if you want to add two BSTRs together, you must use AppendBSTR() rather than Append(). The reason for this is that the former will use SysStringLen() to get the length of the string to append, but the latter will use the LPOLESTR, and the length of the BSTR will be calculated only up to the first NUL.

CComBSTR does not perform reference counting on its data members, and so access to a BSTR is as direct as is possible for a wrapper class: there is an operator BSTR() and an operator&() to give direct access to the data member, so you can use a CComBSTR in all situations where you would use a BSTR.

```
void PassName(BSTR);
BSTR GetFirstName();

CComBSTR name;
CComBSTR surname("Grimes");
name = GetFirstName();
name.Append("T ");
name += surname;
PassName(name);
name.Empty();
GetName(&name);
```

The destructor for the class ensures that the BSTR is freed when the object goes out of scope or is deleted, which prevents resource leaks. You can also attach a BSTR to an existing CComBSTR object, and if you need to free the BSTR before the CComBSTR is destroyed, you can get access to it using the Detach() method. The Copy() and CopyTo() methods allow you to make a copy of the BSTR using; both of these will copy binary data containing embedded NULs.

Finally, there are methods called ToLower() and ToUpper() that convert the BSTR to lower case or upper case letters, and LoadString() that will initialize the BSTR with an application string resource. All three of these will only work on the characters up to the first NUL.

To allow you to use CComBSTRs with STL containers, the class has operator<() and operator==(), but if you want to use a set<> or a list<> you must once again use the CAdapt class:

```
std::set<CAdapt<CComBSTR> > container;
```

Do bear in mind that operator<() (and the equality operator) use wcscmp() to compare strings, thereby assuming that there are no embedded NULs. This means that with a set<> or a map<>, you can only sort string BSTRs, and not BSTRs containing binary data, unless you define your own predicator.

The predicator shown below will handle binary CComBSTRs just fine. However, it doesn't provide true alphabetic ordering, and is not as efficient as using operator<() when you know that the BSTR will contain no NULs. If true alphabetic ordering is an issue, you could enhance this code to provide it, or use whatever rules for sorting that you think are appropriate.

```
struct less<CComBSTR> : binary_function<CComBSTR, CComBSTR, bool>
{
    bool operator()(const CComBSTR& _X, const CComBSTR& _Y) const
    {
        if (_X.m_str == NULL)
            return _Y.m_str ? true : false;

        const unsigned int lX = SysStringByteLen(_X.m_str);
        const unsigned int lY = SysStringByteLen(_Y.m_str);
        int ret = memcmp(_X.m_str, _Y.m_str, min(lX, lY));
        if (ret < 0)
            return true;
        if (ret > 0)
            return false;

        return lX < lY;
    }
};
```

Unlike _bstr_t, CComBSTR has limited parameter checking. To a large extent this is not much of a problem, because the BSTR SDK methods can be passed NULL pointers (but not invalid pointers) with impunity. A facility it has over _bstr_t, on the other hand, is in the two methods ReadFromStream() and WriteToStream(). These allow you to pass an IStream* pointer to the CComBSTR object, which will initialize itself from the stream, or write itself to the stream. These two methods are used by the ATL persistence classes to make object properties persistent. You will see this in use in Chapter 10.

# ATL Conversion Macros

Although you can initialize a CComBSTR with an ANSI string, the class does not have a conversion operator to get an ANSI string from a CComBSTR. Instead, you will need to access the BSTR buffer directly and convert it to a char buffer.

ATL defines a series of macros that allows you to perform this conversion. Because of the variable nature of strings, a buffer will need to be allocated for the conversion. Of course, the buffer must be released at some point to prevent resource leaks – _bstr_t::Data_t does this by holding a char* pointer that's deleted when the object is destroyed.

The ATL macros can't take this course of action because they are not part of any item that has a destructor. Instead, the macros allocate buffers on the *stack* (not the heap) using alloca(). The advantage of this approach is that when the function calling alloca() returns, the allocated memory is freed automatically. Clearly these conversions must therefore be implemented by macros (rather than functions) to ensure that the buffer is allocated in the stack frame in which it will be used.

The conversion macros ultimately call WideCharToMultiByte() or MultiByteToWideChar(), and these take a parameter giving the size of the buffer allocated for the conversion. There are thus two places where the length of the string to be converted is being calculated (the other is in the call to alloca()), and so it makes sense to do this calculation just once and assign it to a variable. However, the macros have been designed to return values, and as such they cannot define a local variable (this would require a code block). Instead, if you use these macros you need to declare this variable within your function, which you can do by calling the USES_CONVERSION macro.

For an example of using the conversion macros, take a look at the LPCSTR version of
CComBSTR::Append() in atlbase.h:

```
void Append(LPCSTR lpsz)
{
    USES_CONVERSION;
    LPOLESTR lpo = A2COLE(lpsz);
    Append(lpo, ocslen(lpo));
}
```

Here the A2COLE() macro is used to convert a LPCSTR into an LPCOLESTR, and the ATL-defined
function ocslen() returns the length of the string. The other conversion macros are:

| | | | |
|---|---|---|---|
| A2BSTR() | OLE2A() | T2A() | W2A() |
| A2COLE() | OLE2BSTR() | T2BSTR() | W2BSTR() |
| A2CT() | OLE2CA() | T2CA() | W2CA() |
| A2CW() | OLE2CT() | T2COLE() | W2COLE() |
| A2OLE() | OLE2CW() | T2CW() | W2CT() |
| A2T() | OLE2T() | T2OLE() | W2OLE() |
| A2W() | OLE2W() | T2W() | W2T() |

In these names, 'A' is an LPSTR, 'OLE' is an LPOLESTR, 'T' is an LPTSTR, 'W' is an LPWSTR, and 'C' is
const. So, A2W() converts an LPSTR to a LPWSTR. Some of these (for example A2BSTR() and
OLE2BSTR()) are actually implemented as inline functions.

You should try to use the const versions of these macros as much as possible, and also remember
that the string returned by the macros is temporary (except in the case of the x2BSTR() macros).

The Win32 conversion functions have a parameter to indicate the code page that will be used. By
default the default ANSI code page will be used (with the identifier CP_ACP), but if you want the
conversion macros to interrogate the system to see what code page it is using, you can define the
symbol _CONVERSION_USES_THREAD_LOCALE. This should be done on systems that do not use the
Latin character set.

# VARIANTs

A VARIANT is a discriminated union that holds data, and the type of that data. This is passed to a
COM object that can, if necessary, convert the data type to another. When you call a method on a
dispinterface with IDispatch::Invoke(), one of the arguments to the latter is a data packet that
contains the arguments to be passed to the former. This data packet is of type DISPPARAMS, and it
passes the parameters through an array of VARIANTs. The VARIANT type is defined in oaidl.idl:

```
typedef [unique] struct _wireVARIANT* wireVARIANT;
typedef [wire_marshal(wireVARIANT)] struct tagVARIANT VARIANT;

struct tagVARIANT
{
    union
    {
        struct __tagVARIANT
        {
```

```
        VARTYPE vt;
        WORD    wReserved1;
        WORD    wReserved2;
        WORD    wReserved3;
        union
        {
            ...
        } __VARIANT_NAME_3;
    } __VARIANT_NAME_2;
    DECIMAL decVal;
  } __VARIANT_NAME_1;
};
```

The anonymous union in the center holds the actual data described by the discriminator vt. VARIANTs are marshaled with the type _wireVARIANT, which is defined as:

```
struct _wireVARIANT
{
    DWORD   clSize;
    DWORD   rpcReserved;
    USHORT  vt;
    USHORT  wReserved1;
    USHORT  wReserved2;
    USHORT  wReserved3;

    [switch_type(USHORT), switch_is(vt)] union
    {
        [case(...)] ...;
    };
};
```

Again, I have missed out the full details of the union; you can look at oaidl.idl to see the actual definition. The clSize parameter holds the size of the data passed, and vt acts as the union discriminator. As with BSTR, the [wire_marshal()] helper functions used to marshal a VARIANT into a wireVARIANT are also exported from oleaut32.dll. Because the Universal Marshaler supports them, VARIANTs can always be marshaled across processes without difficulty.

When you use a VARIANT, you should initialize it with VariantInit(), which clears all the structure except for the union, and sets the discriminator to VT_EMPTY. When the type is VT_EMPTY, any code reading the VARIANT will ignore the contents of the union.

After initialization, you can pass the address of the VARIANT if an [out] parameter is required, or you can initialize the appropriate item in the union with your data and use the discriminator to specify the type of data. oleauto.h defines macros to do this, so to set the BSTR member, for example:

```
VARIANT var;
VariantInit(&var);
BSTR bstr = SysAllocString(L"Richard");
V_BSTR(&var) = bstr;
V_VT(&var) = VT_BSTR;
```

Once you've done this, the VARIANT owns the BSTR, so you should not call SysFreeString(). When the VARIANT is initialized, you can pass it to an object method and the marshaler will read the type of data that the VARIANT holds to ensure that the data is marshaled correctly.

After you have finished with a VARIANT, you *must* call VariantClear(). This method ensures that the item in the variable is properly released, so if the VARIANT has a BSTR, then SysFreeString() will be called. Similarly, if it contains an interface pointer, Release() will be called. You could use vt to determine the data type and then make an informed decision yourself as to how to release the data item, but VariantClear() is much easier.

The types that can be held in a VARIANT are given in this table:

| Type | Meaning | C++ Equivalent |
|---|---|---|
| VT_EMPTY | The VARIANT is empty | |
| VT_NULL | A SQL-type NULL | |
| VT_INT§ | INT | signed int |
| VT_UINT§ | UINT | unsigned int |
| VT_UI1 | BYTE | unsigned char |
| VT_UI2§ | USHORT | unsigned short |
| VT_UI4§ | ULONG | unsigned long |
| VT_I1§ | CHAR | signed char |
| VT_I2 | SHORT | signed short |
| VT_I4 | LONG | signed long |
| VT_R4 | FLOAT | float |
| VT_R8 | DOUBLE | double |
| VT_BOOL | VARIANT_BOOL | VARIANT_BOOL |
| VT_ERROR | SCODE | HRESULT |
| VT_CY | CY | CY |
| VT_DATE | DATE | DATE |
| VT_BSTR | BSTR | BSTR |
| VT_UNKNOWN | IUnknown* | IUnknown* |
| VT_DISPATCH | IDispatch* | IDispatch* |
| VT_ARRAY | SAFEARRAY* | SAFEARRAY* |
| VT_BYREF \| VT_DECIMAL§ | A pointer to a DECIMAL type | |

In addition to these, there are pointer versions of most of the primitive types, represented by ANDing vt with VT_BYREF. If you do put a pointer in a VARIANT, then you have the responsibility of making sure that the memory pointed to is freed – VariantClear() has no idea whether that memory is a pointer to a stack variable or a heap allocated variable. If you're familiar with the VARIANT type, you will notice some additional types (marked with §) – support for these was added in late versions of NT 3.51, and made it in to the Platform SDK for NT 4.0.

The data types that a VARIANT can hold are the usual C primitive data types, with the additional types CY, which is a currency type, DATE, which is a date type, and DECIMAL, which is used to pass a large decimal number with both a sign and exponent.

```
// From wtypes.idl
typedef union tagCY
{
   struct
   {
       unsigned long Lo;
       long          Hi;
   };
   LONGLONG int64;
} CY;

typedef double DATE;

typedef struct tagDEC
{
   USHORT wReserved;
   union
   {
      struct
      {
         BYTE scale;
         BYTE sign;
      };
      USHORT signscale;
   };
   ULONG Hi32;
   union
   {
      struct
      {
         ULONG Lo32;
         ULONG Mid32;
      };
      ULONGLONG Lo64;
   };
} DECIMAL;
```

*This list of variant types happen to be the same data types that the Universal Marshaler can handle. If you're using the Universal Marshaler and you want to pass a* struct *to a method, you have to package it as binary data and send it as a* SAFEARRAY. *Alternatively, you could wrap it up as an object and pass the* IDispatch* *for that object.*

If you receive a VARIANT holding one type and you need to have the data in another type, you may be able to change the VARIANT by calling a **data coercion function**. These are important if you're writing objects for use in untyped languages. The types that can be converted are:

| | | | | |
|---|---|---|---|---|
| unsigned char | char | float | CY | BOOL |
| unsigned short | short | double | BSTR | DECIMAL |
| unsigned long | long | DATE | IDispatch | |

> *You won't find documentation in the platform SDK for coercing from or to* unsigned short, unsigned long *or* DECIMAL *on Win32, although they are documented for WinCE. This documentation has not been updated since the first release of NT 3.51, when these types were not supported in Automation. Support for these types appeared in NT 3.51 service pack 5.*

Any of these types can be converted to any of the others, except for IDispatch, where the conversion is one way: from an IDispatch to another type. The conversion functions have names of the form VarT1FromT2(), where T1 is the new type and T2 is the original type. They take two parameters, the first being an [in] parameter of type T2, and the second an [out] parameter that's a pointer to T1. There is also a general function called VariantChangeType() that takes pointers to two VARIANTs (the source and destination) and a parameter that indicates the data type to coerce to. This function simply calls the appropriate conversion function based on the type held in the source variable and the coerce type. (If the data is VT_BYREF, the value referenced is coerced.)

The types T1 and T2 can be any of these identifiers:

| | | | | | | |
|---|---|---|---|---|---|---|
| UI1 | UI2 | UI4 | I1 | I2 | I4 | R4 |
| R8 | Date | Cy | Str | Disp | Bool | Dec |

Some of these conversion functions are straightforward: converting between the numeric data types works in the way you would expect. Others, like the conversions from DATE or CY to BSTR are more intelligent, in that they make sure that the correct international formatting is used.

The conversions from IDispatch to another type are another matter. These call Invoke() and do a property 'get' for DISPID_VALUE, which is the default member of a dispinterface. The functions then coerce the returned value to the new type. Of course, there may be cases when the conversion will result in an overflow, and in those circumstances the conversion functions return an HRESULT of DISP_E_OVERFLOW.

This procedure of calling VariantInit() when the VARIANT is created, and then calling VariantClear() when it is not longer used, is just crying out to be wrapped in a class constructor/destructor. Similarly, the mechanism of assigning a value to a VARIANT is clearly one that would be handled well by overloaded assignment operators.

# variant_t

In comutil.h, there is a definition for a compiler COM support class called _variant_t that wraps VARIANT access. The class has a copy constructor, and constructors for creating an object initialized with a VARIANT, and from various data types that can be held in a VARIANT. In addition to the BSTR type, you can also construct a _variant_t from a wchar_t* or a char*. These constructors are mirrored with equivalent assignment operators, but note that most of the new types that were introduced in the NT 4.0 Platform SDK are not supported, so you can't create a _variant_t from a ULONG, for example.

The _variant_t class derives from tagVARIANT, and therefore to get a pointer to a VARIANT, you can just upcast a _variant_t pointer. This means that wherever you can use a VARIANT, you can use a _variant_t, so if you want to use a type for which _variant_t does not provide a constructor, you can simply access the discriminator and then get the appropriate union member.

One oddity with this class is that if you call operator IDispatch*() when a _variant_t does not hold an IDispatch or an IUnknown pointer, the operator will attempt to coerce the type to an IDispatch pointer. This is guaranteed to fail with an error of DISP_E_TYPEMISMATCH, but the operator still makes the attempt. I would have expected the method to return the failure without attempting the coercion. The class also has equality operators, a method to clear the _variant_t, and methods called Attach() and Detach() that allow you to pass ownership of the VARIANT to (and extract it from) the object.

You can tell from this description that the class is a fairly thin wrapper around a VARIANT, but the salient point about it is that it makes sure that the VARIANT is initialized properly, and cleared when it's no longer in use.

# CComVariant

Like _variant_t, this ATL class also derives from tagVARIANT. There are constructors for BSTR and for char and wide character strings, and these ensure that the contained BSTR will be a Unicode string. However, they all use SysAllocString(), so embedded NULs are not supported. In addition, there are constructors and assignment operators that can be used to initialize the CComVariant with the various types that you can use in a VARIANT.

You'll notice that the string and VARIANT constructors look rather odd, for example (in atlbase.h):

```
CComVariant(LPCOLESTR lpszSrc)
{
    vt = VT_EMPTY;
    *this = lpszSrc;
}
```

This looks like the type is being set to VT_EMPTY, but the second line calls operator=(BSTR) to initialize the CComVariant (in this context an LPOLESTR can be treated as a BSTR). In fact, setting vt to VT_EMPTY is unnecessary in this constructor because it is almost immediately changed to VT_BSTR.

The class defines an equality operator to compare its data with a VARIANT, but note that although you *initialize* a CComVariant from a BSTR as a string (that is, up to the first NUL), the *comparison* is made on the entire BSTR. If you want a CComVariant to hold a BSTR that contains binary data, you should initialize it through its inherited bstrVal data member directly.

A major difference between this class and _variant_t is that there are no conversion operators in CComVariant to access the VARIANT data, so you have to access the union directly. On the flip side, CComVariant defines operators to read the VARIANT from (and write it to) a stream.

# Exceptions

However careful you are in writing your code, there will always be problems. You may find that your software is executed in situations that you hadn't designed it for, that there is other code running at the same time as yours that has an adverse effect on it, or that (perish the thought!) you have left a bug in your code.

Whatever caused the problem, *something* will return an error code or throw an exception. If an error status code is returned and your code ignores it, this could lead to a system exception being thrown at a later stage.

If exceptions are not caught, the system will handle the situation by closing down your application and presenting the user with the horrible Application Error dialog:

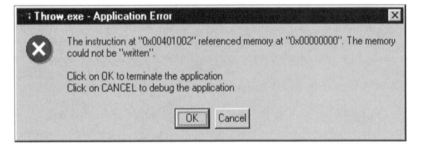

It is poor software that allows the user to see this dialog, because there are a number of ways to stop it appearing. For example, you can use structured exception handling (SEH – Win32 native exceptions) in your module's entry points to catch exceptions thrown by the system. Another approach is to call SetErrorMode(SEM_NOGPFAULTERRORBOX), so that when an exception occurs, this dialog is not shown and the process just dies silently. (Note that if your server is a remote EXE and the modal application error dialog is generated, there may not be anyone to click on OK to dismiss it!)

Of course, these are last chance solutions, and it is much better to stop exceptions propagating out of your code by either preventing or handling software errors. If a fault does occur in your server code, you should handle it and inform the client. Of course, the client was not necessarily written in C++ – it could be Java or Visual Basic, for example – and although other languages have their own exception mechanisms (Java uses classes derived from Throwable, and Visual Basic uses the On Error Goto syntax), they do not understand C++ exceptions. How then are exceptions handled in COM?

# Raw Exception Handling

There are two basic exception-handling mechanisms in COM. The simpler method uses error codes, but to get more information, COM servers can use **error objects**.

## HRESULT

Throwing C++ exceptions from a COM method is completely forbidden. The client may not be written in C++, and even if it is, you cannot guarantee the location of the object – it could be on a different machine or in a different process on the same machine as the client, and C++ exceptions cannot be thrown across processes. Even if the server is in-process, the object may be created in a different apartment (and hence a different thread) from the client, and C++ exceptions can't be caught across threads, either.

For all these reasons, COM methods do not throw exceptions. Instead, they return status codes of type HRESULT, which is a 32-bit value. When you get an HRESULT from a method call you use the SUCCEEDED() and FAILED() macros to check if the code indicates that the method succeeded or failed. A successful method usually returns S_OK, but you should *not* check for this. A method may succeed and use a different HRESULT to send back more information to the client.

A good example of the above is S_FALSE. This is a success code, and SUCCEEDED(S_FALSE) will return true, but the code is used to convey that a method succeeded but returned a Boolean false value. Enumeration interfaces use this code in the implementation of the Next() method that's called by a client to request a number of items. If all of the requested items are returned, the method returns S_OK, but if some or none of the items are returned it returns S_FALSE, not to indicate an error but to say that the enumeration has finished.

The facility of an HRESULT gives an indication of where the status code originated. When you access a COM object in another apartment, the COM runtime gets in between the client and server, and so the HRESULT could come from the object *or* from the COM runtime. Clearly, when an error occurs, it is important to determine who generated the status code.

You can use the HRESULT_FACILITY() macro to get the facility from a HRESULT. Codes in facilities other than FACILITY_ITF are defined by Microsoft, which has complete control over them. Codes in FACILITY_ITF are specific to the interface being called. You will find that most of the codes defined in winerror.h are from this facility, and you can choose either to use these or to create your own. In most cases you will use the Microsoft defined codes because they cover most problems and these error's description strings are compiled into the system DLLs, as you'll see in a moment.

If you decide to define a custom code, you're free to use any value from 0x0000 to 0xffff for the status part of the HRESULT. However, Microsoft has already defined FACILITY_ITF codes in the range 0x0000 to 0x01ff, so it is best to avoid these. Whatever you define though, remember that the code is only unique for the current interface.

Compare this with defining a Win32 error code, when you're allowed to use absolutely any code, as long as the customer bit (29) is set. The Win32 codes existed long before COM appeared on NT, and as such do not fit the COM HRESULT. If you look at the first half of winerror.h you will see that the Win32 codes, though usually representing failure, do not have the top bit set like HRESULT does. It would seem therefore that you cannot use SUCCEEDED() to test a code returned from Win32. To return a Win32 error code from an interface method, you should turn it into a HRESULT; you can do this by adding a success bit and giving it a facility of FACILITY_WIN32 (a value of 7). The HRESULT_FROM_WIN32() macro can be used to perform this task.

As an example, a common status code is 0x800706ba, but you won't find it in winerror.h, so what does it mean? Well, it clearly looks like a HRESULT, but it has been created from a Win32 code. How do I know that? The top bit is set, so it is a failure code and the WORD has a facility code of 7 so that means that it is a Win32 failure code. To get the status code, you need to take the bottom WORD, convert it to base 10 (1722) and finally look it up in winerror.h. This gives the code as RPC_S_SERVER_UNAVAILABLE – DCOM uses RPC to access remote objects, and this indicates that it cannot find the remote object server. The Error Lookup process from the Visual C++ Tools menu can be used to do this decoding.

Note that the description of a code comes from a call to:

```
FormatMessage(FORMAT_MESSAGE_FROM_SYSTEM, NULL, hr, ...)
```

where hr is an HRESULT. This Win32 API will return descriptive text for a system-defined HRESULT or a Win32 error code. If you have defined your own HRESULT, you need to make a message resource file for it and use:

```
FormatMessage(FORMAT_MESSAGE_FROM_HMODULE, hModule, hr, ...)
```

where hModule is a handle to the loaded message resource file. For full details on how to create a message resource file, take a look at *Professional DCOM Programming (Wrox Press; ISBN 186100060X; May 97)*.

In Visual C++ 6.0, the debugger has a neat new feature. If you add the string ",hr" to the name of a variable in a watch window, it will attempt to interpret the value of the variable as an HRESULT, and show the descriptive string if possible. Here, for example, I have a variable called hr with a value of 0x800706ba:

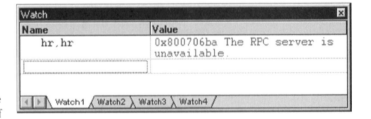

Since the return value of a function is usually returned in the (Intel) processor's EAX register, it is useful to have EAX, hr permanently in a watch window when you debug code.

Visual C++ also provides a pseudo-register called ERR. When you run a process under the debugger this holds the last error value, obtained by calling the Win32 GetLastError(). This is not the same as the value in EAX because not all functions return error codes!

## Status Codes and Exceptions

In the old days of C programs, the usual method of returning error codes from functions was to use a status code. However, the technique has problems that are apparent today in C++ programs that use HRESULTs. For a start, in C/C++ you don't *have* to read the return value from a function, and so the caller can simply ignore a status code. If you're conscientious, you will check the HRESULT from every method and handle the situation of a failure code. However, code that does this often indents its way past the edge of the screen and becomes hard to read.

In the following code, for example, I enumerate all the monikers in the running object table, obtaining the display string for each one. The details are unimportant, but note that it calls several COM API methods. Any of these can fail, and so the code must ensure that all interface pointers are released. To enforce this, I have used many nested if statements. An alternative would be to exit the function at the point of failure, but this would still require clean up either at that point (and hence repeated code throughout the routine), or a goto statement to a generic clean up routine (requiring that you check which resources need to be freed).

```
IRunningObjectTable* pRot;
HRESULT hr;
hr = GetRunningObjectTable(0, &pRot);

if (SUCCEEDED(hr))
{
   IBindCtx* pBC;
   hr = CreateBindCtx(0, &pBC);
   if (SUCCEEDED(hr))
   {
      IEnumMoniker* pEnumMoniker;
      hr = pRot->EnumRunning(&pEnumMoniker);
      if (SUCCEEDED(hr))
      {
         ULONG ulFetched = 1;
         do
         {
            IMoniker* pMoniker;
            hr = pEnumMoniker->Next(1, &pMoniker, &ulFetched);
            if (SUCCEEDED(hr) && ulFetched > 0)
            {
               LPOLESTR oleStr;
               hr = pMoniker->GetDisplayName(pBC, NULL, &oleStr);
               if (SUCCEEDED(hr))
               {
                  // Use the string here
                  CoTaskMemFree(oleStr);
               }
               else
                  OutputDebugString(_T("Cannot get String"));
               pMoniker->Release();
```

```
                }
                else
                {
                    if (FAILED(hr))
                        OutputDebugString(_T("Cannot get Monikers"));
                    else
                        ulFetched = 0;
                }
            }
            while (ulFetched > 0);

            pEnumMoniker->Release();
        }
        else
            OutputDebugString(_T("Cannot get enum"));
        pBC->Release();
    }
    else
        OutputDebugString(_T("Cannot get Bind Context"));
    pRot->Release();
}
else
    OutputDebugString(_T("Cannot get ROT"));
```

Nested if blocks like these make the code very difficult to read, but there would be an easy solution if only the COM calls threw exceptions – then, we could write code like this:

```
// Hypothetical code
try
{
    RunningObjectTablePtr Rot;
    BindCtxPtr BC;
    EnumMonikerPtr EnumMoniker;

    GetRunningObjectTable(0, &Rot);
    CreateBindCtx(0, &BC);
    Rot->EnumRunning(&EnumMoniker);

    ULONG ulFetched = 1;
    do
    {
        MonikerPtr Moniker;
        HRESULT hr = EnumMoniker->Next(1, &Moniker, &ulFetched);
        if (hr == S_FALSE)
            break;
        LPOLESTR oleStr;
        Moniker->GetDisplayName(BC, NULL, &oleStr);
        // Use the string here
        CoTaskMemFree(oleStr);
        Moniker.Release();
    }
    while (ulFetched > 0);
}
catch (COMException& e)
{
    OutputDebugString(e.GetDescription());
}
```

Just to reiterate, this code is hypothetical, but it's the sort of thing that you should expect to see when COM+ becomes available (In fact, you can get an almost identical effect with #import today, as you'll see later). It assumes that if a COM runtime function like CreateBindContext() fails, it will throw an exception of type COMException that can be used to obtain a description of the error. This has eliminated the multiple if (SUCCEEDED(hr)) blocks, and reduced the indentation levels considerably.

The problem of freeing resources has also been covered: the code uses smart pointer wrappers for the interfaces, so that when these objects are destroyed, their interfaces will be released. This happens when execution leaves the try() block, whether normally or through an exception. (In fact, there *are* smart pointer classes for these interfaces defined in comdef.h.)

Exceptions do not come for free: they have a cost both in code size and performance. However, it's clear that code that uses exception handling is far easier to read than code that does not. COM runtime functions might not throw exceptions (this would mean that they would only be usable from C++), but you're free to create your own wrapper functions that do, and I'll show you an example of just that in the section on _com_error in a couple of pages' time.

## Rich Error Handling

An HRESULT describes the status of a method call, and a string can describe that status. Previously, I mentioned that an HRESULT can be converted into a descriptive string using FormatMessage(), provided that a message resource file is provided. However, some status codes are very general – consider this interface method, called CreateAccount():

```
HRESULT CreateAccount([in, string] LPOLESTR strName);
```

This creates a new account object and inserts it into an internally held map<> of account objects. The function could fail if object creation fails (the name could contain invalid characters), or if the insertion into the map<> fails (an account with the same name might already exist). Furthermore, *either* of these operations could fail if there is a low memory condition.

How do you return these errors back to the client? There are no codes for "invalid character" or "already exists", and although there *is* an HRESULT called E_OUTOFMEMORY, how can you specify which operation it refers to? What we require is a far richer error reporting mechanism, and this is handled with **error objects** that support the IErrorInfo interface. (A complete discussion of this interface is left until Chapter 6.)

To use error objects, the object that generates the error should implement the ISupportErrorInfo interface. This has a single method called InterfaceSupportsErrorInfo() that takes a single parameter. Clients call this method passing the IID of a server interface, and if the object can generate error objects for the requested interface, the method should return S_OK. When a client gets an error HRESULT, it should call this method to check whether the faulting interface can generate error objects. The client can then call GetErrorInfo() to get hold of the error object for the current 'logical' thread. This method will return either the IErrorInfo interface on this object, or NULL if no object exists. The client can then call methods on this interface to get more information about the error:

```
    IBank* pBank = GetBankObjectFromSomewhere();
    HRESULT hr;
    hr = pBank->CreateAccount(strMyname);
    if (FAILED(hr))
    {
       ISupportErrorInfo* pSEI;
       HRESULT hr1;
       hr1 = pBank->QueryInterface(__uuidof(ISupportErrorInfo),
          reinterpret_cast<void**>(&pSEI));
       if (SUCCEEDED(hr))
       {
          _tprintf(_T("Error occurred in CreateAccount()\n"));
          // make sure that the interface supports error objects
          hr1 = pSEI->InterfaceSupportsErrorInfo(__uuidof(IBank));
          if (hr1 == S_OK)
          {
             // try to get the error object
             IErrorObject* pEO;
             if (S_OK == GetErrorInfo(&pEO))
             {
                // use the error object
                pEO->Release();
             }
             else
                _tprintf(_T("No rich error info, raw error code = %08x\n"), hr);
          }
          else
             _tprintf(_T("Interface does not support rich error info, ")
                _T("raw error code : %08x\n"), hr);
          pSEI->Release();
       }
       else
          _tprintf(_T("Object does not support rich error info, ")
             _T("raw error code : %08x\n"), hr);
    }
    pBank->Release();
```

You must *not* call GetErrorInfo() to determine if an interface supports error objects; this method is used to determine if an error object exists. If you do call this method on an object that does not support error objects you will get an exception thrown in the COM system – this is clearly a bug.

The server sets the information in an error object. When a method fails for some reason, it should create an error object by calling CreateErrorInfo(); this returns a pointer to an ICreateErrorInfo interface that has methods to set the information that will be passed back to the client. Once the server has set the information, it can call QueryInterface() for IErrorInfo and then pass this pointer to SetErrorInfo(), which associates the current thread of execution with the error object.

```
    // error in method, hr has an error code
    ICreateErrorInfo* pCEI;
    if SUCCEEDED(CreateErrorInfo(&pCEI))
    {
```

```
      pCEI->SetDescription(L"Error happened!");
      IErrorInfo* pEI;
      HRESULT hr1;
      hr1 = pCEI->QueryInterface(__uuidof(IErrorInfo),
         reinterpret_cast<void**>(&pEI));
      if (SUCCEEDED(hr1))
      {
         SetErrorInfo(0, pEI);
         pEI->Release();
      }
      pCEI->Release();
   }
   return hr;
```

Using error objects like this allows the server to pass information back to the client, including a descriptive string, a path to a help file, and a help context within that file that describes the error. The IErrorInfo interface is described in oaidl.idl with:

```
[
   object,
   uuid(1CF2B120-547D-101B-8E65-08002B2BD119),
   pointer_default(unique),
   local
]
interface IErrorInfo: IUnknown
{
   // Methods omitted
}
```

Using the [local] attribute implies that error objects are only accessible on the machine that they are created, which seems rather odd when their entire *raison d'être* is to convey information between object and client. In fact, error objects are transmitted to the client as out-of-band information (that is, it is transmitted along with method data, but it is not an explicit parameter of the method) and do not use standard marshaling. More information will be given in Chapter 6, but basically you can regard an error object as a hidden extra parameter to every method on the interfaces that support them, rather like the this pointer is a hidden parameter of every non-static method in a C++ class.

## com_error

So: COM doesn't throw exceptions. What can you do about it? Well, you can *use* exceptions, as long as you make sure that an exception *never* gets thrown out of an interface method. On the server side, you could make sure that all your interface methods have a catch block that translates all exceptions into HRESULTs, but you must be aware that such code will increase code size and reduce performance. You will therefore have to think carefully about what you gain by using exceptions. An example of such code is:

```
STDMETHODIMP CMyObject::DoWork()   // No exceptions thrown
{
   try
   {
      PerformTask();                 // This can throw a memory exception
   }
```

```
    catch(CMemoryException& e)
    {
        OutputDebugString(e.GetDescription());
        return E_OUTOFMEMORY;
    }
    catch(...)
    {
        OutputDebugString(_T("Unspecified error\n"));
        return E_FAIL;
    }
    return S_OK;
}
```

This is the barest of implementations, and in your code you may decide to create an error object to contain the information contained in your CMemoryException object. This server code ensures that exceptional circumstances are transmitted to the client as HRESULTs. On the client side, you can do the opposite – that is, hide HRESULTs by converting them into exceptions. To do this, you will need to provide a wrapper for all methods that return a HRESULT, which is a lot of work. Thankfully, most of it has been done for you in the #import generated classes.

_com_error is an exception class used by the compiler COM support classes. When an error occurs while you're using _bstr_t, _variant_t, or a class created from _com_ptr_t<>, an exception of type _com_error is thrown. All interface methods will be wrapped with a high-level method that converts HRESULTs into _com_error exceptions.

As an example, the following code will catch any errors generated when creating the object or accessing the interface:

```
// ComError.cpp
#include "stdafx.h"
#import "..\TimeServer\TimeServer.tlb"
using namespace TIMESERVERLib;

int _tmain()
{
    CoInitialize(NULL);
    try
    {
        DATE date = 0;
        IRemoteTimePtr pTime(__uuidof(RemoteTime));
        date = pTime->GetTime();

        SYSTEMTIME st = {0};
        VariantTimeToSystemTime(date, &st);
        _tprintf(_T("%04d-%02d-%02d %02d:%02d:%02d\n"),
            st.wYear, st.wMonth, st.wDay,
            st.wHour, st.wMinute, st.wSecond);
    }
    catch (const _com_error& e)
    {
        _tprintf(_T("Error: 0x%08x %s\n"), e.Error(),
            e.ErrorMessage());
    }
```

```
        CoUninitialize();
        return 0;
}
```

Here, I have wrapped the code from `Native2` in a C++ `try` block. If COM cannot create the object, access the interface, or access the method, or if the method returns an unsuccessful HRESULT, the wrappers will throw a `_com_error` exception that's handled by the `catch` block. To try this out, replace the line declaring the `IRemoteTimePtr` object with:

```
    IRemoteTimePtr pTime;
```

In other words, create a smart pointer with a NULL interface pointer. If you run this, you will get the following output to the command line:

```
    Error: 0x80004003 Invalid Pointer
```

In this particular case, the smart pointer class `IRemoteTimePtr`, which is derived from `_com_ptr_t<>`, generates the exception. If you look at the inline declaration for `operator->()` in `comip.h`, you will find:

```
    Interface* operator->() const throw(_com_error)
    {
        if (m_pInterface == NULL)
        {
            _com_issue_error(E_POINTER);
        }
        return m_pInterface;
    }
```

The smart pointer class checks whether the interface pointer is NULL, and calls the function `_com_issue_error()` if it is. The source for this function is not available (it's provided in `comsupp.lib`), but it's not very hard to work out what it does – it just passes the HRESULT to another method called `_com_raise_error()`. This method is a general exception routine that's prototyped in `comdef.h`:

```
    void __stdcall _com_raise_error(HRESULT hr, IErrorInfo* perrinfo = 0)
                                                        throw(_com_error);
```

If you choose to, you can provide your own version (perhaps if you want to provide a logging mechanism to write all thrown exceptions to an error log) – the default one just creates a `_com_error` and throws it, like this:

```
    void __stdcall _com_raise_error(HRESULT hr, IErrorInfo* perrinfo)
                                                        throw(_com_error)
    {
        _com_error e(hr, perrinfo);
        throw(e);
    }
```

When the preprocessor generates a smart pointer class from a type library, it wraps the method calls with exception handling. As you saw earlier in the chapter, in a different context, the GetTime() method for the IRemoteTimePtr class is:

```
inline DATE IRemoteTime::GetTime()
{
    DATE _result;
    HRESULT _hr = raw_GetTime(&_result);
    if (FAILED(_hr))
        _com_issue_errorex(_hr, this, __uuidof(this));
    return _result;
}
```

The method is declared in IRemoteTime because IRemoteTimePtr is a typedef for the _com_ptr_t<> template based on the IRemoteTime abstract class. It calls the interface method raw_GetTime(), and if the return value is an error code, it calls _com_issue_errorex(). This method has the prototype:

```
void __stdcall _com_issue_errorex(HRESULT, IUnknown*, REFIID)
                                                    throw(_com_error);
```

The last two parameters are the IUnknown of the object and the IID of the interface that returned the error result. The _com_error class wraps HRESULTs, and it can wrap an IErrorInfo interface if the object supports error objects. _com_issue_errorex() does all the work of calling QueryInterface() for the object's ISupportErrorInfo interface to see if there is an error object, and then calls GetErrorInfo() to get the IErrorInfo interface on the current error object. If Microsoft provided us with the source of _com_issue_errorex() it would look something like this:

```
void _com_issue_errorex(HRESULT hr, IUnknown* pUnk, REFIID riid)
                                                    throw(_com_error)
{
    IErrorInfoPtr ErrorInfo;
    if (pUnk)
    {
        try
        {
            ISupportErrorInfoPtr SEI(pUnk);
            HRESULT hr = SEI->InterfaceSupportsErrorInfo(riid);
            if (SUCCEEDED(hr))
                GetErrorInfo(0, &ErrorInfo);
        }
        catch (...)
        {
        }
    }
    _com_error e(hr, ErrorInfo);
    throw(e);
}
```

The methods of _com_error allow you to access the wrapped HRESULT and IErrorInfo interface. The class is shown here:

```
class _com_error
{
public:
    _com_error(HRESULT hr, IErrorInfo* perrinfo = NULL,
                                    bool fAddRef = false) throw();
    _com_error(const _com_error& that) throw();
    virtual ~_com_error() throw();

    _com_error& operator=(const _com_error& that) throw();
    HRESULT Error() const throw();
    WORD WCode() const throw();
    IErrorInfo* ErrorInfo() const throw();

    // IErrorInfo method accessors
    _bstr_t Description() const throw(_com_error);
    DWORD HelpContext() const throw();
    _bstr_t HelpFile() const throw(_com_error);
    _bstr_t Source() const throw(_com_error);
    GUID GUID() const throw();

    // FormatMessage accessors
    const TCHAR * ErrorMessage() const throw();

    // EXCEPINFO.wCode <-> HRESULT mappers
    static HRESULT WCodeToHRESULT(WORD wCode) throw();
    static WORD HRESULTToWCode(HRESULT hr) throw();

private:
    // Implementation details
};
```

The IErrorInfo wrapped methods are explained in more depth in Chapter 6, and give access to the rich error information held in an error object.

You're familiar with HRESULTs, but what are wCodes? You might remember that earlier on I said that codes with FACILITY_ITF are specific to the interface that returns them. I also mentioned that this means you can define your own HRESULTs, but it's best to avoid the status code range from 0x0000 to 0x001f. A wCode is the status code part of a user-defined HRESULT, *relative to* 0x0200. The static methods allow you to create a wCode from a HRESULT and vice versa, so if you call:

```
_com_error::WCodeToHRESULT(0);
```

the return value will be 0x80040200. This makes defining your own HRESULTs quite easy, and if you get an HRESULT, you can readily determine whether it is an object-defined code. The original purpose of wCodes was to provide a means of returning errors from Automation methods in the EXCEPINFO structure used by Automation objects.

The other method you will find interesting in the _com_error class is ErrorMessage(), which calls FormatMessage() to get the descriptive string for the HRESULT. The string returned is allocated by the system with LocalAlloc(), but the _com_error destructor ensures that when the exception object is destroyed, this string is correctly released.

All this is great if you're using smart pointer methods, but if you use COM runtime methods, you still have to check HRESULTs. One thing that you can do is to follow every API call with a check on its HRESULT:

```
HRESULT hr;
IRunningObjectTablePtr pRot;
hr = ::GetRunningObjectTable(0, &pRot);
if (FAILED(hr))
    _com_issue_error(hr);
```

This reduces the error checking required, and therefore the amount of indentation in code listings. In the following, I have defined a new namespace called Except to wrap the COM API that I intend to use:

```
// RotView.cpp
#include "stdafx.h"
#include <comdef.h>

#pragma warning(disable : 4290) // Disable "C++ Exception
                                // Specification ignored"

namespace Except
{
    VOID GetRunningObjectTable(DWORD, IRunningObjectTable** pprot)
        throw(_com_error)
    {
        HRESULT hr;
        if (!pprot)
            _com_issue_error(E_POINTER);
        hr = ::GetRunningObjectTable(0, pprot);
        if (FAILED(hr))
            _com_issue_error(hr);
    }
    VOID CreateBindCtx(DWORD, IBindCtx** ppbc)
        throw(_com_error)
    {
        HRESULT hr;
        if (!ppbc)
            _com_issue_error(E_POINTER);
        hr = ::CreateBindCtx(0, ppbc);
        if (FAILED(hr))
            _com_issue_error(hr);
    }

    VOID CoTaskMemFree(LPVOID pv)
        throw(_com_error)
    {
        HRESULT hr;
        IMallocPtr Malloc;
        hr = ::CoGetMalloc(1, &Malloc);
        if (FAILED(hr))
            _com_issue_error(hr);
        if (1 != Malloc->DidAlloc(pv))
            _com_issue_error(E_FAIL);
        Malloc->Free(pv);
    }
}
```

The functions defined above can now be used in the following code:

```
int _tmain()
{
   CoInitialize(NULL);

   try
   {
      IRunningObjectTablePtr Rot;
      IBindCtxPtr BC;
      IEnumMonikerPtr EnumMoniker;

      Except::GetRunningObjectTable(0, &Rot);
      Except::CreateBindCtx(0, &BC);
      Rot->EnumRunning(&EnumMoniker);

      ULONG ulFetched = 1;
      do
      {
         IMonikerPtr Moniker;
         HRESULT hr = EnumMoniker->Next(1, &Moniker, &ulFetched);
         if (hr == S_FALSE)
            break;
         LPOLESTR oleStr;
         Moniker->GetDisplayName(BC, NULL, &oleStr);
         _tprintf(_T("%S\n"), oleStr);
         Except::CoTaskMemFree(oleStr);
      }
      while (ulFetched > 0);
   }
   catch(const _com_error& e)
   {
      _tprintf(_T("%s\n"),e.ErrorMessage());
   }

   CoUninitialize();
   return 0;
}
```

You can test out these wrapper functions by changing the call to
`Except::GetRunningObjectTable()` to:

```
Except::GetRunningObjectTable(0, NULL);
```

This will stop the program with the message `Invalid Pointer`.

While this allows you to use exception semantics with the COM API, it is extremely tedious to write wrapper functions for all functions. If you decide that this is too much work, your only option is to wait for the COM+ runtime, which should do this work for you!

# ATL Error Handling

ATL has no exception classes. This reflects the fact that the core ATL classes are designed to be used to write small, efficient code: exception handling adds to the code size. This is particularly important if you are writing an inproc server because the server DLL will be loaded into the address space of the client. In fact, although code is more readable with exception support, it is not required – you just need to ensure that all errors are returned as HRESULTs. Throughout the rest of this book I will use the ATL route for writing servers, that is, no exception handling will be used, but I will use exceptions when writing client's to test the code (basically for the convenience of #import).

ATL makes extensive use of assertions, so that exceptional conditions are handled in the debugging phase. The nearest ATL gets to throwing exceptions is in the use of AtlReportError(). This method will be described in Chapter 6, but basically it's used to create error objects so that the client can then use rich error reporting to get this information.

# ATL as a COM Client

Often, you will use the services of other COM objects when you're writing your own COM objects, and you will need to access those objects as a client. The question is, do you access these objects using raw interface pointers, or do you use a smart pointer class like _com_ptr_t<> or CComPtr<>?

The first issue to bear in mind is that when you use a smart pointer template, code will be added to your project. If you are designing a small, lightweight object this may be important, and the extra effort required to manage reference pointers will be rewarded by the smaller server size.

If you do choose to use a smart pointer class, which should you use? Clearly, ATL smart pointer classes will provide smaller code than #import-generated classes, because the former do not use exception handling. In fact, when you create an ATL project, it will turn off exception handling by default.

Note that it is dangerous to use the #import smart pointer classes with exception support turned off. Although you can use the raw interface methods, _com_ptr_t<> defines a number of error throwing operators and it is not necessarily obvious which these are from looking at your client code.

So: is there ever a reason for using #import-generated classes in an ATL project? It all depends on the amount of help you want. The interface structs that are generated by #import by default provide high level methods. These hide HRESULTs by replacing them with exceptions, so that if a problem occurs, you have to handle them. Furthermore, they replace BSTRs, VARIANTs and interface pointer parameters with wrapper classes. This means that you don't have to worry about releasing these resources.

However, if the interfaces that you want to use don't return interface pointers, you don't have to use the smart pointer classes to use the high level methods. Indeed, you can use the #import generated interface classes with CComPtr<> and use it to call the high level methods.

Finally, #import is very useful for the ATL developer because it removes the requirement to use MIDL-generated files for most interfaces and classes. If an interface can be described by type information, then you can get #import to generate the C++ bindings and GUIDs. Since most object servers have their type information bound as a resource (ATL will do this by default), providing the headers for an object is as simple as #importing the object server.

What about interfaces that are not [oleautomation] compatible – that is, they use types or features not compatible with the Universal Marshaler? Type libraries don't hold this type of information, but remember that it's only used by marshalers – as long as you use the MIDL proxy-stub DLLs to marshal the interface, there are no problems with using this *and* #import. The structs generated will be compatible with those in the MIDL-generated header files.

# Summary

This chapter has contrasted the various methods of accessing COM objects. Access to interfaces using raw C++ pointers will always produce the most efficient code, but it is error prone. ATL provides the smart pointer template classes CComPtr<> and CComQIPtr<>, and if you use these your server code may be larger than using the interface pointers directly, but you are more likely to catch interface leaks. The Visual C++ compiler COM support classes can also be used to provide smart pointers, and these not only provide reference count maintenance, but also allow you to write code using the semantics of the interface, rather than the format dictated by the marshaling layer. There is a cost, however: _com_ptr_t<> based smart pointers use exceptions, and this adds to code size and reduces performance.

Now that you've seen the basic support for interface pointers, BSTRs and VARIANTs in ATL, it's time to take a look at the overall architecture of ATL, which is the subject of the next chapter.

# 2

# ATL Architecture

The purpose of this chapter is to provide a very general overview of the main classes used in ATL, and to outline how these classes fit together to give you a robust DLL or EXE server.

To be a viable proposition, a COM template library must provide, at the very least, implementations for the following:

- ❑   IUnknown
- ❑   Class factories
- ❑   The server module's entry points
- ❑   Registration

These must take into account the aggregation and threading models that COM objects can use, and the ways in which objects can be created. The implementations must also be flexible, extensible, and efficient. During the course of the chapter, you'll see how ATL provides for each of these areas.

## IUnknown Implementation

Despite having three methods, IUnknown is responsible for just two features:

- ❑   Handling the lifetime of an interface
- ❑   Returning other interface pointers on the same object

Each of these areas has its own subtleties.

# Lifetime – AddRef() and Release()

At its simplest, implementing AddRef() and Release() – the lifetime methods of IUnknown – is just a matter of incrementing and decrementing a reference count for the object, deleting the object when the object's reference count drops to zero, and locking the server for as long as the object is alive.

*ATL mostly uses multiple inheritance, so a single reference count is shared by all the interfaces of an object. One of the main benefits of multiple inheritance is that it allows a single implementation of the IUnknown methods to be used by all the interfaces on an object. However, this is just an implementation detail – it is* not *a requirement of COM.*

However, this is too simple for real-world use. Objects may be created on the stack or on the heap, the lifetime of an object may or may not have some effect on the lifetime of the server, and the object could be aggregated. Each of these considerations has an effect on the implementation of AddRef() and Release(). (Aggregation also affects the implementation of QueryInterface().)

ATL encapsulates these aspects of the IUnknown implementation in a set of CComObjectxxx<> classes. This allows you to implement your COM objects without limiting them to being used in one particular way. If you want to create an object on the stack, you can use CComObjectStack<>. If you want to create an object that doesn't lock the server, you can use CComObjectNoLock<>. If you want to create an object to be aggregated, you can use CComAggObject<>. More usually, you will create your objects using CComObject<>. CComObject<>s are created on the heap, lock the server during their lifetime, and don't provide support for aggregation.

*Further details of these templates will be given throughout this chapter, and the final section will give a comparison of each.*

Because your implementation may need to be used in any of these situations without you having to change your object-specific code, these classes fit *below* your class in the inheritance hierarchy. In other words, CComObject<CYourATLClass> derives from CYourATLClass.

## *InternalAddRef() / InternalRelease()*

The implementations of the IUnknown methods in the CComObjectxxx<> classes provide code that is specific to the situation in which the class will be used, but much of the implementation is still delegated to methods further up the inheritance tree.

Where the CComObjectxxx<> class maintains the reference count (and isn't used for creating an aggregated object), the AddRef() and Release() implementations delegate to the following methods, which must be provided by your class or one of its base classes:

```
ULONG InternalAddRef();
ULONG InternalRelease();
```

Typically, these methods will be provided by the ATL class CComObjectRootEx<>, from which your own class will derive:

```
template <class ThreadModel>
class CComObjectRootEx : public CComObjectRootBase
{
public:
    typedef ThreadModel _ThreadModel;
    typedef _ThreadModel::AutoCriticalSection _CritSec;
    typedef CComObjectLockT<_ThreadModel> ObjectLock;

    ULONG InternalAddRef()
    {
        ATLASSERT(m_dwRef != -1L);
        return _ThreadModel::Increment(&m_dwRef);
    }

    ULONG InternalRelease()
    {
        ATLASSERT(m_dwRef > 0);
        return _ThreadModel::Decrement(&m_dwRef);
    }

    void Lock() {m_critsec.Lock();}
    void Unlock() {m_critsec.Unlock();}

private:
    _CritSec m_critsec;
};
```

Here you can see that `InternalAddRef()` and `InternalRelease()` just call the static `Increment()` or `Decrement()` methods appropriate to the threading model used. The member that is incremented or decremented (`m_dwRef`) is inherited from the base class `CComObjectRootBase`.

You could decide to override these methods if you wished, perhaps to provide reference count debugging information. However, you really don't need to go to these lengths because ATL provides extensive debugging support, as explained in Chapter 6. You can rely on these methods to do the right thing without any intervention on your part.

> `CComObjectRootBase` *provides a number of other reference-counting methods; these are required for aggregation support, as explained later in the chapter.*

# Returning Interface Pointers – QueryInterface()

As mentioned earlier, the `CComObjectxxx<>` class that you use to create your object provides the implementation of the three `IUnknown` methods. Typically, when you create a COM object, you will use `CComObject<>`, so we'll look at the `QueryInterface()` implementation provided by that class first. Most of the `CComObjectxxx<>` classes follow the same implementation, but later in the chapter, we'll see how the implementation differs when aggregation is thrown into the mix.

`CComObject<>::QueryInterface()` simply calls `_InternalQueryInterface()` which is implemented by the `BEGIN_COM_MAP()` macro applied to your class. If you look at this macro in `Atlcom.h`, you can see that `_InternalQueryInterface()` just calls the `InternalQueryInterface()` function provided by `CComObjectRootBase`. This function provides some debugging support to print out what interfaces are queried and whether the query is successful, then it calls an ATL function called `AtlInternalQueryInterface()`, which does all the hard work.

This diagram summarizes this implementation of `IUnknown`:

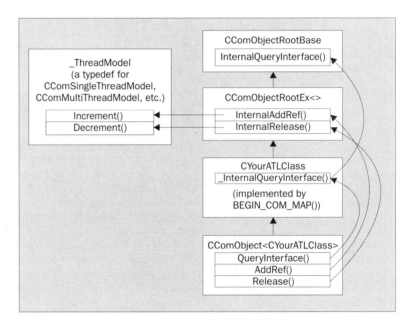

## The COM Map

As mentioned earlier, ATL provides support for `QueryInterface()` through a method called `_InternalQueryInterface()`, this *must* be implemented in your ATL class. You do this by using a **COM map**:

```
BEGIN_COM_MAP(CPinger)
    COM_INTERFACE_ENTRY(IPing)
END_COM_MAP()
```

This list of all the interfaces that the COM class implements would perhaps have been more accurately named the 'interface map', but it's too late to change terminology now. The core of the COM map is an array that contains information about how to get the interface pointer for an interface. The `AtlInternalQueryInterface()` code can simply traverse the array until it gets the IID that has been requested, and then use the other information for that array element to find the pointer for the interface. This makes the querying code generic.

The `BEGIN_COM_MAP()` and `END_COM_MAP()` macros implement `_InternalQueryInterface()` in your class. The `COM_INTERFACE_ENTRY()` macro adds entries in a `static` array that the method will check when a request for an interface is received.

_InternalQueryInterface() obtains a pointer to the array (which you too can obtain by calling the public method _GetEntries()) and passes it to InternalQueryInterface(). InternalQueryInterface() calls the global function AtlInternalQueryInterface() which iterates through all the entries in the array until the required interface is found, or the end of the array is reached.

This interface information is contained in items of type _ATL_INTMAP_ENTRY:

```
struct _ATL_INTMAP_ENTRY
{
   const IID* piid;
   DWORD dw;
   _ATL_CREATORARGFUNC* pFunc;
};
```

This simple struct hides the flexibility that it gives to the COM map. The piid member holds a pointer to the IID of an interface that the object supports. This member is checked by AtlInternalQueryInterface() to see whether the object supports the requested interface. pFunc can have one of three values: NULL, 1 or a valid function pointer. If it is NULL, it indicates that the entry is the end of the COM map. If it is 1 (the constant _ATL_SIMPLEMAPENTRY), it indicates that the dw member is a vptr offset into the object. In this case, ATL can access the vptr using:

```
(IUnknown*)((int)this + dw);
```

If pFunc is a function pointer, then the interface pointer is obtained by calling the function. This (global or class static) function must have the following prototype:

```
HRESULT WINAPI func(void* pv, REFIID riid, LPVOID* ppv, DWORD dw);
```

The this pointer of your ATL class instance is passed as the first parameter, riid is the IID of the interface to find, and if the function is successful, a pointer is returned in ppv. The last parameter, dw, is a value specific to the particular method and comes directly from the dw member of _ATL_INTMAP_ENTRY.

Note that the function should return S_OK, E_NOINTERFACE or S_FALSE. The first two are the acceptable return values from QueryInterface() according to the COM specification, and these stop any further searching for an interface. If the function returns S_OK, then the interface pointer is returned in ppv; if E_NOINTERFACE is returned, it means that the interface is not part of the object, and this error will be returned back to the client. The other value, S_FALSE indicates not that the search for the interface has failed, but only that func cannot find it, so the search continues to the next item in the COM map.

## COM_INTERFACE_ENTRYxxx() Macros

Entries in the array are filled using the COM_INTERFACE_ENTRYxxx() macros, which you place in the COM map in the order that you want them checked. The first entry will always be used when IUnknown is requested.

The ATL headers define 16 macros, which are given in the following table:

| Macro | Notes |
| --- | --- |
| COM_INTERFACE_ENTRY(x) | Most commonly used macro; just requires the interface name |
| COM_INTERFACE_ENTRY_IID(iid, x) | Explicitly give the IID of the interface x |
| COM_INTERFACE_ENTRY2(x, x2) | Used when x is inherited via more than one base class |
| COM_INTERFACE_ENTRY2_IID(iid, x, x2) | A combination of COM_INTERFACE_ENTRY_IID() and COM_INTERFACE_ENTRY2() |
| COM_INTERFACE_ENTRY_AGGREGATE(iid, punk) | Forwards a QueryInterface() for iid to punk |
| COM_INTERFACE_ENTRY_AGGREGATE_BLIND (punk) | Forwards a QueryInterface() for any IID to punk |
| COM_INTERFACE_ENTRY_AUTOAGGREGATE (iid, punk, clsid) | Automatically creates aggregate if required |
| COM_INTERFACE_ENTRY_AUTOAGGREGATE_ BLIND(punk, clsid) | A combination of COM_INTERFACE_ENTRY_AGGREGATE_ BLIND() and COM_INTERFACE_ENTRY_ AUTOAGGREGATE() |
| COM_INTERFACE_ENTRY_BREAK(x) | This is used for debugging. |
| COM_INTERFACE_ENTRY_CHAIN (classname) | Check classname for interfaces |
| COM_INTERFACE_ENTRY_FUNC (iid, dw, func) | Run func to test for the interface iid |
| COM_INTERFACE_ENTRY_FUNC_BLIND (dw, func) | Run func for any interface |
| COM_INTERFACE_ENTRY_NOINTERFACE(x) | Indicates that this object does not implement this interface |
| COM_INTERFACE_ENTRY_TEAR_OFF (iid, x) | Used to specify that an interface is a tear-off |
| COM_INTERFACE_ENTRY_CACHED_TEAR_ OFF(iid, x, punk) | Used to specify that an interface is a tear-off and cached in punk |

- ❑ x is an interface, which is usually a base class of the ATL object
- ❑ x2 is used to specify a base class through which an interface is obtained
- ❑ iid is the IID of the interface
- ❑ punk is a pointer to an IUnknown interface

❑ `clsid` is used in the aggregation macros to specify the CLSID of the object to create if required

❑ `classname` is the C++ class to be checked for an COM map

❑ `func` is a function to run to test for the interface

> Note that I haven't included the `COM_INTERFACE_ENTRY_IMPL()` macros found in ATL 2.1 in this table. Although these macros are present in ATL 3.0 (for compatibility), they are no longer necessary since ATL's implementation classes now derive directly from the interfaces that they implement.

In the table, `COM_INTERFACE_ENTRY_FUNC()` is the generic version of most of the COM map macros. It fills the `_ATL_INTMAP_ENTRY` structure directly with the parameters that you supply.

The difference between `COM_INTERFACE_ENTRY_FUNC()` and `COM_INTERFACE_ENTRY_FUNC_BLIND()` is that the former runs `func` only when a request is made for a specific interface, while the latter will run `func` for all interfaces, so you can use it as a catchall at the end of the COM map. The `_BLIND()` macro sets the `piid` member of the `_ATL_INTMAP_ENTRY` entry to NULL. `AtlInternalQueryInterface()` can test for this and so ensure that the `pFunc` member is set. Note that if a function mentioned in a `_BLIND()` macro fails, the search will continue with the next entry in the COM map. This is in contrast to a function called as a non-blind check.

## Aggregation

Aggregation allows an object to expose the interfaces of another object – the inner object – as if they are its own. Clearly, this inner object must be created at some point, but `COM_INTERFACE_ENTRY_AGGREGATE()` and `COM_INTERFACE_ENTRY_AGGREGATE_BLIND()` assume that the inner object has been already created, and its IUnknown is passed via the `punk` parameter. The auto-aggregation macros allow this inner object creation to be delayed until the interface is actually requested. They indicate that the object should check the `punk` parameter; if it is NULL, the object specified by the `clsid` parameter should be created.

Here's an example of aggregating objects:

```
BEGIN_COM_MAP(CMyObject)
   COM_INTERFACE_ENTRY(IMyObject)
   COM_INTERFACE_ENTRY_AGGREGATE(IItfTwo, pTwo.p)
   COM_INTERFACE_ENTRY_AUTOAGGREGATE(IItfThree, pThree.p, CLSID_Three)
END_COM_MAP()

CComPtr<IItfTwo> pTwo;
CComPtr<IItfThree> pThree;

HRESULT FinalConstruct()
{
   return pTwo.CoCreateInstance(
                     CLSID_Two, GetUnknown(), CLSCTX_INPROC_SERVER);
}
```

As you can see, the pTwo interface pointer must be initialized when the object is created (here I use the member method of the CComPtr<> smart pointer class). The pThree pointer is not initialized in FinalConstruct() because it is auto-aggregated. This highlights another important difference between the two aggregation mechanisms: if the creation of pTwo fails in FinalConstruct(), then the creation of the CMyObject will also fail. However, if the creation of pThree fails when a client calls QueryInterface() for the interface exposed through aggregation, then a failure HRESULT will be returned, but the outer object will still exist.

### Tear-off Interfaces

**Tear-off interfaces** are used in situations where the interface is rarely used, where its initialization requires some expensive resource, or when initialization will take a long time and is best delayed until it's needed. Normally, interfaces are implemented as part of the ATL object, but tear-off interfaces are implemented in a separate C++ object that can be created dynamically when the interface is requested. If you use COM_INTERFACE_ENTRY_TEAR_OFF(), then a new tear-off object will be created whenever the interface is requested. This does not violate the COM rules, which just say that when you QueryInterface() for IUnknown on an instance, the same pointer should always be returned. However, creating a new tear-off can be wasteful, especially if the tear-off uses expensive resources.

A *cached* tear-off will save the interface pointer in an instance variable on the first occasion that the tear-off interface is requested. If that interface is requested again later on, the cached value will be returned. An example of a tear-off interface will be shown in the next chapter.

### Debugging

COM_INTERFACE_ENTRY_BREAK() is helpful in debugging your object because when the specified interface is queried, the _Break() method will be called. The default implementation of this, in CComObjectRootBase, will call DebugBreak() – that is, the debugger will stop the server executing. This implementation doesn't return an interface pointer, but it does return S_FALSE, which means that the AtlInternalQueryInterface() function should continue to look for the interface in the remaining members of the message map. If you are interested in what happens when a client calls QueryInterface() for a particular interface, you should add the COM_INTERFACE_ENTRY_BREAK() macro in the COM map *before* the actual macro that gives access to the interface. More details about debugging can be found in Chapter 6.

### Chaining

If you have several objects in your project that have interfaces in common, you may decide to put these interface implementations together in some base class, and then access this code by deriving your classes from it. Such a scheme is achieved by using the COM_INTERFACE_ENTRY_CHAIN() macro.

What you must do is derive your child classes and then add the interfaces specific to the object to the COM map. You have to implement at least one interface in the derived class so that you can add an entry that will be used for IUnknown. After these interface entries, you should add the COM_INTERFACE_ENTRY_CHAIN() macro to point to the base class. When this entry is reached during a QueryInterface() search, the COM map of the specified base class is checked before moving on to the remaining members of the derived class COM map.

### No Interface

When `AtlInternalQueryInterface()` reaches the end of the COM map without finding the requested interface, it will return `E_NOINTERFACE`. However, you can accelerate this process by using the `COM_INTERFACE_ENTRY_NOINTERFACE()` macro, which specifies that the object does not support the specified interface. The main reason for using this macro rather than letting `AtlInternalQueryInterface()` check the entire map and fail is that it allows you quickly to return `E_NOINTERFACE` for interfaces that you know the object doesn't implement, but for which it is likely to be queried.

If you only implement a few interfaces on your object, then you can easily get away without using this interface – indeed, it can actually *increase* processing if you use it to check for too many interfaces. However, if you have a large COM map, or if you use the `_CHAIN()` macro and the chained class implements an interface that you do not want exposed, or if you use some complicated processing with the `_FUNC_BLIND` macro, then it does become useful. Typically, you place this macro at the top of the COM map, just after the entry for the interface that implements `IUnknown`. The interfaces that you should use it to deny are common ones like `IMarshal`.

## COM Map Functions

The various `func` prototyped functions that are used in these macros are shown in the following table. Although you can write your own versions of these, default versions are inherited as `static` members of `CComObjectRootBase`.

| func | Meaning of dw |
|------|---------------|
| _Break() | n/a |
| _Cache() | The `CreateInstance()` that will create and cache an interface pointer |
| _Chain() | Data used to call `InternalQueryInterface()` |
| _Creator() | An appropriate `CreateInstance()` method to create a tear-off object |
| _Delegate() | The offset within the ATL class of the aggregated object |
| _NoInterface() | n/a |

For some of these, it is clear which macro calls the function, but there are some for which it's not so obvious. `_Creator()` is called for tear-off interfaces, `_Cache()` is called for the cached tear-offs and the auto-aggregated interfaces (where an object is created and then cached for later use), and `_Delegate()` is used for the other aggregated interfaces. Let's take a closer look at these methods.

### _Creator()

As the name suggests, this creates an appropriate object that implements the tear-off interface. This object manages its own lifetime, but delegates `QueryInterface()` requests through the class that implements the COM object.

The COM_INTERFACE_ENTRY_TEAR_OFF() macro uses the following as the dw member of the _ATL_INTMAP_ENTRY. It will be passed in the dw parameter to the _Creator() function:

```
&_CComCreatorData<CComInternalCreator<CComTearOffObject< x > > >::data
```

This is the address of the static data member of the _CComCreatorData<> class, which is declared as:

```
struct _ATL_CREATORDATA
{
    _ATL_CREATORFUNC* pFunc;
};

template <class Creator>
class _CComCreatorData
{
public:
    static _ATL_CREATORDATA data;
};

template <class Creator>
_ATL_CREATORDATA _CComCreatorData<Creator>::data = {Creator::CreateInstance};
```

The _CComCreatorData<> class initializes its static data member by using the address of the CreateInstance() function of the class provided as its template argument. Thus, the dw parameter to _Creator() gives access to an appropriate CreateInstance() function provided by CComInternalCreator<>. The CreateInstance() method in CComInternalCreator<> calls new on its own template argument to create the tear-off (an object of type CComTearOffObject<>) and then FinalConstruct() to initialize it.

### _Cache()

The BEGIN_COM_MAP() macro implements a minimal version of this method to apply thread synchronization locking before calling the member in CComObjectRootBase with the same name. A pointer to the static member of a creator class is passed as the dw parameter to _Cache() in much the same way as with _Creator(). This is called in the two cases of cached tear-off and auto-aggregation.

In the first case, CComCreator<> provides the CreateInstance() that will create the tear-off; the second case is more interesting. In it, the dw parameter is a CComAggregateCreator<> template that is passed the class name of the outer object (so that the IUnknown can be obtained) and the CLSID of the object that should be aggregated.

### _Chain()

The dw parameter of the _Chain() function is passed the address of the data member of the _CComChainData<> class by the COM_INTERFACE_ENTRY_CHAIN() macro. As with _CComCreatorData<>, _CComChainData<> is just provided as a way to initialize a struct based on a template argument – in this case the struct is called _ATL_CHAINDATA:

```
struct _ATL_CHAINDATA
{
   DWORD dwOffset;
   const _ATL_INTMAP_ENTRY* (WINAPI *pFunc)();
};

template <class base, class derived>
class _CComChainData
{
public:
   static _ATL_CHAINDATA data;
};

template <class base, class derived>
_ATL_CHAINDATA _CComChainData<base, derived>::data =
                      {offsetofclass(base, derived), base::_GetEntries};
```

This structure holds the address of the _GetEntries() method in the specified base class, and the
offset of the derived class vptr within the class. _Chain() uses this second item of data to construct a
pointer to the derived class. It then calls this version of _GetEntries(), which returns the COM
map data for the base class. These two items of data are passed to InternalQueryInterface()
which, as you know, starts the search for the interface.

### _Delegate()

Mercifully, this is fairly straightforward. The dw parameter has the offset of the data member that has
been initialized to point to the aggregated object. _Delegate() obtains this IUnknown pointer and
simply calls QueryInterface() to try to obtain the required interface.

## Example: Chaining QueryInterface()

As an example of some of these operations, imagine a problem that requires the creation of
'employee' objects. These will all have an interface called IEmployee that has properties pertinent to
all employees (name, employee number). In this example, there will be two types of employee –
Developer and SalesRep – that have interfaces appropriate to their type. So, the IDeveloper
interface has a property to hold the type of PC the developer uses and her domain username, while
the ISalesRep interface has a property to indicate the type of car he drives. The implementation of
IEmployee is common to both types of employee, making it a good candidate for chaining.

You can start by creating an ATL DLL project called Company. With the Object Wizard, add two
simple objects, Developer and SalesRep. Next, right click on IDeveloper in the ClassView,
select Add Property... from the context menu, and then add a property called Computer that has a
Property Type of BSTR. Then, add another BSTR property called UserName, and make sure that it's
read-only by unchecking the Put Function box. Finally, add a BSTR property called Car to the
ISalesRep interface.

Because this is a very simple example, these interfaces will simply give access to an object instance
variable. So, for IDeveloper, add the following declaration:

```
// IDeveloper
public:
   STDMETHOD(get_UserName)(/*[out, retval]*/ BSTR *pVal);
```

```
    STDMETHOD(get_Computer)(/*[out, retval]*/ BSTR *pVal);
    STDMETHOD(put_Computer)(/*[in]*/ BSTR newVal);
private:
    CComBSTR m_bstrComputer;
};
```

Implement the `Computer` methods like this:

```
STDMETHODIMP CDeveloper::get_Computer(BSTR *pVal)
{
    return m_bstrComputer.CopyTo(pVal);
}

STDMETHODIMP CDeveloper::put_Computer(BSTR newVal)
{
    m_bstrComputer = newVal;
    return S_OK;
}
```

We'll come back to the `UserName` methods in a moment, but for now you can repeat this step for `ISalesRep` and its private member `m_bstrCar`.

So far, so good; now you need to add the `IEmployee` interface. I'll say much more about adding new interfaces to your code in the next chapter, but for now you can just follow these steps. First, use the Object Wizard to create a new object called `Employee`. You don't *need* a new object, but you want the Object Wizard to generate code for you that you can edit.

Next, you need to edit the IDL file and remove the declaration for the `Employee` object in the `library` statement, and then add the `IEmployee` interface to each of the existing `coclass`es. Now open `Company.cpp`, delete the `#include` for `Employee.h`, and delete the entry for `CEmployee` in the object map so that it looks like this:

```
BEGIN_OBJECT_MAP(ObjectMap)
    OBJECT_ENTRY(CLSID_Developer, CDeveloper)
    OBJECT_ENTRY(CLSID_SalesRep, CSalesRep)
END_OBJECT_MAP()
```

The `Employee` class should not be used to create COM objects, so open `Employee.h` and remove the `DECLARE_REGISTRY_RESOURCEID()` macro, and `CComCoClass<>` from the base class list. Last of all, you should remove `IDR_EMPLOYEE` from the `"REGISTRY"` entry in ResourceView.

Now you can use ClassView to add the properties of the `IEmployee` interface: `Name` (BSTR) and `EmployeeNo` (short). Implement these in the `CEmployee` class using a `CComBSTR` and a `short` data member, both *protected*, and initialize the `short` member to 0 in the constructor. This class will be a base for `CDeveloper` and `CSalesRep`, so edit the headers of both of these and replace the mention of `CComObjectRootEx<>` with `CEmployee`, like this:

```
#include "Employee.h"

class ATL_NO_VTABLE CDeveloper :
    public CEmployee,
```

```
    public CComCoClass<CDeveloper, &CLSID_Developer>,
    public IDispatchImpl<IDeveloper, &IID_IDeveloper, &LIBID_COMPANYLib>
{
public:
    CDeveloper()
    {
    }

DECLARE_REGISTRY_RESOURCEID(IDR_DEVELOPER)

DECLARE_PROTECT_FINAL_CONSTRUCT()

BEGIN_COM_MAP(CDeveloper)
    COM_INTERFACE_ENTRY(IDeveloper)
    COM_INTERFACE_ENTRY2(IDispatch, IDeveloper)
    COM_INTERFACE_ENTRY_CHAIN(CEmployee)
END_COM_MAP()
```

So, what exactly has this achieved? Well, for a start, the class now derives from CEmployee and so the methods used to implement IUnknown are inherited from the CComObjectRootEx<> base of CEmployee. Second, since both CDeveloper and CEmployee implement the IDispatch methods, you need to specify which will be used. In this example, I have decided to use the implementation of IDispatch available through the IDeveloper dual interface.

*More details of why this is a problem, and how to solve it, will be given in the next chapter.*

Do you remember the IDeveloper::UserName property? I want to implement this as a string generated from the employee name and number, which is why the data members were protected in CEmployee. Open Developer.cpp and implement the get_UserName() method like this:

```
STDMETHODIMP CDeveloper::get_UserName(BSTR *pVal)
{
    USES_CONVERSION;
    TCHAR userName[256] = {0};
    wsprintf(userName, _T("USR_%S%08x"), m_bstrName, m_sEmployeeNo);
    *pVal = SysAllocString(T2COLE(userName));
    return S_OK;
}
```

This accesses the name and employee number from the base class to generate the username string. Finally, to handle calls on QueryInterface() for IEmployee, I have added the base class to the COM map with the COM_INTERFACE_ENTRY_CHAIN() macro.

With the ATL project compiled, I created this very simple Visual Basic client application. The code listed here implements the dialog you can see on the next page; the two buttons are called cmdCreate and cmdDetails, while the name of the multi-line text box is txtdetails. Don't forget that you'll need to add the **Company 1.0 Type Library** to the project's references to make it work.

```
Dim Fred As SalesRep
Dim Bill As Developer
```

```
Private Sub cmdCreate_Click()
    Dim itf As IEmployee
    Set Fred = New SalesRep

    Fred.Car = "Viper"
    Set itf = Fred
    itf.Name = "Fred"
    itf.EmployeeNo = 12

    Set Bill = New Developer
    Bill.Computer = "PentiumPro 200"
    Set itf = Bill
    itf.Name = "Bill"
    itf.EmployeeNo = 13
    cmdDetails.Enabled = True
End Sub

Private Sub cmdDetails_Click()
    Dim itf As IEmployee
    Set itf = Fred
    txtdetails = itf.Name & " " & Str$(itf.EmployeeNo) & " has a " _
        & Fred.Car & vbCrLf
    Set itf = Bill
    txtdetails = txtdetails & itf.Name & " " & Str$(itf.EmployeeNo) _
        & " has a " & Bill.Computer & vbCrLf
    txtdetails = txtdetails & itf.Name & " uses " & Bill.UserName
End Sub
```

Note that when you call Set in Visual Basic to assign an interface variable to an existing object, you are performing a call to QueryInterface().

When you run this example and click on the **Create Employees** button, two objects will be created – one of each type. When you click on the **Get Details** button, the code queries each object for its IEmployee interface and uses this to obtain the name and employee number details of each employee object.

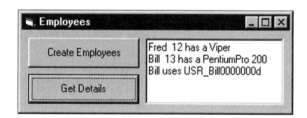

This is a simple example, but you can see the principle. As a final test, try changing the COM map to exclude IEmployee:

```
BEGIN_COM_MAP(CSalesRep)
    COM_INTERFACE_ENTRY(ISalesRep)
    COM_INTERFACE_ENTRY_NOINTERFACE(IEmployee)
    COM_INTERFACE_ENTRY2(IDispatch, ISalesRep)
    COM_INTERFACE_ENTRY_CHAIN(CEmployee)
END_COM_MAP()
```

Notice that the _NOINTERFACE() macro appears as the *second* entry; this is because ATL uses the first entry to implement IUnknown. Compile this and then try to run the client. You will get the following dialog:

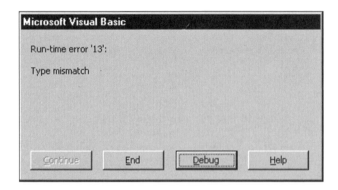

This isn't terribly helpful, but basically it means that this line is failing:

```
Set itf = Fred
```

This line does the `QueryInterface()` for `IEmployee`, which, thanks to our change to the server, now returns `E_NOINTERFACE`.

# Aggregation Support

Code reuse is a subject that gets lots of attention, and with good reason. "If you have already written some code to perform a certain task," the argument goes, "why rewrite it again when you want to do the same task in another project?" However, the very name '*code* reuse' implies that you are reusing code inside other code written in the same language, and typically this is how it is applied: you write classes and either link them statically to a library, or dynamically by using a DLL.

COM allows you to supply code in the form of objects that are used in a language independent way. Taking a wider view, COM objects facilitate *implementation* reuse because any COM-aware language can use that implementation of the interface. The trouble is, we're talking here about granularity and reuse at an object level, but objects often implement many interfaces. How can you reuse code at an interface level?

The last example showed one way to reuse code in ATL, but using the chaining mechanism required that the base class be written in ATL as well, thus making it language bound. However, COM provides its own mechanisms for reuse. In fact, COM offers you two options: containment and aggregation.

In **containment**, you create the reused object within your code and cache an interface pointer as a data member of your object. You can then call methods on this cached pointer. If you decide that the methods of the contained object do all the work that your interface methods need to do, you can just delegate your object's methods to them.

For example, given the following interface:

```
interface IDatabaseProvider : IUnknown
{
    HRESULT GetDatabase([out] IDatabase** ppDatabase);
};
```

You can implement the GetDatabase() method like this, assuming that somewhere you have created the cached object:

```
HRESULT CMyObject::GetDatabase(IDatabase** ppDatabase)
{
    return m_pCachedObject->GetDatabase(ppDatabase);
}
```

The advantage of this approach is that you can choose which methods are delegated to the cached objects, and which ones your object should implement. In particular, you must ensure that the methods of IUnknown are implemented by your *containing* object; this maintains the COM identity rules, which state that a QueryInterface() for IUnknown on an object instance should *always* return the same pointer.

However, if the cached object implements several interfaces that you want to use, or these useful interfaces have many methods, it starts to become tedious to delegate method calls like this; this is where **aggregation** comes in. With aggregation, you pass the QueryInterface() call to the aggregated (or inner) object, so that the interface pointer returned to the client comes directly from the aggregated object rather than from the aggregating (or outer) object.

If you choose, you can implement your outer object's QueryInterface() to check for the interfaces that you have implemented, and pass all other interface requests to the inner object. Such a strategy is called **blind aggregation**. However, you should resist using it because the interfaces on an object should define its behavior. Unless you are absolutely sure what interfaces the inner object implements, blind aggregation means that you really don't know what your object's behavior will be.

Thankfully, there is an alternative to blind aggregation. Interface requests come in via the QueryInterface() of the outer object, and since the implementation of that is your prerogative, you can write it such that QueryInterface() will only pass requests for *some* interfaces to the inner object. From the client's perspective, the whole aggregation is just one object – the fact that the outer object procures the services of the inner object to implement some of its methods is a mere implementation detail.

The difficulty with aggregation comes in solving a problem that wasn't an issue when we were dealing with containment. When a client calls QueryInterface() on the outer object for an interface pointer on the inner object, and then calls QueryInterface() on *this* interface for IUnknown, what will be returned? To be able to satisfy requests for the interfaces that it knows that it implements, the inner object must implement QueryInterface(), and hence it implements IUnknown. However, if the inner object returns its IUnknown pointer to the client, this means that the client can get one of two interface pointers depending on how QueryInterface() is called, violating the COM rules. The COM specification gets round this by requiring that when the outer object creates an object for aggregation, it must pass its own IUnknown (called the **controlling** IUnknown) to the inner object, so that the inner object can delegate IUnknown method calls to the outer object.

But there's a further problem. I just said that the outer object creates the inner object and passes it the outer IUnknown. Then, in the outer object's QueryInterface(), calls to the interfaces that it wants to expose on the inner object are delegated to the inner object's QueryInterface(). The trouble is, to preserve identity, calls on the inner object's QueryInterface() are passed to the QueryInterface() on the outer object. This will inevitably lead to an infinite loop. To fix *this*, the inner object must have *two* versions of IUnknown. The first is the 'non-delegating' IUnknown, and is the interface that the outer object calls when it wants to get hold of an interface on the inner object. The other version is the 'delegating' IUnknown, which just delegates its methods to the IUnknown of the outer object. It is this implementation of the IUnknown methods that is used by clients when they call QueryInterface() on one of the interfaces returned from the inner object.

> **At this point, it's worth mentioning that aggregation is only allowed when the inner object is in-process. To be more specific, the inner object must be in the same apartment as the outer object. If you're writing an object to be aggregated, it is prudent to mark the object as having a threading model of 'Both', so that it can be aggregated into objects running in both single threaded (STA) and multithreaded (MTA) apartments.**

The aggregated object does not have access to the outer object's state, except through public interfaces – an example of this is an aggregated object that's used to provide 'marshal by value' support. This technique is explained in Chapter 7; it's enough to say here that to perform marshal by value, an object needs to implement IMarshal. A generic marshal by value object could provide an implementation of this interface and obtain the aggregating object's state by querying it for one of the IPersistxxx interfaces. In such a situation, the outer object just has to implement an appropriate interface (which it is likely to do anyway), and then aggregate the generic marshal by value object. It will thus get the implementation of IMarshal for free.

So: you have some extra work to do to allow an object to be used as an inner object in aggregation. This is why the Object Wizard gives you the option of Yes, No or Only for aggregation support:

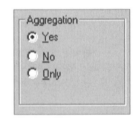

By default, aggregation support is added to every object, because the DECLARE_AGGREGATABLE() macro appears in the declaration for CComCoClass<>. However, if you select No or Only in the Object Wizard, one of these two macros will be applied to your ATL class:

```
DECLARE_NOT_AGGREGATABLE(classname)
DECLARE_ONLY_AGGREGATABLE (classname)
```

There is also a fourth macro called DECLARE_POLY_AGGREGATABLE(), which also allows your class to be aggregated, but which doesn't have an option in the Object Wizard dialog. If you wish to use this, you can add DECLARE_POLY_AGGREGATABLE() to your class.

All of these macros typedef a class called _CreatorClass that creates instances of the object in a manner befitting the aggregation support required. This _CreatorClass provides the implementation of CreateInstance() used by the object's class factory.

## Choosing Aggregation Support

When you write an object that is likely to be aggregated, you have three choices. If you use the DECLARE_AGGREGATABLE() macro (that is, accept the default), then the object can be used as an inner object, or it can be created in its own right. If you use DECLARE_ONLY_AGGREGATABLE(), the object can *only* be used as an inner object as part of an aggregate.

By using the DECLARE_AGGREGATABLE() macro, you're indicating that the object implementation will use either CComObject<> or CComAggObject<> to provide IUnknown. The choice of which is used is made at runtime, and is determined by looking at the parameter of CreateInstance() to see whether a controlling IUnknown was passed. Having both implementations in the same server can increase the module size, and it also means that two copies of the vtable are maintained.

Another option is to replace the aggregation macro with DECLARE_POLY_AGGREGATABLE(), which uses the single CComPolyObject<> class to handle both the aggregated and the non-aggregated case. Clearly, since one class is handling both cases, it cannot be optimum for all situations. It has to maintain a pointer to the controlling IUnknown even when the object is not aggregated (in which case the pointer is NULL). CComObject<> would be optimal for this particular example because it doesn't maintain an extra pointer, but in the right circumstances you can save module size by using this class.

## The Delegating IUnknown Implementation

The inner object of an aggregate needs to have an implementation of IUnknown that delegates to the outer object; these methods are inherited through CComObjectRootBase, from which your class will derive:

```
ULONG OuterAddRef()
ULONG OuterRelease()
HRESULT OuterQueryInterface(REFIID iid, void** ppvObject)
```

The default implementation of these methods delegates the method call to the method on a cached interface pointer called m_pOuterUnknown. This pointer is declared as part of a union:

```
union
{
    long m_dwRef;
    IUnknown* m_pOuterUnknown;
};
```

From this, you'll realize that an instance of a class deriving from CComObjectRootBase can provide a delegating IUnknown implementation or it can manage its own reference count, but not both at the same time. By this, I don't mean that you can't aggregate another object inside an already-aggregated object; just that an inner object cannot manage its own lifetime – this will always be managed by the outer object. If an aggregated object *does* aggregate another, both of these inner objects are managed through the outer object's IUnknown – this is why it's called the *controlling* IUnknown.

The aggregating classes, CComAggObject<> and CComPolyObject<>, have an object of type CComContainedObject<> as an embedded member. The parameter of this template is the ATL class of your object, so in the situation when your object is being aggregated, an instance of your class is held in the aggregating class with its IUnknown methods managed by CComContainedObject<>. This class delegates reference counting calls to the 'Outer' methods described above, and QueryInterface() calls to the outer object's QueryInterface() first, and to your ATL class's QueryInterface() if that fails.

In the figure below, you can see the classes that are used in the standard case of an aggregated object, and the way calls are routed through the hierarchy:

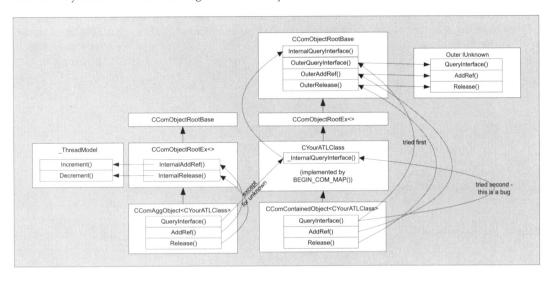

## DECLARE_PROTECT_FINAL_CONSTRUCT

Typically, inner objects are created within the FinalConstruct() of the outer object, but there may be a problem if an inner object wants to access the outer object during the construction phase – an example of this was given earlier with an implementation of a generic 'marshal by value' object that needed to get hold of an IPersistxxx interface of the outer object.

At this point, the outer object is likely to have a reference count of zero, and so to get access to an interface of the outer object, the inner object calls QueryInterface() on the controlling IUnknown, bumping up its reference count to one. Once the inner object has finished using the interface, it should then call Release(), which has the effect of reducing the outer object's reference count to zero. When Release() sees that the reference count is zero it will attempt to delete the outer object!

To get round this, ATL implementations of CreateInstance() bracket calls to an object's FinalConstruct() with calls to InternalFinalConstructAddRef() and InternalFinalConstructRelease(). These methods are inherited through CComObjectRootBase, and do absolutely nothing. However, if you want to stop the outer object being released during a call to its FinalConstruct(), you can use the DECLARE_PROTECT_FINAL_CONSTRUCT() macro that redefines these methods using InternalAddRef() and InternalRelease(). Whenever you create a class through the Object Wizard, it will declare this macro so that FinalConstruct() is always protected.

# Object Map

Each server module must provide access to the class factories of all the externally creatable objects it serves. Servers come in two flavors: DLLs and EXEs. and EXEs. If the server is in a DLL, the object's class factory is accessed when `DllGetClassObject()` is called, whereas if the server is in an EXE, the class factory is registered when the server starts, ultimately with a call to `CoRegisterClassObject()`.

The DLL mechanism checks all the CLSIDs of the objects served by the module and returns a reference to the required class factory, while the EXE mechanism goes through all the class factories and registers each one. To generalize these two mechanisms, ATL provides the **object map**, which is an array of instances of `_ATL_OBJMAP_ENTRY`. This structure is declared in `atlbase.h` as:

```
struct _ATL_OBJMAP_ENTRY
{
    const CLSID* pclsid;
    HRESULT (WINAPI *pfnUpdateRegistry)(BOOL bRegister);
    _ATL_CREATORFUNC* pfnGetClassObject;
    _ATL_CREATORFUNC* pfnCreateInstance;
    IUnknown* pCF;
    DWORD dwRegister;
    _ATL_DESCRIPTIONFUNC* pfnGetObjectDescription;
    _ATL_CATMAPFUNC* pfnGetCategoryMap;
    HRESULT WINAPI RevokeClassObject();
    HRESULT WINAPI RegisterClassObject(DWORD dwClsContext, DWORD dwFlags);
    void (WINAPI *pfnObjectMain)(bool bStarting);
};
```

This `struct` has nine data members, and I've highlighted the six that are pertinent to this discussion. The function pointers are outlined in the following table:

| Member | Function type | Description |
| --- | --- | --- |
| pfnUpdateRegistry | HRESULT (WINAPI)(BOOL) | Used to update the registry with the object's information |
| pfnGetClassObject | _ATL_CREATORFUNC | Returns the class factory for the object |
| pfnCreateInstance | _ATL_CREATORFUNC | Function used to create an object instance |
| pfnGetObjectDescription | _ATL_DESCRIPTIONFUNC | Returns a description of the object |
| pfnGetCategoryMap | _ATL_CATMAPFUNC | Returns the category map for the object |
| pfnObjectMain | void (WINAPI)(bool) | Object initialization routine |

pfnUpdateRegistry is covered in the section on *Registration* later on; pfnGetClassObject and pfnCreateInstance are covered in the next section on class factories; and pfnGetCategoryMap is used to implement the category map, which is covered in the next chapter.

pfnGetObjectDescription holds the address of the GetObjectDescription() method. By default this is NULL, and typically you should leave it this way. The only time you will want to use this is if you are writing a component registrar for MTS: GetObjectDescription() is called by the IComponentRegistrar::GetComponents() method when registering or unregistering individual components.

Your object maps look something like this:

```
BEGIN_OBJECT_MAP(ObjectMap)
    OBJECT_ENTRY(CLSID_MyObject, CMyObject)
END_OBJECT_MAP()
```

BEGIN_OBJECT_MAP() declares a static, module-level array with the same name as the macro argument. The OBJECT_ENTRY() macro provides the object's CLSID, and the ATL C++ class used to implement the object. The macro expands to use this information to fill the data members of the _ATL_OBJMAP_ENTRY.

The object map is accessed through the server module's single CComModule object. This object is global, and it's initialized through AppWizard generated code in DllMain() or _tWinMain() with a call to its Init() method. The Wizard will pass this the name of the object map that it declared with the BEGIN_OBJECT_MAP() macro. You should never want to change the name of the map, so don't be tempted to change this value. Among other things _Module.Init() initializes a public data member, m_pObjMap, to point to the object map. This means that any method that has access to _Module can access the object map; this is why many of the global registration, initialization, and class factory functions have a parameter that takes a pointer to _Module.

In fact, there are two macros that you can use in the object map: OBJECT_ENTRY() and OBJECT_ENTRY_NON_CREATEABLE(). These are for externally creatable objects and those that can only be created within the server respectively.

'Non-creatable' is clearly something of a misnomer, but it's still not immediately apparent why you might want objects that display this behavior. In fact, there are a couple of reasons, the first of which is to 'componentize' your code. In general, object-oriented principles make your code easier to maintain. Your module's algorithms can be written to use objects, reinforcing OOP, but you may not want to expose these to external clients. Such objects are 'non-creatable'. This is not such a wacky idea: Microsoft used COM objects within Office applications for several years before OLE 2 was released.

Another use for 'non-creatable' objects is to implement objects that are created or accessed via method calls on an object that *is* 'creatable'. The interfaces on such objects may need to be marshaled, so their interfaces need to be registered. This is why OBJECT_ENTRY_NON_CREATEABLE() expands to provide NULL pointers for all the function members except for pfnUpdateRegistry, pfnGetCategoryMap and pfnObjectMain. This ensures that the object and its interfaces are registered, but any attempt to create one through a class factory will result in an error.

To prevent the object from being created, while still allowing it to exist in the object map for registration purposes, the macro will give it a pclsid of &CLSID_NULL – that is, a non-NULL pointer. For non-creatable objects, pclsid has to point to an 'invalid' CLSID so that DllGetClassObject() won't create the object, but it can't be NULL since that is used to indicate the end of the object map. The solution is to take the address of the special CLSID value, CLSID_NULL.

> *Note that if you want an object only to be creatable within the server, you should also use the* [noncreatable] *attribute on its* coclass *definition in the project's IDL. This allows tools that understand this attribute to prevent users from trying to create such objects by throwing an error at compile time, rather than leaving the failure to appear at runtime.*

Returning to _ATL_OBJMAP_ENTRY, the pfnObjectMain member points to the ObjectMain() function that's defined in your class to initialize and uninitialize class resources. This method is called twice: once when the server starts (in AtlModuleInit()), and once when the server finishes (in AtlModuleTerm()). The method can tell whether the server is starting or finishing by the parameter passed to it (true for initialization and false for termination). For an EXE server, these methods are called in _tWinMain() through the calls to CComModule::Init() and CComModule::Term(); for a DLL server Init() and Term() are called in DllMain().

You can use ObjectMain() if objects of the class will use some shared class resource that requires lengthy initialization. It allows you to pre-initialize these resources before any object instance is actually requested. If these resources will only be accessed by particular interfaces on an object, and these interfaces are rarely called, you may consider whether using a tear-off interface is appropriate, as explained in the next chapter. The difference between the two methods of resource management is this: ObjectMain() allows you to manage per-class resources, whereas tear-offs allow you to manage per-object resources.

As an example, imagine that your server is used to give access to a piece of laboratory equipment – say, a voltmeter that can provide results from multiple 'channels'. Your Voltmeter object will configure each input channel and return the results from the associated output channel. You can provide a custom class factory (see Chapter 5) so that when a client attempts to obtain a Voltmeter object, the class factory will determine which channel is available. In this situation, ObjectMain() can be used to make the once-only initialization of the voltmeter, when the server is first loaded. Individual initialization of the channels will be carried out when the associated Voltmeter object is created.

# Class Factory Support

> *Before I begin this section, I should say that further details about class factories will be given in Chapter 5, which will explain how to write your own class factory, as well as how to provide licensing support. This section explains how class factories fit into the overall ATL architecture.*

# Class Factories in ATL

When `DllGetClassFactory()` is called, the Object Wizard-generated code will call `CComModule::GetClassObject()`, which in turn calls `AtlModuleGetClassObject()`. This function will iterate through the object map until it finds the object requested by COM. On the other hand, if the server is in an EXE, the Object Wizard places a call to `CComModule::RegisterClassObjects()` in `_tWinMain()`, and this calls `AtlModuleRegisterClassObjects()`. This latter method iterates through all the entries in the object map, and will create and register a class factory for *every* externally creatable object.

These class factories are obtained by calling the `pfnGetClassObject` member of the object map entry. This function pointer is declared in the `OBJECT_ENTRY(clsid, class)` macro as:

    class::_ClassFactoryCreatorClass::CreateInstance

The `_ClassFactoryCreatorClass` is `typedef`'d by the various `DECLARE_CLASSFACTORYxxx()` macros. Your ATL class should derive from `CComCoClass<>`, and so by default `DECLARE_CLASSFACTORY()` will be used. If you want to use one of the other macros, just add it to your class definition to override the `typedef` from the base class. Here are the other macros:

| Macro | Description |
|---|---|
| `DECLARE_CLASSFACTORY()` | Declares an implementation of `IClassFactory` |
| `DECLARE_CLASSFACTORY2()` | Declares an implementation of `IClassFactory2` |
| `DECLARE_CLASSFACTORY_AUTO_THREAD()` | Declares a class factory that can be used to create objects in multiple apartments |
| `DECLARE_CLASSFACTORY_SINGLETON()` | A class factory that only returns references to a single object |
| `DECLARE_CLASSFACTORY_EX()` | Specifies the class used to implement the class factory |

Note that the first four of these are all defined in terms of the `DECLARE_CLASSFACTORY_EX()` macro that's conditionally compiled according to whether you're creating the class factory in a DLL or an EXE server. This is important, because when a class factory is created in an EXE during registration of the class factories, COM puts a reference to the class factory into its own maintained table of class factories. It's this table that is queried when a client wants to create an instance of a coclass. This is in contrast to DLL servers, where the DLL will return a class factory in response to a client's call to `CoGetClassObject()`.

DLLs can be unloaded by the client if the DLL serves no objects, so creation of a class factory should bump up the lock count on the server to ensure that the DLL will not be inadvertently unloaded. For a DLL server, the class factory is implemented using CComObjectCached<>, which increments the module lock count (effectively a call to IClassFactory::LockServer(TRUE)) in AddRef() when the class factory is first created, and decrements it in Release() when the class factory is about to be released:

```
STDMETHOD_(ULONG, AddRef)()
{
    m_csCached.Lock();
    ULONG l = InternalAddRef();
    if(m_dwRef == 2)
        _Module.Lock();
    m_csCached.Unlock();
    return l;
}

STDMETHOD_(ULONG, Release)()
{
    m_csCached.Lock();
    InternalRelease();
    ULONG l = m_dwRef;
    m_csCached.Unlock();
    if(l == 0)
        delete this;
    else if(l == 1)
        _Module.Unlock();
    return l;
}
```

When the class factory object is first created, the IUnknown interface is obtained and AddRef() is called, which increments the reference count to 1. Then, QueryInterface() is called for the class factory interface, and if this is successful the reference count is incremented to 2. Now that the class factory is fully created and useful to the client, the module lock is made. The reverse occurs in Release().

An EXE server is a different case. ATL implements the class factory with CComObjectNoLock<>, which doesn't change the module lock count; this would be unnecessary because when a client calls CoGetClassObject(), COM calls LockServer(TRUE) anyway.

You should choose one of the first four macros according to the type of server and the objects you want to serve. Most objects will use DECLARE_CLASSFACTORY(), but if you want to add licensing support, you should use DECLARE_CLASSFACTORY2().

If you decide to implement your object server using multiple thread-pooled apartments, then you should derive your server's module class from CComAutoThreadModule<>. For each object used in the module, you should add DECLARE_CLASSFACTORY_AUTO_THREAD() to the object's class, which indicates that the objects use CComClassFactoryAutoThread as their class factory implementation. Full details of this technique will be given in Chapter 7.

There are some cases where you may decide that you would prefer the class factory to return a reference to a single instance of an object in response to CreateInstance(). Such an object is called a **singleton**, and is typically used when the object will represent some single resource to which it would be difficult or complicated to apply locking, or which will share data between multiple clients.

For example, if an object gives access to a single piece of equipment – say, a TV set – there will only ever be one of the physical devices, making it a good candidate to be a singleton. There could be multiple clients (each a couch potato with a remote control), and although each has control over the device, they are all actually sharing it. (Note that a singleton is just one way to solve this problem.) To make your object a singleton, you use the DECLARE_CLASSFACTORY_SINGLETON() macro.

Finally, you may decide that you want to implement your own class factory. To do this, you should derive a class from CComClassFactory (overriding the methods you want to change), and then declare this in your ATL class with DECLARE_CLASSFACTORY_EX(). The class factory should implement IClassFactory and whatever other custom interfaces you need. Chapter 5 provides an example of this activity.

# Creating Object Instances

When you create an object instance, it should handle IUnknown according to whether it is being created as an inner or an outer object of an aggregation, or indeed as a standalone object. Bear this in mind in the following discussion.

When a class factory is created, it is passed the address of the CreateInstance() appropriate for the object type it will create. This function is provided by either the CComCreator<> or the CComCreator2<> template, and held as a member of the class's object map entry. To make the code more readable, the class is typedef'd to _CreatorClass by one of the aggregation macros:

```
#define DECLARE_NOT_AGGREGATABLE(x) public:\
    typedef CComCreator2< CComCreator< CComObject< x > >,
                          CComFailCreator<CLASS_E_NOAGGREGATION> >
                          _CreatorClass;
#define DECLARE_AGGREGATABLE(x) public:\
    typedef CComCreator2< CComCreator< CComObject< x > >,
                          CComCreator< CComAggObject< x > > >
                          _CreatorClass;
#define DECLARE_ONLY_AGGREGATABLE(x) public:\
    typedef CComCreator2< CComFailCreator<E_FAIL>,
                          CComCreator< CComAggObject< x > > >
                          _CreatorClass;
#define DECLARE_POLY_AGGREGATABLE(x) public:\
    typedef CComCreator<  CComPolyObject< x > >
                          _CreatorClass;
```

The implementation of CComCreator<>::CreateInstance() effectively calls new on the class that is passed as the single parameter to the template. It then calls FinalConstruct(), and finally it QueryInterface()s for the requested interface. Since CComCreator<> uses new to create COM objects, it typically takes a CComObject<> (or derivative) as the template argument.

`CComCreator<>` is used when the `DECLARE_POLY_AGGREGATABLE()` macro is added to your class. Since a single creator is used in both aggregation cases, the `CreateInstance()` function of this template will delegate to the class passed as its single template parameter. `CComCreator2<>`, which is used in the other cases, has two parameters: one that specifies the class that will be used when the object is being created non-aggregated, and the other when it is being created as an inner object.

```
template <class T1, class T2>
class CComCreator2
{
public:
    static HRESULT WINAPI CreateInstance(void* pv, REFIID riid, LPVOID* ppv)
    {
        ATLASSERT(*ppv == NULL);
        return (pv == NULL) ? T1::CreateInstance(NULL, riid, ppv) :
                              T2::CreateInstance(pv, riid, ppv);
    }
};
```

To prevent an object declared with `DECLARE_NOT_AGGREGATABLE()` from being created as an inner object (and an object declared with `DECLARE_ONLY_AGGREGATABLE()` from being created as an outer object), `CComCreator2<>` is passed `CComFailCreator<>` as one parameter and `CComCreator<>` as the other. `CComFailCreator<>` is defined like this:

```
template <HRESULT hr>
class CComFailCreator
{
public:
    static HRESULT WINAPI CreateInstance(void*, REFIID, LPVOID*)
    {
        return hr;
    }
};
```

Thus, `CreateInstance()` will return the `HRESULT` passed in the template parameter. Looking back at the aggregation macros, you can see that if you try to create a non-aggregatable object as an outer object, a `CComObject<>` is created; otherwise, `CLASS_E_NOAGGREGATION` is returned. If you create an aggregatable object as an outer object, a `CComObject<>` is created; otherwise, a `CComAggObject<>` is created. If you create an only-aggregatable object as an outer object, `E_FAIL` is returned; otherwise, a `CComAggObject<>` is created. Finally, if you create a poly-aggregatable object (in either way), a `CComPolyObject<>` is created.

What does `CComAggObject<>` bring to the party? Well, this class takes the class of the inner object as a parameter. Its version of `CreateInstance()` will pass the `IUnknown` of the outer object to the constructor of the object it creates. Thus, the inner object can use the `IUnknown` of the outer object when appropriate – you can see this in the implementation of `QueryInterface()`:

```
STDMETHOD(QueryInterface)(REFIID iid, void** ppvObject)
{
    HRESULT hRes = S_OK;
    if(InlineIsEqualUnknown(iid))
    {
```

```
        if(ppvObject == NULL)
            return E_POINTER;
        *ppvObject = (void*)(IUnknown*)this;
        AddRef();
    }
    else
        hRes = m_contained._InternalQueryInterface(iid, ppvObject);
    return hRes;
}
```

The implementation of QueryInterface() in CComAggObject<> is the non-delegating implementation. Only the creator of the aggregated object will have access to this implementation. The creator of the aggregated object will use it to get the initial IUnknown interface pointer from the aggregated object, and to service specific interface requests that it forwards from its own QueryInterface() implementation. Clients never get direct access to this implementation of QueryInterface(). As you can see, when interfaces other than IUnknown itself are returned, the client will get hold of an interface that's implemented by the m_contained member of type CComContainedObject<>.

So, if the client has a pointer to an interface implemented on the *inner* object, then calls to QueryInterface() will be handled by CComContainedObject<>::QueryInterface(). This is the delegating implementation of QueryInterface(), and it looks like this:

```
STDMETHOD(QueryInterface)(REFIID iid, void ** ppvObject)
{
    HRESULT hr = OuterQueryInterface(iid, ppvObject);
    if(FAILED(hr) && _GetRawUnknown() != m_pOuterUnknown)
        hr = _InternalQueryInterface(iid, ppvObject);
    return hr;
}
```

> *Unlike* CComAggObject<>, *the* CComContainedObject<> *class derives from its template parameter, which is the ATL class for the inner object.*

The first line of code in this function calls OuterQueryInterface(), which will result in a call to QueryInterface() on the outer object, so that the outer object's COM map is checked for the interface (assuming the outer object is also implemented with ATL). Since the outer object's COM map will have aggregation macros for the interfaces it wants to expose from the inner object, this call should succeed. If it does not, then it means an interface was requested that wasn't mentioned in the outer object's COM map.

The next two lines are confusing, because they suggest that if the interface is not mentioned in the outer object's COM map, the code should try to find the interface in the inner object's COM map. In fact, this is more than confusing, it's wrong. This implementation makes calls to QueryInterface() on the aggregated object unpredictable – calling it on an interface implemented on the outer object will fail for some interfaces, when calls through interfaces implemented on the inner object *for those same interfaces* can succeed. This unpredictability violates the COM specification.

To get the correct behavior, you should comment out these two lines in AtlCom.h so that CComContainedObject<>::QueryInterface() only calls OuterQueryInterface(). This bug is new to ATL 3.0.

# Module Entry Point Support

As explained earlier, COM servers may be packaged in either a DLL or an EXE, so ATL needs to ensure that the correct entry points are provided according to the module type. Incidentally, COM servers may also be intermediate module types, like Java classes or IE scriptlets, but these ultimately end up exposing their COM coclasses through either an EXE or a DLL, via the appropriate interpreter.

The ATL COM AppWizard will generate the entry points appropriate for the module type. If the server is an EXE, it will generate an implementation of _tWinMain(), while for a DLL server it will generate a DllMain() and the four PRIVATE exported functions DllCanUnloadNow(), DllGetClassObject(), DllRegisterServer() and DllUnregisterServer().

To generalize the code, the AppWizard will create a global object of the CComModule class (or a derivative thereof). This object is used by all the module's entry points, and also by many of the common ATL classes to get hold of module-wide resources. Such resources include the server registration information (that is, information about the AppID for the server), description strings for error reporting, server locking, and a global critical section object.

Server locking is managed at a coclass level by IClassFactory::LockServer(). In COM, clients use this to 'lock' a class factory in memory when they want to create many objects of the same class. Servers keep a lock reference count, and a server will only unload itself (or allow itself to be unloaded) when this reference count is zero. Inevitably, this requires a module-wide reference counting scheme, which is implemented through the CComModule::Lock() and CComModule::Unlock() methods.

Because these module-level resources are used by many of the ATL classes, you will always need to have a global instance of CComModule in your project, and this object must be called _Module. The ATL AppWizard will add this object to the project's main source file (where the entry points are implemented).

DLL servers use an instance of CComModule for _Module, while servers implemented in EXEs use a class derived from CComModule. An EXE server that isn't being run as a service needs to shut down the EXE when there are no more outstanding object instances; it does this by sending a WM_QUIT message to the main thread. The derived EXE classes (called CExeModule for standard EXE servers, and CServiceModule for ATL services that aren't being run as such) save the main thread handle and override Lock() to ensure that the server is correctly told to unload. (As you'll see in the next section, an ATL service can be run either as a service or as a local server, depending on how it is registered.)

ATL EXE servers also implement two methods – StartMonitor() and MonitorShutdown() – that are used to monitor the shutdown process when the module reference count becomes zero. StartMonitor() is called when the server starts. It creates an event object and a thread that runs the MonitorProc() function:

```
static DWORD WINAPI MonitorProc(void* pv)
{
    CExeModule* p = (CExeModule*)pv;
    p->MonitorShutdown();
    return 0;
}
```

As you can see, the thread function is passed the this pointer of the _Module object, and it uses this to call the MonitorShutdown() method, which waits for an event to be set. While the server is running, you have the monitor thread and whatever other threads that you or the system has created to service object requests. When the module lock count falls to zero, the event is set, waking up the monitor thread, which initiates the shutdown.

The monitor code exists to allow the server to unload *completely*; there is a small chance that while the unloading occurs, a client could ask a class factory to create an instance before the class factories have all been revoked. The code in MonitorShutdown() prevents this from happening: it calls CoSuspendClassObjects(), which means that the class factories from this server cannot be used to create objects.

# Services

Services are EXEs, but they are started in a different way, and they remain in memory even when no objects are being served. A service can be started up automatically when the NT machine boots, or manually through the Services applet in the control panel. If a COM service has already started, then it will have registered its class factories with COM, so clients can create object instances in the usual way.

If the service has not started, then COM must start it before attempting to get the server to create object instances. To do this, the COM server must be registered to say that it is a service; this is done using the LocalService entry under its AppID entry in the registry. This value gives the name of the NT service that contains the COM server, and COM will use the Win32 service API to start it (this is equivalent to you manually starting the service using the control panel). After the service has started, it will register its class factories, which allows COM to ask for an object instance.

ATL handles all this with several changes to the code it generates for EXE servers. The first change is that the server will check for the -Service command line switch, which is used to register the server as an NT service. The -RegServer switch is used to register the server as a local server (that is, without the LocalService value), and in this case it will be started and will shut down just like a standard EXE server.

If the server is run without a registration switch, _tWinMain() checks for the presence of the LocalService value in the server's AppID. If this exists, it sets CServiceModule::m_bService to TRUE before running CServiceModule::Start(), which looks like this:

```
inline void CServiceModule::Start()
{
    SERVICE_TABLE_ENTRY st[] =
    {
        { m_szServiceName, _ServiceMain },
```

```
        { NULL, NULL }
   };

   if(m_bService && !::StartServiceCtrlDispatcher(st))
   {
      m_bService = FALSE;
   }

   if(m_bService == FALSE)
      Run();
}
```

If the server is being started as a service by the Service Control Manager, then `StartServiceCtrlDispatcher()` is called, passing the service's 'main' function, called `_ServiceMain()`. Otherwise, `CServiceModule::Run()` is called and it starts as a standard EXE server. Calling `StartServiceCtrlDispatcher()` connects the process's main thread to the Service Control Manager (SCM), which uses this connection to send control messages to the process.

`CServiceModule::_ServiceMain()` is a static function so that it has the function signature required by the service architecture, but all it does is call the `CServiceModule::ServiceMain()` method. Note that `CServiceModule::ServiceMain()` also calls `CServiceModule::Run()`, after registering the service's control handler function. It is `Run()` that registers the server's class factories and implements the message pump.

*For more information about the workings of NT services and the roles they can fulfill in the architecture of a system, have a look at* Professional NT Services *by Kevin Miller (Wrox Press; ISBN 1861001304; July 1998).*

# Registration

To be creatable, an object must be registered so that its CLSID is in the `CLSID` key of the registry. For an object's interfaces to be used across apartment boundaries, they must be registered in the `Interface` key of the registry. To set up security, surrogate, and service settings, a server must be registered in the `AppID` key of the registry. Finally, if an object is to be created by scripting languages, it should also have a programmatic ID that maps to the CLSID. These three keys, and the ProgIDs, are found in the `HKEY_CLASSES_ROOT` hive. Thus, at least three different registrations are required.

ATL manages registration through two mechanisms: the project type library and a registration script. (A little bit of direct manipulation of the registry is also used, but we'll treat that as an exception.) Type libraries are tokenized IDL, so (almost) all the information in your IDL file will be compiled into the type library. However, IDL does not have ProgID information, and nor does it have AppID settings, so a secondary mechanism must be used. Furthermore, when you register a type library, the `coclasses` are not registered. This is the reason that registration scripts are used.

# Module Registration

A DLL server self-registers when an application (like `regsvr32`) calls its exported `DllRegisterServer()` function. Likewise, it will unregister itself when an application calls its `DllUnregisterServer()` function. AppWizard will generate these functions for you, and the implementations delegate to the corresponding methods in the global `_Module` object (`RegisterServer()` and `UnregisterServer()`). Among other things, these functions call the COM API functions `RegisterTypeLibrary()` and `UnRegisterTypeLibrary()`, which do most of the work to register an object and its interfaces:

```
STDAPI DllRegisterServer(void)
{
    return _Module.RegisterServer(TRUE);
}

STDAPI DllUnregisterServer(void)
{
    return _Module.UnregisterServer(TRUE);
}
```

An EXE server must check the command line parameters for the `-RegServer` or `-UnregServer` switches (and `-Service` for NT services) to determine whether it should register or unregister the server. As for DLL servers, the registration is carried out through methods on the global `_Module` object. In addition, EXE servers also call `UpdateRegistryFromResource()` to register the AppID for the server.

```
int nRet = 0;
BOOL bRun = TRUE;
LPCTSTR lpszToken = FindOneOf(lpCmdLine, szTokens);
while(lpszToken != NULL)
{
    if(lstrcmpi(lpszToken, _T("UnregServer")) == 0)
    {
        _Module.UpdateRegistryFromResource(IDR_SERVER, FALSE);
        nRet = _Module.UnregisterServer(TRUE);
        bRun = FALSE;
        break;
    }
    if(lstrcmpi(lpszToken, _T("RegServer")) == 0)
    {
        _Module.UpdateRegistryFromResource(IDR_SERVER, TRUE);
        nRet = _Module.RegisterServer(TRUE);
        bRun = FALSE;
        break;
    }
    lpszToken = FindOneOf(lpszToken, szTokens);
}
```

Here, `IDR_SERVER` is a custom resource type that holds multi-line string data; you'll find it in the ResourceView under the **REGISTRY** folder. The data is supplied as a text file with the name of the server and an extension of `.rgs`. `UpdateRegistryFromResource()` calls `AtlModuleUpdateRegistryFromResource()`, which will load this string resource and pass it as a registry script to the Registrar.

## *RegisterServer*

RegisterServer() merely calls the global function AtlModuleRegisterServer(), which is where much of the work is done:

```
ATLINLINE ATLAPI AtlModuleRegisterServer(
                ATL_MODULE* pM, BOOL bRegTypeLib, const CLSID* pCLSID);
```

This function can be used to register any one or all of the classes in the object map. The first parameter points to the project's object map, the second parameter indicates whether the type library should be registered, and the final parameter gives the CLSID of a specific class to register. The argument to CComModule::RegisterServer() is passed as the bRegTypeLib parameter, and pCLSID has a default value of NULL.

AtlModuleRegisterServer() goes through all the entries in the object map. If pCLSID is not NULL, it will check to see whether the specified class is in the object map – if so, it will register it. If pCLSID is NULL (and pfnGetObjectDescription is NULL) then *every member* of the object map is registered (even non-creatable objects). This registration is performed by calling the function member pfnUpdateRegistry, which is set by the appropriate OBJECT_ENTRY() macro; this function is passed TRUE as a parameter to indicate that the class should be registered.

Once the object is registered, the object map's component categories (which are covered in the next chapter) are registered, if present. Finally, when the end of the object map is reached, the bRegTypeLib is checked. If it's TRUE, then AtlModuleRegisterTypeLib() is called to register the type library.

## *UnregisterServer*

CComModule::UnregisterServer() calls the global function AtlModuleUnregisterServer(), which can unregister all classes in the server, or just a particular class.

```
ATLINLINE ATLAPI AtlModuleUnregisterServerEx(
                _ATL_MODULE* pM, BOOL bUnRegTypeLib, const CLSID* pCLSID);
```

This method is very similar to AtlModuleRegisterServer() except that pfnUpdateRegistry and AtlRegisterClassCategoriesHelper() are passed FALSE to indicate that classes should be unregistered.

# Registration Macros

You can alter how the registration works by using the various ATL registration macros, which define the UpdateRegistry() method in your class. The OBJECT_ENTRY() macro specifies that this method should be called when registering an object. The macros are:

| Macro | Description |
|-------|-------------|
| DECLARE_NO_REGISTRY() | Does nothing |
| DECLARE_REGISTRY() | Calls UpdateRegistryClass() |
| DECLARE_REGISTRY_RESOURCE() | Calls UpdateRegistryFromResource() with a resource name |
| DECLARE_REGISTRY_RESOURCEID() | Calls UpdateRegistryFromResource() with a resource ID |

The first of these can be used to disable the registration of an object. The second macro allows you to specify the object's CLSID, ProgIDs and threading model, and these are added into the registry through CComModule::UpdateRegistryClass(), which in turn calls CComModule::RegisterClassHelper(). This method directly manipulates the registry and hence does not use an RGS script.

The final two macros allow you to specify a registry script as a resource (by name or ID) so that the registration is carried out using this script, as explained later in the chapter.

# Type Library Registration

By default, the IDL for all ATL projects will have a library statement, and whenever you add a new ATL object to your project, the Wizard will add that object to the library block. This is the case whether the object uses Automation (that is, dual) interfaces or not. When the object is added, so is the first interface that you specify for the object in Object Wizard. Thus, if you use the ATL Wizards to generate the objects in your project, the type library will describe those objects.

The reason that ATL registers the type library for a server is that this is the simplest way to register all the interfaces used in the project. When RegisterTypeLib() is called, it will read through the type library and add an entry to the registry for every [oleautomation] interface that it finds. Note that although object information is present in the type library, RegisterTypeLib() will *not* add an entry for coclasses.

When you register an [oleautomation] interface like this, COM will use the Universal Marshaler and the type library to marshal the interface – you don't have to register a separate proxy-stub DLL. Dual interfaces are [oleautomation] interfaces, but by default, custom interfaces are not. If your interface uses [oleautomation] compatible parameters, then you can use the attribute on the interface to use the Universal Marshaler – so-called type library marshaling. If such an object is to be activated by a remote client, then the type library must be registered on the client machine as well.

Note that there is a slight problem with this. If your object has a dual interface (and is therefore registered to use type library marshaling), then the interface will have a TypeLib key to specify the type library. If you now register a proxy-stub for the interface, the TypeLib key will exist even though it is no longer needed. If you attempt to unregister the proxy-stub with RegSvr32, the call will fail because of this TypeLib key. Removing this key by hand will allow RegSvr32 to work; another option is to unregister the type library, which will remove the interface key.

### AtlModuleRegisterTypeLib

This method is called to register the type library. It first attempts to load the type library from the module's resources with a call to `LoadTypeLib()`. If this fails, the function assumes that the type library is a separate file with the same name as the project, but with the `tlb` extension. `RegisterTypeLib()` is called to do the registration.

# Registrar

The **registrar** is an object that parses registry scripts and uses this information to add, or remove, information from the registry. You can choose to use the registrar as an external COM object served by `ATL.dll` (the default), or you can statically link the registrar code to your project by defining the `_ATL_STATIC_REGISTRY` symbol.

> *Note that there are two versions of* `ATL.dll`. *One is Unicode (intended for NT), and the other is ANSI (for Windows 9x). You will find these on the Visual Studio disks in* `OS\System` *and* `OS\System\ANSI` *respectively.*

To use the registrar component, you must distribute and register the appropriate `ATL.dll`. If the ATL object you're developing is likely to be downloaded over the internet (perhaps as a control on a web page), `ATL.dll` will complicate matters. It means that any INF file related to the web page should specify that `ATL.dll` must be downloaded, and it must also check that the *correct* version is downloaded and registered. In terms of administration, a simpler option is to statically link the registrar so that only one DLL needs to be downloaded.

The format of registry scripts is documented in the Visual C++ help files, but it's quite simple. These scripts have a list of entries that should be written to, or removed from, the registry. Braces are used to define script blocks, and conceptually, registration goes from outer blocks to inner blocks, while unregistration starts at the inner blocks and works out. This is so that entries are not written to the registry if their parent key does not exist, and so keys are not deleted if they contain entries. There are keywords that relax or enforce this idea: `Delete` specifies that a key should be removed during registration, `ForceRemove` will remove a key and recreate it during registration, and `NoRemove` specifies that a key should remain during unregistration.

The registry scripts have the extension `rgs`, and they are added as resource files to your project. There are two types: one for application registration, and one for each of the `coclasses` in your project.

## Application Registration

The ATL AppWizard will create one RGS file with the same name as your project, into which it will add server AppID information:

```
HKCR
{
    NoRemove AppID
    {
        {BAADF00D-BEEF-BEEF-BEEF-BAADF00DBEEF} = s 'MyServer'
        'MyServer.EXE'
        {
```

```
              val AppID = s { BAADF00D-BEEF-BEEF-BEEF-BAADF00DBEEF }
          }
      }
  }
```

This adds two keys to the `AppID` key. The first entry gives the AppID and its default value, which is the name of the module. The other key has the server's name as its name, and a named value that maps to the server's AppID. This first key is the important one: it's where per-AppID security is held, as well as the `RemoteServerName` (used to specify a remote host if one is not specified in the `COSERVERINFO` structure) and `DllSurrogate` (which is used to specify that a surrogate will be used for a DLL server).

This RGS file will only be created if the project is packaged in an EXE. *Usually* this is OK, because a DLL server does not need an AppID – it will be run under the security context of the client and in the client's memory space. However, if you decide that you will want to access the classes in a DLL server through a surrogate (either to get remote access, or to isolate the DLL from your client) then the DLL server will need to register an AppID.

To do this, you need to create an RGS file to register the AppID, then add it as a `REGISTRY` resource into the project's resources. Finally, you need to call `UpdateRegistryFromResource()` in `RegisterServer()` and `UnregisterServer()`, using this resource ID.

### Service Registration

If the server is an NT service, then the AppWizard will produce code in `CServiceModule::RegisterServer()` to add an entry for the `AppID` key called `LocalService`. This specifies to COM that the server is an NT service, so if the server is not running, it will start it using the Service Control Manager.

Intuition would decree that this manipulation should be done in the AppID-specific RGS file, but the ATL team decided instead to add it directly to the `RegisterServer()` function for the module. The reason for this is that the process can be registered as a service *or* as a local server. If this information were in a `.rgs` script, you would not have this flexibility.

The registration code looks like this:

```
CRegKey keyAppID;
LONG lRes = keyAppID.Open(HKEY_CLASSES_ROOT, _T("AppID"), KEY_WRITE);
if(lRes != ERROR_SUCCESS)
    return lRes;

CRegKey key;
lRes = key.Open(
        keyAppID, _T("{BAADF00D-BEEF-BEEF-BEEF-BAADF00DBEEF}"), KEY_WRITE);
if(lRes != ERROR_SUCCESS)
    return lRes;

key.DeleteValue(_T("LocalService"));

if(bService)
{
    key.SetValue(_T("MyService"), _T("LocalService"));
```

```
        key.SetValue(_T("-Service"), _T("ServiceParameters"));

        // Create service
        Install();
}
```

This opens the server's AppID key, and if the server is being registered as a service, it will add a
`LocalService` entry with the name of the NT service. It will also add a `ServiceParameters`
item with `-Service` as a value. Thus, when an ATL service is started, it can tell whether it is being
started as an NT service or as a local server.

Why does it do this? Well, NT services are designed as background processes and typically run under
privileged accounts (in particular, the `LocalSystem` account). If you run the server as a local server,
it allows you to bypass the service start up code and behave as a normal local server. Thus you can
test and debug your COM objects before you start to worry about testing it as a service. To register it
to be used as a service, you should run the EXE with the `-Service` switch; otherwise, you should
use the usual `-RegServer` switch.

Note that NT services require additional registration to install them into the service database. The
`Install()` method in the above code does this by calling the `CreateService()` Win32 API.

## Object Registration

The second type of RGS file is created for objects. When you add a new ATL object to your project,
the Object Wizard will create an RGS file using the **Short Name** that you have specified:

```
HKCR
{
    MyServer.MyObject.1 = s 'MyObject Class'
    {
        CLSID = s '{BADF00D2-BEEF-BEEF-BEEF-BAADF00DBEEF}'
    }
    MyServer.MyObject = s 'MyObject Class'
    {
        CLSID = s '{BADF00D2-BEEF-BEEF-BEEF-BAADF00DBEEF}'
        CurVer = s ' MyServer.MyObject.1'
    }
    NoRemove CLSID
    {
        ForceRemove {BADF00D2-BEEF-BEEF-BEEF-BAADF00DBEEF}
            = s 'MyObject Class'
        {
            ProgID = s ' MyServer.MyObject.1'
            VersionIndependentProgID = s ' MyServer.MyObject'
            ForceRemove 'Programmable'
            LocalServer32 = s '%MODULE%'
            val AppID = s '{BAADF00D-BEEF-BEEF-BEEF-BAADF00DBEEF}'
            'TypeLib' = s '{BADF00D1-BEEF-BEEF-BEEF-BAADF00DBEEF}'
        }
    }
}
```

This registers the version dependent and version independent ProgIDs, and the CLSID entry. This example shows the entry for an EXE. A DLL server has essentially the same data, except it does not have the entry for the AppID, and instead of `LocalServer32`, it will specify `InprocServer32` with a `ThreadingModel` value:

```
InprocServer32 = s '%MODULE%'
{
    val ThreadingModel = s 'Free'
}
```

## UpdateRegistryFromResource()

This method does the work of registering the object via an RGS file. In fact, if you look in `atlbase.h`, you will find that there are two versions of this function. The version that's called depends on whether the _ATL_STATIC_REGISTRY symbol is set:

```
#ifdef _ATL_STATIC_REGISTRY
    #define UpdateRegistryFromResource UpdateRegistryFromResourceS
#else
    #define UpdateRegistryFromResource UpdateRegistryFromResourceD
#endif
```

The difference between the two is that the S-suffixed method creates a stack based object of type `CRegObject`, while the D-suffixed method calls `AtlModuleUpdateRegistryFromResourceD()`, which in turn creates an instance of the ATL registrar object.

Once the registrar is created, the calls are essentially the same as the calls to the `CRegObject`. The only difference is that the registrar is accessed through a smart pointer to ensure that `Release()` is called when it is no longer needed. The `CRegObject` is stack based, so when *it* is no longer needed, its resources are cleaned up when the variable goes out of scope. (Of course, there is also the fact that one is accessed through the dot operator and the other is accessed through the `->` operator.)

Note that both methods are passed a resource ID and a pointer to an array of _ATL_REGMAP_ENTRY items:

```
struct _ATL_REGMAP_ENTRY
{
    LPCOLESTR szKey;
    LPCOLESTR szData;
};
```

The registrar will go through the `.rgs` script, and every time it sees a string enclosed between `%` characters, it will search the map for a `szKey` with this string. If one exists, it will replace the string with the corresponding data in `szData`. After this replacement has been carried out, the script will be used to change the registry. ATL does not use this facility; it is for your own use. To do so, you should edit the RGS file to contain the items you want replacing, override the `UpdateRegistry()` call in your ATL class to create a static array of these items, and pass this array to the registration method.

For example, if you want to add a key with the date that an object is registered, you could change the object's `.rgs` file and add the following:

```
HKLM
{
    Noremove Software
    {
        NoRemove Wrox
        {
            ForceRemove MyObject = s 'MyObject Class'
            {
                InstallDate = s '%Date%'
            }
        }
    }
}
```

This will add a key to the `HKEY_LOCAL_MACHINE` hive called `Software\Wrox\MyObject`. In that, it will add a string value called `InstallDate`, which is filled with the date during registration. To do this, your `CMyObject` class should not have a registry macro — instead, it must override `UpdateRegistry()`:

```
static HRESULT WINAPI UpdateRegistry(BOOL bRegister)
{
    USES_CONVERSION;
    TCHAR strDate[20];
    SYSTEMTIME st;
    GetLocalTime(&st);
    wsprintf(strDate, _T("%02d-%02d-%04d %02d:%02d:%02d"),
             st.wDay, st.wMonth, st.wYear, st.wHour, st.wMinute, st.wSecond);

    static _ATL_REGMAP_ENTRY MapEntries[2];
    size_t t = sizeof(MapEntries);
    memset(MapEntries, 0, sizeof(MapEntries));
    MapEntries[0].szKey = OLESTR("Date");
    MapEntries[0].szData = T2OLE(strDate);
    return _Module.UpdateRegistryFromResourceD(
                            IDR_NOCREATE, bRegister, MapEntries);
}
```

This gets the current time and formats it into a string. Then it creates an array of `_ATL_MAP_ENTRIES` with an extra entry that has `NULL` pointers to indicate the end of the array. In this example, the first entry associates the key `Date` with the formatted date and then this, together with the resource ID of the RGS script, is passed to a call to `UpdateRegistryFromResourceD()` in the module object.

Note that the appropriate `UpdateRegistryFromResource()` method is used in two contexts. First, it's called when the AppID is registered for an EXE in a call to `_Module.UpdateRegistryFromResource()` in `_tWinMain()`. Second, it is called when the server's `coclasses` are registered by the call to `RegisterServer()` in `_tWinMain()` or `DllRegisterServer()`. As explained earlier, `RegisterServer()` calls `AtlModuleRegisterServer()` which iterates through the object map and calls each object's `pfnUpdateRegistry` method. The `OBJECT_ENTRY()` macro sets this to `UpdateRegistry()`, and so ultimately this ends up in a call to `UpdateRegistryFromResource()` as well.

# Creating Objects with CComObject<>

Your ATL class does not implement the IUnknown methods, so if you try to create an object on the heap or stack, the creation will fail. Instead, you must use your class as a parameter to CComObject<> and create an instance of the generated class. However, there are some things you must be wary of. The CComObject<> constructor does not call FinalConstruct(), so if you initialize resources in this method, you should either call it explicitly or use the class's static CreateInstance() method. Note, though, that the destructor of CComObject<> *does* call FinalRelease().

ATL provides other CComObject<>-like templates, and these all work in a similar way – that is, the template parameter is a CComObjectRoot-derived class (your ATL class), and the new class derives from that parameter. In this way, the new class will contain all the public members of your class, plus the IUnknown members implemented by that class.

| Template | Description |
|---|---|
| CComObject<> | Used for most objects |
| CComObjectCached<> | Used by class factories in DLLs |
| CComObjectNoLock<> | Does not change the module's lock count |
| CComObjectGlobal<> | The reference count of the object is maintained by the module's lock count |
| CComObjectStack<> | Provides only stub methods for reference counting |
| CComContainedObject<> | Used by aggregated objects and tear-offs |
| CComAggObject<> | Used by aggregated objects |
| CComPolyObject<> | Used by aggregated objects and non-aggregated objects |
| CComTearOffObject<> | Used by tear-off interfaces |
| CComCachedTearOffObject<> | Used by tear-off interfaces |

CComObjectNoLock<> will not change the lock count of the module (unlike CComObject<>, which increases the lock count in its constructor and decrements it in the destructor). ATL's EXE class factory templates use this class.

CComObjectGlobal<> is used to implement objects at global scope. The template implements AddRef() and Release() using the module's lock count, so that the module will not be released until all the references on this global object have been released.

Since CComObjectStack<> is designed for use on the stack (that is, an automatic variable in a method), the reference counting methods are not used. You should not pass instances of this template to other methods, as they will assume the COM rules apply and will call Release() when they are finished with the object. To make sure that you know when AddRef() or Release() *are* called, these methods are implemented to assert in debug builds.

If you have an ATL COM class implemented in your server, and you wish to use its services, you can create an instance on the stack without having to call CoCreateInstance(), like this:

```
HRESULT CMyObject::Method()
{
    CComObjectStack<CMyOtherObject> myObject;
    HRESULT hr = myObject.AnotherMethod();
    return hr;
}
```

If you want to use a temporary object in a method, use CComObjectStack<>, but don't call its reference counting methods – the object should be allowed to die naturally as it goes out of scope. If you want to use a global or a shared object, then use CComObjectGlobal<>.

CComContainedObject<> delegates the IUnknown calls to another 'outer' object, and so it's used to implement IUnknown for aggregated objects and for tear-off interfaces that need access to the main object's QueryInterface().

Typically, you will use CComObject<> when you want to create an object and pass an interface reference out to a client – the object should be created with one of the following methods:

```
CComObject< CYourATLClass >::CreateInstance()
CYourATLClass::_CreatorClass::CreateInstance()
CComCreator< CComObject< CYourATLClass > >::CreateInstance()
```

If you use CComObject<>::CreateInstance(), the interface that is passed to the client should be obtained by a call to QueryInterface().

# Summary

This chapter has gone through the general architecture of ATL, explaining how it implements class factories, IUnknown methods, registration, module entry points and lock counts. There is a lot of flexibility built into this architecture, and you can change most of the options by using appropriate macros. Note that much of this has to be done by hand: Visual C++ 6 does not supply Wizards to do it for you.

The next chapter will move on to describe how ATL implements interfaces, and how you can add more interfaces to your object class.

# 3

# Interfaces

COM objects are not accessed directly. Instead, you must obtain a reference to an interface on an object. This has several advantages including **location transparency**, and the enforcement of **interface programming**.

With location transparency, you access an object as if it were implemented in the same apartment as the client, even if the object is actually in another apartment in the process, or in another process, or on another machine. You can do this because when necessary, COM silently creates an in-process proxy object to marshal the interface for you. Since you always access the object through an interface pointer, that pointer can point to any object that implements the required interface, without the user of the pointer knowing exactly what it is pointing to.

Interface programming means that the interface and its implementation are separate. This is important because COM objects are language neutral. Furthermore, since every interface must derive from IUnknown, it means that all COM objects support interface negotiation – at runtime, a client can query an object for the interfaces it supports. Interfaces define the behavior of an object, and through interface negotiation, a client can request only the functionality that it requires.

ATL has support for you to implement different interfaces on your object; you can choose to define and implement new interfaces, or you can implement previously defined interfaces. If you decide that your object should support a standard COM interface, you can implement it yourself, or you can use an ATL-defined default implementation.

## Wizard Generated Interfaces

Despite its name, the ATL Object Wizard allows you to create new COM *classes*. The Object Wizard contains 'templates' of various types of COM class, and it will create all the necessary code for one of these classes. The ATL COM AppWizard creates an application for you, and you add code to fill in the functionality of the application; the Object Wizard creates a class for you, and you fill in the functionality of the class.

*Just as you can create new AppWizards to create a template for the custom projects that you will want to create, you can also create new Object Wizard templates for custom classes. I'll show you how to do that in the next chapter.*

Interfaces define the behavior of a class, so your choice of the interfaces implemented by a class defines its functionality. The classes that Object Wizard creates for you will have all the interfaces required in a particular situation. For many of the standard interfaces, the ATL implementation will suffice, so your task is often limited to adding the extra functionality of your own interfaces.

There are two things that you should be aware of when creating a new class through Object Wizard. The first is that for just about all the items, it will create a new interface for you. The second is that (with the exception of this new interface) the Object Wizard decides all the interfaces that your class supports. Currently, there is no way to use Object Wizard to add support for other pre-defined interfaces; however, adding and removing interfaces from an ATL class is straightforward, and you can do it either by editing the IDL and source files by hand, or by using ClassView.

# ClassView

As you know, ClassView is used primarily to show the existing classes in your project. However, in Visual C++ 6.0 it has some new features used to modify classes, and in particular to add COM features to ATL classes. To change a class, you should select it in ClassView and then right click on it:

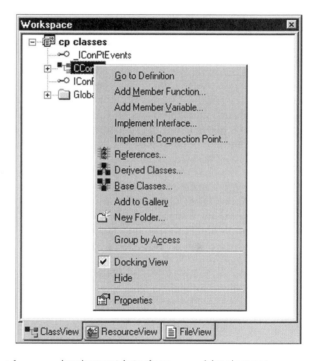

The two context menu items that are relevant here are Implement Interface... and Implement Connection Point..., which allow you to add a new interface or a new connection point to your class respectively.

When you select an *interface* in the ClassView and right-click, you get this context menu:

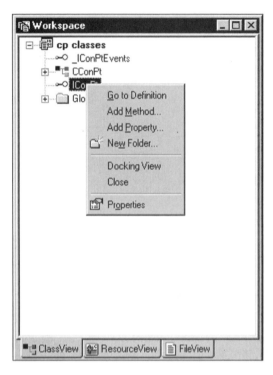

Here, the Add Method... and Add Property... items are the important ones; we'll be looking at all these ClassView options in the sections to come.

## Adding New Interfaces

The Implement Interface... menu item is a new feature in Visual C++ 6.0 that allows you to add a new interface without having to edit the project IDL and object class header by hand. This is a good step forward, but it's not perfect because it only allows you to implement interfaces described in a type library.

If you use this menu item before compiling the original IDL for your project to produce a type library, you will get the following warning:

If you decide that the interface you want to implement is described in another type library, you can click on OK, which will allow you to select a registered type library, or to browse for any unregistered type libraries that you may have. (If you had already compiled the type library for your project, you would go directly to the Implement Interface dialog, as described below.)

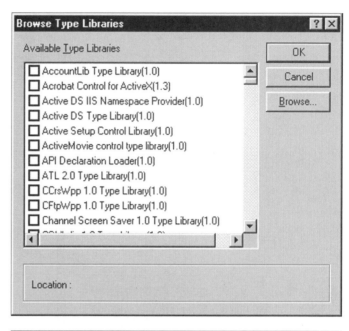

You can use the list box (Available Type Libraries) to select a registered type library, or you can click on Browse... to select a non-registered type library. Once a type library has been selected, you will get this dialog:

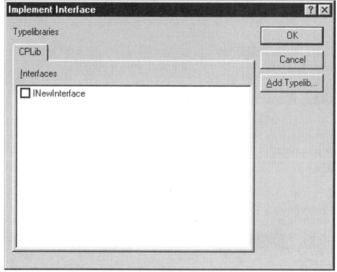

For each type library you add, you'll see a new tab on the dialog. When you select a tab, the Wizard will read all the interfaces defined in the type library and add them to the Interfaces list box. Note that the Wizard will *not* show dispinterfaces because ATL only has support for dual interfaces. If you want to implement a dispinterface, you will have to add and implement the interface by hand, as explained later in this chapter. Note also that the list won't show interfaces already implemented by the class in question.

The Wizard seems to determine which interfaces are already implemented using the same rules as ClassView itself – that is, by looking at the COM map. If ClassView displays an interface as being implemented by a particular class, no interface with the same name will appear in the list of interfaces in a type library.

When you check the box next to an interface and click OK, the Wizard will edit the header for the class you selected in ClassView, derive it from the selected interface, and add the interface to its COM map. Finally, the Wizard will add stub implementations for the interface methods in the *header* for the class, although you may decide to move them to the CPP file.

There are two main purposes to which you can put this Wizard. You can use it to implement an existing interface that's described in a type library, or you can use it to add a new interface to the class.

### Implementing Existing Interfaces

To use an interface that has already been defined, you should use the Browse Type Libraries dialog to select a registered type library, or click its **Browse**... button to select an unregistered type library.

COM-defined interfaces, like IMarshal or IExternalConnection, are not described in a system-supplied type library, but you *can* create your own. To do this, create a new IDL file with a library section that imports the appropriate COM IDL file and declares the interface that you want to use. When you do this, you may find that you have to import several IDL files because of the dependencies between those files.

As an example, if you want to implement IOleItemContainer on your object, you would need to create the following IDL file:

```
// itemcontainer.idl
[
    uuid(A04BEF54-9C73-11D1-9AC9-0060973044A8),
    version(1.0)
]
library RTGStdLIB
{
    import "oleidl.idl";
    interface IOleItemContainer;
};
```

You need to specify the interface that you want to use, and the IDL file where that interface is defined. This imported IDL file must be within the library block, because all you want MIDL to do is compile the definitions into a type library. (If the import is outside the library block, then MIDL will generate the C marshaling files). Since you only want to use it to create the type library, you should not add this IDL to your project. To compile it, you will need to call MIDL by hand from the command line.

*An alternative approach to creating a type library containing many of the system-defined interfaces is simply to #include the system IDL file within the library block. Note that MIDL implicitly imports some IDL files, so although this will not work for all system-supplied IDL files (you'll get redefinition errors), it's quick and easy for the ones that do work.*

Once the ClassView Wizard has read the type library, you can select the interface that you want to use. However, if the interface is derived from interfaces other than IUnknown, then you *must* add those interfaces to your class too. The Wizard only adds the methods and COM map entry for the most derived interface, not for any of its bases.

For example, if you want to implement IOleItemContainer, you must also add the IOleContainer and IParseDisplayName interfaces, because IOleItemContainer derives from IOleContainer, which derives from IParseDisplayName. However, when you do this, the Wizard will derive your ATL class from all three base interfaces, so you will need to edit the ATL class by hand and remove them.

As a final point, type libraries lose some information that's present in the IDL. For example, a BOOL parameter will be added to a type library as long (since BOOL is a typedef for long in wtypes.idl). The ClassView Wizard will interpret this as a LONG. On the other hand, when you compile the IDL to create a header file, MIDL will put the BOOL parameter directly into the header. BOOL is typedef'd in windef.h as int. Another example is that a REFIID will be put into a type library as a _GUID* rather than a REFIID (which is a reference). The net effect of this is that you may have to edit some of the stub methods to have the correct parameter types.

### Implementing New Interfaces

If you want to add a completely new interface to your object, then you need to do some of the work by hand. First, you need to add the interface to the project IDL; in most cases you will want to be able to marshal the interface, and so you must make sure that the interface definition is *outside* the library block. Then, you need to use the GUID generator to create a new IID for the interface, and add a stub definition similar to this:

```
[
    uuid(A04BEF53-9C73-11D1-9AC9-0060973044A8)
]
interface INewInterface
{
};
```

Next, add this interface to the coclass definition in the library block:

```
[
    uuid(A342BA91-9BEC-11D1-9AC8-0060973044A8),
    version(1.0)
]
library MyNewLib
{
    importlib("stdole32.tlb");
    importlib("stdole2.tlb");

    [
        uuid(A342BA9E-9BEC-11D1-9AC8-0060973044A8)
    ]
    coclass MyObject
    {
        [default] interface IMyObject;
        interface INewInterface;
    };
};
```

Now compile the project IDL (either from the command line or from within the IDE) and then use the ClassView Wizard to add the interface to your object. You can then add methods and properties to this interface in the normal way.

## Adding a Connection Point

Another new feature of ClassView in Visual C++ 6.0 is the support for connection points. When you select **Support Connection Points** in the Object Wizard, it will add a dispinterface to the project IDL as the outgoing interface for the connection point mechanism. This interface definition is added to the `library` block of the IDL (not outside it) because the Universal Marshaler uses the type library to marshal dispinterfaces, and so standard marshaling is not required.

The Object Wizard will also derive your class from `IConnectionPointConta inerImpl<>` and add a connection point map to your class. However, note that it does *not* add the outgoing interface to the map. To do this, you need to right click on the class in ClassView and select **Implement Connection Point**. This will read the type library for the project and list all the dispinterfaces in the **Implement Connection Point** dialog:

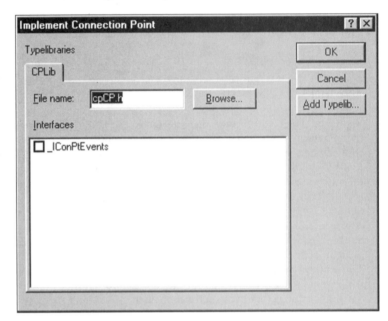

You can use the **Add Typelib...** button to add an outgoing interface defined in another type library. The **File name** will be used as the name of the file in which the Wizard will put the proxy class that it generates. To generate the proxy class, you check the box next to the interface and click on OK. The Wizard will then add the interface to the connection point map:

```
BEGIN_CONNECTION_POINT_MAP(CConPt)
    CONNECTION_POINT_ENTRY(DIID__IConPtEvents)
END_CONNECTION_POINT_MAP()
```

It will also create a proxy class that your code should call to generate the event(s) defined in the outgoing interface, derive your class from this proxy, and `#include` the header for this proxy in the header file for your ATL class. In Visual C++ 5.0, you had to run the ATL Proxy Generator to generate this proxy class.

> *That's all I have to say about connection points in this rapid tour of the Wizards, but certainly not in the book as a whole. Connection points get Chapter 8 all to themselves.*

## Adding Methods

The Add Method context menu item in ClassView is much the same as its predecessor in Visual C++ 5.0. However, in Visual C++ 6.0, the dialog updates the Implementation box as you type characters into the Method Name and Parameters edit boxes; in the Visual C++ 5.0 version, you had to tab out of the edit boxes to get this control to update.

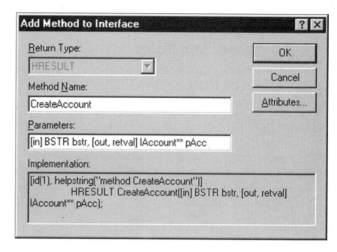

For all interfaces (other than dispinterfaces) the Return Type should be HRESULT; this is because if the interface is marshaled, COM will use the return values of the interface methods to give error results when the marshaling fails. If you do not use an HRESULT, COM will not be able to do this. Even if you decide that the interface will only ever be used on in-process objects, you should still follow the convention – remember that a client has no knowledge of an object's location, and you should write the object code to reflect this.

A dispinterface method does not have to specify HRESULT as the Return Type because the actual method being called by COM is IDispatch::Invoke(), which always returns an HRESULT.

The method name is entirely up to you. If you have designed your object using a modeling tool, you will not have many options about the names and number of methods on an interface. If you decide to design your object without such a tool, then you should read the *Interface Guidelines* section later in this chapter.

The Parameters box is used to enter a comma-separated list of parameters for the method. You must give an indication of whether the data is being passed to the object, or returned from it. If you are sending data to the object, the method should have the [in] attribute (like the bstr parameter above); if the data is allocated by the object then the parameter *must* be a pointer type, and you should use the [out] attribute (like the pAcc parameter). If the client passes data to and obtains data back from the object through a single parameter, this parameter should be a pointer type and marked [in, out].

Finally, if the (last) parameter of a method is used to return data, and you wish knowledgeable clients to be able to use this as the return value of the method, that parameter should be marked with [out, retval]. This means that Visual Basic clients, for example, will treat the method as having one less parameter, and as being a function that returns a value. You will also find that the high-level methods generated by #import will use this parameter as the return type. Such clients have the true return value of the method (the HRESULT) hidden from them, but failure HRESULTs get thrown as exceptions.

### Method Attributes

Methods may have attributes, and to specify what attributes to use, you should click on the Attributes... button:

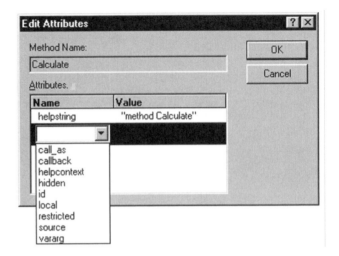

To enter a new attribute, you should double-click on the line below the last attribute in the Attributes list box. You can select an attribute from the list box on the left, and enter the attribute parameter (if any) in the edit box on the right. These are the attributes you can use; some notes on the more interesting ones follow this table:

| Attribute | Description | Parameter |
|---|---|---|
| [call_as()] | For a [local] function, this indicates the remote version | The local method |
| [helpcontext()] | Defines a help file context ID | The ID |
| [helpstring()] | Describes the method | A descriptive string |
| [hidden] | The method is hidden from object browsers | - |
| [id()] | The DISPID for the method | Positive or 0 |
| [local] | Indicates that the function cannot be called through a proxy | - |
| [restricted] | Prevents macro languages from calling the method | - |
| [source] | Indicates that the method returns an object that is the source of events | - |
| [vararg] | Indicates that the method takes a variable number of parameters | - |

### [local] and [call_as()]

Often, methods are called cross-process or cross-machine using different parameters to those that the client or object will use. The [local] attribute is used to indicate the interface method that the client will call (and the object will implement), and the [call_as()] attribute is used to mark the actual method that will be called during marshaling. For example:

```
interface IClassFactory : IUnknown
{
    [local] HRESULT CreateInstance([in, unique] IUnknown* pUnkOuter,
                            [in] REFIID riid,
                            [out, iid_is(riid)] void** ppvObject);
    [call_as(CreateInstance)] HRESULT RemoteCreateInstance(
                            [in] REFIID riid,
                            [out, iid_is(riid)] IUnknown** ppvObject);

    // Other members missed out
};
```

When MIDL compiles this IDL, the C++ header will have a definition for CreateInstance() but not RemoteCreateInstance(). However, the generated proxy-stub code will have marshaling code for RemoteCreateInstance() and not CreateInstance().

The [local] version is the one that a client will call. It has parameters that are relevant to the client code (and to calling the method in the in-process case), and it reflects the method that an object will implement. In this example, the pUnkOuter parameter is used when creating an object that will be aggregated, and its purpose is to pass the IUnknown of the outer (aggregating) object. Aggregation cannot be performed across apartments, so this parameter is not relevant when marshaling across apartments, and hence the [call_as()] version does not have it.

Another situation in which [local]/[call_as()] might be used is to make the parameters of the [local] version more 'natural' for the object caller, but to convert this to a version that can be marshaled. For example, IBindStatusCallback::GetBindInfo() (which you can find in urlmon.idl) has a client-callable version that takes a pointer to a BINDINFO structure, but the data contained is actually marshaled using RemBINDINFO and RemSTGMEDIUM. The marshaler will convert the data from BINDINFO to these parameters.

> *Using a* [local]/[call_as()] *pair requires the interface designer to provide a proxy function (to convert from the* [local] *method to the* [call_as()] *method) and a stub function (to convert from the* [call_as()] *method to the* [local] *method).*

### [id()]

The [id()] attribute is used to associate a DISPID with a method. Note that the **Add Method** dialog will only allow you to give a value that is positive or zero. This is a pain if you have symbols defined for method DISPIDs, or if you are using negative DISPIDs, because you will have to edit the IDL by hand to use those symbols.

### [vararg]

The [vararg] attribute indicates that the method takes a variable number of arguments, a bit like using . . . in a C method. The method must have a final parameter that is of the type SAFEARRAY(VARIANT), so that the client can indicate how many extra parameters there are and pass them in. The object can then use normal SAFEARRAY API functions to read these parameters.

## *Adding Properties*

The Add Property to Interface dialog is
again essentially the same as the one in
Visual C++ 5.0, although (as with the Add
Method dialog) this new version updates the
Implementation box whenever you type in to
the edit boxes.

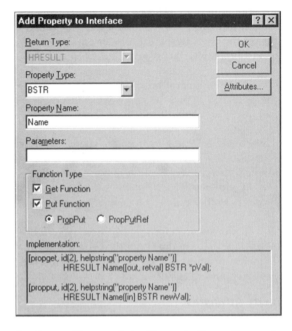

Note that properties have two associated types: the Return Type and the Property Type. Properties
are implemented using methods; MIDL will just add get_ in front of the property name in response
to [propget] and put_ in response to [propput] for the method names that it generates in the
interface header file.

The Return Type is the return value from these methods, and the Property Type is the parameter of
the methods ([in] for the put_ method, and an [out] pointer for the get_ method). For
properties on a dual or a custom interface, the Return Type will be HRESULT.

If the property is on a dispinterface, this dialog will add the property as accessor and mutator
methods in the methods section of the interface (rather than adding the property as a single member
of the properties section). This is so that you can use the radio buttons to determine whether the
property is read- or write-only. If you prefer, you can edit the IDL by hand and create a single
property entry (MIDL will still generate the required put_ and get_ method signatures).

The list boxes contain the types you can use:

| | | | |
|---|---|---|---|
| short | short* | float | float* |
| long | long* | double | double* |
| CURRENCY | CURRENCY* | CY | CY* |
| DATE | DATE* | BSTR | BSTR* |
| LPDISPATCH | LPDISPATCH* | IDispatch* | IDispatch** |
| LPUNKNOWN | LPUNKNOWN* | IUnknown* | IUnknown** |
| SCODE | SCODE* | BOOL | BOOL* |
| VARIANT | VARIANT* | OLE_COLOR | OLE_COLOR* |
| HRESULT | void | | |

HRESULT and void are only listed in the Return Type list box. The list boxes give the synonyms for the various types (e.g. LPDISPATCH and IDispatch*) so that you can choose whichever suits your programming style. The Return Type is a drop down list box, so you are restricted to just these values; however, the Property Type is a combo box for dual and custom interfaces, so you can use one of the types in the list box, or enter your own. This is useful for implementing properties that return typed interfaces (say, ICustomer*).

The Parameters edit box allows you to specify extra parameters to be used when getting or setting the property. Typically, you'll avoid this edit box, but if you're implementing a property that behaves like an array, you will specify the parameter(s) used to subscript that array here.

The Function Type allows you to specify whether the property is read only (just check the Get Function box), write only (just check the Put Function box) or read/write (check both). If you choose to allow the property to have a put_ function, and the property is an object (interface) type, you should choose the PropPutRef radio button, so that it can be used with the Set keyword in Visual Basic. For other types, you should generally use PropPut.

As you can see, you have many options here. My recommendation is to leave the Return Type as HRESULT, and use the Property Type to specify the type of the value used to get and set the property. Typically, I ignore the Parameters box, and use PropPutRef for the put_ method of an interface property, and PropPut for other property types.

### Property Attributes

Just like methods, properties can have attributes too:

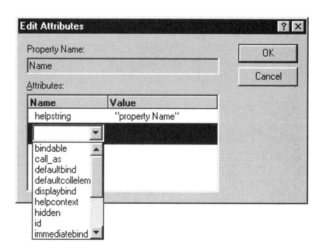

Remember that properties are implemented as methods, so many of the attributes are the same as before. However, there are some attributes that are not applicable to methods:

| Attribute | Description | Parameter |
|-----------|-------------|-----------|
| [bindable] | The property is bindable via IPropertyNotifySink | - |
| [call_as()] | Indicates the method that is called when a [local] property is called remotely | The name of the [local] property |

| Attribute | Description | Parameter |
|---|---|---|
| [defaultbind] | A bindable property that is the default property for the interface | - |
| [defaultcollelem] | An optimization used on collections for Visual Basic, it treats collection members accessed through the ! syntax as properties of the object that implements the collection | - |
| [displaybind] | Indicates to object browsers that a property is bindable | - |
| [helpcontext()] | Gives a help file context ID | The context ID |
| [helpstring()] | Associates a descriptive string with the property | The string |
| [hidden] | The property is hidden in object browsers | - |
| [id()] | The DISPID of the property | Positive or zero |
| [immediatebind] | Indicates that when the property changes, the value is sent to the binding container | - |
| [local] | Indicates that the property is not marshaled | - |
| [nonbrowseable] | Indicates that the property can appear in an *object* browser (like the Visual Basic Object Browser), but not in a *property* browser (like the Visual Basic property box) | - |
| [requestedit] | The property is bound via IPropertyNotifySink::OnRequestEdit() | - |
| [restricted] | Prevents macro languages from accessing the property | - |
| [source] | The property represents an object that generates events and indicates that high level languages should read the type information for this object to determine what those events are | - |
| [vararg] | Indicates that the property's method takes a variable number of parameters | - |

An immediate theme that emerges from these attributes is the idea of **binding**. To bind an object's property, the client must implement the IPropertyNotifySink sink interface, and the object must implement a connection point for this interface (it must support IConnectionPointContainer). When the property changes, it must use the object's connection point mechanism to inform the client that the property is about to change ([requestedit]) or that it has changed. In the former case, the client has the option of canceling the change, so properties with [requestedit] must discard the new value. Data binding is covered in Chapter 10.

As mentioned earlier, methods may have variable numbers of arguments, and since properties are implemented as methods, this attribute indicates that the put_/get_ methods are implemented in this fashion. However, using more than one argument for property methods does remove the distinction between interface methods and properties, so it is probably best not to use the [vararg] attribute on properties.

# _ATL_NO_VTABLE Optimization

When you create a new ATL object using the Object Wizard, you will find that the Wizard declares your ATL class with the ATL_NO_VTABLE symbol. This symbol is defined in Atldef.h, according to whether you have defined the _ATL_DISABLE_NO_VTABLE symbol:

```
#ifdef _ATL_DISABLE_NO_VTABLE
#define ATL_NO_VTABLE
#else
#define ATL_NO_VTABLE __declspec(novtable)
#endif
```

Visual C++ 5.0 introduced the 'no vtable' optimization technique to speed up object creation by preventing the compiler from generating vtable initialization code in a class's constructor. This optimization is applied using __declspec(novtable), and should only be applied to abstract classes. When this optimization is *not* applied, vtable initialization code is executed for each class in an inheritance hierarchy. However, only the vtable for the most derived class is ever used, so each initialization in a base class is wasted effort. Since abstract classes can never be instantiated directly – they can only be used as base classes – the no vtable optimization can be applied safely.

# Tear-off Interfaces

Objects can have many interfaces, but when one of them will be used more often than any of the others, it is usually marked as the [default] interface of the object, so that languages like Visual Basic can access this interface directly without having to specify it.

Some other interfaces on an object will be rarely used. If initialization of these interfaces takes a noticeable amount of time, or consumes resources, then you may decide that it would be better to delay initialization until the interface is actually used and then release the interface's resources when the interface is no longer being used. Imagine, for example, an object that can manage its persistent state in a database via calls to an interface called IPersistDatabase:

```
interface IPersistDatabase : IUnknown
{
    HRESULT Load();
    HRESULT Save();
};
```

Load() will use an ID held as an object member to find the correct record in the database, and then load the object's other data members from this record. Save() just does the reverse – it writes the data into a record in the database.

There are a number of possibilities for implementing this interface. One option would be to create the database connection when the object is created, and release the connection when the object is finally released. However, this clearly involves holding onto resources unnecessarily, especially if the other interfaces on the object don't need a database connection.

Another solution would be to create the connection at the beginning of the call to the Load() or Save() method, and then to release the connection when the method finishes. However, obtaining and releasing database connections is often a time consuming task, and so calls to Load() and Save() will take a long time. This will be a particular problem if the client is likely to do one initial Load() and then multiple Save()s to keep the object state persistent.

A final approach is to create the database connection when the *interface* is first used, and release it when the interface is released. We know exactly when an interface is first used, because a client will call QueryInterface() to get the interface pointer. Furthermore, when the last Release() is called on this interface, reducing the *interface* reference count to zero, we know that the client has finished using it. At this point, the database connection can be released.

An interface that behaves like this is called a **tear-off interface**. Note from the above discussion that a tear-off interface *must* manage its own reference count. When ATL uses multiple inheritance, there is an *object-wide* reference count maintained through the CComObjectRootEx<> template, so tear-off interfaces cannot be implemented by multiple inheritance. Instead, the tear-off must be implemented as a separate C++ object, so that it can manage its own reference count. As you saw in Chapter 2, to create a tear-off interface, you use the COM_INTERFACE_ENTRY_TEAR_OFF() macro.

It is important to point out that this behavior will only occur if the object is being accessed from the same apartment as the client. If the tear-off interface is on an object accessed from another apartment then you will have the reduced (but still useful) behavior of delayed initialization without the benefit of early release of resources.

The reason is that when you access an object cross-apartment, a proxy object is used in the client apartment and a stub object in the server, the proxy caches the reference count changes that the client makes to optimize the calls across apartments. This is generally a good thing, but the downside is that the proxy will not keep a separate reference count for the tear-off, so the object is not informed when the last reference on the tear-off is released.

So, using the above example, if an object implements IPersistDatabase and this object is accessed cross-apartment, then the database connection will not be made until QueryInterface() has been called. This is the behavior that you want. However, since the proxy caches reference counts, it means that the database connection will remain open until the entire object has been released.

If your object just relies on delayed initialization then a tear-off is a good choice for cross-apartment calls. If the object relies on early release of resources (when the tear-off is released) then a tear-off should not be used cross apartment.

# COM_INTERFACE_ENTRY_TEAR_OFF() Macro

Let's take a slightly deeper look at the COM_INTERFACE_ENTRY_TEAR_OFF() macro, which you can find in Atlcom.h:

```
#define COM_INTERFACE_ENTRY_TEAR_OFF(iid, x)\
    {&iid,\
    (DWORD)&_CComCreatorData<\
        CComInternalCreator< CComTearOffObject< x > >\
        >::data,\
    _Creator},
```

This macro ensures that when `QueryInterface()` is called, the
`CComObjectBase::_Creator()` function is called, passing as a parameter
`_CComCreatorData<CComInternalCreator<CComTearOffObject< x > > >::data`. If
you do all the necessary expansions and wind through the code, you'll find that this `data` is the
`CreateInstance()` for the `CComInternalCreator<>` class which, as you know, calls `new` to
create a new `CComTearOffObject<>` object.

The point of this diversion is this: what happens if you call `QueryInterface()` for the tear-off
interface on the object *twice*? The answer is that each time the interface is queried, a new tear-off
object is created:

```
CComPtr<IUnknown> pUnk;
GetPersistableObjectFromSomewhere(&pUnk);

CComQIPtr<IPersistDatabase> pIPDB1;
CComQIPtr<IPersistDatabase> pIPDB2;
pIPDB1 = pUnk;
pIPDB2 = pUnk;
assert(pIPDB1 == pIPDB2);
```

The previous code will assert because the `QueryInterface()` implicit in the assignment operator
will create a new tear-off C++ object for the interface each time it is called. This does not violate the
COM rules, because *only* the `QueryInterface()` for `IUnknown` must return the same interface
pointer (which is true in this case). If you can guarantee that `QueryInterface()` will only be called
once per object, then this behavior is not a problem. However, if it is likely to be called more than
once, and the tear-off takes a long time to initialize or contains data of which there should be only
one copy, then you need a *cached* tear-off.

As the name suggests, a cached tear-off is essentially just a tear-off where the interface pointer is
cached – if `QueryInterface()` is called for the interface again, then instead of a new tear-off
interface being created, the cached pointer is used. To use a cached tear-off, you need to have an
interface pointer as a member of your ATL class, and to use the
`COM_INTERFACE_ENTRY_CACHED_TEAR_OFF()` macro in the COM map.

```
class ATL_NO_VTABLE CPersistableObject :
    public CComObjectRootEx<CComSingleThreadModel>,
    public CComCoClass<CPersistableObject, &CLSID_PersistableObject>,
    public IStandardBehavior
{
public:
    CPersistableObject() {}

DECLARE_REGISTRY_RESOURCEID(IDR_DISKINFO)

DECLARE_PROTECT_FINAL_CONSTRUCT()
```

```
BEGIN_COM_MAP(CPersistableObject)
    COM_INTERFACE_ENTRY(IStandardBehavior)
    COM_INTERFACE_ENTRY_CACHED_TEAR_OFF(
                    IID_IPersistDatabase, CPersistDatabase, m_pUnkTearOff.p)
END_COM_MAP()

// IStandardBehavior
public:
...
private:
    CComPtr<IUnknown> m_pUnkTearOff;
};
```

# Example: Tear-off Interfaces

Let's look at an example using a tear-off interface. In it, we're going to create a COM class that provides information about the local file system. Specifically, we're going to allow the client to specify a directory, and then find out how many files are in that directory.

We're also going to allow the client to retrieve the names of all the directories on a disk. This list of subdirectory names will be built recursively, so the list could be quite large, and it could take some time to build it. The name of the disk for which we'll allow the client to generate a directory list will be hard-coded in this example; in a more realistic case, the disk name would probably be set to some particular value, perhaps based on security information provided by the client.

The important point is that the name of the disk for which we generate a directory list (and, indeed, the directories on the disk itself) *will not change during the lifetime of an object of this class.* This allows us to use a tear-off interface to provide the method that will return the directory list. We can use the FinalConstruct() of the tear-off interface to initialize the directory list.

## FinalConstruct()

FinalConstruct() is the method used in ATL to initialize a fully constructed ATL object. CComObjectRootBase declares it (and an associated method called FinalRelease()), and your ATL class inherits it through CComObjectRootEx<>.

The function is used to provide you with a point at which you can make 'fully' virtual function calls immediately after your object has been constructed. You can't use the constructor of your class for this purpose, because the compiler has to statically resolve calls to virtual functions made from a constructor. In other words, it doesn't use the vtable for such calls. This arises from the fact that a derived class will not be fully constructed during a call to the base class constructor, since classes related by inheritance are constructed in order from base class to most derived class. It would not be safe to call a function in a derived class from a constructor in a base class, so the compiler must resolve such calls to virtual functions at compile time.

FinalConstruct() is called when a class factory creates an instance of the ATL class, and also when CComObject<>::CreateInstance() is called on a heap-based instance of the class. This is an important point, as you'll see if you consider this code:

```
CComPtr<IPing> pItf;

CComObject<CPinger>* pPing;
CComObject<CPinger>::CreateInstance(&pPing);
pPing->QueryInterface(IID_IPing, reinterpret_cast<void**>(&pItf));
// Use pItf
pItf->Release();

CComObject<CPinger>* pPong;
pPong = new CComObject<CPinger>;
pPong->QueryInterface(IID_IPing, reinterpret_cast<void**>(&pItf));
// Use pItf
pItf->Release();
```

These two sections of code may appear to be the same – after all,
`CComObject<>::CreateInstance()` just calls new to create an object, doesn't it? The difference
is that `CreateInstance()` calls the `FinalConstruct()` function defined in `CPinger`, whereas
calling new does not. If you do initialization in `FinalConstruct()`, you must use the former code.

Note that ATL does provide a version of `CComObject<>` called `CComObjectStack<>` that's
designed to be used in this situation. This class calls `FinalConstruct()` of the base class (in this
case, `CPinger`) in its constructor. The following code is therefore acceptable even if `CPinger` has
code in `FinalConstruct()`:

```
CComObjectStack<CPinger> pPong;
pPong.QueryInterface(IID_IPing, reinterpret_cast<void**>(&pItf));
// Use pItf
pItf->Release();
```

`FinalRelease()` is used to release any resources just before an object is destroyed, and typically
releases resources mirroring the allocation in `FinalConstruct()`.

As a final point, note that when you call `CreateInstance()`, it will initialize the object's reference
count to zero. If you call `Release()` on this object (through the `pPing` pointer created above, for
example), the reference count will be decremented to –1, and this *will not* destroy the object (this only
occurs when the reference count is decremented to 0). So, this odd-looking code will delete the object
pointed to by `pPing`:

```
CComObject<CPinger>* pPing;
CComObject<CPinger>::CreateInstance(&pPing);    // ref count is 0
pPing->AddRef();                                 // ref count changes to 1
pPing->Release();                                // ref count changes to 0
```

Obviously, you wouldn't do this on purpose, but there is a situation where it may occur by accident.
If `CPinger` has code in `FinalConstruct()` that passes an interface pointer on the newly
constructed object to another object, then using normal COM reference counting rules, `AddRef()`
must be called when the interface pointer is copied. For the same reason, the object using the
interface pointer will call `Release()` when it is finished with it.

```
HRESULT FinalConstruct()
{
    CComPtr<IAnotherItf> pItf;
```

```
    _InternalQueryInterface(IID_IAnotherItf,
        reinterpret_cast<void**>(&pItf));        // Ref count changes to 1
    g_OtherObject->PassMe(pItf);
    return S_OK;
}
```

The `QueryInterface()` bumps the reference count up to 1, and if the `PassMe()` method doesn't keep a reference count on the object, the reference count will be decremented to zero when the `CComPtr<>` destructor is invoked. This will destroy the `CPinger` object. To safeguard against this, the implementation of `CreateInstance()` should bracket calls to `FinalConstruct()` with the following:

```
    p->InternalFinalConstructAddRef();
    hRes = p->FinalConstruct();
    p->InternalFinalConstructRelease();
```

If the class uses the following macro:

```
    DECLARE_PROTECT_FINAL_CONSTRUCT()
```

These two methods will call `InternalAddRef()` and `InternalRelease()`, temporarily raising the reference count by one during the call to `FinalConstruct()`. (If the macro is not used, then the reference count is not changed.) By default, all classes created by Object Wizard use this macro and hence protect against any code that may change the object's reference count in `FinalConstruct()`.

## Initializing Tear-Offs

Returning to our tear-off interfaces, you might wonder why it's important that the information used to initialize a tear-off interface doesn't change during the lifetime of an object. To find out, consider what would happen if it did. Suppose that a client creates an object, getting its `IUnknown` pointer, and then queries for the `IAmTearOff` interface (which is implemented as a simple tear-off). The tear-off interface then initializes itself with information A, which affects the results of any future method calls on that interface. Now the client subsequently queries the `IUnknown` pointer again for the `IAmTearOff` interface, but this time the information used to initialize the interface has changed to B.

Now the client has two interface pointers to the same interface on the same object, but calling the methods results in completely different behavior depending on which of the interface pointers is used. This is not a good thing! The situation could become even more complicated if marshaling were involved. COM optimizes calls to `QueryInterface()`, so you can't even guarantee which version of the interface a client will get.

You could combat this problem to some extent by using a cached tear-off. Now, the calls to `QueryInterface()` for `IAmTearOff` will result in pointers to the same implementation object (while there's an outstanding reference on that interface). This means that you won't get inconsistent implementations if you call `QueryInterface()` at different times. However, if the change in initialization information is important, the implementation of `IAmTearOff` will become stale. This is something that clients won't expect, and a problem that has no reliable solution even if the clients did know about it.

If the information that you want to use to initialize a tear-off will change during the lifetime of an object (and that change is important to the implementation of the tear-off), you need to reconsider your design decision; there are other optimization techniques that you can use to delay initialization.

## CDirectoryInfo

Start by creating an ATL project called `DirList`, implemented in a DLL. Use the Object Wizard to add a **Simple** object called `DirectoryInfo`, and use the **Attributes** page to specify that the object should have a <u>C</u>ustom interface.

Once the class has been generated, move to ClassView, right-click on IDirectoryInfo, and select **Add** <u>P</u>roperty... from the context menu. Set the property type to `wchar_t*` and call it `Path`, then select **OK**. Now add a read-only property called `NumberOfFiles` of type `long`, using the same procedure.

One of the problems with the **Add Property** dialog is that it doesn't provide any direct access to the attributes or parameter names of the property, so we'll have to make some changes by hand. Once the IDL has been generated, add the `[string]` attribute to the parameter in the `Path` property and change the parameter names in the IDL, header, and source files for this object as shown:

```
interface IDirectoryInfo : IUnknown
{
    [propget, helpstring("property Path")]
    HRESULT Path([out, string, retval] wchar_t** pwszPath);
    [propput, helpstring("property Path")]
    HRESULT Path([in, string] wchar_t* wszPath);
    [propget, helpstring("property NumberOfFiles")]
    HRESULT NumberOfFiles([out, retval] long* pNumber);
};
```

Now you'll need to add some instance data, so change the object header file, `DirectoryInfo.h`:

```
#include "resource.h"        // main symbols
#pragma warning(disable : 4530)   // disable "C++ exception handler used,
                                  // but unwind semantics are not enabled"

#include <string>
typedef std::basic_string<TCHAR> TString;

/////////////////////////////////////////////////////////////////////////////
// CDirectoryInfo
class ATL_NO_VTABLE CDirectoryInfo :
    public CComObjectRootEx<CComSingleThreadModel>,
    public CComCoClass<CDirectoryInfo, &CLSID_DirectoryInfo>,
    public IDirectoryInfo
{
public:
    CDirectoryInfo() : m_Path(_T("C:\\")), m_Disk(_T("C:\\"))
    {
    }

DECLARE_REGISTRY_RESOURCEID(IDR_DIRECTORYINFO)

DECLARE_PROTECT_FINAL_CONSTRUCT()
```

```
BEGIN_COM_MAP(CDirectoryInfo)
   COM_INTERFACE_ENTRY(IDirectoryInfo)
END_COM_MAP()

// Data
private:
   TString m_Path;
   TString m_Disk;

// IDirectoryInfo
public:
   STDMETHOD(get_NumberOfFiles)(/*[out, retval]*/ long* pNumber);
   STDMETHOD(get_Path)(/*[out, string, retval]*/ wchar_t** pwszPath);
   STDMETHOD(put_Path)(/*[in, string]*/  wchar_t* wszPath);
};
```

Here, I've typedef'd TString to be a synonym for the C++ standard library's basic_string<> class. In ANSI builds, TString will be the same as std::string; in Unicode builds, it will be std::wstring.

The #pragma is to disable warnings about exceptions. The standard string classes use exceptions, but for this project, exceptions are turned off by default. The other two additions provide the data members m_Path and m_Disk (which provide the state for our object) and initialize them in the constructor initialization list.

You can add the following implementations for the properties to DirectoryInfo.cpp:

```
STDMETHODIMP CDirectoryInfo::get_Path(wchar_t** pwszPath)
{
   USES_CONVERSION;
   wcscpy(*pwszPath, T2CW(m_Path.c_str()));
   return S_OK;
}

STDMETHODIMP CDirectoryInfo::put_Path(wchar_t* wszPath)
{
   USES_CONVERSION;
   m_Path = W2CT(wszPath);

   // Make sure that the path ends with a backslash
   if(m_Path[m_Path.size() - 1] != _T('\\'))
      m_Path += _T('\\');
   return S_OK;
}

STDMETHODIMP CDirectoryInfo::get_NumberOfFiles(long *pNumber)
{
   USES_CONVERSION;
   *pNumber = 0;

   TString strFilter(m_Path);
   strFilter += _T("*.*");

   WIN32_FIND_DATA FindFileData = {0};
   HANDLE hFind = FindFirstFile(strFilter.c_str(), &FindFileData);
   if(hFind == INVALID_HANDLE_VALUE)
      return HRESULT_FROM_WIN32(GetLastError());
```

```
    long lFileCount = 0;
    HRESULT hr = S_OK;

    while(true)
    {
        // Ignore directories
        if((FindFileData.dwFileAttributes & FILE_ATTRIBUTE_DIRECTORY) == 0)
            lFileCount++;

        if(!FindNextFile(hFind, &FindFileData))
        {
            DWORD err = GetLastError();
            if(err == ERROR_NO_MORE_FILES)
                break;
            else
            {
                hr = HRESULT_FROM_WIN32(err);
                break;
            }
        }
    }

    FindClose(hFind);
    if(SUCCEEDED(hr))
        *pNumber = lFileCount;
    return hr;
}
```

get_NumberOfFiles() gets the path name (set using put_Path()) and then uses the Win32
FindFirstFile() and FindNextFile() functions to find the items in the directory that are *not*
themselves directories. Note that the implementation of put_Path() ensures that the path ends with
a backslash, as expected by the APIs.

## The First Client

You should now be able to build this project and then create a test program. To do this, create a new
Win32 Console Application. Set the Add to current workspace option, and call the new project
ConsoleClient. From the second dialog, select A simple application, and then select Finish and OK to
generate the project.

Now edit StdAfx.h so that you can use the COM API and the C I/O functions:

```
#if _MSC_VER > 1000
#pragma once
#endif // _MSC_VER > 1000

#include <windows.h>
#include <tchar.h>
#include <stdio.h>
```

In ConsoleClient.cpp, we'll use #import to generate a smart pointer, and then access the object
like this:

```
#include "stdafx.h"

#import "..\DirList.tlb"
using namespace DIRLISTLib;

int _tmain(int argc, TCHAR* argv[])
{
    CoInitialize(NULL);

    try
    {
        DWORD dwStart = GetTickCount();
        IDirectoryInfoPtr pDirInfo(__uuidof(DirectoryInfo));

        _tprintf(_T("QueryInterface() for IDirectoryInfo took ")
                  _T("%.2f seconds\n"), (GetTickCount() - dwStart)/1000.0);

        // Set the path to C:\ or the first command line argument
        if(argc == 1)
            pDirInfo->Path = L"C:\\";
        else
            pDirInfo->Path = _bstr_t(argv[1]); // Use _bstr_t to convert

        long lNumFiles = pDirInfo->NumberOfFiles;
        _tprintf(_T("There are %ld files\n"), lNumFiles);
    }
    catch(const _com_error& e)
    {
        _tprintf(_T("Error: 0x%x, %S\n"), e.Error(), e.ErrorMessage());
    }

    CoUninitialize();
    return 0;
}
```

Notice that I #include'd <tchar.h> in stdafx.h, and changed main() to _tmain(). If you're targeting NT, you really should use Unicode, but to be nice to Windows 9x developers who may want to use your code, use the _t macros so that the code will compile for ANSI too. The Visual C++ 6.0 console AppWizard will not do this for you, so you need to do it by hand.

Furthermore, since the command line parameter could be passed in as a LPSTR or a LPWSTR, you may need to convert it – the Path property takes a LPWSTR. Rather than do this conversion myself, I have used the Visual C++ 6.0 class _bstr_t to help me. This class has constructors for both string types, and it has a LPWSTR conversion operator, so creating a temporary _bstr_t will perform the conversion from LPSTR to LPWSTR if required.

Now you can build the client and run it with or without a command line parameter. In the latter case, the test program will return the number of files in the root directory of your C:\ drive.

## IDirectory

Now that you know that the object works, let's add the IDirectory tear-off interface to the DirList project. As mentioned earlier in the chapter, you will have to add this second interface by hand. First, generate a new IID using the GUID Generator, copy the IID to the clipboard and then open the project IDL file. Add the following interface definition using the IID you just generated, and add the interface to the coclass:

```
import "oaidl.idl";
import "ocidl.idl";
    [
        object,
        uuid(2A817790-2086-11D2-A273-0060087B1844),

        helpstring("IDirectoryInfo Interface"),
        pointer_default(unique)
    ]
    interface IDirectoryInfo : IUnknown
    {
        [propget, helpstring("property Path")]
        HRESULT Path([out, string, retval] wchar_t** pwszPath);
        [propput, helpstring("property Path")]
        HRESULT Path([in, string] wchar_t* wszPath);
        [propget, helpstring("property NumberOfFiles")]
        HRESULT NumberOfFiles([out, retval] long* pNumber);
    };

    [
        object,
        uuid(30CE33C4-1CA4-11D2-A273-0060087B1844),
        pointer_default(unique)
    ]
    interface IDirectory : IUnknown
    {
    };

[
    uuid(2A817784-2086-11D2-A273-0060087B1844),
    version(1.0),
    helpstring("DirList 1.0 Type Library")
]
library DIRLISTLib
{
    importlib("stdole32.tlb");
    importlib("stdole2.tlb");

    [
        uuid(0FC16250-9EE0-11D1-9AD2-0060973044A8),
        helpstring("DirectoryInfo Class")
    ]
    coclass DirectoryInfo
    {
        [default] interface IDirectoryInfo;
        interface IDirectory;
    };
};
```

You also need to add the interface implementation to your ATL C++ files. Although there is some support for adding interfaces, there is no Wizard support to add *tear-off* interfaces, so you need to do this by hand as well. Open `DirectoryInfo.h` and add the `CDirectory` definition:

```
#include <string>
typedef std::basic_string<TCHAR> TString;

#include <vector>
typedef std::vector<TString> TStringVector;
```

```
// Forward declaration
class CDirectoryInfo;

///////////////////////////////////////////////////////////////
// CDirectory
class ATL_NO_VTABLE CDirectory :
   public CComTearOffObjectBase<CDirectoryInfo>,
   public IDirectory
{
public:
   CDirectory()
   {
   }

DECLARE_PROTECT_FINAL_CONSTRUCT()

BEGIN_COM_MAP(CDirectory)
   COM_INTERFACE_ENTRY(IDirectory)
END_COM_MAP()

public:
   HRESULT FinalConstruct();

private:
   TStringVector m_Directories;
   HRESULT GetDirectories(LPCTSTR strParentDir);
};
```

This class derives from `CComTearOffObjectBase<CDirectoryInfo>` (hence the forward declaration of `CDirectoryInfo`) and the interface that we are implementing. Notice that the class has a COM map, so that it can manage a reference count and implement `QueryInterface()`.

The COM specification says that if there is a `QueryInterface()` call for `IUnknown` on an object, the object must *always* return the same interface pointer. To ensure that this happens, the tear-off must have access to the object (which is provided as an argument to the `CComTearOffObject<>` constructor via the macro in the COM map) and its class (which is provided as a template argument to the `CComTearOffObjectBase<>` base class).

When objects of this class are created, `FinalConstruct()` will be called. We'll code the function to read the names of all the directories on the disk using the recursive `private` method `GetDirectories()`, and add these directory names to the string vector `m_Directories`.

So that `CDirectory` can access the disk that's held in the `CDirectoryInfo` class, you need to make `CDirectory` a `friend` class of `CDirectoryInfo`. In addition, you need to add the tear-off to the COM map of the `CDirectoryInfo` class.

```
   friend class CDirectory;

BEGIN_COM_MAP(CDirectoryInfo)
   COM_INTERFACE_ENTRY(IDirectoryInfo)
   COM_INTERFACE_ENTRY_TEAR_OFF(IID_IDirectory, CDirectory)
END_COM_MAP()
```

### Implementing GetDirectories()

Now you can add `FinalConstruct()` and `GetDirectories()` to `DirectoryInfo.cpp` like this:

```
HRESULT CDirectory::FinalConstruct()
{
    return GetDirectories(m_pOwner->m_Disk.c_str());
}

HRESULT CDirectory::GetDirectories(LPCTSTR strParentDir)
{
    USES_CONVERSION;

    TString strDir(strParentDir);
    strDir += _T("*.*");

    WIN32_FIND_DATA FindFileData = {0};
    HANDLE hFind = FindFirstFile(strDir.c_str(), &FindFileData);
    if(hFind == INVALID_HANDLE_VALUE)
        return HRESULT_FROM_WIN32(GetLastError());

    HRESULT hr = S_OK;
    while(true)
    {
        // Look for directories
        if((FindFileData.dwFileAttributes & FILE_ATTRIBUTE_DIRECTORY) != 0)
        {
            // We don't want . or ..
            if(lstrcmp(FindFileData.cFileName, _T(".")) != 0 &&
                        lstrcmp(FindFileData.cFileName, _T("..")) != 0)
            {
                TString strSearchDir(strParentDir);
                strSearchDir += FindFileData.cFileName;

                // Add it to the vector, and recurse
                m_Directories.push_back(strSearchDir);
                strSearchDir += _T("\\");
                hr = GetDirectories(strSearchDir.c_str());
                if(FAILED(hr))
                    break;
            }
        }

        if(!FindNextFile(hFind, &FindFileData))
        {
            DWORD err = GetLastError();
            if(err == ERROR_NO_MORE_FILES)
                break;
            else
            {
                hr = HRESULT_FROM_WIN32(err);
                break;
            }
        }
    }

    FindClose(hFind);
    return hr;
}
```

Notice that to get access to the data members of the object class, you can use the m_pOwner member inherited from CComTearOffObjectBase<>. GetDirectories() is designed to be called recursively; it checks the strParentDir for other directories (apart from . and ..), and adds these to the vector.

### Implementing Directories()

Now you can add the Directories() method to the IDirectory interface using the Add Method... item in ClassView's context menu:

```
HRESULT Directories([out, retval] IEnumString** ppEnumDirectories);
```

The function must return an enumerator containing the directories. ATL has several classes that allow you to implement enumerations, and a new feature in ATL 3 is the ability to create an enumeration based on an STL container. Since CDirectory has its information in an STL vector<>, it makes sense to use CComEnumOnSTL<>, which has these parameters:

```
template<class Base, const IID* piid, class T, class Copy,
        class CollType, class ThreadModel = CComObjectThreadModel>
class ATL_NO_VTABLE CComEnumOnSTL;
```

The first parameter is the enumeration interface that you want to implement on the enumerator object, and this is followed by its IID. The next parameter, T, is the type that you are enumerating, and then there's a class with static methods used to copy T items. Finally, CollType is the type of STL container that will provide the data for the enumerator. (Since the enumerator will be a COM object, ThreadModel is required to define the threading model that it will use. The default, which is the threading model of your object, is a good choice here.)

The Copy class is required because when you initialize a class based on CComEnumOnSTL<>, you pass the CollType STL container, and the Next() method of this class will return *copies* of the items in the container. These copies need to be created and destroyed, and they also need to be initialized with the data in the container. If you look in atlcom.h, you will find some examples, including the generalized template _Copy<>:

```
template <class T>
class _Copy
{
public:
    static HRESULT copy(T* p1, T* p2)
    {
        memcpy(p1, p2, sizeof(T));
        return S_OK;
    }
    static void init(T*) {}
    static void destroy(T*) {}
};
```

Notice that this class has only static members, so you are not expected to create instances of it. Indeed, it's really only needed to provide a namespace through which methods are called.

The enumerator object will provide LPOLESTR strings, but our STL collection is a vector<> of TStrings. The _Copy<> template cannot be used, because it copies instances of type T to other, uninitialized, instances of type T. The specialization of this template for LPOLESTR, _Copy<LPOLESTR>, has the same problem, so it can't be used in this case either. To determine how to solve this problem, let's take a look at where these Copy methods are used.

CComEnumOnSTL<> is derived from IEnumOnSTLImpl<>, which is also passed the Copy class. This code comes from IEnumOnSTLImpl<>::Next():

```
hr = Copy::copy(pelt, &*m_iter);
if(FAILED(hr))
{
    while(rgelt < pelt)
        Copy::destroy(rgelt++);
    nActual = 0;
}
```

Here, the types of pelt and m_iter are T* and CollType::iterator, while the type of rgelt is T*. The * operator applied to an STL iterator returns an item in the container, and in this case that means TString. The implication is therefore that the appropriate Copy class should be:

```
class CopyTStringToLPOLESTR
{
public:
    static HRESULT copy(LPOLESTR* p1, TString* p2);
    static void init(LPOLESTR* p);
    static void destroy(LPOLESTR* p);
};
```

Although the Copy classes given in atlcom.h implement copy() by copying a parameter to another parameter of the same type, this does not have to be the case. In our example, the Copy class can be implemented as:

```
class CopyTStringToLPOLESTR
{
public:
    static HRESULT copy(LPOLESTR* p1, TString* p2)
    {
        HRESULT hr = S_OK;
        USES_CONVERSION;
        (*p1) = static_cast<LPOLESTR>(
                    CoTaskMemAlloc(sizeof(OLECHAR) * (p2->size() + 1)));
        if(*p1 == NULL)
            hr = E_OUTOFMEMORY;
        else
            ocscpy(*p1, T2COLE(p2->c_str()));
        return hr;
    }
    static void init(LPOLESTR* p) {*p = NULL;}
    static void destroy(LPOLESTR* p) {CoTaskMemFree(*p);}
};
```

copy() allocates a buffer of OLECHARs big enough to take the number of characters in the TString (including its terminating NUL character), converts the TString to an OLESTR, and finally copies it.

Put this class after the `#includes` in `DirectoryInfo.cpp`, and implement the `Directories()` method like this:

```
STDMETHODIMP CDirectory::Directories(IEnumString** ppEnumDirectories)
{
    typedef CComObject<CComEnumOnSTL<IEnumString, &IID_IEnumString,
        LPOLESTR, CopyTStringToLPOLESTR, TStringVector> > StringEnumerator;

    StringEnumerator* pEnumDirs = NULL;
    StringEnumerator::CreateInstance(&pEnumDirs);
    pEnumDirs->Init(this, m_Directories);

    HRESULT hr = pEnumDirs->QueryInterface(ppEnumDirectories);
    if(FAILED(hr))
        delete pEnumDirs;
    return hr;
}
```

Since the `CComEnumOnSTL<>` class is equivalent to one of your own ATL classes, it needs an implementation of `IUnknown` provided by `CComObject<>`, so we actually create a `CComObject<>` specialized with `CComEnumOnSTL<>` as the template parameter. The enumerator object is then initialized with the STL container that contains the data and the `this` pointer of the `CDirectory` object. Why is the `this` pointer used? The reason can be found in `IEnumOnSTLImpl<>`:

```
template<class Base, const IID* piid, class T, class Copy, class CollType>
class ATL_NO_VTABLE IEnumOnSTLImpl : public Base
{
public:
    HRESULT Init(IUnknown* pUnkForRelease, CollType& collection);
    STDMETHOD(Next)(ULONG celt, T* rgelt, ULONG* pceltFetched);
    STDMETHOD(Skip)(ULONG celt);
    STDMETHOD(Reset)(void);
    STDMETHOD(Clone)(Base** ppEnum);
//Data
    CComPtr<IUnknown> m_spUnk;
    CollType* m_pcollection;
    CollType::iterator m_iter;
};
```

If you look at the implementation of `Init()`, you will find that it initializes the `m_pcollection` by obtaining the address of the container parameter:

```
    m_pcollection = &collection;
```

This is `m_Directories`, a data member of the `CDirectory` class, which means that it exists only as long as the instance of `CDirectory` exists. The enumerator object is passed the `this` pointer of the object so that it has a reference on the `CDirectory` object, ensuring that it remains alive while the enumerator object is alive.

Because the enumerator has a pointer to `m_Directories`, it means that when the enumerator's `Next()` method is called, it gets the data from the STL collection that you pass to `Init()`. Note that `Init()` *doesn't* make a copy of the STL collection that you pass – in fact, no copying of the data is done until `Next()` is called. This does mean, though, that you should not change the contents of the container until the enumerator has been released.

You don't know when the enumerator will be released, but in this example it actually doesn't matter. The data in m_Directories is initialized just once, when the tear-off is created, and the contents remain static after that.

Finally in Directories(), the enumerator is queried for the IEnumString interface, which will be returned to the client. This will bump up the reference count to 1 if the QueryInterface() call is successful; if it fails, the heap-based enumerator will be explicitly deleted.

## The Second Client

To test the tear-off interface, you need to alter the test program to use the IDirectory interface:

```
// Disable "automatically excluding x while importing type library"
#pragma warning(disable : 4192)
#import "..\DirList.tlb"
using namespace DIRLISTLib;
// Enable "automatically excluding x while importing type library"
#pragma warning(default : 4192)

int _tmain(int argc, TCHAR* argv[])
{
    CoInitialize(NULL);

    try
    {
        DWORD dwStart = GetTickCount();
        IDirectoryInfoPtr pDirInfo(__uuidof(DirectoryInfo));

        _tprintf(_T("QueryInterface() for IDirectoryInfo took ")
                 _T("%.2f seconds\n"), (GetTickCount() - dwStart)/1000.0);

        // Set the path to C:\ or the first command line argument
        if(argc == 1)
            pDirInfo->Path = L"C:\\";
        else
            pDirInfo->Path = _bstr_t(argv[1]); // Use _bstr_t to convert

        long lNumFiles = pDirInfo->NumberOfFiles;
        _tprintf(_T("There are %ld files\n"), lNumFiles);

        dwStart = GetTickCount();
        IDirectoryPtr pDir(pDirInfo);

        _tprintf(_T("QueryInterface for IDirectory took ")
                 _T("%.2f seconds\n"), (GetTickCount() - dwStart)/1000.0);

        IEnumStringPtr pEnum(pDir->Directories());

        LPOLESTR pDirs[5] = {0};
        ULONG ulFetched = 0;
        while(SUCCEEDED(pEnum->Next(5, pDirs, &ulFetched)))
        {
            if(ulFetched == 0)
                break;

            for(ULONG x = 0 ; x < ulFetched ; ++x)
            {
                _tprintf(_T("%S\n"), pDirs[x]);
```

```
            CoTaskMemFree(pDirs[x]);
        }
    }
    }
    catch(const _com_error& e)
    {
        _tprintf(_T("Error: 0x%x, %S\n"), e.Error(), e.ErrorMessage());
    }

    CoUninitialize();
    return 0;
}
```

This constructor for `pDir` will perform a `QueryInterface()` for `IDirectory` on the `pDirInfo` smart pointer, and so the tear-off interface will be created. The tear-off takes a while to initialize, and this can be seen by looking at the time that `QueryInterface()` takes: on my Pentium Pro 180MHz with 1300 directories it takes 16.5 seconds, whereas the creation of the object (without the tear-off) takes only takes 0.15 seconds. That's a lot of time saved if you're writing code that uses the object but not this particular interface.

*Note the #pragmas used to disable/enable warning 4192. This warning is displayed when a type library contains a system-defined interface or type, and #import automatically excludes it from the generated files. If the warning were not disabled, you would see a message about the exclusion of the IEnumString interface.*

# Interface Guidelines

Designing interfaces is always a difficult task. In general, interfaces should determine a single, well-defined type of behavior. The methods of an interface should all relate to that behavior. If your object will calculate a value and persist itself, these are two different behaviors, so use one interface for persistence, and another for the calculation.

Even when you have determined the types of interface that an object will support, you still have to decide what methods each interface should have. Should you have many methods that each take a few parameters and perform a small task, or should you amalgamate them into one 'super-method' that takes lots of parameters and does a more complicated task?

You should also consider whether you need to define a new interface at all – perhaps you should implement one of the standard COM interfaces instead? For example, if your object needs to persist itself, ought you to define your own persistence interface, or implement one of the `IPersistxxx` interfaces? Here are some guidelines.

## Interface Names

All interfaces must have a name. The true name is the 128-bit IID that is specified in the `[uuid()]` attribute of an interface. Once you've given an interface an IID, it will always be known by this name; you can never change it. However, you should also give an interface a human-readable name that will typically begin with D for a dispinterface and with I for all others. By convention, interfaces that should not be 'seen' (outgoing interfaces used for event callbacks, for example) should have an initial underscore.

Because an interface is uniquely identified by its IID, it is possible for a developer to ignore the human-readable name given to an interface by its designer completely. For example, if you use `#import` to generate the C++ abstract class used for interface pointers and the interface constant definitions, you could change the common name used for the interfaces. However, doing this could make life difficult for maintainers of your code, not to mention for you yourself, so it's not recommended.

When you create a new interface, you must think carefully about the human-readable name that you will use. While the IID is guaranteed to be unique, the human readable name has no such guarantee. Interface designers should try to make the interface's common name as descriptive as possible (remember it's defining the *behavior* of an object), and as distinctive as they can.

When you're creating a new version of a previously defined interface (for example, an enhanced version of `ICustomer`), you should create a *new* IID and provide a human-readable name that reflects its relationship with the original. To allow for future versions, the recommended method is to use a number suffix, as in `ICustomer2`, rather than `ICustomerEx` or `INewVersionOfCustomer`.

# Number of Methods

Generally, the number of methods in an interface should be kept as low as possible. This will make the meaning of the interface clearer, and generally make it easier to use. However, fewer methods in one interface may mean that the object must implement more interfaces. This in turn will inevitably involve more calls to `QueryInterface()`, which will result in a marshaling overhead for a local or remote object. A good rule of thumb is about 5 or 6 methods per interface.

When defining an interface, you should check carefully to see that the methods are indeed related. If it is clear that some of your prospective methods are independent of the others, these are good candidates for placement in a separate interface.

It is usually good practice to design the interface for the most common situations in which it will be used. If you try to add methods to cover *every* situation, there is a chance that some of them will never be called. The technique we explored above of putting these 'unusual' methods in a new interface and implementing it as a tear-off can be a good alternative.

# Method Names

Methods in an interface are called using their position in the interface, and not the name of the method. To a certain extent, then, method names are irrelevant. However, you'll generally compile the interface IDL to create a C++ header with abstract classes based on the information in the IDL, so pick your method names carefully. If you decide to forgo the convenience of `MIDL`-produced headers, you can define your own interface class and use whatever names you choose. Again, changing method names may cause problems for future maintainers of your code, but this time there are certain advantages too. One good example is the smart pointer classes generated by the Visual C++ 6.0 `#import` directive, which usually rename the interface methods with a `raw_` prefix.

Renaming methods may also be useful for avoiding name clashes between two interfaces implemented by a C++ class through multiple inheritance. However, as you'll see later in the chapter, there are good alternatives to simply renaming the `MIDL`- or `#import`-generated interface names in this situation.

# Method Call Convention

For our purposes, interface methods are just C++ methods, and as such can have any of the calling conventions used by C++ methods: __cdecl, __pascal or __stdcall. You should ask yourself what clients will be using the interface, and whether they support the calling convention you have chosen. By default, MIDL assumes that methods will be defined with __stdcall, as this is available for the largest number of languages.

# Remotable Methods

If an interface will be called cross-process, the method parameters must make sense in the other process. For example, if you want to specify an event kernel object to another (local) process, you should not pass the event handle value, since it is only valid in the originating process. A better approach is to use a named event object and pass the name as a string. Another example is passing GDI information, such as an HWND. These items are only valid on a single machine, so they cannot be passed to another machine. If you decide that only in-process objects will ever use an interface, then you can pass non-remotable parameters, but the interface must be marked [local].

Sometimes, you may decide that the remotable version of an interface method is not what you want your clients to call – that is, it uses data that the client should not see. In this case, you can define two methods in the interface: a [local] version and a [call_as()] version. However, this does mean that you need to change the proxy-stub used to marshal the interface.

# Method Parameters

In addition to determining whether a parameter is remotable, there are other factors to consider. All method parameters must use [in], [out] or [in, out] to specify in which direction the data is being marshaled, and who has the responsibility of allocating and freeing buffers that are passed by reference. [out] and [in, out] parameters must be passed with at least one level of indirection – that is, they cannot be non-pointer types.

If a method takes structs or enums as parameter types, then these must be defined somewhere. If they are specific to this interface, then the definition should be within the interface definition.

# Number of Method Parameters

Every time a method is called (ignoring the marshaling tricks explained in Chapter 7), the object will be accessed. If the object is local or on another machine, marshaling will take up a sizable fraction of the time that the method takes to run. You will have to make a trade-off between adding properties to your interface, and supplying a number of parameters to each method.

It is usually better to pass all the data that a method requires as parameters, rather than forcing users to set up many interface properties first. Each call to set a property will need to be marshaled separately, causing many round trips across the network (each passing a small amount of data), rather than a single marshaling packet containing many data items. However, if data may be used by more than one method, if it affects the behavior of an object, or if it is a true representation of the state of an object, properties start to become more attractive.

You should be wary about using too many parameters in a single method; more than five or six makes documentation unclear, and the method becomes difficult to program. Avoid supplying *reserved* parameters – if you want to extend an interface in the future, just create a new interface.

# Object State

One common method of passing data to an object is to use properties (or an Init()-type method). Separate methods are then called to perform operations on the object. The potential drawback of such a mechanism is that it means the object always has state. In many situations, this is fine, but there may be times when you want an object to be *stateless*.

One particular problem with objects that have state is that they limit scalability, especially for objects intended to be used remotely. Each client will have to have a separate instance of the object to hold client-specific data, and this will take up resources on the server. If the object can be redesigned to be stateless, then you can use a single instance of the object, either through a custom class object or by using a singleton.

# Marshaling Data Items

Some methods will return considerable amounts of data. In non-COM objects, such data is usually passed by reference – a pointer to a buffer containing the data is passed to the method. This works fine for a method implemented in the same memory space as its caller, but if the method will be implemented in another process, the memory pointer will be invalid.

If you're designing an interface that has methods that pass large amounts of data, you need to decide, as part of the design, how this data will be marshaled. If the interface will only ever be used on in-process objects, you can pass a pointer to the buffer. However, if you are going to do this, make sure that the interface (or at the very least, the method) is marked as [local] to indicate that it cannot be marshaled. You will also have to make sure that the resource pointed to can only be used by one thread at a time.

If the data will be marshaled cross-process, you can still pass a pointer, but you need to indicate how much data it is pointing to. After all, a long* parameter can point to a single long, or to a million long items. Although you could decide on some convention to indicate the end of an array, the marshaling layer will not know about it, so you will need to use IDL to specify that the pointer points to an array of items, rather than a single item. You'll also need to specify the number of items. The usual practice is to have a parameter that takes the size of the array, and then mention this parameter in the [size_is()] attribute of the array pointer.

```
HRESULT RegisterCategories(
    [in] ULONG cCategories,
    [in, size_is(cCategories)] CATEGORYINFO rgCategoryInfo[]);
```

Note that string parameters are special, since by convention strings are terminated by a null character (thus, the last item in the wchar_t array will be L'\0'). In this case, the pointer should be marked with the [string] attribute to make sure that the marshaler calls wcslen() on the string pointer to determine how many characters are marshaled.

The side effect of marshaling arrays of data like this is that although the item looks like it is being passed by reference, it is in fact passed by value. The marshaler will *copy* the data to be marshaled, and then pass it to the object where the unmarshaler will create a new buffer and copy the data. The object will get a pointer to this new buffer. Marshaling must work this way because if the object is implemented out-of-process, it will not have access to the client's memory (and vice versa). However, since data is being marshaled by value, the procedure can consume large amounts of memory, and take a considerable amount of time.

> *Note that 'marshal by value' here refers to* parameters*; marshal by value of* interfaces *requires custom marshaling and is explained in Chapter 7.*

Clearly, passing large amounts of data requires careful thought; here are some options:

❑ If the data is an array of similar items, you must avoid passing them individually, as the overhead of the method marshaling will be considerable. You can pass the data in one go using [size_is()] to indicate how much data is being passed, but you will need to have an additional parameter to the method that specifies the size of the array, and this may not fit your programming style.

❑ A second option is to use a SAFEARRAY parameter. A SAFEARRAY is passed as a single parameter because the size of the array is held in the SAFEARRAY structure. The disadvantage with SAFEARRAYs is that they can only be used to hold a restricted range of data types. Although this can be overcome by passing your data as a simple byte array (using the SAFEARRAY type VT_UI1), this puts additional work on the object to 'cast' the byte array back to the actual data type.

❑ A further option is to use a separate enumerator object. In this case, the method will pass one of the IEnumXXXX interface pointers as the parameter. The advantage of enumerators is that they do not need to be initialized before they are used, which means that they can be implemented so that data is copied only when requested, meaning that there is no initial delay. Furthermore, the client specifies how many items are required; a well-behaved client can choose an appropriate number of items to suit how the data is used.

The flip side of using enumerators is that a client could request all the data items in one go, or make multiple requests for a single item. However, at least with an enumerator the interface designer can feel happy that although she has given the client developer the metaphorical rope with which to hang himself, she has not gone to the length of tying the noose!

# Example: Clashing Method Names

Perhaps surprisingly, name clashes between methods are relatively rare. The C++ overloading rules mean that as long as the methods have different parameter types, you can implement two methods with the same name with no trouble at all. Even if the methods do have the same name and parameter list, if they have the same semantics then a single implementation for both methods will suffice. You only get name clashes when two methods in different interfaces implemented by multiple inheritance on the same object have the same signature, but different semantics.

In the example that follows, you'll see how to deal with name clashes when they arise. We'll create a COM class to represent information about a single computer. We'll provide an interface called IMachine to return information about the hardware, and another called IUser to provide information about the user of that computer. Both interfaces will have a read-only Name property that will return a BSTR, but the implementation of the method must be different for each interface.

First, create a new ATL DLL project called
`MachineInfo`. Use the Object Wizard to
insert a **Simple Object** called `Computer` with
an interface called `IMachine`. Now use
ClassWizard's **Add Property...** context menu
item to add the read-only `Name` property to the
`IMachine` interface:

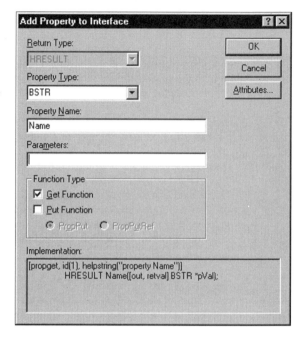

The Wizard adds the method to the IDL, the ATL class header, and the source file. For this interface,
`get_Name()` can be implemented as:

```
STDMETHODIMP CComputer::get_Name(BSTR *pVal)
{
    DWORD dwSize = MAX_COMPUTERNAME_LENGTH + 1;
    TCHAR szMachineName[MAX_COMPUTERNAME_LENGTH + 1] = {0};
    BOOL bSuccess = GetComputerName(szMachineName, &dwSize);
    if(!bSuccess)
        return HRESULT_FROM_WIN32(GetLastError());
    *pVal = CComBSTR(szMachineName).Detach();
    return S_OK;
}
```

Now we want to add a new interface called `IUser`. You must add this by hand, so generate a new
IID using `Guidgen` and edit the IDL to add the interface definition outside the `library` block, and
to add `IUser` to the list of interfaces supported by the `coclass`:

```
    [
        object,
        uuid(C9ABC94F-2212-11D2-99A7-BF62D044AB7E),
        dual,
        helpstring("IMachine Interface"),
        pointer_default(unique)
    ]
    interface IMachine : IDispatch
    {
        [propget, id(1), helpstring("property Name")]
        HRESULT Name([out, retval] BSTR *pVal);
    };
```

```
    [
        object,
        uuid(69C14901-2218-11d2-99A7-BF62D044AB7E),
        dual,
        helpstring("IUser Interface"),
        pointer_default(unique)
    ]
    interface IUser : IDispatch
    {
    };
[
    uuid(C9ABC943-2212-11D2-99A7-BF62D044AB7E),
    version(1.0),
    helpstring("MachineInfo 1.0 Type Library")
]
library MACHINEINFOLib
{
    importlib("stdole32.tlb");
    importlib("stdole2.tlb");

    [
        uuid(C9ABC950-2212-11D2-99A7-BF62D044AB7E),
        helpstring("Computer Class")
    ]
    coclass Computer
    {
        [default] interface IMachine;
        interface IUser;
    };
};
```

Once you save the file, ClassView will be updated to show the new interface. Now add the new interface to CComputer:

```
class ATL_NO_VTABLE CComputer :
    public CComObjectRootEx<CComSingleThreadModel>,
    public CComCoClass<CComputer, &CLSID_Computer>,
    public IDispatchImpl<IMachine, &IID_IMachine, &LIBID_MACHINEINFOLib>,
    public IDispatchImpl<IUser, &IID_IUser, &LIBID_MACHINEINFOLib>
{
public:
    CComputer()
    {
    }

DECLARE_REGISTRY_RESOURCEID(IDR_COMPUTER)

DECLARE_PROTECT_FINAL_CONSTRUCT()

BEGIN_COM_MAP(CComputer)
    COM_INTERFACE_ENTRY(IMachine)
    COM_INTERFACE_ENTRY2(IDispatch, IMachine)
    COM_INTERFACE_ENTRY(IUser)
```

```
END_COM_MAP()

// IMachine
public:
    STDMETHOD(get_Name)(/*[out, retval]*/ BSTR *pVal);
};
```

Don't forget to change the `IDispatch` entry in the COM map from `COM_INTERFACE_ENTRY()` to `COM_INTERFACE_ENTRY2()`. As soon as you add the interface into the COM map, ClassView will be updated to show that `CComputer` implements `IUser` – ClassView keeps a close watch on what you're doing!

The `IUser` interface should also have a read-only `BSTR` property called `Name`, but if you try using ClassView to add this property to the `IUser` interface, you will get this dialog:

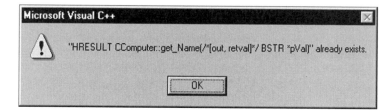

To get around this, we'll have to add the property to the `IUser` interface by hand in the IDL:

```
interface IUser : IDispatch
{
    [propget, id(1), helpstring("property Name")]
    HRESULT Name([out, retval] BSTR *pVal);
};
```

Once you save the file, you'll see ClassView updated once more. Now, if you double-click the `get_Name()` functions listed in ClassView beneath each of the interfaces supported by `CComputer`, you'll see that you are taken to the same implementation. If we could implement `IUser::get_Name()` and `IMachine::get_Name()` with the same code, our work would be done. Unfortunately, we can't – the machine name and the user name should be different – so how do we provide different implementations for these functions?

The solution is to use an intermediate class for each interface. The intermediate classes simply implement each clashing method to call another method with a name that won't clash. Here, I've used non-clashing names of the form `interface_methodname`. The classes are templates so that they can use ATL's 'safe downcasting' trick to get to a method in a class that's derived from them without using virtual functions – the derived class is passed as a template parameter to the base class. Add the following definitions to `Computer.h`, above the definition of `CComputer`.

```
//////////////////////////////////////////////////////////////////////
// Intermediate classes
template <class T>
class /* ATL_NO_VTABLE */ IMachineVtbl : public IMachine
{
public:
    STDMETHOD(get_Name)(/*[out, retval]*/ BSTR *pVal)
    {
```

```
            return static_cast<T*>(this)->IMachine_get_Name(pVal);
        }
    };

    template <class T>
    class /* ATL_NO_VTABLE */ IUserVtbl : public IUser
    {
    public:
        STDMETHOD(get_Name)(/*[out, retval]*/ BSTR *pVal)
        {
            return static_cast<T*>(this)->IUser_get_Name(pVal);
        }
    };
```

Now edit the `CComputer` class to use the intermediate classes:

```
    class ATL_NO_VTABLE CComputer :
        public CComObjectRootEx<CComSingleThreadModel>,
        public CComCoClass<CComputer, &CLSID_Computer>,
        public IDispatchImpl<IMachineVtbl<CComputer>, &IID_IMachine,
                                 &LIBID_MACHINEINFOLib>,
        public IDispatchImpl<IUserVtbl<CComputer>, &IID_IUser,
                                 &LIBID_MACHINEINFOLib>
    {
    public:
        CComputer()
        {
        }

    DECLARE_REGISTRY_RESOURCEID(IDR_COMPUTER)

    DECLARE_PROTECT_FINAL_CONSTRUCT()

    BEGIN_COM_MAP(CComputer)
        COM_INTERFACE_ENTRY(IMachine)
        COM_INTERFACE_ENTRY2(IDispatch, IMachine)
        COM_INTERFACE_ENTRY(IUser)
    END_COM_MAP()

    // IMachine
    public:
        HRESULT IMachine_get_Name(/*[out, retval]*/ BSTR *pVal);

    // IUser
    public:
        HRESULT IUser_get_Name(/*[out, retval]*/ BSTR *pVal);
    };
```

Now there is no name clash. Since the intermediate classes derive from the interfaces, the methods will be virtual, and so when you derive from them, C++ will make sure that the vtable is set up correctly. `IMachine_get_Name()` and `IUser_get_Name()` are not virtual, but are instead called from the intermediate classes using a bit of template hocus pocus. The COM map remains unchanged because `CComputer` still derives from the original interfaces through the intermediate classes.

Now you can implement the non-clashing methods in `Computer.cpp` like this:

```
HRESULT CComputer::IMachine_get_Name(BSTR *pVal)
{
    DWORD dwSize = MAX_COMPUTERNAME_LENGTH + 1;
    TCHAR szMachineName[MAX_COMPUTERNAME_LENGTH + 1] = {0};

    BOOL bSuccess = GetComputerName(szMachineName, &dwSize);
    if (!bSuccess)
        return HRESULT_FROM_WIN32(GetLastError());

    *pVal = CComBSTR(szMachineName).Detach();
    return S_OK;
}

HRESULT CComputer::IUser_get_Name(BSTR *pVal)
{
    DWORD dwSize = 256;
    TCHAR szUserName[256] = {0};

    BOOL bSuccess = GetUserName(szUserName, &dwSize);
    if (!bSuccess)
        return HRESULT_FROM_WIN32(GetLastError());

    *pVal = CComBSTR(szUserName).Detach();
    return S_OK;
}
```

A client could call these interfaces from a console application with the following code

```
#import "..\MACHINEINFO.tlb"
using namespace MACHINEINFOLib;

#include <iostream>
using namespace std;

...

    IMachinePtr pMachine(__uuidof(Computer));
    wcout << static_cast<const wchar_t*>(pMachine->Name)
                                    << L" is the machine name\n";

    IUserPtr pUser(pMachine);
    wcout << static_cast<const wchar_t*>(pUser->Name)
                                    << L" is the user name\n";

...
```

You can find the full console client (complete with error handling) along with the rest of the code for the book on the Wrox Press web site.

# The IDispatch Interface

IDispatch is a mechanism by which an object can provide access to its methods via *dynamic invocation*. With 'regular' COM interfaces (those that ATL calls *custom interfaces*, but which are more accurately described as vtable-based interfaces), the interface methods are part of the immutable interface contract. An interface has a certain number of methods, with specified parameters, and which cannot change once defined.

IDispatch is just such an interface: it has seven methods, which are well documented in the Platform SDK. Since the interface is immutable, you cannot redefine these methods. However, the particular point of IDispatch is that it allows you to relax the immutability constraint (in terms of functionality) by invoking **dispinterface methods** (and **dispinterface properties**) through a vtable method call. These are *not* interface methods, because the interface is IDispatch; rather, they are functionality that's available through an interface method called Invoke().

With a vtable-based interface, COM dispatches a method request to the appropriate interface method. If the client wants to invoke, say, the third method of IMyInterface on object 42, COM will construct a stack frame using the parameters passed from the client, and then invoke the method at that position in the vtable.

With IDispatch, the server developer gets the option of implementing this dispatching mechanism. Invoke() is called with a numeric identifier (a DISPID) that identifies the dispinterface method to invoke. If you decided to implement Invoke() yourself, you would typically use a large switch() statement to dispatch the method calls, but an object can implement Invoke() in whatever way it likes. It could decide, for example, that when a request for the method with the DISPID of 99 is received on a Monday, it will call a function called Apple(), but on a Tuesday, it will call Pear(). In this way, the client would get a different result depending on what day it is.

Invoke() identifies dispinterface methods by their DISPIDs. However, scripting languages (and the programmers that use them) refer to dispinterface methods by textual names, so there must be some mechanism for mapping between names and DISPIDs. That mechanism is IDispatch::GetIDsOfNames(). There are two reasons that Invoke() doesn't simply take a name rather than a DISPID. The first is that names can be locale-dependent – in other words, the dispinterface method Pomme() in France could map to the same DISPID as the dispinterface method Apple() in the US. The second reason is that a DISPID is smaller and easier to handle than a text string – identifying methods by a numeric ID will provide faster access than using a text string once the initial look-up has been done.

A more realistic use for the flexibility of IDispatch than fruit selection is found in the dynamic hierarchy provided by Internet Explorer's HTML object model. At runtime, a Document object may contain any number of sub-objects, each of which can be exposed to script programmers using dispinterface properties. These sub-objects may change or disappear, and the corresponding dispinterface properties will go with them. This flexibility is not available through standard vtable interfaces.

*It's important to understand that scripting environments (and #import-generated classes) make calls to IDispatch-exposed dispinterface methods look just like calls to standard vtable methods using the same tools. Most client programmers will not need to call IDispatch::Invoke() explicitly; it will be handled by their environment or by wrapper classes.*

Despite its benefits, the flexibility of IDispatch is potentially quite anarchic – you could supply access to literally hundreds of dispinterface methods through this single interface, and change them on a whim. However, this is not a good idea. When you group together related methods in dispinterfaces, you are making the statement that for this particular dispinterface, particular method names will always have particular DISPIDs and parameters. In other words, you are taking away some of the uncertainty of the examples given above. (However, you retain complete flexibility over any *extra* dispinterface methods you decide to use at runtime.)

If you are staking a claim for DISPIDs for a particular dispinterface, you need to provide information about the dispinterface in a type library.

# Type Libraries & dispinterfaces

Type libraries are essentially tokenized IDL – the information you put within the library block of an IDL file will be put in the type library. If you want to define items in the IDL and you *don't* want them in the type library, declare them outside the library block and make sure that they are not referenced anywhere within it.

```
import "oaidl.idl";
import "ocidl.idl";
[
    uuid(BADF00D0-BEEF-BEEF-BEEF-BAADF00DBEEF)
]
dispinterface DDispItf
{
    properties:
    methods:
        [id(1)] long Method1([in] long lVal);
};
[
    object,
    uuid(BADF00D1-BEEF-BEEF-BEEF-BAADF00DBEEF),
    pointer_default(unique)
]
interface IVtableItf : IUnknown
{
    HRESULT Method2([in] long lVal, [out, retval] long* lRet);
};

[
    uuid(BADF00D2-BEEF-BEEF-BEEF-BAADF00DBEEF),
    version(1.0)
]
library AUTOLib
{
    importlib("stdole32.tlb");
    importlib("stdole2.tlb");
```

```
    [
        object,
        uuid(BADF00D3-BEEF-BEEF-BEEF-BAADF00DBEEF),
        pointer_default(unique)
    ]
    interface IVtableItf2 : IUnknown
    {
        HRESULT Method3([in] long lVal, [out, retval] long* lRet);
    };
    [
        uuid(BADF00D4-BEEF-BEEF-BEEF-BAADF00DBEEF)
    ]
    coclass CoDispObject
    {
        [default] dispinterface DDispItf;
    };
};
```

In this IDL, the type library will contain descriptions for one object (CoDispObject) and two interfaces (DDispItf and IVtableItf2). The first interface will be included because it is declared as the [default] interface of the object, while the second will be present because it is defined in the library block. Note that MIDL will not create marshaling code for IVtableItf2, because it is not defined *outside* the library block. Conversely, it *will* generate marshaling code for IVtableItf, but it will exclude it from the type library because it's not referenced *within* the library block.

Notice the syntax of declaring a dispinterface: you specify the properties and methods that the dispinterface supports using ODL (object description language) syntax. MIDL will take any properties and implement them with method calls. ODL has now been subsumed by IDL, so ODL code can be compiled with MIDL.

Although there is no explicit mention of CoDispObject supporting IDispatch, it must do so to support the dispinterface. However, even if the object supports more than one dispinterface, it will still only support one IDispatch interface. This is because QueryInterface() called on a single object will only be able to resolve one request for the IID_IDispatch interface.

## Implementing IDispatch

So, how do you implement IDispatch? You could code up GetIDsOfNames() to look up the DISPIDs in a map, and you could write Invoke() to use a large switch statement to dispatch method requests to methods in your object, but this is tedious. An easier option is to let COM provide most of the implementation for you. If your dispinterface can be fully described in a type library (in other words, it has no 'dynamic' dispinterface methods), then the type library contains all the information necessary to implement IDispatch. In this event, COM provides an implementation of the ITypeInfo interface, which can be used to drive your implementation of IDispatch.

The ITypeInfo interface can be obtained from a type library in two stages: first you load the type library with a call to LoadTypeLib() (which takes a filename and returns an ITypeLib interface pointer), then you call ITypeLib::GetTypeInfo(), which returns an ITypeInfo interface pointer.

`ITypeInfo` looks something like this

```
[
    object,
    uuid(00020401-0000-0000-C000-000000000046),
    pointer_default(unique)
]
interface ITypeInfo : IUnknown
{
    [local]  HRESULT GetTypeAttr();
             HRESULT GetTypeComp();
    [local]  HRESULT GetFuncDesc();
    [local]  HRESULT GetVarDesc();
    [local]  HRESULT GetNames();
             HRESULT GetRefTypeOfImplType();
             HRESULT GetImplTypeFlags();
    [local]  HRESULT GetIDsOfNames();
    [local]  HRESULT Invoke();
    [local]  HRESULT GetDocumentation();
    [local]  HRESULT GetDllEntry();
             HRESULT GetRefTypeInfo();
    [local]  HRESULT AddressOfMember();
    [local]  HRESULT CreateInstance();
             HRESULT GetMops();
    [local]  HRESULT GetContainingTypeLib();
    [local]  void ReleaseTypeAttr();
    [local]  void ReleaseFuncDesc();
    [local]  void ReleaseVarDesc();
}
```

I have missed out the method parameters, and I have also missed out the `[call_as()]` versions of the methods marked as `[local]`. But notice the two highlighted methods: the interface has access to the information to map DISPIDs to method names, and to invoke dispinterface methods. Thus, if you can access the type information for an object, you can delegate two of the `IDispatch` methods to `ITypeInfo`. The other two methods of `IDispatch` just give access to the object type information, so they should be trivial to implement.

Of course, ATL provides an implementation of the `IDispatch` methods for you via its `IDispatchImpl<>` class, so you don't need to do even this work yourself. However, if you're willing to go to the lengths of providing an implementation for `Invoke()` and `GetIDsOfNames()`, you can do some interesting things. Later in the chapter, I'll show you how to provide an implementation of `Invoke()` and `GetIDsOfNames()` to allow scripting languages to have access to 'multiple' `IDispatch` interfaces on a single object.

# IDispatchImpl<>

When you specify Dual as the Interface type on the Attributes tab of the Object Wizard, the Wizard will derive your new interface from `IDispatchImpl<>`. The `IDispatchImpl<>` template has six parameters, as you can see from the definition in `atlcom.h`:

```
template <class T, const IID* piid,
    const GUID* plibid = &CComModule::m_libid,
    WORD wMajor = 1, WORD wMinor = 0,
    class tihclass = CComTypeInfoHolder>
```

```
class ATL_NO_VTABLE IDispatchImpl : public T
{
public:
    typedef tihclass _tihclass;
    ... // more code deleted
protected:
    static _tihclass _tih;
    ... // more code deleted
};
```

These parameters are described in the table below:

| Parameter | Description |
|-----------|-------------|
| T | The dual interface that will be implemented |
| piid | A pointer to the IID of the interface |
| plibid | A pointer to the LIBID of the type library that describes the interface |
| wMajor | The major version of the type library |
| wMinor | The minor version of the type library |
| tihclass | The class used to manage the type information for the dual interface |

This last parameter is interesting, IDispatchImpl<> uses tihclass to implement IDispatch and the default class is CComTypeInfoHolder. IDispatchImpl<> creates a static member of this class called _tih. If you look through IDispatchImpl<> you will see that the IDispatch functions are implemented using this object.

The _tih object is initialized with the LIBID of the type library and the IID of the interface that the class is implementing with the following lines:

```
template <class T, const IID* piid, const GUID* plibid,
    WORD wMajor, WORD wMinor, class tihclass>
IDispatchImpl<T, piid, plibid, wMajor, wMinor,
    tihclass>::_tihclass
IDispatchImpl<T, piid, plibid, wMajor, wMinor, tihclass>::_tih =
{piid, plibid, wMajor, wMinor, NULL, 0, NULL, 0};
```

This is initializing a static member of a class, the first few lines declares the type of this static member (template<...> IDispatchImpl<...>::_tihclass), the next line is the name of the member (IDispatchImpl<...>::_tih) and finally the last line gives the member its value. These are the parameters to the IDispatchImpl<> and initialize the eight data members of the class:

```
class CComTypeInfoHolder
{
public:
    const GUID* m_pguid;
    const GUID* m_plibid;
    WORD m_wMajor;
    WORD m_wMinor;
```

```
ITypeInfo* m_pInfo;
long m_dwRef;
struct stringdispid* m_pMap;
int m_nCount;
```

`stringdispid` is a nested structure (not shown here) used to cache the mapping between strings and DISPIDs so that when `GetIDsOfNames()` is called the result is cached so that on a future call the type library is not queried. As you can see, the `static` object now knows about the type library (its LIBID and the version) and the particular interface that the object is associated with.

When one of the `IDispatch` methods is called on `IDispatchImpl<>`, the static `_tih` object is called. The object first checks that the type information for the interface has been loaded and if so it calls the appropriate method. If the type information has not been loaded the the static object does this by calling its `GetTI()` method.

`GetTI()` first loads the type library, which returns a `ITypeLib` pointer, it then calls `GetTypeInfoOfGuid()` to get the type information for the particular interface. Thus, this firmly associates the `_tih` object with a particular interface; this `_tih` object cannot get access to the type information about any other interface. The `COM_INTERFACE_ENTRY2()` macro used with objects that have multiple `dual` interfaces specifies that all queries for `IDispatch` go through one particular `IDispatchImpl<>` base and hence, through its `_tih` object. This only allows access to that specific interface. The problem of multiple dispinterfaces on a single object will be covered, and some solutions suggested, in a later section.

# Binding

To call a method on a dispinterface, you have to call `Invoke()` on `IDispatch` and pass it the DISPID of the method you want to call. Before you can do that, you need to get hold of the DISPID. Programmers write code using text, so at some point there will have to be a call to `GetIDsOfNames()` to convert that text into a DISPID. The time at which the call to `GetIDsOfNames()` is made has a huge impact on the performance of your client.

The call to `GetIDsOfNames()` may be made at runtime, just before the call to `Invoke()`. This is known as **late binding**. Alternatively, the call to `GetIDsOfNames()` could occur at compile time, well before the call to `Invoke()`. This is known as **early binding**.

## Late Binding

Late binding occurs whenever type information for an object or method is unavailable at compile time. In Visual Basic, late binding will also occur when using 'untyped' variables, such as `Variant` or `Object`. (Visual Basic's `Object` data type is equivalent to a reference to the `IDispatch` interface on an object.)

```
Dim mac As MACHINEINFOLib.IMachine
Set mac = New MACHINEINFOLib.Computer

Dim obj As Object
Set obj = mac

MsgBox mac.Name       ' This uses early binding (or better) because the
                      ' type library contains info about the Name property
```

```
MsgBox obj.Name          ' This uses late binding because obj is 'untyped'
MsgBox mac.NotAMethod()  ' This uses late binding because the type library
                         ' doesn't contain info about this (non-existent) method
```

Taking the performance penalty as read, one of the disadvantages of late binding is that it pushes off error handling until runtime. The previous code will compile just fine, but when you execute it, it will give runtime error 438: "Object doesn't support this property or method". Late binding allows you to put all sorts of nasty, hard-to-find bugs in your code that will only be found by extensive testing, which all too often means support calls from your customers.

The message is clear: when you can, avoid late binding. Unfortunately, there is one situation where late binding is unavoidable, and that's when you use scripting languages like VBScript. I'll have more to say about that later.

## Early Binding

Early binding requires the client to have access to the interface's type information to determine the method's DISPID, and the number and types of its parameters. A clever client can check the parameters that it wishes to send to the object before they're actually sent. This allows error handling to be performed by the client at compile time, and not by the object at runtime. Typically, C++, Visual Basic and Visual J++ clients use early binding whenever that's the best solution.

In Visual Basic, you use the References item on the Project menu to load the object's type information. Early binding is used by specifying typed variables – that is, an object is specified to be a particular coclass, or to be accessed through a particular interface. After you have added the object type library to the project, the object and its interfaces are included in the 'Members' list. In the following screenshot, I have added the Microsoft Word 8.0 Object Library to the project's references, so I can access the type information for Word's objects:

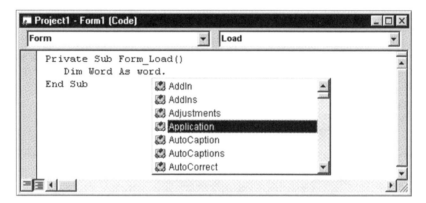

When the Word variable is typed to Word.Application, the Visual Basic IDE can check as you type that the properties and methods you use are indeed implemented on the object, and that you're using the correct number of and types for the parameters.

*As you've seen, using typed variables and providing Visual Basic with type information for an interface is not enough to avoid bugs that can only be caught at runtime. Visual Basic will check the use of methods described in the type library, and give compile time errors if the use doesn't match, but it will still perform late binding for methods that don't appear in the type library. Happily, the 'Members' list and Visual Basic's automatic case correction can help you spot some bugs before you even start to compile.*

On the other hand, if you choose to use Visual J++, you create the Java classes and interfaces for the object using the JActiveX tool (supplied in the Java SDK 2.01). This tool reads an object's type library and creates a Java class for each object, using @com comments to bind DISPIDs into the Java class for the JVM to interpret at runtime. Here are the first few lines of the _Application.java file that's created when JActiveX is passed msword8.olb:

```java
package msword8;

import com.ms.com.*;
import com.ms.com.IUnknown;
import com.ms.com.Variant;
import vbeext1.*;
import mso97.*;

// Dual interface _Application
/** @com.interface(iid=00020970-0000-0000-C000-000000000046, thread=AUTO,
type=DUAL) */
public interface _Application extends IUnknown
{
  /** @com.method(vtoffset=4, dispid=1000, type=PROPGET,
      name="Application", addFlagsVtable=4)
      @com.parameters(
      [iid=000209FF-0000-0000-C000-000000000046,
      thread=AUTO,type=OBJECT] return) */
  public msword8.Application getApplication();

  /** @com.method(vtoffset=5, dispid=1001, type=PROPGET,
      name="Creator", addFlagsVtable=4)
      @com.parameters([type=I4] return) */
  public int getCreator();

  /** @com.method(vtoffset=6, dispid=1002, type=PROPGET,
      name="Parent", addFlagsVtable=4)
      @com.parameters(
      [iid=00020400-0000-0000-C000-000000000046,
      thread=AUTO,type=DISPATCH] return) */
  public Object getParent();

// Other methods missed out

  public static final com.ms.com._Guid iid = new
    com.ms.com._Guid((int)0x20970, (short)0x0, (short)0x0,
      (byte)0xc0, (byte)0x0, (byte)0x0, (byte)0x0, (byte)0x0,
      (byte)0x0, (byte)0x0, (byte)0x46);
}
```

### Vtable Binding and Dual Interfaces

In addition to late binding and early binding, there is a third option. Clients can perform **vtable binding** – that is, call the methods in an interface's vtable. Visual Basic and Visual J++ can access *any* interface described by a type library, whether that interface is an IDispatch interface or not. Internally, these languages use the CoCreateInstance() API and IUnknown::QueryInterface() just as C++ clients do.

All ATL objects created using the Object Wizard will have their interfaces added to the library block. Since access to vtable methods is more direct (therefore giving better performance) than accessing methods through IDispatch, objects really should implement their interfaces as (what the Object Wizard calls) custom interfaces when it's feasible to do so.

However, if scripting clients are important to you, you will still need to provide access to methods via IDispatch. VBScript and JavaScript are typeless languages – the type of a variable is determined by the context of its use. These languages can access COM objects, but typeless COM access means that you can only talk to IDispatch using late binding. This presents you with a dilemma: you want the performance of vtable binding for most clients, while still having the option of allowing VBScript clients to access the methods through IDispatch.

One answer to this problem is to use a **dual interface**. Dual interfaces are derived from IDispatch, and the IDL that defines them uses the [dual] attribute. Like dispinterfaces, they commit to a particular set of dispinterface methods, available through Invoke() with particular DISPIDs. Unlike dispinterfaces, they also pledge to provide the same methods as directly-accessible vtable methods.

Dual interfaces give you all binding options – they allow clients to use late, early or vtable binding – but they aren't a universal solution. As you've already seen, stronger type checking is a reason to prefer pure custom interfaces over duals or dispinterfaces, and as you'll see shortly, there are problems with scripting clients accessing multiple dual interfaces.

> Note that under NT4.0 with Service Pack 3 installed, the maximum number of methods allowed in a dual interface is 1024. With Windows 9*x*, this limit is 512.

## Multiple Dual Interfaces

As you know, COM only allows a single implementation of a particular interface on an object. If your class derives from two dual interfaces, you have a choice as to which of these should provide the implementation for IDispatch. Typically, you will make that choice by using the COM_INTERFACE_ENTRY2() macro in the COM map.

If you look back at the example we developed earlier in the chapter, you'll find that the COM map looked like this:

```
BEGIN_COM_MAP(CComputer)
    COM_INTERFACE_ENTRY(IMachine)
    COM_INTERFACE_ENTRY2(IDispatch, IMachine)
    COM_INTERFACE_ENTRY(IUser)
END_COM_MAP()
```

We decided that the `IDispatch` implementation for the `Computer` coclass was going to be provided by the `IDispatchImpl<IMachine, ...>` class. This means that the implementation of `IDispatch` will match the `[default]` interface declared for the coclass in the type library. If we were to get the `Name` property from `IDispatch`, we'd get the name of the machine rather than the name of the user.

We could change the COM map entries around to let the implementation of `IDispatch` be provided by the other `IDispatchImpl<>` class, but `IDispatch` would still only allow access to one branch of the information that we can get about a computer.

Of course, it isn't always important how `IDispatch` behaves. If a client wants to get information about the computer's user, it can just call `QueryInterface()` for `IID_IUser`, and use the `IUser` interface it gets back. If the client wants hardware information, it can `QueryInterface()` for `IID_IMachine` and use the `IMachine` interface.

Unfortunately, scripting clients *can't* do this. Scripting clients have no way of calling `QueryInterface()`, and no way of indicating which interface they want to call a method on. They always use `IDispatch`.

> *Although the prototype for* `Invoke()` *takes an interface ID as its second parameter, this is currently reserved, and applications must always pass* `IID_NULL`. *Current scripting clients do exactly that.*

Let's look now at how we might try to give scripting clients access to the second interface on our `Computer` coclass.

# Example: Accessor Method

Start by copying the `MachineInfo` project directory that you created earlier in the chapter; you can call the copy `MachineInfoII`. We'll use this as the basis for our changes. Build and register the new version of the project, then test it with the following VBScript code from within Internet Explorer 4. When you click the button, the message box will display the name of your machine.

```
<HTML>
<HEAD>
<TITLE>Client01</TITLE>

<SCRIPT ID=clientEventHandlersVBS LANGUAGE=vbscript>
<!--

Sub button1_onclick
    Dim comp
    Set comp = CreateObject("MachineInfo.Computer.1")

    Dim name
    name = comp.Name
    MsgBox "The machine name is " + name, 0, "Computer Client"
End Sub

-->
</SCRIPT>
</HEAD>
<BODY>
```

```
<P><INPUT id=button1 language=vbscript name=button1 type=button value="Get machine
info"></P>
</BODY>
</HTML>
```

Once you're sure that the code is working, go back to the Visual C++ development environment and add a read-only property called `User` of type `IDispatch*` to the `IMachine` interface. Once the property has been added, you can implement it in `Computer.cpp` as shown:

```
STDMETHODIMP CComputer::get_User(IDispatch** pVal)
{
    return InternalQueryInterface(
            this, _GetEntries(), IID_IUser, reinterpret_cast<void**>(pVal));
}
```

Notice that I'm calling `InternalQueryInterface()` for `IUser`, but assigning it to an `IDispatch*`; this slices off the extra methods of `IUser` which are not needed since VBScript can only use `IDispatch`. Now try the following VBScript code in place of the original:

```
Sub button1_onclick
    Dim comp
    Set comp = CreateObject("MachineInfo.Computer.1")

    Dim name
    name = comp.Name
    MsgBox "The machine name is " + name + Chr(10) + Chr(13) + _
            "The user name is " + comp.User.Name, 0, "Computer Client"
End Sub
```

When you click the button this time, you'll see both the machine name and the user name, so it looks like all our problems with scripting clients are solved, doesn't it. All we need to do is add a new property or method to the default interface that returns a pointer to another interface (cast to `IDispatch*`) and we're all set up.

Unfortunately, life isn't that easy. Apart from the ugliness of the technique (it requires the script client to make an explicit call to get the second interface), this won't work in many circumstances. In fact, as soon as the client and server are in different apartments, our house of cards comes tumbling down. When you make a cross-apartment call to an object, COM will create a proxy to the interface in the apartment of the caller. Whenever calls are made on this interface the proxy will be used. In our case, when you create a `Computer` object and call `QueryInterface()` for `IDispatch`, the client in another apartment will get a proxy for `IDispatch`; this proxy is 'connected' to the `IMachine` interface. When the client calls `get_User()`, the object will return the interface pointer implemented through `IUser`, but try to marshal it back as `IDispatch`. COM will use the `IDispatch` proxy already loaded in the client apartment, and so even though you *think* you have `IDispatch` implemented through `IUser`, you will *actually* have the version implemented through `IMachine`.

> *The code on the Wrox web site for this chapter has a simple example of this problem called* `EXEProblems`. *This has two interfaces:* `IDefault` *(used to implement* `IDispatch`*), and* `ISecondary`*; this second interface is available through a property. When calls are made on this second interface, they result in calls to* `IDefault` *because the same proxy is used in the client.*

How can we go about telling COM that the interface pointer we're returning is an `IUser*` rather than an `IDispatch*`? Well, we could do it by changing our property to return an `IUser*`, but as soon as we do that, the scripting client can't handle it. Another alternative would be to implement the object so that it has a method that you can use to do the `QueryInterface()`; an interesting example of this was written by Valery Pryamikov (the code is available at ftp://ftp.infotron.no/home/vp/public/dispenum.zip). This provides an object that's initialized by passing it the `IDispatch` pointer of your scripting object, and it uses the type information of your object to determine the dispinterfaces that it supports. This object implements a collection whose items are the dispinterfaces on your object, so when you access one of the collection items, the object performs the required `QueryInterface()`.

Let's look at another, simpler, method of solving the problem.

# Example: DISPID Encoding

For this example, go back to the original `MachineInfo` project and copy it again. This time, call the new directory `MachineInfoIII`.

First of all, we're going to add a new read-only property to the `IUser` interface, so right click on the interface in ClassView, select **Add Property...** and add a new read-only BSTR property called `FullName`. Implement the property as shown below:

```
STDMETHODIMP CComputer::get_FullName(BSTR *pVal)
{
    OSVERSIONINFO info = {0};
    info.dwOSVersionInfoSize = sizeof(OSVERSIONINFO);
    BOOL bSuccess = GetVersionEx(&info);
    if(!bSuccess)
        return HRESULT_FROM_WIN32(GetLastError());

    if(info.dwPlatformId != VER_PLATFORM_WIN32_NT)
        return IUser_get_Name(pVal);

    CComBSTR bstrUserName;
    HRESULT hr = IUser_get_Name(&bstrUserName);
    if(FAILED(hr))
        return hr;

    PUSER_INFO_2 pUI2 = NULL;
    if(NetUserGetInfo(
                NULL, bstrUserName, 2, reinterpret_cast<LPBYTE*>(&pUI2)))
        return HRESULT_FROM_WIN32(GetLastError());

    CComBSTR bstrFullName(pUI2->usri2_full_name);
    *pVal = bstrFullName.Detach();
    NetApiBufferFree(pUI2);
    return S_OK;
}
```

Here we check to see if we're running on Windows NT; if we're not, we just return the user name supplied by the `Name` property of the `IUser` interface. If we *are* on NT, however, we can use the Net API to get the full name for a user.

To use the Net API, we need to include the relevant headers, and link to `netapi32.lib`, so add the following code to `Computer.cpp`:

```
#include "stdafx.h"
#include "MachineInfo.h"
#include "Computer.h"

#include <lmaccess.h>
#include <lmapibuf.h>
#pragma comment(lib, "netapi32.lib")
#pragma comment(lib, "delayimp.lib")
#pragma comment(linker, "/DELAYLOAD:netapi32.dll")
```

The last two #pragmas here allow this code to run on both Windows 9x and Windows NT by delaying the loading of `netapi32.dll` until it's actually needed. **Delay loading** is a new feature in Visual C++ 6.0.

The reason why we've gone to the trouble of adding this new property is that we're going to provide a new way of allowing scripting clients to access the methods in two dual interfaces. Unfortunately, it has (at least) one major disadvantage: we can't expose methods or properties with the same name. To see the new technique in action, we had to have a new property in `IUser`.

## DISPID Encoding

So, what is this new technique? The title of this section says it all: **DISPID encoding**. The idea is simply to expose the methods and properties of multiple dual interfaces (or dispinterfaces) via a single implementation of `IDispatch`. Clients will be able to call methods and properties on `IDispatch` that are actually implemented by multiple dual interfaces. The client won't need to do anything special, and the technique is easy to implement for the server. All you need to do is override the implementations of `GetIDsOfNames()` and `Invoke()`.

Currently, `IDispatch::GetIDsOfNames()` is implemented by `IDispatchImpl<IMachine, ...>`. This class only uses the type information for the `IMachine` interface to determine what the ID of a method should be. We need to re-implement this method to use the type information for *all* the available interfaces, and we need to encode the particular interface that supported that method into the DISPID itself, so that we can implement `IDispatch::Invoke()`. This section will describe how you can do just that.

First, add declarations for the `IDispatch` methods that we're going to override to the header for the `CComputer` class:

```
// IDispatch
public:
    // Overrides
    STDMETHOD(GetIDsOfNames)(REFIID riid, LPOLESTR* rgszNames,
        UINT cNames, LCID lcid, DISPID* rgdispid);
    STDMETHOD(Invoke)(DISPID dispidMember, REFIID riid, LCID lcid,
        WORD wFlags, DISPPARAMS* pdispparams, VARIANT* pvarResult,
        EXCEPINFO* pexcepinfo, UINT* puArgErr);
```

Now add the following code to the bottom of `Computer.cpp`:

```
const DISPID INTERFACEMASK = 0xFFFF0000;
const DISPID DISPIDMASK    = 0x0000FFFF;

const DISPID IDISPMACHINE  = 0x00010000;
const DISPID IDISPUSER     = 0x00020000;

typedef IDispatchImpl<IMachineVtbl<CComputer>,
                      &IID_IMachine, &LIBID_MACHINEINFOLib> MachineType;
typedef IDispatchImpl<IUserVtbl<CComputer>,
                      &IID_IUser, &LIBID_MACHINEINFOLib> UserType;
```

The first two `const`s provide bit masks that we can AND with a DISPID to return either an identifier for the interface that corresponds to that DISPID, or the true DISPID for that interface. The next two `const`s are used to identify the interfaces. The `typedef`s will just help to make the later code more readable. Add the following implementation for `GetIDsOfNames()`:

```
STDMETHODIMP CComputer::GetIDsOfNames(REFIID riid,
            LPOLESTR* rgszNames, UINT cNames, LCID lcid, DISPID* rgdispid)
{
    HRESULT hr = DISP_E_UNKNOWNNAME;

    hr = MachineType::GetIDsOfNames(
                                riid, rgszNames, cNames, lcid, rgdispid);
    if(SUCCEEDED(hr))
    {
        rgdispid[0] |= IDISPMACHINE;
        return hr;
    }

    hr = UserType::GetIDsOfNames(riid, rgszNames, cNames, lcid, rgdispid);
    if(SUCCEEDED(hr))
    {
        rgdispid[0] |= IDISPUSER;
        return hr;
    }

    return hr;
}
```

This code first checks `IMachine` to see if it supports the method by calling `GetIDsOfNames()` through the `MachineType` base class. If this interface supports the method, the DISPID is ORed with the constant `IDISPMACHINE`. Otherwise, `IUser` is checked, and if that interface supports the method, then the DISPID is ORed with `IDISPUSER`. If both fail, then an error is returned.

The implementation of `Invoke()` uses these encoded DISPIDs to determine which interface to use for the method:

```
STDMETHODIMP CComputer::Invoke(DISPID dispidMember, REFIID riid,
            LCID lcid, WORD wFlags, DISPPARAMS* pdispparams,
            VARIANT* pvarResult, EXCEPINFO* pexcepinfo, UINT* puArgErr)
{
```

```
    DWORD dwInterface = (dispidMember & INTERFACEMASK);
    dispidMember &= DISPIDMASK;
    switch(dwInterface)
    {
    case IDISPMACHINE:
       return MachineType::Invoke(
                            dispidMember, riid, lcid, wFlags, pdispparams,
                            pvarResult, pexcepinfo, puArgErr);
    case IDISPUSER:
       return UserType::Invoke(
                            dispidMember, riid, lcid, wFlags, pdispparams,
                            pvarResult, pexcepinfo, puArgErr);
    default:
       return DISP_E_MEMBERNOTFOUND;
    }
}
```

Here, the code strips off the encoding and uses the interface part in a `switch` statement to call the appropriate version of `Invoke()`. You can test this code with the following script:

```
Sub button1_onclick
    Dim comp
    Set comp = CreateObject("MachineInfo.Computer.1")

    Dim name
    name = comp.Name
    MsgBox "The machine name is " + name + Chr(10) + Chr(13) + _
           "The full name is " + comp.FullName, 0, "Computer Client"
End Sub
```

There are two main disadvantages with this DISPID encoding method:

❑ The range of DISPIDs that can be stored is reduced – they must be held in a WORD, or however many bits the interface encoding doesn't use

❑ It cannot distinguish between methods on different interfaces that have the same name. (This is even true for clients that can call `Invoke()` through an interface other than `IDispatch` since our encoding implementation replaces the non-encoding one completely)

However, it has the distinct advantage of allowing the client to call methods without using a separate call to get the right interface. This can be a big saving if the object implements many interfaces, as it prevents you from making one interface responsible for all the others. Another advantage with this approach is that it works cross-apartment, because only one `IDispatch` pointer is marshaled. The previous solution, which attempted to change the `IDispatch` pointer when another dispinterface was required, fails for cross-apartment calls.

# dispinterfaces

ATL's IDispatchImpl<> class allows you to implement dual interfaces, but not dispinterfaces. That is to say, if you define a dispatch interface like this:

```
dispinterface DPing
{
    properties:
    methods:
        [id(1)] void OnPing([in] BSTR strReason);
};
```

You cannot implement it like this:

```
IDispatchImpl<DPing, &DIID_IPing, &LIBID_PINGOBJECTLib>
```

However, you *can* implement a dispatch interface using IDispatchImpl<> *if* you define a compatible dual interface:

```
[
    dual  // Other attributes missed out
]
interface IPing : IDispatch
{
    [id(1)] HRESULT OnPing([in] BSTR strReason);
};
```

A 'compatible' dual interface is one that defines a method for every method in the dispinterface, and where each method has the same signature and DISPID as the corresponding method in the dispinterface.

> *Note that the signatures look slightly different because the syntax of the* dispinterface *is ODL rather than IDL. ODL hides the* HRESULT *return type and makes the last* [out, retval] *parameter look like the return type instead.*

Now you can derive your class from this IDispatchImpl<> class:

```
IDispatchImpl<IPing, &IID_IPing, &LIBID_PINGOBJECTLib>
```

To expose the original dispinterface ID to QueryInterface(), you would add COM_INTERFACE_ENTRY_IID() to your COM map:

```
BEGIN_COM_MAP(CPing)
    COM_INTERFACE_ENTRY2(IDispatch, IPing)
    COM_INTERFACE_ENTRY_IID(DIID_DPing, IPing)
END_COM_MAP()
```

Note that you don't need to expose the IID of the dual interface through your COM map if you don't want to. You don't even have to expose IID_IDispatch. The ATL header for this object should look like this:

```
EXTERN_C const IID DIID_DPing;

class ATL_NO_VTABLE CPing :
    public CComObjectRootEx<CComSingleThreadModel>,
    public CComCoClass<CPing, &CLSID_Ping>,
    public IDispatchImpl<IPing, &IID_IPing, &LIBID_PINGOBJECTLib>
{
public:
    CPing()
    {
    }

DECLARE_REGISTRY_RESOURCEID(IDR_PING)

DECLARE_PROTECT_FINAL_CONSTRUCT()

BEGIN_COM_MAP(CPing)
    COM_INTERFACE_ENTRY2(IDispatch, IPing)
    COM_INTERFACE_ENTRY_IID(DIID_DPing, IPing)
END_COM_MAP()

// IPing
public:
    STDMETHOD(OnPing)(/*[in]*/ BSTR bstrReason);
};
```

DPing should be named as an interface of the object in the library block, so that it is included in the type library:

```
library PINGOBJECTLib
{
    coclass PingObject
    {
        [default] dispinterface DPing;
    }
};
```

So, when would you want to implement a pure dispinterface? Typically, objects that use connection points will do so through dispinterfaces – indeed, you have already seen that the ATL Object Wizard will add an outgoing dispinterface to your project when you specify that the object supports connection points. The client must implement this dispinterface.

# Miscellany

The remaining sections in this chapter cover aspects of interface programming that don't really fit into the earlier discussions. In them, we'll take a look at some ways that you can group interfaces and components.

# Component Categories

An object has a certain behavior, and this is defined by the interfaces it supports. However, this behavior is often only usable if the client knows how to use the interfaces *together*. For example, an object may have a behavior (let's call it CAT_Ping) that requires it to support connection points to the IPing outgoing interface. A client that wants to be able to use this behavior must implement the IPing interface, *and* it must know how to use the connection point interface.

A client can determine the interfaces that an object supports by calling QueryInterface() successively for all the interfaces that it is interested in. If the behavior it wants depends on every one of a group of interfaces being supported, and E_NOINTERFACE was returned by at least one of the calls, then the object does not support that behavior.

An immediate problem is apparent here. For a start, to determine what an object can do, you must create a new instance of the object – this can be costly, especially if the object lives across the network or has some expensive initialization. Further, you have to call QueryInterface() for every interface that you require, and each QueryInterface() call results in a round trip to the object. You can minimize these round trips by calling QueryInterface() for IMultiQI, and then calling its QueryMultipleInterfaces() method for all the interfaces required by the behavior. Every proxy to an object will implement IMultiQI.

However, when an interface pointer is returned, it means that the interface has been marshaled, and COM has gone through all the steps of creating the proxy in the client's memory. This is a waste because you may only want to know if the interface is supported. Even if the object supports the necessary set of interfaces, it still does not give all the required information – for example, you cannot tell the outgoing interfaces of an object using QueryInterface(). While it's true that you can query type information for this, if type information is available, or use IProvideClassInfo2 to get the default outgoing interface, this still requires the object to be instantiated.

To solve these problems, COM provides a mechanism called **categories**. Essentially, a category specifies that an object has a particular behavior, and defines its relationship with the client. There are two broad types of categories: **required** and **implemented**. When a server supports a required category, it means that it has all the necessary interfaces to supply the behavior expected by the client but it also means that the object should only be created if the client knows how to use all these interfaces. Often this will mean that the client needs to provide interfaces of its own. For example, if an object supports the interfaces for CAT_Ping and marks this as a required category, then a client will only be able to create the object if it is able to connect to the object with connection points and create notification objects with the IPing interface.

However, if a second object supports the CAT_Ping behavior, but it also has other behavior that *doesn't* require client-side support, it can mark itself as implementing the category. This means that it has the specified behavior, but clients that do not know about this behavior still can create it.

A category is identified by a CATID. This is a UUID, and it's registered as a key under HKEY_CLASSES_ROOT\Component Categories. The entries in this key simply associate a UUID with the category description. The key should have a named value that has a locale and the category description in the language of that locale.

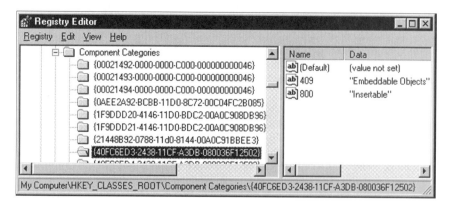

This screenshot shows the category `{40FC6ED3-2438-11CF-A3DB-080036F12502}`, which indicates that an object is insertable (it will appear in the Insert Object dialog). The two named values are `409`, which is the locale for US English, and `800`, which is the system default.

An object that implements a category should add a key to its `CLSID` entry called `Required Categories` or `Implemented Categories`, depending on whether the category support is required on the client to create the object. These keys have subkeys for the CATIDs supported by the object:

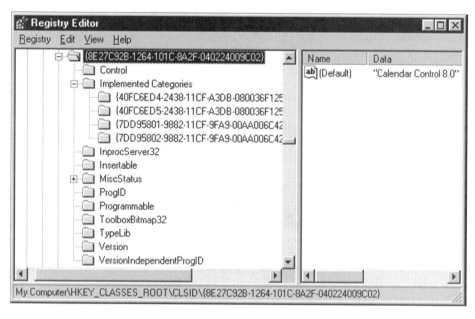

Here, the Calendar Control has the necessary interfaces to be described as `Control`, `Automation Objects`, `Safe for scripting`, and `Safe for initializing`.

Component categories are particularly important when you're writing an ActiveX control container, in which case your container will want to use controls of certain categories. Rather than having to go through the registry yourself to find out which controls support the required categories, you can use the Component Category Manager. This is a system-supplied object that implements two interfaces: `ICatRegister` and `ICatInformation`. The first is used by objects to register the fact that they support a category, while containers use the second to get the CLSIDs of objects that support a particular category.

You can get further information about the Component Category Manager in the Platform SDK, and the code for this chapter on the Wrox web site includes an example called `InsertableList` that lists all the classes installed on your machine that implement the `CATID_Insertable` category. The relevant code (using Visual C++ smart pointers) is shown below:

```
// Create the standard component categories manager
ICatInformationPtr pCatMgr(CLSID_StdComponentCategoriesMgr);

// Get an enumerator object for classes that support CATID_Insertable
CATID cat = CATID_Insertable;
IEnumGUIDPtr pEnum;
pCatMgr->EnumClassesOfCategories(1, &cat, 0, NULL, &pEnum);

CLSID pClsid[5];
ULONG ulFetched = 0;

// Get 5 CLSIDs at a time from the enumerator until there are none left
while(SUCCEEDED(pEnum->Next(5, pClsid, &ulFetched)) && ulFetched > 0)
{
    // Loop through each set of 5 CLSIDs
    for(ULONG ulIndex = 0 ; ulIndex < ulFetched ; ulIndex++)
    {
        // Convert the CLSID to a Prog ID (if possible)
        LPOLESTR lpStr = NULL;
        HRESULT hr = ProgIDFromCLSID(pClsid[ulIndex], &lpStr);
        if(SUCCEEDED(hr))
        {
            // Print whatever Prog IDs we can get
            wcout << lpStr << endl;
            CoTaskMemFree(lpStr);
        }
    }
}
```

However, you don't need to call the Component Category Manager yourself to support categories, because ATL will do it for you. ATL will register the categories supported by your class through the **category map**. As there are no Wizards to do it on your behalf, you must add this yourself, but the process is quite painless – it follows the model of the other ATL maps. Your object can support one of the predefined CATIDs, as declared in `comcat.h` and defined in `uuid.lib`:

```
EXTERN_C const CATID CATID_Insertable;
EXTERN_C const CATID CATID_Control;
EXTERN_C const CATID CATID_Programmable;
EXTERN_C const CATID CATID_IsShortcut;
EXTERN_C const CATID CATID_NeverShowExt;
EXTERN_C const CATID CATID_DocObject;
EXTERN_C const CATID CATID_Printable;
```

```
EXTERN_C const CATID CATID_RequiresDataPathHost;
EXTERN_C const CATID CATID_PersistsToMoniker;
EXTERN_C const CATID CATID_PersistsToStorage;
EXTERN_C const CATID CATID_PersistsToStreamInit;
EXTERN_C const CATID CATID_PersistsToStream;
EXTERN_C const CATID CATID_PersistsToMemory;
EXTERN_C const CATID CATID_PersistsToFile;
EXTERN_C const CATID CATID_PersistsToPropertyBag;
EXTERN_C const CATID CATID_InternetAware;
```

Alternatively, you can define your own CATID (as long as you have a client that is aware of it). You must add the category map and its entries to your ATL object class header by hand, for example:

```
BEGIN_CATEGORY_MAP(CCatCtrl)
    IMPLEMENTED_CATEGORY(CATID_Insertable)
    IMPLEMENTED_CATEGORY(CATID_Control)
    REQUIRED_CATEGORY(CATID_DataSource)
END_CATEGORY_MAP()
```

This indicates an insertable control, and it requires that the container must understand the custom category CATID_DataSource. This made-up category might indicate that the container can access a data source and provide data source interfaces through which the control could bind.

The information in the map is only used when the object is registered (or unregistered). When a class is registered, so must be the categories for the class. Thus, a class's entry in the object map will also have a member that gives access to the category map, so that the registration code can get hold of the map and use the Component Category Manager to register the categories. By default, this is done through a method called GetCategoryMap() that is declared in CComCoClass<> as:

```
static const struct _ATL_CATMAP_ENTRY* GetCategoryMap()
{
    return NULL;
}
```

By default, therefore, a class does not use categories. The BEGIN_CATEGORY_MAP() macro declares an override of this method in your class, which gives access to the map information. When the object is registered or unregistered, the AtlRegisterClassCategoriesHelper() method is called; this creates an instance of the Component Category Manager and uses the ICatRegister methods to register the control as supporting or requiring the specified categories.

As the above discussion has suggested, you can also create your own categories. To do this, you must register that category by calling ICatRegister::RegisterCategories() on the Component Category Manager. This creates a new category that can be used by other classes, and containers can check for classes that support this new category.

*Examples of using the category map can be found in Chapter 10.*

# Services

**Services** in this context are collections of interfaces implemented by a server – they have nothing to do with NT services. A container will use services to indicate to a control that it is capable of providing some particular functionality. It is true that a control could simply call `QueryInterface()` on the container for the necessary interfaces, but this will not always succeed. A container can implement several objects to provide functionality when containing a control, and a particular service (such as "control container") could use several interfaces implemented on several objects. `QueryInterface()` only returns the interfaces implemented on an object of a particular class.

Objects that support services should implement the `IServiceProvider` interface:

```
interface IServiceProvider : IUnknown
{
    HRESULT QueryService(
        [in] REFGUID guidService, [in] REFIID riid, [out] void** ppvObject);
};
```

`QueryService()` is passed the UUID of the service, and the IID of an interface that is a part of the service that the control requires. If the container supports the service, it should return the interface pointer in the `[out]` parameter.

ATL 3.0 provides services through the `IServiceProviderImpl<>` template and the **services map**. To use them, you just derive from the class and then add the map:

```
BEGIN_SERVICE_MAP(CMyObject)
    SERVICE_ENTRY(SID_SContainer)
    SERVICE_ENTRY_CHAIN(m_pObject)
END_SERVICE_MAP()
```

There are two macros that you can use in the service map, and examples of both are shown here. The first indicates that the current object supports the specified service (in this case, `SID_SContainer`).

A class could have an embedded object that will support services, and if this is the case the container object should use the `SERVICE_ENTRY_CHAIN()` macro. This is a 'blind' macro, in that it passes all previously unhandled service requests through to the embedded object through its `IUnknown*` pointer (or a reference to a `CComQIPtr<>`), and so it should always be the last macro in the map.

There is very little documentation about services, but a quick search through the IDL files in the Visual C++ `include` directory gives about a dozen or so defined services. An example of using an object that supports a service will be given in the next chapter.

# Summary

In this chapter, you've seen how interfaces are handled in ATL 3.0. You've seen the new ClassView features, and how to add methods and properties, along with the attributes that they can support.

Interface programming is perhaps the most important aspect of COM. Interface programming means that interface and implementation are separate. A class that implements an interface does not have to be implemented with any particular language (this is an implementation detail), nor does it have a particular location.

COM allows objects to support more than one interface, and through QueryInterface() clients can request a particular interface. An object is not required to initialize all its interfaces when the object is created, but there is a requirement that once a client has obtained a particular interface on an object, that object will always support the interface. This means that you can implement delayed initialization via tear-off interfaces. ATL has good support for tear-offs, and this chapter has presented an example showing how to use this.

Finally, COM provides a dynamic invocation mechanism using the IDispatch interface. The main users of this mechanism are dumb scripting clients, but it does create a problem. Scripting clients only access an object through IDispatch, so if the object implements more than one dispinterface, it means that these are effectively hidden from the client. The only way round this is to provide some extra code that effectively does the QueryInterface() for the client. You've seen two, limited, ways of implementing this.

The next chapter explores the Object Wizard in more depth, looking at the types it supports, and how to enhance it.

# 4

# The ATL Object Wizard

It is, of course, perfectly possible to construct an ATL project entirely by hand, writing the module entry points, the object IDL and the ATL class header yourself. However, such a task is tedious and prone to error. A much better approach is to run the ATL COM AppWizard and allow it to create the starter files for you. Once you have these files, you can use the Object Wizard to add new objects to the project IDL and create the ATL class header files. At this point, you can start thinking about customizing the code for your needs.

This chapter will cover the ATL COM AppWizard and the Object Wizard. In it, I will show you what files these Wizards produce, and how they do it. I will explain the object types that the Object Wizard can create for you, and finally I'll explain how the Object Wizard works, so that you can create your own Object Wizard object types.

# AppWizard

You can't have done ATL development without seeing the AppWizard many times, but I'm going to take this discussion from the top to make sure that I don't miss anything – just join in whenever you feel comfortable. Everything starts with this dialog:

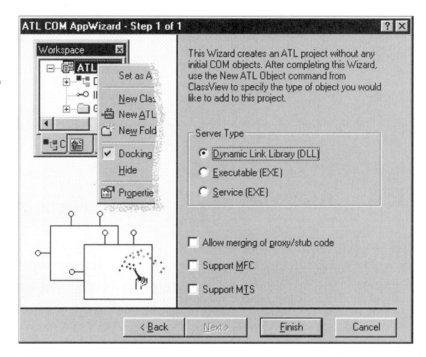

| Item | Meaning |
|------|---------|
| Dynamic Link Library (DLL) | The project will be packaged in a DLL, so the objects can be in-process (usually), or local, or remote (with the aid of a surrogate) |
| Executable (EXE) | The project will be packaged in an EXE, so the objects will be local or remote |
| Service (EXE) | The project will be packaged in an EXE and can be run as a local object, a remote object, or as an NT service |
| Allow merging of proxy/stub code | Merges the interface proxy-stub objects into an in-process server's DLL |
| Support MFC | Adds support for MFC to your project |
| Support MTS | Adds support for the project to use MTS objects |

Notice that the options for merging proxy-stub code and supporting MFC and MTS are only available for DLL servers.

# Merging Proxy-stub Code

Why might you want to merge the proxy-stub objects into your DLL server? Well, if the DLL server you are developing will be used through a surrogate, then the interfaces will need to be marshaled across process boundaries. Also, even if you intend your object to be created in-process, you may decide to allow clients to pass references to your object's interfaces onto other applications. This requires these interfaces to be marshaled.

In both cases, you will need to distribute the proxy-stub DLL to every machine that is likely to use the interfaces. If these machines also have the surrogate or client that uses your object, then you will need to distribute two DLLs, and each of these will have to be registered. You can simplify this administration by merging the proxy-stub objects into your in-process server DLL, making only one DLL to install and register. However, in most circumstances you should *not* merge the proxy-stub code, and that's why an unchecked box is the default setting.

When you merge proxy-stub code into your DLL, you are increasing its size. By their nature, DLL servers should be small and lightweight, and you shouldn't add extra code that is not absolutely necessary. If the server will have objects that support an interface that you have defined, and which is common to other objects in other servers, it is most likely not a good idea to merge the proxy-stub code. This is because you will want to have a single DLL to marshal the interface that all objects will use, regardless of the server. Also, you will not need dedicated proxy-stub code if the interfaces will use type library marshaling, or if they are dual and only get called through IDispatch (if they're to be used by scripting languages, for example). I will have more to say about this option in Chapter 7, but in the meantime, before you check this box, ensure that you really do need it.

# Supporting MFC

You should also think carefully about using MFC support in your project. MFC can bloat your code if you link statically to the MFC libraries, and if you decide to link dynamically then you must ensure that the libraries are installed on the machine where your object will run.

Let's look at a couple of cases where you might think MFC is a good idea. Perhaps you want the ease and simplicity of MFC's CString type, or its collection classes. In these cases, it is better to use the standard library basic_string<> and the STL collection templates. These are easy to use, and the time you spend learning how to use them will repay you many times over in the future. If you're still reticent about using basic_string<> instead of CString, you can download Alex Stockton's NotMFC::CString class from the World of ATL web site (http://www.worldofatl.com/). This gives you CString-like methods but uses basic_string<> for its operation.

Other situations could arise if you have some graphics utility classes written with MFC that you want to use when drawing an ActiveX control, for example, or a database utility class that uses the MFC ODBC classes. Using MFC is a viable option in both of these situations, but remember that ATL does not participate in the MFC document/view architecture, and this may impede your use of this legacy code. Perhaps a better alternative in this case, would be to add ATL support to your MFC application. You can do this using the Object Wizard.

# Supporting MTS

Choosing the Support MTS option links your project with `mtx.lib`, `mtxguid.lib`, and `delayimp.lib`. The AppWizard adds these static libraries so that you can get access to the MTS context objects.

> *In addition, this option adds a reminder in the registration build step to run* `mtxrereg.exe` *before using the component in MTS. It does not run this process.*

`delayimp.lib` is used to allow your project to **delay load** the `mtxex.dll` file. Delay loading is a new feature of Visual C++ 6 that allows you to specify a list of DLLs (using the `/delayload` linker option) that will only be loaded when they are actually called. In previous versions of Visual C++, you had one of two choices: you could use an import library (in which case the DLL is always loaded), or you could use `LoadLibrary()` and `GetProcAddress()` to load a DLL only when it was needed. Visual C++ 6 delay loading is like the second option in that the DLL is only loaded when needed, but like the first in that your application does not need to load the DLL explicitly, nor to obtain the function addresses.

# Generated Files

The AppWizard produces all the files you need to create the server type that you request, but although all the entry points will be set up correctly, your module will not contain any objects. Adding objects to your project requires the Object Wizard, but before we move on to that, let's just take a quick look at the files that the AppWizard generates.

| File | Description | Notes |
|---|---|---|
| `root.h` | Header for the project | |
| `root.def` | Module definition file | DLL projects only |
| `root.rc` | Resource script | |
| `root.idl` | IDL file for the project | |
| `root.clw` | ClassWizard information | MFC only |
| `root.rgs` | Registry script for the project | |
| `rootps.mk` | Proxy-stub makefile | |
| `rootps.def` | Proxy-stub module definition file | |
| `stdafx.h` | Precompiled header | |
| `stdafx.cpp` | Precompiled header support | |
| `resource.h` | Resource header | |
| `dlldatax.c` | Proxy-stub code | Merge proxy-stub only |
| `dlldatax.h` | Proxy-stub code | Merge proxy-stub only |

In this table, `root` is the name of the project. The files you see here are based on templates held in the AppWizard file. When you select items in the AppWizard, details of the project are held as a map of named values. Visual C++'s AppWizard support will parse through the template files, and whenever it finds one of the keys in the template, it will replace it with the value in the map. This is standard Visual C++ AppWizard behavior, and you can find out more if you search MSDN for 'Custom AppWizard'.

If you want to, you can view these template files by loading the AppWizard in Visual C++, and then extracting the resources. To do this, use File | Open... and browse to the `Common\MSDev98\Bin\IDE` subdirectory of the Visual Studio directory. Change Open as to Resources, and open `AtlWiz.awx`.

You can extract a resource by right-clicking on it and then selecting Export....

`newproj.inf` has information about the actual files that are added to the new project, `confirm.inf` generates the confirmation dialog, and the rest are template files. Here is an extract from `root.cpp`:

```
#include "stdafx.h"
#include "resource.h"
#include <initguid.h>
#include "$$root$$.h"
$$BEGINLOOP(CONTROLCOUNT)
#include "$$ctl_hfile$$"
$$ENDLOOP
$$IF(MERGEPS)
#include "dlldatax.h"
$$ENDIF

#include "$$root$$_i.c"

$$IF(MERGEPS)
#ifdef _MERGE_PROXYSTUB
extern "C" HINSTANCE hProxyDll;
#endif
$$ENDIF

$$IF(PROJTYPE_DLL)
CComModule _Module;
$$ENDIF
```

The items *surrounded* by $$ marks are keys in the map of replaceable strings, while the items *prefixed* by $$ are directives that the AppWizard uses. Thus, if you select DLL as the project type in the AppWizard, then PROJTYPE_DLL will be set and so the line CComModule _Module; will be added to the file.

If you decide you would like to write your own AppWizard to add more options, you can do so using the Custom AppWizard, using the templates in the ATL AppWizard as a basis.

# Object Wizard

The Object Wizard now supports considerably more object types than it did in Visual C++ 5. The screenshot shows just a few of these, but I'll describe all of them in this section.

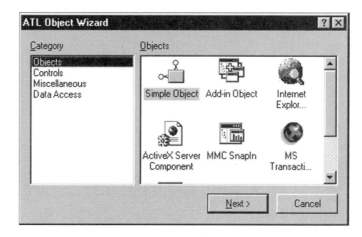

| Objects | | |
|---|---|---|
| Simple Object | Minimal COM Object | All server types |
| Add-in Object | Visual C++ Add-in object | DLL server only |
| Internet Explorer Object | UI-less IE object | DLL server only |
| ActiveX Server Component | An object that can be used by Active Server Pages | All server types |
| MMC Snap-in | Microsoft Management Console snap-in object | DLL server only |
| MS Transaction Server Component | A non-aggregatable object with the MTS headers | DLL server only |
| Component Registrar Object | Object that implements IComponentRegistrar | DLL server only |

A striking thing about this table is that although most objects are only applicable for DLL servers, they still appear in the Object Wizard dialog even when the server type is an EXE. Although it's harmless to add an object to an incompatible server type, you won't be able to create those objects.

If you're developing business objects, you are likely to use Simple Object. This is the simplest and therefore the most flexible of the object types. The Internet Explorer Object type is a Simple Object that also supports `IObjectWithSite` and has a test HTML file, while the MS Transaction Server Component includes `mtx.h` so that you can access the context object. It also gives you the option of implementing `IObjectControl`. The component registrar is also used with MTS, to allow you to register particular classes in a server. The snap-in object allows you to create a new snap-in for the Microsoft Management Console, while the add-in allows you to add a new command to the Visual C++ development environment.

| Controls | |
|---|---|
| Full Control | Supports control interfaces used by all control containers |
| Lite Control | 'Lite' version of the Full Control |
| Composite Control | Control that hosts other ActiveX controls |
| Lite Composite Control | 'Lite' version of the Composite Control |
| HTML Control | DHTML control |
| Lite HTML Control | 'Lite' version of the HTML Control |
| Property Page | Property page |

Controls, of course, can *only* live in DLLs, so you will have to use your discretion here. Notice that there are two versions of all the control types: a normal version, and a 'lite' version. The normal versions are 'heavy' in that they support the full range of interfaces required for the control, and typically this will include interfaces that many containers do not use.

A case in point is the `IPersistxxx` set of interfaces. Most containers will initialize and save a control's state by using `IPersistStreamInit`, and thus both normal and 'lite' versions support this interface. However, a few containers may use the more heavyweight `IPersistStorage`. Since this is not so common, it is not provided on the 'lite' control, but for completeness it is provided on the normal version. To decide which version you want, you really must know your container.

| Miscellaneous | |
|---|---|
| Dialog | A dialog object |

The Dialog type is not a COM type at all, but it's provided to give you a lightweight C++ wrapper class around the dialog API. The Object Wizard will give you a dialog resource to design your dialog. Visual C++ 6 has an MFC-style message handler dialog that allows you to add message handlers for the controls on the dialog, and I'll show you an example of using this a little later on.

| Data Access | |
|---|---|
| Provider | An OLE DB provider |
| Consumer | An OLE DB consumer |

The Consumer type isn't a COM object either – it's a method of creating a wrapper class to give access to a data source via OLE DB. These classes can be used by any project that has initialized COM, but unfortunately there's a deficiency in the Object Wizard that means when you try to run it in non-ATL compliant projects, it refuses to start. The workaround is to create a dummy ATL project first, and then copy the files across, as I'll demonstrate a little later on. The Provider type allows you to create a new OLE DB provider.

# Standard Objects

The section contains details of all the standard types provided with Visual C++ 6. The Object Wizard for most of the objects uses the Names and Attributes pages that you're familiar with, although a few will disable some of the items, and a couple have new pages all of their own.

# Objects

In general these do not have user interfaces, although some, like the MMC snap-in and the Visual C++ Add-in types, *do* provide some visual elements through toolbars and control bars.

## Simple Objects

This is a general-purpose object type. You can use this to create an object with a single interface that can be either custom or dual. If you want the object to support other interfaces, you will have to add this support using ClassView, as explained in the last chapter.

## Add-in Objects

The Add-in object option allows you to define a new object that supports the IDSAddIn interface. Add-in objects must be implemented in DLL projects.

With an Add-in object, you can extend the Visual C++ IDE. Your Add-in can add new commands to Visual C++, and it can respond to events generated by some of the existing Visual C++ objects. When you specify that an Add-in should be used (through the Tools | Customize... | Add-ins and Macro Files tab), Visual C++ accesses the object's IDSAddIn interface and calls OnConnection(), passing it the IApplication interface pointer to Visual C++'s Application object. Through this interface you can tell Visual C++ what commands, toolbars and buttons the Add-in supports.

A command can be invoked by starting msdev at the command line using the -ex switch:

```
> msdev -ex MyCommand
```

Note that commands do not take parameters, so if a command needs some data, it should obtain it from another source – the registry, for example, or by presenting a dialog.

Once the command has finished executing, Visual C++ will continue to run. If this is not what you want, you must explicitly tell Visual C++ to stop. The Add-in object is passed an interface pointer to the Visual C++ Application object, and if you call its Quit() method, Visual C++ will close down.

If you just want to add commands, all you need to do is add those commands as methods to your object's dual interface. (The Object Wizard doesn't give you a choice: the new interface must be dual.) The Wizard-generated code tells Visual C++ about this interface by calling `IApplication::SetAddInInfo()`, passing it the `IDispatch` part of your object's interface. Visual C++ can then use this interface pointer to get your object's type information to determine what commands you are providing.

Why would you want to provide a command without a toolbar button? Well, these commands are available through the Visual Studio macros, so you can write utility routines to be used by scripts. Another situation is when you want to do tasks that are not possible in VBScript or Jscript; for example I have written Add-ins that perform archive maintenance checking out files from Visual Source Safe and then performing raw file manipulations that would be impossible to do with a scripting language.

Adding a command to a toolbar or creating a new toolbar is a little more work. To add a command button, you need to call `IApplication::AddCommand()`, passing the name of the command (that is, the method on your interface) and information that will be used on the button itself: the text, a tooltip, a status bar string and a bitmap for the button. To add a toolbar *and* a button, you need to call `IApplication::AddCommandBarButton()` and pass the button information.

Although you can call these Add-in command methods in your own code, it is easier to allow the Object Wizard to generate the code to do it – this is the purpose of the DevStudio Add-in tab:

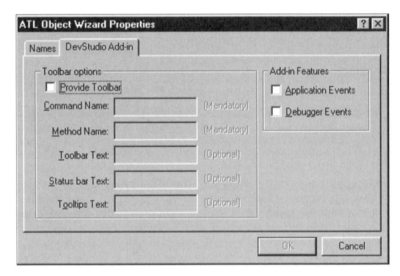

If you don't select the Provide Toolbar checkbox, you will only add a command. Otherwise, a toolbar is added with the single button that you specify using Command Name and Method Name. The former is the method that will be added to the Visual Studio object model, while the latter refers to the method that the Wizard will add to your object to perform the command.

The Add-in Features allow you to provide support for sinking events from Visual C++ or the debugger. The Wizard will add the `IApplicationEvents` or `IDebuggerEvents` interfaces to your objects, along with stub methods. The events that you can respond to are:

| Event | Description | Object |
|---|---|---|
| BeforeApplicationShutDown() | Called just before Visual C++ shuts down. | |
| BeforeBuildStart() | Called just before a build is to start. | |
| BeforeDocumentClose() | Called before a document closes; a pointer to the document is passed to the method. | Document |
| BuildFinish() | Called when a build has finished. The method is passed the number of errors and warnings that occurred. | |
| DocumentOpen() | Called when the specified document is opened. | Document |
| DocumentSave() | Called when the specified document is saved. | Document |
| NewDocument() | Called after the specified document has been created. | Document |
| NewWorkspace() | Called after a new workspace has been created. | |
| WindowActivate() | Called after the specified window becomes activated. | Window |
| WindowDeactivate() | Called after the specified window is deactivated. | Window |
| WorkspaceClose() | Called when a workspace is closed. | |
| WorkspaceOpen() | Called after a workspace is opened. | |

The IDebuggerEvents interface has one method, BreakpointHit(), which is called when a breakpoint is hit. This method is passed a BreakPoint object, and you can read its properties to determine where in the source code the breakpoint was hit.

In the table I refer to several types of Visual Studio objects. As with many Microsoft applications the top object in the hierarchy is the Application object and from that you can access other objects or collections of objects. Collections are characterized by having plural names, so the Application.Projects property can be used to access all the Project objects open in the current workspace.

A `Document` object represents an open document in the IDE and you can regard it as a 'typed' text file, that can be saved to disk. `Document` objects have a `Language` property that can be C++, VBScript, HTML or any of the other types of document that you can open in Visual Studio. If the document represents an editable text file then through its `Selection` property you can obtain a `TextSelection` object that allows you to change the text in the `Document`. A `TextSelection` object has methods like `CharLeft()`, `PageDown()` and `StartOfDocument()` which you can use to move around the document. You can also use its `Text` property to replace or add text to the document.

If you want to change the window aspects of an open `Document`, for example its size and position, you can do so by accessing the `Windows` property that is a collection of `Window` objects. If `Window` object is a window on a text document then you can access it as a `TextWindow`, and this also has a `Selection` property through which you can get access to a a `TextSelection` object. Because you can get to a single object via various routes like this it means that it can get confusing.

The `IApplicationEvent` methods are also passed a pointer to the object to which they refer. For example, when a window is activated, the `WindowActivate()` event is generated, and this method is passed the `IDispatch` pointer to the `Window` object.

### A Sample Add-in Project

As an example of an Add-in, the Copyright project handles the `NewDocument()` event to add a copyright message to the top of every newly created file. To create this project, run the **ATL COM AppWizard** and choose the **Dynamic Link Library (DLL)** option, since this is required for Add-ins. Once the AppWizard has finished creating the files, you can insert the object using **Insert | New ATL Object...** and select **Add-in Object** from the Object Wizard.

In the **Names** tab, supply a **Short Name** of `FileCopyright`. Then, select the **DevStudio Add-in** tab and select **Application Events** and **Provide Toolbar**. Add these values:

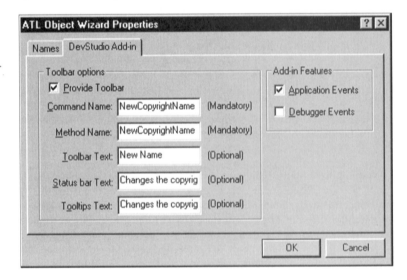

This will add a new command to Visual C++ called `NewCopyrightName`; the command is implemented by the `NewCopyrightName()` method which is added to the `IFileCopyright` interface. Here's the header file:

```
class ATL_NO_VTABLE CFileCopyright :
    public CComObjectRootEx<CComSingleThreadModel>,
    public CComCoClass<CFileCopyright, &CLSID_FileCopyright>,
    public IDispatchImpl<
        IApplicationEvents, &IID_IApplicationEvents, &LIBID_COPYRIGHTLib>,
    public IDSAddIn,
    public IDispatchImpl<IFileCopyright, &IID_IFileCopyright,
&LIBID_COPYRIGHTLib>
{
public:
    CFileCopyright() {}

DECLARE_REGISTRY_RESOURCEID(IDR_FILECOPYRIGHT)

DECLARE_PROTECT_FINAL_CONSTRUCT()

BEGIN_COM_MAP(CFileCopyright)
    COM_INTERFACE_ENTRY(IFileCopyright)
    COM_INTERFACE_ENTRY2(IDispatch, IFileCopyright)
    COM_INTERFACE_ENTRY(IDSAddIn)
    COM_INTERFACE_ENTRY(IApplicationEvents)
END_COM_MAP()

    CComPtr<IApplication> m_spApplication;
    DWORD m_dwAddInID;
    DWORD m_dwAppEvents;

// IDSAddIn methods
public:
    STDMETHOD(OnConnection)(IApplication* pApp, VARIANT_BOOL bFirstTime,
                            long dwCookie, VARIANT_BOOL* bOnConnection);
    STDMETHOD(OnDisconnection)(VARIANT_BOOL bLastTime);

// IApplicationEvents methods
public:
    // Several of these methods omitted for brevity
    STDMETHOD(NewDocument)(IDispatch *pDocument);

// IFileCopyright
public:
    STDMETHOD(NewCopyrightName)();
};
```

The class implements the IApplicationEvents interface so that it can respond to events generated by the Application object. I have left out most of the IApplicationEvents sink interface methods, since the only one we're interested in is NewDocument(). The class also implements the IDSAddIn interface that Visual C++ will call to allow your Add-in to add new commands and new toolbars to the IDE.

Whenever a new document is created, this Add-in should place a copyright notice at the top of the file. This notice has the form:

```
// Copyright 1998 Richard Grimes
```

There are several points to notice here, the first of which is the comment symbol '//'. I want the Add-in to test the document to see what type it is and then use an appropriate symbol (like '′' for VBS and the pair '<!--' and '-->' for HTML). Obviously, the year should be the current year, and the copyright name (here, 'Richard Grimes') should be a value that you can supply.

This Add-in will access the copyright name from the registry – a value called Name in a key called \Wrox\VC Addins\Copyright in HKEY_CURRENT_USER – so that different users can have different copyright notices. When the Add-in starts, it will test for this value in the registry. If the value doesn't exist, you will be given the option of adding a new name; the Add-in gets this name from you by calling the NewCopyrightName command.

To get user input, you'll need to add a dialog to the project. So run the Object Wizard again, select **Dialog** from the **Miscellaneous** category, and call it ChangeName. This will add new source and header files to the project, as well as a dialog resource. So that you can use the ATL window classes, it will also add atlwin.h to your stdafx.h file – if you take a look, you should find the Visual C++ object model headers have been added:

```
#include <atlcom.h>
#include <ObjModel\addauto.h>
#include <ObjModel\appdefs.h>
#include <ObjModel\appauto.h>
#include <ObjModel\blddefs.h>
#include <ObjModel\bldauto.h>
#include <ObjModel\textdefs.h>
#include <ObjModel\textauto.h>
#include <ObjModel\dbgdefs.h>
#include <ObjModel\dbgauto.h>
#include <atlwin.h>
```

These headers define the interfaces and constants used to access the Visual C++ objects. Edit the dialog resource to have an edit box with the symbol IDC_COPYRIGHTNAME:

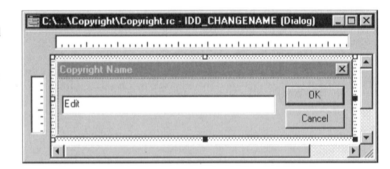

Open ChangeName.h and add a public data member to hold the copyright name:

```
LRESULT OnCancel(WORD wNotifyCode, WORD wID, HWND hWndCtl, BOOL& bHandled);
{
    EndDialog(wID);
    return 0;
}

CComBSTR m_bstrName;
};
```

This dialog is really simple, but just to get a feel of the new message handler Wizard, right click on the CChangeName class in the ClassView and select Add Windows Message Handler... from the context menu:

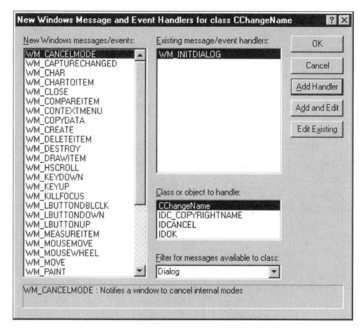

This is very similar to the ClassWizard that MFC programmers use. You can add message handlers for the various controls on the dialog (or for the dialog itself) by selecting the control in the Class or object to handle list box, and then choosing a message from the left-hand list box. In this case, we want to edit the WM_INITDIALOG handler, so select this item and click on the Edit Existing button. This will take you to the OnInitDialog() handler in ChangeName.h! OK, this isn't a wonderful example, but if you want to add a *new* handler for a control, the Wizard will ensure that the correct entry is added to the message map, as well as a suitable stub for the message handler.

Use OnInitDialog() to initialize the edit control with the value in the m_bstrName member, so that users of the class can set a value that the end user can edit:

```
LRESULT OnInitDialog(UINT uMsg, WPARAM wParam, LPARAM lParam, BOOL& bHandled)
{
    USES_CONVERSION;
    SetDlgItemText(IDC_COPYRIGHTNAME, OLE2CT(m_bstrName));
    return 1;  // Let the system set the focus
}
```

Then, change OnOK() so that the value in the edit box is saved:

```
LRESULT CChangeName::OnOK(WORD wNotifyCode, WORD wID,
                                       HWND hWndCtl, BOOL& bHandled)
{
    GetDlgItemText(IDC_COPYRIGHTNAME, m_bstrName.m_str);
    SysFreeString(bstr);
    EndDialog(wID);
    return 0;
}
```

Next, open `FileCopyright.h` and add a data member for the copyright name:

```
// IFileCopyright
public:
    STDMETHOD(NewCopyrightName)();
private:
    CComBSTR m_bstrName;
};
```

Now you should implement the Add-in, so open `FileCopyright.cpp`, and add the following header:

```
#include "stdafx.h"
#include "Copyright.h"
#include "FileCopyright.h"
#include "ChangeName.h"
```

Implement `NewCopyrightName()` like this:

```
HRESULT CFileCopyright::NewCopyrightName()
{
    USES_CONVERSION;
    CChangeName dlg;

    dlg.m_bstrName = m_bstrName;

    if (dlg.DoModal() == IDOK)
        m_bstrName = dlg.m_bstrName;

    CRegKey copyrightName;
    copyrightName.Create(HKEY_CURRENT_USER,
                          _T("Software\\Wrox\\VC AddIns\\Copyright"));
    copyrightName.SetValue(OLE2CT(m_bstrName), _T("Name"));
    return S_OK;
}
```

This puts any existing name into the dialog, and after the user has clicked the OK button, the value is saved in the `Name` value in the registry. Notice that I'm using `CRegKey::Create()`; this will open a key if it already exists, and create one if it doesn't.

When the Add-in is loaded into Visual C++, including when Visual C++ starts, and when you first add it through the **Customize** dialog, the `OnConnection()` method of the Add-in's `IDSAddIn` interface is called. We will use this to check the registry for the copyright name, and if it doesn't exist we'll call `NewCopyrightName()`:

```
HRESULT CFileCopyright::OnConnection(IApplication* pApp,
      VARIANT_BOOL bFirstTime, long dwAddInID, VARIANT_BOOL* bOnConnection)
{
    HRESULT hr = S_OK;
    m_spApplication = pApp;
    m_dwAddInID = dwAddInID;

    // Connect up to application event sink
    AtlAdvise(pApp, GetUnknown(), IID_IApplicationEvents, &m_dwAppEvents);
```

```
    hr = pApp->SetAddInInfo((long)_Module.GetModuleInstance(),
                            static_cast<IFileCopyright*>(this),
                            IDB_TOOLBAR_MEDIUM_FILECOPYRIGHT,
                            IDB_TOOLBAR_LARGE_FILECOPYRIGHT, dwAddInID);
    LPCTSTR szCommand = _T("NewCopyrightName");
    VARIANT_BOOL bRet;
    if (SUCCEEDED(hr))
    {
        hr = pApp->AddCommand(CComBSTR(_T("NewCopyrightName\n")
                    _T("New Name\nChanges the copyright name\n")
                    _T("Changes the copyright name")),
                    CComBSTR(_T("NewCopyrightName")), 0, dwAddInID, &bRet);
    }

    if (bFirstTime)
    {
        if (SUCCEEDED(hr))
        {
            hr = pApp->AddCommandBarButton(dsGlyph,
                            CComBSTR(_T("NewCopyrightName")), dwAddInID);
        }
    }
```

```
    CRegKey copyrightName;
    TCHAR strName[256];
    DWORD dwSize = 256;
    DWORD dwRet;
    copyrightName.Create(HKEY_CURRENT_USER,
                            _T("Software\\Wrox\\VC AddIns\\Copyright"));
    dwRet = copyrightName.QueryValue(strName, _T("Name"), &dwSize);
    if (dwRet != ERROR_SUCCESS || lstrlen(strName) == 0)
        NewCopyrightName();
    else
        m_bstrName = strName;
```

```
    *bOnConnection = SUCCEEDED(hr) ? VARIANT_TRUE : VARIANT_FALSE;
    return hr;
}
```

The Wizard-generated code calls `AddCommand()` to give the application the Add-in's command. If you want to add more commands, you need to call this method for each one. The implementation also calls `AddCommandBarButton()` to add the command to a new toolbar.

Finally, you need to implement the `NewDocument()` method to add the copyright notice:

```
HRESULT CFileCopyright::NewDocument(IDispatch* theDocument)
{
    CComQIPtr<ITextDocument, &IID_ITextDocument> pTextDoc(theDocument);
    HRESULT hr = S_OK;
    CComBSTR bstrLang;
    hr = pTextDoc->get_Language(&bstrLang);
    if(FAILED(hr))
        return hr;

    CComBSTR bstrComment;
    if(bstrLang == DS_CPP)
        bstrComment = L"// ";
    else if(bstrLang == DS_HTML_IE3 || bstrLang == DS_HTML_RFC1866)
```

```
        bstrComment = L"<!-- ";
    else if(bstrLang == DS_IDL)
        bstrComment = L"// ";
    else if(bstrLang == DS_VBS)
        bstrComment = L"\' ";
    else if(bstrLang == DS_JAVA)
        bstrComment = L"// ";
    else bstrComment = L"// ";

    CComBSTR bstrType;
    hr = pTextDoc->get_Type(&bstrType);
    if(FAILED(hr))
        return hr;

    if(bstrType == DS_TEXT_DOCUMENT)
    {
        ATLTRACE(_T("This is an editable window!"));
        CComQIPtr<ITextSelection, &IID_ITextSelection> pTextSel;
        CComPtr<IDispatch> pDisp;
        hr = pTextDoc->get_Selection(&pDisp);
        if(FAILED(hr))
            return hr;

        pTextSel = pDisp;
        hr = pTextSel->StartOfDocument(CComVariant());
        if(FAILED(hr))
            return hr;

        CComBSTR bstrText;
        bstrText = bstrComment;
        bstrText += L"Copyright ";

        SYSTEMTIME st;
        GetLocalTime(&st);
        TCHAR strYear[5];
        wsprintf(strYear, _T("%ld"),st.wYear);

        bstrText += strYear;
        bstrText += L" ";
        bstrText += m_bstrName;
        if(bstrLang == DS_HTML_IE3 || bstrLang == DS_HTML_RFC1866)
            bstrText += L" -->";
        bstrText += L"\n";

        hr = pTextSel->put_Text(bstrText);
    }
    else
        ATLTRACE(_T("Not an editable window!"));
    return hr;
}
```

To get access to the document type, you need to access the ITextDocument interface, and to do that the first line creates a CComQIPtr<> smart pointer, initializing it with the IDispatch* parameter that points to the document's IGenericDocument interface. CComQIPtr<> is used because it automatically performs a QueryInterface() for ITextDocument.

I determine the type of the file through the Language property, which I access in the code to determine the comment string to insert. If you use the **New Text File** button on the **Standard** toolbar, the document will not have a type, so I assume that it will be used as a C++ file. Notice that there are text strings defined in textdefs.h with the prefix DS_, and that I use CComBSTR::operator ==() to check the language type.

After identifying the language, the code accesses the Type property, which determines whether you can edit the file. For this to be possible, it should have the value DS_TEXT_DOCUMENT.

Now the code is ready to construct the copyright notice and add the text to the document. To do this, it needs to access the Selection object of the document. ITextDocument::get_Selection() returns an IDispatch pointer, so I must first access this pointer and then call QueryInterface() for the ITextSelection interface. The actual QueryInterface() call is done in the assignment:

```
pTextSel = pDisp;
```

After that, the code moves to the start of the document, constructs the copyright notice and writes it to the document by accessing the Text property. You should now be able to compile this code.

Once the Add-in is built and registered, you need to install it into Visual C++. Select the Customize... item from the Tools menu, select the Add-ins and Macro Files tab, and use the Browse... button to add the Copyright.dll Add-in (you will have to change the Files of type to Add-ins (.dll)).

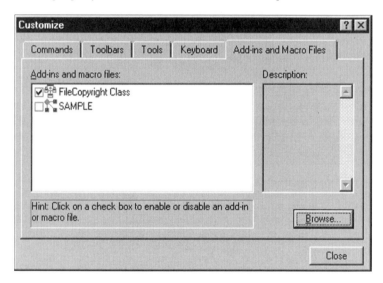

When you click on the Close button, the Add-in will be loaded and you will see the **Copyright Name** dialog:

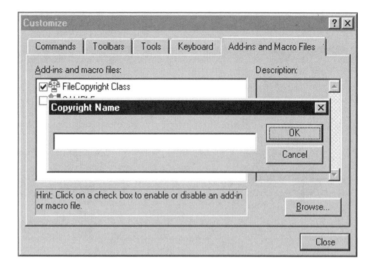

Once you've entered a name, the Customize dialog will disappear. Open it again, select the Commands tab, and then choose All commands in the Category box. You should find that NewCopyrightName has been added to the Commands box:

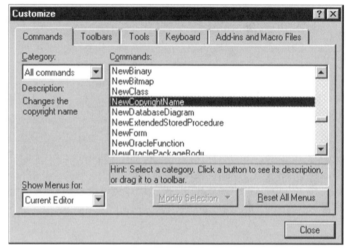

You will also find that a new toolbar will has been added to the IDE:

By default, this toolbar will be called Toolbar1, and unfortunately there's no way of changing it through code. Instead, you have to use the Customize Toolbars tab and change it by hand. The reason that you can't make this change through code is that there is no Toolbar object in the Visual C++ object model. You'll notice that there *are* ToolsCustomize and ToolsCustomizeToolbars commands, but these don't allow you to change the toolbar name – as you know, commands don't take a parameter. Instead, these commands open the specified dialog, and you need to edit the items by hand.

To test the add-in, click on the New Text File button on the Standard toolbar. You should see something like this:

You'll notice that Visual C++'s context coloring hasn't changed the color of the text, the reason is that the document is a text document, not a C++ document. To create a file with a specific type, use the File | New... menu item, pick the Files tab, and select C++ Source File:

```
// Copyright 1998 Richard Grimes
|
```

Better still, if you use the same dialog to create an HTML Page, you'll get something like this:

```
<!-- Copyright 1998 Richard Grimes -->
<HTML>
<HEAD>
<META NAME="GENERATOR" Content="Microsoft Developer Studio">
<META HTTP-EQUIV="Content-Type" content="text/html; charset=iso-8859-1">
<TITLE>Document Title</TITLE>
</HEAD>
<BODY>

<!-- Insert HTML here -->

</BODY>
</HTML>
```

You can see that the correct comment symbols are being used, as intended.

There are other things that you can do with Add-ins, but remember that the commands you add do not have any parameters, so they are most suitable for commands that, for example, you would add as menu items. Since your Add-in has access to the Application object it means that you can always access the current active Window or Document object, this makes it particularly useful for Add-ins that manipulate or format text. However, the object model doesn't expose the collection of files in the project, so you cannot write an Add-in to work on project files that are not open in the IDE (you can use CreateFile() to open a file in the project directory, but there is no easy way to determine if it is actually part of the project).

## Internet Explorer Objects

These are objects without user interfaces that can be scripted from Internet Explorer. The difference between an Internet Explorer Object and a Simple Object is that the former implements IObjectWithSite through the ATL class IObjectWithSiteImpl<>. This interface acts as a lightweight version of IOleObject, in that it provides a mechanism for an object's container to provide the object with its IUnknown pointer. The object can then use this pointer to gain access to the container's services.

For example, if you have an object called `Quitter` that has a method called `QuitMe()`, you can use this to close down Internet Explorer 4:

```
#include <exdisp.h>
STDMETHODIMP CQuitter::QuitMe()
{
    CComQIPtr<IServiceProvider> spSP(m_spUnkSite);
    CComPtr<IWebBrowser2> pWebBrowser2;
    spSP->QueryService(IID_IWebBrowserApp, IID_IWebBrowser2,
                              reinterpret_cast<void**>(&pWebBrowser2));
    if (pWebBrowser2)
        pWebBrowser2->Quit();
    return S_OK;
}
```

When the object is created, Internet Explorer will call the object's `IObjectWithSite::SetSite()` method and pass its `IUnknown` pointer. The ATL implementation then caches this in the public `m_spUnkSite` member, which this code uses to call `QueryInterface()` for the `IServiceProvider` interface (the first line). It then asks Internet Explorer for its `IWebBrowser2` interface with a call to `QueryService()`.

If the container *has* the `IWebBrowser2` interface, this code calls its `Quit()` method. The object can be used with the following HTML:

```
<HTML>
<BODY>
<OBJECT ID="Quitter" CLASSID="CLSID:5176BD94-1808-11D2-8D0C-0060973044A8">
</OBJECT>
</BODY>
<BUTTON ID="Quit">Quit</BUTTON>
<SCRIPT LANGUAGE="VBS">
sub Quit_onclick
    Quitter.QuitMe
end sub
</SCRIPT>
</HTML>
```

Pretty pointless, I agree, but it does illustrate how to use `IObjectWithSite`. As a final tip, and as you've probably already guessed, Internet Explorer Objects should be DLL servers.

## ActiveX Server Component

ActiveX server components are server-side components used by IIS. Like Internet Explorer objects they do not have a user interface, however, unlike an IE object they are not intended to be used from a client-side web page, instead, you load them based on code in server-side Active Server Pages loaded into IIS. The ASP page is a server-side script that is run by IIS to generate web pages to be sent back to the client. ASP provides many facilities (including database access and context objects) and you can customize and extend this object model by developing ActiveX Server Components.

Effectively, the component is an object with a dispinterface that you load using the `<OBJECT>` tag or the VBScript `CreateObject()` function (or its equivalent in other scripting languages) on the ASP page. Since a scripting language is accessing your object, you shouldn't implement more than one interface on it. If you decide to do this, you'll have all the problems of accessing the non-default interfaces that I explained in the last chapter.

ASP components can be DLLs or EXEs, but I recommend that you package them as DLLs, because IIS will be able to load the component quicker. To a large extent, you can treat ASP components as **Simple Objects** that must have a dual interface. The Object Wizard has an **ASP** tab that is specific to this object type:

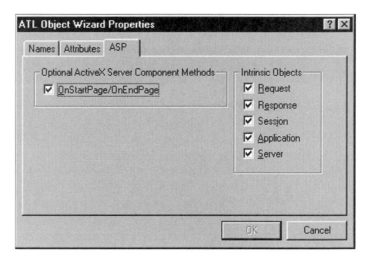

The `OnStartPage()` and `OnEndPage()` methods are event handlers that are called by IIS when an ASP page is created, and when the script has finished. If you check the <u>O</u>nStartPage/OnEndPage box, the Wizard will add these methods to your dispinterface. When the object is created, IIS will do a `GetIDsOfNames()` for `OnStartPage`. If the object returns a DISPID, IIS will call the method, passing the `IUnknown` pointer of the `ScriptingContext` object, which you can query for the `IScriptingContext` interface. If you do not need access to the IIS intrinsic objects then you may decide to leave this check box unchecked.

This first checkbox enables the **Intrinsic Objects** frame, and you can select which of these objects you want to use in the component. For each object you select, the Wizard will add a `CComPtr<>` for the appropriate interface in your class. These objects are obtained by calling methods on the `IScriptingContext` interface of the ASP `ScriptingContext` object, and the Wizard will add the appropriate code for you. If you check all the intrinsic objects, the Object Wizard will add the following code to the ATL class:

```
public:
    STDMETHOD(OnStartPage)(IUnknown* IUnk);
    STDMETHOD(OnEndPage)();

private:
    CComPtr<IRequest> m_piRequest;
    CComPtr<IResponse> m_piResponse;
    CComPtr<ISessionObject> m_piSession;
    CComPtr<IServer> m_piServer;
    CComPtr<IApplicationObject> m_piApplication;
    BOOL m_bOnStartPageCalled;
```

These are initialized in `OnStartPage()`:

```
STDMETHODIMP CMyASP::OnStartPage(IUnknown* pUnk)
{
    if(!pUnk)
        return E_POINTER;
```

```
      CComPtr<IScriptingContext> spContext;
      HRESULT hr;

      // Get the IScriptingContext Interface
      hr = pUnk->QueryInterface(IID_IScriptingContext, (void **)&spContext);
      if(FAILED(hr))
         return hr;

      // Get Request Object Pointer
      hr = spContext->get_Request(&m_piRequest);
      if(FAILED(hr))
      {
         spContext.Release();
         return hr;
      }

      // Get Response Object Pointer
      hr = spContext->get_Response(&m_piResponse);
      if(FAILED(hr))
      {
         m_piRequest.Release();
         return hr;
      }

      // Get Server Object Pointer
      hr = spContext->get_Server(&m_piServer);
      if(FAILED(hr))
      {
         m_piRequest.Release();
         m_piResponse.Release();
         return hr;
      }

      // Get Session Object Pointer
      hr = spContext->get_Session(&m_piSession);
      if(FAILED(hr))
      {
         m_piRequest.Release();
         m_piResponse.Release();
         m_piServer.Release();
         return hr;
      }

      // Get Application Object Pointer
      hr = spContext->get_Application(&m_piApplication);
      if(FAILED(hr))
      {
         m_piRequest.Release();
         m_piResponse.Release();
         m_piServer.Release();
         m_piSession.Release();
         return hr;
      }
      m_bOnStartPageCalled = TRUE;
      return S_OK;
   }
```

ATL takes the all-or-nothing approach: if the code fails to get one of the objects, it will release all the others. If you don't want this behavior, you're perfectly entitled to edit the generated code. Bear in mind, though, that if you fail to get one of these intrinsic objects, there must be something bad going on!

Although the ScriptingContext object is available in IIS 4, it is provided only for backward compatibility. IIS 4 provides the equivalent functionality through the ObjectContext object. You may be familiar with this object as the transaction context of an object registered with MTS. The context for an object is obtained by calling GetObjectContext(), and this will return the IObjectContext interface, on which you can call the SetComplete() or SetAbort() methods for transactions.

MTS 2.0 (which is included with IIS 4) provides the context object with an additional interface, IGetContextProperties, and therefore to get the intrinsic objects you should call:

```
CComPtr<IObjectContext> pObjContext;

hr = ::GetObjectContext(&pObjContext);
if(SUCCEEDED(hr))
{
    CComPtr<IGetContextProperties> pProps;
    CComBSTR bstrObj;
    CComVariant varObj;

    hr = pObjContext->QueryInterface(&pProps);
    if(SUCCEEDED(hr))
    {
        bstrObj = L"Request";
        hr = pProps->GetProperty(bstrObj, &varObj);
        hr = varObj.pdispVal->QueryInterface(&m_piRequest);
    }
    if(SUCCEEDED(hr))
    {
        bstrObj = L"Response";
        hr = pProps->GetProperty(bstrObj, &varObj);
        hr = varObj.pdispVal->QueryInterface(&m_piResponse);
    }
    if(SUCCEEDED(hr))
    {
        bstrObj = L"Session";
        hr = pProps->GetProperty(bstrObj, &varObj);
        hr = varObj.pdispVal->QueryInterface(&m_piSession);
    }
    if(SUCCEEDED(hr))
    {
        bstrObj = L"Server";
        hr = pProps->GetProperty(bstrObj, &varObj);
        hr = varObj.pdispVal->QueryInterface(&m_piServer);
    }
    if(SUCCEEDED(hr))
    {
        bstrObj = L"Application";
        hr = pProps->GetProperty(bstrObj, &varObj);
        hr = varObj.pdispVal->QueryInterface(&m_piApplication);
    }
}
```

This is the preferred method with IIS 4. At present, ATL 3.0 takes the safe, backward-compatible route of obtaining these intrinsic objects through the ScriptingContext object. If you are sure that your object will always run under IIS 4 you should use the IGetContextProperties method.

## MMC Snap-in

The Control Panel has been the friendly front-end of Windows system management for many years, and it is easily extended by using DLL applets (with the extension .cpl) that export the CPlApplet() function. The Control Panel can then call this function to pass requests to the applets. Unfortunately, this is very restrictive, because the API defines what actions the applet can take, and there is no way that these can be extended. The Control Panel is one of those few areas of NT 4 that stubbornly remind you of its evolution from 16-bit Windows.

Now, Microsoft has decided that it's time for a change. The new tool for administration is the **Microsoft Management Console** (MMC), which can be added to NT 4 with the Option Pack. MMC is just a container, to which you can add URLs (and hence provide Java applets), shortcuts to EXEs, or MMC extensions called **Snap-ins**. The latter are COM objects that provide functionality to MMC via COM interfaces.

> There is not space here for a complete discussion about MMC and for more details I recommend you refer to Professional DCOM Application Development (ISBN 1-861001-31-2) and Professional NT Services (ISBN 1-861001-30-4) both published by Wrox.

This screenshot shows the Microsoft Management Console with the MTS snap-in:

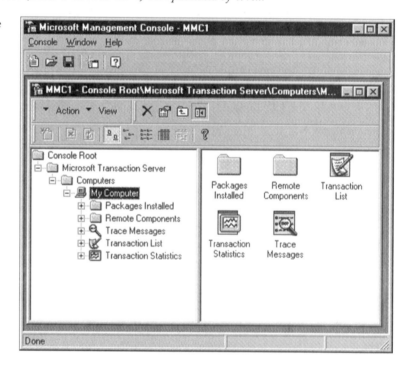

MMC snap-ins can have three sections – a **command bar**, a **scope pane**, and a **result pane** – and you can see examples of all three in the screenshot. The command bar has toolbars, to which you can add menus and controls. The scope pane is a tree view that displays the snap-in's **namespace**, which is made up of **nodes** that represent some task, object or view. The console provides the scope pane to which a snap-in can add nodes, when a user selects a node the snap-in should update the contents of the result pane according to the node. In the screenshot I have clicked on the My Computer node and in this case the result pane has items for its child nodes. Other nodes might use the result pane to give access to a management task, for example.

As you can see, MMC is an MDI application. Each window is called a **tool**, and can contain one or more snap-ins. MMC gives the user the option of saving tools to an MSC (Management Saved Console) file that can be loaded at a later stage, or even passed to another user. To enable this, snap-ins can support persistence, allowing them to save a configured state to the MSC file.

There are effectively two types of snap-ins that you can develop: a standalone snap-in, and an extension snap-in. As the name suggests, a standalone snap-in does not depend on any other, and so it can be loaded into MMC on its own. Extensions require a parent snap-in, and are used to extend the functionality of that parent. However, a given extension can only extend a particular node type.

As you can see the architecture is very flexible, the screenshot above shows the items added for MTS, which you get when you click on the Transaction Server Explorer item added to the Start Menu by the Option pack setup, which is a collection of tools saved in an MSC file. You can create small snap-ins that perform administrative tasks that can be added as a tool to other MSC files. For example you could write a snap-in to show events logged to the NT Event Log. This could be provided as a tool in its own right, or as an extension node that will show only those events generated by a particular application. Such an extension node would add value to the Transaction Server Explorer.

Let's take a look at some of the parts of MMC, the facilities that they provide, and the various interfaces that you need to implement to use them.

### The Scope Pane

Each item in the scope pane implements the `IComponentData` interface and its methods are called by the console in response to particular events. In particular, when the console adds a new snap-in it will call `CoCreateInstance()` to create it, then it calls `QueryInterface()` for `IComponentData` and then calls `Initialize()`. Conversely, when the snap-in is removed, the console calls `Destroy()`. When some action is performed on a node (for example the user expands a branch) the console informs the snap-in by calling `Notify()`.

One important aspect of `Initialize()` is that it is passed the `IUnknown` pointer of the console, through this the snap-in can query for the various interfaces that it needs to talk to the console. In particular, the snap-in can get the `IConsoleNameSpace` interface and the `IConsole` interface. The former allows the snap-in to add and delete nodes from the scope pane and to get access to existing nodes. The latter allows the snap-in to get access to particular console user interface objects like the scope pane image list.

### Nodes

There are three types of node that can be added to the scope pane, and these are categorized by what they represent, and the code that implements them:

| Node Type | Description |
| --- | --- |
| Built-in | These can be shortcuts, HTML pages or ActiveX controls. They do not interact with your snap-in. |
| Static | These nodes are displayed when the snap-in is loaded. Static nodes can only have enumerated nodes as children. |
| Enumerated | These nodes are added to the tree view dynamically when a user expands a static node in the scope pane tree. |

Enumerated nodes can be folders or items, but they are characterized by the fact that they are loaded into the tree view dynamically when their parent is expanded. Note that when you select an *enumerated* node, the notification goes to the *static* node, which has the responsibility of providing the node task. So using the previous example with the NT Event Log, the System, Security and Application logs could be implemented as static nodes and when you expand each node it will enumerate all the event log sources that have events in the particular log, presenting each as an enumerated node. When the user clicks on one of these the snap-in should then add all the events for that source into the result pane.

As another example, here are examples of the nodes provided by the MTS snap-in:

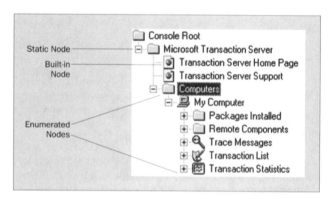

Each type of snap-in node has a GUID which is registered. Each snap-in also has a GUID and in its registry entry has a key which lists all the nodes that it provides.

You add nodes to the scope pane by filling the SCOPEDATAITEM structure that gives information about how the node is added to the pane and gives its relationship with other nodes. In particular this structure has a HSCOPEITEM handle, which is used to identify the node.

### Result Pane

When a user selects a node in the scope pane the result is shown in the result pane. If the node is a container node (it has child nodes) then the usual action is to fill the result pane with the child items. For other nodes the result pane is used to display the results of whatever task that node performs. By default, the console provides a list view, however, you can provide your own user interface. For example, the Transaction Statistics node on the MTS snap-in displays the number of active transactions using a bar chart.

To manage items in the result pane the snap-in should implement the `IComponent` interface, as with `IComponentData` this has `Initialize()`, `Destroy()` and `Notify()` methods. `Initialize()` is passed the `IConsole` interface of the console and through this the snap-in can call `QueryResultView()` to obtain the `IResultData` interface of the result view. The snap-in uses this interface to add and delete items to the result pane, and to access existing items.

You add items to the result pane with the `RESULTDATAITEM` structure, which has an `HRESULTITEM` that identifies the item.

### Data Objects

The data managed by a snap-in is maintained by using data objects that implement the standard `IDataObject` interface. Whenever data is passed between the snap-in and the console it is done using data objects. In particular, your snap-in should provide clipboard support, through the following clipboard formats:

| Format | Description |
|---|---|
| CCF_NODETYPE | The GUID of your snap-in |
| CCF_SZNODETYPE | The snap-in's GUID in string format |
| CCF_DISPLAY_NAME | The name displayed by MMC's snap-in manager |
| CCF_SNAPIN_CLASSID | The CLSID of the object implementing the snap-in |

The data for each of these is declared as a `static` member of your snap-in item class, and the ATL Object Wizard will initialize them to appropriate values. Of these, the snap-in manager will obtain the node type to determine the other snap-ins that a snap-in extension will extend.

### Other Snap-in Interfaces

The previously mentioned interfaces are the basic support for snap-ins, however, there are several others that you may or may not decide to support depending on the functionality that your snap-in supports. One interface that it *must* implement is `ISnapInAbout`, which provides the console with version information about the snap-in. This is used by the console when you add a new snap-in it.

Your snap-in can provide a context menu extension. This is the menu that appears when you right click on a node in the scope pane or an item in the result pane. To add items to the context menu your snap-in should support `IExtendContextMenu`, this has two methods: `AddMenuItems()` that provides information about the menu items that should be added, and `Command()` that is called when the user clicks on the item.

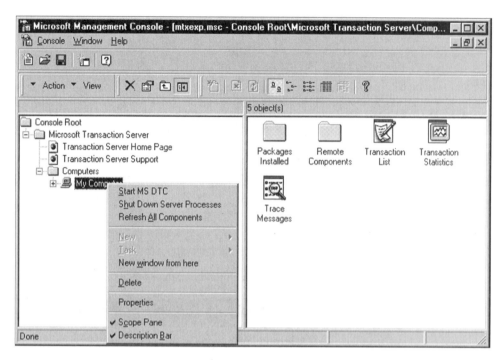

Here you can see the context menu obtained by right-clicking on the My Computer node. This node has added the top three items to the menu, the rest are provided by MMC.

The context menu can also have a Properties menu item that displays a property dialog. To add new pages to this dialog your snap-in should support IExtendPropertySheet. Finally, the console can add items to the control bar, menus and other controls. To do this the snap-in should support IExtendContextControlbar, which the console will call to pass its IControlBar interface for the snap-in to add items. The console will also use this interface to pass notifications when the user selects or clicks on an item. The following screenshot shows the controlbar:

Finally, snap-ins can support persistence so that a user can save a configured state to the MSC file. To do this, the snap-in will support one of the standard IPersistxxx interfaces. When it is closed, the MMC console will call QueryInterface() on the snap-in to see if it supports persistence, and if so, it calls the appropriate method to save the state. Subsequently, when the MSC file is loaded, the snap-in will be created, queried for the appropriate persistence interface, and initialized with the saved data.

### Creating a Snap-in

Now that you have an idea about the various features of the console and the interfaces that your snap-in needs to implement, let's look at what ATL will do for you.

When you select the MMC SnapIn type in the Object Wizard, you'll find that apart from the usual Names tab, you also get an MMC Snapin tab:

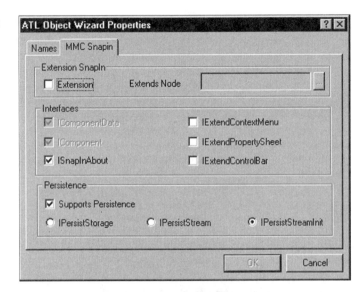

If you check the Extension box, the ... button is enabled and you can select the snap-in node that you want to extend. My machine has the NT 4 Option Pack (and therefore the MTS snap-in) installed, and these are the nodes I can extend:

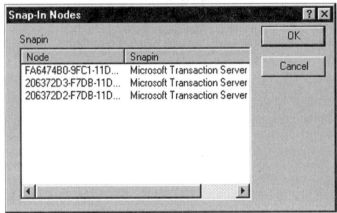

Remember that an extension node can only extend an existing node type and cannot be run stand alone.

Returning to the Object Wizard, the Interfaces frame determines what snap-in related interfaces you will support. ISnapInAbout should be checked; this interface gives the MMC console access to the version and copyright notice of your snap-in. The other interfaces should be supported if you want to extend the user interface of the snap-in, as I have already mentioned, through the IExtendContextMenu, IExtendPropertySheet and IExtendControlBar interfaces. At the bottom of the dialog you specify which persistence interface you will use: IPersistStorage, IPersistStream or IPersistStreamInit.

The classes produced by the Object Wizard for an object with the Short Name of ShortName are:

| Class | Description |
|---|---|
| CShortNameAbout | This class gives information about the snap-in, mainly from strings held as resources. |
| CShortNameComponent | Implements the IComponent interface and persistence for the snap-in. |
| CShortNameData | This is the class used to implement the nodes of the snap-in. |
| CShortName | The main class that manages the scope pane. It is used to create the nodes and to implement IComponentData. |
| CShortNamePage | This is the class used to provide a property page if you select support for IExtendPropertySheet. |
| CShortNameExtData | If the snap-in extends another node, this class holds information data to give access to the extended node. |

The default persistence methods in the main project and the component classes are not implemented, so it's up to you to replace the ATLTRACENOTIMPL() macro with an implementation. One option would be to derive these classes from IPersistStreamInitImpl<>, and then to add any data members to a property map, just as you would do with an ActiveX control.

The main class (CShortName in the table above) exposes just two interfaces: IComponentData, and the interface you use for persistence. There is no interface generated from the Short Name in the Names tab. This is in contrast to most of the other object types, which generate a new interface for you based on this string. The reason that a new interface is not generated is that no client other than the console will use the object, and so it should only implement interfaces that the console knows about.

CShortName is derived from CSnapInObjectRoot<>, which derives from CSnapInObjectRootBase. This latter class has data members for the control bar interface, (which is passed to the snap-in by the console) and a map used to hold the items that the snap-in will add to the control bar. These items implement the IToolbar interface, and hence, the map is called the toolbar map and is an instance of CSimpleMap<>, which is a lightweight associative container class. If your snap-in supports IExtendControlBar, the Object Wizard will add IExtendControlbarImpl<> as a base class, and this will add and remove toolbars to and from the map. It also uses the map to notify all the toolbars when the user does something in the user interface of the console.

The class where all the action occurs is the one whose name ends in Data. This is derived from CSnapInItemImpl<> and represents the snap-in in both the scope and result panes. This class encapsulates both a SCOPEITEMDATA member (which represents how the item is added to the scope pane), and a RESULTITEMDATA (which indicates how it is added to the result pane). The snap-in object implements a method called GetDataClass() that gives access to the snap-in items that it contains.

If your snap-in extends another node, you'll get a class with the `ExtData` suffix that gives access to the node that is being extended. This class has a method called `InitDataClass()` that initializes the `m_pDataObject` data member to point to the snap-in object that is being extended. An instance of this extension snap-in object is added to the main snap-in class with the `EXTENSION_SNAPIN_DATACLASS()` macro. This object is accessed through the **extension node snap-in map** by adding it with the `EXTENSION_SNAPIN_NODEINFO_ENTRY()` macro. The map implements the `GetDataClass()` method that searches the entries in the map for appropriate extension data.

The main class is also derived from `IComponentDataImpl<>`. Unsurprisingly, this implements the `IComponentData` interface, which is the main interface for the snap-in. This interface is called when the snap-in is initialized, and also to create new components, so the template takes the name of the project's `Component` class as a parameter.

### Context Menus

If you add support for a context menu, you will get a menu resource with the following items:

These are:

| Menu | Used for |
|------|----------|
| TOP | Adds menu items to the top of the context menu |
| NEW | Adds menu items to the New... submenu |
| TASK | Adds menu items to the Task submenu |
| VIEW | Adds menu items to the bottom of the View menu when you obtain the context menu in the result pane |

To handle a user clicking on one of these menu items, you implement a **snap-in command map**. This is similar to the message maps that you use to handle window messages in controls (as you'll see in Chapter 9), except that you don't get Wizard support. You add to this map in the data item class (that is, the class derived from `CSnapInItemImpl<>`), for example:

```
BEGIN_SNAPINCOMMAND_MAP(CAdminData, FALSE)
    SNAPINCOMMAND_ENTRY(ID_TOP_RECALCULATE, Recalculate)
    SNAPINCOMMAND_ENTRY(ID_NEW_NEWITEM, NewItem)
END_SNAPINCOMMAND_MAP()
```

This will handle the situations when a user clicks on the Recalculate menu item, which I have added to the top of the main context menu, and when they choose the New Item member of the New submenu. These are handled by the member functions `Recalculate()` and `NewItem()`. In general, these functions should have the following prototype:

```
HRESULT func(bool& bHandled, CSnapInObjectRootBase* pObj)
```

bHandled should be set to false if you want the command handling to continue. It is set to true when your handler method is called, so it is your responsibility to set it to false if you want command handling to continue. The macros that you can use in the map are:

| Macro | Description |
|-------|-------------|
| SNAPINCOMMAND_ENTRY | Specifies a member function that will handle a particular command. |
| SNAPINCOMMAND_RANGE_ENTRY | Specifies a member function that will handle a range of commands. |
| CHAIN_SNAPINCOMMAND_MAP | Specifies the name of another class with a snap-in command map. This class will be given the option to handle commands not handled by the present map. |

### Adding Scope Pane Items

You will, of course, want to add items to the scope pane and (when a scope item is selected) to the result pane as well. ATL helps here by creating for you the Notify() method of the Data class, which is inherited through the CSnapInItem class. Earlier on I mentioned that both the IComponentData and IComponent interfaces have a Notify() method. The CSnapInItem::Notify() is called by the Notify() methods on both IComponentDataImpl<> and IComponentImpl<> and centralizes notification code:

```
HRESULT Notify( MMC_NOTIFY_TYPE event, long arg, long param,
    IComponentData* pComponentData, IComponent* pComponent,
    DATA_OBJECT_TYPES type)
```

Within this method, you will find the following switch:

```
switch(event)
{
case MMCN_SHOW:
    // Other code
    break;

case MMCN_EXPAND:
    // Other code
    break;

case MMCN_ADD_IMAGES:
    // Other code
    break;
}
```

This method is called when various actions occur, including the user clicking on the + symbol to expand a tree, and clicking on an item to see the results. In the MMCN_EXPAND case, you should add the items to the tree. You'll find that the Wizard has generated some of this code for you:

```
CComQIPtr<IConsoleNameSpace, &IID_IConsoleNameSpace>
                                 spConsoleNameSpace(spConsole);
// TODO : Enumerate scope pane items
hr = S_OK;
break;
```

You can add items by calling `InsertItem()` through this `spConsoleNameSpace` smart pointer. The function takes a parameter of type `SCOPEITEMDATA*`, and the easiest way get this data is to create a new instance of the `Data` class, because this encapsulates both a `SCOPEITEMDATA` and a `RESULTITEMDATA`. Items added to a scope tree are identified by a `HSCOPEITEM` value, and the value for the parent item is passed as the `param` parameter of `Notify()`. To add a new item, you can write this code for a snap-in called `Admin`:

```
CAdminData* pData = new CAdminData;
pData->m_scopeDataItem.mask |= SDI_PARENT;
pData->m_scopeDataItem.relativeID = (HSCOPEITEM)param;
pData->m_scopeDataItem.nImage = 0;
pData->m_scopeDataItem.nOpenImage = 1;
pData->m_bstrDisplayName = "New Item";
hr = spConsoleNameSpace->InsertItem(&pData->m_scopeDataItem);
```

The `relativeID` and `mask` indicate how the item is inserted into the tree. In this case, the mask has `SDI_PARENT` and the `relativeID` is the parent, and so the new item is added as a child (in fact, `SDI_PARENT` has a value of 0 and is therefore the default).

The `lParam` member of a `SCOPEITEMDATA` item is the 'cookie' that the console will use when it needs to obtain information about an item. The Wizard will add this code to the constructor of your `Data` class:

```
m_scopeDataItem.lParam = (LPARAM) this;
```

In other words, whenever you obtain a cookie, you can cast it to a pointer to your `Data` class. If you look at the `displayname` item, you will see that it is passed the value of `MMC_CALLBACK`. This indicates that when it wants to get a display name, the console will obtain the value put in the `m_bstrDisplayName` variable, which is an inherited member of `CSnapInItemImpl<>`.

Finally, the two image parameters determine the bitmap used for the item in the scope pane. You can have two values: one for the item 'closed' and another for it 'opened' (compare this to the folder item in Explorer). The value you supply is the 0-based index of the images in the bitmap added to your project by the Wizard. This bitmap will have a single image initially, but it is a painless task to extend it to add more items. Note that you are given both a 16x16 and a 32x32-pixel bitmap, and if you add new images, you need to change both.

The data that you pass to `InsertItem()` is saved by the console in a map. The console associates this data with a `HSCOPEITEM` value and it is this value that the console uses to specify a node to your snap-in. To get the `SCOPEDATAITEM` from this `HSCOPEITEM` you can call `IConsoleNameSpace::GetItem()`:

```
HSCOPEITEM hscope; // you get sent this from the console
SCOPEDATAITEM item;
item.ID = hscope;
item.mask = SDI_PARAM;
spConsoleNameSpace->GetItem(&item);
```

In this code, `GetItem()` is passed the address of a `SCOPEDATAITEM` whose `ID` member is assigned the `HSCOPEITEM` that you are interested in. The method will fill all the items specified by the mask member. Most of the time you'll specify at least `SDI_PARAM`, since the `lParam` member of the structure containes the `this` pointer of the data item.

When your snap-in is added to the console you will have a static node for the snap-in. The first time that a user expands this node you will get a `MMCN_EXPAND` event generated in `Notify()` and you can use this to add the enumerated nodes to the namespace. When the user expands these items you will get another `MMCN_EXPAND` event and you can use this to add more nodes. However, since the same code handles the event how do you know what nodes you should add?

The answer lies in the `param` and `arg` parameters passed to the `Notify()` method. These take different values depending on the event that is being handled (you can get the full list from `mmc.idl`):

| Event | arg | param |
|-------|-----|-------|
| MMCN_EXPAND | true for expand, false for contract | Parent's HSCOPEITEM |
| MMCN_SELECT | Top WORD is true if an item is selected, false if it is deselected; bottom WORD is true for an item in the scope pane, false if it is in the result pane | not used |
| MMCN_SHOW | 0 if the item is deselected, non-zero if it is selected | HSCOPEITEM of selected or deselected item |

The `case` for `MMCN_EXPAND` generated by the wizard will give you an `IConsoleNameSpace` interface pointer, and you can call the `GetParentItem()` passing `param` to get the parent of an item. Note that this call will fail if the root node is being expanded:

```
HSCOPEITEM parent;
LONG cookie;
if (FAILED(spConsoleNameSpace->GetParentItem((HSCOPEITEM)param,
                                             &parent, &cookie)))
{
    // Must be root, so add top level node
    CAdminData* pData = new CAdminData;
    pData->m_scopeDataItem.mask |= SDI_PARENT | SDI_CHILDREN;
    pData->m_scopeDataItem.relativeID = (HSCOPEITEM)param;
    pData->m_bstrDisplayName = "Top Level";
    hr = spConsoleNameSpace->InsertItem(&pData->m_scopeDataItem);
}
```

If this call succeeds then the node that is expanding has a parent and so it must be a node that you have already added (or the node that you are extending) otherwise it is the root. In this code I use this knowledge to add the `"Top Level"` node beneath the root.

If the call to `GetParentItem()` succeeds, you'll want to determine where in the tree the node is, and in particular get access to the `Data` class of the parent, to do this you need to call `GetItem()`:

```
else
{
    SCOPEDATAITEM parent;
    memset(&parent, 0, sizeof(SCOPEDATAITEM));
    parent.mask = SDI_PARAM;
    parent.ID = (HSCOPEITEM)param;
    spConsoleNameSpace->GetItem(&parent);
    CAdminData* pData = (CAdminData*)parent.lParam;
    // access the members of pData to decide where we are in the tree
    // and if necessary add other nodes
}
```

Of course, in this code I have added heap objects to the scope pane and these need to be deleted at some point. One way to do this is maintain a list of all the items that you add to the scope pane and then override the `IComponentDataImpl<>::Destroy()` method to iterate through this list and delete the items. If you do decide to override this method make sure that you call the inherited version, which performs other clean up.

Another way to do this is to get hold of the top node and then enumerate all the child items and from each call `GetItem()` to get the actual data item.

## Adding Result Pane Items

Adding items in the result pane is a similar process to adding nodes to the scope pane: you add code into the `case` for `MMCN_SHOW`. Here's the code the Wizard will have added for you:

```
CComQIPtr<IResultData, &IID_IResultData> spResultData(spConsole);
// TODO : Enumerate the result pane items
hr = S_OK;
break;
```

Items are added to the result pane by calling `InsertItem()` through the `spResultData` smart pointer, passing a pointer to a `RESULTDATAITEM`:

```
spHeader->InsertColumn(0, L"Item", LVCFMT_LEFT, 200);
CAdminData* pData = new CAdminData;
pData->m_bstrDisplayName = L"Result";
hr = spResultData->InsertItem(&pData->m_resultDataItem);
```

Here, I have added a new column into the result pane for the item I am adding. This column is 200 pixels wide and uses left justification. The result pane will be drawn with a single column and the string given in `m_bstrDisplayName` will be shown next to the item. If you want to use more than one column you should add more columns using `InsertColumn()`. The actual data that goes into the second column is returned when the console calls `IComponent::GetDisplayInfo()` on your `Data` object, this ends up in the `GetResultPaneColInfo()` that the wizard adds to your class:

```
LPOLESTR CAdminData::GetResultPaneColInfo(int nCol)
{
    if (nCol == 0)
        return m_bstrDisplayName;
    // TODO : Return the text for other columns
    return OLESTR("Override GetResultPaneColInfo");
}
```

As you can see, the wizard generated code returns the m_bstrDisplayName in the first column. If you need to return data for a second column, you can do this by returning a value when nCol has a value of 2. For example, if you add a CComBSTR data member called m_bstrValue to the Data class (called CAdminData here) then you can add the item to the result pane with:

```
spHeader->InsertColumn(0, L"Item", LVCFMT_LEFT, 200);
spHeader->InsertColumn(1, L"Value", LVCFMT_LEFT, 200);
CAdminData* pData = new CAdminData;
pData->m_bstrDisplayName = L"Result";
pData->m_bstrValue = L"Item value";
hr = spResultData->InsertItem(&pData->m_resultDataItem);
```

To get this value shown in the second column of the result pane you need to make this change:

```
LPOLESTR CAdminData::GetResultPaneColInfo(int nCol)
{
    if (nCol == 0)
        return m_bstrDisplayName;
    if (nCol == 1)
        return m_bstrValue;
    return NULL;
}
```

Whenever you click on a node, Notify() will be called with MMCN_SHOW for both the node that is being deselected as well as for the new node that is being selected. You should check to see if the event is for selection or deselection:

```
case MMCN_SHOW:
    if (arg)
    {
        // item selected
    }
    else
    {
        // item deselected
    }
    break;
```

Typically you will only want to have code for selection. However, note that the result pane is *cleared* when you handle this event, and so you must add the appropriate items to the pane. This means that if you create Data objects in the heap you must make sure that you keep a record of the pointers elsewhere so that when the user clicks on a node a second time, you can reuse the previously created object.

For example, in the following code I have a STL map data member in the `Component` class:

```
std::map<CComBSTR, CAdminData*> m_map;
```

When a node is selected, I check to see if a `CAdminData` object has already been created for the result pane item. If so, I delete it:

```
CAdminData* pData = NULL;
std::map<CComBSTR, CAdminData*>::iterator it;
it = ((CAdminComponent*)pComponent)->m_map.find(bstrName);
if (it != ((CAdminComponent*)pComponent)->m_map.end())
{
    CAdminData* pData = (*it).second;
    ((CAdminComponent*)pComponent)->m_map.erase(it);
    delete pData;
}

pData = new CAdminData;
pData->m_bstrDisplayName = bstrName;
pData->m_bstrValue = strValue;
hr = spResultData->InsertItem(&pData->m_resultDataItem);
((CAdminComponent*)pComponent)->m_map[bstrName] = pData;
```

Notice in this code I just cast the `pComponent` argument passed to `Notify()` to get the `Component` object for the snap-in.

These items are destroyed in the `Destroy()` method:

```
STDMETHODIMP CAdminComponent::Destroy(long cookie)
{
    std::map<CComBSTR, CAdminData*>::iterator it;
    for (it = m_map.begin(); it != m_map.end(); it++)
        delete (*it).second;

    return IComponentImpl<CAdminComponent>::Destroy(cookie);
}
```

### Registering a Snap-in

Each node has a unique GUID, which indicates its type, these GUIDs are registered in `HKEY_LOCAL_MACHINE\Software\Microsoft\MMC\NodeTypes`. Your snap-in should be registered under `HKEY_LOCAL_MACHINE\Software\Microsoft\MMC\Snapins` – again, with a GUID. This entry has values that give the name and CLSID of an object used to get 'About' information for the snap-in. In addition, the registry entry should have a key called `NodeTypes` that has all the GUIDs of the types of node that this snap-in supports. It also needs a key called `StandAlone` if the snap-in is standalone, and one called `RequiredExtensions` that contains the GUIDs of all the extension snap-ins that this snap-in needs to function, the Object Wizard will ensure that the correct registration code is provided.

You do not have to worry about these registry values because the Object Wizard will make sure that you have the appropriate registration script.

### Debugging MMC Snap-ins

Debugging snap-ins is a little different to debugging normal inproc servers. Chapter 6 has more details about debugging ATL classes, so I will restrict myself to the pertinent points. Usually when you want to debug an inproc server, you use the Project Settings dialog and from the Debug tab use the General Category to specify the executable that you want to use to test the server, then you set your break points and start debugging. With MMC snap-ins you use the Debug tab to specify the debug executable (in this case mmc.exe in %systemroot%\System32) but if you set breakpoints then you'll find that that the code will not stop.

MMC wraps the code that loads the snap-in with exception handling with the consequence that when a Visual C++ breakpoint is hit, the exception handler will gobble it up and you will not see it. The solution is to use DebugBreak() or _asm int 3 in your code to force an exception that the Visual C++ debugger can catch. I prefer the latter of these two because the exception will be thrown in your function, whereas the former requires you to step out of DebugBreak() to get back to your function. Of course, you must be careful when you litter your code with either of these. At the very least, you should bracket them with conditional compilation to prevent them creeping into release builds:

```
#ifdef _DEBUG
    // lets debug this sucker!
    _asm int 3;
#endif
```

## MS Transaction Server Component

At first sight, the transaction server component may seem a bit redundant – after all, the AppWizard has already asked if you want to use MTS, so why do you have this Object Wizard type too? In fact, there are two main reasons, the more important of which is to determine at what time the MTS DLLs should be loaded: are they loaded when the object server loads, or when an object first uses them? The other reason is that this object type allows you to implement IObjectControl, which allows an object to indicate whether it can be pooled, and to perform initialization and clean up when activated or deactivated.

When you select Support MTS in the AppWizard, your project is linked with mtx.lib and mtxguid.lib. This allows *any* object in the server to use objects running under MTS to call GetObjectContext() in order to obtain the context for the current object. In this way, an object can manage the transaction under which it is running. In addition, the project also links with delayimp.lib using the /delayload linker option on mtxes.dll. All objects in the server can use this DLL, but it is only loaded the first time it is actually called, and so the object server will initially load more quickly. If you don't select this option, the libraries are not added to the link line.

When you select that you want to insert an MTS component, you get this page:

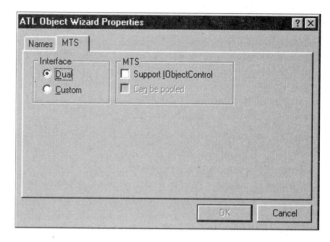

The important item here is the Support IObjectControl option. If you leave this clear, the Wizard will effectively just create a simple object and #include <mtx.h>. If you check this box, however, the object will implement IObjectControl, and the Wizard will add the following lines to the bottom of your class:

```
// IObjectControl
public:
    STDMETHOD(Activate)();
    STDMETHOD_(BOOL, CanBePooled)();
    STDMETHOD_(void, Deactivate)();
    CComPtr<IObjectContext> m_spObjectContext;
};
```

The implementations of these methods are quite simple. Activate() calls GetObjectContext() and caches the context object in m_spObjectContext, while Deactivate() releases this context object. If you check Can be pooled, then CanBePooled() will return TRUE, otherwise it returns FALSE.

Since this object calls GetObjectContext(), you're probably wondering whether you can add a transaction server component to a project in which you didn't select Support MTS in the AppWizard. In fact, you can. Mtx.h has these lines:

```
#ifndef _MTX_NOFORCE_LIBS
#pragma comment(lib, "mtx.lib")
#endif
```

The #pragma comment effectively adds the library to the linker command line. This is the import library for the MTS DLLs, and because the /delayload linker option is *not* being used, the MTS DLLs will be loaded when the object server is loaded.

So the choice is yours. If you think the objects in your server *might* use MTS, you can add support through the AppWizard and the MTS DLLs will only be loaded when they are actually called. If the first object created in the server doesn't use MTS, the DLLs won't be loaded, and you will gain in load time. If you *know* that an object will use MTS, you can create an **MTS Transaction Server Component**, in which case the MTS DLLs will be loaded when the DLL server is loaded, because by definition they are required.

## Component Registrar Object

When you run `regsvr32` on your DLL server, the `DllRegisterServer()` exported function is called. Similarly, when `regsvr32 /u` is executed, `DllUnregisterServer()` is called. The COM specification says that these methods should register (and unregister) *all* the coclasses in the server, so if you decide that you would prefer just to (un)register one coclass, you have to use a different approach.

This is the purpose of the Component Registrar Object, which supports the `IComponentRegistrar` interface:

```
[
    object,
    uuid(a817e7a2-43fa-11d0-9e44-00aa00b6770a),
    dual,
    helpstring("IComponentRegistrar Interface"),
    pointer_default(unique)
]
interface IComponentRegistrar : IDispatch
{
    [id(1)] HRESULT Attach([in] BSTR bstrPath);
    [id(2)] HRESULT RegisterAll();
    [id(3)] HRESULT UnregisterAll();
    [id(4)] HRESULT GetComponents(
            [out] SAFEARRAY(BSTR)* pbstrCLSIDs,
            [out] SAFEARRAY(BSTR)* pbstrDescriptions);
    [id(5)] HRESULT RegisterComponent([in] BSTR bstrCLSID);
    [id(6)] HRESULT UnregisterComponent([in] BSTR bstrCLSID);
};
```

Although this interface is declared in your IDL `library` statement, it is not a new interface – the IID being used is the standard IID for `IComponentRegistrar`. In fact, it doesn't matter that the interface is declared in your IDL; because it is declared in the `library` statement, so no proxy-stub is created. The methods are:

| Method | Description |
|---|---|
| `Attach()` | This is called when a server is first loaded |
| `RegisterAll()` | This registers all components in the server, effectively the same as `DllRegisterServer()` |
| `UnregisterAll()` | This unregisters all components in the server, effectively the same as `DllUnregisterServer()` |

*Table Continued on Following Page*

| Method | Description |
|---|---|
| GetComponents() | This returns a SAFEARRAY with the CLSIDs of all the components in the server, and a corresponding SAFEARRAY with a description of each component |
| RegisterComponent() | This will register a single component |
| UnregisterComponent() | This will unregister a single component |

The description that is returned in GetComponents() is added to a component using the DECLARE_OBJECT_DESCRIPTION() macro.

When you add a component registrar to your project, you get the following dialog, to remind you that there should only be one component registrar in each server.

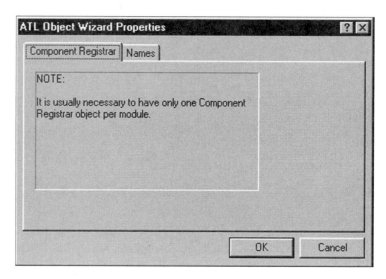

This is all you need to do. The Wizard will provide all the code that is required to implement this object.

Component registrars are typically used in inproc servers that will be used for components which will be added to packages in MTS.

# Controls

There are many different control types, but a common feature is that they can only be implemented in DLL servers. The controls offered by the Object Wizard can be split into three main groups. The first group (Full and Lite) contains controls that comply with the OC96 standard. The second group (Composite and Lite Composite) consists of controls that are themselves control containers, so you can create controls using a similar technique to the one you use with Visual Basic CCE (Control Creation Edition). The final group (HTML and Lite HTML) allows you to create a control based on a DHTML script.

Also included in this category is the Property Page, but although these are used by controls, they are not controls themselves. I will be covering controls in much greater depth in Chapter 10, but I will take the opportunity in this section to show you the different available types.

## Full and Lite Controls

As its name suggests, a full control has support for all the possible interfaces that you may need when implementing a control. Inevitably, this will mean that the control implements interfaces that may not be used by all containers, so the control may be larger than it needs to be. This is a problem if the control is to be used on a web page, and is therefore likely to be downloaded over the Internet. However, if you want to make your control as flexible as possible, a full control is a good place to start.

'Lite controls were called 'IE controls' in Visual C++ 5, but the new name is more apt. A lite control has all the interfaces required for it to be used as a control in most control containers, but it does not have the interfaces for property pages, or for persisting itself to a storage.

So: when would you create a full control, and when would you create a lite control? The choice is not clear-cut. The additional interfaces that are implemented on a full control could be added piecemeal to a lite control. However, if you know that the control will have property pages and will be used by a variety of containers, it may be prudent to create a full control in the first place. Chapter 10 lists some of the containers that require a full control, and the ones that will accept a lite control.

Of course, full and lite controls both have user interfaces, and so they must respond to window messages, which they handle by means of a message map. A new feature in Visual C++ 6 is a ClassView context menu item that allows you to add a message handler to the message map. This Wizard looks and works very like the MFC ClassWizard.

Controls can have **properties** that are used by a client (the container itself, or client code that accesses the control through scripting) to change the state of the control. Typically, you would do this either to change the behavior of a control (its color, the text displayed, etc.), or to initialize something before asking the control to perform an action (setting the contents of a shopping cart before asking the control to calculate the total bill, perhaps). In the second case, the state is only required until the action is performed; in the first case, you may decide that this state ought to be made persistent, so that every time the control is run, it can initialize its properties from this persistent state.

Controls can implement several IPersistxxx interfaces to make their state persistent. ATL supplies the property map and various Impl classes, so that all you have to do is specify the properties that you want to make persistent in the map, and the Impl classes will do the rest of the work. You'll find more information about these classes in Chapter 10.

## Composite Controls

Visual Basic 5.0 and Visual Basic CCE (Control Creation Edition) introduced the facility to take a Visual Basic form and repackage it as an ActiveX Control. This is a very useful feature, because a developer could take existing controls (both native Windows controls and ActiveX controls) and, using scripting, add these together to create a new ActiveX control. The Visual Basic developer could 'add value' to existing controls.

ATL 2.1 didn't prevent you from doing this, but it didn't offer much in the way of support. If you wanted to use ActiveX controls then you had to write the required control site code yourself. In ATL 3.0, the composite control in Object Wizard allows you to do a similar thing without any of this pain.

When Object Wizard creates a composite control, it gives you a dialog resource to hold the controls that you want to use. You can position controls and set their properties at design time. At runtime, the composite control creates itself and its child controls based on the information in the dialog template.

Dialog resource templates can use the CONTROL resource type, which means that you can add an ActiveX control to the dialog. Further, dialog resources can also use the DLGINIT resource type and associate it with an ActiveX control. This binary type is a stream of data that will be passed to the control (through IPersistStreamInit) when it is created. Thus, using the dialog editor you can set control properties at design time and the control will be initialized with these properties at runtime *without you having to write any extra code*. Note that both lite and full controls implement IPersistStreamInit.

## HTML Control

Internet Explorer 4.0, believe it or not, is a small program. The functionality that you get in IE4 is implemented by the *web browser* control that covers the client area of IE4. IE4 is just a container for this control.

The web browser control has a great deal of functionality: it has all the logic to allow you to browse the Internet (using one of several protocols), to obtain the resource you require, and then to render it. For example, if the resource type is an Active Document (like a Word document), the web browser control will obtain the correct rendering engine and show the document. If it's an HTML page, the control will interpret the HTML, obtain any referred graphics or frames, and render those.

The web browser control can also run DHTML scripts written in a scripting language. This means that you can create an HTML page that contains various controls, and a script that responds to the events of these controls. Unlike the composite control, where the controls are added using Visual C++'s dialog editor and the control events were managed in C++, the web browser control allows you to do all this in DHTML. You can use your favorite HTML editor to create a page, and then handle events using VBScript or JavaScript. Furthermore, the script could be on a server machine, which means that the script code will always be kept up to date. (Imagine that as a concept: when you get a bug report on your code, you can update it immediately, so that when another customer uses the code they get the updated version without knowing that it has recently been changed.)

Wouldn't it be great to be able to use all this functionality as part of your ATL control? Well you can. The ATL HTML control type hosts the IE4 web browser control and through your ATL code you can provide a URL to a web page or script that the web browser control will run. By default, the Object Wizard will create a DHTML script that can handle events or 'bubble them up' to your wrapper C++ code and this script is added to your control's resources. Chapter 11 explains how ATL performs this magic and what you can do through the web browser control.

## Property Page

Property pages allow you to provide a collection of controls on a page to manipulate single or multiple properties of a control. Typically, you will add a property page to your control if you have a complicated property type that is not one of the types managed by control containers.

For example, in the book *Beginning ATL COM Programming*, we developed a control based on the Win32 tree control. The branches of the tree (and the data associated with the branches) were held in an array property. This property could be accessed through scripting as a SAFEARRAY, but for design time access the array was accessed through a property page. Another use of a property page is to group associated properties that should be set together.

The ATL property page does a lot of the hard work for you. The Object Wizard will create a dialog resource, and you can then add Windows controls (and ActiveX controls) to it. When the property page is created, it is passed the IUnknown interface of the object that it is associated with, so you can QueryInterface() for the interface that implements the object's properties in the page's initialization code. Once you have this interface, you can initialize the controls on the page to reflect the current values. When the user closes the page (or clicks on the Apply button), your page will be informed, and you can write the property values back to the object.

# Miscellaneous

The Dialog type is not a COM object. However, there are times when you will need to use a dialog, and this provides a relatively simple way of creating one. You have already seen an example of how to use the Dialog type in the add-in example earlier in this chapter, so I won't discuss dialogs further here. You can find out more about ATL's other window classes in Chapter 9.

# Data Access

The ATL Object Wizard gives you the opportunity of creating an OLE DB provider, or an OLE DB consumer. OLE DB, as a topic, is too large to cover here, but basically it provides access to a data source through some standard COM interfaces. The data source can be any type, and isn't constrained to relational databases accessed through SQL, for example. You could write an OLE DB provider that gives access to e-mail messages, an e-mail reader's address book, directory services, or the file system, as well as to relational or object databases. This enables heterogeneous joins, so (for example) you could search for all e-mails sent on the same day that you created the file "Future Prospects.doc".

The Object Wizard supports two object types for OLE DB under the Data Access category: Provider and Consumer. The former allows you to create a new data source type, while the latter creates classes that give access to a data source.

## Consumer

The Consumer type does not create a COM class. Instead, it creates a specialized class to access tables and commands on a particular data source. You may choose to use this class in an ATL object, or you can use it in another project. Note, however, that the Wizard will only run under certain circumstances: when you're writing an ATL project or an MFC project. When you try to launch Object Wizard in other circumstances, you will get a dialog saying that it won't work.

This is a bit of a pain. If you're writing, say, a console application and you want to use the ATL consumer classes, you have one of two choices. Firstly, you can eschew the Object Wizard completely and write the classes yourself. Of course, this is only an option if you completely understand the classes and the various maps that they use. The other option is to create a dummy ATL project, and then use the Object Wizard to create your classes. You can then copy these classes to your real, console project.

For the following example, I will use the ODBC text driver. Obviously, a text-based database is not the best choice for a production system, but it does at least demonstrate the versatility of OLE DB. The database file is called `Addresses.txt`, and has this data:

```
Richard Grimes,"30 Lincoln Road, Birmingham"
Bill Clinton,"White House, Washington DC"
Tony Blair,"10 Downing Street, London"
Boris Yeltsin,"Kremlin, Moscow"
```

I used the ODBC applet in the control panel to select the Microsoft Text Driver, and then used the Configure... option to create the `schema.ini` file:

```
[addresses.txt]
ColNameHeader=False
Format=CSVDelimited
MaxScanRows=25
CharacterSet=OEM
Col1=NAME Char Width 255
Col2=ADDRESS Char Width 255
```

You can install this database on to your system by copying both files to a single directory, and then running the ODBC applet from the Control Panel:

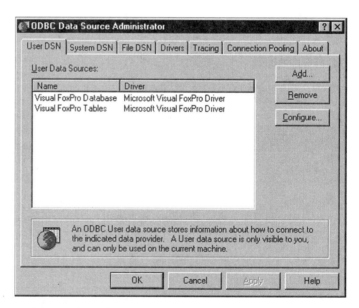

Select the Add... button, and from the resulting dialog, choose Microsoft Text Driver (*.txt; *.csv) to get the following:

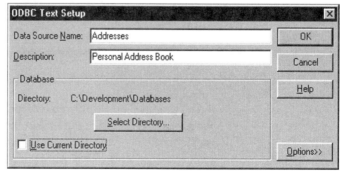

Fill in the values shown here, uncheck the Use Current Directory check box, and then use the Select Directory... button to navigate to the directory that has the Addresses.txt and schema.ini files. After you have done this, the directory will be treated as a database with a single table called Addresses.txt, and you can use ODBC to access it. In this example, you will use the OLE DB ODBC provider.

Now create a dummy ATL project and insert a new Consumer data access object. You will see this dialog:

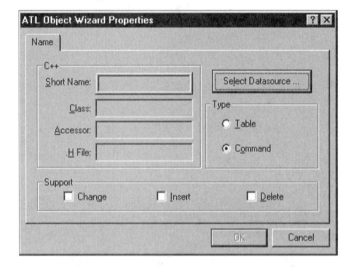

Before you can do anything else, you must use the Select Datasource... button to select the Addresses.txt table. This is what you'll see:

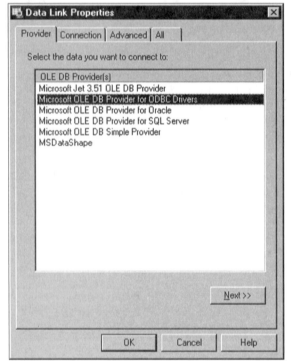

This gives the names of all the provider objects registered under the CLSID key that have the OLE DB Provider key. From this list, select Microsoft OLE DB Provider for ODBC Drivers. Then, Next> will move you to here:

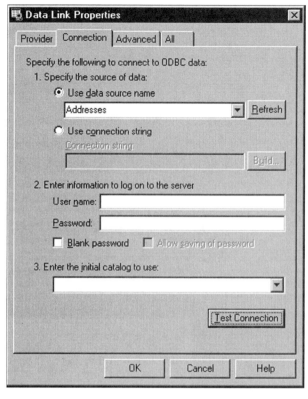

If the database you want to access is on another machine, you can choose Use connection string to give details. In this case, you just need to supply the data source name on the current machine, so pull down the dropdown list and select Addresses. If your database requires authentication information, you can provide this on second part of this page, but it's not necessary for this simple example.

You can now use the Test Connection button to check that the data source exists, and that OLE DB can connect to it. Furthermore, you can switch to the Advanced tab to change some of the settings used to make the connection, and to the All tab to get a summary of the OLE DB parameters that will be used.

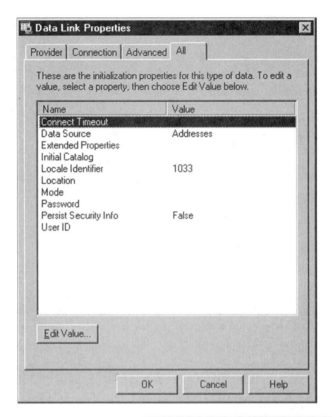

When you close this dialog, the Wizard will connect to the data source and obtain information from it. In the example shown above, the Wizard will read information from `schema.ini` and display the following dialog that shows all the tables in the database:

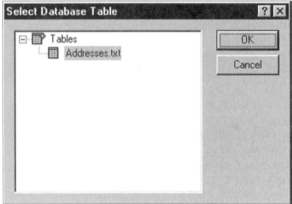

If the database has stored procedures (like SQL Server, for example), then they will also be shown in this box; if you select a stored procedure, the accessor class that will be created will have any relevant output variables, and any input/output parameters. In this example, select Addresses.txt, and the Wizard will fill in the rest of the Object Wizard property page for you:

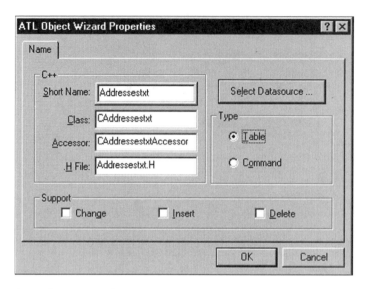

In this dialog, you have the option of specifying the type of classes that will be added: Table for straightforward table access, or Command for more complex commands that allow you to use input parameters as well as statement prepare and execute (that is, construct and execute a query in two separate steps).

In this example, we will just read the data, so leave the Change, Insert and Delete check boxes unchecked. Also, for this first test the access will be to *all* fields on *all* rows – you don't need to prepare a command, so make sure that the Type is set to Table. (You'll see an example of using a command later on, but note that doing so does result in larger code.) When this dialog is dismissed, the Wizard will generate two classes: CAddressestxtAccessor (which represents a row in the table) and CAddressestxt (which gives access to such a row). Here's the first of the two:

```
class CAddressestxtAccessor
{
public:
    TCHAR m_NAME[256];
    TCHAR m_ADDRESS[256];

BEGIN_COLUMN_MAP(CAddressestxtAccessor)
    COLUMN_ENTRY(1, m_NAME)
    COLUMN_ENTRY(2, m_ADDRESS)
END_COLUMN_MAP()

    void ClearRecord(); //clears all members
};
```

The first thing to notice is that there are two data members, one for each of the fields in the table. These will hold data when a rowset is read from the database. In addition, there is a column map that provides information for binding one of the data members to a column in the table. The CAddresstxt class looks like this:

```
class CAddressestxt : public CTable<CAccessor<CAddressestxtAccessor> >
{
public:
    HRESULT Open();
    HRESULT OpenDataSource();
    HRESULT OpenRowset();

    CSession m_session;
};
```

The CTable<> template provides access to the data as a table, while the actual access is carried out through the methods of the CAccessor<> template. The Open() method opens the data source and then opens a rowset on the table:

```
HRESULT Open()
{
    HRESULT hr;

    hr = OpenDataSource();
    if (FAILED(hr))
        return hr;

    return OpenRowset();
}

HRESULT OpenDataSource()
{
    HRESULT hr;
    CDataSource db;
    CDBPropSet dbinit(DBPROPSET_DBINIT);

    dbinit.AddProperty(DBPROP_AUTH_PERSIST_SENSITIVE_AUTHINFO, false);
    dbinit.AddProperty(DBPROP_INIT_DATASOURCE, OLESTR("Addresses"));
    dbinit.AddProperty(DBPROP_INIT_PROMPT, (short)4);
    dbinit.AddProperty(DBPROP_INIT_LCID, (long)1033);
    hr = db.Open(_T("MSDASQL"), &dbinit);
    if (FAILED(hr))
        return hr;
    return m_session.Open(db);
}
```

This sets up the OLE DB properties and then opens the database session. OpenRowSet() is simple:

```
HRESULT OpenRowset()
{
    return CTable<CAccessor<CAddressestxtAccessor> >
                                ::Open(m_session, _T("Addresses.txt"));
}
```

Notice how the Open() method is passed the name of the table (Addresses.txt) and the session object that represents this transaction. The consumer classes have now been created; you don't have to write any more code to access the OLE DB data source.

Now for an example that uses it: create a console project and select the "Hello, World" type. Since this project will use COM and the OLE DB consumer classes, you should edit `stdafx.h` to add `windows.h` and `atldbcli.h`:

```
#include <windows.h>
#include <atldbcli.h>
#include <tchar.h>
#include <stdio.h>
```

Next, you need to copy the consumer class header file, `Addressestxt.h`, to the project and edit the `main()` function:

```
#include "stdafx.h"
#include "Addressestxt.h"
int _tmain()
{
    CoInitialize(NULL);

    CAddressestxt* myAddresses = new CAddressestxt;
    HRESULT hr;
    hr = myAddresses->Open();
    if(SUCCEEDED(hr))
    {
        while(myAddresses->MoveNext() == S_OK)
        {
            _tprintf(_T("%s : %s\n"), myAddresses->m_NAME, myAddresses
>m_ADDRESS);
        }
    }

    delete myAddresses;

    CoUninitialize();
    return 0;
}
```

I've chosen to create an instance of `CAddressestxt` on the heap; in most cases it will work just as well as a stack variable, but in this example I want the destructor to be called *before* the call to `CoUninitialize()`, which can be done by deleting the object. This will produce the following output:

```
C:\>Addresses
Richard Grimes : 30 Lincoln Road, Birmingham
Bill Clinton : White House, Washington DC
Tony Blair : 10 Downing Street, London
Boris Yeltsin : Kremlin, Moscow

C:\>
```

This is just the beginning! If you select Command instead of Table in the Object Wizard, you will also get two classes, but the Accessor class will have the following line added:

```
DEFINE_COMMAND(CAddressestxtAccessorC, _T(" \
    SELECT \
    NAME, \
    ADDRESS \
    FROM Addresses.txt"))
```

Here, I have appended the letter C to the names of the classes and files to distinguish them from the table versions. Since this is an ODBC provider, you can query it for data using SQL – this command just accesses all data from the table. The other changes are that CAddressestxtC will be derived from CCommand<> rather than CTable<>:

```
class CAddressestxtC : public CCommand<CAccessor<CAddressestxtAccessorC> >
```

The OpenRowSet() method also reflects this:

```
HRESULT OpenRowset()
{
    return CCommand<CAccessor<CAddressestxtAccessorC> >::Open(m_session);
}
```

Of course, if you want a different command, you just change the string in the DEFINE_COMMAND() macro. For example:

```
DEFINE_COMMAND(CAddressestxtAccessorC,
               _T("SELECT NAME, ADDRESS FROM Addresses.txt")
               _T("WHERE NAME=\'Richard Grimes\'"))
```

All this does is add a static method to your rowset class called GetDefaultCommand() that returns this command string as a static string. The Open() method called by OpenRowset() calls this method to get the command. This SQL will just return my address and it can be used with this client code:

```
CAddressestxtC* myAddress = new CAddressestxtC;
hr = myAddress->Open();
if(SUCCEEDED(hr))
{
    myAddress->MoveNext();
    _tprintf(_T("My Address (%s) is %s\n"), myAddress->m_NAME,
                                            myAddress->m_ADDRESS);
}
delete myAddress;
```

To make this more flexible, you can change the command to take a parameter:

```
DEFINE_COMMAND(CAddressestxtAccessorC, _T(" \
      SELECT \
      NAME, \
      ADDRESS \
      FROM Addresses.txt \
      WHERE NAME = ?"))

BEGIN_PARAM_MAP(CAddressestxtAccessorC)
   COLUMN_ENTRY(1, m_NAME)
END_PARAM_MAP()
```

The parameter map provides the binding information between the data member and the parameters in the command. By default, data is passed *in* via a command, but you can specify that data is passed *out* through the data member by using the SET_PARAM_TYPE() macro before COLUMN_ENTRY().

With the above changes to the CAddressestxtAccessorC class, you can use it in this code:

```
CAddressestxtC* myAddress = new CAddressestxtC;
lstrcpy(myAddress->m_NAME, _T("Richard Grimes"));
hr = myAddress->Open();
if(SUCCEEDED(hr))
{
    myAddress->MoveNext();
    _tprintf(_T("My Address (%s) is %s\n"), myAddress->m_NAME,
                                            myAddress->m_ADDRESS);
}
delete myAddress;
```

Notice that I'm passing in the value of the parameter using the m_NAME member.

## Provider

The OLE DB Provider item in the Object Wizard is a different kettle of fish. This option *does* produce a COM object, and this provides the OLE DB object that a consumer will use. When you select this object type, you get this dialog:

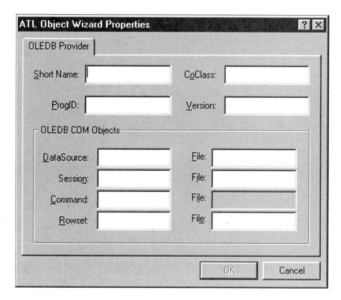

There are a lot of items here, but you really only need to fill in the Short Name – the page will fill in the rest. As you can see, you're not creating one object, but four: DataSource, Session, Command and Rowset.

When the user wants to access a data source, they create an instance of the DataSource object. To perform some work, the user must obtain a Session object from the DataSource object, and this essentially represents an OLE DB transaction. To make a query on a DataSource, the user must create a Command object from a Session. A Command object is a text command that is specific to the particular data source. In the previous example, for instance, the command was a SQL statement, because the provider wrapped ODBC data sources. When a command has been executed, the data is returned via RowSet objects.

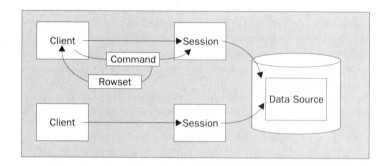

In this schematic you can see that the database is managed by the Data Source object and one or more clients get access to it via Session objects. The client creates a Command object from the Session and, when it is executed, will be returned a Rowset object.

The Wizard creates eight classes for you. If you use a <u>S</u>hort Name of ShortName, they'll look like this:

| Class | Description |
|-------|-------------|
| CShortNameWindowsFile | The **user record**. This represents the column data for a rowset. Note that the Wizard creates a sample user record for a provider that gives access to the file system. |
| CShortNameSource | Class for the DataSource object. |
| CShortNameSession | A Session object for the provider. |
| CShortNameSessionColSchemaRowset | Provides column schema information. |
| CShortNameSessionPTSchemaRowset | Provides schema information about the provider type. |
| CShortNameSessionTRSchemaRowset | Provides schema information about the tables supported in the data source. |
| CShortNameCommand | Class used to provide a Command object. |
| CShortNameRowset | The implementation of the Rowset object. |

These classes will be described in the following sections. But note that in addition to the classes for the OLE DB objects described above there are also schema rowset classes (used to provide information about the database) and a user record class. The former has all the data and code required to implement an OLE DB rowset, whilst the latter contains the data that is returned.

## User Record

The first thing you need to do is change the `CShortNameWindowsFile` class to reflect the rowset that you will return from this data source. The sample user record is an OLE DB provider for the Win32 file system, hence the name `CShortNameWindowsFile` and the fact that it derives from `WIN32_FIND_DATA`. Your user record most likely will *not* provide this data, and so you should change the class accordingly. Thus, you should search for and replace all occurrences of `CShortNameWindowsFile` with an appropriate class name for your data source. Then, edit the new class to have data members for each column in your rowset, and provide a **provider column map** that maps these data members to the columns in the rowset.

For example, if you want a rowset that has two strings in each row, the user record should be:

```
class CMyUserRecord
{
public:
    TCHAR szKey[255];
    TCHAR szValue[255];

BEGIN_PROVIDER_COLUMN_MAP(CMyUserRecord)
    PROVIDER_COLUMN_ENTRY("Key", 1, szKey)
    PROVIDER_COLUMN_ENTRY("Value", 2, szValue)
END_PROVIDER_COLUMN_MAP()
};
```

The first parameter in the map entry is the name of the column (you don't have to worry about the Unicode/ANSI issue because the macro applies `OLESTR()` to this name), the second item is the column number, and the third is the data member of the user record.

## Data Source

The data source class has three main purposes. Firstly, it is used to describe the **properties** of the database – that is, to give a consumer information about the database. This is done through the `IDBPropertiesImpl<>` base class, which uses the data provided by the property maps, as described below. The second role of the class is to allow the data source to be initialized. This is done through the `IDBInitializeImpl<>` template that initializes the data source using the data source properties. The third responsibility of the data source class is to create `Session` objects. Thus, it is derived from `IDBCreateSessionImpl<>`, a template that takes the data source class *and* the session class as parameters.

The Wizard also derives the class from `IInternalConnectionImpl<>`. This implements the `IInternalConnection` interface, which maintains a count of how many `Session` objects are attached to the data source, as explained in the next section.

## Session

When a consumer wants to get access to the database, it must create a session. This gives consumers direct access to the data source as a table through a rowset object. The consumer gets a rowset object by calling `IOpenRowset::OpenRowset()`, and the ATL session object provides support for this by deriving from the `IOpenRowsetImpl<>` interface and giving an implementation of `OpenRowset()` that calls `IOpenRowsetImpl<>::CreateRowset()`. This method creates an instance of the project's rowset class.

Session objects also provide schema information about the provider (that is information about the data source). By default, you get implementations of the three required schemas (which are declared in the **schema map**): tables, columns and provider types. These schemas are returned to the user when they call `IDBSchemaRowset::GetRowset()`, and ATL provides an implementation of this in `IDBSchemaRowsetImpl<>` that accesses the schema map and creates an instance of the specified schema class.

For our ATL OLE DB provider called `ShortName`, these classes are called `CShortNameSessionTRSchemaRowset`, `CShortNameSessionColSchemaRowset`, and `CShortNameSessionPTSchemaRowset`. The classes are rowsets, so they should also have a user record to provide a **provider column map** specifying the columns that they contain. The Wizard provides these maps for you; they're provided in the classes `CTABLESRow`, `CCOLUMNSRow` and `CPROVIDER_TYPERow` respectively (which are used as template parameters in your schema classes), and they're declared in `atldb.h`.

Information about the session is provided by implementing `ISessionProperties`, which is carried out by deriving from `ISessionPropertiesImpl<>`. This obtains information stored in the **property set map** (see later) for the session, and by default the Object Wizard will give support for the transaction isolation level used by this session.

You will notice that the ATL class also derives from `IObjectWithSiteSessionImpl<>`. This might seem a little odd, because `IObjectWithSite` (which it implements) is normally associated with controls, for which it provides communications with a container site. However, all this interface *really* does is provide a method to get and set an `IUnknown` pointer on the container site cached in the object. You're free to pass any interface, and this is what the OLE DB classes do: they pass the `IInternalConnection` interface, which is implemented by the data source. The `IObjectWithSiteSessionImpl<>` class uses this interface to maintain the session object count on the data source object.

The final two base classes to the session class are `IGetDataSourceImpl<>` and `IDBCreateCommandImpl<>`. The former allows a consumer to get the data source for the session, while the latter is perhaps the *raison d'être* of the `Session` object: it allows a consumer to create a new `Command` object.

## Command

`Command` objects are used to make queries on the data source. These commands are textual queries, and use whatever querying language your data source supports. An ODBC data source, for example, supports SQL queries, but you are not restricted to those. The `Command` object supports the `ICommand` interface, which has the `Execute()` method that the consumer actually calls to perform the command. When the command is completed, the results are held in a rowset, and the consumer gets access to the data in the rowset through an **accessor**. An accessor object has information about how the data is stored, and so consumers need to create an accessor before making any query.

The ATL-generated `Command` class will derive from `ICommandTextImpl<>` (which implements the `ICommandText` interface, which derives from `ICommand`) and also from the `IAccessorImpl<>` class to provide the `IAccessor` interface. Of course, the accessor needs to know about the data in a rowset, and it obtains this by calling the static method `GetColumnInfo()`. This last function calls the identically named method in the user record class that obtains the information placed into the provider column map.

Commands must implement the `IConvertType` interface to indicate to a consumer whether they can convert data from one type to another, and to this end the ATL class derives from `IConvertTypeImpl<>`. Other information provided by a `Command` is dealt with by the `ICommandProperties` and `IColumnsInfo` interfaces, which are provided by ATL in the appropriate `Impl` classes. The former provides the `Command` properties, which are declared in the property set map, while the latter provides information about the columns that will feature in the rowsets returned by the `Command`. Predictably, this uses the user record `GetColumnInfo()` method that I have already mentioned.

Finally, to provide communication between the `Session` and the `Command` object, the ATL class derives from the `IObjectWithSiteImpl<>` class as well.

### Rowset

Regardless of whether the consumer accesses the data source as a table or through a `Command`, the data is returned through a rowset object. The Object Wizard generates a `Rowset` class that has a method called `Execute()` that's used when generating a rowset. Note that the code generated for you is just sample code concerned with returning data from the file system; you should replace the `Execute()` method with your own rowset creation code.

### Property Maps

In the sections above, I have consistently talked about properties, without *really* explaining what they are. In OLE DB terms, properties are attributes of an object that describe its capabilities. Properties are grouped together into **property sets**, and each property set has a GUID. Properties within a property set are further identified by an integer value. You can use the OLE DB defined properties (which you can find in the *OLE DB Programmer's Reference*), or even define your own.

The Wizard adds a property set map into your `DataSource`, `Session` and `Command` classes. The data source property set map, for example, has two property sets:

```
BEGIN_PROPSET_MAP(CShortNameSource)
   BEGIN_PROPERTY_SET(DBPROPSET_DATASOURCEINFO)
      // Property entries
   END_PROPERTY_SET(DBPROPSET_DATASOURCEINFO)
   BEGIN_PROPERTY_SET(DBPROPSET_DBINIT)
      // Property entries
   END_PROPERTY_SET(DBPROPSET_DBINIT)
   CHAIN_PROPERTY_SET(CShortNameCommand)
END_PROPSET_MAP()
```

The two property sets give information about the data source, and the initialization of that data source. I've omitted the Wizard-generated entries here, but they are entered using the `PROPERTY_INFO_ENTRY()` macro, and give information about things like the number of active sessions allowed, whether the database is read only, and information about the username used internally by the database. As you can see this map uses the usual ATL trick of chaining maps so that the maps of other classes (in this case `CShortNameCommand`) are also read.

Your OLE DB Provider must implement property maps because they provide information about the data source, its capabilities and features.

# Creating a Custom Object Wizard

Just as you can create new AppWizards, so you can create new Object Wizards, although the process is slightly different. Object Wizard object types are created from templates, and a script that's run by the Object Wizard determines the items inserted into the templates. Object Wizard templates are simple text files, while custom AppWizards are compiled DLLs.

In case it had slipped your mind, here's the dialog you get when you request to insert an ATL object:

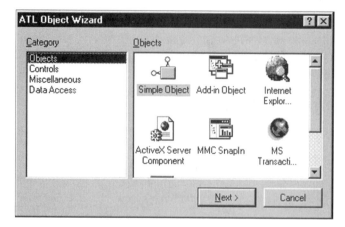

Every item in the Object Wizard has a corresponding entry in the registry under the key `HKEY_LOCAL_MACHINE\Software\Microsoft\DevStudio\6.0\ATLWizard`

> **Visual C++ 5 put these keys under `HKEY_CURRENT_USER`, but this caused problems, especially for automatic set-ups over a network where the installation would be done under a different account to the final user. This situation would lead to an empty Object Wizard. Thankfully, Visual C++ 6 has addressed the problem by moving the values to `HKEY_LOCAL_MACHINE`.**

The following screenshot shows this registry key:

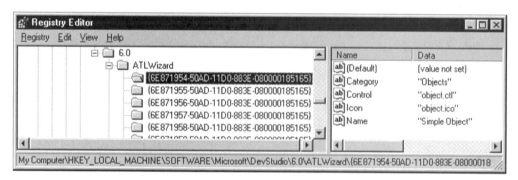

Each entry under the `ATLWizard` key is a GUID used to identify an Object Wizard entry. GUIDs are used here simply because they guarantee that each has a unique name, they don't correspond to any COM ID.

Under this key are values that are used by the Object Wizard to show the object type. Category is the category type in the left-hand pane of the Object Wizard, and this can be one of the existing categories (Objects, Control, Miscellaneous or Data Access), or an entirely new one. Name is the name of the object type that Object Wizard will place under the object's icon. The other values give the names of files found in the `Microsoft Visual Studio\Common\MSDev98\Template\ATL` folder that's usually installed under `Program Files`. Icon specifies the icon file used in the right hand pane for the object, and Control is the script used to create the Object Wizard dialog and interpret the results.

The script that will be run to generate the files for the object is an Object Wizard script with the extension CTL. The script controls the process for a particular item and is used to manipulate template files that will be used to create the files that will be added to your projects.

# Template Files

These template files can be absolutely anything you like. Let's take the Objects | Simple Object type as an example; it has the following files which are used by the `object.ctl` script to create the new object:

| File | Contents |
|------|----------|
| Object.cpp | Template for the CPP file |
| Object.h | Template for the header |
| Object.rgs | Template for the registrar script |
| Objco.idl | Template for the coclass part of the object IDL file |
| Objint.idl | Template for the interface part of the object IDL file |

Take a look at `Object.cpp`:

```
[!if=(FileExists, "FALSE")]
// [!CPPName] : Implementation of [!ClassName]

#include "stdafx.h"
#include "[!ProjectName].h"
#include "[!HeaderName]"
[!else]
[!AddIncludeFile(TargetFile, "stdafx.h")]
[!AddStringToSymbol(ProjectName.h, ProjectName, ".h")]
[!AddIncludeFile(TargetFile, ProjectName.h)]
[!AddIncludeFile(TargetFile, HeaderName)]
[!endif]
[!crlf]

/////////////////////////////////////////////////////////////////////
// [!ClassName]
[!crlf]
[!if=(ErrorInfoEnabled, "TRUE")]
STDMETHODIMP [!ClassName]::InterfaceSupportsErrorInfo(REFIID riid)
{
```

```
      static const IID* arr[] =
      {
         &IID_[!InterfaceName]
      };

      for(int i = 0 ; i < sizeof(arr) / sizeof(arr[0]) ; i++)
      {
         if(InlineIsEqualGUID(*arr[i],riid))
            return S_OK;
      }
      return S_FALSE;
   }
[!endif]
```

You can see that it's similar to an AppWizard script, in that it has C++ code interspersed with script code. In this case, the script code is enclosed between [! and ] delimiters, rather than $$.

In fact, there are two types of script code: **commands** (which I'll discuss later on) and **replacement text**. The latter are held in a symbol map managed by Object Wizard. The values in this map are taken from the property pages displayed to the user or added by the CTL script. Most of these are self-descriptive – for example, ClassName is the name of the class from the Class edit box on the Names tab. Also from this tab come HeaderName and InterfaceName, while ProjectName is the name of the DLL or EXE project.

# Object Wizard Scripts

When you select an Object Wizard object type, the Object Wizard script interpreter runs the appropriate CTL file. Obviously, this script needs to present a user interface to get values from the user – this interface comes in the form of property pages. You can create your own pages, or you can use pages used by the existing Visual C++ Object Wizard types.

The script uses the Dialog() command to specify up to 9 property pages. This dialog is modal, so the script is suspended until the dialog is dismissed with a click of the OK button. At this point, each property page should write any values entered in its controls to the Object Wizard symbol map. We'll look more closely at the Dialog() command a little later in the chapter.

The symbol map is simply an associative container that has pairs of keys and values. Both of these are strings, although you can add a key with an empty string to act like a manifest symbol in C (using #define). Object Wizard scripts can read and write entries in the symbol map, and the various ways to do this will be shown later. Property pages can *also* read and write entries in the symbol map by calling methods on the ISymbolMap interface:

```
[
   object,
   uuid(C6D58201-1FA3-11D0-BF1E-0000E8D0D146),
   pointer_default(unique)
]
interface ISymbolMap : IUnknown
{
```

```
    HRESULT Set([in] LPCOLESTR strSymbol, [in] LPCOLESTR strValue);
    HRESULT Get([in] LPCOLESTR strSymbol, [out, retval] BSTR* pstrValue);
    HRESULT Clear();
    HRESULT SetStatus([in] const CLSID* pclsid, [in] BOOL bEnableOK);
};
```

The interface is simple: you use the Get() method to obtain values from the map, and the Set() method to create new entries, or replace existing entries. The SetStatus() method is called by individual property pages to specify whether the OK button should be enabled or not.

In the normal course of initialization, a property page is passed the IUnknown of the object it is associated with. In this case, the property pages are passed the IUnknown interface of an object that implements the ISymbolMap interface. The page can call QueryInterface() to get a pointer to this interface for later use.

## Command Theory

The following section gives a list of the commands that that you can use. Note that these can be used both in the CTL file, and in template files. The reason for this is that a CTL script opens an output stream for the project file it is generating, and any command that produces output will write to this stream. Template files are added to this stream in an analogous way to how header files are #included in .cpp files during preprocessing. Just as the C preprocessor parses header files, so the Object Wizard parses template files, and the results are sent to the output stream.

Note that if you miss out the '!' in a command, the whole command is treated as text, so

```
[set(MySymbol, "Hello")]
```

will write the string [set(MySymbol, "Hello")] to the output stream, whereas

```
[!set(MySymbol, "Hello")]
```

will set the symbol MySymbol in the map to the value "Hello". Also note that the script is case sensitive: Set() will produce an error. Unfortunately, the error returned by the Object Wizard is not very helpful:

This dialog is produced whenever an error occurs, which is a bit like the C++ compiler saying there was an error in your C++ file, but not telling you where or what it was. It is clear that if you want to write your own scripts, you should test small pieces of code, so that you can identify where errors occur. You can get more information about the error that occurred if you add the Debug() command into your script, as explained later.

You should also be aware that most of the commands listed later take a symbol rather than a string as a parameter, so you will need to set the symbol first before using it:

```
[!set(MyFile,"bozo.txt")]
[!target(MyFile)]
This is [!MyFile]
[!target()]
```

Another point you should bear in mind is that if the target file exists, the output text will be appended to the end of the existing file. However, there are ways to get round this, as you will see later.

## Commands

Symbols in the symbol map are string values, but you can use them to hold bit values by making a symbol hold a string representation of a binary number. Also, you can use a symbol as a Boolean either by testing for its presence in the map, or settling on an agreed value like TRUE or 1. Testing is carried out using the if directive:

```
[!if(MySymbol)]
[!MySymbol]
[!else]
MySymbol does not exist
[!endif]
```

This code tests for the existence of the symbol MySymbol in the map. If the symbol does exist, its value is added to the output stream, otherwise the string "MySymbol does not exist" is used. You use the set() command to set a symbol like this:

```
[!set(MySymbol,"TRUE")]
```

You can test for a specific value:

```
[!if=(SayPing,"TRUE")]
Ping!
[!endif]
[!if!=(SayPong,"do not say pong")]
Pong!
[!endif]
```

The if=() directive tests the value of a symbol with the specified value, and if they are the same performs the following script. Likewise, if!=() tests that the symbol's value does not equal the specified value.

You can temporarily suspend output to the output stream with the OutputOff directive and resume output with OutputOn.

### Files

There are two sorts of files you need to be concerned with: **target files** and **template files**. Most of the commands are concerned with target files, which you'll typically create in the project directory. Template files are in the template directory. In both cases, you need to specify the full path to the file. The GalleryPath symbol is set by Object Wizard to point to the template directory and the ProjectDirectory symbol is set to point to the project directory.

It is usually trivial to construct a full path to a template file. For example, the following is from `object.ctl`:

```
[!AddStringToSymbol(HeaderTemplate, GalleryPath, "object.h")]
[!AddStringToSymbol(CPPTemplate, GalleryPath, "object.cpp")]
[!AddStringToSymbol(RGSTemplate, GalleryPath, "object.rgs")]
```

This creates three symbols called `HeaderTemplate`, `CPPTemplate` and `RGSTemplate` and each is created by adding the string in the final parameter to the path held in `GalleryPath`.

To associate the output stream with a particular file, you use the `target()` command. You should use this in pairs: the first has a symbol as the parameter and opens the file, and the second has no parameter and closes the file. If you are feeling lazy, you can omit the closing `target()`, but only if you have an opening `target()` following it. The last opening `target()` in a script *must* have a closing `target()`, otherwise the file will not be created. Consider the following script:

```
[!set(File1,"1.txt")]
[!set(File2,"2.txt")]
[!set(File3,"3.txt")]
[!target(File1)]
this is the first file
[!target(File2)]
this is the second file, the first file is closed
[!target()]
[!target(File3)]
this is the third, and last file
```

The code for `File2` is the preferred form, but note that `File1` is closed when `File2` is opened. However, since `target()` is not called for `File3`, the stream buffer is not flushed and the file `3.txt` is not created.

As noted before, if the file mentioned in `target()` exists, it is opened and the output stream is appended to the end of the file. This is often not what you want. To delete an existing file, you can use the `DeleteFile()` command, and if you want to make a copy of a file before deleting it you can use `CopyFile()`.

```
[!AddStringToSymbol(BackupFile, FileName, ".bak")]
[!CopyFile(FileName,BackupFile)]
[!DeleteFile(FileName)]
[!target(FileName)]
This text is in a new file, the old version is in [!BackupFile]
[!target()]
```

Sometimes, you will want to create a temporary file, for example when you want to merge several files together. To ensure that the name of the file is unique, you can call `GetTemporaryFileName()` and pass the command a symbol. The command will give this symbol the value of the temporary name:

```
[!GetTemporaryFileName(TempFile)]
[!target(TempFile)]
Stuff for the temporary file
```

```
[!target()]
Later delete the file
[!DeleteFile(TempFile)]
```

The template files are added to an output stream with the `include()` command:

```
[!target(HeaderFileTarget)]
[!include(HeaderFile)]
[!target()]
```

Here, the symbol `HeaderFile` has the name of a template file, which is loaded as if it was part of the script, so that any embedded commands are performed. The output from this file is sent to the file indicated by the `HeaderFileTarget` symbol.

After you have created a file, you will want to add it to the project so that it is included in builds and the dependency list. To do this, you need to use the `AddFileToProject()` command. The single parameter is the name of the file in the project directory. This file is added to the appropriate FileView folder according to the extension of the file. Note that the file is added with the Settings option of Use precompiled header file (.pch); this is because `stdafx.cpp` has been set to Create precompiled header file (.pch) through header stdafx.h. If you decide that you want to prevent this file from using precompiled headers, you can call `SetNoPCH()` with a symbol containing the name of the file.

When you have created a header file for a new object, you will need to include the header in any file that will use the object (if it is created internally to the server). You should certainly include the header in the project's CPP file, since this file has the object map. The `AddIncludeFile()` command will do this for you; its parameters are symbols set to the name of the file to which the `#include` is to be added, and to the header file. This new `#include` directive will be added after any existing `#include`s. The advantage you get in using this command is that you do not have to change the file yourself.

An associated command is `AddClassInclude()`, which allows you to specify a class (in a symbol or a string) and whether you want the header or CPP file altered. The command will find the correct file and add the specified include line. In similar fashion, you can use the `AddImportFile()` command to add an `import` statement after any other existing `import` statements in an IDL file.

### Symbol Manipulation

Symbols are added to the map, or existing ones changed, using the `set()` command. The contents of a symbol are generally used as parameters to the other commands, but you can send the contents of a symbol to the output stream using `[!Symbol]`. For example:

```
[!set(Greeting, "Hello")]
[!Greeting]
```

This sends the string `"Hello"` to the output stream. If you want to add a new line, use `[!crlf]`. You can remove an existing symbol with the `RemoveSymbol()` command:

```
[!set(DoSomething, "TRUE")]
[!RemoveSymbol(DoSomething)]
[!if(DoSomething)]
[!Error("Don't know whether I can do anything")]
[!endif]
```

Here, the code checks to see if the symbol DoSomething is in the map. If it isn't (and it shouldn't be, as it has been removed), an error will be generated and you'll get a dialog produced.

You can manipulate the strings held in a symbol. To change the case, you can use toupper() and tolower(), and to write over one symbol with another you can use strcpy() (or simply set()). In addition, there are the confusingly-named AddSymbolToString() and AddStringToSymbol(). The former creates a new symbol by adding the value of an existing symbol onto the end of a string, and the latter creates a new symbol by adding a string onto the end an existing symbol. This script:

```
[!set(SymbolOne,"a new symbol")]
[!SymbolOne]
[!crlf]
[!AddSymbolToString(SymbolTwo,"This is ",SymbolOne)]
[!SymbolTwo]
[!crlf]
[!AddStringToSymbol(SymbolThree,SymbolTwo," and more!")]
[!SymbolThree]
[!crlf]
```

produces this in the output stream:

```
a new symbol
This is a new symbol
This is a new symbol and more!
```

One final command in this section is DoubleSlash(). This command is useful if you are likely to add symbol strings to code, and those strings contain backslashes as directory separators. In C++ code, these backslashes should be replaced with double backslashes to prevent them being mistaken for escape characters:

```
[!set(FileName,"..\OtherDir\file.txt")]
[!DoubleSlash(FileName)]
HANDLE hFile;
hFile = CreateFile(_T([!FileName]), 0, 0, NULL, OPEN_EXISTING, 0, NULL);
```

This will ensure that the string "..\\OtherDir\\file.txt" is used.

## Property Pages

You present your Object Wizard's user interface to the user via a property page; each property page is a tab on the Object Wizard dialog. To create this dialog, you call the Dialog() command and pass the names of the property pages that you want to use. The command takes a variable number of parameters, up to a maximum of nine. Each property page is assumed to have a version-independent ProgID in the form name.name; the Dialog() command just takes half of this ProgID, so to open the Names98.Names98 property page, you use Dialog("Names98").

The property page will be able to access the symbol map through the Object Wizard's `ISymbolMap` interface, so you can set symbol values to indicate initial values for the page. In particular, some of the standard pages read the symbol map on initialization to check for values passed in. For example, the `ObjDlg98` property page (which provides the **Attributes** tab) has a symbol called `Attributes`, and the `Names98` property page (which serves the **Names** tab) has a symbol called `ComponentType`. Both of these symbols hold binary data in string form that determine which item on the page is *disabled* – that is, they hold strings like `"00001000"`, which by setting the 4th bit indicate that a particular item should be disabled. These symbols are covered later.

When the property page is first displayed (even before `Activate()` is called), Object Wizard will call the `Apply()` method of the property page. It will also call this method when the user switches away from a property page or **OK**s the Object Wizard dialog. You can use this method to set symbols in the symbol map, or pass back data entered in the property page. There is nothing special about Object Wizard property pages, so you can use the Object Wizard property page type to create one!

These are the standard pages that you can use:

| Property Page | Description |
| --- | --- |
| AddInDlg98 | Visual C++ Add-in |
| CompRegDlg98 | Component Registrar |
| ConsProp98 | Database Names |
| CtlDlg98 | Miscellaneous |
| Denali98 | ASP pages |
| Names98 | Names |
| ObjDlg98 | Attributes |
| PropDlg98 | Strings (for property pages) |
| ProvName98 | OLE DB provider |
| SnapInObj98 | MMC Snap-in |
| StockProps98 | Stock Properties |
| ViperDlg98 | MTS |

> **To get more information about the symbols that are set by these pages, see the World of ATL web site (http://www.worldofatl.com/).**

As an example of how you can pass data to and get data from property pages, let's look at two of the most widely used: the **Names** and **Attributes** pages. The `Names98` property page serves the first of these, and you can disable items on it by setting the appropriate bit position of the `ComponentType` symbol before calling `Dialog()`:

| Bit Pattern | Enables |
|---|---|
| 10000000 | Nothing |
| 01000000 | Class |
| 00100000 | Short Name, Class and .H File |
| 00010000 | .H File and .CPP File |
| 00001000 | Short Name and CoClass |
| 00000100 | Class, .CPP File and Interface |
| 00000010 | .H File, .CPP File and Type |
| 00000001 | Prog ID |

The Names page sets the following symbols when it closes, but note that you cannot set these values before calling Dialog().

| Symbol | Description |
|---|---|
| ShortName | The short name that you give in the dialog |
| ClassName | The ATL class that will be generated |
| HeaderName | The header used |
| CPPName | The CPP implementation file |
| CoClassName | The object's coclass name |
| InterfaceName | The interface generated |
| TypeName | The object type |
| ProgID | The ProgID |
| VersionIndependentProgID | Version independent ProgID |
| ObjectGUID | A GUID generated for the object |

It is interesting that this page generates a GUID for the object coclass (ObjectGUID), but not for the interface – you have to call newguid() in your script to do that.

The ObjDlg98 property page manages the **Attributes** page. The controls on this page can be disabled by setting the following bit positions in the Attributes symbol before calling Dialog():

| Bit pattern | Disables this control |
|---|---|
| 10000000000 | Single Threading Model |
| 01000000000 | Apartment Threading Model |
| 00100000000 | Both Threading Model |
| 00010000000 | Free Threading Model |
| 00001000000 | Dual Interface |
| 00000100000 | Custom Interface |
| 00000010000 | Yes to Aggregation |
| 00000001000 | No to Aggregation |
| 00000000100 | Only Aggregation |
| 00000000010 | Support ISupportErrorInfo |
| 00000000001 | Free Threaded Marshaler |

There doesn't seem to be a bit pattern to disable Support Connection Points. The results from the page are passed to the script via the following symbols but, as before, setting these values before calling `Dialog()` has no effect on the dialog.

| Symbol | Values |
|---|---|
| ThreadingModel | Single, Apartment, Both, Free |
| Dual | TRUE, FALSE |
| Aggregatable | YES, NO, ONLY |
| ErrorInfoEnabled | TRUE, FALSE |
| ConnectionPointsEnabled | TRUE, FALSE |
| FreeThreadedMarshaler | TRUE, FALSE |

### Resources

When you create a new object type, you may well have to create some new resources to add to the project's resource script. `AddRegistryToRC()` will add an RGS file as a `REGISTRY` resource; it has two parameters, both symbols. The first of these is the name of the RGS file, while the second is the name of the symbol to be used. The command will add the (already created) RGS file to the project, and it will add the resource to the resource script:

```
[!Dialog("Names98")]
[!AddStringToSymbol(RGSName, ShortName, ".rgs")]
[!AddSymbolToString(RGSResourceID, "ID_", ShortName)]
[!target(RGSName)]
[!include(MyRGSTemplate)]
[!target()]
[!AddRegistryToRC(RGSName, RGSResourceID)]
```

This will allow the user to enter a short name into the standard `Names` tab, which it will use to create two new symbols. The first is the name of the RGS file to create, while the second is a new resource ID. It then includes a template to create the RGS file, and adds the file to the project resources. If you enter "MyObj" as a short name, then the RGS file will be called `MyObj.rgs`, and an ID called `ID_MyObj` will be created as well. The Wizard will generate the actual value of the resource ID.

`AddStringResource()` adds a new string resource to the project. The ID of the string resource is given as the first parameter, and the actual string is given as the second parameter. Both parameters, of course, are symbols. For example:

```
[!set(ErrorFileNotFound, "File Not Found")]
[!set(IDS_NoFile, "IDS_NoFile")]
[!AddStringResource(IDS_NoFile, ErrorFileNotFound)]
```

If you want to add other resource types, you can use `AddResourceFromFile()`. This allows you to add a resource of a particular type, with a specified ID, from a specified file. The resource types that you can add are those that you would get in the Insert Resource dialog:

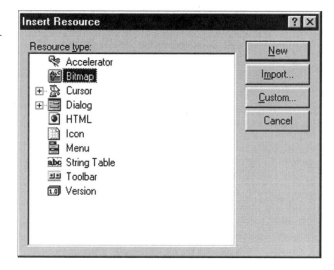

If you add a dialog resource to a project, you might decide to open that resource once the Wizard has finished, so that the user can start editing it straight away. This is done with the `OpenDialog()` command. Here's an example taken from the CTL file for composite controls:

```
[!strcpy(UpperShortName, ShortName)]
[!toupper(UpperShortName)]
[!AddSymbolToString(IDD_DIALOGID, "IDD_", UpperShortName)]
[!AddStringToSymbol(DLGTemplate, GalleryPath, "cmposite.rc")]
[!AddResourceFromFile(DLGTemplate, IDD_DIALOGID, "DIALOG")]
[!OpenDialog(IDD_DIALOGID)]
```

Here, the `GalleryPath` symbol is set up with the path to the template directory, as I mentioned above. When this script is run, the dialog template is opened in the dialog editor. This is the only resource type that you can open this way.

### COM Commands

Of course, most of the object types that you want to add will need to have a GUID or manipulate the project IDL, and so there are several commands that let you do this. In fact, I have already mentioned the `AddImportFile()` command that allows you to add an `import` statement after any other existing `import` statements in the IDL file.

To create a new GUID, you can call `newguid()`. This takes a symbol as a parameter and the new GUID (in 'bare' registry form – that is, the same form as a CLSID in the registry but without the braces) is written to that symbol. Once you have a GUID, you can merge this into the necessary statements for an `interface` statement in an IDL file, and pipe the results to a temporary file. This file can then be used with `AddInterfaceToIDL()` to add the interface definition to the project's IDL file. Here is an example from the CTL file for Simple Objects:

```
[!newguid(InterfaceGUID)]
[!Dialog("Names98", "ObjDlg98")]
[!AddStringToSymbol(IDLInterface, GalleryPath, "objint.idl")]
[!AddInterfaceToIDL(IDLProject, IDLInterface)]
```

Clearly, this is hiding most of the work. `IDLProject` will point to the project's IDL, but the file `objint.idl` looks like this:

```
[
[!if=(Dual, "TRUE")]    object,[!endif]
   uuid([!InterfaceGUID]),
[!if=(Dual, "TRUE")]    dual,[!endif]
   helpstring("[!InterfaceName] Interface"),
   pointer_default(unique)
]
interface [!InterfaceName] :
   [!if=(Dual, "TRUE")]IDispatch[!else]IUnknown[!endif]
{
[!if=(OnStartPage, "TRUE")]
   //Standard Server Side Component Methods
   HRESULT OnStartPage([in] IUnknown* piUnk);
   HRESULT OnEndPage();
[!endif]
};
```

The `Dual` symbol is set by the `ObjDlg98` tab, `InterfaceName` is set by the `Names98` tab, and `OnStartPage` is set if the user is creating an ASP object. Hence, the `AddInterfaceToIDL()` command effectively loads the IDL template, parses it, and merges the results into the specified IDL file *outside* any `library` block. `AddCoClassToIDL()` works in a similar way, but the parsed IDL is put *inside* the `library` block. To ensure that the correct build settings are used, you can call `IDLSettingsForATL()`; this is useful when adding ATL objects to MFC projects, where it is used to provide the settings for `MIDL`.

Once an object has been created, you will want to add it to the object map, and this is carried out by calling `AddToObjectMap()`. This takes two symbols as parameters: the `coclass` for the object, and the name of the ATL class that implements the object (both of which can be obtained from the `Names98` tab).

Of course, ATL projects contain many other maps, and to manipulate these you can use the `AddToMap()` command. This takes the name of the class to change, and the map name. To understand how it works, remember that most maps are declared with a pair of macros, for example:

```
BEGIN_COM_MAP(CMyObject)
END_COM_MAP()
```

This is the COM map, and to add a new entry to it, you pass the string `"COM"` to `AddToMap()`. In addition, you need to give the macro the name of the entry that you want to add to the map, and its parameters. Different map entries have a different number of parameters, so you also need to give the number of parameters to add to the entry. Hence, to add a new interface to `CMyObject`, you can call:

```
[!AddToMap(MYOBJECT, "COM", "COM_INTERFACE_ENTRY", 1, "IMyInterface")]
```

### Other Commands

As I mentioned above, Object Wizard scripts are parsed by an interpreter that has a rather limited error output capability. The only command that you have in your arsenal to display errors to the user is `Error()`. If an incorrect value is detected, you can stop all processing of the script and display a modal dialog with the error text using:

```
[!Error("Use a non-empty string for the name!")]
```

To track down errors in your scripts while you're debugging, you can add the `Debug()` statement at the top of the script:

```
[!Debug()]
```

If an error occurs after this line, the Object Wizard will produce a modal dialog with more information about the error. Once the script has been debugged you should remove this line.

The Object Wizard script parser also allows the `comment()` command, which takes a string parameter. However, this does not appear to affect the output stream, and so its sole purpose is to place comments in the script.

The `Commit()` command is called to commit any changes made by the script. This is particularly important for scripts that create a dialog resource and then attempt to open that resource using `OpenDialog()`, because it ensures that the dialog resource is actually saved and is thus accessible.

When you add a feature to a class, you may decide that you need to derive it from another class (for example, when you add support for stock properties, you need to derive the ATL class from `CStockPropImpl<>`). You can do this by using the `AddBaseClass()` command, which takes two symbols and a string as arguments. The two symbols are the name of the class to change and the name of the base class to add, and the string is the access level of the derivation. At present, the third parameter is ignored, since only public derivation is allowed.

### Existing Symbols

These are symbols set by the Object Wizard:

| Symbol | Description |
|---|---|
| CWinApp | This contains the name of the `CWinApp`-derived class, if it exists |
| FileExists | Allows you to check if a file exists on disk |
| GalleryPath | The path to the template files |
| IDLProject | The name of the IDL for the project |
| LibGUID | The LIBID of the type library |
| LibName | The name of the type library in the IDL |
| MFC | Set to "1" for MFC projects |
| MFCCTL | Set to "1" if the project is an MFC control, "0" otherwise |
| MFCOLE | Set to "1" if the project is an MFC control |
| NULLSTR | Set to "" |
| ObjectMap | Set to "1" if there is an object map |
| ProjectDirectory | The path to the project's directory |
| ProjectHadIDL | Set to "TRUE" if the project has an IDL file |
| ProjectName | The name of the project |
| ProjectNameCPP | The name of the main CPP file in the project |
| ProjectNameHeader | The name of the project's header file |
| ProjectNameRC | The name of the RC file for the project |
| ProjectNameSafe | If the project name has unusual characters, this contains the project name with those characters removed |
| ProjectType | The project type ("EXE" or "DLL") |
| ProjectAppID | For EXE projects, this is the AppID |
| stdafx.cpp | Set to "stdafx.cpp" |

*Table Continued on Following Page*

| Symbol | Description |
|--------|-------------|
| stdafx.h | Set to "stdafx.h" |
| STDAFXCPP | Set to "stdafx.cpp" |
| STDAFXH | Set to "stdafx.h" |
| VC | Set to "6.0" in Visual C++ 6 |
| VCINCDIR | Points to the Visual C++ include directory |

### Adding an ATL Object to an MFC Project

You can add ATL objects to an MFC project. To do this, the project needs to be changed, and when you select New ATL Object..., you will get this dialog:

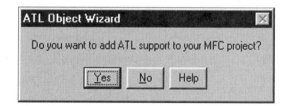

If you click on **Yes**, the Object Wizard will run the AddAtl.ctl script. This adds all the code needed in an MFC project to have ATL and it adds an object map to the CWinApp file of the project. This is required, of course, for registration of objects and their class factories. For the map to be of any use, there must be a global object called _Module, so the Object Wizard derives a class from CComModule in stdafx.h (where atlbase.h and atlcom.h are included), and creates an instance of this class in the CWinApp file.

Object Wizard also changes the project's CWinApp to have a private method called ATLInit() called from InitInstance(). ATLInit() (for an EXE project) initializes COM and makes sure that the class factories are registered. ATLInit() also calls the Init() method on _Module to initialize it, and to clean up when it is no longer needed, the Object Wizard adds ExitInstance() to CWinApp to revoke the ATL class factories (again, for an EXE) and to call the Term() method.

At this point, the project has all the support needed to add an ATL object, so the Object Wizard brings up the familiar dialog showing the objects that can be inserted.

The Object Wizard clearly does a lot of work here, and there are several commands that are called to do it. ExistsMemberFunction() checks to see if a class has a particular method, while ExistsInMemberFunction() checks to see if a particular string is contained within a specified function. AddAtl.ctl calls AddMemberVariable() and AddMemberFunction() to add data members and methods to a specified class.

You should note that MFC projects have ODL files rather than IDL files, so when you add a new ATL object, it will be added to the ODL. A particular consequence of this is that interface definitions will be added to the library statement in the ODL, which means that *no* proxy-stub code will be generated, even if the project is an EXE project. Thus, you should make sure that your objects have dual interfaces, so that you can use type library marshaling.

### Custom Object Wizard Type

As a quick example, let's create an Object Wizard template that will add a new interface to your IDL file. This will just place the interface definition at an appropriate point in your IDL file and will save you the hassle of generating a new UUID for the interface.

The CTL file should look like this:

```
[!newguid(InterfaceGUID)]
[!set(ComponentType, "00001100")]
[!Dialog("Names98")]

[!AddStringToSymbol(IDLInterface, GalleryPath, "objint.idl")]
[!AddInterfaceToIDL(IDLProject, IDLInterface)]
[!AddImportFile(IDLProject, "oaidl.idl")]
```

Save this file in the `Template\ATL` directory as `AddItf.ctl`.

The CTL file uses the `newguid()` command to generate the IID for the new interface and store it in the symbol `InterfaceGUID`. Next, it uses `set()` to set the `ComponentType` symbol that is used by the `Names98` page to enable/disable controls. The `Names98` page isn't ideal for this task since we can't get it to enable only the **Interface Name** box, but it will do for this simple example. You could write your own property page if you wanted a more appropriate user interface. The `Dialog()` command is used to display the property page to the user.

The next three lines of code are taken from the `Object.ctl` file that controls the **Simple Object** type in Object Wizard. This uses the `AddInterfaceToIDL()` command to add the `objint.idl` file as an interface to the project's IDL file. `Objint.idl` uses symbols set by the `Names98` page to provide the interface name.

Now you need to register the CTL file. You could use `.reg` file shown below for this purpose:

```
REGEDIT4

[HKEY_LOCAL_MACHINE\Software\Microsoft\DevStudio\6.0\ATLWizard\{871CF1E0
BB2E-11d0-BC16-002018349816}]
"Category"="Wrox"
"Control"="AddItf.ctl"
"Icon"="Object.ico"
"Name"="Add Interface to IDL"
```

Now if you run the Object Wizard, you'll see a new category called **Wrox** containing an item labeled **Add Interface to IDL**. Selecting this item will allow you to easily add a new interface to your IDL file.

# Summary

The ATL Object Wizard is clearly a complex and useful tool. This chapter has shown you the object types that are present in the Visual C++ 6 Object Wizard, and also how the Wizard works, so that you can add your own object types if you so choose.

# 5

# Class Factories

Objects have to be created before you can use them, and although COM can locate and run an object server by using information from the registry, it must still be the job of the server actually to create the objects. This implies that when the server starts, there is already some code devoted to creating objects, and indeed this is the case. The code in question is the **class factory**.

In this chapter, I will explain precisely what a class factory is and how ATL provides them. I will also describe the different kinds of class factories, and how you can provide your own.

## Creating Objects

There are essentially two ways to create an object. The first way is to ask an existing, non-class factory object to create the object, and the second is to use a class factory. In both cases, there is a running object in the server capable of creating other objects.

Let's take a look at an example of the first case. Consider this code for the _NewEnum property that provides an enumerator for a collection object:

```
class ATL_NO_VTABLE CRainbow :
        public CComObjectRootEx<CComSingleThreadModel>,
        public CComCoClass<CRainbow, &CLSID_Rainbow>,
        public IDispatchImpl<IRainbow, &IID_IRainbow, &LIBID_COLOURSLib>
{
public:
   CRainbow() {}
   HRESULT FinalConstruct()
   {
```

```
            m_vecColors.push_back(L"Red");
            m_vecColors.push_back(L"Orange");
            m_vecColors.push_back(L"Yellow");
            m_vecColors.push_back(L"Green");
            m_vecColors.push_back(L"Blue");
            m_vecColors.push_back(L"Indigo");
            m_vecColors.push_back(L"Violet");
            return S_OK;
        }

    DECLARE_REGISTRY_RESOURCEID(IDR_RAINBOW)

    BEGIN_COM_MAP(CRainbow)
        COM_INTERFACE_ENTRY(IRainbow)
        COM_INTERFACE_ENTRY(IDispatch)
    END_COM_MAP()

    // IRainbow
    public:
        STDMETHOD(get_Count)(long* pVal);
        STDMETHOD(Item)(VARIANT Index, LPVARIANT pItem);
        STDMETHODIMP get__NewEnum(LPUNKNOWN* pVal)
        {
            typedef CComObject<CComEnumOnSTL<IEnumVARIANT, &IID_IEnumVARIANT,
                    VARIANT, _Copy<VARIANT>, std::vector<CComVariant> > > EnumVar;
            EnumVar* pVar = new EnumVar;
            pVar->Init(NULL, m_vecColors);
            return pVar->QueryInterface(IID_IUnknown, (void**)pVal);
        }

    private:
        std::vector<CComVariant> m_vecColors;
    };
```

The _NewEnum property is used in scripting languages with the `for each` syntax to access all elements in the collection:

```
Private Sub Form_Load()
    Dim colors As Rainbow
    Set colors = New Rainbow
    Dim var As Variant
    For Each var In colors
        lstColors.AddItem var
    Next
End Sub
```

I could have used the new ATL 3.0 class `ICollectionOnSTLImpl<>` in this code, but what you see here illustrates the principle more clearly – I'll demonstrate the new class in Appendix C. The `get__NewEnum()` function has to create a enumerator object, which it does by using the multiply-nested parameterized types you can see. `CComEnumOnSTL<>` is an ATL class that creates an enumerator from an STL collection; however, as mentioned in Chapter 2, `CComObject<>` is also required to supply the `IUnknown` methods.

The actual object is created using new, which is quite safe since the enumerator class does not use FinalConstruct(). When new creates the object, the reference count on the object is zero. This object is *not* returned to the client, because when the client has finished with the object and calls Release(), the object reference count will fall to -1 and so will never be released! In any case, the client wants an IUnknown pointer, so QueryInterface() is called to get this pointer, which has the happy side effect of bumping up the reference count to 1.

The best thing about returning an object that supports the IUnknown interface is that you can blithely create it with new in a method and return a pointer to it as a parameter, safe in the knowledge that the object will manage its own lifetime. delete will be called when the reference count falls to zero in response to a call to Release().

Anyway, the point is that a client that calls get__NewEnum() will be returned a reference to a new object. This method creates objects, but to get access to it, you must have already created the Rainbow object. What creates that? This, of course, is where we come to the second way to create objects. A **class factory**, also known as a **class object**, is a COM object that creates other COM objects. What creates the class factory? The server does.

# In-process Servers

When COM creates an in-process server for the purpose of creating an object, it will call DllGetClassObject() to obtain the class factory object. In response to this call, the server creates the specified class factory object, and returns it back to COM. COM can then either pass the class factory to the client (if the client called CoGetClassObject()) or use the class factory to create an object instance (if the client called CoCreateInstanceEx()). ATL implements DllGetClassObject() like this:

```
STDAPI DllGetClassObject(REFCLSID rclsid, REFIID riid, LPVOID* ppv)
{
    return _Module.GetClassObject(rclsid, riid, ppv);
}
```

The implementation of GetClassObject() looks like this:

```
HRESULT CComModule::GetClassObject(
                        REFCLSID rclsid, REFIID riid, LPVOID* ppv)
{
    return AtlModuleGetClassObject(this, rclsid, riid, ppv);
}
```

As you have seen already, AtlModuleGetClassObject() takes a pointer to an _ATL_MODULE object (which is the base class of CComModule), and through this obtains a pointer to the object map in the data member _ATL_MODULE::m_pObjMap. AtlModuleGetClassObject() can move through the object map until it finds the CLSID for the object that COM requested, and then it can create the class factory. One of the members in the object map contains a pointer to the static CreateInstance() method of the class factory class; AtlModuleGetClassObject() uses this pointer to create the class factory instance.

# EXE Servers

An EXE cannot export functions like DLLs can, so a COM server packaged in an EXE must create its class factories when it is first started up. Here is some code from the _tWinMain() function for an EXE server:

```
const DWORD dwPause = 1000;
extern "C" int WINAPI _tWinMain(
                  HINSTANCE hInstance, HINSTANCE, LPTSTR lpCmdLine, int)
{
   // Other stuff
   HRESULT hRes;
   int nRet = 0;
   BOOL bRun = TRUE;
   // Other stuff
   if(bRun)
   {
      _Module.StartMonitor();
#if _WIN32_WINNT >= 0x0400 & defined(_ATL_FREE_THREADED)
      hRes = _Module.RegisterClassObjects(
               CLSCTX_LOCAL_SERVER, REGCLS_MULTIPLEUSE | REGCLS_SUSPENDED);
      _ASSERTE(SUCCEEDED(hRes));
      hRes = CoResumeClassObjects();
#else
      hRes = _Module.RegisterClassObjects(
                              CLSCTX_LOCAL_SERVER, REGCLS_MULTIPLEUSE);
#endif
      _ASSERTE(SUCCEEDED(hRes));

      MSG msg;
      while(GetMessage(&msg, 0, 0, 0))
         DispatchMessage(&msg);

      _Module.RevokeClassObjects();
      Sleep(dwPause); // Wait for any threads to finish
   }

   _Module.Term();
   CoUninitialize();
   return nRet;
}
```

I mentioned StartMonitor() and Term() in Chapter 2. Notice that the way class factories are registered depends on whether the server has an MTA or uses STAs. Before looking at the significance of the parameters, though, let's look at what RegisterClassObjects() does:

```
HRESULT RegisterClassObjects(DWORD dwClsContext, DWORD dwFlags)
{
   return AtlModuleRegisterClassObjects(this, dwClsContext, dwFlags);
}
```

AtlModuleRegisterClassObjects() is passed a pointer to an _ATL_MODULE object, and it iterates through *all* the members of the object map, calling the RegisterClassObject() function of each item. This method creates an instance of the class factory for the item (using the same function pointer that the in-process server does) and then calls CoRegisterClassObject(), caching the cookie that this function returns.

# Registering Class Factories

An EXE server ultimately calls `CoRegisterClassObject()` for each of the class factories that it implements. This passes the CLSID, a class factory pointer and some flags to COM, which caches the class factory pointer in an internally maintained table and returns a cookie value back to the server. This cookie identifies the class factory when its passed to `CoRevokeClassObject()`, which is called in response to a call to `CComModule::RevokeClassObjects()` to tell COM that the server no longer wants to create objects.

The flags that are passed to `CoRegisterClassObject()` give COM information about *how* the server intends to create objects. The first flag is a context flag, and the second is a registration flag. The context flag can be:

| Flag | Description |
|---|---|
| CLSCTX_INPROC_SERVER | The class factory can be used to create instances of the specified class within the server process |
| CLSCTX_LOCAL_SERVER | The class factory can create instances of the specified class for out-of-process clients |

It may seem a bit odd to have a context flag, since this function will be called by a *local* server, but really the idea is sound – a server could provide some utility objects that clients *or* the server could use. If CLSCTX_LOCAL_SERVER is used and the server process calls `CoCreateInstanceEx()` to create an instance of a utility object, COM will respond by creating another instance of the server. You will not necessarily want this behavior, so you can use the in-process flag to indicate that the same process should be used both for out-of-process clients, and for when the server itself is a client.

The registration flag can be:

| Flag | Description |
|---|---|
| REGCLS_SINGLEUSE | Once one client obtains the class factory, the class factory is not available to any other clients |
| REGCLS_MULTIPLEUSE | Once the server is running, multiple processes can be clients |
| REGCLS_MULTI_SEPARATE | A new instance of the server is created when there is an in-process request to activate an object |
| REGCLS_SUSPENDED | Suspends registration until COM is told to resume registration |
| REGCLS_SURROGATE | The class is in a surrogate and will forward requests for a class factory object to an object in a DLL server |

If CLSCTX_LOCAL_SERVER and REGCLS_MULTIPLEUSE are used, the server can provide multiple clients with a reference to the class object. In addition, there is an implicit CLSCTX_INPROC_SERVER, so that a request from the server for one of the objects it serves will be handled in-process, rather than through a new instance of the server. If this behavior is not required, then REGCLS_MULTI_SEPARATE can be used.

When the REGCLS_SUSPENDED flag is used, COM 'remembers' the class factory that is passed to it, but does not register it. Registration will only occur when CoResumeClassObjects() is called. This ensures that all class factories are registered at the same time, and is especially useful in the case where one object depends on other objects provided by the server, and there is a possibility that object activation will fail because the other objects have not yet been registered.

Thus, referring to the _tWinMain() code given above, if the server is apartment threaded (the main thread is in an STA) class factory registration will not be suspended. This is perfectly safe, because at this stage there is just one thread and the message queue has not yet been serviced, so any client requests for objects will be held in the message queue. If the server is free threaded, then COM will create threads to service the object creation requests. This means that potentially, a client request could come in before the class factory of another object on which it depends has been registered. In this case, therefore, all class factories are registered as suspended, and only when all class factories have been registered is CoResumeClassObjects() called to complete the registration.

The flags in this second table are exclusive except for REGCLS_SUSPENDED, which can be applied with the other flags. REGCLS_MULTIPLEUSE and REGCLS_MULTI_SEPARATE can be used with either (or both) of the context flags, but REGCLS_SINGLEUSE can only be used with CLSCTX_LOCAL_SERVER. REGCLS_SINGLEUSE means that when another request for a class factory is made, another instance of the server is created, and this makes no sense for the in-process case.

# Class Factory Interfaces

When a client calls CoCreateInstanceEx(), COM will look for the class factory for the object type, either by starting up the EXE server and waiting for the server to register the class factories and then querying its table of registered class factories, or by loading a DLL server and calling DllGetClassObject(). COM will look for a class factory with either the IClassFactory or the IClassFactory2 interface; it only knows about these two interfaces.

Once COM has got an interface pointer to one of these interfaces, it can create the object instance it requires by calling CreateInstance() on the class factory interface, and then passing the obtained interface pointer back to the client.

However, you are not constrained to using these interfaces on your class factory. If you decide that you want to use a different interface, that's fine, but your *clients* must know about the class factory interface, and rather than using CoCreateInstanceEx() to let COM manage the communication with the class factory, your client must call CoGetClassObject() to talk directly to the class factory. The final example in this chapter illustrates this procedure.

This adds great flexibility to your server, because you can do wacky things like caching object references, and load balancing. The downside of this approach is that your client is effectively forced to use C++, because Visual Basic and Java both use CoCreateInstanceEx().

## IClassFactory

IClassFactory has five methods: the IUnknown triplet, CreateInstance() and
LockServer(). CreateInstance() is passed the IID of the interface that is required on the
object, and if the object will be aggregated, it's also passed the IUnknown of the outer object. If the
class factory can create the object, and the requested interface exists on it, the interface pointer is
returned in an [out] pointer. Since CreateInstance() is passed the outer object's IUnknown
during aggregation, the ATL implementation of this method depends on the aggregation support for
the object. Chapter 2 explained how this process works: the implementation of CreateInstance()
is determined by the _AGGREGATABLE() macro used.

LockServer() is used to change the global server lock count, which holds the server in memory
even when it isn't serving any objects. The client uses this for performance reasons: if it knows that it
will need to create objects in the near future, there is no point in allowing an EXE server to die, or a
DLL server to be unloaded, only to have to be loaded again at a later stage. LockServer() is
passed TRUE to increment the lock count, and FALSE to decrement it.

ATL implements LockServer() through the two methods Lock() and Unlock(). Default
implementations of the methods are supplied by CComModule, but EXE servers override Unlock().
When the lock count falls to zero, an EXE server can die and a DLL server will be able return S_OK
to DllCanUnloadNow(). EXE servers override Unlock() because they use a monitor thread to
ensure that all the class factory objects have been completely revoked. The process is effectively the
reverse of using the REGCLS_SUSPENDED flag: the monitor thread calls
CoSuspendClassObjects() to prevent any client activation requests getting through to the class
factory objects before they can be revoked.

## IClassFactory2

In addition to the methods inherited from IClassFactory, IClassFactory2 has methods to do
with **licensing**. The concern here is one of legitimate use: how can you, an impoverished developer
writing objects, control what people can use those objects? To a certain extent, ATL helps software
thieves, because all objects have their type library bound in as a resource, so that if a thief obtains an
object server, he can find out exactly what the object will do and how to call the object's methods.

Controls present a particular problem, in that a developer will buy a control from a vendor
specifically to distribute to their customers. In this case, there must be a mechanism to prevent the
control from being used in an application other than the one from the licensed developer. These
issues are covered by the licensing support in IClassFactory2, whose interface looks like this:

```
interface IClassFactory2 : IClassFactory
{
    typedef struct tagLICINFO
    {
        LONG cbLicInfo;
        BOOL fRuntimeKeyAvail;
        BOOL fLicVerified;
    } LICINFO; .

    HRESULT GetLicInfo([out] LICINFO* pLicInfo);
    HRESULT RequestLicKey([in] DWORD dwReserved, [out] BSTR * pBstrKey);
```

```
[local] HRESULT CreateInstanceLic([in] IUnknown* pUnkOuter,
                [in] IUnknown* pUnkReserved, [in] REFIID riid,
                [in] BSTR bstrKey, [out, iid_is(riid)] PVOID* ppvObj);
}
```

I have missed out the marshaled version of `CreateInstanceLic()`, and left the `[local]` version that you will have to implement.

> *Remember that in IDL, you can give two versions of a method (or even an interface). The one that clients will use (the `[local]` version) can have parameters that normally cannot be marshaled, while the one that the marshaler will implement (the `[call_as]` version) will have parameters that can be marshaled. It is the marshaler's job to convert the unmarshalable parameters into a form that can be marshaled. Unless you intend to write a marshaler, you do not need to worry about the `[call_as]` versions.*

Licensing recognizes two situations. The first is when the control is being used in a design tool (like Visual Basic) to create a new application using the control. This requires that the developer has a **design time license**. The second situation occurs when a client is attempting to create the control as part of an application; this is a **runtime license**.

Typically, design time licenses impose a restriction that only a single machine will have the license, by making the license depend in some way on the machine on which it is installed. Tools used to design applications will create the control, and the class factory will specifically check for the design time license. This tool will create an application that uses the control, and it will place the runtime license in the application so that anyone who has a licensed version of the application will be able to use the control. This effectively means that *anyone* can create the control, as long as it is being created as part of an application, and they are not using it to design a new application. You can change the behavior if you decide that you want to force runtime license checks. Let's look at the two licensing situations in detail.

### Design-time License

A design tool should call `GetLicInfo()` to get a copy of the `LICINFO` structure for the object. In response, the class factory will determine whether the object is licensed for use in a design time tool, and it will return this result in the `fLicVerified` member of the structure. The class factory should also determine whether it can return a string that will be used as the runtime license (that is, whether licensing is available), and return this Boolean value in the `fRuntimeKeyAvail` member. A value of `TRUE` in `fLicVerified` indicates that the design tool can call `CreateInstance()` to create the object.

Older objects use a `.LIC` file to hold the design time license, and `GetLicInfo()` can verify that the appropriate file exists, and read it to ensure that it contains the correct licensing information. More recent objects use the `HKEY_CLASSES_ROOT\Licenses` key in the registry. This key contains keys that are named with a GUID; the purpose of this is to name a particular license, and has no connection to object GUIDs. In fact, you should make an effort to ensure that a license GUID isn't at all similar to your object CLSID. Each of these keys has the license as its (Default) value.

In the following screenshot, I have created a design time license that has the string "xxyyzz-=this is the license=-zzyyxx"; your own license will most likely be some encrypted text or a random string known only to the class factory. If a software thief copies the object server from your machine, they can also make a copy of the Licenses values in the registry. If you are careful not to use the object's CLSID as the license GUID, the thief will not be able to identify which is used by your object, but that wouldn't stop him from copying the entire Licenses key.

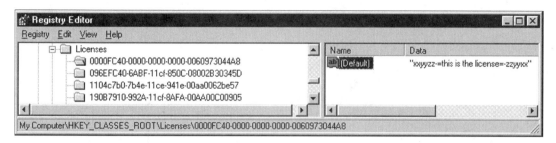

To get round this, your object installation code can create a license specific to the machine. You could, for example, encrypt a string with the machine name, so that when validating the license, you can decrypt it and compare it against the current machine name. Of course, only the class factory will know the key used for the encryption. You can extend this idea further, so that (for example) the license key could contain the installation date, enabling you to put a time limit on the object. Alternatively, it could have a number that indicates a usage count that is decremented every time the object is created. Both of these techniques are useful for products distributed as shareware.

As I mentioned above, the fRuntimeKeyAvail member specifies whether the class factory can return a runtime license string. If it can, the design time tool can call RequestLicKey() to get a copy of this string and cache it in the application. This key is passed at runtime to CreateInstanceLic() when creating the object. This string can be anything you like, but note that it is generated by the class factory running on the application designer's machine, and passed to the class factory running on your customer's machine, so don't generate a machine-specific string.

The design time tool uses CreateInstance() if it needs to create the object, and this method should check that the design time license is valid before creating the object. If a design time license does not exist, the class factory should return CLASS_E_NOTLICENSED.

### Runtime License

When an object is created at runtime (that is, within an application and not within a design tool) the CreateInstanceLic() method is called. This method has two parameters in addition to those it has in common with CreateInstance(). One of these is a reserved pointer that should be NULL, and the other is used to pass the runtime license string to the class factory. The string that is used here is the string obtained by the design tool with RequestLicKey(), and the object just has to compare it with the string it has cached to see if the application can use the object. The application should *not* call CreateInstance(), because unless the application is run on the same machine as the design time tool, the method will fail.

The design time tool will embed the runtime license in the application in an encrypted form, so no one will be able to use reverse engineering tools to get hold of it. No other application will be able to create the control, since they will have neither the design time license (so CreateInstance() will fail) nor the runtime license (and so will CreateInstanceLic()).

# The Default ATL Class Factories

ATL provides several class factories, and even allows you to define your own. Selecting a class factory is as simple as providing the appropriate macro in your ATL class:

| Macro | Description |
|---|---|
| DECLARE_CLASSFACTORY() | Declares an implementation of IClassFactory |
| DECLARE_CLASSFACTORY2() | Declares an implementation of IClassFactory2 |
| DECLARE_CLASSFACTORY_AUTO_THREAD() | Declares a class factory that can be used in multiple apartments |
| DECLARE_CLASSFACTORY_SINGLETON() | A class factory that only returns references to a single object |
| DECLARE_CLASSFACTORY_EX() | Specifies the class used to implement the class factory |

Your ATL class will derive from CComCoClass<>, and so by default DECLARE_CLASSFACTORY() will be declared. If you are creating a control, you may decide to use DECLARE_CLASSFACTORY2() instead. This defines the class factory in terms of IClassFactory2, which adds licensing support, but note that you will have to supply some extra code yourself, as will be described below. Using these class factory macros overrides the one used by the base class, and you can place them anywhere in your class.

If you choose to use thread pooling in your server, you will have to use a class factory that takes this into account. Chapter 7 will go into the details of thread pooling, but basically the CComAutoThreadModule<> class will create a specified number of threads, each in an STA. When a request comes in to create an object instance, it will use a round-robin routine to select a thread from the pool and create the object on that thread. Of course, this complicates the module code because lock counts have to be per-apartment, and the code has to make sure that all the threads are properly closed down when the server unloads. Since object activation requests will come in on the main thread, and the object will be created an a different thread, this means that the class factory will need to manage cross thread communications, and this is the reason for a separate class factory macro.

There are some cases when there will only ever be one instance of a class, and so the class factory will only ever return references to this instance. For example, consider the situation where you have a logging application that will accept messages and log these to a single resource – say, a file. Since there is just one instance of this resource, it means that when two clients say, "Create me a logger object," the class factory should return an interface pointer to the same object. Such an object is called a singleton, and requires a special class factory that will only return a reference to this single object.

Finally, the `CreateInstance()` method on `IClassFactory` only allows you to pass information about the interface of the object you are interested in, *and nothing else.* If you want to pass other information, then you will need to provide your own class factory. Note that this is your own implementation of `IClassFactory` (or a class derived from it, like `IClassfactory2`), and not an implementation of your own class creation interface. If you decide that you want to provide your own class creation interface, you will need to provide stub versions of the `IClassFactory` methods (that is, return `E_NOTIMPL`) on the class factory, and add your custom class factory interface. The final example in this chapter illustrates how to do this.

# Class Factory

The default class factory supplied through `DECLARE_CLASSFACTORY()` is suitable in most situations. The only point you need to be aware of is that `CreateInstance()` will create your object on the heap using `new`, and then call `FinalConstruct()` to allow the object to complete its construction. Thus, you have to ensure that any construction code that uses virtual methods must be placed in `FinalConstruct()`, because the object vtable will not be created when the constructor is called.

# Licensed Objects

Licensed objects must implement `IClassFactory2`, as explained earlier. Any calls to `CreateInstance()` should fail with `CLASS_E_NOTLICENSED` if the design time license has not been validated. If an application is creating the object at runtime it should call `CreateInstanceLic()` and pass a runtime license key. If this key is correct, then the object will be created.

You add support for `IClassFactory2` by using `DECLARE_CLASSFACTORY2()` in your ATL class. This will supply your class factory through `CComClassFactory2<>`. The macro takes a class name as a parameter, because `CComClassFactory2<>` depends on three methods:

```
class CMyLicense
{
protected:
    static BOOL VerifyLicenseKey(BSTR bstr);
    static BOOL GetLicenseKey(DWORD dwReserved, BSTR* pBstr);
    static BOOL IsLicenseValid();
};
```

These methods are described here:

| Method | Description |
| --- | --- |
| `VerifyLicenseKey()` | Returns TRUE if the passed-in runtime license key is correct |
| `GetLicenseKey()` | Returns the runtime license for this object in a BSTR |
| `IsLicenseValid()` | Returns TRUE if the design time license is present and correct |

Thus, you need to create a class that has these three `static` methods, and pass its name to `DECLARE_CLASSFACTORY2()`. Furthermore, note that an object that implements `IClassFactory2` should use the `[licensed]` attribute on its `coclass`. The Object Wizard will not do this for you, and so you will have to edit the project's IDL by hand.

As I mentioned earlier, you will generally use the `Licenses` key to store license keys, associating them with a GUID. The *installation* program that you use to install the object on your customer's machine should set this registry key. To do this, I have written the `LicenseGen` utility that you will find with the code for this chapter. This utility has the following command line:

```
LicenseGen [-uuid:uuid] [-output:file] -key:encrypt "string"
```

Here, the `key` switch and the quoted string are mandatory. The `string` is encrypted by a simple `XOR` routine, using the string passed in as `encrypt`. This is then written either to a registry script, or directly to the registry.

If a `uuid` is supplied and is valid (that is, in registry format including the braces `{ }`), then this will be used as the GUID for the license string. Otherwise, a GUID will be generated for you. If the `output` switch is present, a registry script will be generated in the file named in `file`; if not, the data is written to the registry.

I usually generate a GUID and add a line in my installation script like this:

```
LicenseGen -uuid:{8B06C8C0-BF4E-11D1-9B16-0060973044A8}
           -key:RTGrimes %COMPUTERNAME%
```

The GUID has been generated separately, and is used by `IsLicenseValid()` to obtain the license on the current machine and compare it with what the object thinks the license should be. I pass `%COMPUTERNAME%` as the string to encrypt, so that the name of the machine on which the installation script is run is used, and so the string will be useless on any other machine.

To use this data, I implement `IsLicenseValid()` like this:

```cpp
LPCTSTR CMyLicense::m_strLic = _T("8B06C8C0-BF4E-11D1-9B16-0060973044A8");
LPCTSTR CmyLicence::m_strEncryptKey = _T("RTGrimes");

BOOL CMyLicense::IsLicenseValid()
{
    TCHAR strMachine[MAX_COMPUTERNAME_LENGTH + 1];
    DWORD dwSize = MAX_COMPUTERNAME_LENGTH + 1;
    GetComputerName(strMachine, &dwSize);

    TCHAR strEncrypt[MAX_COMPUTERNAME_LENGTH * 2 + 1];
    Encrypt(_T(m_strEncryptKey), strMachine, strEncrypt);

    // Get the data from the registry
    HKEY hKey;
    if(RegOpenKey(HKEY_CLASSES_ROOT, _T("Licenses"), &hKey) != ERROR_SUCCESS)
        return FALSE;

    HKEY hKeyNew;
    if(RegOpenKey(hKey, m_strLic, &hKeyNew) != ERROR_SUCCESS)
    {
        RegCloseKey(hKey);
        return FALSE;
    }
```

```
        TCHAR strRegVal[MAX_COMPUTERNAME_LENGTH * 2 + 1];
        LONG lSize = MAX_COMPUTERNAME_LENGTH * 2 + 1;
        if(RegQueryValue(hKeyNew, NULL, strRegVal, &lSize) != ERROR_SUCCESS)
        {
            RegCloseKey(hKeyNew);
            RegCloseKey(hKey);
            return FALSE;
        }

        RegCloseKey(hKeyNew);
        RegCloseKey(hKey);
        return(_tcsicmp(strEncrypt, strRegVal) == 0);
    }
```

In the first part of the code I get hold of the computer name and encrypt it, just as `LicenseGen` does. `Encrypt()` looks like this:

```
int CMyLicense::Encrypt(LPCTSTR strKey, LPCTSTR strString, LPTSTR strReturn)
{
    LPCTSTR ptr = strKey;

    while(*strString != 0)
    {
        TCHAR ch;
        ch = strString[0] ^ ptr[0];
        strReturn[1] = (ch & 0xf) > 9 ? '7' + (ch & 0xf) : '0' + (ch & 0xf);
        ch = ch >> 4;
        strReturn[0] = (ch & 0xf) > 9 ? '7' + (ch & 0xf) : '0' + (ch & 0xf);
        strString++;
        strReturn += 2;
        if(ptr[1] == 0)
            ptr = strKey;
        else
            ptr++;
    }

    *strReturn = 0;
    return 1;
}
```

The routine is simple. I just iterate through the string to encrypt, and XOR each character with a corresponding character in the key. Since this may return an unprintable character, I convert the character to a hexadecimal value in string format. This means that the encrypted string will be twice the length of the string that is to be encrypted.

Once the computer name has been encrypted, `IsLicenseValid()` reads the default value of the license from the registry and then compares the two. If they are the same, then the license is valid.

## Example: An Object that uses IClassFactory2

For this example, I created a DLL ATL COM server called `Licensed`. To demonstrate the principles, I added a Lite Control, so that I could test it out with Visual Basic 6 and Internet Explorer 4. The control's Short Name is `Status`.

Within the control header file (Status.h), I added this class:

```
//////////////////////////////////////////////////////////////////
// CMyLicense
class CMyLicense
{
protected:
    static BOOL VerifyLicenseKey(BSTR bstr);
    static BOOL GetLicenseKey(DWORD, BSTR* pBstr);
    static BOOL IsLicenseValid();
    static int Encrypt(LPCTSTR strKey, LPCTSTR strString, LPTSTR strReturn);

    static LPCTSTR m_strLic;
    static LPCTSTR m_strEncryptKey;
    static CComBSTR m_bstrRuntime;
};
```

This is used in CStatus:

```
public:
    CStatus()
    {
    }

DECLARE_REGISTRY_RESOURCEID(IDR_STATUS)
DECLARE_CLASSFACTORY2(CMyLicense)
```

The implementations of these methods are in Status.cpp:

```
LPCTSTR CMyLicense::m_strLic = _T("8B06C8C0-BF4E-11D1-9B16-0060973044A8");
LPCTSTR CMyLicense::m_strEncryptKey = _T("RTGrimes");
CComBSTR CMyLicense::m_bstrRuntime = L"This control is licensed";

BOOL CMyLicense::VerifyLicenseKey(BSTR bstr)
{
    return (wcscmp(bstr, m_bstrRuntime.m_str) == 0);
}

BOOL CMyLicense::GetLicenseKey(DWORD, BSTR* pBstr)
{
    return m_bstrRuntime.CopyTo(*pBstr);
}
```

IsLicenseValid() and Encrypt() have been given earlier. The two methods given above simply retrieve the static string "This control is licensed", and compare a parameter with this string. The DECLARE_CLASSFACTORY2() macro in the control class ensures that the class factory is implemented by CComClassFactory2<>, and that this class has access to CMyLicense.

These methods will suffice, but to get a better insight into what is happening, we need a bit more code. To test to see whether the license has been checked, the OnDraw() method (which I have moved from Status.h to Status.cpp) needs to determine if the licenses have been checked and whether the check returned TRUE or FALSE. To do this, I have added two public static data members to CMyLicense:

```
    static CComBSTR m_bstrRuntime;

public:
    static LONG m_bRuntimeValid;
    static LONG m_bDesigntimeValid;
};
```

These are initialized at the top of Status.cpp:

```
LONG CMyLicense::m_bRuntimeValid = 0;
LONG CMyLicense::m_bDesigntimeValid = 0;
```

> *Note that these members are only here for debugging purposes: I have added them so that you can*
> *see when the licenses of this control are being checked. They have to be* static *so that the*
> *methods in* CMyLicense *can access them. However, because they are* static*, they are*
> *effectively global and so you should only ever access them from one object. In the following tests,*
> *you will only create one instance of the control, so their* static *nature is not a problem.*

I use the least significant bit to establish whether the license has been checked, and bit 1 to take the result of that check:

```
BOOL CMyLicense::VerifyLicenseKey(BSTR bstr)
{
    BOOL bChecked;
    m_bRuntimeValid = 1;
    bChecked = (wcscmp(bstr, m_bstrRuntime.m_str) == 0);
    if(bChecked)
        m_bRuntimeValid |= 0x2;
    return bChecked;
}
```

IsLicenseValid() is changed accordingly:

```
BOOL CMyLicense::IsLicenseValid()
{
    m_bDesigntimeValid = 1;
```

and

```
    BOOL bChecked;
    bChecked = (_tcsicmp(strEncrypt, strRegVal) == 0);
    if(bChecked)
        m_bDesigntimeValid |= 0x2;
    return bChecked;
}
```

Finally, the OnDraw() method looks like this:

```
HRESULT CStatus::OnDraw(ATL_DRAWINFO& di)
{
    USES_CONVERSION;
    TEXTMETRIC tm;
```

```
      GetTextMetrics(di.hdcDraw, &tm);
      int iHeight = tm.tmHeight;
      int iWidth = tm.tmAveCharWidth;

      RECT& rc = *(RECT*)di.prcBounds;
      Rectangle(di.hdcDraw, rc.left, rc.top, rc.right, rc.bottom);

      CComBSTR bstrText;
      int yPos = rc.top + iHeight / 2;
      int xPos = rc.left + iWidth / 2;
      if(CMyLicense::m_bDesigntimeValid & 1)
      {
         bstrText = L"Designtime checked";
         ExtTextOut(di.hdcDraw, xPos, yPos, 0, NULL,
                          OLE2CT(bstrText.m_str), bstrText.Length(), NULL);
         yPos += iHeight;
         if(CMyLicense::m_bDesigntimeValid & 2)
            bstrText = L"Designtime valid";
         else
            bstrText = L"Designtime not valid";
         ExtTextOut(di.hdcDraw, xPos, yPos, 0, NULL,
                          OLE2CT(bstrText.m_str), bstrText.Length(), NULL);
         yPos += iHeight;
      }
      else
      {
         bstrText = L"Designtime not checked";
         ExtTextOut(di.hdcDraw, xPos, yPos, 0, NULL,
                          OLE2CT(bstrText.m_str), bstrText.Length(), NULL);
         yPos += iHeight;
      }

      if(CMyLicense::m_bRuntimeValid & 1)
      {
         bstrText = L"Runtime checked";
         ExtTextOut(di.hdcDraw, xPos, yPos, 0, NULL,
                          OLE2CT(bstrText.m_str), bstrText.Length(), NULL);
         yPos += iHeight;
         if(CMyLicense::m_bRuntimeValid & 2)
            bstrText = L"Runtime valid";
         else
            bstrText = L"Runtime not valid";
         ExtTextOut(di.hdcDraw, xPos, yPos, 0, NULL,
                          OLE2CT(bstrText.m_str), bstrText.Length(), NULL);
      }
      else
      {
         bstrText = L"Runtime not checked";
         ExtTextOut(di.hdcDraw, xPos, yPos, 0, NULL,
                          OLE2CT(bstrText.m_str), bstrText.Length(), NULL);
      }

      return S_OK;
   }
```

I simply write out on the control surface whether the licenses have been checked, and whether the check was validated. To install the control, you need to run `LicenseGen`:

```
LicenseGen -uuid:{8B06C8C0-BF4E-11D1-9B16-0060973044A8}
           -key:RTGrimes %COMPUTERNAME%
```

To test the control, I created an incredibly simple Visual Basic application whose form just has a `Status` control on it. When I add the control to the form, I see this:

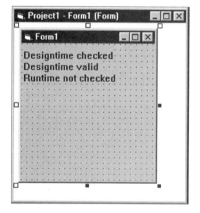

That is, when Visual Basic adds the control to the form, it checks the design time license. In this case, it found it was valid. If you haven't installed the control correctly – if one of the parameters to `LicenseGen` was not correct, for example – the control will not be created. Notice that the runtime license is *not* checked.

When I run this application in the Visual Basic IDE, I get:

In other words, when the application is run in the IDE, the *design time* license must be valid. If you make an EXE for this application, the Visual Basic compiler calls `IsLicenseValid()` to ensure that you can create a project based on this control, and then `GetLicenseKey()` to get the runtime license. This key is placed in the executable in an encrypted form. When you run the executable, you get this:

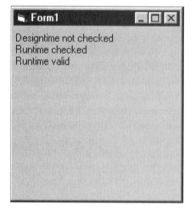

An interesting further check is to run the control under Internet Explorer 4. To do this, load the Wizard-generated page, `Status.htm`:

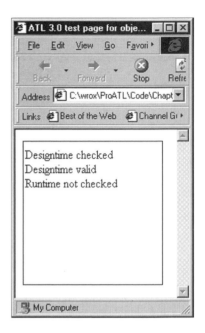

This probably isn't the result you were expecting – you'd have thought that a control on a web page would use a runtime license. The reason why these values are shown is that Internet Explorer doesn't know that the control has a license, and so it blindly calls `IClassFactory::CreateInstance()`, which checks for the design time license. Since my machine has the design time license, the control creation succeeds, but if the design time license is not valid (or not present) then the control will not be loaded.

What you want is for Internet Explorer to call `IClassFactory2::CreateInstanceLic()`, passing the runtime license. However, that would mean embedding the runtime license somewhere on the web page, so that Internet Explorer can extract it to pass to `CreateInstanceLic()`. Because HTML files can be viewed by any client once downloaded, this would make the runtime license insecure: anyone could copy the control and its license key (whether encrypted or not) and use it on their page. This wasn't a problem with the Visual Basic application, because the runtime license key was saved encrypted in the compiled executable. Even looking through the executable with a hex file viewer, it is not clear where the key is stored.

Help is at hand: Microsoft has recognized that there is a problem and come up with a secure mechanism for providing runtime licenses. Instead of embedding the information on the web page, it is held in a separate file called the **license package** (**LPK**) **file**. This file contains the runtime licenses for one or more controls in an encoded form, and is held on the web server. To use the LPK file, an HTML page should create an instance of the **license manager**, and give it a reference to the LPK file using a relative or absolute URL. The license manager loads the LPK file, checks it for the license for the control, decrypts the license, and caches it. When Internet Explorer 4 comes across an `<OBJECT>` tag to load a control on the page, it will see from the license manager that a license is available. Thus, it can create the control by calling `IClassFactory2::CreateInstanceLic()` with the cached key.

The LPK file is created with the `LPK_Tool.exe` tool, which is supplied with the Internet Client SDK. This tool merely calls `IClassFactory2::GetLicenseKey()` on a specified control and then creates the LPK file:

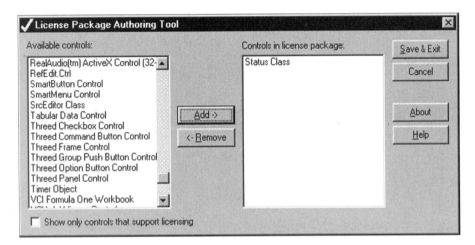

When you click on <u>S</u>ave & Exit, the tool will create this file:

```
LPK License Package
//////////////////////////////////////////////////////////////////////
//   WARNING:  The information in this file is protected by       //
//   copyright law and international treaty provisions.           //
//   Unauthorized reproduction or distribution of this file, or  //
//   any portion of it, may result in severe criminal and civil  //
//   penalties, and will be prosecuted to the maximum extent     //
//   possible under the law.  Further, you may not reverse       //
//   engineer, decompile, or disassemble the file.               //
//////////////////////////////////////////////////////////////////////
{3d25aba1-caec-11cf-b34a-00aa00a28331}
UGKnvkLC0RGbGgBglzBEqg=
AQAAAA=
kLmcptS/0RGbFwBglzBEqBgAAAB
UAGgAaQBzACAAYwBvAG4AdAByAG8AbAAgAGkAcwAgAGwAaQBjAGUAbgBzAGUAZAA=
```

The GUID is a version string for the license manager, and the rest is the license information in uuencoded form. You can change the HTML file to reference this:

```
<HTML>
<HEAD>
<TITLE>ATL 3.0 test page for object Status</TITLE>
</HEAD>
<BODY>
<OBJECT CLASSID="CLSID:5220CB21-C88D-11CF-B347-00AA00A28331">
<PARAM NAME="LPKPath" VALUE="Status.lpk">
</OBJECT>
<OBJECT ID="Status" CLASSID="CLSID:A69CB990-BFD4-11D1-9B17-0060973044A8">
</OBJECT>
</BODY>
</HTML>
```

The first <OBJECT> tag creates the license manager, and Status.lpk is the (single) LPK file for the page. If there are several licensed controls on the page, they should all be included in the same LPK file. The second <OBJECT> tag then creates the control.

Here is the result of using the HTML file shown above:

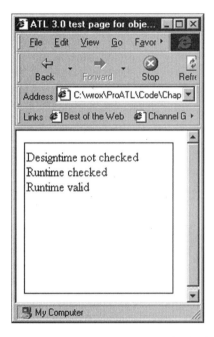

This time, you can see that the design time license is ignored, but that the runtime license is checked and found to be valid, as we wanted.

# Singleton Objects

Singleton objects are useful when you're modeling an object of which there absolutely *must* be just one instance. This is achieved with a class factory that will only create one instance of the object; for all subsequent requests for the same object, the class factory will just return a reference to the single object it has cached.

Sometimes, singleton behavior can be simulated in other ways. For example, if you're writing a logging component that must have exclusive access to a persistent resource (a file, for example), you could argue that this is a good candidate for a singleton. Whenever a client tries to get a reference to the component, the singleton class factory will ensure that the returned reference will be to the single resource. Synchronization of the access to the resource will be achieved by the message queue in the server (if apartment threading is used) or by your own synchronization mechanism (if the server is free threaded).

Another design could be to allow multiple instances of the *component*, but to use a synchronization method when a component attempts to access the *resource*. So, for example, you could obtain a mutex at the start of the AddMessage() method to write data to the log, and release the mutex at the end of the method. If the server is free threaded, then you will have already written such a mechanism.

Note also that if you want there to be one object *per machine*, the object server must be packaged in an EXE. If the server is packaged in a DLL, then every client that loads the DLL will get the singleton class factory, and thus the singleton is now ensuring that there is only one object instance *per process*.

Once you have decided to use a singleton, the actual coding is simple: you include the DECLARE_CLASSFACTORY_SINGLETON() macro in the ATL class. This uses CComClassFactorySingleton<> for the class that implements the class factory:

```
template <class T>
class CComClassFactorySingleton : public CComClassFactory
{
public:
    void FinalRelease();
    STDMETHOD(CreateInstance)(LPUNKNOWN pUnkOuter,
                                            REFIID riid, void** ppvObj);
    CComObjectGlobal<T> m_Obj;
};
```

The singleton object is a data member of the class factory, so when the class factory object is first created, an instance of the singleton object is created. The constructor of CComObjectGlobal<> calls the FinalConstruct() method of the singleton class, so you do not have to call the static CreateInstance() as is necessary when you use CComObject<>. When a client calls IClassfactory::CreateInstance(), rather than creating a new instance of an object, the requested interface pointer is obtained from the embedded object, m_Obj.

When there is more than one client, they will all have a reference to the single object, but each will have a separate stub object to manage the connection to the proxy in the client. When the server shuts down, it needs to ensure that all these stub objects are destroyed, indicating to any connected proxies that the object has died. To do this, FinalRelease() calls the API function CoDisconnectObject() on the cached object.

Stub objects are managed by the stub manager that COM creates in the object apartment. When the object server calls CoDisconnectObject(), COM will destroy the stub manager, which means that if there are any connected clients, the stub objects that their proxies are connected to will be destroyed. The client will discover this the next time that it makes a call to the object, but this is perfectly safe because although the proxy will try to call a non-existent stub, it will handle the problem by returning a failure HRESULT to the client.

This method of implementing a singleton object is useful in most cases. However, be aware that an object server should start up as quickly as possible, and this start up includes registering all the class factories in the server. Singleton class factories create an instance of the object, and if this object has a lengthy start up – creating objects within FinalConstruct(), for example – then this may cause an unacceptable delay.

You should also note, though, that no QueryInterface() is called until CreateInstance() has completed, so you can implement a tear-off interface on the object and put the resource initialization in the constructor of the tear-off class. If you do this, then the resource initialization will be carried out *after* the server has started, when COM is happy that the server has initialized correctly.

## *Example: Logger Object*

The example in this section is quite simple: it implements a logger object that saves messages to a file with a date stamp. To ensure that only one client has access to the file at a time, it is implemented as a singleton object. To begin this example, create an EXE COM server, and call the project LoggerEXE. Once AppWizard has finished, insert a Simple Object with the Short Name of Logger; give it a Dual interface, and opt to Support Connection Points. Clients will use this last feature to get notifications of when new items are added to the log.

By default, Wizard-generated classes use CComClassFactory. To get the singleton class factory, add the following line to CLogger; then all you need to do is implement the ATL object class.

```
public:
    CLogger()
    {
    }
```

```
DECLARE_CLASSFACTORY_SINGLETON(CLogger)
```

> This is in contrast to **DECLARE_CLASSFACTORY2()** where to get the class
> factory support, you had to provide extra code of your own.

When the object is created, it will open its log file using the Win32 API CreateFile(). Then, when the object is destroyed (which happens when the last client releases its interface reference) it will close the file again. To deal with this, add FinalConstruct() and FinalRelease() methods, a data member for the file handle, and a data member to hold the file name:

```
public:
    CLogger()
    {
    }

    HRESULT FinalConstruct();
    void FinalRelease();

    // Rest of the class...

// Other members
private:
    HANDLE m_hFile;
    static LPCTSTR m_strFile;
};
```

These are implemented like this:

```
LPCTSTR CLogger::m_strFile = _T("LoggerEXE.dat");

HRESULT CLogger::FinalConstruct()
{
    m_hFile = CreateFile(m_strFile, GENERIC_READ | GENERIC_WRITE,
                                    0, NULL, OPEN_ALWAYS, 0, NULL);

    if(m_hFile == INVALID_HANDLE_VALUE)
    {
```

```
        m_hFile = NULL;
        return HRESULT_FROM_WIN32(GetLastError());
    }
    return S_OK;
}
```

```
void CLogger::FinalRelease()
{
    if(m_hFile)
        CloseHandle(m_hFile);
}
```

Since only this object will have access to the file, it is opened in such a way as to deny access to anyone else. The file is called `LoggerEXE.dat`, but you could make it more configurable by reading the file name from a key in the registry. I have resisted the temptation of adding a `FileName` property because writing to this property would make no sense. A client getting a reference to the singleton object will not know if it is the first to do so, and so there will be no concept of initialization. In fact, the filename is an implementation detail, because the singleton could implement the same functionality with a database, and a client would have no interest in reading the filename.

I have used `LoggerEXE.dat` with no path, which means that if COM starts the EXE, then the file will be created in your system directory (on NT this is usually `\winnt\system32`) since this is the 'current directory' for the SCM. If you start the server yourself (to debug it, for example) then the 'current directory' will be your project directory. I mention this so you're not surprised that the results are different when you debug the application compared to allowing COM to start the server.

The `ILogger` interface needs a method to add messages to the log file. This method is called `AddMessage()`, and you should add it using ClassView:

```
STDMETHOD(AddMessage)(/*[in]*/ BSTR strMsg);
```

I have decided to restrict the log file to contain only 10 messages, and so only the last 10 will be held. This value is another implementation detail, and for convenience it is held as a constant in the class, but you could very easily load the value from the registry in `FinalConstruct()` to allow it to be configurable. Thus, the class declaration has:

```
private:
    HANDLE m_hFile;
    static const ULONG m_lMaxRecords;
    static LPCTSTR m_strFile;
```

And the implementation file has:

```
const ULONG CLogger::m_lMaxRecords = 10;
```

The messages are added to the file along with the time that the message was received by the component. You can imagine that the file is made up of records like this:

| DWORD dwSize |
| --- |
| FILETIME stLogged |
| TCHAR string[] |

This is intended to indicate that the data is held as a DWORD, followed by a FILETIME, and then a variable length string. These records vary in length: the first member is the total size in bytes, and this is followed by the time that the message was logged. After that is the NUL-terminated string that holds the message. The length of the string, in bytes, is therefore dwSize - sizeof(FILETIME) - sizeof(DWORD).

To allow a client to have access to the data in the file, the Logger object implements a collection. I'll provide full details of this later on, but you can rest assured that it will have a Count property that gives the number of items. The get_Count() method will be useful in writing data to the file, so the read-only Count property should be added to ILogger using ClassView. The type of the property is long, and it's implemented like this:

```
STDMETHODIMP CLogger::get_Count(long *pVal)
{
    // Get to the start of the file
    SetFilePointer(m_hFile, 0, NULL, FILE_BEGIN);

    // Now read all the records using the size to skip over each
    *pVal = 0;
    DWORD dwSize;
    DWORD dwBytesRead;
    while(ReadFile(m_hFile, (LPVOID)&dwSize,
                                    sizeof(DWORD), &dwBytesRead, NULL))
    {
        if(dwBytesRead > 0)
        {
            SetFilePointer(m_hFile, dwSize - sizeof(DWORD),
                                        NULL, FILE_CURRENT);
            (*pVal)++;
        }
        else
            break;
    }
    return S_OK;
}
```

This code reads each record and increments a count. Notice that the actual *data* of each record is not read – all that's retrieved is the size, which is used to skip to the next record. Now you can implement AddMessage():

```
STDMETHODIMP CLogger::AddMessage(BSTR strMsg)
{
    USES_CONVERSION;
    DWORD dwSize;

    get_Count((long*)&dwSize);
    if(dwSize >= m_lMaxRecords)
    {
```

```
    // Need to delete excess records and move the other records forward
    DWORD dwRecSize;
    DWORD dwBytesRead;

    // Get to the start of the file
    SetFilePointer(m_hFile, 0, NULL, FILE_BEGIN);

    // Move past the number of records we want to discard
    DWORD dwCount = dwSize - m_lMaxRecords + 1;
    while(dwCount > 0)
    {
        ReadFile(m_hFile, (LPVOID)&dwRecSize, sizeof(DWORD),
                                                    &dwBytesRead, NULL);
        // Move forward that number of bytes
        SetFilePointer(m_hFile, dwRecSize - sizeof(DWORD),
                                                    NULL, FILE_CURRENT);
        dwCount--;
    }

    // Get the size of a page
    SYSTEM_INFO sysInfo;
    GetSystemInfo(&sysInfo);
    LPBYTE pPageFile = new BYTE[sysInfo.dwPageSize];

    // Create a temporary file
    TCHAR strTemp[MAX_PATH + 1];
    TCHAR strTempFile[MAX_PATH + 1];
    GetTempPath(MAX_PATH, strTemp);
    GetTempFileName(strTemp, _T("LOG"), 0, strTempFile);
    HANDLE hTempFile;
    hTempFile = CreateFile(strTempFile, GENERIC_READ | GENERIC_WRITE,
                                    0, NULL, OPEN_ALWAYS, 0, NULL);
    while(ReadFile(m_hFile, pPageFile, sysInfo.dwPageSize,
                                                    &dwBytesRead, NULL))
    {
        if(dwBytesRead == 0)
            break;
        DWORD dwBytesWritten;
        WriteFile(
                hTempFile, pPageFile, dwBytesRead, &dwBytesWritten, NULL);
    }

    CloseHandle(m_hFile);
    m_hFile = hTempFile;

    // Delete old file and rename temporary file
    DeleteFile(m_strFile);
    MoveFile(strTempFile, m_strFile);
    delete [] pPageFile;
}

// Move to the end of the file
SetFilePointer(m_hFile, 0, NULL, FILE_END);
CComBSTR bstrMsg(strMsg);
dwSize = sizeof(FILETIME) + sizeof(DWORD) +
                                (bstrMsg.Length() + 1) * sizeof(TCHAR);
```

```
    // Write the data to the file
    DWORD dwBytesWritten;
    WriteFile(m_hFile, &dwSize, sizeof(DWORD), &dwBytesWritten, NULL);

    FILETIME now;
    SYSTEMTIME st;
    DWORD dwBytesWritten;
    GetLocalTime(&st);
    WriteFile(m_hFile, &dwSize, sizeof(DWORD), &dwBytesWritten, NULL);
    SystemTimeToFileTime(&st, &now);
    WriteFile(m_hFile, &now, sizeof(FILETIME), &dwBytesWritten, NULL);
    WriteFile(m_hFile, OLE2CT(bstrMsg.m_str),
        (bstrMsg.Length() + 1) * sizeof(TCHAR), &dwBytesWritten, NULL);
    return S_OK;
}
```

This starts by getting the number of records in the file, and if this is greater than (or equal to) the maximum number allowed, then the excess records are discarded. The code does this by moving past all the records we want to discard, and then creating a temporary file. The records that we want to preserve are copied in chunks the size of the system page size to the temporary file. Once this is done, the old file is deleted, and the temporary file renamed.

Next, the file pointer is moved to the end of the file and the record data is written. First the record size is calculated and written to the file, then the time is obtained and written too. Notice that I call `GetLocalTime()` to take into account time zones and daylight saving; I convert this to a `FILETIME` because it is a compact form to save in the file. Finally, the message is written to the file.

A client will want to obtain the message text and the time that the message was logged. To give access to this data, I have added an enumerator property to the `Logger` object and this, combined with the `Count` property, allows the object to be treated as a collection of messages. To give access to both the message text and the time, the project has another object type called `Msg`.

So, you need to add a new **Simple Object** to the project with a **Short Name** of `Msg`. Use ClassView to add two read only properties called `Message` and `Time`. The former is of type `BSTR` and the latter is of type `DATE`. The reasons why these are read only are that `AddMessage()` is just used to log a value, and the `Msg` object is only used to return data.

Edit `Msg.h` to have two data members for these properties:

```
// IMsg
public:
    STDMETHOD(get_Time)(/*[out, retval]*/ DATE *pVal);
    STDMETHOD(get_Message)(/*[out, retval]*/ BSTR *pVal);

private:
    CComBSTR m_Message;
    DATE   m_Date;
};
```

This object is implemented like this:

```
STDMETHODIMP CMsg::get_Message(BSTR *pVal)
{
    return m_Message.CopyTo(*pVal);
}

STDMETHODIMP CMsg::get_Time(DATE *pVal)
{
    *pVal = m_Date;
    return S_OK;
}
```

> *At this point, it is interesting to look at the IDL generated. Adding the* Logger *object with connection point support will add* ILogger *outside the* library *block, and* _ILoggerEvents *inside the* library *block. When you added the* Msg *object, Object Wizard will have added the* IMsg *interface inside the* library *block. This is a bug – Object Wizard should have added the* IMsg *interface to the IDL outside the* library *block. If you only intend to use type library marshaling, however, this is not a problem.*

The next task is to add a read-only property called _NewEnum to ILogger. Use ClassView to add this property with the type LPUNKNOWN, and to have the [restricted] attribute. The IDL for ILogger should look like this:

```
interface ILogger : IDispatch
{
    [id(1)] HRESULT AddMessage([in] BSTR strMsg);
    [propget, id(2)] HRESULT Count([out, retval] long *pVal);
    [propget, id(-4), restricted] HRESULT _NewEnum(
                                    [out, retval] LPUNKNOWN *pVal);
};
```

Notice that the DISPID of _NewEnum has to be changed to DISPID_NEWENUM (a value of -4) by hand. The Add Property... Wizard will not allow you to add a negative DISPID.

Add a #include for Msg.h to the top of Logger.h so that you can create Msg objects in the Logger code. The access method for _NewEnum is implemented like this:

```
STDMETHODIMP CLogger::get__NewEnum(LPUNKNOWN *pVal)
{
    // Get the data in an array
    long lSize;
    *pVal = NULL;
    get_Count(&lSize);
    VARIANT* varArray = new VARIANT[lSize];

    // Get to the start of the file
    SetFilePointer(m_hFile, 0, NULL, FILE_BEGIN);
    long lCount = 0;
    while(lSize > lCount)
    {
        DWORD dwSize;
```

```
      DWORD dwBytesRead;
      FILETIME FileTime;
      ReadFile(m_hFile,(LPVOID)&dwSize, sizeof(DWORD),
                                              &dwBytesRead, NULL);
      ReadFile(m_hFile,(LPVOID)&FileTime, sizeof(FILETIME),
                                              &dwBytesRead, NULL);
      LPTSTR str = new TCHAR[(dwSize - sizeof(DWORD) -
                                 sizeof(FILETIME))/sizeof(TCHAR)];
      ReadFile(m_hFile,(LPVOID)str, dwSize - sizeof(DWORD) -
                             sizeof(FILETIME), &dwBytesRead, NULL);

      // Create a Msg object
      CComObject<CMsg>* pObj;
      CComObject<CMsg>::CreateInstance(&pObj);

      SYSTEMTIME SystemTime;
      FileTimeToSystemTime(&FileTime, &SystemTime);
      DATE Date;
      SystemTimeToVariantTime(&SystemTime, &Date);
      pObj->m_Date = Date;
      pObj->m_bstrMessage = str;

      CComPtr<IMsg> pMsg;
      pObj->QueryInterface(&pMsg);
      pMsg->put_Message(CComBSTR(str));

      // Write the object to the array
      CComVariant var(pMsg);
      VariantInit(&varArray[lCount]);
      var.Detach(&varArray[lCount]);
      lCount++;
   }

   typedef CComObject<CComEnum<IEnumVARIANT,
                          &IID_IEnumVARIANT,
                          VARIANT,
                          _Copy<VARIANT> > > EnumVar;
   EnumVar* pVar = new EnumVar;

   pVar->Init(&varArray[0], &varArray[lSize], NULL, AtlFlagCopy);
   HRESULT hRes;
   hRes = pVar->QueryInterface(pVal);

   lCount = 0;
   while(lSize > lCount)
   {
      VariantClear(&varArray[lCount]);
      lCount++;
   }

   delete [] varArray;
   return hRes;
}
```

The ATL `CComEnum<>` template has a method called `Init()` that is used to initialize the enumerator with the data. This method assumes that it is passed two pointers: a pointer to the first item, and a pointer to an item *after* the last item. It further assumes that all the other items are consecutive in memory between these two pointers.

So, the code gets the number of items and then creates an array of `VARIANT`s. It reads all the records in the file, creating a new `Msg` object from each, and these are put in the array as `VARIANT`s containing `IDispatch` pointers. Notice that I initialize the `Msg` object by accessing its public `data` members. The code then creates an enumerator that contains `VARIANT`s, initializing it with the array. The `AtlFlagCopy` flag ensures that a copy of the data is made, so before the function finishes it clears the `VARIANT`s in the array.

So far, the object will allow a client to add a new message and to view the messages in the log. There is one final section of code to write. This object implements connection points, so that when a message is added to the log, the object can inform all connected clients of this so that they can take appropriate action. When you added support for `IConnectionPointContainer`, the Wizard added a dispinterface called `_ILoggerEvents` to the `library` section of the IDL. This is marked as the default `outgoing` interface of the `Logger` object.

The first thing to do is to add a new method to this interface with ClassWizard. This method will be the event that the `Logger` object will generate, and connected clients will respond to. The method is called `OnNewMessage()` and it has no parameters.

Once you have added this method, compile the IDL to update the project's type library before implementing the event firing mechanism (you can do this by right clicking on the IDL in FileView and selecting **Compile LoggerEXE.IDL**). To add a connection point for this outgoing interface you need to use the connection point Wizard, so right click on the `CLogger` class in the ClassView and from the context menu select **Implement Connection Point...** When the Wizard starts, it will list the dispinterfaces in the type library, so check the box next to `_ILoggerEvents` and click **OK**.

Your connection point map should look like this:

```
BEGIN_CONNECTION_POINT_MAP(CLogger)
CONNECTION_POINT_ENTRY(DIID__ILoggerEvents)
END_CONNECTION_POINT_MAP()
```

> **I have found that occasionally, the Wizard will put the wrong constant in the connection point map, although I haven't been able to determine what circumstances cause this problem. Use this rule of thumb: if the outgoing interface is a dispinterface, then the constant should be prefixed with a D.**

This Wizard has generated the proxy class called `CProxy_ILoggerEvents<>` to implement the connection point and to provide event firing methods. To use it, edit `AddMessage()` to include this line:

```
  Fire_OnNewMessage();
  return S_OK;
}
```

Now you need a client to test this out, and the easiest way to do this is to use Visual Basic 6. Create an EXE project, and use the Project | References... menu item to add the LoggerEXE 1.0 Type Library. The form looks like this:

The command button is called cmdLog, the list box is called lstMessages, and the text box is called txtMsgToLog. The application should get a reference to the Logger singleton object, so add a form-level variable called LoggerObject:

```
Dim LoggerObject As Logger
```

The code for loading the form should obtain this reference and update the list box:

```
Private Sub UpdateListbox()
    Dim obj As Msg
    lstMessages.Clear
    For Each obj In LoggerObject
        lstMessages.AddItem Str$(obj.Time) + " : " + obj.Message
    Next
End Sub

Private Sub Form_Load()
    Set LoggerObject = New Logger
    cmdLog.Enabled = False
    UpdateListBox
End Sub
```

This accesses the class factory for the Logger object and calls CreateInstance() to get access to the singleton object. Then it calls UpdateListBox, which clears the list box and accesses the messages collection using the For Each loop.

To add a message to the log, you need to implement the click event of the command button:

```
Private Sub txtMsgToLog_Change()
    cmdLog.Enabled = True
End Sub

Private Sub cmdLog_Click()
    LoggerObject.AddMessage txtMsgToLog
    txtMsgToLog = ""
```

```
        cmdLog.Enabled = False
        UpdateListBox
    End Sub
```

The first method enables the command button when there is data in the text box (to prevent you from logging empty strings), and the click handler gets the text from the text box and calls `AddMessage()` on the `Logger` object, before updating the display. You can now compile the project and run a couple of instances of the application. When you add a new message, the list box in that application will be updated with the new contents of the log. However, when you add a message through one instance, the other instance is not updated. To do this, the application should respond to the `OnNewMessage()` event.

To do this, change the declaration of the `LoggerObject` to:

```
    Private WithEvents LoggerObject As Logger
```

Now you will be able to select **LoggerObject** from the **Object** dropdown list, and the Visual Basic IDE will add the event to the form. The handler code here will merely update the list box:

```
    Private Sub LoggerObject_OnNewMessage()
        UpdateListBox
    End Sub
```

When you add items from one instance of the application, the displays of the other instance will also be updated:

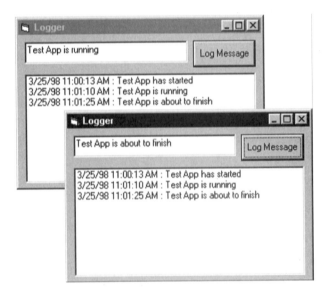

# Auto Thread Class Factories

I'll describe thread pooling in detail in Chapter 7, but a server that uses thread pooling must have at least one object that uses the thread pooling class factory. If the object class does not use the thread pooling class factory, then instances of the object will be created on the main thread of the object server (if the server is apartment threaded) or on an RPC-allocated thread (if the server is free threaded).

To mark that the class should be created on the thread pool threads, you use the
DECLARE_CLASSFACTORY_AUTO_THREAD() macro in the class. This macro ensures that
CComClassFactoryAutoThread is used as the class factory. The interesting thing about this
implementation is that when CreateInstance() is called, it obtains a method pointer to create the
object instance and passes this to the _Module's CreateInstance() function, rather than calling
the method pointer directly:

```
// From atlcom.h

STDMETHODIMP CreateInstance(LPUNKNOWN pUnkOuter, REFIID riid, void** ppvObj)
{
    ATLASSERT(m_pfnCreateInstance != NULL);
    HRESULT hRes = E_POINTER;
    if(ppvObj != NULL)
    {
        *ppvObj = NULL;
        // Cannot aggregate across apartments
        ATLASSERT(pUnkOuter == NULL);
        if(pUnkOuter != NULL)
            hRes = CLASS_E_NOAGGREGATION;
        else
            hRes = _Module.CreateInstance(m_pfnCreateInstance, riid, ppvObj);
    }
    return hRes;
}
```

The module implements CreateInstance() to create the specified object on one of the threads in
the thread pool in a round robin fashion:

```
// From atlcom.h

template <class ThreadAllocator>
HRESULT CComAutoThreadModule<ThreadAllocator>::CreateInstance(
                    void* pfnCreateInstance, REFIID riid, void** ppvObj)
{
    _ATL_CREATORFUNC* pFunc = (_ATL_CREATORFUNC*)pfnCreateInstance;
    _AtlAptCreateObjData data;
    data.pfnCreateInstance = pFunc;
    data.piid = &riid;
    data.hEvent = CreateEvent(NULL, FALSE, FALSE, NULL);
    data.hRes = S_OK;
    int nThread = m_Allocator.GetThread(m_pApartments, m_nThreads);
    ::PostThreadMessage(m_pApartments[nThread].m_dwThreadID,
                    CComApartment::ATL_CREATE_OBJECT, 0, (LPARAM)&data);
    AtlWaitWithMessageLoop(data.hEvent);
    CloseHandle(data.hEvent);
    if(SUCCEEDED(data.hRes))
        data.hRes = CoGetInterfaceAndReleaseStream(
                                        data.pStream, riid, ppvObj);
    return data.hRes;
}
```

The default class used as `ThreadAllocator` is `CComSimpleThreadAllocator`. This keeps a note of the current thread, and an instance of this class is held in `m_Allocator`. The `GetThread()` method increments the thread index up to the maximum passed as the second parameter (which is the number of threads in the thread pool), rolling round to 0. Once an appropriate thread has been found, it is told to create an object instance: `PostThreadMessage()` is used as a inter-thread communication mechanism. One advantage of using a message queue like this is that if the thread is working on something else, the request is queued until the thread is free.

Since this method must return an interface pointer, it must wait for the thread to serve the request. To do this, it creates an event kernel object and passes it to the pool thread. When the thread has created the object instance, it will signal the event. `CreateInstance()` uses `AtlWaitWithMessageLoop()` to wait for the event to become signaled, as well as for serving the thread's message queue.

Once the object has been created, it has to be returned back to the client. Since the interface pointer will be returned to the client from an apartment other than the one that created it, `CoGetInterfaceAndReleaseStream()` is called to marshal the pointer between apartments.

The effect of all this is that your server's main thread gets the object requests, which it dispatches to the threads in the pool. These other threads create the objects, and the interface pointer is returned back to the client. This means that there is more than one thread handling method requests on these objects. The architecture is quite flexible, as you'll see in Chapter 7, because you can provide code to determine which thread is used to create the object, and hence provide your own load balancing algorithm.

# Implementing Your Own Class Factories

Despite all that has gone before, you may decide that the default class factories provided by ATL do not meet your needs. For example, `IClassFactory::CreateInstance()` is passed the IID of the interface that the client is interested in, but there is no way to pass any other parameter to this method to influence *how* the class factory should create the object. If you want to pass more information, then you should provide your own class factory class. To do so, you should derive a class from `CComClassFactory`, and override `CreateInstance()`. This class factory class must then be declared in the ATL object class using `DECLARE_CLASSFACTORY_EX()`.

The above will allow you to create your own version of `IClassFactory`, but what if you want to implement your own interface? The ATL architecture assumes that the object will have `IClassFactory`, but since the class factory is just a COM object, you can simply add your new interface to the ATL class. When you provide a custom class factory interface, it means that the client will not be able to call `CoCreateInstanceEx()` to create an object. Instead, it must call `CoGetClassObject()` specifying the custom interface, and then call the appropriate method to get access to the objects. This effectively restricts the client to being implemented in C++.

## *Example: A Custom Class Factory Object*

This example simulates an experiment that has four voltmeters. These meters always exist, so the COM objects representing them should be created when the server starts. The class factory for the object implements the following interface:

```
interface IGetMeter : IUnknown
{
    HRESULT GetMeter([in] short sMeter, [out] IVoltmeter** ppTheMeter);
};
```

The client calls this interface on the class factory object, passing in the index of the required meter, and obtaining an interface pointer to the meter as an [out] parameter.

The example is an EXE COM server called MeterEXE. The voltmeter objects will be instances of a **Simple Object** added with the Object Wizard, using the **Short Name** of Voltmeter. The class factory class is called CExperimentCF, and you should add the code for it to the bottom of the Voltmeter.h header.

```
class CExperimentCF : public CComClassFactory
{
public:

BEGIN_COM_MAP(CExperimentCF)
END_COM_MAP()

    // IClassFactory
    STDMETHOD(CreateInstance)(LPUNKNOWN pUnkOuter, REFIID riid, void** ppvObj)
    {
        *ppvObj = NULL;
        return E_NOTIMPL;
    }
};
```

Notice that it derives from CComClassFactory so that it implements LockServer(). This class is then used in the CVoltmeter class:

```
// Forward declaration
class CExperimentCF;

/////////////////////////////////////////////////////////////////////////
// CVoltmeter
class ATL_NO_VTABLE CVoltmeter :
    public CComObjectRootEx<CComSingleThreadModel>,
    public CComCoClass<CVoltmeter, &CLSID_Voltmeter>,
    public IDispatchImpl<IVoltmeter, &IID_IVoltmeter, &LIBID_METEREXELib>
{
public:
    CVoltmeter()
    {
    }

DECLARE_CLASSFACTORY_EX(CExperimentCF)
```

The IGetMeter interface should be added to the COM map of the class factory. There is a Wizard to do this, but first you need to make sure that the interface is in the project's type library. So, edit MeterEXE.idl to declare the interface *outside* the library statement (so that the proxy is generated), and give a reference *inside* the library statement so that it is included in the type library:

```
[
   object,
   uuid(AC856EB1-C3D2-11D1-9B1D-0060973044A8),
   pointer_default(unique)
]
interface IGetMeter : IUnknown
{
};

[
   uuid(AC856EA1-C3D2-11D1-9B1D-0060973044A8),
   version(1.0)
]
library METEREXELib
{
   importlib("stdole32.tlb");
   importlib("stdole2.tlb");
   interface IGetMeter;
```

Next, you need to compile the IDL so that a type library is generated. Once this is done, you can add the interface to the CExperimentCF class by right clicking on the class in ClassView and selecting Implement Interface.... You will get this dialog, which lists the interfaces described in the type library:

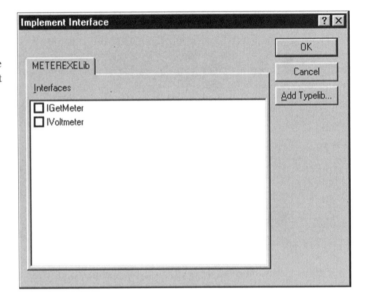

Check the box next to IGetMeter and click on OK. The next task is to add the GetMeter() method of the interface using ClassView. After doing so, the class factory should look like this:

```
class CExperimentCF : public CComClassFactory,
                      public IGetMeter
{
public:

BEGIN_COM_MAP(CExperimentCF)
   COM_INTERFACE_ENTRY(IGetMeter)
END_COM_MAP()
   // IClassFactory
   STDMETHOD(CreateInstance)(LPUNKNOWN pUnkOuter, REFIID riid, void** ppvObj)
   {
```

```
        *ppvObj = NULL;
        return E_NOTIMPL;
    }

public:
// IGetMeter
    STDMETHOD(GetMeter)(/*[in]*/ short sMeter,
                        /*[out]*/ IVoltmeter** ppTheMeter);
};
```

The GetMeter() method will return a reference to the specified meter. In an actual application, the constructor and destructor of the CVoltmeter class would make and break the connection to the physical meter. Depending on the hardware interface used, there will be some mechanism to distinguish between the meters, probably by accessing different DMA addresses. In this example, passing a value to the constructor of the object simulates this address.

Remember that you cannot just instantiate an ATL class – it has to be used as a parameter to one of the CComObjectxxx<> templates. The object creation methods of these templates (the constructor or CreateInstance()) create the ATL object using the default constructor, so a constructor parameter on CVoltmeter would be useless, and it wouldn't compile anyway.

What we need is some way of passing a value during object construction that can be accessed within the object to make the connection. The CComObjectxxx<> template that we will use is CComObjectGlobal<>, but since this has a parameter-less default constructor, we will derive a new class from it. Put this code before the declaration of CExperimentCF in Voltmeter.h:

```
template <class Base>
class CGlobalMeter : public CComObjectGlobal<Base>
{
public:
    CGlobalMeter(short sNumber)
    {
        m_sAddr = sNumber;
    }
};
```

m_sAddr is a data member of the CVoltmeter class, which is inherited through CComObjectGlobal<CVoltmeter>:

```
public:
    short m_sAddr;
};
```

The meters can now be data members of the class factory class:

```
    STDMETHOD(GetMeter)(/*[in]*/ short sMeter,
                        /*[out]*/ IVoltmeter** ppTheMeter);
private:
    CGlobalMeter<CVoltmeter> m_One;
    CGlobalMeter<CVoltmeter> m_Two;
    CGlobalMeter<CVoltmeter> m_Three;
    CGlobalMeter<CVoltmeter> m_Four;
};
```

These can be initialized in the constructor of CExperimentCF:

```
public:
   CExperimentCF() : m_One(1), m_Two(2), m_Three(3), m_Four(4)
   {
   }
```

When the class factory object is created, these Voltmeter objects will also be created. GetMeter() is straightforward:

```
STDMETHODIMP CExperimentCF::GetMeter(short sMeter, IVoltmeter **ppTheMeter)
{
   *ppTheMeter = NULL;
   if(sMeter < 1 || sMeter > 4)
      return E_FAIL;

   switch(sMeter)
   {
   case 1:
      return m_One.QueryInterface(IID_IVoltmeter, (void**)ppTheMeter);
   case 2:
      return m_Two.QueryInterface(IID_IVoltmeter, (void**)ppTheMeter);
   case 3:
      return m_Three.QueryInterface(IID_IVoltmeter, (void**)ppTheMeter);
   case 4:
      return m_Four.QueryInterface(IID_IVoltmeter, (void**)ppTheMeter);
   default:
      return E_FAIL;
   }
}
```

As with the singleton class factory, we must ensure that when the server shuts down, all connections to the objects are broken. This is done in the FinalRelease() method of the class factory:

```
void FinalRelease()
{
   CoDisconnectObject(m_One.GetUnknown(), 0);
   CoDisconnectObject(m_Two.GetUnknown(), 0);
   CoDisconnectObject(m_Three.GetUnknown(), 0);
   CoDisconnectObject(m_Four.GetUnknown(), 0);
}
```

The very last action is to implement the IVoltmeter interface. This will have a single method called GetReading() that returns the current reading of the meter as a long, which you should add to IVoltmeter in the usual way using ClassView. Here's the prototype:

```
STDMETHOD(GetReading)(/*[out, retval]*/ long* pVal);
```

The implementation here just generates a random number using the C runtime rand() function. The seeding of the random number generator is done in the FinalConstruct() function of the CVoltmeter class:

```
HRESULT FinalConstruct()
{
    srand((unsigned int)GetTickCount());
    return S_OK;
}
```

And `GetReading()` is implemented as:

```
STDMETHODIMP CVoltmeter::GetReading(long *pVal)
{
    *pVal = rand() + (0x10000 * m_sAddr);
    return S_OK;
}
```

The largest number that `rand()` will return is `0x7fff`, so I have used the top word to indicate which meter is returning the value.

Since this is an EXE server and the class factory uses a custom interface, you need to compile and register the proxy-stub DLL before you can test this server.

The test application is simple. I created a Win32 Console Application and used the "Hello, World!" application option. So that I could use COM, `stdafx.h` had to be edited like this:

```
#include <windows.h>
#include <stdio.h>
#include <tchar.h>
```

Unfortunately, the AppWizard assumes that you will want to write an ANSI console application. To remedy this, I changed the `main()` method like this, so *you* can decide whether the project is ANSI or Unicode:

```
int _tmain(int argc, TCHAR* argv[])
{
    return 0;
}
```

The entire `_tmain()` function is given here:

```
#include "stdafx.h"
#import "..\MeterEXE\MeterEXE.tlb" no_namespace
int _tmain(int argc, TCHAR* argv[])
{
    CoInitialize(NULL);

    try
    {
        HRESULT hr;
        IGetMeterPtr pClassFactory;
        hr = ::CoGetClassObject(__uuidof(Voltmeter), CLSCTX_ALL,
                    NULL, __uuidof(IGetMeterPtr), (void**)&pClassFactory);
        if(FAILED(hr))
            _com_issue_error(hr);
        IVoltmeterPtr pMeterOne;
```

```
            IVoltmeterPtr pMeterTwo;
            IVoltmeterPtr pMeterThree;
            IVoltmeterPtr pMeterFour;

            pClassFactory->GetMeter(1,&pMeterOne);
            pClassFactory->GetMeter(2,&pMeterTwo);
            pClassFactory->GetMeter(3,&pMeterThree);
            pClassFactory->GetMeter(4,&pMeterFour);

            // Get some readings
            _tprintf(_T("One\tTwo\tThree\tFour\n"));
            for(int x = 0 ; x < 10 ; x++)
            {
                _tprintf(_T("%x\t%x\t%x\t%x\n"),
                        pMeterOne->GetReading(),    pMeterTwo->GetReading(),
                        pMeterThree->GetReading(), pMeterFour->GetReading());
            }
        }
        catch(_com_error e)
        {
            _tprintf(_T("Error: 0x%x %s\n"), e.Error(), e.ErrorMessage());
        }

        CoUninitialize();
        return 0;
    }
```

This code calls `CoGetClassObject()` with the CLSID of the `Voltmeter` object, but requesting the `IGetMeter` interface. This is used to get access to the `Voltmeter` objects by calling `GetMeter()`, passing the index of the required meter. A small test is then done, by taking 10 readings from each meter and printing them on the screen. A sample result is shown here:

```
C:\wrox\PROATL\CODE\CHAPTER6\MeterTest\DEBUG>metertest
One     Two     Three   Four
10865   205c9   379f1   4240d
16341   25175   374a6   46217
14482   27e75   371c2   44428
13b8d   24cda   32f85   467da
1594a   27084   31094   47053
15e20   2072e   30f4b   46522
10421   22fab   37b54   4786b
13981   2266e   33579   47844
15f4d   20b50   35db6   46f5e
16059   2348e   32793   438e8

C:\wrox\PROATL\CODE\CHAPTER6\MeterTest\DEBUG>
```

Looking at the top word, you can verify that each reading does indeed come from the required meter.

# Summary

In this chapter, we've discussed class factories and how ATL implements them. I have explained what a class factory object is, how COM obtains them from your server, and how ATL implements the required methods. I have also described the class factory interfaces that COM recognizes, and how to use them in your own ATL classes by using one of the ATL class factory macros. Finally, through three examples, I have shown how you can implement a licensed object, a singleton object and a server that uses a custom class factory.

# 6

# Debugging and Error Handling

We all try to write bug-free code, but there are still times when subtle problems appear. Maybe there's a glitch that didn't surface despite your extensive testing phase, or perhaps you have two pieces of code that work perfectly on their own, but just won't behave when you put them together. There's always a need to have debugging support in your code so that you can get an idea of exactly what is going on.

Debugging messages come in two forms: assertions and trace messages. The former ensure that the object is consistent, and that pre- and post-conditions are met – if they're not, an assertion will inform the user with a dialog or some other message. The latter are used to write diagnostic messages to a debug stream – this can be useful for identifying where a problem occurs during the debugging phase, and (with some constraints) within a released product.

Diagnostic messages in a released product are a special case. Usually, you will want to make sure that such messages take the form of readable strings, rather than a user-unfriendly status code, and this is where **error objects** become useful. These originated in Visual Basic to convey OLE errors in a way that a Visual Basic program could catch, but in fact any client can use them.

When you're dealing with COM, one of the things you really have to look out for is leaked reference counts, about which COM is notoriously unforgiving. During your testing period, it is important to ensure that reference counts are not leaked, and so you need to get some information when such a situation occurs.

In one way or another, ATL has provisions for all of these issues. In this chapter, I'll explain what those facilities are, and how to use them.

# Trace Messages

There are two sorts of trace messages: those that are used during the debugging phase, and those that provide diagnostic messages in the released product. The temptation of trace messages is to insert them in many places in the program, and I would encourage you to do this *in your debug version*. In your release version, you should restrict the number of trace messages you use.

Release versions of software should only have trace messages when absolutely necessary, and even then you should question whether the output stream that the trace messages you generate will go to is ever likely to be read. The following sections will give an indication of where the trace messages will go, and what type of builds will include them.

# OutputDebugString

Win32 has a function called `OutputDebugString()` that sends a string to the debugging stream. Typically, a debugger attached to this stream will decide what to do with the strings that get sent to it – showing them on the screen for the developer to see is a common action. However, it is not *only* a debugging tool, because it works in release builds as well.

It might look a little like black magic at first, but in fact `OutputDebugString()` just uses a memory mapped file (MMF) and some event kernel objects to pass data from one process to another. The debugger creates a named MMF called DBWIN_BUFFER, and two events called DBWIN_BUFFER_READY and DBWIN_DATA_READY. The first event is set when the MMF can be written to, and the second event is set when data has been written to the MMF.

Thus, when the debugger creates the MMF it should set DBWIN_BUFFER_READY to indicate that a process can call `OutputDebugString()`. The debugger should then wait on DBWIN_DATA_READY to find out when a client has logged a message. The `OutputDebugString()` function writes the string and its process ID to the MMF, and then sets DBWIN_DATA_READY to indicate that a message has been logged. The debugger can then read the MMF and process the data.

Rather than writing your own application to process debug messages, however, you can just use Visual C++. Any messages that come from a process being debugged with the Visual C++ debugger will be shown in the Output window. Note that the first four bytes in the MMF contain the process ID of the process that generated the message, so the debugger will ignore any messages from other processes. If you are *interested* in messages from other processes (If you're using a local server, for example), then you can run the DBMon utility supplied with the Platform SDK, which does not filter messages according to process ID.

It's important to note that `OutputDebugString()` will write a string to the debug stream whether the project is compiled in **Debug** or **Release** mode. I advise, therefore, that you only use the function in development code, by enclosing it with conditional compilation if necessary. Otherwise, you will have the problem of generating diagnostic messages that will probably never be read, and (more worrying) since `OutputDebugString()` waits on DBWIN_BUFFER_READY, this event may be held by another process, creating problems with performance.

# ATLTRACE

`OutputDebugString()` takes an `LPCTSTR` as a parameter, and so it's up to you to allocate this buffer and format the string. To help you, ATL defines several methods and macros.

Most output is carried out by calling `ATLTRACE()`; this macro is defined as `AtlTrace()` if `_DEBUG` is defined, and `(void)0` otherwise (that is, it does nothing). `AtlTrace()` has this prototype:

```
void AtlTrace(LPCSTR lpszFormat, ...)
```

The method is overloaded with `lpszFormat` declared as an `LPCWSTR` as well. `AtlTrace()` takes a variable number of parameters, and behaves much like `printf()` does, The implementation of the method uses `_vsnprintf()` to fill a 512-character array, so be careful how you use it. In particular, if you want to send multiple lines to the output window, call `ATLTRACE()` several times rather than packing all the messages into one call.

`ATLTRACE()` has very little granularity: if `_DEBUG` is defined, all messages written with `ATLTRACE()` will be sent to the debug stream. For code written cautiously, this can mean a lot of messages, which sometimes makes it difficult to pick out the ones you're interested in. To get round this problem, ATL also provides the `ATLTRACE2()` macro that logs a message with a category, as defined by the `atlTraceFlags` enumeration, the first four members of which are for your own use:

```
enum atlTraceFlags
{
    atlTraceUser        = 0x00000001,
    atlTraceUser2       = 0x00000002,
    atlTraceUser3       = 0x00000004,
    atlTraceUser4       = 0x00000008,
    atlTraceGeneral     = 0x00000020,
    atlTraceCOM         = 0x00000040,
    atlTraceQI          = 0x00000080,
    atlTraceRegistrar   = 0x00000100,
    atlTraceRefcount    = 0x00000200,
    atlTraceWindowing   = 0x00000400,
    atlTraceControls    = 0x00000800,
    atlTraceHosting     = 0x00001000,
    atlTraceDBClient    = 0x00002000,
    atlTraceDBProvider  = 0x00004000,
    atlTraceSnapin      = 0x00008000,
    atlTraceNotImpl     = 0x00010000,
};
```

ATL uses two symbols to determine whether a message will be sent to the debug stream: `ATL_TRACE_CATEGORY` and `ATL_TRACE_LEVEL`. The former is a bitmask that combines the categories in `atlTraceFlags` that will be traced; by default this is `0xFFFFFFFF`, which means that all categories are traced. You can change this as long as you define `ATL_TRACE_CATEGORY` in `stdafx.h` *before* `atlbase.h` is included, so to get only COM messages traced, you can use this:

```
#define ATL_TRACE_CATEGORY 0x00000040
```

If you would prefer to use members of the enumeration to set which categories to trace, you will need to define ATL_TRACE_CATEGORY *after* including atlbase.h, and since this header file will define the symbol, you will need to undefine it before you can use it:

```
#ifdef ATL_TRACE_CATEGORY
#undef ATL_TRACE_CATEGORY
#endif
#define ATL_TRACE_CATEGORY atlTraceCOM
```

This is rather messy compared to the previous version.

The **message level** determines the importance of the message, with 0 being the most important. The symbol ATL_TRACE_LEVEL determines globally the level of messages that will be traced. The default value of 0 means that only the most important messages will be traced. By setting this value to a higher number, you will get less important messages traced.

As with ATLTRACE(), ATLTRACE2() preprocesses to (void)0 in non debug builds, while in debug builds it will preprocess to AtlTrace2(). Here's its prototype:

```
void AtlTrace2(DWORD category, UINT level, LPCSTR lpszFormat, ...)
```

The first parameter is the category, which again should be a member (or a combination of members) of the atlTraceFlags enumeration. The second parameter is the level of the message, where the lower the value, the more important it is. When writing your components, you should apply 0 for important messages, and progressively greater values for less important messages. When debugging the component, you should set ATL_TRACE_LEVEL to an appropriate level, as explained above.

Most authorities on COM will tell you that if your object implements an interface, it should implement all methods in that interface. On the occasions when this is not possible, the method should return E_NOTIMPL. ATL defines a macro called ATLTRACENOTIMPL() that you should use instead of the return statement in these cases. This macro will preprocess to return E_NOTIMPL for non-debug builds, but for debug builds it calls ATLTRACE2() to *indicate* that the method is not implemented, and then returns E_NOTIMPL.

For example, IPersistStreamInitImpl has this for GetSizeMax():

```
STDMETHOD(GetSizeMax)(ULARGE_INTEGER FAR* /* pcbSize */)
{
   ATLTRACENOTIMPL(_T("IPersistStreamInitImpl::GetSizeMax"));
}
```

# Event Log

If you're developing on Windows NT, then another way to log messages is to use the **Event Log**. This is a logging service that is provided by the system and accessed through a rather arcane API. The Event Log should *not* be used for debugging trace messages because these will quickly fill the log, obscuring other, more important messages that other processes will place there. The event log is really intended for diagnostic messages during runtime – in particular it acts as a central repository for event messages, so that an administrator can determine inter-process contributions to a problem.

Imagine you have several processes that rely on, and communicate with, each other. If there is a failure in one process, it may have its root in one of the other processes that it communicates with, but all of these processes can report events to the Event Log. When a failure occurs, an administrator can trace this failure through the events in the Event Log back to its actual source.

Although events are typically sent to the Event Log on the local machine, the Event Log API allows them to be logged on another machine in the domain, and also to be accessed remotely by administrators with appropriate privileges. Thus, if you are developing a distributed application, the Event Log is a useful tool when trying to solve problems that may be caused by processes on several machines.

The sorts of messages you should *not* log are things like, "The object was activated," or, "The object was released." These are events that will always happen, and are just noise in the Event Log. Instead, you should log exceptional events, indicating to the administrator when something catastrophic happened. If you use exception handling in your process, for example, you may decide to log the result from the `catch` block into the Event Log.

The Event Log is actually implemented in files with the EVT extension that are held in the `%systemroot%\System32\Config` directory (the environment variable `%systemroot%` is often `C:\Winnt`, but it depends on where you installed NT). You should *not* attempt to access these files yourself, and in fact you won't be able to, because the `EventLog` service will open them denying access to anyone else. Instead, you should use the Event Log API, which is designed for access by multiple users.

By default, there are three event logs – `System`, `Security` and `Application` – and these are used by NT system processes, the security subsystem and other applications respectively. Normally you will log events to the `Application` log, but you can log to the `System` or `Security` logs if you are running under the `SYSTEM` account. You can also add other logs of your own, but they will not be supported by the Event Log Viewer.

## Reporting Events

Whenever you report an event, you should do so with a registered **event source**. If your COM server (whether an NT service, or an in-process or local server) generates events, then you should register and unregister the event source in `RegisterServer()` and `UnregisterServer()`. The API is forgiving in that it will allow you to use an unregistered event source, but I recommend against it. If you don't use a registered source name, then you will not be able to use **resource strings**. I'll get back to these later, but they are integral to the efficient working of the Event Log.

A registered event source has a key within one of the keys in `HKEY_LOCAL_MACHINE\SYSTEM\CurrentControlSet\Services\EventLog`. This key has three subkeys whose names correspond with those of the event logs – typically your event source key will be in the `Application` key. You can use whatever name you want as long as it is unique; it is a good idea to use your application's name. Note that within each of these keys there is a named value called `Sources` that has the names of all the keys under that key. *Do not be tempted to edit this value.* This is dynamically maintained by the `EventLog` service, and if you change its value you may do horrible damage to the system: I once did edit this value, and the `EventLog` service behaved very oddly until I reinstalled NT!

To report an event, you must first obtain an event source handle by calling
RegisterEventSource(). This function has a rather unfortunate name, as you are *not* registering
an event source, but getting hold of a handle to the Event Log. It takes two parameters: the name of
the machine where you want the event logged (or NULL for the current machine) and the name of the
event source. By default the source you specify is assumed to be in the Application log, but you
can prefix the source name with System\ or Security\ to get a source in those logs.

Note that although you access the Event Log through a HANDLE, you must not use CloseHandle()
when you have finished with the Event Log – instead, you should use
DeregisterEventSource(). Again, let me reiterate that this function just closes your handle to
the Event Log; it does not deregister your event source.

Once you have a handle to the Event Log, you can log a message with ReportEvent(). Events are
logged with a severity code of 'informational', 'warning' or 'error', and the difference is just a flag
added to the Event Log (there are also audit severity codes used by events in the Security Event Log).
An Event Log viewer, like the system-provided EventVwr.exe, will be able to filter messages by the
severity code.

These severities have the following symbols; the icons shown here are the ones used by the NT Event
Log Viewer utility:

| Icon | Value | Description |
|---|---|---|
| | EVENTLOG_ERROR_TYPE | Error event |
| | EVENTLOG_WARNING_TYPE | Warning event |
| | EVENTLOG_INFORMATION_TYPE | Information event |
| | EVENTLOG_AUDIT_SUCCESS | Success Audit event |
| | EVENTLOG_AUDIT_FAILURE | Failure Audit event |

A finer level of granularity is offered by categorizing the events. This is determined by an application,
and could involve breaking down events into subdivisions like "Billing" or "Order". Again, the
Event Log viewer will be able to filter messages by category. However, unless you provide a message
resource file, categories will show up as fairly meaningless numbers in the Event Log Viewer.

So, how are messages logged? If entire messages were logged, this would bloat the Event Log,
particularly if there were many repeated messages. Further, logging entire messages would mean that
the message would be specific to a particular locale and hence to a particular language. The problem
with this is that only an administrator who understands the default language of the locale of the
machine that generated the error will be able to decipher the event. In these days of international
corporations, it is unwise to assume that a single language will be used across the enterprise.

A much better scheme is to use resource strings to describe the event, and placeholders within those strings to take data specific to a particular event. This way, the description can be locale-dependent and the Event Log just needs the resource string ID and the insertion strings for the placeholders. This has the dual effect of allowing a locale-dependent format string to be used, and making the data sent to the Event Log as small as possible. For example, if you have an event (say, #123), the resource string in English could be "Drive %1 has failed". When the event occurs, the Event Log would have the ID of this format string and the insert string: 123, "C:". You could then create a resource file containing translations of this string into all major languages, so that the Event Log Viewer could obtain the right format string for the locale.

## Resource Files

Event Log resource strings are of type RT_MESSAGETABLE (a value of 11), but if you try to create one in ResourceView, you will be disappointed: Visual Studio does not support resources of this type. Instead, you are provided with the MC.exe utility that will create the binary string resource from text source files; you can then bind this resource into a project. MC.exe can be found in the Visual C++ bin directory together with a small help file.

You have two options regarding to how to use this tool. First, you can add the binary resource to an existing project through the **Resource Includes** dialog on the Visual C++ **View** menu. Alternatively, you can create a DLL that has no code other than a minimal DllMain() (an AppWizard "simple DLL project", for example) and add the resource to that. This second option requires less effort because MC will create a resource script for you, and all you need to do then is add it to your project. The example I'll demonstrate later on uses this approach.

> *If you're interested, the source files of the* MC.exe *utility are available as an example in the Platform SDK.*

The source files for MC are basically text files that have two parts: header and the message sections. The items in the **header section** are global, and apply to all the message definitions that follow them. There are two particular items in the header section that you should know about: MessageIdTypedef and LanguageName.

MC will define manifest constants for you from the message IDs that you supply. Generally, the message IDs are 32-bit values; in the source file, you specify the bottom 16 bits and MC will determine the top 16 bits, usually using default values. If you specify a type with MessageIdTypedef, MC will cast these constants to that type. If you are defining message IDs then the type should be DWORD, but for category IDs the type should be WORD.

The most important item of all is LanguageName, which allows you to state that the messages in the source file will have more than one language.

```
LanguageName=(British=0x809:MSG00809)
LanguageName=(French=0x40c:MSG0040c)
```

Placing the above lines in the header section would indicate that the source file contained messages in *three* languages: International English, British English and French. The parameters indicate the locale IDs that will be used, and the resource files that MC will create – respectively, MSG00001.bin, MSG00809.bin and MSG0040C.bin. It is these files that your resource DLL should add to its resources.

In the **message section**, you have to specify the ID and the format string for the message. If you specify more than one language in the header section, then you *must* provide a version of each message for each language *and* for International English. There are three items pertinent to defining message IDs:

| Item | Description |
|------|-------------|
| MessageId | Message ID |
| SymbolicName | The #define symbol for the message ID |
| Language | The language of the format string |

Each message must have a `MessageId` line, but there does not have to be an associated value: if there isn't, then the last `MessageId` value is incremented. The C++ header that `MC` generates will use the `SymbolicName` for the name of the constant that it defines for this message, cast to the type defined with `MessageIdTypedef`, and with a value generated from the `MessageId`.

The really important part is the `Language` item. Each message must have one of these for every language to be used in the file. The `Language` line has the name of a language specified in the header section, and then the format string. The string is terminated by a period on a line by itself. For example:

```
LanguageNames=(British=0x809:MSG00809)
LanguageNames=(French=0x40c:MSG0040c)

MessageId=0x1000
SymbolicName=HELLO
Language=English
Hello! %1
.

Language=British
Alright! %1
.

Language=French
Salut! %1
.
```

This defines a message with an ID of `0x1000` that has format strings in the three different languages. Notice that the string has just one insert string, represented by the `%1` placeholder. If you have more than one insert string, then just increment the placeholders (`%1`, `%2`, `%3`, ...). For more details, see the Platform SDK entry for `FormatMessage()`.

When this file is run through `MC`, you will get a resource script, a header, and the three BIN resource files. Typically, you would copy the values from the resource script into the **Compile Time Directives** of the **Resource Includes** dialog. The previous file will produce the following resource script:

```
LANGUAGE 0xc,0x1
1 11 MSG0040c.bin
LANGUAGE 0x9,0x1
1 11 MSG00001.bin
LANGUAGE 0x9,0x2
1 11 MSG00809.bin
```

The header file will have this single entry:

```
#define HELLO   0x00001000L
```

Thus, when you want to refer to the hello message (in whatever language) you can use the constant HELLO.

When you have created a resource DLL containing format strings, you should register it under the registry entry for your event source. This key should have the named values `TypesSupported` and `EventMessageFile`; the former is the types of events that the source can generate ORed together (typically 7 for error, warning and informational), while the latter is the path to the resource file DLL on your system.

## Categories

I mentioned earlier that you could report an event with a category. These can also have descriptive strings defined in a resource file: you just treat the category as a message without any parameters. Note, however, that categories are specified in `ReportEvent()` as `WORD` values, so you will have to use a different `MessageIdTypedef` for categories than for message format strings. For example:

```
LanguageNames=(British=0x809:MSG00809)
LanguageNames=(French=0x40c:MSG0040c)

;// Categories
MessageIdTypedef=WORD

MessageId=1
SymbolicName=GREETING
Language=English
Greeting
.
Language=British
Greeting
.
Language=French
Salutation
.


;// Message format Strings
MessageIdTypedef=DWORD

MessageId=0x1000
SymbolicName=HELLO
Language=English
Hello! %1
.
Language=British
Alright! %1
.
Language=French
Salut! %1
.
```

Notice that the comment lines start with `;//`. The reason for this is that MC will remove the semicolon and put the rest of the line into the header verbatim, and so the `//` is required to make sure that the rest of the text is treated as a comment.

Once you have generated a resource file for categories, you need to register that too – the named values to use are `CategoryCount` and `CategoryMessageFile`. The first is the number of categories (in this case 1), which is used because categories and format strings can be in the same file, and categories should come first. The second value is the path to the resource file that has the category.

## Reporting Events

To report an event, you use the `ReportEvent()` function:

```
BOOL ReportEvent(HANDLE hEventLog, WORD wType, WORD wCategory,
                 DWORD dwEventID, PSID lpUserSid, WORD wNumStrings,
                 DWORD dwDataSize, LPCTSTR* lpStrings, LPVOID lpRawData);
```

The first parameter is the handle obtained by calling `RegisterEventSource()`, and the second is the severity of the event as discussed earlier (for example, `EVENTLOG_INFORMATION_TYPE`). Then follows the category and event ID, which you have defined in your MC source file and compiled into a header and message resource file. `lpUserSid` is the security ID of the user that logged the event, although you can use `NULL` if you don't want to specify the user (I'll show you how to get a SID later in this section).

The remaining parameters comprise the data that will be sent to the Event Log. First, you need to supply an array with all the strings that will be inserted into the format string by an Event Log viewer, and since you can pass as many strings as the format string requires, you also need to supply how many strings there are in the array. In addition, every event can be associated with some binary data; `lpRawData` contains this data, and `dwdataSize` gives the size of this buffer in bytes.

You should be particularly careful about what raw data you send to the Event Log: keep it pertinent, and try to make sure the size is as small as possible. If you want to log that a method has been passed invalid parameters, then if these parameters are strings (or easily convertible to strings), you should insert them into the main message. The raw data is intended for parameters that cannot be formatted, or that are meaningless when printed. For example, I was once involved in writing an application that made TCP connections, and when the application failed to make the connection I used the raw data to hold the IP address. While an IP address is meaningful when printed, it would have been too much effort to extract each byte and use it as an insert string, and so it made sense to log it as raw data.

> Note that insert strings are passed using an array of type **LPCTSTR** – that is, each member is a pointer to a string. This will be significant later on.

Here's an example taken from the code that the Object Wizard generates for NT services in `CServiceModule::LogEvent()`. As you can see, this function does not use a registered event source, so there is no resource file.

```
HANDLE hEventSource;
hEventSource = RegisterEventSource(NULL, m_szServiceName);
if(hEventSource != NULL)
{
    ReportEvent(hEventSource, EVENTLOG_INFORMATION_TYPE, 0, 0,
                        NULL, 1, 0, (LPCTSTR*)&lpszStrings[0], NULL);
    DeregisterEventSource(hEventSource);
}
```

Since Object Wizard does not create a message resource file, it uses zero for the category and the event ID. This ATL code just wants to log a single message, without using a format string, and so `lpszStrings[0]` contains a single pointer to that string. It produces results like this:

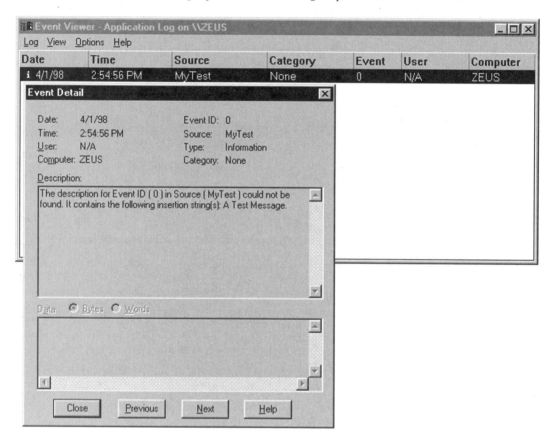

The message "The description for Event ID (0) in Source (MyTest) could not be found..." is not likely to inspire the confidence of your customers in your product. If you choose to use the Event Log in your application, or if you create an ATL NT service COM server, then I urge you to register a source properly and use resource files so that you can provide proper, locale-dependent format strings.

Notice that this dialog gives a User of N/A; this is because the SID passed to ReportEvent() was NULL. To get a SID for an account name, you should use LookupAccountName():

```
BOOL LookupAccountName(LPCTSTR lpSystemName, LPCTSTR lpAccountName,
                PSID Sid, LPDWORD cbSid, LPTSTR ReferencedDomainName,
                LPDWORD cbReferencedDomainName, PSID_NAME_USE peUse);
```

This is passed the account name and the name of the machine where the account is defined (NULL for the local machine), and two buffers that it will be filled with the SID and the name of the domain where the account is defined. Because these values can be any size you also must pass the size of the buffers; if you pass a value of 0 for either size, the function will return the *required* size in this parameter, and will not attempt to fill the buffer. Thus, you often call this function *twice*: once to get the required size of the buffers, which you should then allocate, and a second time to fill the buffer. The final parameter returns the type of SID returned: a user account, a group, a domain account, etc.

So, if my account is RichardGrimes and I want to log an event to the Billing event source, I can use this function:

```
void FailedValidation(LPCTSTR strName)
{
    LPCTSTR strUser = _T("RichardGrimes");
    HANDLE hEventLog;
    hEventLog = RegisterEventSource(NULL, _T("Billing"));
    PSID pSid = NULL;
    DWORD dwSidSize = 0;
    SID_NAME_USE eUse;
    LPTSTR strDomainName = NULL;
    DWORD dwDomainSize = 0;

    LookupAccountName(NULL, strUser, pSid, &dwSidSize,
                                    strDomainName, &dwDomainSize, &eUse);
    pSid = new BYTE[dwSidSize];
    strDomainName = new TCHAR[dwDomainSize];

    LookupAccountName(NULL, strUser, pSid, &dwSidSize,
                                    strDomainName, &dwDomainSize, &eUse);
    ReportEvent(hEventLog, EVENTLOG_INFORMATION_TYPE, CAT_ORDER,
                        MSG_VALIDATION, pSid, 1, 0, &strName, NULL);
    DeregisterEventSource(hEventLog);

    delete [] pSid;
    delete [] strDomainName;
}
```

## Example: Creating a Resource file

Creating a resource file is really quite straightforward, but it's worth seeing a quick demonstration. I will take the Billing example from the last section and produce format strings for just one locale. (My French is not good enough to do the translations!)

Use Visual Studio to create a Win32 Dynamic-Link Library and call it `Billing`; use the A simple DLL project AppWizard type, because you will not add any code. Now add a text file with the name `Billing.mc`, and place the following into the file:

```
;//Billing message file
MessageIdTypedef=WORD

MessageId=1
SymbolicName=CAT_ORDER
Language=English
Order
.

MessageIdTypedef=DWORD

MessageId=0x1000
SymbolicName=MSG_VALIDATION
Language=English
Failed to validate %1
.
```

In FileView, right click on this file and select **Settings**. Change the **Custom Build** setting so that the **Command** is `mc Billing.mc` and the **Output** is `Billing.rc`. Next, compile the MC file, click on the **Source Files** folder, select **Add Files to Folder** and add `Billing.rc`. Finally, you can build the project.

Copy the DLL you've just created to the `System32` directory, and add the `Billing` key to the `HKEY_LOCAL_MACHINE\SYSTEM\CurrentControlSet\services\EventLog\Application` key in the registry. Then, add the values shown in the following screenshot (`CategoryCount` and `TypesSupported` are `DWORD` values, the other two are `String` values):

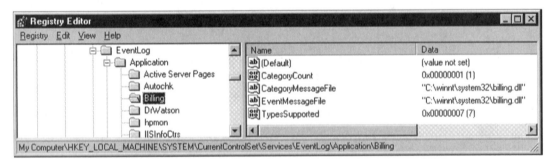

Now you can create a test application that calls the `FailedValidation()` method given earlier and call it a few times with a few names, then run the Event Log Viewer, and you should get something like this:

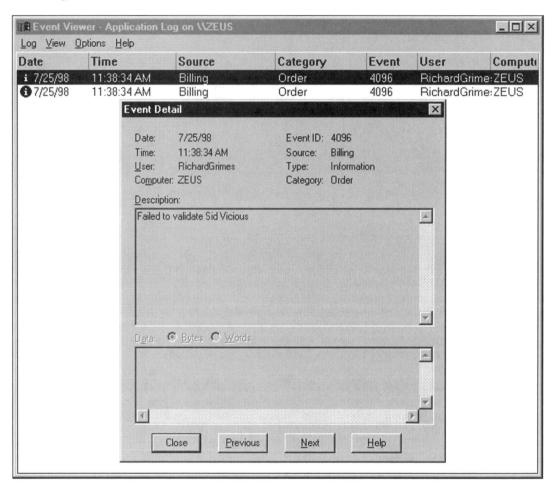

You can see that the Category is correctly given as Order, and when you view the event the message will be formatted with the format string.

## Reading the Event Log

Just for completeness, I'll outline how to read events from the Event Log. The Win32 function to use is called `ReadEventLog()`:

```
BOOL ReadEventLog(HANDLE hEventLog, DWORD dwReadFlags,
        DWORD dwRecordOffset, LPVOID lpBuffer, DWORD nNumberOfBytesToRead,
        DWORD* pnBytesRead, DWORD* pnMinNumberOfBytesNeeded);
```

The first parameter is the handle to an Event Log that was opened using OpenEventLog() with one of the event log names (Application, System or Security). The other parameters are given in this table:

| Parameter | Description |
| --- | --- |
| hEventLog | A handle to an open event log |
| dwReadFlags | How to read from the event log |
| dwRecordOffset | Where to start reading from |
| lpBuffer | Buffer to take the data |
| nNumberOfBytesToRead | Size of the buffer |
| pnBytesRead | Returns the actual number of bytes read |
| pnMinNumberOfBytesNeeded | Number of bytes required for the next record |

The function returns data in records that vary in size but always contain EVENTLOGRECORD structures, and these are put in the buffer pointed to by lpBuffer. The function can read the Event Log record from a particular record number, or forward or backward from the last record read – this direction is specified in the dwReadFlags parameter. If the read is to be from a particular record number, then that number must be specified in the dwRecordOffset parameter, and the direction of the read must also be given.

The records can vary in length because they depend on the number and size of the insert strings, the size of the raw data, and whether a user SID was logged. The only way to tell how many records was read during a call to ReadEventLog() is to read the Length member and compare it with the value pointed to by pnBytesRead. The EVENTLOGRECORD structure looks like this:

| Member | Description |
| --- | --- |
| DWORD Length | Total size of the record, including the variable portion |
| DWORD Reserved | Reserved |
| DWORD RecordNumber | Record number |
| DWORD TimeGenerated | Time the record was generated |
| DWORD TimeWritten | Time the record was actually written to the Event Log |
| DWORD EventID | The format string ID |
| WORD EventType | The event severity |
| WORD NumStrings | Number of insert strings |
| WORD EventCategory | Category |

*Table Continued on Following Page*

| Member | Description |
|---|---|
| WORD ReservedFlags | Reserved |
| DWORD ClosingRecordNumber | Reserved |
| DWORD StringOffset | Offset from the beginning of the record to the insert strings |
| DWORD UserSidLength | Size of the SID |
| DWORD UserSidOffset | Offset from the beginning of the record to the SID |
| DWORD DataLength | Size of the raw data |
| DWORD DataOffset | Offset from the beginning of the record to the raw data |

This is the fixed-size portion of the record; after the EVENTLOGRECORD comes the variable portion:

| Item | Description |
|---|---|
| TCHAR SourceName[] | The name of the event source |
| TCHAR Computername[] | The computer that logged the event |
| SID UserSid | The SID of the user that logged the event |
| TCHAR Strings[] | The insert strings |
| BYTE Data[] | The raw data |
| CHAR Pad[] | |
| DWORD Length | Length of the entire record including the fixed portion |

These are not members of EVENTLOGRECORD; they are given just to identify the data that the variable portion contains. The variable portion is actually just a byte buffer following the fixed portion of the record in memory. The insert strings are placed one after the other in this buffer (each is NUL terminated), and *not* as an array of string pointers, so to use them you need to obtain the string pointer yourself.

For example, if you have a record pointed to by pelr, then the source name is at:

```
LPTSTR SourceName = (LPTSTR)((LPBYTE)pelr + sizeof(EVENTLOGRECORD));
```

That is, it is in the memory immediately after the EVENTLOGRECORD. The first insert string is at:

```
LPTSTR strInsert = (LPTSTR)((LPBYTE)pelr + pelr->StringOffset);
```

While the second one (assuming there is one) is determined in the following way:

```
strInsert = strInsert + lstrlen(strInsert) + 1;
```

If the buffer passed to `ReadEventLog()` is too small to take the data, then the function fails. However, if the buffer is too big, the function will fill it with as many whole records as it can. This unusual behavior can complicate enumerating the messages in the event log, because it means that you always need to check how many records have been returned.

Of course, once you have this event data, you will want to construct a fully readable, locale dependent string. This is done with `FormatMessage()`:

```
DWORD FormatMessage(DWORD dwFlags, LPCVOID lpSource, DWORD dwMessageId,
    DWORD dwLanguageId, LPTSTR lpBuffer, DWORD nSize, va_list* Arguments);
```

You have seen this before in the `HRESULT` discussion of Chapter 1: the `dwMessageId` can be an `HRESULT` or a message format string ID. `lpBuffer` can be passed a pointer to a caller-allocated buffer (the size is in `nSize`), or you can pass a pointer to a `LPTSTR` pointer and the *function* will allocate a buffer for you. If you want to do this, you must also set the `dwFlags` to contain `FORMAT_MESSAGE_ALLOCATE_BUFFER`, and the buffer must be freed with `LocalFree()` when you have finished with it.

If `dwFlags` contains the `FORMAT_MESSAGE_FROM_SYSTEM` flag, the function will search the Win32 DLLs for the `dwMessageId`. If you use the `FORMAT_MESSAGE_FROM_MODULE` flag, then you should load a DLL (with `LoadLibrary()`) and pass the `HINSTANCE` parameter in `lpSource` – typically, this is your resource string DLL (the NT Event Log Viewer does this using the paths in `CategoryMessageFile` and `EventMessageFile`).

The insert strings are usually passed in the `Arguments` parameter as a pointer to an array of `LPTSTR` pointers, but to do this you need to also add `FORMAT_MESSAGE_ARGUMENT_ARRAY` to `dwFlags`. Note that `ReadEventLog()` does not give you an array of insert string pointers, and so you have to create this array yourself.

# Assertions

Assertions are a common technique in C++ development for checking class invariance. The idea is that the class has conditions that should always be true for the object to be consistent. For example, your class may have an embedded object which is created in `FinalConstruct()`, and released in `FinalRelease()`. All other methods in the class will then assume that the data member holding the object interface pointer will always be valid. This is an **invariant** of the class, and if it is not true for an object instance, that object is said to be inconsistent.

To ensure that the invariant condition is met, you can test it at the start of each method, and **assert** – that is, generate an error – if the condition is not true. In ATL, you can do this with `ATLASSERT()`.

This macro is actually #define'd as _ASSERTE(), which is the standard C runtime library assertion macro, but it's *only* defined if _DEBUG is defined, so the expression in ATLASSERT() is only evaluated in debug builds. If the result of the expression is FALSE, the CRT routine _CrtDbgReport() is called to report that the expression failed. After the report, the macro will usually call _CrtDbgBreak() to break at the position where the assertion failed.

If the application is compiled in release mode, the ATLASSERT() macro preprocesses to 0. Any expression in the macro will not be evaluated, so you should be careful to make sure that the expression in the macro just checks values, and does not change them. Of course, this is true for assertions in general, but you may sometimes be tempted to call functions that return values, and then assert on the value. In this situation, you should save a copy of the return value, rather than putting the function call into the assert macro.

When ATLASSERT() fails, the default action is to create a dialog containing the file, line number and expression that failed. This dialog has three buttons: **Abort**, **Retry** and **Ignore**. The first of these will stop the process, the second will enter the debugger at the position where the assertion failed, and the third will continue execution. This is why I said above that the _ASSERTE() macro will *usually* call _CrtDbgBreak() – in fact, this will only happen if the user clicks on **Retry**.

You are not constrained to reporting assertions to a dialog; instead, you can redirect the output either to a file, or to the debug stream (as used by OutputDebugString()). To do this, you call the _CrtSetReportMode() function, which takes two parameters. The first is the type of the message (for ATLASSERT() this will always be _CRT_ASSERT), and the second is the new output mode:

| Mode | Description |
| --- | --- |
| _CRTDBG_MODE_DEBUG | Output is send to the debug stream, as used by OutputDebugString() |
| _CRTDBG_MODE_FILE | Output is sent to a file |
| _CRTDBG_MODE_WNDW | Output is presented in a dialog |

By default, _CRTDBG_MODE_WNDW is used, which is why a modal dialog is shown. To change this so that ATLASSERT() sends output to the Visual C++ **Output** window is trivial:

```
_CrtSetReportMode(_CRT_ASSERT, _CRTDBG_MODE_DEBUG);
```

After this function is called, the setting (which affects all threads in the process) will last until _CrtSetReportMode() is called again. Note that if a 'debug build' object server is run without the Visual C++ debugger, you can use a tool like DBMon (mentioned earlier) to pick up these assert messages. Another thing you need to remember about redirecting assertions is that when one fails and the message is sent to the output stream, there is then no way to use the debugger to examine the code that failed. However, you *are* told where the assertion failed, and what the expression was.

As an example, when I put this line in my code:

```
_ASSERTE(0 == 1);
```

The following line will appear in the output window:

```
C:\Chapter7\DebugTest\DebugTest.cpp(36) : Assertion failed: 0==1
```

To get the output sent to a file, you need to use the _CRTDBG_MODE_FILE mode. However, there is a little more to it than that: you need to specify the file that will be used, and to do *that* you must call _CrtSetReportFile(). This function has two parameters as well: the first is the type of the messages that will be sent to the file (for ATLASSERT() it will always be _CRT_ASSERT), and the second is a handle to an open file:

| Value | Description |
|---|---|
| file handle | The output is sent to the file opened with file handle |
| _CRTDBG_FILE_STDOUT | Output is sent to stdout |
| _CRTDBG_FILE_STDERR | Output is sent to stderr |

If your in-process object is used in a console application, you can do this:

```
_CrtSetReportMode(_CRT_ASSERT, _CRTDBG_MODE_FILE);
_CrtSetReportFile(_CRT_ASSERT, _CRTDBG_FILE_STDERR);
```

Now, all asserts will go to the stderr stream. To get the output sent to a file, you need to open that file:

```
HANDLE hFile;
hFile = CreateFile(
        _T("debug.txt"), GENERIC_WRITE, 0, NULL, OPEN_ALWAYS, 0, NULL);
_CrtSetReportMode(_CRT_ASSERT, _CRTDBG_MODE_FILE);
_CrtSetReportFile(_CRT_ASSERT, hFile);
```

Then, when an assertion fails, the message is sent to the specified file. Remember that you will need to make a call to CloseHandle() when the logging is no longer required, or when the object server unloads.

Note that if you do redirect output in this way, *only* the assertions will go to the file – trace messages generated with OutputDebugString() (and hence those generated with ATLTRACE()) will go to the debug stream. If you want trace messages sent to the same stream as asserts (in this case, a file) then you can call _CrtDbgReport() to report a string (and the file and line number). This function takes variable parameters so that you can report a message with a format string, rather like printf():

```
_CrtSetReportMode(_CRT_WARN, _CRTDBG_MODE_FILE);
_CrtSetReportFile(_CRT_WARN, hFile);
_CrtDbgReport(
   _CRT_WARN, __FILE__, __LINE__, NULL, "Ref count is %ld\r\n", m_dwRef);
```

The above code will result in the following being sent to `debug.txt`:

```
C:\AssertionsTest\Assertions.cpp(49) : Ref count is 2
```

The `crtdbg.h` header file defines a set of macros called `_RPTFn()` that behave like this, but ensure that the file and line number are added. `n` refers to the number of parameters, so the following is the same as the previous call:

```
_RPTF1(_CRT_WARN, "Ref count is %ld\r\n", m_dwRef);
```

If you don't want the file and line number reported, you can use the `_RPTn()` macros instead. Note that `_CrtDbgReport()` does not convert `\n` into `\r\n`, and so to get `Notepad` or other text readers to interpret ends of lines correctly, you need to use `\r\n` as I have here.

It may occur to you that you could rewrite `ATLTRACE()` and `ATLTRACE2()` to use `_CrtDbgReport()`, and hence redirect trace messages to a file. However, this will not be 100% successful, because ATL sometimes calls `OutputDebugString()` directly, and you will 'miss' this data when it does so. If you're interested in saving trace messages to a file, the best solution is to write your own version of `DBMon` to do this, and continue to use the existing version of `ATLTRACE()`.

# HRESULTs

COM doesn't allow you to throw an exception out of an object with the intention of it being caught by a client. If you throw a C++ exception in an EXE-packaged server, the most likely result is that the server will die. If you throw an exception in a DLL-packaged server, then it is possible that the client will be able to catch the exception, but this behavior is regarded as antisocial and is strongly discouraged. Remember this simple fact: C++ exceptions are language dependent, and COM objects are language neutral.

You might argue that the object could raise SEH (structured exception handling) exceptions, since these are part of Win32. However, most languages (and some C++ compilers) cannot handle SEH, and even if they could, it would still limit COM to Win32 platforms. Another of COM's goals is to be platform neutral.

I'm headed, of course, toward HRESULTs, which are an excellent way of propagating error values, but can be a little hard to decipher. To get the meaning of a HRESULT, you can rummage through `winerror.h` to find the appropriate description, but there are ways to ease this process. The following is taken from `comdef.h` for `_com_error`:

```
inline const TCHAR* _com_error::ErrorMessage() const throw()
{
    if(m_pszMsg == NULL)
    {
        FormatMessage(FORMAT_MESSAGE_ALLOCATE_BUFFER |
                    FORMAT_MESSAGE_FROM_SYSTEM, NULL, m_hresult,
                    MAKELANGID(LANG_NEUTRAL, SUBLANG_DEFAULT),
                    (LPTSTR)&m_pszMsg, 0, NULL);
        if(m_pszMsg != NULL)
        {
```

```
            int nLen = lstrlen(m_pszMsg);
            if(nLen > 1 && m_pszMsg[nLen - 1] == '\n')
            {
                m_pszMsg[nLen - 1] = 0;
                if(m_pszMsg[nLen - 2] == '\r')
                    m_pszMsg[nLen - 2] = 0;
            }
        }
        else
        {
            m_pszMsg = (LPTSTR)LocalAlloc(0, 32 * sizeof(TCHAR));
            if(m_pszMsg != NULL)
            {
                WORD wCode = WCode();
                if(wCode != 0)
                    wsprintf(m_pszMsg, TEXT("IDispatch error #%d"), wCode);
                else
                    wsprintf(m_pszMsg,TEXT("Unknown error 0x%01X"), m_hresult);
            }
        }
    }
    return m_pszMsg;
}
```

When the `FormatMessage()` function is passed the `FORMAT_MESSAGE_FROM_SYSTEM` flag, it will search the Win32 DLLs for the `HRESULT` contained in `m_hresult`, and return the message description. It is also used to get the formatted message from an Event Log ID and array of insert strings. Note that this code is part of the COM compiler support classes, and not ATL. There is no mechanism in ATL to manipulate `HRESULT`s.

All your interface methods should return a `HRESULT`. The reason is clear: if the interface is likely to be marshaled, COM will return the status of the marshaling layer in the `HRESULT`. If the method does not return an `HRESULT`, COM will not be able to inform the client of a marshaling problem.

If you're writing COM client code, you should always check the `HRESULT` returned from a COM API function or a COM object method, and take an appropriate action if a failure status is returned. This can be tedious, and often it leads to code that has many levels of indentation. This issue has been covered in an earlier chapter, but basically, although you can get more readable code by using the COM compiler support classes and exception handling, you will get fatter code with a corresponding decrease in performance.

# Error Objects

COM has a much richer mechanism of propagating results than the rather basic `HRESULT`, using a concept called **error objects**. These have their roots in Automation: the last but one parameter of `IDispatch::Invoke()` is a pointer to an `EXCEPINFO` structure that holds all the information about an error. It has a `BSTR` with a textual description of the error, a `BSTR` and a `DWORD` that are used to point to a help context in a particular help file, and a separate status code. `EXCEPINFO` is only used by `Invoke()`, which is a little restrictive, but it is fairly trivial to wrap a structure into a COM object. This is exactly what was done with `EXCEPINFO` to produce an error object.

Error objects are COM objects that have the data members of EXCEPINFO, and an additional GUID to indicate the interface that generated the error. They have some quite peculiar properties as you'll see later, but note that if you use an error object within your implementation of a dual interface, and then a client accesses the object through IDispatch::Invoke(), COM will write any data in the error object into the EXCEPINFO structure, so the error object provides error information for both methods of accessing the interface. However, note that error objects are not restricted to IDispatch in particular or dual interfaces in general – you can use them with custom interfaces too.

To use an error object, you have to ask COM to create one for you through a call to CreateErrorInfo(). This returns a pointer to the ICreateErrorInfo interface on the error object:

```
interface ICreateErrorInfo: IUnknown
{
    HRESULT SetGUID([in] REFGUID rguid);
    HRESULT SetSource([in] LPOLESTR szSource);
    HRESULT SetDescription([in] LPOLESTR szDescription);
    HRESULT SetHelpFile([in] LPOLESTR szHelpFile);
    HRESULT SetHelpContext([in] DWORD dwHelpContext);
}
```

You should fill the appropriate members, but remember that szDescription is supposed to be a string that is user-readable – that is, it should be a written in a way that the end user will be able to read and understand. Note that these variables do not have any default values.

Once the object has been initialized, you call SetErrorInfo() to make it the current error object for the **logical thread**. What is a logical thread? Well, the idea is that a client running on one thread will create an object and call a method. The object server may well be an EXE, which means that it will be running in another thread. When the method is called and a problem occurs, the error object created must be associated with the thread in the server *and* the thread in the client. Together, these two threads form the logical thread:

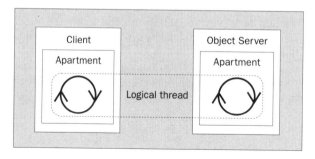

When you call **SetErrorInfo()**, any previous error object will be released.

To indicate that an error object has been set for the logical thread, the object should return an unsuccessful HRESULT to the client. Doing so indicates that a problem occurred and that an error object *may* be available. In other words, a successful HRESULT indicates that the client should not attempt to obtain an error object, but a failure code indicates that it can check to see if one is available.

When the client sees that there's a problem, it can use the HRESULT to get limited information, but before it can access any error object, it must first determine whether the server supports them. To do this, the client will call QueryInterface() on the interface pointer it holds for the ISupportErrorInfo interface. If a valid interface pointer is returned, then the object supports error objects.

In order to use error objects, therefore, your ATL class must implement ISupportErrorInfo. The easiest way to do this is to check the Support ISupportErrorInfo box in the Object Wizard:

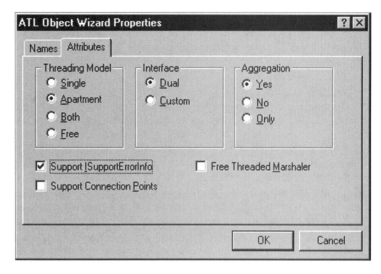

Once the client knows that the *object* supports error objects, it then needs to know if the *interface* that generated the error supports error objects. To do this, it calls InterfaceSupportsErrorInfo() on the ISupportErrorInfo interface, passing the IID of the interface that generated the error. If the interface supports error objects, the function will return S_OK; otherwise it should return S_FALSE. The Object Wizard will add an implementation of this method for you, using the IID of the default interface:

```
STDMETHODIMP CMyObject::InterfaceSupportsErrorInfo(REFIID riid)
{
    static const IID* arr[] =
    {
        &IID_IMyInterface
    };

    for(int i = 0 ; i < sizeof(arr) / sizeof(arr[0]) ; i++)
    {
        if(InlineIsEqualGUID(*arr[i], riid))
            return S_OK;
    }
    return S_FALSE;
}
```

If you add more interfaces to your object and arrange for these to generate error objects, you should add their IIDs to the arr array.

The client can now try to obtain the error object for the logical thread by calling GetErrorInfo(). Note that this method will return either S_OK or S_FALSE – the former to indicate that an error object was created, and the latter to say that the interface supports error objects but there was not one available. There is no return value to say that the interface does not support error objects, so if you call GetErrorInfo() in this case, an access violation will occur and your client will most likely die, unless you have code to catch this exception.

The code for accessing and setting error objects, and then making them current, is rather tedious. Thankfully, ATL helps with several methods. The global AtlSetErrorInfo() function has this prototype:

```
ATLINLINE ATLAPI AtlSetErrorInfo(const CLSID& clsid, LPCOLESTR lpszDesc,
                         DWORD dwHelpID, LPCOLESTR lpszHelpFile,
                         const IID& iid, HRESULT hRes, HINSTANCE hInst)
```

The first parameter is the CLSID of the object, while the second is the description of the problem. You should use a properly descriptive string here – if you don't, it will hardly be worthy of the name 'rich error information'. The next two parameters indicate a help context within a help file that IDEs like Visual Basic's will use to load and display further information. After that comes the IID of the interface that caused the problem and the HRESULT that the calling method wants to return. Finally, so that you can use string resources, a module instance can be passed.

AtlSetErrorInfo() will take the information that you pass to it and create, initialize and set an error object. The HRESULT that you pass will also be its return value, so that it can be used in this context:

```
STDMETHODIMP CMyInterface::SquareRoot(double val, double* ret)
{
   if(val < 0)
      return AtlSetErrorInfo(CLSID_MyObject,
                         _T("Value cannot be negative"), 0, NULL,
                         IID_IMyInterface, E_INVALIDARG, NULL);
   *ret = sqrt(val);
   return S_OK;
}
```

You can call the function and simply pass a string to lpszDesc, or you can pass a string resource ID in the low WORD of the same parameter (in the range 0x0200 to 0xffff). If you do the latter, the method will look for this string ID in the module given by hInst.

This is not the most convenient of functions to use, so ATL has provided a global function called AtlReportError() with various overloaded forms that make life a bit easier:

```
HRESULT WINAPI AtlReportError(const CLSID& clsid, UINT nID,
                         const IID& iid, HRESULT hRes,
                         HINSTANCE hInst);
HRESULT WINAPI AtlReportError(const CLSID& clsid, UINT nID,
                         DWORD dwHelpID, LPCOLESTR lpszHelpFile,
                         const IID& iid, HRESULT hRes,
                         HINSTANCE hInst);
```

```
HRESULT WINAPI AtlReportError(const CLSID& clsid, LPCSTR lpszDesc,
                    DWORD dwHelpID, LPCSTR lpszHelpFile,
                    const IID& iid, HRESULT hRes);
HRESULT WINAPI AtlReportError(const CLSID& clsid, LPCSTR lpszDesc,
                    const IID& iid, HRESULT hRes);
HRESULT WINAPI AtlReportError(const CLSID& clsid, LPCOLESTR lpszDesc,
                    const IID& iid, HRESULT hRes);
HRESULT WINAPI AtlReportError(const CLSID& clsid, LPCOLESTR lpszDesc,
                    DWORD dwHelpID, LPCOLESTR lpszHelpFile,
                    const IID& iid, HRESULT hRes);
```

The first and second of these use a description string from a resource, the third and fourth take ANSI strings, and the last two take wide character strings. However, `AtlReportError()` *still* involves unnecessary coding: because it is a global function, it requires that you pass the object's CLSID. To help you further, `CComCoClass<>` (which should be a base class of your ATL class) provides overloaded versions of `Error()`:

```
HRESULT WINAPI Error(LPCOLESTR lpszDesc, const IID& iid = GUID_NULL,
                    HRESULT hRes = 0);
HRESULT WINAPI Error(LPCOLESTR lpszDesc, DWORD dwHelpID,
                    LPCOLESTR lpszHelpFile, const IID& iid = GUID_NULL,
                    HRESULT hRes = 0);
HRESULT WINAPI Error(UINT nID, const IID& iid = GUID_NULL,
                    HRESULT hRes = 0,
                    HINSTANCE hInst = _Module.GetResourceInstance());
HRESULT WINAPI Error(UINT nID, DWORD dwHelpID,
                    LPCOLESTR lpszHelpFile, const IID& iid = GUID_NULL,
                    HRESULT hRes = 0,
                    HINSTANCE hInst = _Module.GetResourceInstance());
HRESULT WINAPI Error(LPCSTR lpszDesc, const IID& iid = GUID_NULL,
                    HRESULT hRes = 0);
HRESULT WINAPI Error(LPCSTR lpszDesc, DWORD dwHelpID,
                    LPCSTR lpszHelpFile, const IID& iid = GUID_NULL,
                    HRESULT hRes = 0);
```

This method just calls `AtlReportError()` with appropriate values. It makes life a bit easier, particularly if you want to use string resources, because the default parameters will ensure that the module `HINSTANCE` is used. However, note that you will still have to pass an IID if you want to use a value for `ICreateErrorInfo::SetGUID()`. This is because `CComObject<>` is applicable to the *entire* object, and thus will have no knowledge of what interface is being called.

The simplest way of using `Error()` is like this:

```
STDMETHODIMP CMyInterface::SquareRoot(double val, double* ret)
{
   if(val < 0)
      return Error(_T("Value cannot be negative"));
   *ret = sqrt(val);
   return S_OK;
}
```

As I have said previously, when you set an error object for the current thread, any previously set error object will be released. This is fine, because it means that when the client calls `GetErrorInfo()`, it gets the current error object. However, if you have an object method that calls other methods on the current object (or other methods on other objects) then these secondary methods may fail and set an error object. You can detect this and only create a new error object if one has not already been set, but this has the further problem that the information in the error object will refer to a different method from the one the client called.

In this situation, it is better to read the error object set by the other methods, copy the string, append any other information that is relevant to your method, and then create and set a new error object for the thread. For example:

```
CComPtr<IBank> pBank = GetBankObjectFromSomewhere();
HRESULT hr;
hr = pBank->CreateAccount(strMyname);
if(FAILED(hr))
{
    CComBSTR bstrError;
    CComPtr<ISupportErrorInfo> pSEI;
    HRESULT hr1 = pBank->QueryInterface(&pSEI);
    if(SUCCEEDED(hr))
    {
        bstrError = _T("Error occurred in CreateAccount()");

        // Make sure that the interface supports error objects
        hr1 = pSEI->InterfaceSupportsErrorInfo(__uuidof(IBank));
        if(hr1 == S_OK)
        {
            // Try to get the error object
            CComPtr<IErrorObject> pEO;
            if(S_OK == GetErrorInfo(&pEO))
            {
                CComBSTR bstrDesc;
                pEo->GetDescription(bstrDesc);
                bstrError += bstrDesc;
            }
        }
    }
    return Error(bstrError.m_str, IID_ThisInterface, hr);
}
```

Since the error object mechanism returns just the *current* error object, it means that there is no record of the errors that have been generated over a period of time. This is a shame, because that kind of long-term picture would be useful information if you wanted to see *how often* a method fails, and the reason for failure. One approach here is to override `Error()` so that whenever it is called, the error is logged to the Event Log. You can then either use the NT Event Log viewer or write your own tool to read these errors. Remember, however, that in general you should try to keep the number of logged messages low, and if `Error()` is likely to be called often, you will need to use another solution.

In any case, if the error information is specific to this object and unlikely to be read on a regular basis, it may be better for the object to handle the information and return it only when requested.

One way to do this is to provide a collection on your object that returns all the error objects that have been created. On the surface this looks quite straightforward, but there are some issues that you will have to address. For example, your object could maintain an STL list<>, and put an error object into it whenever one is created. This is fine, because the error object is just a COM object, and provided that a *copy* of the interface pointer is made (that is, AddRef() is called), then the error object will remain even after the system frees its copy when a subsequent call to SetErroInfo() is made. You could then add the Count and _NewEnum properties to your object, and use the list to provide values for these.

In this scenario, Count could be implemented by calling std::list<>::size(), and you could use the ATL CComEnumOnSTL<> template to create the _NewEnum property. However, one small problem exists. IErrorInfo is marked with the [local] attribute, so you cannot marshal this interface, which means that if you return an enumerator with the IUnknown of these objects, the client would not be able to call QueryInterface() for IErrorInfo unless the enumerator was in-process. To solve this problem, you would either have to provide your own version of IErrorInfo that can be marshaled, or enumerate strings that have all of the items from IErrorInfo packed together.

# Example: ErrorList

This example will provide one possible solution to the previous problem. I will make things a little easier for myself here and just return an enumerator with strings that contain the *contents* of the error objects that have been generated, but you'll see the principle involved, and you shouldn't find it difficult to extend the idea.

The example will feature two objects. The first of these is Math, which is an object that can do some mathematical operations and will test its parameters to make sure that they have valid values. If the values are not valid, the methods will create an error object and 'throw' it so that the client can get rich error information. When it does this, the Math object will add the rich error information to the second object, ErrorList. This has a STL vector<> to hold the data passed to it, and also has the Count and _NewEnum properties so that VBA clients can obtain its data as a collection.

To make this object's functionality available to the Math object, I have decided to aggregate it. This is a natural choice because the error information is integral to the Math object, and so it makes sense to make one available through the other.

## The Basic Server

Start by creating a DLL project called MathSvr and then add a simple object called Math that has support for error objects (check Support ISupportErrorInfo). Add to it the following methods:

| Method | Parameters |
|---|---|
| Add | [in] double d1, [in] double d2, [out, retval] double* dRet |
| Subtract | [in] double d1, [in] double d2, [out, retval] double* dRet |
| Multiply | [in] double d1, [in] double d2, [out, retval] double* dRet |
| Divide | [in] double d1, [in] double d2, [out, retval] double* dRet |
| Sqrt | [in] double d, [out, retval] double* dRet |

Include support for math routines at the top of `Math.cpp`:

```
#include <cmath>
```

And implement the methods like this:

```
STDMETHODIMP CMath::Add(double d1, double d2, double *dRet)
{
    if(dRet == NULL)
        return Error(OLESTR("Add: invalid pointer for return value"),
                                               IID_IMath, E_POINTER);
    *dRet = d1 + d2;
    return S_OK;
}

STDMETHODIMP CMath::Subtract(double d1, double d2, double *dRet)
{
    if(dRet == NULL)
        return Error(OLESTR("Subtract: invalid pointer for return value"),
                                               IID_IMath, E_POINTER);
    *dRet = d1 - d2;
    return S_OK;
}

STDMETHODIMP CMath::Multiply(double d1, double d2, double *dRet)
{
    if(dRet == NULL)
        return Error(OLESTR("Multiply: invalid pointer for return value"),
                                               IID_IMath, E_POINTER);
    *dRet = d1 * d2;
    return S_OK;
}

STDMETHODIMP CMath::Divide(double d1, double d2, double *dRet)
{
    if(dRet == NULL)
        return Error(OLESTR("Divide: invalid pointer for return value"),
                                               IID_IMath, E_POINTER);
    *dRet = 0;
    if(d2 == 0)
        return Error(OLESTR("Divide: denominator must not be zero"),
                                               IID_IMath, E_INVALIDARG);
    *dRet = d1 / d2;
    return S_OK;
}

STDMETHODIMP CMath::Sqrt(double d, double *dRet)
{
    if(dRet == NULL)
        return Error(OLESTR("Sqrt: invalid pointer for return value"),
                                               IID_IMath, E_POINTER);
    *dRet = 0;
    if(d == -1)
        return Error(OLESTR("Sqrt: parameter must not be -1"),
                                               IID_IMath, E_INVALIDARG);
    *dRet = sqrt(d);
    return S_OK;
}
```

This is pretty straightforward stuff: if there are any problems with the parameters, then an error object is created. You should compile this server and test it out with a Visual Basic client (I'll show you a C++ client in a moment).

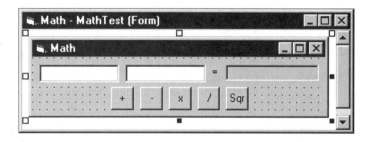

This has two text boxes (`txtLeft` and `txtRight`) for the operands and a label (`lblResult`) for the result. The operations are performed by clicking on the buttons (`cmdAdd`, `cmdSubtract`, `cmdMultiply`, `cmdDivide` and `cmdSqrt`). Add the type library for the `MathSvr`, and implemnent the code like this:

```
Dim obj As MATHSVRLib.Math

Private Sub cmdAdd_Click()
    Dim d As Double
    d = obj.Add(Val(txtLeft), Val(txtRight))
    lblResult = Str$(d)
End Sub

Private Sub cmdSqrt_Click()
    Dim d As Double
    d = obj.Sqrt(Val(txtLeft))
    lblResult = Str$(d)
End Sub

Private Sub Form_Load()
    Set obj = New MATHSVRLib.Math
End Sub
```

I have missed out the implementations for the subtract, divide and multiply buttons because they are so straightforward. To test this out, you can run the example and attempt to get the square root of −1 − you should get this dialog:

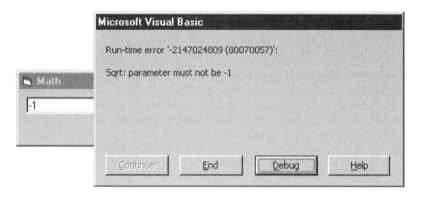

In other words, Visual Basic is catching the error object and giving you the description string. To make this client a bit more robust, you could add another label and error handling code, for example:

```
Private Sub cmdAdd_Click()
    Dim d As Double
    lblError = ""
    On Error GoTo addError
    d = obj.Add(Val(txtLeft), Val(txtRight))
    lblResult = Str$(d)
    Exit Sub
addError:
    lblError = Err.Description
End Sub
```

This simply puts the description into the label.

## The ErrorList Object

Now go back to the MathSvr project. Insert a simple object called ErrorList and make it *only* aggregatable. Add two read-only properties: Count (type long) and _NewEnum (type LPUNKNOWN). Make this last property [restricted] and then edit the IDL to change its id() attribute to DISPID_NEWENUM.

This example will hold the data in an STL vector<>, so add the following lines to the top of ErrorList.h:

```
#pragma warning(disable : 4530)
#include <vector>
```

Also add the following data member:

```
private:
    std::vector<CComVariant> m_coll;
};
```

The error object's contents will be added to the vector as CComVariants containing a BSTR. The Count property is implemented like this:

```
STDMETHODIMP CErrorList::get_Count(long *pVal)
{
    if(pVal == NULL)
        return E_POINTER;
    *pVal = m_coll.size();
    return S_OK;
}
```

And _NewEnum should look like this:

```
STDMETHODIMP CErrorList::get__NewEnum(LPUNKNOWN *pVal)
{
    if(pVal == NULL)
        return E_POINTER;
```

```
    *pVal = NULL;
    HRESULT hRes = S_OK;
    typedef CComEnumOnSTL<IEnumVARIANT,
                          &IID_IEnumVARIANT,
                          VARIANT,
                          _Copy<VARIANT>,
                          std::vector<CComVariant> > EnumType;

    CComObject<EnumType>* p;
    hRes = CComObject<EnumType>::CreateInstance(&p);
    if(SUCCEEDED(hRes))
    {
        hRes = p->Init(NULL, m_coll);
        if(hRes == S_OK)
            hRes = p->QueryInterface(IID_IUnknown, (void**)pVal);
    }

    if(hRes != S_OK)
        delete p;
    return hRes;
}
```

This uses the new `CComEnumOnSTL<>` template, the parameters to which are pretty self-explanatory. The one that interests us here is the final parameter that gives the STL container type that will have the data. The enumerator is created using `CreateInstance()`, and then initialized by calling `Init()` passing the collection data member.

Next, you need a method to add data into the container, and to do this you need to add a method called `AddString()` that takes a `BSTR` and has the `[hidden]` attribute (so that Visual Basic cannot see it). This method is implemented like so:

```
STDMETHODIMP CErrorList::AddString(BSTR bstr)
{
    CComVariant var(bstr);
    m_coll.push_back(var);
    return S_OK;
}
```

The next task is to use this in the `Math` object, so the first thing to do is add a data member for the object's `IUnknown` pointer:

```
private:
    CComPtr<IUnknown> m_spErrors;
};
```

And aggregate this object in `FinalConstruct()`:

```
HRESULT FinalConstruct()
{
    return m_spErrors.CoCreateInstance(
                    CLSID_ErrorList, GetUnknown(), CLSCTX_INPROC_SERVER);
}
```

You will also need to add the `IErrorList` interface to the COM map:

```
BEGIN_COM_MAP(CMath)
    COM_INTERFACE_ENTRY(IMath)
    COM_INTERFACE_ENTRY(IDispatch)
    COM_INTERFACE_ENTRY(ISupportErrorInfo)
    COM_INTERFACE_ENTRY_AGGREGATE(IID_IErrorList, m_spErrors.p)
END_COM_MAP()
```

The final change to the header is to add a new `Error()` method to log the error object into `ErrorList`:

```
HRESULT Error(LPCOLESTR lpszDesc, HRESULT hRes);
```

This is implemented like so:

```
HRESULT CMath::Error(LPCOLESTR lpszDesc, HRESULT hRes)
{
    CComBSTR bstr(lpszDesc);
    CComQIPtr<IErrorList> pError(m_spErrors);
    pError->AddString(bstr);
    return AtlReportError(GetObjectCLSID(), lpszDesc, IID_IMath, hRes);
}
```

I've decided just to add the error description into the `ErrorList` object, but you can see the principle. This method is called in the other methods to generate the error, for example in `Sqrt()`:

```
STDMETHODIMP CMath::Sqrt(double d, double *dRet)
{
    if(dRet == NULL)
        return Error(OLESTR(
                    "Sqrt: invalid pointer for return value"), E_POINTER);
    *dRet = 0;

    if(d == -1)
        return Error(OLESTR(
                        "Sqrt: parameter must not be -1"), E_INVALIDARG);

    *dRet = sqrt(d);
    return S_OK;
}
```

You can now compile this project again. To test the server, change the Visual Basic client to have a list box called `lstErrors` and add this method:

```
Private Sub UpdateListbox()
    Dim errList As IErrorList
    Set errList = obj
    lstErrors.Clear
    lstErrors.AddItem "There are " & Str$(errList.Count) & " errors"
```

```
    Dim v As Variant
    For Each v In errList
        lstErrors.AddItem v
    Next
End Sub
```

This gets hold of the aggregated `ErrorList` object by querying for the `IErrorList` interface. The code then clears the list box and adds the number of errors to it before obtaining the enumerator with `For Each` and adding each `BSTR` to the list box. If you run this a few times and make a few errors you should see something like this:

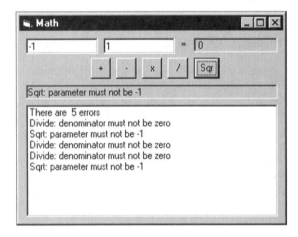

## The C++ Client

The last example only tested for the value of the `[in]` parameters, because Visual Basic will always make sure that the `[out]` parameters are passed a valid pointer. To test that an error will be generated if a `NULL` pointer is passed, you need to create a C++ client.

Create a console "Hello, World!" Application called `MathTest`, and change `stdafx.h` as usual to allow you to use COM:

```
#define _WIN32_DCOM
#include <windows.h>
#include <stdio.h>
#include <tchar.h>
```

At the top of the CPP file, I added this function:

```
void ReportError(_com_error& e)
{
   _tprintf(_T("Error: %08x %s\n"), e.Error(), e.ErrorMessage());
   _bstr_t desc = e.Description();
   if(desc.length() > 0)
   {
      // Must be error info
      _tprintf(_T("Description: %s\n"), static_cast<LPTSTR>(desc));
      _tprintf(_T("From: %s\n"), static_cast<LPTSTR>(e.Source()));
      LPOLESTR lpolestr;
      IID iid = e.GUID();
```

```
      StringFromIID(iid, &lpolestr);
      _tprintf(_T("Interface: %S\n"), lpolestr);
      CoTaskMemFree(lpolestr);
   }
}
```

This prints out the error object information. To get smart pointer support, I use this:

```
#import "..\MathSvr\MathSvr.tlb" no_namespace
```

Finally, _tmain() is implemented like this:

```
void _tmain()
{
    CoInitialize(NULL);

    try
    {
        IMathPtr ptr(__uuidof(Math));
        double d;
        try
        {
            d = ptr->Divide(0, 0);
        }
        catch(_com_error e)
        {
            _tprintf(_T("Divide by zero error:\n"));
            ReportError(e);
        }
        try
        {
            HRESULT hr;
            hr = ptr->raw_Divide(0, 0, NULL);
            if(FAILED(hr))
                _com_issue_errorex(hr, ptr, __uuidof(ptr));
        }
        catch(_com_error e)
        {
            _tprintf(_T("Bad pointer error:\n"));
            ReportError(e);
        }

        IErrorListPtr pErrList;
        pErrList = ptr;

        IEnumVARIANTPtr pEnum;
        IUnknownPtr pUnk;
        pUnk = pErrList->Get_NewEnum();
        pEnum = pUnk;

        _tprintf(_T("\nGetting Error List\n"));
        VARIANT pVar[5];
        for(int i = 0 ; i < 5 ; i++)
            VariantInit(&pVar[i]);
```

```
         ULONG fetched = 0;
         while(SUCCEEDED(pEnum->Next(5, pVar, &fetched)) && fetched>0)
         {
            for(ULONG z = 0 ; z < fetched ; z++)
            {
               _bstr_t bstr(pVar[z]);
               _tprintf(_T("%s\n"), static_cast<LPTSTR>(bstr));
               VariantClear(&pVar[z]);
            }
         }
      }
      catch(_com_error e)
      {
         _tprintf(_T("General problem\n"));
         ReportError(e);
      }
      CoUninitialize();
   }
```

First I create the `Math` object and then attempt to call `Divide()` with a zero denominator. This should throw an exception. The next test is to try and pass a `NULL` pointer for the `[out]` parameter; to do this I have to call `raw_Divide()`, because `Divide()` ensures that this parameter is not `NULL`. Since I'm calling the raw interface method, I have to throw the exception myself with a call to `_com_issue_errorex()`.

Finally, I obtain the errors in the enumerator object. To do this I first call `QueryInterface()` for the `IErrorList` interface, using the assignment operator:

```
         IErrorListPtr pErrList;
         pErrList = ptr;

         IEnumVARIANTPtr pEnum;
         IUnknownPtr pUnk;
         pUnk = pErrList->Get_NewEnum();
         pEnum = pUnk;
```

Then I call `Get_NewEnum()` to get the `IUnknown` of the enumerator object, and finally call `QueryInterface()` on that for the `IEnumVARIANT` interface. The code should produce the following results:

```
C:\>mathtest
Divide by zero error:
Error: 80070057 The parameter is incorrect.
Description: Divide: denominator must not be zero
From: MathSvr.Math.1
Interface: {821BA332-2320-11D2-8D1C-0060973044A8}
Bad pointer error:
Error: 80004003 Invalid pointer
Description: Divide: invalid pointer for return value
From: MathSvr.Math.1
Interface: {821BA332-2320-11D2-8D1C-0060973044A8}

Getting Error List
Divide: denominator must not be zero
Divide: invalid pointer for return value

C:\>
```

# Interface Checking and Reference Count Debugging

Perhaps the worst aspect of COM, as it stands, is the fact that when you have finished using an interface pointer, you absolutely, utterly and incontrovertibly *must* release it. There are no ifs or buts: once the interface pointer has been used, it must go. The problem, of course, is that most code isn't as simple as:

```
IMyInterface* pInt;
GetMyInterface(&pInt);
pInt->SomeMethod();
pInt->Release();
```

More often, interface pointers are cached as data members, or passed to methods where they get copied (and `AddRef()` will be called), or used in large functions full of spaghetti code. Frequently, objects implement a single reference count for *all* the interfaces they implement, so when you're debugging an object and an interface is not released, how can you tell which interface it is? Furthermore, how can you tell whether an interface pointer is being excessively `AddRef()`'d, or that it is not being `Release()`'d? Another related problem is that of being able to determine the interfaces that are being queried for. This is useful, because you can get an idea of what order the interfaces are `QueryInterface()`'d in, and indeed whether they are being `QueryInterface()`'d at all.

ATL provides all this information through **interface debugging**. Normally, this is not provided even in debug builds, so to get this support you must define the `_ATL_DEBUG_INTERFACES` symbol, either in the **Preprocessor** section of the C/C++ tab of the project settings, or by `#define`ing it before the `#include` for `atlbase.h` in `stdafx.h`. Note that you can use this symbol regardless of whether the project is a debug build or a release build – in both cases, the information it provides will be sent to the debug stream. This is an important point, so you must remember to remove the definition of this symbol in release builds that you distribute to your customers.

> *ATL 2.1 supported a restricted version of reference count debugging that was designed only to count references on ATL interface implementations, and not on any of the ones that the user defined. This used the `_ATL_DEBUG_REFCOUNT` symbol, which now just defines `_ATL_DEBUG_INTERFACES` so that old ATL code will still work.*
>
> *In addition, ATL 2.1 used a symbol called `_ATL_DEBUG_QI` that made sure that whenever an interface was requested, its human-readable name was written to the debug stream. This symbol is still valid in ATL 3.0.*

This one little symbol provides you with a lot of functionality. It adds additional members to the `CComModule` class, and it also defines a new class called `_QIThunk`. The idea of a **thunk** is that some code is placed 'in between' the interface pointer and the method code in the object. This is done in such a way that the user of an interface pointer sees no change, and the object methods that are accessed through the thunk are also the same as before the thunk was applied.

The thunk code has access to the parameters that the client passed, expecting to call an interface method directly, and it can manipulate these if it chooses to do so. The thunk does this by manipulating the stack, which inevitably involves some machine code. In a way, you can think of a proxy and stub as being a 'distributed thunk', in that the client calls the proxy as if it is the interface pointer, and then the stub manipulates the stack to call the actual interface method. Thunks are used by ATL in interface debugging because they can be used to 'inject' code that monitors the reference count changes on an interface. However, it does mean that the thunk must be set up at some point and this happens when an interface pointer is returned, as you'll see in a moment.

The new public data members in CComModule due to the _ATL_DEBUG_INTERFACES symbol are:

```
UINT m_nIndexQI;
UINT m_nIndexBreakAt;
CSimpleArray<_QIThunk*>* m_paThunks;
```

m_nIndexQI keeps a running count of the number of thunks that have been allocated, while m_nIndexBreakAt is a thunk index that when reached will cause the program to stop in the debugger. Once you've identified an interface request that you're interested in, you can set m_nIndexBreakAt to this thunk index. Since this data member is public, you can set it from anywhere in the program – perhaps in DllMain() or _tWinMain(). Note that since m_nIndexQI is a *count* and not the index in the array, a value of 0 means that there are no thunks. Correspondingly, a value of 0 for m_nIndexBreakAt means that a break will not occur for any thunk creation. The thunks themselves are held in the array pointed to by m_paThunks, which is created in CComModule::Init().

Using _ATL_DEBUG_INTERFACES will also add some methods to CComModule to manipulate this array of thunks: AddThunk(), AddNonAddRefThunk(), DeleteNonAddRefThunk(), DeleteThunk() and DumpLeakedThunks(). The first four add a new thunk to, or remove a specific thunk from the array. The final method checks the array, and if there are any items in it, calls _QIThunk::Dump() on each item. This method is called in CComModule::Term() when the server shuts down. In an ideal case, there shouldn't be any items in the array; if there are, then _QIThunk::Dump() will print out the name of the interface and the class that implements it to the debug stream, and give information about the reference counts on the interface.

As you can see, there are two types of thunks used: AddRef()'d thunks and non-AddRef()'d thunks. Most of the time, AddRef()'d thunks will be used, because you will want to monitor the reference count. However, if the object's reference count is maintained by another object, then the thunk should *not* keep a separate reference count, and so a non AddRef()'d thunk is used. This situation arises in the cases of aggregated objects and objects that are used to implement tear-off interfaces, and these are characterized by the fact that they are derived from CComContainedObject<>.

Any method that returns an interface pointer will need to return a thunk rather than the interface requested. The main mechanism to return an interface pointer is QueryInterface(), which in ATL ends up in a call to InternalQueryInterface(), as we discussed in Chapter 2. Here are the relevant lines in atlcom.h:

```
static HRESULT WINAPI InternalQueryInterface(void* pThis,
        const _ATL_INTMAP_ENTRY* pEntries, REFIID iid, void** ppvObject)
{
    ATLASSERT(pThis != NULL);
    // First entry in the com map should be a simple map entry
    ATLASSERT(pEntries->pFunc == _ATL_SIMPLEMAPENTRY);
    #if defined(_ATL_DEBUG_INTERFACES) || defined(_ATL_DEBUG_QI)
        LPCTSTR pszClassName = (LPCTSTR)pEntries[-1].dw;
    #endif // _ATL_DEBUG_INTERFACES
    HRESULT hRes = AtlInternalQueryInterface(
                                    pThis, pEntries, iid, ppvObject);
    #ifdef _ATL_DEBUG_INTERFACES
        Module.AddThunk((IUnknown**)ppvObject, pszClassName, iid);
    #endif // _ATL_DEBUG_INTERFACES
    return _ATLDUMPIID(iid, pszClassName, hRes);
}
```

*Note that the method returns a value based on* _ATLDUMPIID(), *which has* pszClassName
*as a parameter, but that this is only declared if either* _ATL_DEBUG_QI *or*
_ATL_DEBUG_INTERFACE *is defined. However, if you look at the definition of*
_ATLDUMPIID() *in* atlcom.h, *you'll find that if* _ATL_DEBUG_QI *is not defined, the
macro will preprocess to* hRes *and this code will compile.*

In the first highlighted section, the class name is obtained from the pEntries array. This array
usually holds information about the interfaces that the object implements, but notice that the index
used is –1. If you look at the definition of BEGIN_COM_MAP() in atlcom.h, you'll find that the lines
relevant to the array of interface pointers are:

```
const static _ATL_INTMAP_ENTRY* WINAPI _GetEntries() { \
static const _ATL_INTMAP_ENTRY _entries[] = { DEBUG_QI_ENTRY(x)
```

Here, x is the parameter of BEGIN_COM_MAP() that is the class name. DEBUG_QI_ENTRY() is
defined as:

```
#ifdef _ATL_DEBUG
#define DEBUG_QI_ENTRY(x) \
    {NULL, \
    (DWORD)_T(#x), \
    (_ATL_CREATORARGFUNC*)0},
#else
#define DEBUG_QI_ENTRY(x)
#endif //_ATL_DEBUG
```

_ATL_DEBUG is defined if _ATL_DEBUG_INTERFACES is defined, so this will add another entry to
the map that has a pointer to the class named in the dw member of _ATL_INTMAP_ENTRY. The
problem here, of course, is that the first entry in the map should be the interface that's used to
implement IUnknown, so how does this work? Well, the map is obtained by calling the
_GetEntries() method, the first part of which is shown above (it's inserted by
BEGIN_COM_MAP()), while last part is inserted by END_COM_MAP():

```
#ifdef _ATL_DEBUG
#define END_COM_MAP() {NULL, 0, 0}}; return &_entries[1];} \
    virtual ULONG STDMETHODCALLTYPE AddRef( void) = 0; \
    virtual ULONG STDMETHODCALLTYPE Release( void) = 0; \
    STDMETHOD(QueryInterface)(REFIID, void**) = 0;
#else
#define END_COM_MAP() {NULL, 0, 0}}; return _entries;} \
    virtual ULONG STDMETHODCALLTYPE AddRef( void) = 0; \
    virtual ULONG STDMETHODCALLTYPE Release( void) = 0; \
    STDMETHOD(QueryInterface)(REFIID, void**) = 0;
#endif // _ATL_DEBUG
```

The interesting part is the first line of the macro. If _ATL_DEBUG is defined, the *second* entry in the array is returned. This is why, when _ATL_DEBUG_INTERFACES is defined, you can access a negative index on pEntries: _entries[1] has been obtained from _GetEntries().

Let's go back to InternalQueryInterface(). After the class name is obtained, AtlInternalQueryInterface() is called as usual to obtain the requested interface, and this interface pointer will be put into the location pointed to by ppvObject. Next, the thunk is created for this interface with a call to _Module.AddThunk().

CComModule holds the thunks in an array pointed to by m_paThunks; this is implemented by CSimpleArray<>, which (as the name suggests) offers basic array support, including Add() and Remove() and an operator[]() to access the items it contains. I'll talk more about _QIThunk in the next section, but its data members include the IUnknown pointer and IID of the interface, and a reference count. AddThunk() traverses this array to see if the interface has already been added, and if so the reference count it holds is incremented. Notice that this count is associated with the *interface* in the thunk, and this is how interface debugging gives you the per-interface reference count rather than the per-object reference count that ATL objects implement.

If the interface is not in the array, then a new thunk is created and added to the array, with the thunk count, m_nIndexQI, incremented (it is *not* incremented if the interface already has a thunk, because this is an index of the number of thunks in the array). If you have set m_nIndexBreakAt and m_nIndexQI reaches this value, then DebugBreak() will be called – the application will reach a breakpoint even if the COM server was compiled in release mode.

> **Because of this behavior, you must be diligent about removing**
> **_ATL_DEBUG_INTERFACES when you make a release build.**

In the figure below, a client has references on three interfaces: IUnknown, IMyItfOne and IMyItfTwo. The client accesses the interfaces through thunks that maintain the reference counts on those interfaces, while the object maintains the *total* reference count applied through *all* interfaces.

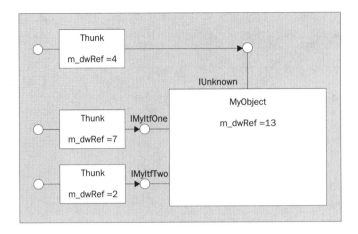

The interface pointer passed to AddThunk() is cached in the thunk object, and replaced with the address of the thunk. Thus, when InternalQueryInterface() returns, the variable pointed to by ppvObject will contain a pointer to the thunk. Now that the thunk is in place, it means that whenever methods are called by the client on this "interface pointer", the thunk methods will be called. Exactly how this works will be explained in the next section.

Of course, interface pointers can be obtained by methods other than QueryInterface(). In particular, if a method wants to get hold of its own IUnknown pointer, it should call GetUnknown(), which effectively makes a copy of an interface pointer. This method is defined by the _ATL_DECLARE_GET_UNKNOWN() macro called by BEGIN_COM_MAP():

```
#ifdef _ATL_DEBUG_INTERFACES
#define _ATL_DECLARE_GET_UNKNOWN(x)\
    IUnknown* GetUnknown() \
    { \
        IUnknown* p; \
        _Module.AddNonAddRefThunk(_GetRawUnknown(), _T(#x), &p); \
        return p; \
    }
#else
#define _ATL_DECLARE_GET_UNKNOWN(x) IUnknown* GetUnknown()\
    {return _GetRawUnknown();}
#endif
```

_GetRawUnknown() obtains the IUnknown pointer, and if you're using interface debugging, a non-AddRef()'d thunk is added.

# QI Thunks

_QIThunk is defined with the following methods and data members:

```
struct _QIThunk
{
    STDMETHOD(QueryInterface)(REFIID iid, void** pp);
    STDMETHOD_(ULONG, AddRef)();
    STDMETHOD_(ULONG, Release)();
```

```
    // Other methods (see below)

    STDMETHOD(f3)();
    STDMETHOD(f4)();
    STDMETHOD(f5)();

    // etc

    STDMETHOD(f1022)();
    STDMETHOD(f1023)();
    STDMETHOD(f1024)();

    IUnknown* pUnk;
    long m_dwRef;
    long m_dwMaxRef;
    LPCTSTR lpszClassName;
    IID iid;
    bool bBreak;

    // Other members
};
```

STDMETHOD declares a method as `virtual`, so this class has a vtable with 1025 entries, and the first three entries have the same signatures as the IUnknown methods.

> *It is interesting to see that there is space for 1025 methods and not 1024. Under NT 4.0 with Service Pack 3 installed, the maximum number of methods allowed in a dual interface is 1024; with Windows 95 this limit is 512.*

Let's look at these first three methods:

```
STDMETHOD(QueryInterface)(REFIID iid, void** pp)
{
    ATLASSERT(m_dwRef >= 0);
    return pUnk->QueryInterface(iid, pp);
}
STDMETHOD_(ULONG, AddRef)()
{
    if(bBreak)
        DebugBreak();
    pUnk->AddRef();
    return InternalAddRef();
}
STDMETHOD_(ULONG, Release)()
{
    if(bBreak)
        DebugBreak();
    ATLASSERT(m_dwRef > 0);
    ULONG l = InterlockedDecrement(&m_dwRef);
    ATLTRACE(_T("%d< "), m_dwRef);
    AtlDumpIID(iid, lpszClassName, S_OK);
    pUnk->Release();
    if(l == 0 && !bNonAddRefThunk)
        _pModule->DeleteThunk(this);
    return l;
}
```

As you can see, `QueryInterface()` delegates to the actual `QueryInterface()` of the interface. `AddRef()` checks to see if it should break, and if so calls `DebugBreak()`, which will stop the process in the debugger. `AddRef()` then delegates to the wrapped interface's `AddRef()`, and increments its own managed reference count through `InternalAddRef()`. In addition to this behavior, `InternalAddRef()` also prints out debugging information with `ATLTRACE()`:

```
ULONG InternalAddRef()
{
    if(bBreak)
        DebugBreak();
    ATLASSERT(m_dwRef >= 0);
    long l = InterlockedIncrement(&m_dwRef);
    ATLTRACE(_T("%d> "), m_dwRef);
    AtlDumpIID(iid, lpszClassName, S_OK);
    if(l > m_dwMaxRef)
        m_dwMaxRef = l;
    return l;
}
```

The `m_dwMaxRef` data member keeps a count of the maximum reference count that the interface has had.

> *At this point, it is worth reviewing the Platform SDK documentation for* `InterlockedIncrement()`, *which states that under Windows 95, you cannot rely on the return value to be the actual value of the incremented variable. The check here should be like this:*
>
> ```
>     if(m_dwRef > m_dwMaxRef)
>         m_dwMaxRef = m_dwRef;
> ```
>
> *If you do a lot of development on Windows 95, it may be prudent to change this code.*

There is no `InternalRelease()` because `Release()` itself contains the delegating and debugging code. If the result of the call to `Release()` will free the interface, then the thunk must be destroyed, which is why we get the call to `DeleteThunk()`. This function has the effect of deleting the thunk and removing it from the module's thunk list.

In general, of course, interfaces have more than just the `IUnknown` methods, so what happens when the client calls one of these? Well, the method call ends up as a call through one of the function pointers in the vtable (either directly if the object is in-process, or via a stub object). For example, if the first method in the interface after the `IUnknown` interface is called, then this will result in `_QIThunk::f3()` being called. In `atlbase.h`, you will find a series of declarations:

```
IMPL_THUNK(3)
IMPL_THUNK(4)
IMPL_THUNK(5)

// etc

IMPL_THUNK(1022)
IMPL_THUNK(1023)
IMPL_THUNK(1024)
```

`IMPL_THUNK()` is a macro defined as:

```
#define IMPL_THUNK(n)\
__declspec(naked) inline HRESULT _QIThunk::f##n()\
{\
    __asm mov eax, [esp+4]\
    __asm cmp dword ptr [eax+8], 0\
    __asm jg goodref\
    __asm call atlBadThunkCall\
    __asm goodref:\
    __asm mov eax, [esp+4]\
    __asm mov eax, dword ptr [eax+4]\
    __asm mov [esp+4], eax\
    __asm mov eax, dword ptr [eax]\
    __asm mov eax, dword ptr [eax+4*n]\
    __asm jmp eax\
}
```

Let's look at this in greater detail, starting with the function signature. Normally, the C++ compiler will generate code that manipulates the stack to get the function parameters and to allocate space for local variables. This is called **prolog code**, and it's added at the start of the function. Similarly, **epilog code** is added at the end of the function to clear up local variables, add the return value to the stack, and call the return address. The `__declspec(naked)` attribute prevents the compiler from adding this prolog/epilog code, so that the inline assembly code can manipulate the stack for its own purposes.

We'd better take a look at what this code is actually doing, then. The first bit of code checks that the thunk is valid; if it isn't, the code asserts. The interesting code comes after `goodref`:

```
__asm mov eax, [esp+4];
__asm mov eax, dword ptr [eax+4];
```

These lines load the `eax` register with the `IUnknown` pointer cached earlier; this is because `[esp+4]` is the `_QIThunk this` pointer, and the second data item in the `_QIThunk` object is the wrapped interface pointer (the first item is the vptr for the object). The next line:

```
__asm mov [esp+4], eax;
```

makes the data in the `eax` register the `this` pointer, which is held on the stack. It then loads the vptr of the wrapped interface with:

```
__asm mov eax, dword ptr [eax];
```

A vptr, of course, points to an array of function pointers, so the following line puts the nth pointer into `eax`:

```
__asm mov eax, dword ptr [eax+4*n];
```

This is the function pointer of the method on the wrapped interface that the client wants to call. The stack is now set up to call this method, since it still has the return address and the method parameters that the client sent, but it now has the hidden `this` pointer of the interface that the client wants to call as well. So finally, the assembler code calls:

```
__asm jmp eax;
```

which calls the required interface method.

One final warning is needed here. The `_ATL_DEBUG_INTERFACES` symbol is independent of `_DEBUG`. That is, you do not need a debug build to use `_ATL_DEBUG_INTERFACES`. If you do use it, thunks will be created that have the enormous vtables you see here, and you will have greater memory usage. Furthermore, because the thunk gets in the way of interface access, you will have slower performance. The message is clear: make sure that you remove the `_ATL_DEBUG_INTERFACES` symbol when you make your release builds!

# IID Dumping

A macro that you have seen several times in the previous sections is `_ATLDUMPIID()`. This is defined as:

```
#ifdef _ATL_DEBUG_QI
#define _ATLDUMPIID(iid, name, hr) AtlDumpIID(iid, name, hr)
#else
#define _ATLDUMPIID(iid, name, hr) hr
#endif
```

The three parameters are the IID of the interface, the name of the class, and an `HRESULT`. This macro is most often used to provide a return value, which is part of the reason for the `HRESULT` parameter, but this parameter has another purpose too. If the `HRESULT` doesn't contain a success code, `AtlDumpIID()` will send the string `" - failed"` to the debug stream after the interface name; this is particularly useful for the result of a call to `QueryInterface()`.

The `AtlDumpIID()` function does all the work: if the `ATL_TRACE_CATEGORY` includes the `atlTraceQI` flag, then the class name and the interface name are sent to the debug stream. Notice that it will try to print the interface name, rather than the IID in string form, so `AtlDumpIID()` will read this from the default value of the interface's registry entry. If the function cannot find the GUID in the `Interface` key, it will look for the GUID in the `CLSID` key; failing that it will use the IID in string form. For example:

```
CTest - IUnknown
CTest - IMalloc - failed
```

# Reference Count Monitoring

As mentioned previously, `_QIThunk`'s `InternalAddRef()` and `Release()` methods print the changed thunk reference count to the debug stream; they also print the name of the interface that the thunk wraps, and the name of the class on which the interface is implemented. Significantly, however, they *don't* give any indication of the object instance. If you have code like this:

```
try
{
    ITestPtr pTest(__uuidof(Test));
    pTest->DoSomething();
}
catch(...)
{
}
```

You will get lines like this in the Output window of Visual C++ (or whatever is capturing the debug stream):

```
1> CComClassFactory - IUnknown
1> CComClassFactory - IClassFactory
1> CTest - IUnknown
0< CComClassFactory - IClassFactory
2> CTest - IUnknown
1< CTest - IUnknown
1> CTest - ITest
0< CTest - IUnknown
0< CTest - ITest
0< CComClassFactory - IUnknown
```

These debug statements show the reference count *after* is has been changed, so a value of 0 means that the interface will be released.

The sample code calls CoCreateInstance() for the ITest interface of an in-process Test object. In the first line, the DLL server is asked for the class factory, and the IUnknown of the class factory is returned; this interface is held for as long as the DLL server is loaded. Next, the class factory is queried for IClassFactory, and since this is successful both interfaces now have a reference count of 1. The class factory is then asked for the Test object, which results in the IUnknown of the object being obtained. The class factory's IClassFactory interface is no longer needed, so it released.

Finally, the Test object is queried for the ITest interface and the IUnknown is released; the client does what it wants with the ITest interface and then this is released, followed by the IUnknown of the class factory.

Notice that a _QIThunk is applied to an *interface*, and so the reference count that a thunk maintains is that *interface's* reference count. Many objects use just one reference count for all interfaces on the object, so printing out CComObjectRootBase::m_dwRef will not give an accurate count of how many times AddRef() and Release() had been called on a particular interface. Each _QIThunk is specific to a particular interface on a particular object, and so the reference count printed out in Dump() is an accurate value of the interface's reference count. This is shown in the trace above, where the IUnknown and ITest interfaces appear to have independent reference counts.

What happens if you create another instance of the object, using Visual C++'s compiler COM support classes?

```
try
{
   OutputDebugString("Creating first instance of Test\n");
   ITestPtr pTest(__uuidof(Test));
   OutputDebugString("Creating second instance of Test\n");
   ITestPtr pTest2(__uuidof(Test));
}
catch(...)
{
}
```

Now the debug output looks like this:

```
Creating first instance of Test
1> CComClassFactory - IUnknown
1> CComClassFactory - IClassFactory
1> CTest - IUnknown
0< CComClassFactory - IClassFactory
2> CTest - IUnknown
1< CTest - IUnknown
1> CTest - ITest
0< CTest - IUnknown
Creating second instance of Test
1> CComClassFactory - IClassFactory
1> CTest - IUnknown
0< CComClassFactory - IClassFactory
2> CTest - IUnknown
1< CTest - IUnknown
1> CTest - ITest
0< CTest - IUnknown
0< CTest - ITest
0< CTest - ITest
0< CComClassFactory - IUnknown
```

Again, you can see that the IUnknown of the class factory is held throughout the lifetime of the server, and IClassFactory is queried anew every time CoCreateInstance() is called. However, notice the last few lines. Here, both Test objects are released at the end of the try block, but which is released first – pTest or pTest2? This trace gives no indication of which instance the changing reference count refers to. I would have preferred it if _QIThunk was passed the this pointer of the object, so that InternalAddRef() and Release() could print it out to identify the object instance. As it stands, this reference count debugging is only useful when you are debugging a process that will only ever create one instance of a particular object.

# Interface Leaks

Two of the most common problems in COM programs are having too many calls to AddRef() on an interface, or insufficient calls to Release(). Such bugs can be quite serious. If you are implementing tear-off interfaces that manage some resource, and you do not completely free them, the tear-off object will remain and the resource it manages will not be freed. Even if you do not have interface-specific resources, not releasing an interface pointer will mean that the object will not be released, and so its resources will be leaked.

If you get hold of an object via `CoCreateInstance()`, COM will create resources to manage the object – if you do not release the interface correctly, these resources will leak. In particular, I have noticed that when a DLL server is loaded, several section kernel objects are created. If an interface is leaked, one of these section objects will also be leaked. You can monitor this with the NT Performance Monitor (`PerfMon`) by watching the system's Sections count, as shown in the dialog below that's used to add a new counter to the `PerfMon` chart.

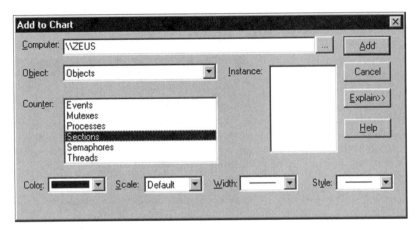

Needless to say, leaking interfaces should be avoided. Smart pointers help a bit, but you must be careful how you use them. The _com_ptr_t<> compiler COM support class is a little brain-dead about reference counting: it allows access to the wrapped interface's `AddRef()` and `Release()` functions through `operator ->()`, and so you can change the reference count without the smart pointer knowing it. `CComPtr<>` is a different case, and, as you have already seen, it protects against you making calls to the wrapped interface pointer's reference counting methods: code that does this will not compile.

> *Note, however that the wrapped interface pointer is a public member of* CComPtr<>, *so* AddRef() *can be called by perverse code like:*
>
> ```
>     pTest.p->AddRef();
> ```
>
> *But then, you wouldn't write code like this, would you?*

The key to checking that your code is not leaking interfaces is in `CComModule::DumpLeakedThunks()`. As mentioned earlier, this is called in `CComModule::Term()` when the server is shutting down. When the final `Release()` is called on an interface, it should cause the thunk to be deleted and removed from the thunk array held by the `CComModule` object. At shutdown, this array should be empty, and so any items remaining in the array are leaked interfaces. The `DumpLeakedThunks()` method goes through the thunk array and calls `Dump()` on any thunks it finds to ask them to identify themselves.

If a section of code calls `AddRef()` four times and `Release()` twice, you will get the following in the debug stream:

```
INTERFACE LEAK: RefCount = 2, MaxRefCount = 5, {Allocation = 4}
   CTest - ITest
```

This says that the ITest interface on an object of the CTest class has had two unreleased reference counts. The maximum number of reference counts at any one time was 5 (this was after the last of the four AddRef()s, because the class factory also did one AddRef() in response to the CoCreateInstance() in the ITestPtr constructor). The Allocation value is the m_nIndexQI index within the array of thunks, and hence indicates through which thunk the leak is reported. (Despite its name, it has nothing to do with reference counts.)

# Interface Map Debugging

There are three ways to debug an interface, and I will outline them in this section. The first way is the most brutal: you place DebugBreak() or __asm int 3 call in the interface method. This will mean that when the call is reached, the application will stop in the debugger. If a debugger is not running, you will get the following dialog:

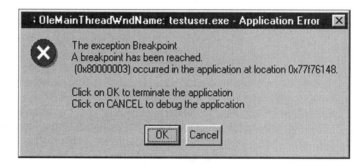

Clicking on Cancel will start the system debugger. Under Windows NT, the system debugger is registered in HKEY_LOCAL_MACHINE\Software\Microsoft\Windows NT\ CurrentVersion\AeDebug, and under Windows 9x it is registered in the win.ini file under the [AeDebug] section.

DebugBreak() calls __asm int 3, so the program will stop in this method:

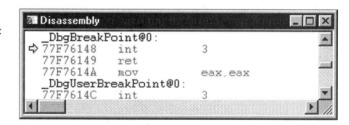

Because the debugger is stopped in DebugBreak(), you will have to single-step past the ret statement to get to the place where the actual breakpoint was set. Using __asm int 3 is a bit more convenient, because the debugger will break within the code where you placed the line.

Note that you should bracket both of these calls in conditional compilation, otherwise the breakpoint will be hit in the release version of the application. This is of limited usefulness, because the release version will not have all the required debugging information!

```
#ifdef _DEBUG
    __asm int 3;
#endif //_DEBUG
```

The second way to debug an interface needs _ATL_DEBUG_INTERFACES to be defined, since it uses the m_nIndexBreakAt member of CComModule and the bBreak member of _QIThunk. Remember that m_nIndexBreakAt indicates that the program should break when a thunk with this index is created in the array of thunks, while bBreak means that the program should break when the specified interface's AddRef() or Release() is called. Both of these members are public, but you still need to get access to them and determine what value to set them to.

In the following code, m_nIndexBreakAt will make the application stop when the first thunk is created; this will be for the IUnknown of the first class factory requested:

```
#ifdef _ATL_DEBUG_INTERFACES
    _Module.m_nIndexBreakAt = 1;
#endif // _ATL_DEBUG_INTERFACES
```

Before you set this index, it is often useful do one debugging session and look at the output stream to see which interfaces are returned, and hence determine the right value to use. If you are interested in an interface that is leaking, you can use the Allocation value returned in Dump().

_QIThunk::bBreak determines whether the program should break in its reference counting methods; if m_nIndexBreakAt is the current thunk number, it is set to TRUE when the thunk is created, but since bBreak is a public member, it means that as long as you can get hold of a thunk, you can change its value. For example:

```
#ifdef _ATL_DEBUG_INTERFACES
    for(int i = 0 ; i < _Module.m_paThunks->GetSize() ; i++)
        _Module.m_paThunks->operator[](i)->bBreak = true;
#endif // _ATL_DEBUG_INTERFACES
```

Setting bBreak for every thunk like this can make a debugging session extremely tedious, because even the most simple access to a COM object will involve many changes of the reference counts of the object and its class factory, and each change will cause a breakpoint. However, you can see the principles involved.

I mentioned the final technique for debugging interfaces briefly in Chapter 2: COM map debugging. This does not need _ATL_DEBUG_INTERFACES to be defined, and in fact it doesn't even require a debug build (although it *is* more useful in debug builds). To use it, you need to place the COM_INTERFACE_ENTRY_BREAK() macro in the COM map before the interface that you want to debug:

```
BEGIN_COM_MAP(CTest)
    COM_INTERFACE_ENTRY(ITest)
#ifdef _DEBUG
    COM_INTERFACE_ENTRY_BREAK(ITest2)
#endif // _DEBUG
    COM_INTERFACE_ENTRY(ITest2)
END_COM_MAP()
```

When a `QueryInterface()` occurs for `ITest2`, the `_Break()` method will be called. You can produce your own version of this; if you don't, you'll inherit the version from `CComObjectRootBase`:

```
static HRESULT WINAPI _Break(void* /* pv */, REFIID iid,
                                 void** /* ppvObject */, DWORD /* dw */)
{
    iid;  // Unreferenced variable
    _ATLDUMPIID(iid, _T("Break due to QI for interface "), S_OK);
    DebugBreak();
    return S_FALSE;
}
```

Under debug builds, this will dump the string to the debug stream, but whatever build you are using, `DebugBreak()` will be called. Notice that the method returns `S_FALSE`, which means that `AtlInternalQueryInterface()` will continue to query for the interface. As with many of the debugging macros, you must make sure that you remove `COM_INTERFACE_ENTRY_BREAK()` for release builds, which is why I have enclosed it in conditional compilation in the previous example.

You can produce your own version of `_Break()`, particularly if you want to do something like call `_CrtSetReportMode()` to send the debug output to a different stream. However, remember that the whole purpose is to allow you to debug the interface querying mechanism, so you will almost always want to call `__asm int 3` and return `S_FALSE`.

# Other Visual C++ Debugging Features

Visual C++ provides many debugging features that are helpful when you're developing ATL objects. In this section, I will give a brief overview of these features so that you become familiar with them. Further details can be found in the online documentation.

## Watch and Variable Windows

You can view some really quite interesting information in the Visual C++ Watch and Variable windows, which will generally make an attempt to show you what a variable refers to. If you have a parameter that holds an IID or a CLSID, they will display the human-readable name of the interface, rather than the GUID in string format:

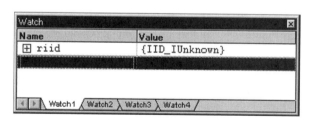

I find this very useful, because in the past I have had to read the individual members of the IID variable and then try to interpret which interface it refers to. (You soon get to remember what the IIDs of common interfaces are, but it's not really the kind of thing that you want to put your mind to!) This trick works for the tooltips that appear when the cursor hovers over a variable while you're debugging, too:

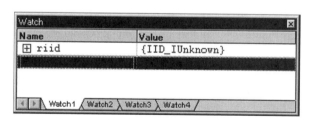

The formatting that occurs in the Watch window is managed by the file `autoexp.dat`, which you can find in the `Microsoft Visual Studio\Common\MSDev98\Bin` directory. This file has comments that explain how to add new formatting strings of your own, and it is best to read through and look at the values in that file. However, just as an example, you can add the following line:

```
ATL::CComObjectRootEx<*>=ref count=<m_dwRef,u>
```

This states that whenever an object derived from the template `ATL::CComObjectRootEx<>` is shown in the Watch window, it will show the value of the object with the string `ref count=x`, and replace x with the value of the member variable `m_dwRef` (which holds the object reference count) and interpret the value as an unsigned integer. For example:

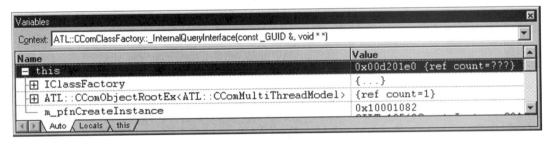

Here, the object (a class factory object) has a single reference count of 1. Note that the file also has these lines:

```
ATL::CComBSTR=<m_str,su>
_bstr_t=<m_Data->m_wstr,su> (<m_Data->m_RefCount,u>)
```

The formatting code `su` indicates that whenever you view `CComBSTR`s and `_bstr_t`s in the debugger, you will see the string that they contain, rather than the `short` arrays that they hold. Another thing to remember is that on Intel machines, the `EAX` register will contain the return value, so if your code omits to get a return value from a function, you can get the value in the Watch window by watching the `EAX` register (and maybe using `,hr` as well, which we saw in Chapter 1, to get the `HRESULT` descriptive string).

A final feature that you should consider using is the `ERR` pseudo-register. This will have the value from calling `GetLastError()`, which is useful if you make Win32 calls. For example, look at this call:

```
HANDLE h = CreateFile("", 0, 0, NULL, 0, 0, 0);
```

This should fail. The handle h will be `INVALID_HANDLE_VALUE`, and `ERR` will show the following value:

| Name | Value |
|------|-------|
| ERR,hr | 0x00000057 The parameter is incorrect. |

Watch1 / Watch2 / Watch3 / Watch4

Remember, ERR is not a real variable: it only exists during debugging sessions, and if you want to use its value in your code, you should call `GetLastError()`.

# Debugging with Visual C++

Visual C++ allows you to debug object servers. This is very neat, because not only can you load an in-process server and debug it, but you can also start an EXE server on the same machine and step through that code. You can even step through code on a remote machine (although this may involve you getting longer arms, or maybe moving back and forth between machines!).

I won't go into the details of remote COM debugging (and issues like `DllDebugRemoteRPCHook()`), because there's some pretty wacky code involved – you can find more information in the COM specification under *Support for Remote Debugging* in the *Interface Remoting* chapter. Suffice to say that if you have Visual C++ set up appropriately, you can step into a function call on a client machine and get a debugging session started on the server machine. For now, let's look at debugging piecemeal.

> *You can find the COM specification on the Microsoft web site at* http://www.microsoft.com/com, *in the* Resources *section.*

## DLL Server

If the server is a DLL, then typically it will be on the local machine. Once you've created the object (using `CoCreateInstance()` or equivalent), the server DLL will be loaded. Visual C++ will allow you to step into methods on the object even if the object is running in a different apartment from the client. However, if the client and server *are* in different apartments, you don't get any visual indication that the thread context is changing as you step into the server code.

Of course, if your client is using smart pointers, you will have to negotiate through the wrapper classes before you get to the server code. This is particularly important with the `#import`-generated smart pointers, because often you will have both a smart pointer *and* a high level method wrapping your interface method.

What about setting breakpoints in the code, and debugging the class factory code before an object is created? To do this, you need to be able to set breakpoints before the object is loaded, but Visual C++ won't allow you to set breakpoints unless it has the debugging information for the code. To resolve this, you must go into the client's project settings and on the Debug tab select a Category of Additional DLLs, and add the DLL server to the list. You should now be able to set breakpoints in your server code and in ATL code too.

## Controls and DLL Servers

Controls are packaged in DLLs, and a DLL cannot run on its own – it needs an executable. You can specify which one using the Project | Settings... Debug tab. When you select the General Category, you will be presented with a page of edit boxes, the topmost of which allows you to specify the executable that will be run. Depending on the type of object that you are debugging, you have several options here.

If you're debugging a control, then you need to use an executable that knows about the control site interfaces. Next to the edit box is a button that gives you three options: Browse, ActiveX Control Test Container and the Default Web Browser. Let's take them in reverse order.

The Default Web Browser means whatever is registered as your web browser, and for these purposes I will assume it is Internet Explorer 4. If you click on this option, the dialog will fill the edit box with the full path to the browser. However, when you start a debug session you won't see the control immediately because you need to provide a web page that contains has the control. The Object Wizard creates such a web page for you, and you need to specify this in the Debug tab – there's an edit box called Program arguments into which you should type the *full path* to the web page. Unfortunately, Object Wizard will not fill this for you (for good reason: your server could have more than one control, and therefore more than one HTML page), so you have to type the full path here.

I find this tedious, and often I get it wrong, so here's a handy tip: if you right click on the web page in Windows Explorer and select the Properties option, you will get details about the file, including its location. This information is presented in read-only *edit boxes*, and so you can select the string and copy it to the clipboard. You can then paste this into the Program arguments box and append the name of the page.

The ActiveX Control Test Container is a process designed to test controls, and you can use it to call control methods, to persist a control (or load it from persisted data), to test how it responds to changes to ambient properties, and to run VBScript macros. More details will be given in Chapter 10, but note that you need to tell it to load your control. The first time that you run the test container, you can select Insert New Control from the Edit menu to get the standard insertable controls page (there is also a toolbar button to do this). However, it can get tedious to do this every time you want to start a debug session, and so the solution is to load the control and then save the session from the File menu. This will persist the control to a file, so it's usually sensible to save the session just after the control is first loaded, so that you store its just loaded, initialized state. You can then use the name of this session file (TCS file) in the Program arguments box. Note that you do not need to type the full path to this file, or specify a Working directory.

The final option for an executable for the debugging session is to use the Browse option to browse for the executable (or to type the path into the edit box). Note once again that the edit box must have the *full* path to the executable, and you must give the file extension too (Visual Studio does not assume the EXE extension). You can use any executable that will use your object, including Visual Basic executables, or programs that you have written in C++.

If you want to test how the Visual Basic IDE responds to your control when it's loaded on a page in design mode, then you will first need to create a Visual Basic project and save it to disk. Then you need to browse for VB6.EXE as the executable, and give the name of the project as the Program arguments. If you want Visual Basic to compile and run the project, then use the /run or /runexit switches. These will both compile and run the executable, but while the first will put you into design mode when you stop execution, the second will close down Visual Basic at that time.

## Local EXE Server

To debug local servers, you need to ensure that the OLE RPC Debugging option is set on the Debug tab of the Tools | Options... dialog. Once this is set, you can run the client, and when you step into an object method Visual C++ will launch a new instance and load the server code. If that code has debugging information, then Visual C++ will load the source and you will be able to single-step through the code.

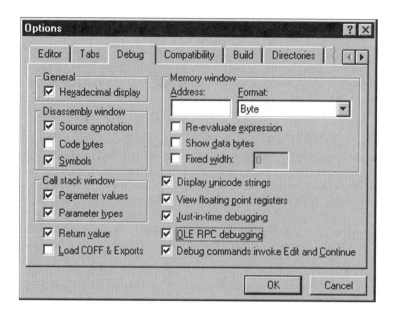

> Unlike Visual C++ 5.0, where you often had to single-step through several
> lines of marshaler code before getting to the actual method that you were
> debugging, Visual C++ 6.0 takes you directly to the method.

If you choose to set breakpoints, then you must start a separate instance of Visual C++ yourself and
load the server project. Then you should start the server, which will register its class factories so that
when the client creates a new object, COM will use your debugging server.

## Remote EXE Server

The first time you remotely debug a server, it comes as quite a surprise. In fact, you are not
debugging the process remotely at all – rather, you run a debugger on the remote machine. Assuming
that you have the correct launch and access permissions for the server on the remote machine, and
that the OLE RPC Debugging option is set, then when you step into an object method on the *client*
machine, Visual C++ will run on the *server* machine and start a debug session.

If you have a debug version of the server on the remote machine, and access to the source files, then
you will be able to single step through the server. Note that if you do not have access to the remote
machine, then your client will be effectively blocked until the COM call times out.

# Summary

In this chapter, I have shown you the debugging support present in ATL 3.0. There is a new technique for debugging, using _QIThunks, which provides information about the reference count changes on interfaces. The other techniques were present in previous versions of ATL, although they have been enhanced in ATL 3.0.

I have also shown you how to send debugging and diagnostic messages to the debug output stream, and how to change this stream. Furthermore, I have demonstrated how to create error objects to provide rich error reporting.

Throughout this chapter, I have been careful to point out to you the behavior of particular debugging techniques according to whether the build is in release or debug more. As my final act in this summary, let me reiterate those warnings:

| Technique | Debug | Release |
|---|---|---|
| __asm int 3 | ✔ | ✔ |
| DebugBreak() | ✔ | ✔ |
| ATLASSERT() | ✔ | ✘ |
| _ATL_DEBUG_INTERFACES | ✔ | ✔ |
| CComModule::m_nIndexBreakAt | ✔ | ✔ |
| _QIThunk::bBreak | ✔ | ✔ |
| COM_INTERFACE_ENTRY_BREAK() | ✔ | ✔ |
| ATLTRACE() | ✔ | ✘ |
| OutputDebugString() | ✔ | ✔ |
| Error Objects | ✔ | ✔ |
| Event Log | ✔ | ✔ |

✔    The technique produces output, or will break in the debugger
✘    The technique produces no output, and will not break in the debugger

# 7

# Threading and Marshaling

Every thread represents an execution context that is scheduled by Windows. If you have a single-processor machine, you can have more than one routine running at once, and Windows arranges for them to be run in a coordinated sequence, each with a slice of the CPU time. The net effect is that the code will *appear* to be running concurrently. If you have a multiprocessor NT machine, Windows will schedule different threads to run on different processors, and the concurrency will be *real*, at least for some of the threads. As the application developer, you don't have to worry about issues like sectioning the execution time into time slices, prioritizing threads, scheduling threads, or determining which thread runs on which processor. Windows manages all this for you.

So what *do* you have to do? Well, the number of threads running on the system will always exceed the number of processors, so the system will use its scheduling algorithm to run each thread for a short amount of time (a time slice). However, it cannot guarantee that it will leave a global or static resource in a consistent state at the end of the time slice, and so it is up to you to ensure that such a resource cannot be used by more than one thread. This brings up the issues of **synchronization**, where you are responsible for applying locks on resources, and **reentrancy**, where you ensure that a routine can be run by more than one thread at a time.

Then there is the issue of how COM interacts with threads. If you have more than one thread, can they all access a single object at the same time? COM enforces the restriction that an object will live in exactly one **apartment**, which specifies the execution context for that object. Currently, COM defines two types of apartment: single-threaded apartments (STA) and multithreaded apartments (MTA). When you create a thread in your process to use COM objects, that thread must join an apartment. Sensibly, an STA can only contain one thread, while an MTA may contain several threads.

The other subject for this chapter is **marshaling**, which is related to threading. The threading model determines the apartments used, and marshaling allows objects to communicate *between* apartments. There are several issues here. For a start, interface pointers need to be marshaled across apartment boundaries – sometimes this has to be done explicitly, and other times it is done implicitly. By and large, the code that's used to marshal interfaces is generated for you, but there are cases when you need to write your own marshaling code, or to use some of the marshaler objects that COM supplies. We'll be looking at these, and the circumstances in which you'll want to use them, later in the chapter.

# Threading and COM

If there is more than one thread running, Windows will section the execution time of each thread into **time slices** and, depending on the priority of each thread, it will schedule the time that each thread runs on the processor(s) of the system. The immediate problem is that a thread may be accessing a variable when its time slice runs out and it gets put to sleep, leaving the variable in an inconsistent state. This spells disaster if another thread tries to access the variable, because the value it holds will be invalid. On the other hand, the first thread may leave the variable in a known, valid state when its time runs out, but it could depend on that value being unchanged when it is scheduled to run again. Without protection applied on this variable, another thread may change its value, affecting the behavior of the first thread.

Such problems are not restricted to variables – a function may be implemented in such a way that only one thread should execute it. For example, it could contain a static variable, which has the same synchronization problems that a global variable has. Further, a function might access a resource in such a way that the routine must be completed before another thread can use it.

Like objects used in many programming languages, COM objects have behavior and typically also have state. COM objects will always have at least one data member to hold the reference count (the object as a whole may have a single reference count, or it may have a separate reference count for each interface), and if an object instance will be used by more than one thread, then the reference counter must be protected.

An object's behavior is implemented by its methods, and if multiple threads can access a single instance of the coclass (or even if multiple threads can access multiple instances of this coclass), then its methods should be reentrant. Reentrancy means that a section of code can be run by more than one thread at a time without adverse effects. Access to global or static data should be protected during the section of code where it is used, so that another thread running the same piece of code cannot change its value. This usually involves writing a section of code in such a way that only one thread at a time can run it.

Of course, when you activate an object using `CoCreateInstance()`, COM will be accessing that object with the intention of returning an interface pointer to you. You have no control over the code that is used in `CoCreateInstance()`, and so your client and object code must be compatible with whatever code Microsoft has provided.

# Apartments

To make life easier, Microsoft has produced the concept of an **apartment**. An apartment is an execution context in which an object can be run or accessed – that is, you call CoCreateInstance() in one apartment to create an object, and it will run in the same or another apartment. In the case of some in-process objects, the calling and called apartments will be the same. For other in-process objects, and for all objects accessed from another process (on the local or on a remote machine), the calling and called apartments will be different.

To some extent, you can take the attitude that the idea of COM calls being purely 'client-server' is a little outdated – instead you could say that they are 'inter-apartment'. This concept is fine in some cases, and certainly if an object implements bi-directional connections it can become difficult to determine which is the client and which is the server. However, in most cases the distinction *is* evident, so I will continue to use the former terminology for simplicity.

A process can have zero or more STAs and/or zero or one MTA. Code in a thread can only access the COM API if it is part of an apartment, and so accessing or serving an object can only be done in an apartment thread. Objects can run in only one apartment, and if code in another apartment wants to access one of those objects, the interface pointer that's used to do so must be marshaled. There are no restrictions on the number of running objects within an apartment.

A thread joins an apartment by calling CoInitializeEx(); the second parameter of this function determines the apartment type:

| Value | Description |
|---|---|
| COINIT_APARTMENTTHREADED | A new STA is created for the thread |
| COINIT_MULTITHREADED | The thread joins the process's MTA |

The legacy CoInitialize() function just calls CoInitializeEx() with COINIT_APARTMENTTHREADED. The first STA to be created is called the **main STA**. If a COM object is not apartment-aware, or an in-process object does not specify its threading model, this is where it will be created. The net effect of this is that all access to such apartment-unaware objects will be serialized: only one of them will run at any one time.

Since an STA can only have one thread, when you call CoInitializeEx() with COINIT_APARTMENTTHREADED from within a thread, a new STA is created. However, a process can only have *one* MTA, so if you use COINIT_MULTITHREADED and an MTA already exists, the thread will join that apartment. If not, a new MTA is created.

From the server's point of view, an STA can run one or more objects, and these objects get direct access to each other because the call is intra-apartment. From the client's point of view, an STA can access more than one object with no special code – you can pass interface pointers from one object to another object in the apartment, and if the objects are in-process, no marshaling will be used.

If you have more than one STA in your process (whether client or server), then access to an object in one STA from another STA can only be done through a marshaled pointer. Details of how to do this will be given later, but basically the process happens either explicitly by calling an API, or implicitly by passing an interface pointer as a COM method parameter.

The multiple threads of an MTA can access or serve any number of objects. Any object in an MTA can access any other object in the MTA – this is what an apartment is all about. However, if an object that's running on one thread tries to access an object on another thread, you will have all the problems of multithreaded access that I identified earlier. Objects designed for use within an MTA must protect their instance and class data members from multithreaded access, and any concurrency-sensitive methods should likewise be protected.

# Marshaling

Marshaling is important. Whenever a COM call is made across an apartment boundary, marshaling will be used. If the call occurs between processes on the same machine, or between processes on different machines, then marshaling will package up the data into packets that can be transmitted to the other process.

These packets may contain data in the same format as the parameters of the methods, or they may contain extra data to make these parameters more useful to the called object. An example of the first case is passing a `long` – the actual data is sent to the object. An example of the latter is passing an interface pointer – the actual value of the pointer is only valid in one process, so it can't be passed directly. Take, for example, this pseudo-code:

```
IDriver* pDriver;
CoCreateInstance(CLSID_CoDriver, ... reinterpret_cast<void**>(&pDriver));
ICar* pCar;
CoCreateInstance(CLSID_CoCar, ... reinterpret_cast<void**>(&pCar));
pCar->OpenCar(pDriver);

// Driver in car, so we can release our reference
pDriver->Release();

// Get the car to do something
pCar->DriveToWork();
pCar->Release();
```

A new `Driver` and `Car` object are created, and the pointer to the `Driver` object is passed to the `Car`. `pDriver` is just a memory pointer, and if the `Car` object is in a different process to this code, a memory pointer will be useless. This is where marshaling steps in. The marshaler for the `ICar` interface will realize that the pointer is to an interface, and so it will generate a packet that will allow the `Car` object to access the `Driver` object wherever it happens to be. When I say "wherever", I really mean that the client, `Driver` and `Car` objects could be:

- ❑ In the same apartment
- ❑ In different apartments in the same process
- ❑ In different processes on the same machine
- ❑ Or even in different processes on different machines

This last situation, of course, stretches virtual reality to its limit, with a `Driver` in a totally different location to the `Car` he is driving!

The point is that the client neither knows nor cares where these objects are – the code is the same in all cases. It is true that if you are interested in specifying the locations of these objects, you can do so in the call to `CoCreateInstanceEx()`, but the actual access to the objects would still be the same.

Note that in most cases marshaling is carried out for you automatically, but in some cases, you may need to marshal interface pointers yourself. For example, if you have an object in one apartment thread and want to pass an interface pointer to it to another apartment without using a COM method call, you will have to marshal it manually (details of how to do this will be given later). However, once this interface has been marshaled between apartments, you can call its methods, and even pass interface pointers as parameters, without any more explicit marshaling.

Marshaling is clearly important, and the marshaling code has a lot of work to do. There are several ways that you can carry out marshaling, but in all cases there will be a proxy object on the client side obtained somewhere, and most likely a stub object on the server side.

In most cases, COM is helpful if you try to use an interface pointer in a different apartment from the one where it was created without marshaling. Any method calls on such a pointer will return `RPC_E_WRONG_THREAD` (0x8001010E). However, there are exceptions to this. If you try to register an interface pointer with the GIT that does not have a registered proxy-stub DLL, for example, an access violation exception will be thrown in `OLE32.dll`, in an undocumented function called `FindStdMarshal()`. A helpful failure `HRESULT` would have been much nicer.

When you're creating EXE servers, you automatically think about proxy-stub registration. Although it's not explicitly part of the Visual C++ build process, over time it gets inserted into a COM developer's psyche. Objects packaged in DLLs, however, are a different matter – after all, in-process objects are created in the address space of the client, so they will never use marshaling, right? Wrong! If you pass an interface between apartments, the interface pointer will be marshaled.

Compare the following two cases. Imagine you have an in-process (in-apartment) object and a local object created from your client's apartment. Because the in-process object has been created as such, the interface pointer will be a direct pointer to the object interface – no proxy is used. On the other hand, since the local object is out-of-process, the `CoCreateInstance()` call will have resulted in the proxy-stub DLL for the interface being loaded, and the interface pointer returned will be a pointer to a proxy object. Thus, creating the local object will have the possible expense of launching a new process (so that the client will have the access to the server), and it will involve loading another DLL. But then, you knew that: no one expects access to a local object to be fast.

Now imagine that these two interface pointers are marshaled to another apartment within the process. When the local object interface pointer is marshaled, it uses the interface's proxy-stub DLL, which is already loaded. However, when the in-process object's interface is marshaled, its proxy-stub DLL must be loaded, so now *two* DLLs are needed for your super-fast, in-process object.

You can merge the proxy-stub code within your in-process server DLL to prevent an extra DLL from being loaded. ATL gives you this option, but note that it is not always needed, as you will see later in this chapter. There are essentially three types of marshaling: standard marshaling, type library marshaling and custom marshaling, I will cover the first two here, and leave the delight of custom marshaling for later.

# Standard Marshaling

Every interface that doesn't use custom marshaling uses standard marshaling, which involves having a proxy in the calling apartment and a stub in the called apartment. To the caller, the proxy looks like the object; to the object, the stub looks like the caller. The proxy ensures that parameters are correctly marshaled across the apartment boundary, while the stub ensures that the stack is correctly constructed with the unmarshaled parameters sent by the proxy, and that the method is called.

Regardless of whether you create a dual or a custom interface in the Object Wizard, you will get an IDL file generated. The difference between the two is that in the first case the interface will be derived from `IDispatch`, while in the second, derivation will be from `IUnknown` directly. In both cases, you can choose to use either type library or standard marshaling.

The main thing to remember about standard marshaling is that a proxy is required in the client apartment and a stub is required in the object apartment, and the **marshaling layer** deals with loading them. As with all other objects, they need to be built and registered, so if you intend to use standard marshaling you should add the proxy-stub makefile to your project. Then, if your project is called `CarDrivers`, you should do this from a command line:

```
nmake CarDriversps.mk
regsvr32 /s CarDriversps.dll
```

The `/s` switch stops the registration notification dialog from appearing, so it's useful if you want to perform command line and batch builds.

Registering this DLL will add an entry to the registry in the `Interface` section for the interface IID with a value called `ProxyStubClsid32`, and this will contain the CLSID that's used for both the proxy and the stub object. It will also add an entry for these proxy-stub objects in the `CLSID` key, which will have an `InprocServer32` key that has the path to the proxy-stub DLL. Thus, when an interface is marshaled, COM will be able to find the proxy-stub DLL.

# Type Library Marshaling

I have identified type library marshaling as one of my three cases, but in fact it's just a special case of standard marshaling – rather than being specific to an interface, the proxy and stub are just generic objects implemented in `OLEAUT32.dll`.

Any interface that can be described by a type library can be type library marshaled. Whether your object's interface is custom or dual, the Object Wizard ensures that it has an entry in the `library` section of the IDL file. Furthermore, the registration code for an ATL server will register the type library. For a DLL server, the code looks like this:

```
STDAPI DllRegisterServer(void)
{
    // Registers object, typelib and all interfaces in typelib
    return _Module.RegisterServer(TRUE);
}
```

The TRUE argument to `RegisterServer()` gets passed to `AtlModuleRegisterServer()`, which uses it to determine whether it should call `AtlModuleRegisterTypeLib()`. If so, this final method will call the COM API `RegisterTypeLib()`, this will register all `[oleautomation]` interfaces as using the Universal Marshaler, and this includes all dual interfaces and dispinterfaces, as well as custom interfaces with the `[oleautomation]` attribute.

This adds an entry to the interface's key in `Interface`. The `ProxyStubClsid32` value is now `{00020424-0000-0000-C000-000000000046}`, and there is a new key, called `TypeLib`, that contains the LIBID of the registered type library for the object. The CLSID is for an object called `PSOAInterface`, an in-process object implemented in `OLEAUT32.dll`. This object is the **Universal Marshaler**, and it uses the information in the type library to determine how interface methods are marshaled.

> Note that if you want to use a proxy-stub DLL rather than type library marshaling, you should change the call to `RegisterServer()` to have a parameter of **FALSE** to prevent the **TypeLib** entry being added to the interface's key.

Note that using the Universal Marshaler does *not* mean that methods are called using `IDispatch::Invoke()` (although dispinterface methods called in this way do use the Universal Marshaler), nor does it mean that the interface has to be dual. However, when you're using the Universal Marshaler with a custom interface, you need to make sure that the data types you use are Automation compatible, and that it's marked with the `[oleautomation]` attribute in the IDL file. This last requirement is needed to make sure that `RegisterTypeLib()` will register the interface to use the Universal Marshaler.

So, since there is all this interface registration occurring does it mean that when you create an object with a new interface, you can call the object from another machine without any registration on the client machine? Unfortunately, the answer is 'no'. Registration is still required, because COM has to know that the interface is marshaled through the Universal Marshaler, and so it will need a registered type library.

> *If you do want to be able to call an object without having to register it on the client machine, there are two options. You can use standard marshaling, and merge the proxy code in to the client (which will be covered later in this chapter), or you can use late binding. Late binding is the simpler of the two, and it's used by scripting clients like VBScript. In this case, the client calls* `IDispatch::GetIDsOfNames()` *to get method DISPIDs, and then calls the method it wants through* `IDispatch::Invoke()`.

Basically, the choice of whether you use standard or type library marshaling is resolved at registration. If you're using type library marshaling, you need to register the type library on the client machine, ensure that the `ProxyStubClsid32` entry for the interface contains the CLSID for `PSOAInterface` and verify that there is a `TypeLib` key. All of this can be done on the client through a registry script, or by calling `RegisterTypeLib()`. If you want to use standard marshaling, then you need to generate the proxy-stub DLL and register that on the client machine.

Naturally, the server machine also needs to have a registered proxy-stub, so that the server gets access to the stub object. As mentioned earlier, ATL will make sure that the type library is registered.

# EXE Servers

When you create an ATL EXE project, the AppWizard will choose a threading model for you: single threaded apartment model. This means that whatever threading model you select in Object Wizard for your objects you will have just a single thread in the server. Of course, this is not always the best choice. However, the AppWizard and Object Wizard code does help you, because although an initial threading model is chosen, the code is designed to allow you to change the threading model with relative ease.

Once you have chosen a threading model you also need to think about how you manage worker threads. The issue here is that an object method may spin a new thread to perform some background task. In this case you will have to decide whether the worker thread will access the object. If so, this will influence your threading model choice. In most cases, the best way to do this is for the worker thread to be part of the same apartment as the object and this means that the server will have to support an MTA.

> *As a side issue, if your object spins worker threads that will access the object, you will have to make sure that when the object dies, the workers are told to die as well. Otherwise, they may attempt to access an object that no longer exists.*

## Single STA Server

A server with a single STA can create more than one object, and more than one client can access a single object, or multiple objects, in the server. However, if the server has a single STA, it means that only one object can be accessed at a time: multiple objects cannot run concurrently, and nor will multiple accesses to a single object be concurrent. All calls into the STA have to be serialized. COM automatically serializes the calls through a thread message queue.

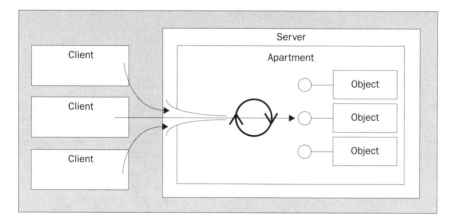

I have tried to illustrate this serialization in the diagram by indicating that there is only one way into the apartment and this has room for only one access: the other client accesses are blocked during this call even if they are to a different object.

To enable this mechanism, the single thread must have a message loop that waits for requests and dispatches messages in the normal way. COM accepts these dispatched requests and accesses the various objects implemented in the STA. But note that while COM is accessing an object, the message loop will no longer accept requests, because its single thread is already doing work. Any subsequent request will be queued by Windows as messages in the thread queue until the STA thread can service the queue.

When the server thread has finished servicing a request, it can resume polling the queue, where it can pick up the next request. Requests are thus carried out in the strict order dictated by the FIFO thread queue.

In addition, EXE servers typically use the message queue to manage the server shutdown. When some server code determines that the server can shut down, it can post a WM_QUIT to the thread queue. This has the effect of breaking the message loop, which leads to the main() function returning, and hence the server dies.

If objects create worker threads then these will have to join an apartment to be able to use COM. However, these new threads will be in a different apartment to the objects, so they will only be able to access the parent object through a marshaled interface pointer. Any access to the object will be treated like any other client access: the request is serialized using the main STA's message queue.

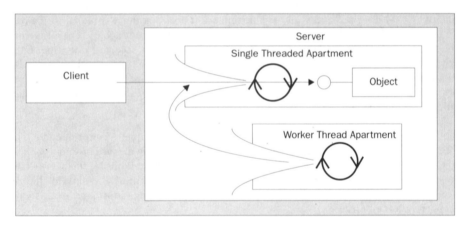

## *MTA Server*

A server with an MTA will have threads created by the RPC runtime. When a client request comes in, whether to create an object or to call an object method, the RPC runtime will choose a thread from a pool it manages. This means that you cannot guarantee that calls to the same object will come in on the same thread, so you *must not* use any thread-specific resources like thread local storage (TLS), for example.

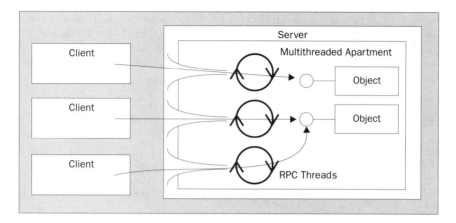

In the diagram above I have tried to indicate the action of an MTA by illustrating that the RPC runtime will provide threads for each client access, and thus no client access is blocked, even if the access is to the *same* object.

Requests can come in at any time, and if there is a pool thread available, the request will be handled immediately. COM does not apply any synchronization between these threads, so if two requests come in to access a single object, those threads will have concurrent access. On a machine with more than one CPU, this may actually mean two threads will access an object at one time. Otherwise, the threads will be scheduled, but there will be no guarantee that one thread will have finished its work with the object before the other thread is reactivated. The developer is responsible for making sure that data members are protected from multiple thread access, and that concurrency-sensitive methods are similarly protected.

Since the developer manages synchronization, a thread message queue is not needed. This simplifies the code, and it improves performance because the server can use a more efficient mechanism than a message loop to determine that the server should shut down. For example, the server could have an event kernel object and use `WaitForSingleObject()` to determine if it should shut down. `WaitForSingleObject()` is much more efficient than a message loop, and so this will give your server a performance boost.

If your objects use worker threads then these must join an apartment, and it makes sense to have them join the MTA. If the new thread joins the MTA, then it will have direct access to the object.

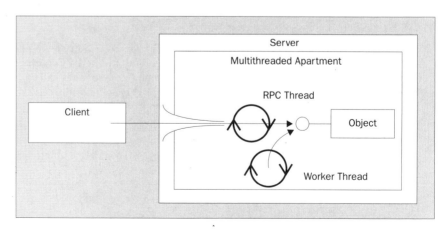

### Thread Pool STA Server

There is an intermediate type of server between one with a single STA and one with an MTA, and that's a server with a *pool* of STAs. The scheme works like this: the server starts with a single main STA that implements a message loop, and all requests will come in on this thread. However, during initialization, the main thread will create a pool of worker threads, each a member of an STA. When a request comes in to create an object, the server can create the object on one of the pooled threads, according to a load-balancing algorithm.

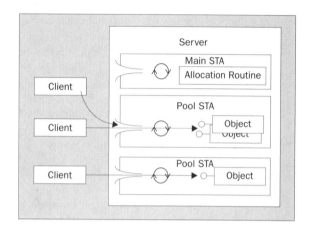

The advantage of this approach over a single STA is that if the server serves multiple objects, access to them will be determined by Windows' thread scheduling rather than by the time it takes to complete a method request. The advantage over an MTA server is that the objects don't have to be written with explicit instance data synchronization, since all object access will be to an STA, and COM will implement an implicit thread queue to serialize the requests. In addition, the developer has control over the number of threads used in the server.

The disadvantage is that the server handles *external* COM requests through an STA, and so the thread within this apartment must have a message loop. Further, this scheme requires a special class factory that can create objects on different threads. However, if you have objects written without synchronization, but you don't want the bottleneck of a single STA server, a thread pool STA server is a good compromise.

## DLL Servers

A DLL server is loaded into a client's process. It cannot call `CoInitializeEx()` to select the kind of apartment it wants to join because the client has already done that. The DLL server is thus constrained to using the apartments that exist in the client, but if COM detects that this may cause a problem, it can intervene.

As you have already seen, an object designed for use in an MTA has certain responsibilities that objects designed for STAs do not have. Objects designed for use in an STA should not be loaded into an MTA because they won't have the required synchronization mechanisms. When an MTA client attempts to create such an object, COM will silently create an STA and load the object into that. In this example, the client code to access the object will be in the MTA, so access to the object will be cross-apartment to the STA. However, since COM has created the new apartment, *it* will ensure that the interface pointer that you receive will be correctly marshaled.

All of this begs a rather obvious question: how does COM know that an object is designed for use in an MTA or an STA? The answer is that it cannot determine this from the object code, and so instead it reads the object's registry entry for this information. The relevant entry is the `ThreadingModel` value given in the object's CLSID key, which can have one of four values: `Single`, `Apartment`, `Both` or `Free`. If the value does not exist, a value of `Single` is assumed.

❑ `Single` means that the object is apartment-unaware – typically, it is an object written before apartment models were introduced to COM. Such an object will only run in the main STA of the client. If necessary, COM will create an STA for you.

❑ `Apartment` means that the object does not synchronize access to its data members or protect thread sensitive methods. To protect this object from concurrent access, COM will create this object in an STA.

❑ `Both` means that the object is designed for concurrent access, and that it contains code to protect itself from multiple threads. Such an object is meant to be loaded into an MTA, but will work fine in an STA, although the synchronization code will impair performance a little.

❑ `Free` means that the object is designed for use in an MTA. The difference between `Free` and `Both` is that the former is used to specify that the object will create worker threads, and since these will want direct access to the object, best performance will only occur if the object is created in an MTA. If necessary, COM will create an MTA for the object and its threads.

So, if the client apartment is incompatible with the threading model of the server, COM will create an appropriate apartment. Since this will require a cross-apartment call, COM will ensure that a correctly marshaled pointer is returned to the client apartment.

Note that the `Single` threading model is generally used for objects that are not reentrant, or that use a library that's not reentrant. Access to all such objects within the process will always be serialized, and it is therefore not a very scaleable solution.

`Both` is a good choice for a threading model, because if it is used in an STA, COM will ensure that only one thread will access the object at a time. Although synchronization code will be called, this should not impair performance by too much. If the object is created by a client in an MTA, then it will have all the necessary synchronization code, and can be accessed by multiple threads. In both cases, the object is created in the apartment that creates it, so no cross-apartment marshaling is needed. The object, if you like, is apartment neutral.

If the object will create worker threads then typically (although not necessarily) these threads will want to have direct access to the object. If this is the case, the object and its worker threads should be run in an MTA. You can mark your object as `Free` to ensure that it's created in the MTA; the worker threads will make an appropriate call to `CoInitializeEx()` to specify that they want to join the MTA. In this case, the access between the worker threads and the object will be direct.

However, if the client will be in an STA, access from the client to the object will be cross-apartment through a proxy. In this case you may decide to mark your object as `Both` rather than `Free` so that it is created in the same apartment as the client. Your choice between using `Both` or `Free` should take into account how many times the client will access the object compared to the number of times the worker threads will access the object.

One other issue you must consider is if the `Both` object has worker threads that make callbacks to the client, for example generating events. If the `Both` object is created in an MTA then there are no problems because the client sink object will also be created in the MTA and so the worker threads can generate the event. If the `Both` object is created in an STA it will mean that to pass the client sink interface to the worker threads it must marshal it.

# Client

As I have mentioned above, COM client code will need to run in an apartment – you should call `CoInitializeEx()` in all threads that will use the COM API and access objects. Your choice of which apartment to use depends on what you intend to do. Note that all access to *out-of-process* objects will be carried out through proxies, so the threading model of the server here is not relevant to the client. Even in the case of in-process servers, where the threading model is more important to the client, COM will never *refuse* to create an object due to incompatible threading models – it will just create an apartment compatible with the server and marshal the interface pointer.

If your client will use multiple threads, then an MTA is usually a good choice. In particular, if one thread will want to access the objects created in another thread, using an MTA will allow you (in cases when the objects are in-process and compatible with the client apartment) to have direct access to the objects. If the object is marked as `Apartment` or `Single`, then you should try to access the object only within the STA where it is created, otherwise a proxy will be used. Note, however, that in performance terms STA to STA communication is just as bad as MTA to STA.

# Threading Models in ATL

There are two issues to be aware of regarding the threading model used for your object. The first issue concerns the module that you will use for the server (EXE or DLL), and the effect this has on how or whether threads are created and COM is initialized. The second issue is how the threading model affects the object's data members and methods.

If the server is packaged in an EXE, you can specify the threading model by defining either `_ATL_APARTMENT_THREADED` or `_ATL_FREE_THREADED` symbol in your `stdafx.h` header, before the ATL headers are included. This ensures that `CoInitializeEx()` is called appropriately, and that class factory registration and shutdown are correct for the threading model. If the server is packaged in a DLL, then it will not call `CoInitializeEx()`, and in this case these symbols are used to specify how locking is applied, as you'll see later.

If the object is single-threaded (and therefore designed to run in an STA), no further protection of its members is needed because object access is synchronized by the STA. In this case, you should use either `Single` or `Apartment` as the threading model on the **Attributes** tab of Object Wizard. Which you choose depends in part upon whether the server is a DLL or an EXE. If the server is a DLL, you will most likely want to use `Apartment`, unless the object *must* run in the client's main STA (for example it if must access data in the main STA), in which case `Single` should be used. If the server is an EXE, it makes no difference which one you choose.

If the object is likely to be accessed by more than one thread – that is, it will be created in an MTA – you should use `Free` or `Both` and it will need to be written to allow safe access from multiple threads. Again, the choice depends on the server package: for an EXE, there's no difference between `Free` or `Both`, but for a DLL you have to decide whether the object is likely to create other worker threads. If so, you will more likely want to use `Free`, as explained earlier.

When you select a threading model, the ATL Object Wizard will derive your class from
`CComObjectRootEx<>`. `CComObjectRootEx<>` is used to provide `AddRef()` and `Release()`
implementations. These implementations use the `Increment()` and `Decrement()` methods of the
class supplied as the parameter to `CComObjectRootEx<>` – either `CComSingleThreadModel` or
`CComMultiThreadModel`. The first of these uses the quicker (but thread-unsafe) `++` and `--`
operators, while the second uses the equivalent (but thread-safe) Win32 functions
`InterlockedIncrement()` and `InterlockedDecrement()`.

In addition, `CComSingleThreadModel` and `CComMultiThreadModel` also `typedef` three
further classes – `AutoCriticalSection`, `CriticalSection` and `ThreadModelNoCS` – to
appropriate implementations. `AutoCriticalSection` is used to implement the
`CComObjectRootEx<>` `Lock()` and `Unlock()` methods, which are either implemented using a
critical section, or perform no operation. You should bracket any thread-sensitive code between calls
to `Lock()` and `Unlock()`, so that if the object is compiled for an STA no synchronization is applied,
but if it's compiled for an MTA you get a critical section.

It's worth remembering that `Lock()` and `Unlock()` for your object will use a *single* critical section,
which is declared in `CComObjectRootEx<>`:

```
template <class ThreadModel>
class CComObjectRootEx : public CComObjectRootBase
{
public:
    typedef _ThreadModel::AutoCriticalSection _CritSec;

... // code omitted

    void Lock() {m_critsec.Lock();}
    void Unlock() {m_critsec.Unlock();}
private:
    _CritSec m_critsec;

};
```

You could apply the critical section in two methods on two different data members, with the intention
of preventing two threads changing one of these data members at the same time, like this:

```
STDMETHODIMP CMyObject::put_X(int x)
{
    Lock();
    m_x = x;
    Unlock();
    return S_OK;
}

STDMETHODIMP CMyObject::put_Y(int y)
{
    Lock();
    m_y = y;
    Unlock();
    return S_OK;
}
```

However, this will cause a problem when one thread tries to access put_X() while another is running put_Y(). This is because when one thread has the critical section, the other will not be able to obtain it until the first thread has called Unlock(). In this case, you will most likely want to use a separate AutoCriticalSection object:

```
STDMETHODIMP CMyObject::put_X(int x)
{
   AutoCriticalSection cs;
   cs.Lock();
   m_x = x;
   cs.Unlock();
   return S_OK;
}

STDMETHODIMP CMyObject::put_Y(int y)
{
   AutoCriticalSection cs;
   cs.Lock();
   m_y = y;
   cs.Unlock();
   return S_OK;
}
```

Now, one thread can call put_X() while another calls put_Y(), and the two methods will run concurrently. However, two threads will not be able to execute one of these methods concurrently. Note that the difference between AutoCriticalSection and CriticalSection is that the former initializes the kernel object in its constructor and deletes it in its destructor, whereas the latter requires you to call member methods Init() and Term() to do this. Initializing a critical section does not come for free, so you can use a CriticalSection object if you want to control when this initialization and cleanup occurs.

The ThreadModelNoCS class is a threading model class that will be used to provide appropriate Increment() and Decrement() methods without any critical section classes defined and this is used for aggregated objects because aggregation cannot occur across apartments so there is not a synchronization issue.

As a final point in this section, if the server is an EXE, then you know what threading model will be used for the objects – they will only ever be created in the server process, and you will have defined one of the threading model symbols described earlier. However, the Object Wizard is apparently oblivious to this, and will allow you to insert an object without synchronization when the server is free threaded, so you have to be disciplined.

In fact, in most cases this oversight won't matter, because objects on different RPC threads will not interact with each other. However, it *will* be important if you write a singleton object in a free threaded server. In this case, more than one client may access the same object at one time on different RPC threads and so synchronization to the object's data members is required.

If the server is a DLL, there is no way that the Object Wizard can know what type of apartment will create the object – indeed, in many cases neither will you!

# EXE Servers

When you create your ATL project, you are committing yourself to how the server is to be packaged. While it is possible to take an object out of one project and put it into another, the work is tedious and error prone. This means that even more than usual, you should think about the threading model that you're going to use right at the start of your project. ATL gives you three options: a server with a single STA (which I have called an Apartment Threaded Server), a server with an MTA (which I have called a Free Threaded Server), and an intermediate model (which I have called a Thread Pool Server).

## Apartment Threaded Server

By default, when you create an EXE server with the ATL COM AppWizard, it will be apartment-threaded – that is, it will have a single STA. The Wizard will add the following line to your project's `stdafx.h` file:

```
#define _ATL_APARTMENT_THREADED
```

This means that `CoInitialize()` is called in `_tWinMain()` to make the main thread join an STA. All the server's class factories will be created and registered in this thread, so that all objects created by these class factories will be created in the same STA. The net effect of this is that all requests to create and access objects managed by this server will be serialized. Thus, if 5 clients create 5 objects, the objects will be created one at a time, in the order that the requests are made to the server.

Furthermore, if each client makes a method call on its own object, these will also be serialized. The effect is a bottleneck:

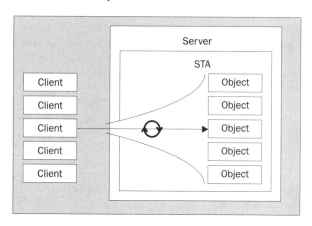

If an object in the server wants to create a worker thread, this thread must join either another STA or the server MTA (the first thread to join the MTA will create it), and the worker thread will only be able to talk to the object through a marshaled pointer.

When you create objects for this server, you should use the **Attributes** page to select a threading model of either **Single** or **Apartment** – which one you choose isn't important. This will derive your class from `CComObjectRootEx<CComSingleThreadModel>`, which implements the `IUnknown` methods `AddRef()` and `Release()` with C++ increment and decrement operators. These are perfectly safe, because the methods will never be called concurrently from different threads. The class factory, however, will use `CComMultiThreadModel`, which uses `InterlockedIncrement()` and `InterlockedDecrement()`. This is because of the following lines from `atlbase.h`:

```
#if defined(_ATL_SINGLE_THREADED)
    typedef CComSingleThreadModel CComObjectThreadModel;
    typedef CComSingleThreadModel CComGlobalsThreadModel;
#elif defined(_ATL_APARTMENT_THREADED)
    typedef CComSingleThreadModel CComObjectThreadModel;
    typedef CComMultiThreadModel CComGlobalsThreadModel;
#else
    typedef CComMultiThreadModel CComObjectThreadModel;
    typedef CComMultiThreadModel CComGlobalsThreadModel;
#endif
```

Generally, you will not use _ATL_SINGLE_THREADED because it is designed for legacy code. Notice that you have two typedefs CComObjectThreadModel and CComGlobalsThreadModel defined according to the threading model of your server. The former is used as a default parameter for templates that require a threading model and you omit to supply one. CComGlobalsThreadModel is used to define what sort of locking will be applied when an object tries to access a global object. In all cases except for the single threaded server, this class uses a critical section; this is needed because in both apartment and free threaded servers there may be more than one thread running (in the case of an apartment threaded server these other threads will be in other apartments) and so some synchronization must be applied to accesses to global objects. In the case of a single threaded server there will only ever be a single thread in the process, so no synchronization is required. Note that CComClassFactory is derived from CComObjectRootEx<CComGlobalsThreadModel>.

## ThreadServer

Let's try an example to get a better grasp about how the choice of apartment threaded server affects its performance. This example will have an EXE server that will be used to create simple objects. These objects only have one purpose: to give you an indication of what time they were created and what thread they are running in. The example will be extended in the later sections to show how the other server threading models compare.

Use the Wizard to create an executable server called ThreadServer, and then add an ATL object using the **Short Name** of ThreadInfo with the default values in the **Attributes** tab. Use the ClassView to add a single method called GetInfo() to the IThreadInfo interface. This method has the following prototype:

```
HRESULT GetInfo([out, retval] BSTR* pbstrInfo);
```

The method is simple:

```
STDMETHODIMP CThreadInfo::GetInfo(BSTR *pbstrInfo)
{
    USES_CONVERSION;
    TCHAR str[31];
    SYSTEMTIME st;
    GetLocalTime(&st);
```

```
    wsprintf(str, _T("%02d:%02d:%02d.%03d %08x:%08x"),
            st.wHour, st.wMinute, st.wSecond, st.wMilliseconds,
            this, GetCurrentThreadId());
    *pbstrInfo = ::SysAllocString(T2CW(str));
    ATLTRACE(_T("%s\n"), str);

    Sleep(500); // Half a second delay
    return S_OK;
}
```

I've put in a half-second delay, so that you can see more clearly what's going with some timing tests that I'll conduct later. In addition, so that you can observe the synchronization that's occurring through the thread message queue, add the following to _tWinMain():

```
MSG msg;
while (GetMessage(&msg, 0, 0, 0))
{
    ATLTRACE(_T("%ld %0x, %08x, %08x\n"),
            msg.time, msg.message, msg.lParam, msg.wParam);
    DispatchMessage(&msg);
}
```

Now you can compile the project. (The interface is dual, and therefore uses type library marshaling by default. You do not have to compile a proxy-stub DLL.)

Next you need a client, so create a **Win32 Console Application** called `ThreadServerClient` and check the **A "Hello, World!" Application** option. Before you can use COM in this project, you need to edit `stdafx.h`:

```
#define _WIN32_DCOM
#include <windows.h>
#include <stdio.h>
#include <tchar.h>
```

The client will use the compiler COM support classes, so here's a skeletal _tmain() function:

```
#import "..\ThreadServer\ThreadServer.tlb" no_namespace

int _tmain(int argc, TCHAR* argv[])
{
    DWORD dwStart = GetTickCount();

#ifdef _FIRST_TEST
    CoInitialize(NULL);
#endif

    try
    {
    }
    catch(_com_error e)
    {
        _tprintf(_T("Error in main thread: %x\n\t%s\n"),
                                    e.Error(), e.ErrorMessage());
    }
```

```
#ifdef _FIRST_TEST
   CoUninitialize();
#endif
   _tprintf(_T("That took %2.3f seconds\n"),
                        (float)(GetTickCount() - dwStart) / 1000);
   return 0;
}
```

The purpose of this test program is to give you an indication of the amount of time that the test takes. The client will create several threads, and can perform one of two tests – the test that will be used is selected by defining a preprocessor symbol.

In the first test, the main thread will create one object and marshal the interface pointer to the other threads; the thread function will access the object through GetInfo() and print the string. So that all the threads try to access the object at the same time, I will use an event that is not initially signaled, when the event becomes signaled, all the threads will attempt to access the object. In the second test, each client thread will create an object and then call GetInfo().

CoInitialize() is only called in the first test, and you'd be forgiven for thinking that this would present a problem: _com_error uses a COM object, so surely we need COM to be initialized? As it turns out, the answer is no, because in the second test an exception of _com_error cannot be thrown – as you will see, the try block will have no COM code.

The test to be conducted is determined by the _FIRST_TEST symbol. The project needs an event synchronization object so that all the threads will access the server at the same time. The handle to the object is declared global, as is the array of threads to which the interface pointer will be marshaled:

```
HANDLE g_hEvent = NULL;
#define NO_THREADS 5
#ifdef _FIRST_TEST
IStream* g_pMarshalPtr[NO_THREADS];
#endif
DWORD WINAPI AccessServer(LPVOID lpParameter);
```

These variables are initialized within _tmain(), before the try block:

```
DWORD x;
HANDLE hThreads[NO_THREADS];
ZeroMemory(hThreads, sizeof(hThreads));
#ifdef _FIRST_TEST
   CoInitialize(NULL);
   ZeroMemory(g_pMarshalPtr, sizeof(g_pMarshalPtr));
#endif
   g_hEvent = CreateEvent(NULL, TRUE, FALSE, "");
```

The clean up code comes straight after the `catch` block:

```
    // Wait for threads to die
    WaitForMultipleObjects(NO_THREADS, hThreads, TRUE, INFINITE);
    _tprintf(_T("Releasing thread handles\n"));
    for(x = 0 ; x < NO_THREADS ; x++)
    {
        // Release handles
        if(hThreads[x])
            CloseHandle(hThreads[x]);
    }
    CloseHandle(g_hEvent);
```

```
#ifdef _FIRST_TEST
    CoUninitialize();
#endif
```

The `try` block looks like this:

```
    #ifdef _FIRST_TEST
    IThreadInfoPtr pObj(__uuidof(ThreadInfo));
    for(x = 0 ; x < NO_THREADS ; x++)
    {
        HRESULT hr;
        hr = CreateStreamOnHGlobal(NULL, TRUE, &g_pMarshalPtr[x]);
        if(FAILED(hr))
            _com_issue_error(hr);

        hr = CoMarshalInterface(g_pMarshalPtr[x], __uuidof(pObj),
                        pObj, MSHCTX_INPROC, NULL, MSHLFLAGS_NORMAL);
        if(FAILED(hr))
        {
            g_pMarshalPtr[x]->Release();
            g_pMarshalPtr[x] = NULL;
            _com_issue_error(hr);
        }
    }
    #endif

    _tprintf(_T("Creating threads\n"));
    DWORD dwThreadID;
    for(x = 0 ; x < NO_THREADS ; x++)
    hThreads[x] = CreateThread(NULL, 0,
        (LPTHREAD_START_ROUTINE)AccessServer, (LPVOID)x, 0, &dwThreadID);

    // Start the action
    SetEvent(g_hEvent);
```

In the first test an object is created and the `IThreadInfo` pointer is marshaled into the stream array. Notice that these streams are created with `CreateStreamOnHGlobal()` that creates a new stream object in global memory. In both tests, the code creates all the threads and then sets the event so that all the threads start their work at one time.

The thread function, `AccessServer()`, looks like this:

```
DWORD WINAPI AccessServer(LPVOID lpParameter)
{
    HRESULT hr = S_OK;
    CoInitialize(NULL);
    DWORD dwThreadNumber = (DWORD)lpParameter;
    try
    {

#ifdef _FIRST_TEST
        IThreadInfoPtr pObj;
        LARGE_INTEGER l;
        l.QuadPart = 0;
        g_pMarshalPtr[dwThreadNumber]->Seek(l, STREAM_SEEK_SET, NULL);
        hr = CoUnmarshalInterface(g_pMarshalPtr[dwThreadNumber],
                        __uuidof(pObj), reinterpret_cast<void**>(&pObj));
        g_pMarshalPtr[dwThreadNumber]->Release();
        g_pMarshalPtr[dwThreadNumber] = NULL;
        if(FAILED(hr))
            _com_issue_error(hr);
#else
        IThreadInfoPtr pObj(__uuidof(ThreadInfo));
#endif

        WaitForSingleObject(g_hEvent, INFINITE);
        _bstr_t bstrInfo;
        bstrInfo = pObj->GetInfo();
        _tprintf(_T("For client thread %ld (%08x) ")
                    _T("the server returned\n%S\n"), dwThreadNumber,
                    GetCurrentThreadId(), (LPWSTR)bstrInfo);
    }
    catch(_com_error e)
    {
        _tprintf(_T("Error in thread %ld: %x\n\t%s\n"), dwThreadNumber,
                                        e.Error(), e.ErrorMessage());
        hr = e.Error();
    }
    CoUninitialize();

    return hr;
}
```

In the first test, the interface pointer is unmarshaled out of the appropriate stream; since normal marshaling is used, the stream cannot be used to marshal the interface another time, so it is released. If the second test is being carried out, a new object is created in this thread. The information string is obtained from the object and printed.

Make sure you define _FIRST_TEST near the top of the source file. Before you compile it, make sure that the CRT used is a multithreaded version (use the C/C++ tab of the project settings dialog and select the Code Generation category).

Compile this, and then run it *twice* from the command line. I say twice because the first time you run it, the client and server will be placed in the page cache, so the second time the client is run, the access is likely to be quicker. Remember, in this test the server has a single thread. The client creates 5 worker threads, and then it creates a single object in the main thread and marshals the interface pointer from the main thread STA to each worker STA where the object is accessed.

On my 180MHz Pentium Pro, I get these results:

```
Creating threads
For client thread 0 (0000002e) the server returned
13:58:47.614 00c10040:0000010b
For client thread 1 (000000e4) the server returned
13:58:48.135 00c10040:0000010b
For client thread 2 (000000cf) the server returned
13:58:48.636 00c10040:0000010b
For client thread 3 (0000010f) the server returned
13:58:49.137 00c10040:0000010b
For client thread 4 (00000110) the server returned
13:58:49.637 00c10040:0000010b
Releasing thread handles
That took 2.724 seconds
```

Notice that the string obtained from the server shows that the `this` pointer is always the same (there is only one object at `0xc10040`), and the thread ID is also the same (`0x0000010b`; there is only one thread in the server). Now check the times – although the threads were all told to access the object at the same time, they actually access it at 500ms intervals: the length of the `Sleep()` used in `GetInfo()`.

As an extra test, I ran the DBMon utility from the Platform SDK. As explained in the last chapter, this prints out the strings sent to `OutputDebugStream()`. The trace I get from the previous test is:

```
242: 20421514 54a, 00142190, 0000babe
242: 20421514 54a, 001422e8, 0000babe
242: 20421574 54a, 00142598, 0000babe
242: 20421594 54a, 00142848, 0000babe
242: 20421594 54a, 00142af8, 0000babe
242: 20421604 54a, 00142da8, 0000babe
242: 13:58:47.614 00c10040:0000010b
242: 20421604 54a, 00142f00, 0000babe
242: 13:58:48.135 00c10040:0000010b
242: 20421614 54a, 00143058, 0000babe
242: 13:58:48.636 00c10040:0000010b
242: 20421634 54a, 001431b0, 0000babe
242: 13:58:49.137 00c10040:0000010b
242: 20421634 54a, 001435b8, 0000babe
242: 13:58:49.637 00c10040:0000010b
242: 20422145 54a, 00143710, 0000babe
242: 20422646 54a, 001439c0, 0000babe
242: 20423146 54a, 00143c70, 0000babe
242: 20423647 54a, 00143f20, 0000babe
242: 20424148 54a, 00142190, 0000babe
```

Most of these are coming from the message loop, but the others are the information strings from `GetInfo()`. The message loop strings give the time, message, `lParam` and `wParam`. A Windows message of `0x054a` with a `wParam` of `0x0000babe` is COM synchronizing object calls to the STA; the address of the marshaling packet is in the `lParam`. (For more information about marshaling packets see *Professional DCOM Programming*.)

Now let's try the second test. Comment out the definition of `_FIRST_TEST` and recompile. Again, run the example twice. Remember that in this case the server is still single threaded; the client creates 5 STA threads, and each one creates an object and then calls the object method.

This time the output is:

```
Creating threads
For client thread 1 (0000002e) the server returned
14:07:14.043 00c11fa0:00000102
For client thread 3 (00000043) the server returned
14:07:14.553 00c11f60:00000102
For client thread 2 (000000f1) the server returned
14:07:15.054 00c10040:00000102
For client thread 4 (000000f0) the server returned
14:07:15.555 00c11fe0:00000102
For client thread 0 (00000110) the server returned
14:07:16.096 00c11f20:00000102
Releasing thread handles
That took 2.684 seconds
```

This time the `this` pointer is different in the information string, but the thread ID is still the same for each call. However, as before, the thread accesses are 500ms apart.

What should be clear from these tests is that the server only has one thread regardless of how many objects are created – all accesses to a single object or to multiple objects are serialized. If your server will only serve one object, and there will only be one client of that object – that is, only one apartment accessing it – then a server with a single STA is fine. For all other cases, a more scaleable solution is required.

## Free Threaded Server

To make the server free threaded (that is, to create the server's class factories in an MTA and accept method calls on RPC-allocated threads), you need to comment out the definition of `_ATL_APARTMENT_THREADED` and replace it with one for `_ATL_FREE_THREADED`. Now that multiple threads can access your object, you need to change the ATL class so that it derives from `CComObjectRootEx<CComMultiThreadModel>`, so that access to the reference count is protected. If you're inserting an ATL class afresh, make sure that you check the **Both** or **Free** threading model from the **Attributes** tab; for the purposes of this test, it doesn't matter which you choose.

Making the server free threaded means that when a request comes in to create an object or to call a method, COM will pick an RPC-managed pool thread:

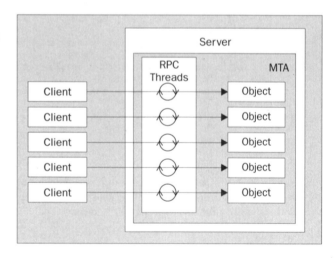

Make these changes to ThreadServer, and recompile it. Now try the first test with ThreadServerClient (remember to define _FIRST_TEST). The output is:

```
Creating threads
For client thread 0 (000000f4) the server returned
14:18:50.454 00c10030:00000111
For client thread 4 (0000011d) the server returned
14:18:50.494 00c10030:0000011b
For client thread 3 (000000f6) the server returned
14:18:50.494 00c10030:00000113
For client thread 2 (00000102) the server returned
14:18:50.474 00c10030:000000cf
For client thread 1 (0000011a) the server returned
14:18:50.464 00c10030:000000f2
Releasing thread handles
That took 0.611 seconds
```

The this pointer is the same, because there is just one object, but there are at least five server threads. Now look at the times: as near as makes no odds, they are the same – access to the object is *concurrent*. This is further confirmed by the total access time by the client being 0.6 seconds, compared with 2.7 seconds in the apartment model server. The output from DBMon is also revealing:

```
284: 14:18:50.454 00c10030:00000111
284: 14:18:50.464 00c10030:000000f2
284: 14:18:50.474 00c10030:000000cf
284: 14:18:50.494 00c10030:00000113
284: 14:18:50.494 00c10030:0000011b
```

There are *no* debug strings from the message loop. This is because COM does not need to synchronize access to the object. In this case, the message loop is only used to indicate that the server process should die when the last object instance is released.

Now for another go at the second test. Comment out the definition of _FIRST_TEST and recompile the client. Here are the results I get:

```
Creating threads
For client thread 1 (00000051) the server returned
14:27:09.942 00c11f80:00000121
For client thread 2 (00000101) the server returned
14:27:09.942 00c10030:00000120
For client thread 3 (00000114) the server returned
14:27:09.942 00c11ee0:00000123
For client thread 0 (0000010f) the server returned
14:27:09.952 00c11f30:00000124
For client thread 4 (00000115) the server returned
14:27:09.962 00c11fd0:0000011f
Releasing thread handles
That took 0.631 seconds
```

Once again, this is exactly what you would expect: the this pointers are all different, as are the thread IDs, but the time that the client accesses each object is the same. The trace from DBMon also is the same as in the first test with the MTA server.

With this example, I have tried to demonstrate that the default threading model – the apartment model (a single STA) – is not scaleable in situations where you have multiple clients (whether you have a single or multiple objects). In both cases, there is just one thread in the server, and all accesses to the object (or objects) are serialized using the thread message queue.

The free threaded server is a far more scaleable solution. COM uses a separate thread in the server to service each object request, and you don't have to worry about the details of doing this as COM will get the threads from a pool that the RPC runtime creates. If more threads are required, RPC will create them, relieving you of that responsibility too.

The following diagram shows a trace from the NT performance monitor to show the total number of threads in the system. The increase in the number of threads is a result of me running an adapted version of `ThreadServerClient` using the second test to create 150 client threads and an object on each of those threads. The vertical line shows when the client died.

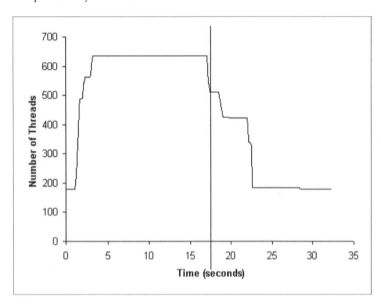

It is instructive to see that the number of threads has risen from 179 to a maximum of 639 – in other words, the increase of 456 threads is more than *three times* the number of objects created. 151 of these threads come from the client, and I guess that the other 405 threads are being created in the server or by COM for its own uses. The steps in the chart for the 5 seconds after the client finishes show that COM has realized that the huge number of threads is no longer required, and so it releases them.

## Free Threaded Server Without a Message Queue

The last section showed that the thread message queue is not needed to synchronize access to the object when the server supports multiple threads, and so it can be removed. However, removing the message queue *completely* will mean that the server will not stay in memory long enough to serve any objects. Here's the generated code from `_tWinMain()`:

```
if (bRun)
    {
        _Module.StartMonitor();
#if _WIN32_WINNT >= 0x0400 & defined(_ATL_FREE_THREADED)
        hRes = _Module.RegisterClassObjects(CLSCTX_LOCAL_SERVER,
            REGCLS_MULTIPLEUSE | REGCLS_SUSPENDED);
```

```
        _ASSERTE(SUCCEEDED(hRes));
        hRes = CoResumeClassObjects();
#else
        hRes = _Module.RegisterClassObjects(CLSCTX_LOCAL_SERVER,
            REGCLS_MULTIPLEUSE);
#endif
        _ASSERTE(SUCCEEDED(hRes));

        MSG msg;
        while (GetMessage(&msg, 0, 0, 0))
            DispatchMessage(&msg);

        _Module.RevokeClassObjects();
        Sleep(dwPause); //wait for any threads to finish
    }

    _Module.Term();
    CoUninitialize();
    return nRet;
```

If the message loop is removed, the main thread will register the class factories and then immediately revoke them and return. For a free threaded server, the message loop exists to keep the main thread alive until the WM_QUIT message is sent to indicate that the server should die.

To perform a similar task *without* a message loop, the program needs to wait for another sort of message, and an efficient mechanism is to use a Win32 event kernel object. To do this, edit the CExeModule class in stdafx.h:

```
class CExeModule : public CComModule
{
public:
    LONG Unlock();
    DWORD dwThreadID;
    HANDLE hEventShutdown;
    HANDLE hEventKillMe;
    void MonitorShutdown();
    bool StartMonitor();
    bool bActivity;
};
```

This event object can be created and destroyed in _tWinMain():

```
    if (bRun)
    {
        _Module.StartMonitor();
        _Module.hEventKillMe = CreateEvent(NULL, TRUE, FALSE, NULL);
#if _WIN32_WINNT >= 0x0400 & defined(_ATL_FREE_THREADED)
        hRes = _Module.RegisterClassObjects(CLSCTX_LOCAL_SERVER,
                REGCLS_MULTIPLEUSE | REGCLS_SUSPENDED);
        _ASSERTE(SUCCEEDED(hRes));
        hRes = CoResumeClassObjects();
#else
        hRes = _Module.RegisterClassObjects(CLSCTX_LOCAL_SERVER,
                REGCLS_MULTIPLEUSE);
#endif
        _ASSERTE(SUCCEEDED(hRes));
```

```
WaitForSingleObject(_Module.hEventKillMe, INFINITE);

    _Module.RevokeClassObjects();
    Sleep(dwPause); //wait for any threads to finish
    CloseHandle(_Module.hEventKillMe);
}
```

To indicate that the server should die, you need to change `CExeModule::MonitorShutdown()` in the same source file as `_tWinMain()`. When your server is running, this method is running in a monitor thread, waiting on the `hEventShutdown` event. When `CExeServer::Unlock()` detects that the last lock on the server has been released, it sets this event to allow `MonitorShutdown()` to start the shutdown process. At the bottom of this method is

```
    CloseHandle(hEventShutdown);
    PostThreadMessage(dwThreadID, WM_QUIT, 0, 0);
}
```

You should change it to:

```
    CloseHandle(hEventShutdown);
    SetEvent(hEventKillMe);
}
```

This allows `_tWinMain()` to finish, and it's all you have to do. Now the server no longer has a message queue, but instead uses the more efficient `WaitForSingleObject()`.

## Thread Pool Server

In the midst of this discussion, it is important to keep in mind that threads are not a panacea for all performance ills. The last two sections have demonstrated that for an unusually-stressed system on a single processor machine, it takes five times longer for a server with a single thread to serve five clients than it does for a server with five threads. But what happens if there are 150 clients? The only way to find out is to give it a try.

With the code for this chapter, you will find an adapted version of `ThreadServerClient` (called `ThreadServerClientMany`) that allows you to specify the number of threads the client should use as a command line parameter. The only special thing to note about this version is that `WaitForMultipleObjects()`, which is used to determine when all the worker threads have died, can only wait for a maximum of `MAXIMUM_WAIT_OBJECTS` objects (a value of 64), so I have had to use a loop to check for groups of threads at a time.

I used this application to get the data for the graph at the end of the last section; for that test I created 150 threads, and the test took 21 seconds. This is consistent with the performance obtained earlier, when 5 threads took 0.6 seconds. *However*, the big difference between the two tests was that when the server had 150 threads, I could not do anything else on my machine for those 21 seconds. The RPC runtime must have created those threads with a sufficiently high priority to prevent any threads managing the user interface to run.

It is not a good idea to have a server that regularly runs 150 threads unless you have a multiprocessor machine with a large amount of memory, but what if you expect your server to have 30 or 40 clients? Is creating 30 or 40 threads a good idea? Not if you can avoid it. Thread context switching imposes an overhead on your processor, so judging the number of threads to use is a balancing act between responsivity and performance.

However, in a free threaded server, it's the RPC runtime that creates the threads, and you have no control over how many are created, nor what priority they have. What can you do to change this? The answer is to use a Thread Pool Server. ATL gives you this facility with the `CComAutoThreadModule<>`, `CComApartment`, and `CComClassFactoryAutoThread` classes.

### CComAutoThreadModule<>

To create a thread pool, you must derive your EXE server `CExeModule` class from `CComAutoThreadModule<>`. You will find this latter class declared in `atlbase.h`, but the implementation is in `atlcom.h`. This template class takes an allocator class as a parameter, and by default `CComSimpleThreadAllocator` is used. This allocator class should have a method called `GetThread()`, the purpose of which is to implement the algorithm to return the thread index that should be used when an object request is made:

```
int GetThread(CComApartment* pApt, int nThreads);
```

The first parameter is an array of **apartment objects,** and the second parameter is the number of members in this array. `CComSimpleThreadAllocator` implements a simple round-robin algorithm that keeps a count of the previously returned value, incrementing it on each call to `GetThread()` and wrapping to zero when the size of the array is reached. You are free to implement your own algorithm – to implement a load balancing routine, perhaps.

To create the thread pool, your server should call `CComAutoThreadModule<>::Init()`; the Wizard-generated code will do this automatically in `_tWinMain()`:

```
_Module.Init(ObjectMap, hInstance, &LIBID_THREADSERVERLib);
```

This call is not specific to thread pooled servers; the Wizard adds it for all server types. The `CComAutoThreadModule<>` version of `Init()`, however, has four parameters – the final one is the number of threads to create in the pool, and has a default value of `GetDefaultThreads()`, which is defined as:

```
static int GetDefaultThreads()
{
    SYSTEM_INFO si;
    GetSystemInfo(&si);
    return si.dwNumberOfProcessors * 4;
}
```

In other words, it creates four times the number of processors in the system, which is a reasonable value. If you want to change the number of threads that will be created, you can do so by changing the call in `_tWinMain()` to include the number that you require.

However it determines what size it should be, Init() creates an array of CComApartment objects. This class effectively wraps the necessary code to manage an STA. After creating the CComApartment objects, one for every thread in the pool, Init() then creates the threads

```
for(int i = 0 ; i < nThreads ; i++)
   m_pApartments[i].m_hThread = CreateThread(
                          NULL, 0, CComApartment::_Apartment,
                          (void*)&m_pApartments[i], 0,
                          &m_pApartments[i].m_dwThreadID);
```

Thus, the thread procedure is the static _Apartment() method, and this is passed the this pointer of the appropriate CComApartment object. _Apartment() merely uses this pointer to call the Apartment() method, which looks like this:

```
DWORD Apartment()
{
   CoInitialize(NULL);
   MSG msg;
   while(GetMessage(&msg, 0, 0, 0))
   {
      if (msg.message == ATL_CREATE_OBJECT)
      {
         _AtlAptCreateObjData* pdata = (_AtlAptCreateObjData*)msg.lParam;
         IUnknown* pUnk = NULL;
         pdata->hRes = pdata->pfnCreateInstance(
                          NULL, IID_IUnknown, (void**)&pUnk);
         if (SUCCEEDED(pdata->hRes))
            pdata->hRes = CoMarshalInterThreadInterfaceInStream(
                             *pdata->piid, pUnk, &pdata->pStream);
         if (SUCCEEDED(pdata->hRes))
         {
            pUnk->Release();
            ATLTRACE2(atlTraceCOM, 2,
            _T("Object created on thread = %d\n"), GetCurrentThreadId());
         }
         SetEvent(pdata->hEvent);
      }
      DispatchMessage(&msg);
   }
   CoUninitialize();
   return 0;
}
```

At this point, a new thread has been created and is running, so the first thing that the thread procedure does is to call CoInitialize() to enter an STA. Each STA has to have a message loop for synchronization, and the loop in Apartment() only handles two messages: WM_QUIT, which breaks the loop and returns from the thread procedure, and the private message ATL_CREATE_OBJECT, which is registered by Init():

```
CComApartment::ATL_CREATE_OBJECT =
                    RegisterWindowMessage(_T("ATL_CREATE_OBJECT"));
```

This message is sent by `CreateInstance()` to create an object, as you'll see in a moment. The `lParam` of this message is a pointer to an object of type `_AtlAptCreateObjData`:

```
class _AtlAptCreateObjData
{
public:
    _ATL_CREATORFUNC* pfnCreateInstance;
    const IID* piid;
    HANDLE hEvent;
    LPSTREAM pStream;
    HRESULT hRes;
};
```

The first member is a pointer to the `CreateInstance()` of the class factory for the object, `piid` is the IID of the interface to create, and `hRes` is used to obtain the result of the object creation.

The sender of this message is on a different thread to the receiver of the message, so this message is effectively an inter-thread communication mechanism. However, although the sender has a message loop, the message is actually sent from a method embedded several layers down in the call stack, so Windows messages cannot be used to communicate results from the receiving thread to the original sender. Instead, this communication is done using an event object. `hEvent` is created in the sender thread and is set by the receiver thread (in `Apartment()`) when the object creation has completed. Since the sender and receiver are on two different threads and consequently in two different apartments, the object's interface pointer must be marshaled, and this is the reason for `pStream`.

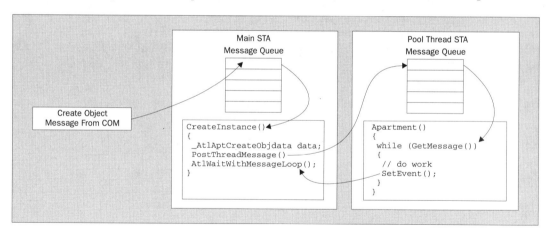

If you look back to `Apartment()`, you can see this object creation in action. First, the class factory `CreateInstance()` is called for the object's `IUnknown`, and then the `CoMarshalInterThreadInterfaceInStream()` API helper function is called to marshal the requested interface into the stream. At this point, the event is set and the message loop continues. The sender can obtain the `hRes` member of `_AtlAptCreateObjData` to see if the creation was successful, and if so it can call the `CoGetInterfaceAndReleaseStream()` API helper to unmarshal the interface pointer.

### Module Locks

Since there are now several threads, each running in a separate STA, you need to coordinate them to determine whether the server can shut down. The class factories use _Module.Lock() and _Module.Unlock() to implement IClassFactory::LockServer(), and the various CComObjectxxx<> classes use these to keep a count of the number of objects created. Although _Module.Lock() is a process-wide method, it is useful to keep a count of the number of objects created in an apartment: you can use this as an ingredient in your load balancing algorithm in a custom allocator class.

Since a class factory's CreateInstance() will be called on various pool threads, the implementations of Lock() and Unlock() should determine which thread is calling the method, and then increment or decrement the appropriate CComApartment's lock count, for example Lock():

```
template <class ThreadAllocator>
inline LONG CComAutoThreadModule<ThreadAllocator>::Lock()
{
    LONG l = CComModule::Lock();
    DWORD dwThreadID = GetCurrentThreadId();
    for(int i = 0 ; i < m_nThreads ; i++)
    {
        if(m_pApartments[i].m_dwThreadID == dwThreadID)
        {
            m_pApartments[i].Lock();
            break;
        }
    }
    return l;
}
```

The Lock() and Unlock() methods of CComApartment call the Increment() and Decrement() methods of CComGlobalsThreadModel.

CComAutoThreadModule<>::Lock() is inherited by your CExeModule class, but the AppWizard, during its normal actions, overrides the Unlock() method, assuming that it was inherited from CComModule. Thus you need to make sure that this code (in the same source file as _tWinMain()) calls CComAutoThreadModule::Unlock():

```
LONG CExeModule::Unlock()
{
    LONG l = CComAutoThreadModule<CComSimpleThreadAllocator>::Unlock();
    if(l == 0)
    {
        bActivity = true;
        SetEvent(hEventShutdown);
    }
    return l;
}
```

### Class Factories

An object that wants to make use of the thread pool must have () declared in its ATL class. Furthermore, aggregation is not allowed, so it should also DECLARE_NOT_AGGREGATABLE() through the Object Wizard. The effect of the former is to ensure that CComClassFactoryAutoThread is used as the class factory class rather than CComClassFactory. This class is special because it doesn't create objects in its CreateInstance() method; instead it calls the CreateInstance() method supplied by _Module:

```
STDMETHODIMP CComClassFactoryAutoThread::CreateInstance(
                         LPUNKNOWN pUnkOuter, REFIID riid, void** ppvObj)
{
   ATLASSERT(m_pfnCreateInstance != NULL);
   HRESULT hRes = E_POINTER;
   if(ppvObj != NULL)
   {
       *ppvObj = NULL;

       // Cannot aggregate across apartments
       ATLASSERT(pUnkOuter == NULL);
       if(pUnkOuter != NULL)
         hRes = CLASS_E_NOAGGREGATION;
       else
         hRes = _Module.CreateInstance(m_pfnCreateInstance, riid, ppvObj);
   }
   return hRes;
}
```

You'll remember from Chapter 2 that the OBJECT_ENTRY() in the object map for an object stores a pointer to the CreateInstance() function that's used to create the object: class::_CreatorClass::CreateInstance() (where class is your object's ATL class). _CreatorClass is typedef'd by the aggregation macro:

```
#define DECLARE_NOT_AGGREGATABLE(x) public:\
   typedef CComCreator2<CComCreator<CComObject<x> >,
               CComFailCreator<CLASS_E_NOAGGREGATION> > _CreatorClass;
```

When the class factory is registered, the pointer to _CreatorClass::CreateInstance() is passed to CComCreator<>::CreateInstance(), which passes it to the class factory via a call to SetVoid(). This initializes the m_pfnCreateInstance of CComClassFactoryAutoThread. Looking back at CreateInstance() above, you can see that all it does is call _Module::CreateInstance(), passing this function pointer. The version of this method that appears in CComAutoThreadModule<> looks like this (from atlcom.h):

```
template <class ThreadAllocator>
HRESULT CComAutoThreadModule<ThreadAllocator>::CreateInstance(
                  void* pfnCreateInstance, REFIID riid, void** ppvObj)
{
   _ATL_CREATORFUNC* pFunc = (_ATL_CREATORFUNC*)pfnCreateInstance;
   _AtlAptCreateObjData data;
   data.pfnCreateInstance = pFunc;
   data.piid = &riid;
   data.hEvent = CreateEvent(NULL, FALSE, FALSE, NULL);
   data.hRes = S_OK;
```

```
      int nThread = m_Allocator.GetThread(m_pApartments, m_nThreads);
      ::PostThreadMessage(m_pApartments[nThread].m_dwThreadID,
                    CComApartment::ATL_CREATE_OBJECT, 0, (LPARAM)&data);
      AtlWaitWithMessageLoop(data.hEvent);
      CloseHandle(data.hEvent);
      if(SUCCEEDED(data.hRes))
          data.hRes = CoGetInterfaceAndReleaseStream(data.pStream, riid, ppvObj);
      return data.hRes;
   }
```

This is the sender of the `ATL_CREATE_OBJECT` message mentioned earlier. As you can see, it creates an `_AtlAptCreateObjData` object and initializes it with the `CreateInstance()` pointer, the IID of the required interface, and the handle of the event that is used to indicate that the object has been created.

Next, it calls `GetThread()` to determine the index in the `CComApartment` array for the appropriate thread to use. As mentioned before, the default implementation is a round-robin algorithm. `CreateInstance()` then calls `PostThreadMessage()` to post the `ATL_CREATE_OBJECT` message to the appropriate thread.

As mentioned above, the `Apartment()` routine in the pool thread accepts this message and creates the object using the passed function pointer. It then marshals the interface into a stream. `CreateInstance()` waits (using `AtlWaitWithMessageLoop()`) for the event to be set. At this point, the object is created (or has failed to be created), and the method can unmarshal the interface pointer into the current apartment, so that it can be passed back to the client.

Notice that the change of the state of the event object is determined by calling `AtlWaitWithMessageLoop()`. This calls the Win32 `MsgWaitForMultipleObjects()` function, which will return either when the kernel object is signaled or there is a Windows message in the thread queue. If it returns because of messages in the queue, these are dispatched and the routine waits for the kernel object to become signaled again. `AtlWaitWithMessageLoop()` is called because `CreateInstance()` is called on the class factory in the main thread, and this will have a thread message queue to accept synchronized calls to create objects dispatched from COM. If the message queue were not maintained, it would mean that during object creation, other requests for objects would be queued, blocking those clients.

### Thread Pool Example

Let's look at an example. This server is to be called `AutoThreadServer`, so create an executable server and add a single, non-aggregatable object with a **Short Name** of `ThreadInfo2`. Then, open `stdafx.h` and derive `CExeModule` from `CComAutoThreadModule<>`:

```
   class CExeModule : public CComAutoThreadModule<CComSimpleThreadAllocator>
   {
   public:
      LONG Unlock();
      DWORD dwThreadID;
      HANDLE hEventShutdown;
      void MonitorShutdown();
      bool StartMonitor();
      bool bActivity;
   };
```

Now open the main project file and change `CExeModule::Unlock()`:

```
LONG CExeModule::Unlock()
{
    LONG l = CComAutoThreadModule<CComSimpleThreadAllocator>::Unlock();
    if(l == 0)
    {
        bActivity = true;
        SetEvent(hEventShutdown); // Tell monitor that we transitioned to 0
    }
    return l;
}
```

The next task is to edit the object's ATL class. Add this line:

```
class ATL_NO_VTABLE CThreadInfo2 :
            public CComObjectRootEx<CComSingleThreadModel>,
            public CComCoClass<CThreadInfo2, &CLSID_ThreadInfo2>,
            public IDispatchImpl<IThreadInfo2, &IID_IThreadInfo2,
                                        &LIBID_AUTOTHREADSERVERLib>
{
public:
    CThreadInfo2()
    {
    }

DECLARE_REGISTRY_RESOURCEID(IDR_THREADINFO2)
DECLARE_NOT_AGGREGATABLE(CThreadInfo2)
DECLARE_CLASSFACTORY_AUTO_THREAD()
```

Once again, this interface has a single method called `GetInfo()` that returns a `BSTR`. The method is implemented like this:

```
STDMETHODIMP CThreadInfo2::GetInfo(BSTR *pbstrInfo)
{
    USES_CONVERSION;
    TCHAR str[31];
    SYSTEMTIME st;
    GetLocalTime(&st);
    wsprintf(str, _T("%02d:%02d:%02d.%03d %08x:%08x"),
            st.wHour, st.wMinute, st.wSecond, st.wMilliseconds,
            this, GetCurrentThreadId());
    *pbstrInfo = ::SysAllocString(T2CW(str));
    ATLTRACE(_T("%s\n"), str);

    // Delay
    Sleep(500);
    return S_OK;
}
```

As with `ThreadServer`, add a line to the main thread message queue to print the received message to the debug stream. You can then compile the project.

```
MSG msg;
while (GetMessage(&msg, 0, 0, 0))
{
    ATLTRACE(_T("%ld %0x, %08x, %08x\n"),
                      msg.time, msg.message, msg.lParam, msg.wParam);
    DispatchMessage(&msg);
}
```

The client is the same as ThreadServerClient, except that IThreadInfo2 replaces all references to IThreadinfo, and references to ThreadInfo are replaced with ThreadInfo2. (Remember that the #import line needs changing too.)

As before, run the client *twice* so that the timings reflect the server and client being loaded from the page cache. Here are the results I get for the first test:

```
Creating threads
For client thread 0 (0000013c) the server returned
14:01:17.935 00c10030:00000135
For client thread 1 (0000013d) the server returned
14:01:18.436 00c10030:00000135
For client thread 2 (0000013e) the server returned
14:01:18.937 00c10030:00000135
For client thread 3 (0000013f) the server returned
14:01:19.438 00c10030:00000135
For client thread 4 (00000140) the server returned
14:01:19.938 00c10030:00000135
Releasing thread handles
That took 2.584 seconds
```

Notice that the this pointer is the same for each client thread, and the server thread is the same too. Since only one object is created, this is exactly what you would expect. Now look at the debugging output sent to DBMon:

```
307: 22160925 54a, 001423b0, 0000babe
307: 14:01:17.935 00c10030:00000135
307: 14:01:18.436 00c10030:00000135
307: 14:01:18.937 00c10030:00000135
307: 14:01:19.438 00c10030:00000135
307: 14:01:19.938 00c10030:00000135
```

There really isn't much here. Most of the output comes from GetInfo(); the only other line comes from the client request to create the object. What has happened to the other messages, in response to the client calls to GetInfo()? Well, since the object was created on a thread other than the main thread, the requests to GetInfo() and the object's IUnknown methods are sent by COM as messages to the message queue of the apartment in which the object is created. There isn't a trace message in that apartment's message queue (implemented in Apartment()), so you don't see those messages.

Following on, the results I get for the second test are:

```
Creating threads
For client thread 0 (00000170) the server returned
14:10:30.880 00c11e20:00000177
```

**387**

```
For client thread 4 (00000189) the server returned
14:10:30.880 00c11e60:00000178
For client thread 3 (0000018a) the server returned
14:10:30.880 00c11ea0:00000175
For client thread 2 (0000018b) the server returned
14:10:30.890 00c11ee0:00000176
For client thread 1 (0000016f) the server returned
14:10:31.391 00c10030:00000177
Releasing thread handles
That took 1.412 seconds
```

The this pointers are different, as are the server threads... except for client threads 0 and 1, which are the same. The reason is that the server creates a thread pool of 4 threads (my machine only has one processor), but the client creates five worker threads, each of which creates one object. The round-robin algorithm will create two objects in one pool thread, and one in each of the others.

Running the client using the second test and 150 worker threads (and therefore 150 objects) gives the following trace in PerfMon:

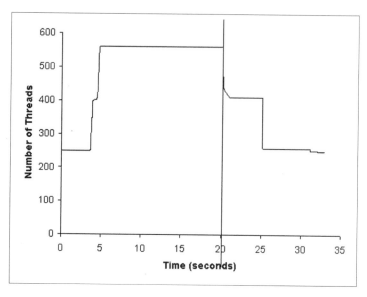

As before, the vertical line on the graph shows when the client ends. The change in the number of threads is from 251 to a peak of 561, a difference of 310 threads. 150 of these are in the client, and COM will use a further 150 to implement the STAs. The server only creates 5 threads – one as the main thread, and four others for the pool (COM creates 5 threads to mirror these as part of the synchronization it provides for STAs).

## Real Server Behavior

Remember, though, that while examples like this are all very well, you're looking at data for a very unusual case. Although you may come across a situation where your server will create 150 objects, it is *not* likely that all 150 will be accessed at exactly the same time. Furthermore, even if your server is likely to have 150 different clients, it is still unlikely that they will want to create objects at exactly the same time. Some of the clients may release their objects before other clients create theirs, so RPC will not necessarily create a new RPC thread, but will reuse a freed thread in the pool. I have used this unusual stress test to indicate to you as clearly as possible how threads are used.

A rather more likely situation is shown here:

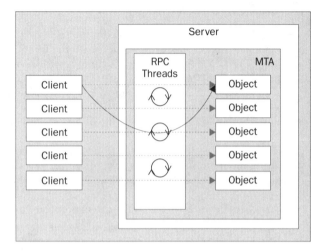

Each client has a reference to an object, and when a method call is made on an object, RPC picks a thread from the pool and the request goes through that thread to the object. It is unlikely that all clients will try to access all the objects at the same time, and so the thread pool is likely to contain fewer threads than there are objects. Another point that can be seen in this diagram is that a single client making more than one call to the object will not necessarily get the same server thread on each call.

## EXE Server Summary

This section has shown you the various COM server types that you can create with ATL. The default server type is apartment-threaded, which is not scaleable and should be avoided. The other types of server you can create are a free threaded server and a thread pool server.

With a free threaded server, RPC creates the server threads for you. It will create an initial pool of threads, and if the number of client requests exceeds the number of threads in the pool, RPC handles this dynamically by creating extra temporary threads, which are released later when the rush is over.

If you want to have control over the number of threads created in a server, you can create a thread pool server. This option supplies a special class factory that creates objects in STA worker threads, according to a load balancing mechanism that you can supply. The number of worker threads is specified by the developer, and is kept constant throughout the lifetime of the server.

Thread pool servers are useful if you want to use objects that do not have synchronization code. In particular, if you create an object that aggregates an object with a threading model of Apartment, then you will not want to create this in an MTA, even if the outer object is thread safe because another thread in the MTA will be able to access the methods on this aggregated object and hence use code that is potentially thread unsafe. This server type is a good compromise.

# DLL Servers

As I explained earlier, DLL servers do not call `CoInitializeEx()`, and instead rely on the client to do so. The object should be written with the intended client apartment in mind. If the client apartment is an MTA, then multiple threads will have access to the object, which will have to be written to protect itself from concurrent access to its data members. The only way that COM knows whether an object has been written correctly for access in an MTA is to look at the `ThreadingModel` value for the object in the registry. If this value is `Free` or `Both`, the object can be created in an MTA. Otherwise, the object will be created in an STA.

To specify that you want an object to be used in a particular apartment, you should select the threading model in the Attributes tab of Object Wizard. The four types have been given before, and in response to this setting Object Wizard will do the following:

- ❏ Change the RGS file for the object to register the `ThreadingModel`
- ❏ Derive the object's ATL class from either `CComObjectRootEx<CComMultiThreadModel>` or `CComObjectRootEx<CComSingleThreadModel>`

`CComObjectRootEx<>` is used to provide `AddRef()` and `Release()` implementations, and the template parameter determines how these work according to the object threading model, as explained earlier.

# Threading and MTS

Microsoft Transaction Server takes most of the problems of threading away from you. However, it does impose some restrictions with which you must comply – specifically, that you cannot create worker threads. Your client will create an object using `CoCreateInstance()`, and the magic of MTS will ensure that the object is created using the MTS surrogate process `mtx.exe`. Such an object is created in an **activity**, which is a distributed logical thread. This means that although MTS objects may be running on different machines, and thus in different threads, MTS ensures that they behave as if they are running in a single thread. This simplifies your code considerably because you do not have to worry about making your code thread safe: any object created within the activity (using `IObjectContext::CreateInstance()`) will be synchronized with all the other objects within the activity, regardless of what actual machine it is running on.

> **Objects can only communicate with each other within an activity: you cannot pass interface pointers across an activity boundary. This does not mean, however, that a client is restricted to a single activity; the client can create more than one activity, and pass data obtained from one activity to another. It just means that objects in different activities cannot talk to each other directly.**

MTS effectively creates a thread for the activity in which the object runs (if the `Apartment` threading model is used), so this is equivalent to the STA thread pool server as explained earlier. I say effectively, because as an optimization, MTS 2.0 does allow for there to be more than one activity on a single thread to cut down on the number of threads created. However, in this case calls into an activity are still serialized.

MTS components must be DLLs and can be written as `Single`, `Apartment` or `Both`:

## Single

This threading model is useful for objects that are not reentrant, or use functions from libraries that are not reentrant. These objects are run within the main STA – in other words, all objects with a `ThreadingModel` set to `Single` will run in the same apartment, so serialization occurs across all these objects. This model is good for objects that know nothing about threads, but it is not at all scaleable. Deadlocks can occur when you have several single-threaded objects running at once.

## Apartment

In this case, each object will have a new STA for its lifetime, which means that you don't have the serialization problem that `Single` has. The MTS object's activity is defined by this apartment, so if another object joins the activity – that is, the first object creates a new object using `IObjectContext::CreateInstance()` – it will be running in the same logical thread.

## Both

If the `Both` threading model is used, the object will still be created in an STA. Even if the server is registered with a threading model of `Free`, MTS ignores this and creates its instances within an activity.

# Marshaling

When an object is created in one apartment and you want to use it in another apartment, the object's interface pointer must be marshaled. This will ensure that a proxy is created in the client's apartment so that the client can access the object through an interface pointer valid for its memory context.

The way to do this manually is to call `CoMarshalInterface()` in an apartment that has access to that interface. This API function takes the interface pointer that you want to marshal and its IID, and it will create a marshaling packet in a stream allocated by the caller. This `IStream` pointer should be made available to the destination apartment which will call `CoUnmarshalInterface()` to create the proxy and provide an interface pointer for the apartment.

```
STDAPI CoMarshalInterface(
    IStream* pStm,           // Pointer to the stream used for marshaling
    REFIID riid,             // Reference to the identifier of the interface
    IUnknown* pUnk,          // Pointer to the interface to be marshaled
    DWORD dwDestContext,     // How far away the other apartment is
    void* pvDestContext,     // Reserved for future use
    DWORD mshlflags          // How the marshaling packet will be used
);
```

In addition to the interface, `CoMarshalInterface()` takes some flags from the `MSHCTX` enumeration to indicate how far away the other apartment is (in-process, local, or remote):

| Flag | Description |
| --- | --- |
| MSHCTX_INPROC | The other apartment is within the same process |
| MSHCTX_LOCAL | The other apartment is within a process on the same machine |
| MSHCTX_<br>DIFFERENTMACHINE | The other apartment is within a process on a different machine |

To indicate how the marshaling packet will be used, values from the MSHLFLAGS enumeration are passed as well. This latter flag indicates whether the stream will be used once or many times to unmarshal the interface:

| Flag | Description |
| --- | --- |
| MSHLFLAGS_NORMAL | Marshal once, unmarshal once |
| MSHLFLAGS_TABLESTRONG | Marshal once, unmarshal many times |
| MSHLFLAGS_TABLEWEAK | Marshal once, unmarshal many times |
| MSHLFLAGS_NOPING | Disable DCOM garbage collection |

Normal marshaling means that once the interface has been unmarshaled from the stream, it cannot be unmarshaled again. Instead, the source apartment must call CoMarshalInterface() to fill a new stream. This inevitably means that the marshaling is only ever carried out once.

Table marshaling is used when interface pointers are being cached in internal tables. As an example, consider the Running Object Table (ROT) – a table typically used by OLE document servers. When you register an object with the ROT, you pass it an interface pointer. At that point, the object will be running (hence the name), and the interface will be marshaled to the ROT, which will result in a stub object being created. This is managed in the server by an object called the stub manager, which manages the stub objects for each individual server object.

The stub manager object can increment the stub's reference count to get a **strong reference**, which means that the object will remain alive even if there is no client. On the other hand, if the stub manager doesn't increment the stub's reference count, and just hands out a pointer to the object's interface to clients, it means that as soon as the last client releases the interface, the reference count in the stub manager will fall to zero and the object will die. This is a **weak reference**.

Note that interface proxies cannot be marshaled using MSHLFLAGS_TABLEWEAK or MSHLFLAGS_TABLESTRONG, but they *can* be marshaled with MSHLFLAGS_NORMAL. An interface proxy is generated when you create a local or a remote object, or when you marshal an interface between apartments. In both of these cases, if you do not use MSHLFLAGS_NORMAL, then CoMarshalInterface() will fail with E_INVALIDARG. Thus, if you have a client that creates a local object, you can marshal this pointer to another apartment in the client as long as you use MSHLFLAGS_NORMAL. You'll see an example of this later in this chapter.

The MSHLFLAGS_NOPING value is useful when the object is remote and you want to turn off **remote garbage collection**. Garbage collection is used to ensure that a server only lives as long as there are clients to it. Normally, DCOM sends pings from the client machine to the server machine every 2 minutes, to indicate to the server machine that the client for a COM server is still alive. These pings are machine to machine, not client to object, nor client to server. The ping packet simply has an identifier to indicate the client machine from which it originated, and the server machine uses this identifier to determine which objects it serves are used on the client. When new objects are created or released, this change is placed in the ping packet.

You have no control over the length of this ping period, and the only action you can take is to turn it off completely for a particular coclass. You may decide to do this if the object is stateless and exists on the server essentially as a service to client (for example, a calculator object where the operands and results are passed as method parameters), or if the object is purposely long-lived. If you turn off remote garbage collection, it means that when a client calls Release() on an interface pointer, it will not release the object – indeed Release() implemented on the interface proxy is essentially a no-op.

When garbage collection is turned off, the server gets no information about whether the client is alive or not. Normally, if the server does not receive a ping packet from the client after 3 ping periods (6 minutes), it knows that there is a problem: either the network is down or the client machine is dead. An object that turns off garbage collection has opted out of this mechanism – if the client dies, the object will not be told. If you turn off garbage collection, you need to manage the object lifetime in another way: specifically, when the server dies it should call CoDisconnectObject() on the interface pointers it holds to disconnect any existing object-client connections.

## ATL Helper Functions

Before you call CoMarshalInterface(), you have to create a stream object and pass this to the function; when you unmarshal an interface, you have to release the stream. These jobs have to be done every time, and they can quickly get tedious. ATL helps you in both these cases by providing two methods designed to be called in-process – that is, to marshal an interface between apartments within a single process.

AtlMarshalPtrInproc(), declared in atlbase.h, returns a stream pointer:

```
ATLINLINE ATLAPI AtlMarshalPtrInProc(
                    IUnknown* pUnk, const IID& iid, IStream** ppStream)
{
    HRESULT hRes = CreateStreamOnHGlobal(NULL, TRUE, ppStream);
    if(SUCCEEDED(hRes))
    {
        hRes = CoMarshalInterface(*ppStream, iid, pUnk, MSHCTX_INPROC,
                                        NULL, MSHLFLAGS_TABLESTRONG);
        if(FAILED(hRes))
        {
            (*ppStream)->Release();
            *ppStream = NULL;
        }
    }
    return hRes;
}
```

Notice that MSHLFLAGS_TABLESTRONG is used, which means that any number of users can unmarshal the interface from the same stream. The other corollary of using this flag is that the interface to be marshaled must *not* have been marshaled already, since this flag cannot be used on interface proxies. The function can be called like this:

```
AtlMarshalPtrInProc(pCustomer, IID_ICustomer, &g_pStream);
```

Here, g_pStream is some IStream pointer that both the marshaling thread and the unmarshaling thread have access to. The code will return a stream with a marshaling packet that can be used to unmarshal the interface. To do this, you can call AtlUnmarshalPtr():

```
ATLINLINE ATLAPI AtlUnmarshalPtr(
                         IStream* pStream, const IID& iid, IUnknown** ppUnk)
{
    *ppUnk = NULL;
    HRESULT hRes = E_INVALIDARG;
    if(pStream != NULL)
    {
        LARGE_INTEGER l;
        l.QuadPart = 0;
        pStream->Seek(l, STREAM_SEEK_SET, NULL);
        hRes = CoUnmarshalInterface(pStream, iid, (void**)ppUnk);
    }
    return hRes;
}
```

This sets the stream's seek pointer to the beginning of the stream, and then unmarshals the interface. When you don't want to marshal the interface any more, you must release the stream by calling AtlFreeMarshalStream():

```
ATLINLINE ATLAPI AtlFreeMarshalStream(IStream* pStream)
{
    if(pStream != NULL)
    {
        LARGE_INTEGER l;
        l.QuadPart = 0;
        pStream->Seek(l, STREAM_SEEK_SET, NULL);
        CoReleaseMarshalData(pStream);
        pStream->Release();
    }
    return S_OK;
}
```

COM provides the helper API CoMarshalInterThreadInterfaceInStream(), which is essentially the same as AtlMarshalPtrInproc(), except that it uses normal marshaling. The combination of AtlUnmarshalPtr() and AtlFreeMarshalStream() is equivalent to a call to the helper API CoGetInterfaceAndReleaseStream(). Since both these APIs use normal marshaling, they are safe to use when marshaling interface pointers between client apartments when used with a local or remote object.

## *The Global Interface Table*

You have probably already noticed the problem with using `CoMarshalInterface()`: if you want to pass a proxy pointer between apartments, you must use `MSHLFLAGS_NORMAL`, which means that when the marshaling packet has been unmarshaled once, it cannot be unmarshaled again. `MSHLFLAGS_TABLESTRONG` cannot be used, because it is not applicable to marshaling proxy pointers. The solution is the **Global Interface Table** (GIT).

The GIT is a facility that's available for Windows NT when Service Pack 3 has been applied; it is also available in DCOM '95 1.1 and higher. The GIT holds a list of marshaled interface pointers that, on request, can be unmarshaled any number of times to any apartment in your process, regardless of whether the pointer is for an object or a proxy. The GIT solves many marshaling problems and it is considerably easier than marshaling interfaces into streams yourself. If you have an operating system that supports it, you are well advised to use it.

There is a single GIT for each process, and to get access to this system-supplied object you call `CoCreateInstance()` for `CLSID_StdGlobalInterfaceTable`:

```
CoCreateInstance(CLSID_StdGlobalInterfaceTable, NULL,
        CTSCLX_INPROC_SERVER, IID_IGlobalInterfaceTable, (void**)&pGIT);
```

Naturally, since the GIT is process-specific, it should be created in-process. The `IGlobalInterfaceTable` interface looks like this:

```
[
    local,
    object,
    uuid(00000146-0000-0000-C000-000000000046)
]
interface IGlobalInterfaceTable : IUnknown
{
    HRESULT RegisterInterfaceInGlobal([in] IUnknown* pUnk,
                            [in] REFIID riid, [out] DWORD* pdwCookie);
    HRESULT RevokeInterfaceFromGlobal([in] DWORD dwCookie);
    HRESULT GetInterfaceFromGlobal([in] DWORD dwCookie, [in] REFIID riid,
                            [out, iid_is(riid)] void** ppv);
};
```

Once the GIT has been created, you can place interfaces in it using `RegisterInterfaceInGlobal()`. When you do this, the GIT will try to marshal the interface. Be careful when you choose your parameters to this method, as the error handling is not too good. For example, since the interface will be marshaled, it must have registered a proxy-stub DLL. If you forget to do this, you will get an exception thrown in `OLE32.dll`, rather than the method failing with a helpful `HRESULT`. I have also found that passing invalid parameters results in an exception being thrown rather than a failure `HRESULT` being returned. You have been warned!

The pointer to `IGlobalInterfaceTable` is special, because you can pass it across apartment boundaries within a single process without marshaling. You cannot pass the pointer to another *process*, because the GIT in one process is not valid in another. Also, you will find that this interface is not registered in the registry, because no marshaling code exists for it.

When you register an interface with the GIT, the method will return a DWORD cookie; this is used to identify the interface in later calls to the GIT. You can pass the GIT pointer to another apartment, which can call GetInterfaceFromGlobal() with the cookie to get an unmarshaled interface pointer. This apartment can then call on the proxy pointer to access the object. When the interface is no longer needed in the other apartments, you can call RevokeInterfaceFromGlobal() using the cookie to identify the interface. This method can be called in any apartment, but after doing so, you will not be able to unmarshal the interface.

## Example of the GIT

As an example of using the GIT, lets take the previous example (ThreadServerClient) and change it to use the GIT rather than CoMarshalInterface(). You will find this example in the project called GITClient that comes with the code for this chapter.

First, I define a class called GIT that can be used to hold the data for the GIT:

```
class GIT
{
public:
    GIT() : dwCookie(0) {}
    IGlobalInterfaceTablePtr pGit;
    DWORD dwCookie;
};
```

Here I hold a data member called pGIT, which is a smart pointer to the IGlobalInterfaceTable interface, and a DWORD that will have the cookie for a marshaled interface. When objects of this class are destroyed, the destructor of the smart pointer will release the interface. One thing you must remember with such code is that if you create an instance of this class within main() as a local variable, it will be destroyed when main() finishes – that is, after CoUninitialize() is called – and so COM will not be able to release the object. In this test, I create an instance of this class on the heap so that I can decide when the destructor is called by calling delete. The start of _tmain() looks like this:

```
int _tmain(int argc, char* argv[])
{
    DWORD dwStart = GetTickCount();
    DWORD x;
    CoInitialize(NULL);
    HANDLE hThreads[NO_THREADS];
    ZeroMemory(hThreads, sizeof(hThreads));
    g_hEvent = CreateEvent(NULL, TRUE, FALSE, "");
    GIT* MyGIT = new GIT;
```

The try block looks like this:

```
    try
    {
        HRESULT hr;
        MyGIT->pGit.CreateInstance(CLSID_StdGlobalInterfaceTable);

        IThreadInfoPtr pObj(__uuidof(ThreadInfo));
        hr = MyGIT->pGit->RegisterInterfaceInGlobal(
                            pObj, __uuidof(pObj), &MyGIT->dwCookie);
```

```
        if(FAILED(hr))
           _com_issue_error(hr);

        _tprintf(_T("Creating threads\n"));
        DWORD dwThreadID;
        for(x = 0 ; x < NO_THREADS ; x++)
        {
            hThreads[x] = CreateThread(
                            NULL, 0, (LPTHREAD_START_ROUTINE)AccessServer,
                            (LPVOID)MyGIT, 0, &dwThreadID);
        }
        SetEvent(g_hEvent);
    }
    catch(_com_error e)
    {
        _tprintf(_T("Error: %x\n\t%s\n"), e.Error(), e.ErrorMessage());
    }
```

Notice that I use the smart pointer `CreateInstance()` method to create the GIT. After I have
created the `ThreadInfo` object, I register it with the GIT, which will call `AddRef()` on the interface
pointer so that the object will not be released when `pObj` goes out of scope. Next, the threads are
created and passed a pointer to the GIT object created earlier. I do this because I want to illustrate to
you that an `IGlobalInterfaceTable` pointer can be passed between threads without marshaling.

The cleanup code looks like this:

```
    // Wait for threads to die
    WaitForMultipleObjects(NO_THREADS, hThreads, TRUE, INFINITE);
    _tprintf(_T("Releasing thread handles\n"));
    for (x = 0 ; x < NO_THREADS ; x++)
    {
        // Release handles
        if(hThreads[x])
            CloseHandle(hThreads[x]);
    }
    if (MyGIT->dwCookie != 0)
        MyGIT->pGit->RevokeInterfaceFromGlobal(MyGIT->dwCookie);
    delete MyGIT;
    CoUninitialize();
    _tprintf(_T("That took %2.3f seconds\n"),
                        (float)(GetTickCount() - dwStart) / 1000);
    return 0;
}
```

As before, the code waits for all threads to die, and then it releases the thread handles. The next line
revokes the interface from the GIT, so that the object will be released. Finally, I delete the GIT object
so that the pointer to the GIT is released.

The thread function looks like this:

```
DWORD WINAPI AccessServer(LPVOID lpParameter)
{
    GIT* MyGIT = (GIT*)lpParameter;
```

```
    HRESULT hr = S_OK;
    CoInitialize(NULL);
    try
    {
        IThreadInfoPtr pObj;
        hr = MyGIT->pGit->GetInterfaceFromGlobal(MyGIT->dwCookie,
                          __uuidof(pObj), reinterpret_cast<void**>(&pObj));
        if(FAILED(hr))
            _com_issue_error(hr);
        WaitForSingleObject(g_hEvent, INFINITE);
        _bstr_t bstrInfo;
        bstrInfo = pObj->GetInfo();
        _tprintf(_T("%S\n"), (LPWSTR)bstrInfo);
    }
    catch(_com_error e)
    {
        _tprintf(_T("Error from worker thread: %x\n\t%s\n"),
                                        e.Error(), e.ErrorMessage());
        hr = e.Error();
    }
    CoUninitialize();

    return hr;
}
```

This obtains the marshaled pointer from the GIT by calling `GetInterfaceFromGlobal()`, and then the object is accessed. Notice that you do not have to marshal the interface explicitly, or worry about creating and releasing stream objects – the GIT does all that for you. You should be able to compile and run this project as it stands.

## The Free Threaded Marshaler

Imagine the situation where you have an EXE server that has an MTA and one or more STAs. In this server's MTA, there is an object, and all client access to the object will be through a proxy, as you would expect. However, imagine further that there is an STA in the server process that also wants access to the object. This STA will access the object through a proxy, because the call will be between apartments. The MTA object will have synchronization applied to protect itself from access by other threads in the MTA, but since the STA has a separate thread, this implies that the proxy is unnecessary. If we can be sure that cross-apartment calls are safely synchronized by some other means, the proxy no longer has a purpose.

Custom marshaling could be used to overcome this problem, because instead of going through the expensive process of marshaling the interface, a custom `IMarshal` interface could be written to pass the raw interface pointer to the MTA object. Although this is possible, it is not a complete solution because the custom marshaling code will also be used when a client tries to access the MTA object across processes. A more complete solution is to use custom marshaling that has the intelligence to determine whether the call is in-process or cross-process. Such code is an effort to write but possible to generalize. Fortunately, this work has already been done for you in the form of the **Free Threaded Marshaler** (FTM).

The FTM is an object that provides a custom implementation of IMarshal designed to be aggregated as part of your object. When COM requests that an interface on the object be marshaled cross-apartment, it will check to see if the object has an IMarshal interface. Through the aggregation, COM will obtain IMarshal from the FTM. This interface is implemented to determine whether the call is in-process or cross-process, and will marshal the interface accordingly.

Building on the work COM has already done, ATL helps you here as well. One of the options on the Attributes tab is Free Threaded Marshaler, and if you select this, the Object Wizard will aggregate the FTM into your ATL class. Note that you will rarely want to use this option, and you must think very carefully before you select it. There is no check that the object is implemented in an EXE server, or that the object is designed to run in an MTA; if you try to use the FTM when it is not needed, you will get unpredictable results.

# Custom Marshaling

When an interface is marshaled, COM queries the object for the IMarshal interface. If no interface is returned, COM knows that it should use standard marshaling, which will mean using either a proxy object from an interface-specific proxy-stub DLL, or the Universal Marshaler.

If the object returns a valid IMarshal pointer, it says that it wants to take more control of the marshaling process. Although marshaling is usually carried out on a per-interface level (proxy and stub objects are specific to a particular interface), when an object returns a valid IMarshal pointer, it means that it will handle *all* interface marshaling. Smart proxies ease this responsibility, because they can create a standard marshaler and use it for a particular interface, but there will inevitably be a performance cost while the smart proxy decides whether it will handle an interface or not.

If your object is told to marshal an interface, it is given details of the context of the marshaling (marshaling is done in response to a call by CoMarshalInterface(), and its flags determine the context of the marshaling). The object will also be asked to provide information about how the interface will be marshaled. Remember that the client will have to have an in-process proxy to call, and COM will have to create it, so IMarshal on the object is asked for the CLSID of the proxy object. Even if this is known, the client must make a connection to the object. Normally COM will do this and choose an appropriate transport. However, when you decide to handle marshaling yourself, you get to choose the transport but you have to write all the necessary code to initialize it, transmit data using it, and then close down this transport. I didn't say marshaling was easy!

On the server side, COM will want to send a packet of data to the proxy in the client to tell it how to make the connection to the object. COM knows about the CLSID of the proxy, so that can go into the marshaling packet, but it also needs data to send to the proxy so that it can make the connection: such data will be, perhaps, the endpoint of an IPC mechanism. The marshaling packet is accessed via a stream, so first COM will ask how big the information sent to the proxy will be, and then it will pass a stream to the object and ask it to fill the stream with the marshaling information.

This packet is then passed to the client machine where COM creates the proxy and passes it the marshaling packet. How does the proxy get the packet? Well, the proxy also implements IMarshal, although it only provides the methods important for unmarshaling interfaces. COM thus uses these methods to pass the marshaled packet to the proxy, which unmarshals it and obtains the necessary information to make the connection to the object.

Now that the object and client are connected, COM gracefully disappears – all method calls on the object will be made on the proxy, which will use the IPC mechanism to transmit the request to the object.

If you choose, you can implement a stub object that the proxy talks to, but bear in mind that you will have to write it yourself. Most likely, you will have some listening mechanism that will pass the request to the appropriate method via a `switch` statement.

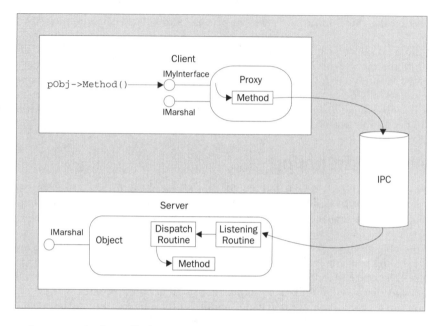

This diagram illustrates how a method is called using custom marshaling; the inter-process communication mechanism could be TCP/IP, UDP/IP, named pipes, or indeed any mechanism that allows two processes to talk to one another. The proxy has to implement `IMarshal` to make the connection to the object, but it also needs to implement the interface that it is a proxy for, so that method requests can be packaged and sent to the actual object via the IPC mechanism.

The object needs to implement `IMarshal` to take part in custom marshaling, but note that it need not implement the interface that will be marshaled. This is because the object does not take part in COM marshaling of methods, and so will have its own listening and method dispatch routines. If you look at the figure again, it becomes apparent that if you're the developer writing the proxy, it means that you have an opportunity to implement some of an object's methods in the proxy rather than in the object. This can offer a distinct advantage if the object lives on another machine.

You may decide that some of the methods use immutable data – that is, data that cannot change – and that when this data has been accessed once from the object, subsequent accesses should use the same data. In this situation, it makes sense to cache the immutable data in the proxy; then, when another request is made, the proxy can return the data rather than making a round trip to the object.

In fact, this is a well-known technique, and there are two main strategies for implementing it. In the first, you can have the proxy make the choice as to whether the round trip should be made or whether the cached value should be used. This is a smart proxy, and has the advantage that you get the best of both worlds. In the second strategy, you can tell the proxy the value of the immutable data when it is first created, and then implement the entire object with the proxy. The best way to do this is to tell the proxy the state of the object in the interface marshaling packet. Because the entire state is marshaled to the client, this technique is known as **marshal by value**.

The key to custom marshaling is the IMarshal interface:

```
[
    local,
    object,
    uuid(00000003-0000-0000-C000-000000000046)
]
interface IMarshal : IUnknown
{
    HRESULT GetUnmarshalClass([in] REFIID riid,
        [in, unique] void* pv, [in] DWORD dwDestContext,
        [in, unique] void* pvDestContext, [in] DWORD mshlflags,
        [out] CLSID* pCid);
    HRESULT GetMarshalSizeMax([in] REFIID riid,
        [in, unique] void* pv, [in] DWORD dwDestContext,
        [in, unique] void* pvDestContext, [in] DWORD mshlflags,
        [out] DWORD* pSize);
    HRESULT MarshalInterface([in, unique] IStream* pStm,
        [in] REFIID riid, [in, unique] void* pv,
        [in] DWORD dwDestContext, [in, unique] void* pvDestContext,
        [in] DWORD mshlflags);
    HRESULT UnmarshalInterface([in, unique] IStream* pStm,
        [in] REFIID riid, [out] void** ppv);
    HRESULT ReleaseMarshalData([in, unique] IStream* pStm);
    HRESULT DisconnectObject([in] DWORD dwReserved);
}
```

Notice the [local] attribute at the beginning of the interface definition section. The IMarshal interface is never marshaled.

As you have seen, both the object and proxy implement IMarshal, but they only implement those methods applicable to the context. Objects implement GetUnmarshalClass(), GetMarshalSizeMax(), MarshalInterface() and DisconnectObject(), while proxies implement UnmarshalInterface() and ReleaseMarshalData().

Most of these methods accept a 'destination' context and a 'marshal' flag, and these have the same meaning as the flags passed to CoMarshalInterface() and CoUnmarshalInterface(). Indeed, the methods of IMarshal are called in response to those API calls.

When CoMarshalInterface() is called, the system calls GetUnmarshalClass() to get the CLSID of the proxy object, it then calls GetMarshalSizeMax() to determine how much data the object needs to write to set up the connection to the proxy and finally, it then calls MarshalInterface() to get the object to supply this information. It then constructs a packet with the proxy CLSID and the marshaling information, which it sends to the client apartment. There, COM creates the proxy object and calls UnmarshalInterface() passing the marshaling information from the object. The proxy can then make the custom marshaling connection with the object and now COM no longer has anything to do with this relationship.

Custom marshaling is more work than you might at first imagine. As the diagram above indicates, the object must implement a listening routine of some kind. So for example, if you used sockets as the IPC, then you could create a new thread to handle each request (or even use a thread pool through an IO completion port). The socket accepting the request has a direct connection to the proxy, so that the proxy thread is blocked until the object has served the request, and so there is no synchronization issue.

If your proxy and object will run on a single machine, then you can use window messages as an IPC mechanism. In this case, requests and replies are sent as messages, but if two proxies have a connection to a single object, then the object must ensure that it can distinguish between them when sending back results. One way to do this is to pass the thread ID of the proxy in the message, so that the results will be sent back to the correct one.

Other IPC mechanisms could require even more synchronization code than the previous example. For example, if you used shared memory via a memory mapped file, then you would have to use some messaging to indicate that a request is in the shared memory, and later that the object has written a result. This could be done with event kernel objects.

Furthermore, you must also synchronize access to the memory, so that no two threads have access at any one time. In particular, you must solve the problem of having multiple proxies with access to the same object. Although a mutex kernel object will help here, a simple scheme that uses a shared memory buffer for the requests and results will not solve the kind of problem that's caused by one proxy making a request and releasing the mutex, and then another proxy coming along and making a request that overwrites the previous one before the object can accept the first request and gain the mutex. To overcome this, you could implement a FIFO queue for requests and have a tagged list for the results. The requests could pass a unique ID with the request, and the object could tag each result in the results list so that the proxy could access the correct result in the list and then remove it.

Even for these relatively simple examples, things are already getting quite complicated. Before you consider implementing custom marshaling to replace the existing COM RPC layer, you should think very carefully about it, and especially consider whether you will cover all uses of the custom proxy.

There are issues on the client-side too. Remember that the IUnknown pointer of an object defines its identity. If you have two IUnknown pointers and they have the same value then they are pointers to the same object. Standard marshaling ensures this, but when you implement custom marshaling, *you* must ensure that your proxies exhibit this behavior. Thus if a client makes more than one call in an apartment to QueryInterface() to get a proxy to IUnknown then IMarshal::UnMarshalInterface() should return the same pointer.

## *Marshal by Value*

Objects that contain immutable data and get accessed across apartments are a performance problem. The issue here is that once the client has accessed a piece of immutable data, it should not use the object to get the data again, because the cross-apartment call will take more time than accessing a local variable. Unfortunately, you can't always assume that the user of an object will realize this, and so they will happily make more calls on the object when the data is required subsequently.

To remedy this, you can create a **marshal by value** (MBV) object. The interesting thing about doing this is that the MBV object and the proxy are implemented *by the same code*. It works like this: when the client makes a request for an object, the server creates it and COM will ask for IMarshal. Then, COM will call GetUnmarshalClass(), and the object should pass its own CLSID as the CLSID of the proxy. Next, COM calls MarshalInterface(), and the object can copy its internal state into the marshaling packet. At this point, the object is no longer required, and it is free to delete itself.

The information in the marshaling packet is passed back to the client apartment, which then creates a new instance of the object. This time, COM will call UnMarshalInterface() passing the marshaling packet as an argument, and the proxy object will now initialize itself with this data, to become a clone of the original object. Proxy objects are in-process, so the methods will be accessed directly.

Imagine the situation of a data source object that returns data from some query. This data could be wrapped up in an in-process data object created inside the data source object. If the data source object is local or remote, then when the data object is returned back to the client, the object's interface will be marshaled and the client will get a proxy. If marshal by value is used, the entire state of the data object will be returned to the client and used to create a custom proxy. The client will now have direct access to the results rather than having to make a cross-apartment call.

*There is an example of using marshal by value with ATL later on in this chapter.*

## Mixed Custom and Standard Marshaling

IMarshal is just one of the interfaces on an object – the object will always have at least one more, and it may have many others. Whenever one of these interfaces is marshaled, methods of IMarshal are used – when GetUnmarshalClass() is called, you will have to return the correct CLSID; likewise, when the GetMarshalSizeMax() and MarshalInterface() methods are called, these should check what interface is being marshaled and return appropriate values.

What happens if the object only wants to provide custom marshaling of a specific interface? Well, since all of the methods of IMarshal are passed the IID of the interface being marshaled, they can make decisions about the interface being marshaled. Objects can call CoGetStandardMarshal() to obtain a COM object that implements IMarshal for a specified interface. Thus, your implementation can check to see if the interface being marshaled is one that you're handling, and if not, it can create the standard marshaling object and delegate the call to its methods:

```
HRESULT CMyObject::MarshalInterface(IStream* pStm, REFIID riid,
    void* pv, DWORD dwDestContext, void* pvDestContext, DWORD mshlflags)
{
    if(riid == IID_IMyInterface)
    {
        // Custom marshal the interface
    }
    else
    {
        // Standard marshal the rest
        CComPtr<IMarshal> pStd;
        CoGetStandardMarshal(
                        riid, pv, dwDestContext, NULL, mshlflags, &pStd);
        return pStd->MarshalInterface(
                    pStm, riid, pv, dwDestContext, pvDestContext, mshlflags);
    }
}
```

# Marshal by Value in ATL

To implement marshaling by value, your object needs to implement whatever interface you decide the client will use to access the object's state, and IMarshal. The latter tells COM that the object will use custom marshaling, and therefore, except for the initial creation and initialization of the proxy object, it will not use COM's IPC. As explained above, an MBV object uses the marshaling packet that was created by a call to IMarshal::MarshalInterface() to pass its state to the proxy. This packet is formed by writing data into a stream object that was created by the marshaling layer.

Since you're writing data to and then reading it from a stream, it's only sensible to implement `IPersistStream` on your object and use that for the purpose. ATL helps here, because the `IPersistStreamInitImpl<>` class serializes the data mentioned in the property map to a stream. `IPersistStreamInitImpl<>` can be added to any class. We'll look at how to do that in the following discussion.

> *In ATL 2.1, any object using* `IPersistStreamInitImpl<>` *had to derive from* `CComControl<>` *which made no sense if the object was not a control. This is no longer the case.*

This section will present to you a template called `IMarshalByValueImpl<>` that you can use to implement `IMarshal` on your ATL class so that objects can be marshaled by value.

> **The `IMarshalByValueImpl<>` template was originally posted on the DCOM mailing list by Jon Borden, and my thanks go to him.**

The `IMarshalByValueImpl<>` class is shown here:

```cpp
#pragma once

template <class T>
class ATL_NO_VTABLE IMarshalByValueImpl : public IMarshal
{
public:
  // IMarshal
  STDMETHODIMP GetUnmarshalClass(REFIID riid, void* pv,
    DWORD dwDestContext, void* pvDestContext, DWORD mshlflags,
    CLSID* pCid)
  {
    T* pT = static_cast<T*>(this);
    *pCid = pT->GetObjectCLSID();
    return S_OK;
  }

  STDMETHODIMP GetMarshalSizeMax(REFIID riid, void* pv,
    DWORD dwDestContext, void* pvDestContext, DWORD mshlflags,
    DWORD* pSize)
  {
    T* pT = static_cast<T*>(this);
    HRESULT hr = E_FAIL;
    ULARGE_INTEGER uli;
    // Access IPersistStreamInit::GetSizeMax()
    hr = pT->GetSizeMax(&uli);
    if(SUCCEEDED(hr))
        *pSize = uli.LowPart;
    return hr;
  }

  STDMETHODIMP MarshalInterface(IStream* pStm, REFIID riid,
    void* pv, DWORD dwDestContext, void* pvDestCtx,
    DWORD mshlflags)
  {
    T* pT = static_cast<T*>(this);
    HRESULT hr = E_FAIL;
```

```
        // Use IPersistStreamInit::Save()
        hr = pT->Save(pStm, FALSE);
        return hr;
    }

    STDMETHODIMP UnmarshalInterface(IStream* pStm, REFIID riid, void** ppv)
    {
        T* pT = static_cast<T*>(this);
        // Use IPersistStreamInit::Load()
        HRESULT hr = pT->Load(pStm);
        if(FAILED(hr))
            return hr;
        return pT->QueryInterface(riid, ppv);
    }

    STDMETHODIMP ReleaseMarshalData(IStream* pStm)
    {
        return S_OK;
    }

    STDMETHODIMP DisconnectObject(DWORD dwReserved)
    {
        return S_OK;
    }
};
```

You can see that most of these methods just delegate to appropriate methods of
IPersistStreamInit that were inherited by the ATL class (passed as the parameter T) through
IPersistStreamInitImpl<>. Notice that MarshalInterface() and
UnmarshalInterface() *don't* test the interface type, and so it is assumed that the object will only
have *one* interface that *will* be marshaled; this is generally the case with MBV objects.

To use this template, you will need to create an object with a dual interface and derive from
IMarshalByValueImpl<> and IPersistStreamInitImpl<>, passing your class as the template
parameter to both. Then, there are two changes you need to make for the persistence code to work.

First, you need a BOOL (or bool) public data member called m_bRequiresSave. This is used by
IPersistStreamInitImpl<>::IsDirty() and it's reset by Load().
IPersistStreamInitImpl<> doesn't declare this member, so you need to do it. Also, the default
implementation of GetSizeMax() does nothing, so if you want to use this in
IMarshal::GetMarshalMaxSize(), you must provide an implementation, as you'll see in a
moment.

The persistence code takes data mentioned in the property map and writes it to the stream, or else it
reads data from the stream and writes it to the properties in the property map. There are three ways
that you can specify such properties. First, you can use the PROP_DATA_ENTRY() macro, which will
specify one of your C++ class data members. Second, you can use PROP_ENTRY(), which specifies
COM properties in the map (and will place an item's DISPID into the map). Finally, you can use
PROP_ENTRY_EX(), which works like PROP_ENTRY(), but also allows you to specify the IID of a
dual interface supported by your object; this is useful if you have several interfaces on the object.

If you haven't dealt with property maps before, just take this as read for now – you'll see them in detail in Chapter 10.

When you use PROP_DATA_ENTRY() to add an item to the property map, the macro will determine the actual size of the item and save that information in the property map, The problem with PROP_DATA_ENTRY() is that it uses sizeof() to determine the number of bytes to write, and although this is fine for simple types like DWORD or float, there is a problem for types like string pointers, which will only get a size at runtime. You'll find out how to get around this problem when we construct an example later on.

Dispatch properties are a different case: their sizes are not added to the map. Instead, when you use PROP_ENTRY() their DISPID is added, so that the code can get the type of the property at runtime, and from this determine the size of the data. While this works with most property types, it doesn't necessarily work with objects added to the property map as an IDispatch pointer. To ensure that such an embedded object is serialized, it too should implement IPersistStreamInit.

The big problem with putting properties in the map is that it gives read/write access to them. IMarshalByValueImpl<> will call IPersistStreamInitImpl<>::Save() to write the marshaling packet, and will therefore read items from the property map. However, when unmarshaling the interface, it will call Load(), which will write property values. If this class can write properties, then so too can the client of the interface, and that shouldn't be allowed to happen to an immutable object.

To prevent this, you could add data members to the property map, and use read-only properties to access them. This will mean that IMarshalByValueImpl<> will create the marshaling packet from data members, but the client of the marshaled interface will only be given access to read-only properties. The disadvantage of this is that it restricts the data types that you can use – in particular, you need to handle strings carefully. The approach that I will take here is to declare them as arrays in the class so that their sizes are known at compile time.

This example obtains information about a directory on your drive. You call the Directory object and tell it the directory that you are interested in. It will then return to you an enumerator object that you can call to get hold of File objects, each of which has data about the files in the directory. The data in these objects is assumed to be immutable, and so these objects are marshaled by value.

Start by creating an ATL COM DLL object server called FileData. Add a simple object with a **Short Name** of File. Edit the header file to derive from the two base classes mentioned previously. Don't forget the comma after IDispatchImpl<>!

```
#include "IMarshalByValueImpl.h"


/////////////////////////////////////////////////////////////////
// CFile
class ATL_NO_VTABLE CFile :
    public CComObjectRootEx<CComSingleThreadModel>,
    public CComCoClass<CFile, &CLSID_File>,
    public IDispatchImpl<IFile, &IID_IFile, &LIBID_FILEDATALib>,
    public IMarshalByValueImpl<CFile>,
    public IPersistStreamInitImpl<CFile>
```

Next, your ATL class needs to add members for `IPersistStreamInitImpl<>`, so add the following:

```
// Property map
BEGIN_PROP_MAP(CFile)
END_PROP_MAP()

// IPersistStreamInit
public:
    STDMETHOD(GetSizeMax)(ULARGE_INTEGER FAR* puli);
    BOOL m_bRequiresSave;

// IFile
public:
};
```

`GetSizeMax()` returns the total size of the space required in the marshaling packet for property map data members, and for properties:

```
STDMETHODIMP CFile::GetSizeMax(ULARGE_INTEGER FAR* puli)
{
    ATL_PROPMAP_ENTRY* pMap = GetPropertyMap();
    puli->LowPart = sizeof(DWORD);
    for(int i = 0 ; pMap[i].pclsidPropPage != NULL ; i++)
    {
        if(pMap[i].dwSizeData)
            puli->LowPart += pMap[i].dwSizeData;
        else
        {
            puli->LowPart += sizeof(VARTYPE);
            CComVariant var;
            CComPtr<IDispatch> pDispatch;
            _InternalQueryInterface(IID_IDispatch, (void**)&pDispatch);
            CComDispatchDriver::GetProperty(pDispatch, pMap[i].dispid, &var);

            switch(var.vt)
            {
            case VT_UI1:
            case VT_I1:
                puli->LowPart += sizeof(BYTE);
                break;

            case VT_I2:
            case VT_UI2:
            case VT_BOOL:
                puli->LowPart += sizeof(short);
                break;

            case VT_I4:
            case VT_UI4:
            case VT_R4:
            case VT_INT:
            case VT_UINT:
            case VT_ERROR:
                puli->LowPart += sizeof(long);
                break;
```

```
            case VT_R8:
            case VT_CY:
            case VT_DATE:
                puli->LowPart += sizeof(double);
                break;

            case VT_BSTR:
                puli->LowPart += sizeof(DWORD);
                puli->LowPart +=
                      (CComBSTR(var.bstrVal).Length() + 1) * sizeof(OLECHAR);
                break;

            default:
                break;
            }
        }
    }
    return S_OK;
}
```

Some of this code is used to take into account the extra data that `IPersistStreamInitImpl<>`
will add to the stream. Firstly, it will add the ATL version number as a `DWORD`, and this is the reason
for the initial increase in the size of the packet. Next, the code obtains the property map and iterates
through the items in it. The last entry in the map is a dummy entry and has a `NULL` value for
`pclsidPropPage` (other entries may have `&CLSID_NULL`, which is not `NULL`). The code then
checks to see if the member is a property or a class data member. If it's the latter, the size is in the
map and so no more work needs to be done.

If the entry is a property, the code gets access to it by calling `_InternalQueryInterface()` for
the `IDispatch` interface, and then passing this and the property DISPID to the static
`GetProperty()` function. I need the `IDispatch` interface and to get this I need to call
`QueryInterface()` but since this calls `_InternalQueryInterface()` and I'm making the call
from within the object, I can bypass `QueryInterface()` and call
`_InternalQueryInterface()` directly.

The code can then test the type of the property and increment the size accordingly. Notice that the
size is also incremented by `sizeof(VARTYPE)`; this is because the serialization code for
`IPersistStreamInitImpl<>::Save()` adds the type of the property to the stream.

Finally, you need to add the following to the COM map:

```
BEGIN_COM_MAP(CFile)
    COM_INTERFACE_ENTRY(IFile)
    COM_INTERFACE_ENTRY(IDispatch)
    COM_INTERFACE_ENTRY(IMarshal)
    COM_INTERFACE_ENTRY(IPersistStreamInit)
END_COM_MAP()
```

Now you are ready to implement the object. This will be used to pass data about a file on the disk,
which will come from a `WIN32_FIND_DATA` item returned from the Win32 `FindFirstFile()` and
`FindNextFile()` functions. Take a look at this structure:

```
typedef struct _WIN32_FIND_DATA
{
    DWORD dwFileAttributes;
    FILETIME ftCreationTime;
    FILETIME ftLastAccessTime;
    FILETIME ftLastWriteTime;
    DWORD nFileSizeHigh;
    DWORD nFileSizeLow;
    DWORD dwReserved0;
    DWORD dwReserved1;
    TCHAR cFileName[MAX_PATH];
    TCHAR cAlternateFileName[14];
} WIN32_FIND_DATA;
```

As I mentioned before, you can't use string pointers for items added with PROP_DATA_ENTRY(), but you *can* add a string array. Add the following private data members:

```
private:
    DWORD m_dwFileAttributes;
    FILETIME m_ftCreationTime;
    FILETIME m_ftLastAccessTime;
    FILETIME m_ftLastWriteTime;
    DWORD m_dwFileSize;
    TCHAR m_strFileName[MAX_PATH];
    TCHAR m_strAlternateFileName[14];
```

As you can see, WIN32_FILE_DATA actually has two DWORDs for the size of the file. However, since a DWORD can represent a size of up to 4Gb, it's pretty safe to assume at this point in time that nFileSizeHigh will be zero, and so in the class I only use one DWORD.

These data members are then added to the property map; the last parameter isn't used, so I have given it a value of VT_NULL:

```
BEGIN_PROP_MAP(CFile)
    PROP_DATA_ENTRY("FileAttributes", m_dwFileAttributes, VT_NULL)
    PROP_DATA_ENTRY("CreationTime", m_ftCreationTime, VT_NULL)
    PROP_DATA_ENTRY("LastAccessTime", m_ftLastAccessTime, VT_NULL)
    PROP_DATA_ENTRY("LastWriteTime", m_ftLastWriteTime, VT_NULL)
    PROP_DATA_ENTRY("FileSize", m_dwFileSize, VT_NULL)
    PROP_DATA_ENTRY("FileName", m_strFileName, VT_NULL)
    PROP_DATA_ENTRY("AlternateFileName", m_strAlternateFileName, VT_NULL)
END_PROP_MAP()
```

The client will access the data members through read-only properties, but since properties use VARIANT types, you must convert them. This operation can be done in the property get_ method. Add the following read-only properties to the object using ClassView, unchecking the Put function box as you do so:

| Name | DISPID | Type |
|------|--------|------|
| FileAttributes | 1 | long |
| CreationTime | 2 | DATE |
| LastAccessTime | 3 | DATE |
| LastWriteTime | 4 | DATE |
| FileSize | 5 | long |
| FileName | 6 | BSTR |
| AlternateFileName | 7 | BSTR |

The get_ functions are implemented like this:

```
STDMETHODIMP CFile::get_FileAttributes(long *pVal)
{
    *pVal = m_dwFileAttributes;
    return S_OK;
}

STDMETHODIMP CFile::get_CreationTime(DATE *pVal)
{
    SYSTEMTIME st;
    FileTimeToSystemTime(&m_ftCreationTime, &st);
    SystemTimeToVariantTime(&st, pVal);
    return S_OK;
}

STDMETHODIMP CFile::get_LastAccessTime(DATE *pVal)
{
    SYSTEMTIME st;
    FileTimeToSystemTime(&m_ftLastAccessTime, &st);
    SystemTimeToVariantTime(&st, pVal);
    return S_OK;
}

STDMETHODIMP CFile::get_LastWriteTime(DATE *pVal)
{
    SYSTEMTIME st;
    FileTimeToSystemTime(&m_ftLastWriteTime, &st);
    SystemTimeToVariantTime(&st, pVal);
    return S_OK;
}

STDMETHODIMP CFile::get_FileSize(long *pVal)
{
    *pVal = m_dwFileSize;
    return S_OK;
}
```

```
STDMETHODIMP CFile::get_FileName(BSTR *pVal)
{
    return CComBSTR(m_strFileName).CopyTo(pVal);
}

STDMETHODIMP CFile::get_AlternateFileName(BSTR *pVal)
{
    return CComBSTR(m_strAlternateFileName).CopyTo(pVal);
}
```

There is one final issue: how do the data members in this object get initialized? This object is not really designed for ordinary users to create; rather, it will be created by another object, as I'll explain later. This latter object should create the `File` object in-process and have 'write' access to it; the easiest way to do this is to create a new interface with the sole responsibility of initializing the object. Run the `Guidgen` utility to get a new IID, and paste it into a new interface in the IDL file, after `IFile`:

```
[
    object,
    local,
    uuid(9686D1BF-D3D7-11D1-9B43-0060973044A8),
    pointer_default(unique)
]
interface IInitializeFile : IUnknown
{
};
```

To use this interface, you need to derive `CFile` from it, and add it to the COM map:

```
    public IPersistStreamInitImpl<CFile>,
    public IInitializeFile
{
public:
    CFile()
    {
    }

DECLARE_REGISTRY_RESOURCEID(IDR_FILE)

DECLARE_PROTECT_FINAL_CONSTRUCT()

BEGIN_COM_MAP(CFile)
    COM_INTERFACE_ENTRY(IFile)
    COM_INTERFACE_ENTRY(IInitializeFile)
    COM_INTERFACE_ENTRY(IDispatch)
```

This interface will have a single method called `Init()` that will initialize all the private data members. Use ClassView to add this method (you will need to compile the IDL first to see it in ClassView):

```
HRESULT Init([in] DWORD dwFileAttributes,
            [in] FILETIME ftCreationTime, [in] FILETIME ftLastAccessTime,
            [in] FILETIME ftLastWriteTime, [in] DWORD dwFileSize,
            [in, string] LPOLESTR strFileName,
            [in, string] LPOLESTR strAlternateFileName);
```

This is implemented like so:

```
USES_CONVERSION;
m_dwFileAttributes = dwFileAttributes;
m_ftCreationTime = ftCreationTime;
m_ftLastAccessTime = ftLastAccessTime;
m_ftLastWriteTime = ftLastWriteTime;
m_dwFileSize = dwFileSize;
lstrcpy(m_strFileName, OLE2CT(strFileName));
lstrcpy(m_strAlternateFileName, OLE2T(strAlternateFileName));
return S_OK;
```

Once you've added this code, you can compile the project.

I mentioned earlier that clients should not create instances of this object. If they do, it will be created in-process, and hence the marshal by value code won't be used. Instead, a new object should be returned as an [out] parameter from a local object that we'll create now.

Create an executable ATL COM project called DirectoryInfo, and add a simple object with a **Short Name** of Directory. The idea is that you will create a Directory object and pass a directory name to it via the GetDir() method. It will then return an enumerator containing the File objects for all the entries in that directory. The first thing to do is add the method:

```
HRESULT GetDir([in] BSTR bstrDir, [out, retval] IEnumUnknown** ppUnk);
```

Then, to the Directory.h header, add this line:

```
#include "..\FileData\FileData.h"
```

And add these to the .cpp file:

```
#include "..\FileData\FileData_i.c"
#pragma warning(disable : 4530)
#include <vector>
```

This is done so that you can use the interfaces defined in the previous project (and the pragma ensures that you do not get warnings about the <vector> code using exceptions). The GetDir() method will return an enumerator, so for this I will use the trusty CComEnum<> template and initialize it with a STL vector; hence the reason for the other two includes. Note that I have decided *not* to use CComEnumOnSTL<> because this class does not allow you to make a copy of the data in the STL container. If we used CComEnumOnSTL<>, the vector<> container would have to be an instance variable, which is not the behavior that I want here.

```
STDMETHODIMP CDirectory::GetDir(BSTR bstrDir, IEnumUnknown **ppUnk)
{
    USES_CONVERSION;
    *ppUnk = NULL;
    std::vector<IUnknown*> vec;
    WIN32_FIND_DATA wfd;
    HANDLE hFind;
    HRESULT hr;
    std::basic_string<WCHAR> strDir;
```

```
         strDir = bstrDir;
         strDir += L"\\*.*";
         hFind = FindFirstFile(W2CT(strDir.c_str()), &wfd);

         if(hFind == INVALID_HANDLE_VALUE)
            return HRESULT_FROM_WIN32(GetLastError());

         while(true)
         {
            CComPtr<IInitializeFile> pInitFile;
            hr = CoCreateInstance(CLSID_File, NULL, CLSCTX_INPROC_SERVER,
                                  IID_IInitializeFile, (void**)&pInitFile);

            if(FAILED(hr))
            {
               FindClose(hFind);
               return hr;
            }

            pInitFile->Init(wfd.dwFileAttributes, wfd.ftCreationTime,
                            wfd.ftLastAccessTime, wfd.ftLastWriteTime,
                            wfd.nFileSizeLow,       T2OLE(wfd.cFileName),
                            T2OLE(wfd.cAlternateFileName));

            IUnknown* pUnk = NULL;
            pInitFile.QueryInterface(&pUnk);
            vec.push_back(pUnk);

            if(!FindNextFile(hFind, &wfd))
            {
               DWORD err = GetLastError();
               if(err == ERROR_NO_MORE_FILES)
                  break;
               else
               {
                  hr = HRESULT_FROM_WIN32(err);
                  break;
               }
            }
         }

         FindClose(hFind);
         if(FAILED(hr))
            return hr;

         typedef CComObject<CComEnum<IEnumUnknown, &IID_IEnumUnknown,
                            IUnknown*, _CopyInterface<IUnknown> > > EnumVar;
         EnumVar* pEnumerator = new EnumVar;
         pEnumerator->Init(vec.begin(), vec.end(), NULL, AtlFlagCopy);
         hr = pEnumerator->QueryInterface(ppUnk);
         if(FAILED(hr))
            delete pEnumerator;

         std::vector<IUnknown*>::iterator it;
         for(it = vec.begin() ; it < vec.end() ; it++)
         {
            (*it)->Release();
         }
         return hr;
      }
```

Here, I'm using an STL `vector<>` as an array that can grow in size dynamically, using its property of keeping all items contiguous, and in order, in memory. I assume that the name passed is a directory, so the code constructs a search string and calls `FindFirstFile()` and then `FindNextFile()` in a loop. For each file that it finds, the code creates a `File` object: accessing the `IInitializeFile` interface, it initializes the object with the `WIN32_FILE_DATA` members, and then puts the `IUnknown` pointer into the `vector<>`. Although the `IUnknown` pointer is obtained using `QueryInterface()`, which means an implicit `AddRef()`, I do not call `Release()` in this part of the code – I want the interface pointer to live for a while!

When all the items have been read, I create an enumerator object, initialize it with the items in the `vector<>`, and since this container is a local variable, I specify that a copy should be made. In any case this is the behavior that I want because it means that a client can use a single `Directory` object to create several enumerations, and so I do not want the data to be held in an instance variable.

Then, I call `QueryInterface()` for the required interface and finally clean up by releasing the interfaces in the `vector<>`.

> When you compile this project you will get a warning from MIDL saying that the interface is not [oleautomation] compatible. The reason for this is the **IEnumUnknown** interface parameter, but it's harmless for this test because the client will be C++ and not VB.

It's about time we had a client. This is a Win32 Console Application called MBVClient, and it uses smart pointer classes. Once you've made the same changes to `stdafx.h` that you had to make for our last example, the code is pretty simple, so here it is in its entirety:

```
#include "stdafx.h"
#import "..\DirectoryInfo\DirectoryInfo.tlb" no_namespace,
                                              exclude("IEnumUnknown")
#import "..\FileData\FileData.tlb" no_namespace

int _tmain(int argc, TCHAR* argv[])
{
    CoInitialize(NULL);

    try
    {
        IDirectoryPtr pDir(_uuidof(Directory));
        IEnumUnknownPtr pEnum;
        if(argc == 2)
            pEnum = pDir->GetDir(_bstr_t(argv[1]));
        else
            pEnum = pDir->GetDir(_bstr_t(_T("C:\\temp")));

        IUnknown* Unk[5];
        ULONG ulFetched;
        while(true)
        {
            pEnum->Next(5, Unk, &ulFetched);
            if(ulFetched > 0)
            {
                for(ULONG i = 0 ; i < ulFetched ; i++)
                {
```

```
                    IFilePtr pFile;
                    HRESULT hr;
                    hr = Unk[i]->QueryInterface(&pFile);
                    if(SUCCEEDED(hr))
                    {
                        BSTR bstrName;
                        pFile->get_FileName(&bstrName);
                        _tprintf(_T("%S\n"), bstrName);
                        SysFreeString(bstrName);
                    }
                    Unk[i]->Release();
                }
            }
            else
                break;
        }
    }
    catch(_com_error e)
    {
        _tprintf(_T("Error: %08x\n\t%s\n"), e.Error(), e.ErrorMessage());
    }

    CoUninitialize();
    return 0;
}
```

The first thing to note is the exclude() on the #import directive; this is because IEnumUnknown is in an included header, so this prevents a warning from being generated. Other than that, the code is straightforward. When you run it, you should get output like this:

```
C:\wrox\PROATL\CODE\CHAPTER8\MBVClient\DEBUG>mbvclient c:\wrox\ProATL\Code\Chapt
er8\MBVClient

..
..
StdAfx.cpp
ReadMe.txt
MBVClient.dsp
MBVClient.dsw
MBVClient.ncb
Debug
StdAfx.h
MBVClient.opt
MBVClient.plg
MBVClient.cpp

C:\wrox\PROATL\CODE\CHAPTER8\MBVClient\DEBUG>
```

But how do you know that marshal by value is being used? The simplest way is to place a breakpoint in MarshalInterface() in the server and UnmarshalInterface() in the client. Remember that the proxy implements IMarshal and is loaded into the client; since we are using MBV this means that the File object will be used as the proxy.

So load DirectoryInfo into one instance of Visual Studio and change the project settings so that on the **Debug** tab, FileData.dll is mentioned in the **Additional DLLs**. Then, you can open IMarshalByValueImpl.h and place your breakpoint in MarshalInterface(). Finally, run the process, which will register its class factories with the system and wait for object requests.

Start another instance of Visual Studio and load `MBVClient`. Change the project settings to include `FileData.dll` as an **Additional DLL** and then set a breakpoint in `UnmarshalInterface()`. When you run the client, you should find that when `IEnumUnknown::Next()` returns data, the breakpoint will be hit in the server and the state of the first `File` object will be written to a stream. When you continue execution, the other 4 `File` objects that are returned in the call to `Next()` are written to marshaling streams. After the fifth object is written to the stream, the breakpoint will be hit in the client and you can then watch as these five `File` objects are initialized from their marshaling streams.

Before I leave this section, it is worth making one final point. Since the MBV object *is* the proxy, it means that it is called inproc in the client and so no standard marshaling proxy nor type library marshaling information is needed for the client. However, the `File` object does need its interfaces registered because the server needs to get access to the `File` object's `IInitializeFile` interface.

# Merging Proxy-Stub Code

The final part of this section concerns the AppWizard option that allows you to merge the proxy-stub code in with your DLL server. The first point to make about this is that it is never *necessary* to do it – if you don't, your objects will still work. The question then becomes, "*Why* would you want to do it?" As I explained earlier, when you create an in-process object and then pass it between apartments, the interface will be marshaled. If your object uses standard marshaling, then the proxy-stub DLL will be loaded in the server *and* the client to create the stub and proxy respectively.

Obviously, loading a new DLL will take time and memory, so if you can include the proxy-stub code in the same DLL as your in-process object, you will gain in both respects because the combined DLL will be smaller than the total size of the other two DLLs. However, if you are marshaling to another machine, you will have to register the proxy-stub DLL on that, and so you may want to build this separately. Of more concern is that if you marshal the interface between processes on a single machine, your whole object server DLL will be loaded into the client process, because it contains the proxy and stub objects for the interface. This has a potentially sizable cost in memory.

There is a way to prevent this however: you can merge proxy code into the *client*, and then use the COM API `CoRegisterPSClsid()` to dynamically register a class implemented in the client, as the class factory to create the interface proxy object. To use this you need to add to your client the proxy code that `MIDL` generates for you (the file with `_p.c`) and the DLL entry points (`dlldata.c`), note that you are just using this DLL code to obtain the proxy class factory and not to provide normal DLL initialization (your client is most likely an EXE, anyway). Since these files use the interface constants, you also need to add the `MIDL`-generated constants file too (the file with `_i.c`).

To merge the proxy in the client you need to add the following code before you attempt to marshal the interface (here `ICompName` is the interface that you want to marshal):

```
ICompNamePtr pObj;
IUnknownPtr pUnk;
DWORD dwNotUsed;
DllGetClassObject(__uuidof(pObj), __uuidof(pUnk),
    reinterpret_cast<void**>(&pUnk));
CoRegisterClassObject(__uuidof(pObj), pUnk, CLSCTX_INPROC_SERVER,
    REGCLS_MULTIPLEUSE, &dwNotUsed);
CoRegisterPSClsid(__uuidof(pObj), __uuidof(pObj));
```

Since the proxy-stub code has been merged into the client, it means that you can obtain the class factory of the required interface by calling `DllGetClassFactory()`. However, since the client is an EXE, you need to register these class factories so that when COM wants to create the proxy object it can get hold of its class factory. (Remember this happens because during marshaling COM asks the object for the CLSID of the proxy object, which it then uses to create the proxy in the client process.)

The interface that you are trying to marshal is *not* registered on the client machine so this would normally cause a fault when COM tries to marshal the interface. To temporarily register the interface this code calls `CoRegisterPSClsid()`. For a registered interface all that the `ProxyStubClsid32` key does is associate the interface with the CLSID of the proxy object used to marshal it, and this is exactly what `CoRegisterPSClsid()` does.

Notice that in the above code, I do not use any CLSIDs. For example, the first parameter of `DllGetClassObject()` usually has the CLSID of the object that you want the class factory for, but in this code I use the IID of the interface that I am interested in. The reason is that the CLSID of the `MIDL`-generated proxy object (and the stub object too) is the same as the IID of the interface that it marshals.

Although merging proxy code into a client reduces the administration on a client machine (and is good for downloaded components), it does become a problem if you have several client processes on a single machine that will use the same interface, because each will have the proxy code and hence there will be a duplication. In this situation it is better to register a separate proxy-stub as is the normal practice.

## Merging in the Server

Merging proxy-stub code into the server is a similar process, but you do not have to worry too much about the details because the AppWizard will do the work for you. In particular, since the server is a DLL then there is a possible clash between the DLL entry points that your server defines and the ones that `MIDL` creates for you (through the `dlldata.c` file). The AppWizard gets round this by `#define`ing the entry point names to prevent the clash.

There is one small thing to be aware of here. When you check Allow merging of proxy/stub code in the ATL COM AppWizard, it will add `dlldatax.c` and `dlldatax.h` to your project, which add stub methods for what would have been the entry points of the proxy-stub DLL. The RPC headers expect to find these, and project's DLL entry points will call them. `dlldatax.c` also includes the `_p.c` proxy file created by `MIDL`.

However, although AppWizard has added `dlldatax.c` to your project, it does not include it in builds. To do this, you need to right click on the file in FileView, and then select Settings.... In the General tab, you need to uncheck Exclude file from build. In addition, you should also move to the C/C++ tab, choose Precompiled Headers as the category, and then select Not using precompiled headers. Finally, you need to define the _MERGE_PROXYSTUB symbol for the project. Now, when you compile the project, the proxy-stub code will be part of your DLL.

## Stubless Proxies

One further point is worth mentioning. You will see the USE_STUBLESS_PROXY symbol defined in dlldatax.c, which means that MIDL will be called with the /Oicf optimization switch. This specifies that the interface will be marshaled with an operating system marshaling interpreter. MIDL generates marshaling data (called 'fast format data') in the _p.c file to tell the interpreter how to marshal the interface. This is not quite the same as the Universal Marshaler, which is a generic marshaler *object*; here, the marshaling interpreter is called by your *proxy object*. I would suspect that the Universal Marshaler will most likely be code that converts type information into the marshaling data required by the interpreter.

The marshaling interpreter is only available on more recent operating systems. In particular, the /Oicf switch cannot be used for code that is intended for NT 3.51 or raw Windows 95 (the /Oic switch should be used for these). There is a small bug in Visual Studio in that there are two places on the Project Settings dialog where you can specify whether stubless proxies will be used: the MIDL tab for the entire project, and the MIDL tab for the IDL file. If you want to use stubless proxies, check the box on the page for the IDL file. If you check the box for the entire project, you do not get the USE_STUBLESS_PROXY symbol defined in the MIDL-generated proxy file.

'Stubless proxies' are essentially an optimization (which is why they are enabled with a /O switch). Since you are using system provided code to marshal the interface, the proxy-stub files will be smaller and hence quicker to load. The Platform SDK uses the term 'codeless proxies', which better describes their action since the code is provided by the system and not your DLL.

## Example: Merging Proxy-Stub files into Client and Server

Let's create a very simple example with an in-process object called CompName. This will just return the name of the computer on which it is running and the process ID of the process that is running the object. This object will have a custom interface, without the [oleautomation] attribute. This will mean that a proxy-stub must be used for standard marshaling. I will use the ATL AppWizard to merge the proxy-stub code into the object's DLL so that only one DLL is loaded. In the tests, I will run the object on a machine remote to the client and since it is implemented in a DLL I will use the system surrogate. On the client-side, I will merge the proxy-stub code into the client so that no interface registration is required on the client machine.

The first thing to do is create a new DLL project called CompSvr and make sure that you check Allow merging of proxy/stub code. Then insert a simple object called CompName and use the Attributes tab to specify that it is a Custom interface. Use ClassView to add this method:

```
HRESULT GetName([out, string, retval] wchar_t** strName);
```

Implement the method like this:

```
STDMETHODIMP CCompName::GetName(wchar_t * * strName)
{
    USES_CONVERSION;
    TCHAR strCompName[MAX_COMPUTERNAME_LENGTH + 1];
    DWORD dwSize = MAX_COMPUTERNAME_LENGTH + 1;
    GetComputerName(strCompName, &dwSize);
    TCHAR str[MAX_COMPUTERNAME_LENGTH + 21];
```

```
    dwSize = wsprintf(str, _T("%s in process %08x"), strCompName,
        GetCurrentProcessId());
    *strName = (LPWSTR)CoTaskMemAlloc((dwSize + 1) * sizeof(WCHAR));
    wcscpy(*strName, T2W(str));
    return S_OK;
}
```

Notice that I get the current process ID, so that you can tell whether the object is in-process or not.

Now you need to add `dlldatax.c` to the build, so right click on the file in FileView, and then select Settings…. Make sure that you select All Configurations in the Settings for box and then in the General tab uncheck Exclude file from build. Next move to the C/C++ tab, choose Precompiled Headers as the category, and then select Not using precompiled headers. Finally, select the project (`CompSvr`) and then Preprocessor as the category and add `_MERGE_PROXYSTUB` symbol for the project.

To make sure that the type library for the object is *not* registered change `DllRegisterServer()` to pass `FALSE` as the argument to `RegisterServer()`.

```
STDAPI DllRegisterServer(void)
{
#ifdef _MERGE_PROXYSTUB
    HRESULT hRes = PrxDllRegisterServer();
    if (FAILED(hRes))
        return hRes;
#endif
    // registers object, typelib and all interfaces in typelib
    return _Module.RegisterServer(FALSE);
}
```

I don't want the type library registered to ensure that there is no possible chance of type library marshaling being used. This does mean that the type library need not be bound to the server, so from the View menu, select Resource Includes and remove the reference to the type library from the Compile time directives box. Next, right click on the IDL file (`CompSvr.IDL`) in FileView and select Settings, and then remove the type library name from the Output file name box. Finally, open the RGS file for the project and remove the line that mentions the TypeLib in the `CLSID` section. You should have now removed all references to the type library, so there is no way that type library marshaling can be used.

Now you can compile the project.

Next you need to write a client. Create a Win32 console application called `CompClient`. Make sure that `_WIN32_DCOM` symbol is defined because you will call `CoCreateInstanceEx()`.

The code for `_tmain()` is shown here.

```
#import "..\CompSvr\CompSvr.tlb" no_namespace

int _tmain(int argc, TCHAR* argv[])
{
    CoInitialize(NULL);
```

```
    try
    {
        ICompNamePtr pObj;
        HRESULT hr = S_OK;

        if (argc == 1)
        {
            hr = pObj.CreateInstance(__uuidof(CompName));
            if (FAILED(hr))
                _com_issue_error(hr);
        }

        LPWSTR strName;
        strName = pObj->GetName();
        _tprintf(_T("Computer %S\n"), strName);
        _tprintf(_T("Called from %08x\n"), GetCurrentProcessId());
        CoTaskMemFree(strName);
    }
    catch (const _com_error& e)
    {
        _tprintf(_T("Error (%08x): %s\n"), e.Error(), e.ErrorMessage());
    }

    CoUninitialize();
    return 0;
}
```

The first test is to run this code on the local machine. You should find that the client will run and you will get a result like this:

```
Computer ZEUS in process 000000da
Called from 000000da
```

In this case, the object will be created in-process, the two process IDs will be the same and the interface will not need to be marshaled.

Now add the following code:

```
if (argc == 1)
{
    hr = pObj.CreateInstance(__uuidof(CompName));
    if (FAILED(hr))
        _com_issue_error(hr);
}
else if (argc == 2)
{
    hr = pObj.CreateInstance(__uuidof(CompName), NULL,
                                            CLSCTX_LOCAL_SERVER);

    if (FAILED(hr))
    _com_issue_error(hr);
}
```

If you rebuild the project, and run the client using a command line argument, S (for 'Surrogate'), you will get an error complaining that the object is not registered as a local server:

```
Error (80040154): Class not registered
```

This makes sense since our server is an inproc server, so change the server to run in a surrogate to ensure that it can be loaded as a local server. The simplest way to do this is to use the OLE/COM Object Viewer. Make sure that you have Expert Mode checked on the View menu and then from All Objects in the tree select CompName Class (but don't click on the + next to it). Select the Implementation page and on the Inproc Server page check Use Surrogate Process. Do not put anything in the Path to Custom Surrogate so that the default system surrogate is used. Finally, click on the Registry tab so that OLEView will write these changes to the registry.

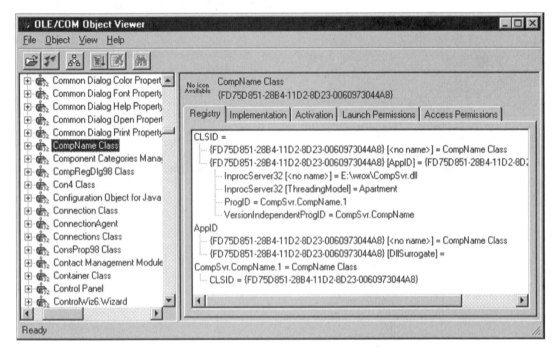

You can see that OLEView has created an AppID and a named value called DllSurrogate.

Now run the client again with a command line argument. This time the call will succeed; you will get something like this:

```
Computer ZEUS in process 0000007e
Called from 000000e3
```

Notice that the process IDs are *not* the same, this is because when CreateInstance() is called with CLSCTX_LOCAL_SERVER COM will load the default surrogate DllHost.exe and load the server in that. This is a different process and yet the call still succeeds, why? Take a look in the Interface branch in OLEView and you'll find the answer:

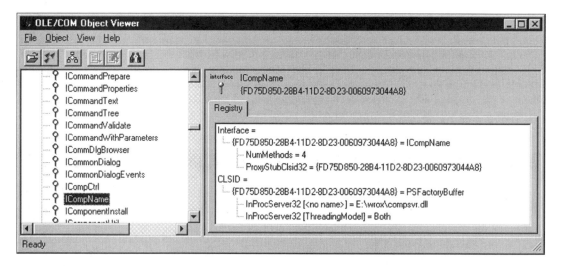

Here you can see that the UUID in the `ProxyStubClsid32` is different to the interface IID, the lower section tells you why: the object that marshals the interface is the `PSFactoryBuffer` in `compsvr.dll`, which is the result of merging the proxy-stub into the server.

Now add the following code to the client to register the proxy as explained earlier:

```
try
{
    ICompNamePtr pObj;
    HRESULT hr = S_OK;
    IUnknownPtr pUnk;
    DllGetClassObject(__uuidof(pObj), __uuidof(pUnk),
        reinterpret_cast<void**>(&pUnk));
    DWORD dwNotUsed;
    CoRegisterClassObject(__uuidof(pObj), pUnk, CLSCTX_INPROC_SERVER,
        REGCLS_MULTIPLEUSE, &dwNotUsed);
    CoRegisterPSClsid(__uuidof(pObj), __uuidof(pObj));
```

Add a new test on the command line arguments:

```
else if (argc == 3)
{
    COSERVERINFO csi = {0, NULL, NULL, 0};
    MULTI_QI qi = {&__uuidof(ICompName), NULL, S_OK};
    _bstr_t bstrName(argv[2]);
    csi.pwszName = bstrName;
    hr = CoCreateInstanceEx(__uuidof(CompName), NULL,
                            CLSCTX_REMOTE_SERVER, &csi, 1, &qi);
    if (FAILED(hr))
        _com_issue_error(hr);
    pObj = static_cast<ICompName*>(qi.pItf);
}
```

Thus if you pass two command line arguments (e.g. R Athena) the code will take the second parameter as the name of a remote machine to call.

To merge the proxy-stub into the client you need to add the files generated by MIDL to the project. So use the Project | Add to project | Files... menu item to add CompSvr_i.c, CompSvr_p.c, and dlldata.c to the project. Go into the project settings and select All Configurations and then make sure that none of these files use precompiled headers.

Since they do not use precompiled headers, they do not know that _WIN32_DCOM is used. So select CompSvr_p.c and add this symbol to its preprocessor settings. Finally, add RpcRt4.lib to the list of libraries in the Link tab. You can now compile the project.

To test it out copy the client to another machine, one that has never seen ICompName. Run DCOMCnfg on the server and make sure that EveryOne can launch and access the CompName Class. Then run the client on the remote machine with two parameters, the first should be R (for 'remote') and the second should be the name of the machine where the server is registered. You should find that the client succeeds, and returns the name of the remote server together with the process ID of that instance of DllHost on that machine. The interface has not been registered on the client machine, and you are not accessing a dispinterface, nor using type library marshaling – the interface marshaling code is in the client.

# Summary

Win32 operating systems have support for threads, which can be used in COM code to improve performance by eliminating bottlenecks. COM defines an apartment as an executable context in which COM objects can run. A COM object can only run in one apartment, and all access from another apartment must be carried out through a marshaled interface pointer. Current versions of COM have two types of apartment: single threaded apartments (STAs) and multithreaded apartments (MTAs). Threads in your client that intend to use COM objects, and threads in your server that provide access to objects must join an apartment. Threads in EXE servers explicitly indicate what apartment type they join by calling CoInitializeEx(), whereas DLL servers do this by a value in a coclass's registry entry.

You don't have to worry too much about writing thread synchronization code; you just need to bracket thread-sensitive code between calls to Lock() and Unlock(), and ATL will ensure that the appropriate mechanism is used for the server type and threading model involved. ATL also provides support for single-threaded and multithreaded EXE servers, and it also provides code for thread pooled STA EXE servers. This chapter has given an example of each, and compared their performance under a severe stress test.

To use an object in a different apartment, an interface pointer must be marshaled. Standard and type library marshaling come almost for free: with the latter you just have to make sure that the interfaces are Automation compatible and that the type library is registered. Custom marshaling involves a lot more work, and in this chapter I have introduced you to the subject with an example that uses marshal-by-value as an optimization for immutable objects.

The final section of the chapter addressed the issue of providing standard marshaling proxy-stub code. MIDL will generate the necessary files to create a separate proxy-stub DLL, but often it complicates administration to have yet another file to register. If you have just one server that will provide implementations of the interface then you may decide to merge the proxy-stub code in the server DLL, similarly if you have just one client that uses this interface, then it is possible to merge the proxy code in the client. In both cases this can reduce the number of files that need to be registered.

# 8

# Connection Points

Connection points are a mechanism for providing bi-directional communication between COM objects. You don't *have* to use connection points for this communication, but if you don't, you will still have to solve some of the problems that connection points have solutions for, and you will find that the only applications that will talk together will be your own. If this is what you want, that's fine. However, if you want to provide events for Visual Basic or scripting clients, or if you are writing a control, you will need to use connection points. If that's you, then read on.

When a client gets an interface on an object, it has unidirectional communication with that object: the client can tell the object to do things. To get bi-directional communication, you need to implement a **sink object** in the client, and pass an interface pointer from this to the object. In this situation, your client has an interface pointer to the object, and your object has an interface pointer to the client's sink object. The client can talk to the object and the object can talk to the client, independently.

If the client is itself an object (for example if it is a control) then it can merely implement the sink interface iself so that it will be the actual sink object; if the client is not an object then it will have to create a lightweight object that implements the sink interface to handle the notifications.

Of course, this raises a rather awkward question: which is the client, and which is the object? The answer is that they both are. In this chapter, I will try to distinguish between the sink object in the client, and the connectable object in the server. "Client" here means the code that initiates the connection, and "server" is the code that has the connectable object.

If you are writing the client and the server objects, and you don't intend to have more than one client, then you don't need connection points. You can get by with passing an interface pointer to the client sink object to the connected server object. However, if there is any likelihood that more than one client will make a connection, then your server object will need to implement some 'map' of connected clients. Further, if the object can provide notifications to more than one sink interface, then you will need to implement multiple maps of connected objects: one for each sink interface type.

It is at this point, when things are beginning to get complicated, that you need to consider using connection points. Indeed, with all the ATL connection point support that implements these maps of connected clients for you, it makes good sense to decide to use them at the outset!

Visual C++ 6.0 and ATL 3.0 have added new support over and above what was available in Visual C++ 5. In particular, ClassView now integrates what used to be called the proxy generator, and there are classes to write event sinks. Before I describe these changes, however, I will briefly outline what connection points are, and how they are used.

# Connection Points

An object that generates events is essentially calling a method on an interface on a client. Because it's a method, the event can have parameters, so if you are implementing (say) a distributed chat program, the server object could inform all clients when a new message is received by sending them the `OnNewMessage()` event, and passing them the message text. Within the client, the interface that's called by the server is known as a **sink interface**, since it is a sink for events.

The server object will have one or more interfaces, and unidirectional communication occurs when a client connects to one of them – the communication is from the client to the object. From the server's perspective, such an interface is an **incoming interface**, since clients call methods on it and calls come *into* the object.

When an object generates an event, it calls a method on the client's sink interface. From the server's perspective, this is an **outgoing interface**, because the call is going *out* of the object. Let me make this quite clear: objects do not *implement* outgoing interfaces, they *call* them.

Think about this a little more. The client knows about the object's incoming interfaces because it wants to connect to them. The client's developer has either obtained the header (describing the C++ bindings for the interface generated by MIDL), or has the type library for the object. For bi-directional communication, the client must implement a sink interface, and the connected object must know about this interface. If you are writing client and object, you can define both interfaces, and make the MIDL-generated header files available to both projects.

How, though, will the sink interface be defined if your client has a virtual machine, like Microsoft Java or Visual Basic, which do not use MIDL (or rather, do not generate C++ header files)? The client's sink interface will be defined in the object's IDL as an outgoing interface, and this will be placed in the object's *type library* for language tools to read. To mark an outgoing interface, you must use the [source] attribute on the interface when declared in the coclass within the library block. Outgoing interfaces are marked with [source], because you are saying that your object is the *source* of events from this interface. For example:

```
coclass EventSource
{
    [default] interface IEventSource;
    [default, source] dispinterface _IEvent;
};
```

In this example the EventSource object implements IEventSource and generates events described by the _IEvent interface, it does not implement this interface.

The client IDE, or some other developer tool, can read the type library of the connectable object to find the interfaces that are marked as [source]. These are the interfaces that the client should implement in order to *sink* events. The outgoing interface can be a custom interface, a dual interface, or a dispinterface. Note, however, that if the client will be Visual Basic, then the sink interface should be a custom interface or a dispinterface; it cannot implement dual interfaces.

The reason that the [source] interface shouldn't be a dual is that dual interfaces implement their methods both as part of the vtable and as dispinterface methods. To handle an event, Visual Basic has to be able to implement the sink interface, and in order to support duals it would have to implement both parts (although in reality, Invoke() could just delegate to the vtable methods). The real problem is to do with the connection point itself, which would have two choices – either call the vtable method, or IDispatch::Invoke() – and there is no standard to decree which should be used. Visual Basic sidesteps this dilemma by sinking dispinterface *or* custom events, and not duals.

Recall that a dispinterface is a named collection of Automation methods with specific DISPIDs, and that these methods are *only* available by calling IDispatch::Invoke(). Visual Basic will look for a [source] interface in a type library, and if it finds a dual interface, it will simply ignore it. This is not a problem if your clients will always be written in Visual Basic, because you can just make sure that your outgoing interface is custom or a dispinterface. It *becomes* a problem, though, if at some point you decide to write an ATL client, because you simply can't create an object with a dispinterface – ATL will insist that it is a dual. However, as I showed you in Chapter 3, you *can* use a dual interface to implement a dispinterface.

If the client is Internet Explorer or ASP (in other words, it uses scripting) then the outgoing interface must be a dispinterface. Thus, for your object to be usable by the largest possible number of clients, the outgoing interface should be a dispinterface, and this is the approach taken by ATL.

# Connection Point Container

A client's connections to an object are made on a per-interface basis, and so it must be that one or more of the incoming interfaces on an object will be the source of events. The client can ask for all the events of a particular outgoing interface to be sent to a sink interface on a sink object that it implements. As I mentioned earlier, more than one client could decide to connect to a single object, so there must be a mechanism to hold all these client sink interface references. That way, when the event occurs in the object, it can call the appropriate method on all the clients' sink interfaces.

An object that can generate events is called a **connection point container**, and as such should implement the `IConnectionPointContainer` interface:

```
[
    object,
    uuid(B196B284-BAB4-101A-B69C-00AA00341D07),
    pointer_default(unique)
]
interface IConnectionPointContainer : IUnknown
{
    HRESULT EnumConnectionPoints([out] IEnumConnectionPoints** ppEnum);
    HRESULT FindConnectionPoint([in] REFIID riid,
                                [out] IConnectionPoint** ppCP);
}
```

This interface has two methods: `FindConnectionPoint()` and `EnumConnectionPoints()`. The former is used to find the connection point object for a particular object's outgoing interface. Thus, if your client implements the `IChatEvents` sink `dispinterface`, it should call `FindConnectionPoint()` passing the IID of this interface. If this is one of the object's outgoing interfaces, the object should return an interface pointer to a connection point object that handles all connections to sink these events.

The `EnumConnectionPoints()` function will return an enumerator on the `IEnumConnectionPoints` interface, which gives you access to all the connection point objects in the connectable object.

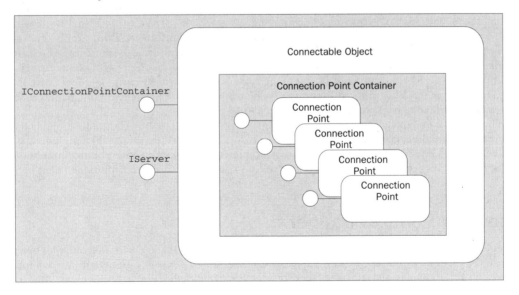

# Connection Points

A connection point object implements the `IConnectionPoint` interface:

```
[
    object,
    uuid(B196B286-BAB4-101A-B69C-00AA00341D07),
    pointer_default(unique)
]
interface IConnectionPoint : IUnknown
{
    HRESULT GetConnectionInterface([out] IID* pIID);
    HRESULT GetConnectionPointContainer(
                        [out] IConnectionPointContainer** ppCPC);
    HRESULT Advise([in] IUnknown* pUnkSink, [out] DWORD* pdwCookie);
    HRESULT Unadvise([in] DWORD dwCookie);
    HRESULT EnumConnections([out] IEnumConnections** ppEnum);
}
```

Once a client has a reference to this interface, it can make the connection by calling `Advise()`. It uses this method to pass the sink interface on the client sink object to the connection point object, which saves it in an internal map and returns a unique cookie. The client should hold on to this cookie, because it is used in a later call to `Unadvise()` to break the connection. The connection point object should implement an array or some other container to hold this and other interface pointers passed through `Advise()`.

When an event occurs in the connectable object, that object can obtain the connection point for the outgoing interface, and call the appropriate method for each entry.

The other methods are for information purposes. Recall that the client can ask the connection point container to enumerate all its connection points. To determine what each of these connection points are, the client can call `GetConnectionInterface()` to get the IID of the outgoing interface that the connection point object supports. If this matches the client's sink interface, it can then call `Advise()`. `GetConnectionPointContainer()` does what you'd expect: it returns an interface pointer to the container.

Finally, `EnumConnections()` returns an enumerator object with the `IEnumConnections` interface for all the connections in the current connection point object. The enumerator will return CONNECTDATA structures:

```
typedef struct tagCONNECTDATA
{
    IUnknown*  pUnk;
    DWORD      dwCookie;
} CONNECTDATA;
```

Thus, a caller of this method will have potential access to all the client sink interface pointers.

> *Note that if these sink interfaces are on different clients accessed via DCOM then security will be applied and hence the caller of* `EnumConnections()` *must be explicitly given access permissions by the client.*

# Other Issues

Before I explain how to implement connection points and sink interfaces in ATL, let me first describe a couple of ATL helper methods, and also point out some security and network issues.

## ATL Helper Functions

ATL provides two helper functions that are used to make and break connections. Both of these are called by the client. The first is AtlAdvise():

```
ATLINLINE ATLAPI AtlAdvise(IUnknown*  pUnkCP, IUnknown* pUnk,
                       const IID& iid, LPDWORD pdw)
{
   CComPtr<IConnectionPointContainer> pCPC;
   CComPtr<IConnectionPoint> pCP;
   HRESULT hRes = pUnkCP->QueryInterface(
                       IID_IConnectionPointContainer, (void**)&pCPC);
   if(SUCCEEDED(hRes))
      hRes = pCPC->FindConnectionPoint(iid, &pCP);
   if(SUCCEEDED(hRes))
      hRes = pCP->Advise(pUnk, pdw);
   return hRes;
}
```

Here you can see connection points in action. The method is passed an interface pointer to the connectable object (pUnkCP) obtained elsewhere, the interface pointer of the sink object (pUnk), and the IID of the object's outgoing interface. The code is straightforward: it calls QueryInterface() for IConnectionPointContainer, and, on success, it asks for the required connection point object before calling Advise(). The cookie from the connection point object is returned via the pdw pointer.

When the client no longer wants to be informed of events, it should call AtlUnadvise():

```
ATLINLINE ATLAPI AtlUnadvise(IUnknown* pUnkCP, const IID& iid, DWORD dw)
{
   CComPtr<IConnectionPointContainer> pCPC;
   CComPtr<IConnectionPoint> pCP;
   HRESULT hRes = pUnkCP->QueryInterface(
                       IID_IConnectionPointContainer, (void**)&pCPC);
   if(SUCCEEDED(hRes))
      hRes = pCPC->FindConnectionPoint(iid, &pCP);
   if(SUCCEEDED(hRes))
      hRes = pCP->Unadvise(dw);
   return hRes;
}
```

This is passed a pointer to the connectable object, the IID of the object's outgoing interface, and the cookie returned from a previous call to AtlAdvise(). The method gets the IConnectionPointContainer interface, finds the connection point object and then calls Unadvise(), breaking the connection. These two methods are designed to be called using raw pointers:

```
IMySink* pSink = GetMySinkFromSomewhere();
IUnknown* pUnk = GetConnectableObjectPointer();
DWORD dwCookie;
AtlAdvise(pUnk, pSink, __uuidof(pSink), &dwCookie);
pSink->Release();
pUnk->Release();
```

If you are using smart pointers, you can call `CComPtr<>::Advise()`:

```
CComPtr<IMySink> pSink = GetMySinkFromSomewhere();
CComPtr<IUnknown> pUnk = GetConnectableObjectPointer();
DWORD dwCookie;
pSink->Advise(pUnk, __uuidof(pSink), &dwCookie);
```

These two blocks of code are equivalent. Note that there is no `Unadvise()` method on `CComPtr<>`, the reason is that `CComPtr<>::Advise()` is used to say that you want to make the interface wrapped by the smart pointer the sink interface for an object, and hence you must pass the `IUnknown` of this sink interface to the connection point; `Unadvise()` breaks the connection using the cookie and not the sink interface and hence is not relevant to `CComPtr<>`.

# Circular References

If you're really concentrating hard, you may have noticed a potential circular reference here. When a client calls `Advise()`, the connection point object in the server will be passed a copy of the client sink object's interface, and that connection point object will increment the reference count on this interface (as should always be done when you make a copy of an interface pointer). The relevant code in `IConnectionPointImpl<>::Advise()` does this by calling `QueryInterface()` for the sink interface on the `IUnknown` pointer passed in from the client. A successful call to `QueryInterface()` results in an implicit call to `AddRef()`.

The sink object will now have a reference count of at least one, whatever the client code does. To release this sink object, the client must call `AtlUnadvise()` to tell the connected object to release its interface pointer on the sink object, and thereby release the extra reference count. You should therefore be wary of putting a call to `AtlUnadvise()` in `FinalRelease()` or in an object's destructor, because these methods will not be called while the sink object is still connected to the server object. Such a circular reference will result in a client sink object refusing to die.

To get round such circular references, you can either explicitly call `AtlUnadvise()` from some shutdown method (the sink object could implement a `ShutDown()` method to be called when the client wants the connection broken), or you can remove the sink object's lifetime dependence on `IUnknown` (by making it a stack object, for example). Then it will be possible to put `AtlUnadvise()` in `FinalRelease()` or the object's destructor.

# Security Issues

Inherent in the nature of connection points is that the connectable object will be able to call an interface on an object in the client. In fact, the call to `AtlAdvise()` results in the server calling the client. To see why, take a look at the ATL implementation of `IConnectionPoint::Advise()`; I'll explain more of this code later, but for now I've highlighted the line that's important to this discussion:

```
template <class T, const IID* piid, class CDV>
STDMETHODIMP IConnectionPointImpl<T, piid, CDV>::Advise(
                                    IUnknown* pUnkSink, DWORD* pdwCookie)
{
    T* pT = static_cast<T*>(this);
    IUnknown* p;
    HRESULT hRes = S_OK;
    if(pUnkSink == NULL || pdwCookie == NULL)
        return E_POINTER;
    IID iid;
    GetConnectionInterface(&iid);
    hRes = pUnkSink->QueryInterface(iid, (void**)&p);
    if(SUCCEEDED(hRes))
    {
        pT->Lock();
        *pdwCookie = m_vec.Add(p);
        hRes = (*pdwCookie != NULL) ? S_OK : CONNECT_E_ADVISELIMIT;
        pT->Unlock();
        if(hRes != S_OK)
            p->Release();
    }
    else if(hRes == E_NOINTERFACE)
        hRes = CONNECT_E_CANNOTCONNECT;
    if(FAILED(hRes))
        *pdwCookie = 0;
    return hRes;
}
```

The interface pointer passed to the connection point is IUnknown. It is also marshaled as IUnknown, so for the object to be able to generate events, it must obtain the sink interface. (Note that if you call AtlAdvise() with a sink interface pointer, it will *still* be marshaled as IUnknown.) This code calls IConnectionPoint::GetConnectionInterface() to obtain the IID of the sink interface this connection point connects to, and then it calls QueryInterface() on the IUnknown* pointer to get this sink interface.

If the client is in a different process from the server, then the client *must* allow the security context of the server to access it. This complicates matters, because it means that if the client uses declarative security, it must have an AppID key in the registry, and the access permissions under it must be changed to give access to the server account. (The launch permissions *don't* have to be changed, because at this point the client process will be running.) The ATL AppWizard will add the code to create an AppID in the RGS script for an EXE server, but not for DLLs, so if you're using declarative security, you must do it by hand.

Alternatively, you can use programmatic security, where the client calls CoInitializeSecurity() before it marshals any interfaces. The client can then specify which accounts will have access to objects in the client. The key phrase here, though, is, "before it marshals any interfaces," which means that the client will need to know when it starts that it must allow the server account to call back. It also means that any object running under this account will be able to call any object implemented in the client.

Setting `AppID` values or calling `CoInitializeSecurity()` is certainly relatively easy to do if you have written the client, but what happens if you *haven't* written the client process – if the client is a control to be used in Internet Explorer, for example? In this case, the control is implemented in a DLL, so the call to `CoInitializeSecurity()` (whether explicit or implicit) will have already been made before the control was created – it will have to live with those settings. This means that the APPID of the client will have to reflect the possible remote servers that will be used with connection points. The problem here is that to give the remote account access to a control in Internet Explorer, you will have to give that account access to the entire process and all the controls loaded in it; this is not very good security practice.

The solution is to use an intermediate local object on the client machine. This **middleman object** will look like the remote server to the control, and like the control to the remote server. However, because it is specific to this particular connectable server, it means that any security changes are made on this one server for access to the single control, and not to all controls that may be running in Internet Explorer. If you want to allow anonymous access across the network, the APPID of the middleman object's server process can be configured to give access to `Everyone`, or else you can write the server to turn off authentication with `CoInitializeSecurity()` (as I'll demonstrate later in this chapter).

When the Internet Explorer control wants to connect to the remote object, it should create the middleman object and make a connection to a connection point in that object. The middleman can be configured to allow the Internet Explorer control to access it, so that a connection can be made between the Internet Explorer control and the middleman. When it is created, the middleman can create the remote object, and since you can administrate its security, you can give permissions for the remote object to access it, and hence make the connection.

Now all the middleman object needs to do is delegate all method calls to the remote object, and delegate all events to the control. This mechanism is shown in the following diagram, and I'll show you an example in code later on.

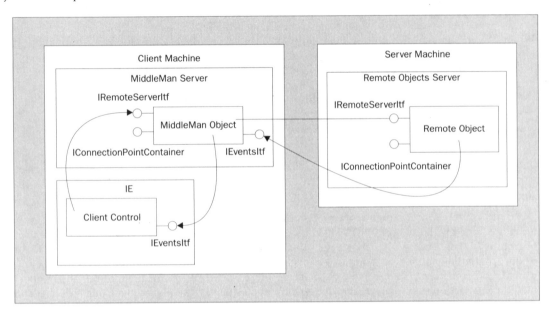

# Network Efficiency

Before looking at how ATL implements connection points, there is one final issue that needs to be covered. As you have seen, when you make a connection to a remote connectable object it takes four round trips across the network and when you break the connection it also takes four calls. These calls across a network take time and hence you should minimize the number of calls you have to make. To see where these calls are made, let's review how `IConnectionPointContainer` and `IConnectionPoint` are used.

To make a connection the client has to query for `IConnectionPointContainer` and then call `FindConnection()`, it then has to call `IConnectionPoint::Advise()` and pass the `IUnknown` pointer of the sink object. This represents three round trips, but note that because the `Advise()` takes an `IUnknown` and the connection point object will want the actual sink interface it will call back to the sink object and query for the sink interface – this is the fourth round trip.

When the connection is broken, the client will query for `IConnectionPointContainer` and then call `FindConnection()` to get the connection point object (two round trips). It then calls `IConnectionPoint::Unadvise()` which results in the connection point object calling `Release()` on the appropriate sink interface (two more round trips).

These calls are relatively inexpensive for the inproc case, so the connection point mechanism is part of the specification for an ActiveX control. However, these calls could impede the efficiency of your application if called across a network. If you do want to reduce the number of network calls, then you should replace the connection point mechanism with your own custom mechanism. Two network calls can be saved by adding `Advise()` and `Unadvise()` to your object's main interface (hence reducing the requirement to query for `IConnectionPointContainer` and obtaining a connection point object). A further round trip can be passing a typed pointer for the sink interface passed to `Advise()`, eliminating the requirement for the object to query the client for the sink interface.

# Event Source

When you create your object using the Object Wizard, and you check the Support Connection Points box on the Attributes tab, four things happen. First, your class is derived from `IConnectionPointContainerImpl<>`, which provides your object with the `IConnectionPointContainer` interface, so making it a connection point container. So that the client can call `QueryInterface()` for this interface, the Wizard adds it to the COM map.

Next, the Wizard adds a connection point map:

```
BEGIN_CONNECTION_POINT_MAP(CConnectableObject)
END_CONNECTION_POINT_MAP()
```

These macros add a method called `GetConnMap()` that returns a static array of `_ATL_CONNMAP_ENTRY` structures, although the actual map that is created is empty. The items in the array are added with the `CONNECTION_POINT_ENTRY()` macro, which adds the offset from the beginning of the `IConnectionPointContainerImpl<>` object within the connectable ATL object of the appropriate connection point object to the map. These connection point objects are *not* created using COM, and cannot be created externally, so there are no entries for them in the object map. In fact, the connection point objects are all implemented as part of the instance of your ATL class, as you'll see in a moment.

For example, if you have an object that generates events on two interfaces _IEvent1 and _IEvent2 then the object will contain vptrs to the base objects; the connection point map entries will point to the appropriate 'proxy' base object. The proxy class (as will be explained in a moment) is not used for marshaling; rather, it is used to generate events through a particular outgoing interface.

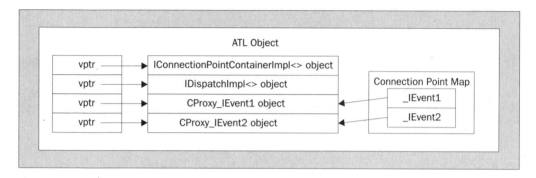

Finally, the Object Wizard adds a `dispinterface` to the `library` section of the IDL file, for example:

```
[
    uuid(96E4AA10-2174-11D2-8D1A-0060973044A8)
]
dispinterface _IConnectableObjectEvents
{
    properties:
    methods:
};
```

And then this interface is added as the default outgoing interface for the component:

```
coclass ConnectableObject
{
    [default] interface IConnectableObject;
    [default, source] dispinterface _IConnectableObjectEvents;
};
```

The Object Wizard gives the `dispinterface` the same name as the interface on your component, but with a leading underscore and the suffix `Events`. This is not declared outside the `library` block because `dispinterfaces` do not need standard marshaling – the Universal Marshaler is used instead. However, it has to be declared in the `library` section so that it will be included in the type library of the component, making tools like Visual Basic able to determine what events the component will generate, so that they can create an appropriate sink interface.

The interface doesn't have to be a `dispinterface`. If you decide that you want to use a custom interface, then you will still be able to connect to Visual Basic clients (but *not* to scripting clients). For example, to change the previous outgoing interface, you would need to make these changes:

```
[
    object,
    uuid(96E4AA10-2174-11D2-8D1A-0060973044A8),
    pointer_default(unique)
]
interface _IConnectableObjectEvents : IUnknown
{
};
```

That is, give the interface [object] and [pointer_default(unique)] attributes, delete the properties: and methods: lines, and make sure that the interface derives from IUnknown. Furthermore, you need to modify the [default, source] line that refers to this interface to specify that it is an interface rather than a dispinterface:

```
[default, source] interface _IConnectableObjectEvents;
```

This outgoing interface is created empty, but it will show up in the ClassView, so you can add methods for the events that can be generated. However, although the interface has been added to the IDL, it has not been added to your object – the connection point map is empty. To add it to the map, you need to run the Implement Connection Point Wizard through the ClassView context menu.

> **Before doing this, you should add all the events that can be generated through this outgoing interface and compile the IDL. The Wizard will generate code from the type library, so the type library must contain this interface.**

*Note that the Implement Connection Point Wizard actually adds*
IConnectionPointContainer *to your COM map for a second time – the Object Wizard added it once using* COM_INTERFACE_ENTRY(), *and the Implement Connection Point Wizard adds it again using* COM_INTERFACE_ENTRY_IMPL(). *Although unnecessary, this bug is harmless. You can remove the second entry by hand.*

If your component is a control that's to be used in a container, you should add support for the IProvideClassInfo2 interface by deriving the class from IProvideClassInfo2Impl<> and adding the interface to the COM map. This interface provides a control container with a mechanism to get the IID of the default outgoing interface for the control. The container could obtain this information by accessing the type information through IDispatch, but IProvideClassInfo2 gives this IID with a single call.

To run the Wizard, right-click on the object that you want to implement the connection point, and you'll see this context menu:

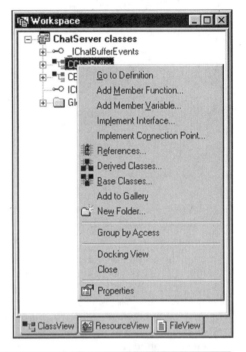

The Implement Connection Point... item will read the type library for the object and display all the outgoing interfaces declared. Note that this shows *all* interfaces marked with [source], whether they are custom or dispinterfaces. You can add support for other outgoing interfaces declared in other type libraries by clicking on the Add Typelib... button; each new type library will get a new tab:

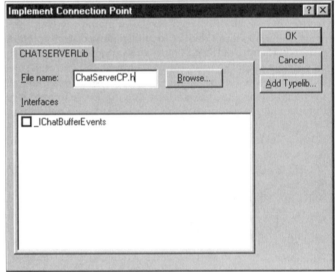

This screenshot comes from the ChatServer project that I'll develop later in this chapter. _IChatBufferEvents is the outgoing interface that was added to the ChatBuffer object by the Object Wizard. The File name box allows you to specify a header file that will be used for the proxy classes. To create a proxy class, check whichever outgoing interface you want to use in the Interfaces box, and click on OK.

This Wizard will do three things. First, it will add the outgoing interface to the connection point map, allowing `FindConnectionPoint()` to obtain the right connection point object. Second, it will generate a proxy class. Here's an example:

```
template <class T>
class CProxy_IChatBufferEvents : public IConnectionPointImpl<
                              T, &DIID__IChatBufferEvents, CComDynamicUnkArray>
{
public:
    VOID Fire_OnNewMessage(BSTR bstrMsg)
    {
        ...
    };
};
```

> *Note that this class derives from* `IConnectionPointImpl<>`, *which implements a connection point object.*

Finally, the Wizard will derive your ATL class from this proxy class, and in doing so does two things. Firstly, it gives access to the `Fire_` method, so that other methods in your class can generate these events to be handled by all the connected clients (in this case, the `OnNewMessage()` event). Secondly, thanks to multiple inheritance, an instance of your class will derive from the `CProxy_IChatBufferEvents` class, which is a connection point object. It is this object whose offset is calculated in the static array maintained by `GetConnMap()` and accessed through the connection point map.

Notice the `CComDynamicUnkArray` argument to the template. Sink interfaces will be added to an array when `Advise()` is called, and removed from it when `Unadvise()` is called. This template parameter specifies the class that will implement this array, and in this case the `CComDynamicUnkArray` array will grow and shrink dynamically. This is flexible, but involves calls to the CRT memory allocator (and if you want to remove dependencies on the CRT this will be a problem). If you don't want this behavior, you can use `CComUnkArray<>` as a parameter instead; this template takes a parameter that specifies the maximum number of interface pointers it will hold.

Getting back to the proxy class, the `Fire_` method looks like this:

```
VOID Fire_OnNewMessage(BSTR bstrMsg)
{
    T* pT = static_cast<T*>(this);
    int nConnectionIndex;
    CComVariant* pvars = new CComVariant[1];
    int nConnections = m_vec.GetSize();

    for (nConnectionIndex = 0; nConnectionIndex < nConnections;
                                              nConnectionIndex++)
    {
        pT->Lock();
        CComPtr<IUnknown> sp = m_vec.GetAt(nConnectionIndex);
        pT->Unlock();
        IDispatch* pDispatch = reinterpret_cast<IDispatch*>(sp.p);
        if (pDispatch != NULL)
        {
```

```
        pvars[0] = bstrMsg;
        DISPPARAMS disp = { pvars, NULL, 1, 0 };
        pDispatch->Invoke(0x1, IID_NULL, LOCALE_USER_DEFAULT, DISPATCH_METHOD,
                                              &disp, NULL, NULL, NULL);
    }
  }
  delete[] pvars;
}
```

This has been generated from the method information in the type library, and in this case the method is declared in a `dispinterface` as:

```
    [id(1)] void OnNewMessage([in] BSTR bstrMsg);
```

The `Fire_OnNewMessage()` code obtains the array of interface pointers (called m_vec, which is a member of the proxy class inherited from `IConnectionPointImpl<>`), and then iterates through each one calling the appropriate event method. Since in this case the outgoing interface is a `dispinterface`, the sink interface pointer will be `IDispatch`, so a DISPPARAMS structure is created and filled with the parameters, and `Invoke()` is called with the method's DISPID (in this case 0x1).

Thus, to generate an event, all your code needs to do is call the `Fire_` method:

```
    Fire_OnNewMessage(bstrMessage);
```

# Example: Chat Server

This example implements a simple chat server. The `ChatBuffer` object will be a singleton that all clients will attach to. The object's `IChatBuffer` interface will be called by clients to send a message. These clients will also connect to `ChatBuffer`'s connection point object for the `_IChatBufferEvents` dispinterface. The `ChatBuffer` singleton generates the single event `OnNewMessage()` to inform all connected clients that it has received a new message. The message will be passed as a parameter of the event. The connected clients can then display the message, making this a simple mechanism for broadcasting a message between several connected clients.

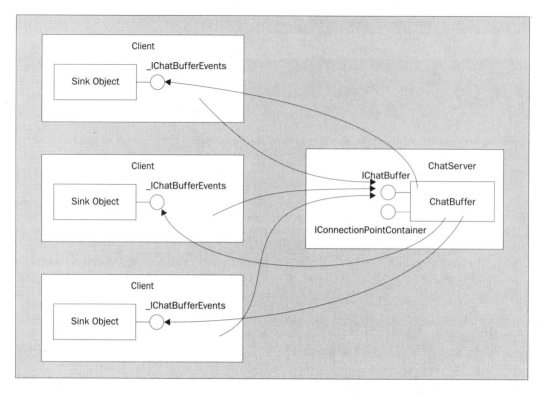

Since the `ChatBuffer` object has a `dispinterface` for its outgoing interface (and not a `dual`), it means that Visual Basic can be used to create a client. This will be my method in the first example, but later in the chapter you will also develop an Internet Explorer control, an ATL composite control, and an ATL simple object to sink events from the `ChatBuffer`.

Start by creating an EXE server called `ChatServer` with a **Simple Object** that has a **Short Name** of `ChatBuffer`. Remember to check the **Support Connection** **Points** box on the **Attributes** tab. The next thing to do is to add the event method to the outgoing interface, so use ClassView to add the following method to `_IChatBufferEvents`:

```
[id(1)] void OnNewMessage([in] BSTR bstrMsg);
```

Now, add the following method to `IChatBuffer`, so that the client can send a message:

```
[id(1)] HRESULT Say([in] BSTR bstrMsg);
```

At this point, you should compile the IDL. After you've done that, you can use ClassView to add support for the outgoing interface. Right click on `CChatBuffer` in ClassView and select the **Implement Connection Point...** item. Then, in the resulting dialog, check the **_IChatBufferEvents** interface.

The Wizard should now add the outgoing interface to the connection point map. I have found that it occasionally gets this step wrong, so open ChatBuffer.h and check that the map looks like this:

```
BEGIN_CONNECTION_POINT_MAP(CChatBuffer)
    CONNECTION_POINT_ENTRY(DIID__IChatBufferEvents)
END_CONNECTION_POINT_MAP()
```

*You may find that the Wizard has used* IID__IChatBufferEvents; *if so, change it now to have the right IID.*

Now you need to implement the Say() method. All this will do is tell all the connected clients about the new message by firing the event:

```
STDMETHODIMP CChatBuffer::Say(BSTR bstrMsg)
{
    Fire_OnNewMessage(bstrMsg);
    return S_OK;
}
```

Finally, so that there is just one chat server object created, make the class a singleton by adding the following to the class definition:

```
DECLARE_CLASSFACTORY_SINGLETON(CChatBuffer)
```

You can see that the object is behaving a bit like a broadcast mechanism, in that it receives a message from one client and then broadcasts it to all the connected clients through the connection point mechanism. Now you can build the project.

## Visual Basic Client

The client is written in Visual Basic 6.0, and it's a Standard EXE project. Once the form has been created, select the References... item from the Project menu and check ChatServer 1.0 Type Library. The form has these controls:

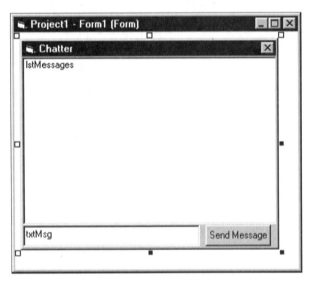

The command button is called `cmdSend`. Double click on the form to get the code window, and add the following above `Form_Load`:

```
Private WithEvents ChatServer As ChatBuffer
```

The `WithEvents` keyword instructs the Visual Basic IDE to read the type library for the outgoing interfaces of the object. This will allow Visual Basic to determine what events the application should handle. Now if you select `ChatServer` from the (left-hand) Object list, you will find that the OnNewMessage event is added to the (right-hand) Procedure list:

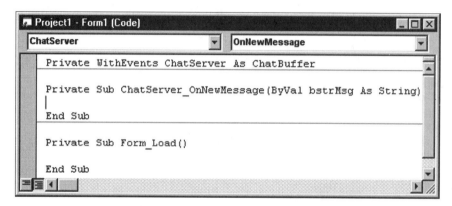

If, on the other hand, you add a control to the VB form (and that control generates events) then you will not have a separate object in the declarations section of the form code. However, in this case, Visual Basic will show the control in the Object box and you'll still be able to implement the event handlers.

Implement `ChatServer_OnNewMessage` like this:

```
Private Sub ChatServer_OnNewMessage(ByVal bstrMsg As String)
    lstMessages.AddItem bstrMsg
End Sub
```

This is the event handler that's called by the server when the event is generated, and it simply adds the message to the list box. Add a form-level variable for the name of the user:

```
Dim strUser As String
```

The `Form_Load` procedure should initialize it like this:

```
Private Sub Form_Load()
    strUser = InputBox("Your Name?", "Chatter", "User")
    Caption = Caption + " - " + strUser
    Set ChatServer = New ChatBuffer
End Sub
```

This code also gets access to the singleton `ChatBuffer` object. Finally, to send a message to the server, double-click on the command button and implement it like this:

```
Private Sub cmdSend_Click()
    ChatServer.Say strUser + "> " + txtMsg
    txtMsg = ""
End Sub
```

When the server gets this message, it will inform all connected clients.

You should now make the executable and then run several copies. As each starts up, give it a different name. If you want to improve on the `ChatBuffer` server, you could change it to have a name registration service so that each connected client will have a different name. However, I have decided to keep the example simple.

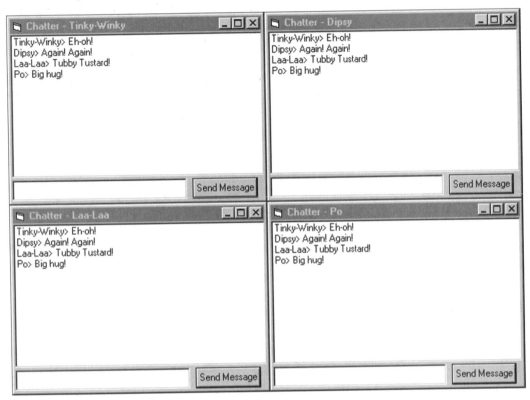

You will find that whenever you type a message and click on Send Message, the message is sent to all of the clients.

It's quite possible to run the server on a different machine from the client. To do this, the client should use the following in the `Form_Load` procedure:

```
Private Sub Form_Load()
    strUser = InputBox("Your Name?", "Chatter", "User")
    Caption = Caption + " - " + strUser
    Set ChatServer = CreateObject("ChatServer.ChatBuffer", "Zeus")
End Sub
```

This is a new feature in Visual Basic 6.0. The second parameter to the `CreateObject()` function is the machine name where the server should be run, in this case `Zeus`. However, you may well find that this fails on your machine with an error of `0x80070721`, indicating a security fault.

Your first reaction would probably be to use `DCOMCnfg` on the server machine to allow `Everyone` to launch and access the server, but in fact that's not the cause of the problem. When the Visual Basic client makes the connection, it passes the `IUnknown` of the sink interface. The server will then `QueryInterface()` for the `dispinterface`, and it is *this* call that fails – the server does not have access to the client.

The problem here is that by default (and for compatibility with legacy applications), DCOM servers are configured to run under the identity of the **Launching User**. The problem with this is that COM has obtained the security token of the remote, launching user, and then called out of the remote host using this token. This action requires support for delegation, which won't be available until Windows NT 5.0.

There are several ways to fix this problem. The first is to use `DCOMCnfg` to change the **Identity** of the server to be the same as the client – that is, select the **This User** option and type in the account that's used by the client. COM on the remote machine creates a *new* security token for this account, so there is not a problem with delegation.

Try this out to see that it works; if you're running on a domain and the client is logged on as a domain account, then you will be able to use this client name in **This User**. If you're running the client and server machines peer-to-peer, then you should create an account on the server machine with the same account name and password as the account that you use on the client. Use this account in the **This User** edit box.

The problem with this approach is that if there will be many clients, all on different machines, they will all have to use the same account. This is not desirable, and we'll look at another solution later in this chapter.

# Handling Events in IE4

It's also possible to catch the events generated by an in-process object embedded on a web page. To do this, however, you need to make sure that the object implements `IProvideClassInfo2`, and exposes both `IProvideClassInfo2` and `IProvideClassInfo`. To see how this works, create a simple DLL server called `Callback`, and add a **Simple Object** called `Sinker`. Remember to make sure that this object implements `IConnectionPointContainer`!

To `ISinker`, add a method called `CallMe()` that takes no parameters. Then, add a method called `Notify()` to `_ISinkerEvents`; this takes no parameters either, but its return type should be `void`. Next, compile the IDL and use ClassView to add support for the outgoing interface, and then implement `CallMe()` like this:

```
STDMETHODIMP CSinker::CallMe()
{
    Fire_Notify();
    return S_OK;
}
```

So that Internet Explorer can handle these events, you need to add support for
`IProvideClassInfo2`:

```
public IDispatchImpl<ISinker, &IID_ISinker, &LIBID_CALLBACKLib>,
public CProxy_ISinkerEvents< CSinker >,
public IProvideClassInfo2Impl<&CLSID_Sinker, &DIID__ISinkerEvents>,
public IObjectSafetyImpl<CSinker, INTERFACESAFE_FOR_UNTRUSTED_CALLER>
```

> *The object will be used for scripting, so to indicate to Internet Explorer that the control is safe for
> untrusted callers, the control supports* `IObjectSafety`. *We'll look more closely at object
> safety in Chapter 10.*

So that you can derive from `IObjectSafetyImpl<>` you need to include the following:

```
#include "resource.h"
#include "CallbackCP.h"
#include <atlctl.h>
```

Also, add the following to the COM map:

```
BEGIN_COM_MAP(CSinker)
    COM_INTERFACE_ENTRY(ISinker)
    COM_INTERFACE_ENTRY(IDispatch)
    COM_INTERFACE_ENTRY(IConnectionPointContainer)
    COM_INTERFACE_ENTRY(IProvideClassInfo)
    COM_INTERFACE_ENTRY(IProvideClassInfo2)
    COM_INTERFACE_ENTRY(IObjectSafety)
END_COM_MAP()
```

I have deleted the second mention of `IConnectionPointContainer` which the Object Wizard
adds by mistake, and made sure that the connection point map has the correct interface – that is,
`DIID__ISinkerEvents`. Now compile this project.

The next thing to do is to create a client. The client will be IE4 running a web page with the `Sinker`
object created using the `<OBJECT>` tag. IE4 will call `QueryInterface()` for
`IProvideClassInfo2` to get information about the default outgoing interface, and then it will
check your script for event handlers and expose these through `IDispatch`. Notice that this
`IDispatch` will only implement `Invoke()` there is no mapping of names to DISPIDs via
`GetIDsOfNames()`.

The client script is implemented in the following HTML file:

```
<HTML>
<BODY>
<OBJECT ID="Callback"
    CLASSID="CLSID:0FE9E4ED-2209-11D2-8D1B-0060973044A8">
</OBJECT>
<INPUT TYPE="BUTTON" ID="bn" VALUE="Call Me">
<SCRIPT LANGUAGE="VBS">
sub Callback_Notify()
```

```
    MsgBox "You called me!"
end sub
sub bn_OnClick()
    Callback.CallMe
end sub
</SCRIPT>
</BODY>
</HTML>
```

When you click on the Call Me button, it will call the object's `CallMe()` method. The code provides an event handler called `Callback_Notify()`; notice the syntax that VBScript uses: `object_event`. The result should be the following:

# Event Sinks

The `ChatServer` example showed you how to generate events in an ATL object, and you saw how to use Visual Basic to create a suitable client. But what if you want to use ATL to create a client that can sink events?

Let's assume that you need to sink events on a `dispinterface`. That means that the client will need to implement that dispinterface. There are three main ways of doing this:

❑   Implement the dispinterface by hand
❑   Implement it using a compatible dual interface and `IDispatchImpl<>`
❑   Use ATL 3.0's new `IDispEventImpl<>` class

The advantage of the first method is that you can make your code as tight as you need. You only need to implement the `Invoke()` method (the other vtable methods can return `E_NOTIMPL`) since this is the only method that will be called. You also have the option of removing any reliance on a type library describing the interface. However, this means writing code yourself to extract the parameters from the `DISPPARAMS` sent to `Invoke()` and taking appropriate action based on the DISPID. If there are events that you're not interested in handling, you can just throw the DISPID away.

The second method is quick and easy to implement for small interfaces. You saw how to implement a dispinterface in terms of a dual interface back in Chapter 3. Unfortunately, this method can become a chore for larger interfaces where you're only interested in a couple of the events. Although Visual C++ now provides a Wizard to help you implement an interface, this Wizard does not work with dispinterfaces, so you're on your own having to type everything out by hand, including dummy methods for uninteresting events. The `IDispatchImpl<>` class relies on the type information contained in a type library.

The third option is perhaps the best choice for implementing event interfaces since it's been designed specifically for that purpose. The class does rely on type information, but doesn't require the creation of a compatible dual interface, nor does it force you to implement methods for events that you're not interested in. Let's take a closer look.

# Event Sinks in Composite Controls

The `IDispEventImpl<>` class is designed to be used by **composite controls** (although you can use it independently, as you'll see later in the chapter), so let's examine it in that context. Be warned, though – this code is used to synthesize event-handling methods on the fly using non-`dispinterface` class methods to provide the implementation. This means that there is some complex code being called. Studying how this works, however, will help you get a grasp on the entire connection point mechanism.

## *Composite Controls*

Composite controls were introduced in Chapter 4, and they will be covered in more depth in Chapter 10. A composite control is a bit like a Visual Basic form, in that it's a control made up of other controls. When you develop a composite control, all you have to do is create a dialog resource, and add to that resource the controls that you want to use. Then, as in Visual Basic, you handle the notifications from the controls, or call methods on them.

The controls that you use may be Windows controls, or they could be ActiveX controls. If they are Windows controls, they will communicate using window messages – for example, you add an item to a list box by sending it a `LB_ADDSTRING` message. Similarly, the control tells you of events by sending its parent window a notification message: if a user double clicks on a list box, it will send its parent the `LBN_DBLCLK` message.

If the child control is an ActiveX control, then the composite control will talk to the control using its COM interfaces, and notifications will come from the child control in the form of events. Thus, the composite control should determine the outgoing interface of the control and implement a version of this interface, so that the composite control developer can write event handler code.

However, a `dispinterface` is just a named version of `IDispatch` that has specific methods with DISPIDs. A control can only have one `IDispatch` interface, and so if the composite has more than one control, they will all have access to the same sink interface. The problem here is that the event with a DISPID of 1 generated by one control will have a different meaning from the event with DISPID 1 generated by another control. Indeed, these two events will most likely have totally different parameters.

Because of this potential problem, you will find that some of the Microsoft-provided controls have custom as well as `dispinterface` outgoing interfaces, but you cannot guarantee that this will be the case. Indeed, because many controls are designed with scripting in mind, you will find that most of them just have outgoing `dispinterfaces`.

So, how can you handle more than one control with outgoing `dispinterfaces`? Chapter 3 showed one way to do this: you can implement `IDispatch::GetIDsOfNames()` and `IDispatch::Invoke()` in such a way that the component exposes `IDispatch` and yet gives access to more than one `dispinterface`. ATL extends this idea with a **sink map**. Like the implementation of connection points, this requires two parts: entries in the map, and corresponding base classes. The sink map needs additional methods in your class to provide the event handlers. These methods are not part of an interface, and they're associated to a sink interface method via the map. This allows you to make sure that the event handlers have unique names.

To create a composite control, you use the Object Wizard in the normal way. It will create the necessary headers and source files, but in addition it will create a dialog template, which you should use to place and position the controls that make up the composite control. To add controls, you should right click on the dialog template and select Insert ActiveX Control from the context menu. This will produce a dialog containing all the controls registered on your machine.

The following shows a simple dialog template:

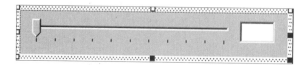

It has two child controls: on the left is the Microsoft Slider Control version 6.0, and on the right is the Microsoft Forms 2.0 TextBox. Both are ActiveX controls; the former is described by the type information in mscomctl.ocx, while the latter has type information in fm20.dll. Adding these two controls to the composite dialog resource does not change the composite's code – that happens when you decide to add event handlers for the child controls. In this case, the Wizard will add entries to the sink map and, if necessary, derive your control class from an appropriate base class (if other events for the sink interface have not already been handled).

To add a handler, you should right click on the ATL control class in ClassView, and select Add Windows Message Handler... from the context menu. Yes, I *know* that you have no intention of adding a message handler, and that you actually want to add an event handler, but in fact this Wizard does both:

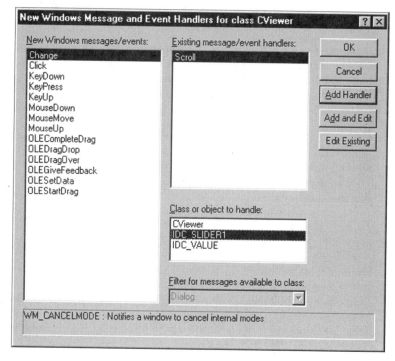

Here, I have selected IDC_SLIDER1 as the object to handle. The Wizard reads the outgoing interface for the control and places the names of the events in the left-hand box. You can select an event from this box, and use Add Handler to add it to the top right hand box, as I have done with the Scroll event. In response to this, the first thing that the Wizard does is derive the control class from:

```
IDispEventImpl<IDC_SLIDER1, CSlider>
```

Obviously, this is only done once. The base class handles the events for the control with the ID of
IDC_SLIDER1; when you add event handlers for other controls, a base class will be added for each
even if you add several instances of the same control (the first parameter to the template is used to
distinguish between them). The Wizard then adds a member to the sink map:

```
BEGIN_SINK_MAP(CSlider)
    SINK_ENTRY(IDC_SLIDER1, 0x1, OnScrollSlider1)
END_SINK_MAP()
```

The first parameter is the control ID, the second is the DISPID of the event, and the third is the name
of a member of the class that will handle the event:

```
VOID __stdcall OnScrollSlider1()
{
    // TODO : Add Code for event handler.
}
```

Notice that the handler is __stdcall, and does not return a HRESULT. This is not a COM method,
and it is not called directly by the control when generating the event. Instead, this function is called
through the event handling mechanism that will synthesize a dispinterface member, that is
create the correct stack frame for this method based on the stack frame created by COM with the
intention of calling a dispinterface method.

The map creates an array of _ATL_EVENT_ENTRY instances:

```
template <class T>
struct _ATL_EVENT_ENTRY
{
    UINT nControlID;              // ID identifying object instance
    const IID* piid;             // dispinterface IID
    int nOffset;                 // offset of dispinterface from this pointer
    DISPID dispid;               // DISPID of method/property
    void (__stdcall T::*pfn)();  // class method to invoke
    _ATL_FUNC_INFO* pInfo;
};
```

The first entry is the ID of the control on the template so that you can have different methods
handling the same event from different controls; the second is the IID of the sink interface and the
third is the offset of the IDispEventImpl<> base class that implements IDispatch for this event.
dispid is the DISPID of the event method and a pointer to your handler is given in pfn. Finally, to
synthesize a dispinterface method from the handler method you need to get information about
the stack frame that COM will have generated when it calls the dispinterface method. This
information is held by ATL in an _ATL_FUNC_INFO structure, which is created by Invoke(). As an
optimization, this structure is cached through the pointer pInfo so that the information is only
generated once.

The SINK_ENTRY() macro will use IID_NULL for the dispinterface IID and hence assumes that only one of the control's outgoing interfaces (the default source interface) will be sinked. If you want to sink events from another outgoing interface, you can use the SINK_ENTRY_EX() macro that has an additional parameter that allows you to specify the IID of the sink interface. If you use this macro then you will need to specify the third template parameter of IDispEventImpl<> to give this IID. For example, if you have a composite control with a control that has two outgoing interfaces, _IEvents1 and _IEvents2 then you can handle events generated on these interfaces by deriving from these two templated classes:

```
public IDispEventImpl<IDC_CTRL1, CMyComposite, &DIID__IEvents1>,
public IDispEventImpl<IDC_CTRL1, CMyComposite, &DIID__IEvents2>
```

And using a sink map that looks like this:

```
BEGIN_SINK_MAP(CMyComposite)
    SINK_ENTRY_EX(IDC_CTRL1, DIID__IEvents1, 0x1, OnEventFromItf1)
    SINK_ENTRY_EX(IDC_CTRL1, DIID__IEvents2, 0x1, OnEventFromItf2)
END_SINK_MAP()
```

When the control is created, ATL creates the visual part by passing the dialog resource to CreateDialogIndirectParam(). The dialog resource contains information about the ActiveX controls that are used in the composite control – in particular, the resource will have the CLSID of the control, and a separate resource of type DLGINIT that contains the initialization values passed to the control using its IPersistStreamInit interface (more details of this will be given in Chapter 10). ATL does some preparation of this data to convert the resources into a form that can be passed to CreateDialogIndirectParam(), but the details are not important here.

## The Advise Mechanism

After creating the dialog template, ATL sets up the connections to the controls. This is done in a call to CComCompositeControl<>::AdviseSinkMap(), which is called immediately after the dialog is shown. This method calls AtlAdviseSinkMap(), which iterates over the sink map. The code in this method is quite interesting, so let's take a look at how it works. Here's the code from atlcom.h, with error handling removed:

```
template <class T>
inline HRESULT AtlAdviseSinkMap(T* pT, bool bAdvise)
{
    const _ATL_EVENT_ENTRY<T>* pEntries = T::_GetSinkMap();
```

This obtains the sink map from the class; the rest of the code then iterates through all the members in the map:

```
while(pEntries->piid != NULL)
{
    _IDispEvent* pDE = (_IDispEvent*)((DWORD)pT + pEntries->nOffset);
    hr = E_FAIL;
    HWND h = pT->GetDlgItem(pEntries->nControlID);
    if(h != NULL)
    {
```

```
            CComPtr<IUnknown> spUnk;
            AtlAxGetControl(h, &spUnk);
            if(spUnk != NULL)
            {
                if(bAdvise)
                {
                    if(!InlineIsEqualGUID(IID_NULL, *pEntries->piid))
                        hr = pDE->DispEventAdvise(spUnk, pEntries->piid);
                    else
                    {
                        AtlGetObjectSourceInterface(spUnk, &pDE->m_libid,
                                            &pDE->m_iid, &pDE->m_wMajorVerNum,
                                                        &pDE->m_wMinorVerNum);
                        hr = pDE->DispEventAdvise(spUnk, &pDE->m_iid);
                    }
                }
                else
                {
                    if(!InlineIsEqualGUID(IID_NULL, *pEntries->piid))
                        hr = pDE->DispEventUnadvise(spUnk, pEntries->piid);
                    else
                        hr = pDE->DispEventUnadvise(spUnk, &pDE->m_iid);
                }
            }
        if(FAILED(hr))
            break;
        pEntries++;
    }
```

Similar to the way that the connection point map gives access to connection point objects by holding the offsets of these connection points from the start of a base class of your control, the sink map holds the offsets of the sink objects within the map. The initial code will therefore be familiar to you. Sink objects are derived from the _IDispEvent abstract base class that's used to provide basic IUnknown methods, and 'advise' and 'unadvise' methods.

By default, there is nothing in the sink map or the sink object that indicates what the outgoing interface is for the control. There is only information about the event and the event handler for a particular control, not what dispinterface the event is part of. The sink map is used only to map the DISPID of an event onto the actual handler function. It is possible to put the name of the dispinterface into the map by hand, however the Wizard code is usually sufficient so I will assume here that you have not done this.

The code in AtlAdviseSinkMap() obtains the window handle for the control, and from this obtains the IUnknown* for the control through a call to AtlAxGetControl(). This call sends an ATL-registered WM_ATLGETCONTROL message to the control, which replies by returning its IUnknown interface. This may seem a little odd: how does the ActiveX control know that it needs to handle this message, when it is a private message registered by ATL? It can achieve this feat because the code that initializes the composite control will wrap each contained control with CAxHostWindow (you can find this in atlhost.h), with a rather convoluted mechanism that we'll be examining in the later chapters of this book.

Basically, a window is created for every ActiveX control that you have added to the dialog template, and the window procedure is set to `AtlAxWindowProc()`. This creates an instance of `CAxHostWindow` for the control. This object uses `IUnknown` to manage its lifetime, but it cannot be created externally. It is used to link a window and a COM object, so it has a message map (which we'll discuss in more detail in the next chapter) and a pointer to the `IUnknown` of the object. Thus, when this window is sent the `WM_ATLGETCONTROL` message, it can reply by returning the `IUnknown` of the object.

If your class *did* put the IID of the control's outgoing interface into the map, then this IID is used. If it's not there, the `AtlAdviseSinkMap()` code calls `AtlGetObjectSourceInterface()` to obtain the outgoing interface and the control's type information. This is quite a large function, but basically it obtains the outgoing interface by calling `QueryInterface()` for `IProvideClassInfo2`, and then calling `GetGUID()`. Controls will usually implement this interface, which makes containers' work much easier. If a control doesn't implement this interface, then it will hunt through the type information for the control's outgoing interface. Once it has been obtained, the IID is cached in the sink object for future use.

Now the code can call `_IDispEvent::DispEventAdvise()`, which simply calls `AtlAdvise()` with appropriate values. The child control, of course, calls `QueryInterface()` on the sink object for the outgoing interface, and this call succeeds because `AtlGetObjectSourceInterface()` has already stored the IID in the sink object, so it can check this IID when the `QueryInterface()` is made.

## Sinking Events

Now the connections have been made between the composite control and its children, what happens when an event is generated in one of the child controls? After all, the interface returned to the child control when it calls `QueryInterface()` for a sink interface is an `IDispatch` interface pointer.

Your composite control class is derived from `IDispEventImpl<>`, and it is a pointer to this interface that is returned as the sink object. The class gets its implementation of `IDispatch::Invoke()` from its base class `IDispEventSimpleImpl<>`; this function is shown here:

```
STDMETHOD(Invoke)(DISPID dispidMember, REFIID riid, LCID lcid, WORD,
        DISPPARAMS* pdispparams, VARIANT* pvarResult, EXCEPINFO*, UINT*)
{
    T* pT = static_cast<T*>(this);
    const _ATL_EVENT_ENTRY<T>* pMap = T::_GetSinkMap();
    const _ATL_EVENT_ENTRY<T>* pFound = NULL;
    void (__stdcall T::*pEvent)() = NULL;
    while(pMap->piid != NULL)
    {
        if((pMap->nControlID == nID) &&
                (pMap->dispid == dispidMember) && (pMap->piid == pdiid))
        {
            pFound = pMap;
            break;
        }
        pMap++;
    }
    if(pFound == NULL)
        return S_OK;
```

```
        _ATL_FUNC_INFO info;
        _ATL_FUNC_INFO* pInfo;
        if(pFound->pInfo != NULL)
            pInfo = pFound->pInfo;
        else
        {
            pInfo = &info;
            HRESULT hr = GetFuncInfoFromId(*pdiid, dispidMember, lcid, info);
            if(FAILED(hr))
                return S_OK;
        }
        InvokeFromFuncInfo(pFound->pfn, *pInfo, pdispparams, pvarResult);
        return S_OK;
    }
```

This packs a lot into a few lines of code, so let's go through it slowly. First of all, it goes through the sink map and checks to see if the control ID is the same as the parameter passed to `IDispEventImpl<>`; this ensures that the code is handling the event for the right control. It checks that the `DISPID` passed to `Invoke()` is the same as in the map, and that the IID member in the sink map is the same as the IID passed to `IDispEventImpl<>`, which ensures that the generated event is indeed handled by this code.

Note that by default, the two previously mentioned IIDs are both `IID_NULL`. However, if the control has more than one outgoing interface that you will want to handle, you can distinguish between them by using the IID parameter to `IDispEventImpl<>`, and by specifying the sink interface for an event in the map. The ATL code ensures that this IID is used in the call to `AtlAdvise()`, rather than querying for the default outgoing interface as explained above.

When this method is satisfied that the event has a handler in the sink map, it will need to call the handler function. There is a special, system-supplied Automation function to do this, but it needs to know information about the method that it will call, so that it can unpack the event parameters and create a correct stack frame. To get this information, `Invoke()` calls `GetFuncInfoFromId()` (which is overridden by `IDispEventImpl<>`); this will return an `_ATL_FUNC_INFO` structure that describes a method:

```
    struct _ATL_FUNC_INFO
    {
        CALLCONV cc;                            // Calling convention
        VARTYPE vtReturn;                       // Return type
        SHORT nParams;                          // Number of parameters
        VARTYPE pVarTypes[_ATL_MAX_VARTYPES];   // Types of the parameters
    };
```

*Notice that* pVarTypes *is a fixed size array of* _ATL_MAX_VARTYPES *elements (by default this is 8). If you intend to call methods with more than 8 parameters, you should redefine this symbol to a larger value.*

`GetFuncInfoFromId()` is quite a large method, but it's pretty straightforward nonetheless; it just obtains the FUNCDESC structure for the method by using type information, and then uses that to fill the `_ATL_FUNC_INFO` structure.

Armed with this information, `IDispEventSimpleImpl<>::Invoke()` then calls
`IDispEventSimpleImpl<>::InvokeFromFuncInfo()` to call the handler:

```
HRESULT InvokeFromFuncInfo(void (__stdcall T::*pEvent)(),
        _ATL_FUNC_INFO& info, DISPPARAMS* pdispparams, VARIANT* pvarResult)
```

The parameters of this method are the handler function pointer placed in the sink map, the event
method description (initialized earlier), the parameters passed as part of the event, and the buffer to
take the return value. Remember that the event handler you have in your class is a member function,
and so the information sent to `Invoke()` must be translated to the parameters that that member
function expects.

## The Thunk

To call the handler, `InvokeFromFuncInfo()` creates a thunk object from `CComStdCallThunk<>`.
This natty little class has data members that hold values that will be interpreted as machine code:

```
template <class T>
class CComStdCallThunk
{
public:
   typedef void (__stdcall T::*TMFP)();

   void* pVtable;
   void* pFunc;
   DWORD m_mov;                          // mov dword ptr [esp+4], pThis
   DWORD m_this;                         //
   BYTE  m_jmp;                          // jmp func
   DWORD m_relproc;                      // relative jmp
   void  Init(TMFP dw, void* pThis);
};
```

The significant things here are the data members: the first two are a vptr and a function pointer.
Then, the members starting with m_mov hold machine code. `InvokeFromFuncInfo()` calls the
`Init()` method, passing the address of the function implemented in your class that will handle the
event, and the `this` pointer of your control:

```
void Init(TMFP dw, void* pThis)
{
   union
   {
      DWORD dwFunc;
      TMFP pfn;
   } pfn;

   pfn.pfn = dw;
   pVtable = &pFunc;
   pFunc = &m_mov;
   m_mov = 0x042444C7;
   m_this = (DWORD)pThis;
   m_jmp = 0xE9;
   m_relproc = (int)pfn.dwFunc - ((int)this + sizeof(CComStdCallThunk));
   FlushInstructionCache(GetCurrentProcess(), this, sizeof(CComStdCallThunk));
}
```

Here a union is used to convert a function pointer to a DWORD. This code initializes the function pointer pFunc to point to the machine code members, and then it fills these members with machine code and pointers to the handler function. At the end of this method, pFunc will point to this code:

```
mov dword ptr [esp+4], pThis
jmp pHandlerFunc
```

pThis is the this pointer of the ATL class, and pHandlerFunc is the address of the member that will handle the event. This sets up the stack for a call to the handler function. InvokeFromFuncInfo() then passes the thunk object, the event description (in the _ATL_FUNC_INFO structure) and the event parameters to DispCallFunc(). This is an undocumented function that comes in OLEAut32.dll and is used to call interface functions. The method calls the handler and returns the handler return value to the connected object. Thus, the event is handled.

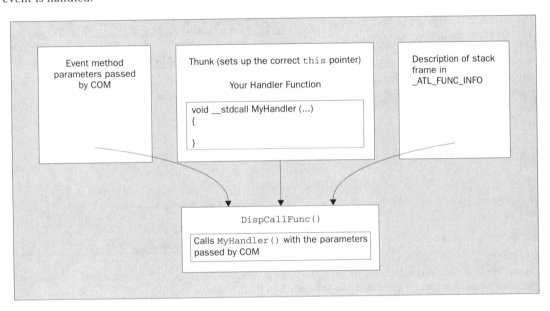

## The Unadvise Mechanism

When the control is unloaded, the implementation of IOleInPlaceObject::InPlaceDeactivate() calls AdviseSinkMap(false) to break the connections between the child controls and the composite control. Remember the warning I gave earlier: the call to Unadvise() is not put in FinalRelease() or the control destructor, because the reference count will not be zero and so these methods will not be called.

# Sinking Events: An Example

The event sink map is integral to the composite control, which assumes that the items added to the sink map are events generated by controls in the dialog resource. Since ChatBuffer is not a control, AtlAdviseSinkMap() will fail if we try to put it in the map. Specifically, it will fail at this line:

```
HWND h = pT->GetDlgItem(pEntries->nControlID);
```

The method is trying to get the window handle of the control so that it can get to its `IUnknown` pointer.

Instead of using the sink map, this example will use a simpler mechanism: I'll implement the sink interface on the client control itself. The `ChatClient` project will be a composite control that communicates with a `ChatBuffer` object. The control will look like the Visual Basic client you saw earlier, with a list control, a text box and a button. This is the reason that a composite control is used.

Start by creating a DLL COM server project called `ChatClient`. Into this project, insert a composite control with the **Short Name** of `Chatter`. However, make sure that you change the interface name to `IChatBufferEvents`, the control will need to implement the sink interface to handle events from the server and this will be done by implementing a `dispinterface` through `COM_INTERFACE_ENTRY_IID()`. It will make the code clearer if the dual interface has a similar name to the `dispinterface`.

When the Wizard has finished its work, you will see the dialog resource. Resize this appropriately, and add a list box (`IDC_MESSAGES`), an edit box (`IDC_MSG`), and a button (`IDC_SEND`) from the toolbox. Make sure that the list box *doesn't* sort entries.

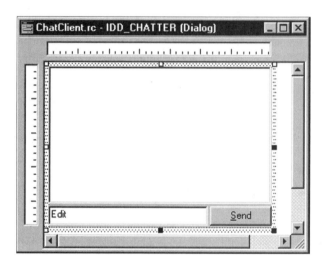

Since these are all Windows controls, the sink map will not be used, and notifications will be sent as window messages through handlers in the message map.

This control should connect to the singleton `ChatBuffer` object, and to distinguish the messages sent by this client from those sent by other clients, it should obtain a name from the user. This name could be sent to the control via the `<PARAM>` tag in Internet Explorer, or as a property initialized through `IPersistStreamInit`. For details of how to do these, I suggest you consult *Beginning ATL COM Programming*. Because it's not the focus of this example, I will use a simpler mechanism here: like the Visual Basic client, I'll create a dialog when the control is created into which the user can enter their name. More of that later.

Let's start by creating the connection to the `ChatBuffer` object. To the `CChatter` class, add a private data member to talk to the server:

```
private:
    CComPtr<IChatBuffer> m_pServer;
};
```

CComPtr<> needs the definition of the interface, so there needs to be the following line at the top of the header:

```
#import "..\ChatServer\ChatServer.tlb" no_namespace, \
                    named_guids, raw_interfaces_only, raw_native_types
```

This uses #import to get the interface and GUID constants from the ChatServer project without having to use the MIDL-generated files.

The server needs to be created when the control is first created, and then released when the control is unloaded. At first glance, FinalConstruct() may seem to be the best place to do this. However, at this point the control is not completely constructed: the interface pointer has not been returned to the container. If you create the server in this method and make the connection, then the reference count on the control will be non-zero (the server will be holding a reference on it). ATL will balk when it attempts to return the interface pointer to the container because it will expect the reference count to be zero.

I will come back to this issue of what method to use to initialize a control in Chapter 10. For now, I will just use CComControl<>::InPlaceActivate(), which is called whenever the control is activated and (the behavior we're interested in) when a new instance is created:

```
HRESULT CChatter::InPlaceActivate(LONG iVerb, const RECT* prcPosRect)
{
    HRESULT hr;
    hr = CComControlBase::InPlaceActivate(iVerb, prcPosRect);
    if(iVerb == OLEIVERB_INPLACEACTIVATE)
    {
        hr = m_pServer.CoCreateInstance(CLSID_ChatBuffer);
    }
    return hr;
}
```

The check for OLEIVERB_INPLACEACTIVATE ensures that the server creation code is not called when, for example, this control gets the focus. You need to add the method to the header, and when you do this you should also add InPlaceDeactivate(), which will be used for cleanup:

```
public:
    HRESULT InPlaceActivate(LONG iVerb, const RECT* prcPosRect);
    STDMETHOD(InPlaceDeactivate)(void);
```

Of course, once the server is created, the control must make a connection. It does this by passing its IUnknown interface to AtlAdvise(). First, add a member to hold the cookie:

```
private:
    CComPtr<IChatBuffer> m_pServer;
    DWORD m_dwCookie;
};
```

Then, add the following to InPlaceActivate(), after the call to CoCreateInstance():

```
if(iVerb == OLEIVERB_INPLACEACTIVATE)
{
    hr = m_pServer.CoCreateInstance(CLSID_ChatBuffer);
    if (SUCCEEDED(hr))
        hr = m_pServer.Advise(GetUnknown(), DIID__IChatBufferEvents,
                                                        &m_dwCookie);
}
```

When the control is unloaded, the connection to the server should be broken. This can be done in InPlaceDeactivate():

```
STDMETHODIMP CChatter::InPlaceDeactivate(void)
{
    if (m_pServer)
        AtlUnadvise(m_pServer, DIID__IChatBufferEvents, m_dwCookie);
    return IOleInPlaceObjectWindowlessImpl<CChatter>::InPlaceDeactivate();
}
```

Now you need to implement the sink interface. As mentioned above, ATL implements dual interfaces, but since a dispinterface is effectively the IDispatch part of a dual, there is no problem: we can use the interface that was added to the control by the Object Wizard. This is done by adding the dispinterface to the COM map and specifying that IDispatch will implement it:

```
BEGIN_COM_MAP(CChatter)
    COM_INTERFACE_ENTRY(IChatBufferEvents)
    COM_INTERFACE_ENTRY(IDispatch)
    COM_INTERFACE_ENTRY_IID(DIID__IChatBufferEvents, IDispatch)
```

Finally, you need to add the event handler, so use ClassWizard to add this method to the IChatBufferEvents dual interface:

```
    [id(1)] HRESULT OnNewMessage([in] BSTR bstrMsg);
```

The [id()] here is important, and must match the same method in _IChatBufferEvents. This method is called when an event is generated through _IChatBufferEvents, and it simply adds the parameter as a string to the list box:

```
STDMETHODIMP CChatter::OnNewMessage(BSTR bstrMsg)
{
    USES_CONVERSION;
    CWindow ListBox(GetDlgItem(IDC_MESSAGES));
    ListBox.SendMessage(LB_ADDSTRING, 0, (LPARAM)OLE2CT(bstrMsg));
    return S_OK;
}
```

This uses the ATL CWindow class to access the list box on the control. I'll explain this class in more detail in the next chapter, but basically it's a thin wrapper around the Win32 GDI commands, and is used to maintain a HWND.

If you choose, you can compile the project now and load the control in Internet Explorer using the HTML page that the Object Wizard has created for you. You won't be able to send a message, though, so to test it out, run the Visual Basic client we developed earlier and send a few messages. This will confirm that the control can accept events.

Next, we need to write the code that sends a message to the server. There are two things that need to be done. Firstly, you need to write code to initialize the client's name so that all messages are identified. The second task is to handle the click event on the button, and hence send the message.

You will need to get a string from the user, and to do this you should add a dialog through the Object Wizard. I called this class CUserName, and the dialog template looks like this:

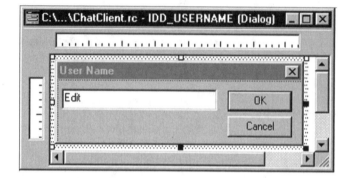

The edit box has an ID of IDC_USERNAME. To return data entered into the dialog, add a data member called m_bstrName to CUserName:

```
public:
    CComBSTR m_bstrName;
};
```

Next, use the context menu item <u>A</u>dd Windows Message Handler... in ClassView to add a handler for the OK button. This should copy the value in the text box into the data member:

```
LRESULT OnOK(WORD wNotifyCode, WORD wID, HWND hWndCtl, BOOL& bHandled)
{
    CWindow pEdit(GetDlgItem(IDC_USERNAME));
    BSTR bstr = NULL;
    pEdit.GetWindowText(bstr);
    m_bstrName.Attach(bstr);
    EndDialog(wID);
    return 0;
}
```

This dialog will be used when the control is first created, and the code should cache the user name in a data member in the control class, so add a similar data member to CChatter:

```
private:
    CComPtr<IChatBuffer> m_pServer;
    DWORD m_dwCookie;
    CComBSTR m_bstrName;
};
```

So that the dialog can be used, the `UserName.h` header must be `#include`'d at the top of `Chatter.h`:

```
#include "UserName.h"
```

The code to create the dialog can appear in `InPlaceActivate()`, before the server object is created:

```
HRESULT CChatter::InPlaceActivate(LONG iVerb, const RECT* prcPosRect)
{
    HRESULT hr;
    hr = CComControlBase::InPlaceActivate(iVerb, prcPosRect);
    if(iVerb == OLEIVERB_INPLACEACTIVATE)
    {
        CUserName dlg;
        if(dlg.DoModal())
            m_bstrName = dlg.m_bstrName;
        else
            m_bstrName = _T("User");
```

Finally, you need to add a handler for the button's click event, so that you can send messages to the buffer. To do this, use the ClassView Wizard to add a handler for the `BN_CLICKED` message of the `IDC_SEND` button. Then add the following body:

```
LRESULT OnClickedSend(WORD wNotifyCode, WORD wID,
                                        HWND hWndCtl, BOOL& bHandled)
{
    CWindow TextBox(GetDlgItem(IDC_MSG));
    BSTR bstr = NULL;
    TextBox.GetWindowText(bstr);
    CComBSTR bstrSend;
    bstrSend = m_bstrName;
    bstrSend += L"> ";
    bstrSend += bstr;
    m_pServer->Say(bstrSend);
    TextBox.SetWindowText(_T(""));
    return 0;
}
```

You can now compile the code and test it out either by running multiple instances of the HTML page created by the AppWizard, or by using it alongside the Visual Basic client:

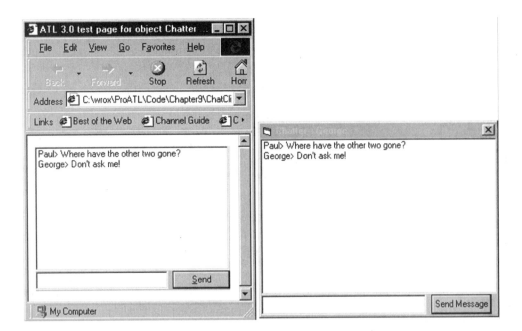

# IDispEventImpl<> Example

In the previous example, we couldn't use the sink map to capture the events from the chat server because we needed to use a composite control for the user interface. The `CComCompositeControl<>` class assumes that the ID used for the sink entry is the resource ID of a control.

However, we *can* use the sink map and `IDispEventImpl<>` from any other type of ATL class as a quick and easy way of sinking events. `IDispEventImpl<>` doesn't rely on `CComCompositeControl<>` in any way. We can use the sink map without worrying about composite controls, resource IDs, or any other complications. Let's see how we can do that by creating a simple event sink to log the messages broadcast by the chat server.

Start by creating an ATL EXE project called `ChatLogger`. Now add a new Simple Object to this project called `ChatterLogger`. This class will act as the event sink.

At the top of `ChatterLogger.h`, add the following code:

```
#import "..\ChatServer\ChatServer.tlb" \
        no_namespace, named_guids, raw_interfaces_only, raw_native_types
```

This will introduce the necessary `ChatServer` interface and GUID definitions into the project.

Now derive `CChatterLogger` from `IDispEventImpl<>` as shown:

```
class ATL_NO_VTABLE CChatterLogger :
    public CComObjectRootEx<CComSingleThreadModel>,
    public CComCoClass<CChatterLogger, &CLSID_ChatterLogger>,
    public IDispatchImpl<IChatterLogger, &IID_IChatterLogger,
                                         &LIBID_CHATLOGGERLib>,
    public IDispEventImpl<42, CChatterLogger, &DIID__IChatBufferEvents,
                                 &LIBID_CHATSERVERLib, 1, 0>
```

Although `IDispEventImpl<>` provides default values for most of its template parameters, all the arguments supplied here are vital.

The first template parameter is an ID. When using the `IDispEventImpl<>` class separately from `CComCompositeControl<>`, this ID is arbitrary – it is simply used to link a particular `IDispEventImpl<>` base class with the corresponding entries in the sink map. You can think of this as an ID representing the source of an event interface. Here I've chosen to use the value 42, to show just how arbitrary this ID can be.

The second template parameter is the class that derives from `IDispEventImpl<>` and contains the sink map. In this case, that's the `CChatterLogger` class.

Next is the interface ID for the event interface. We're interested in receiving events from the `ChatBuffer` so we pass the IID of the `_IChatBufferEvents` interface.

The IID is followed by the LIBID and the major and minor version numbers for the type library. Without this information, `IDispEventImpl<>` wouldn't have the necessary type information for the event interface, so it's vital that you supply this.

Now you can add the sink map to `CChatterLogger`:

```
BEGIN_SINK_MAP(CChatterLogger)
    SINK_ENTRY_EX(42, DIID__IChatBufferEvents, 0x1, OnNewMessage)
END_SINK_MAP()
```

The sink entry specifies the ID of the event source (that is, the same ID as was used for the first template parameter to `IDispEventImpl<>`), the interface ID, the DISPID of the method we're interested in handling, and the handler function.

You can add the `OnNewMessage()` handler function as shown below:

```
void __stdcall OnNewMessage(BSTR bstrMsg)
{
    USES_CONVERSION;
    // Monitoring is basic - just display a message box
    MessageBox(NULL, OLE2CT(bstrMsg), _T("Message Logged"), MB_OK);

    // Monitor m_lLimit messages then stop
    // If m_lLimit is zero, monitor indefinitely
    static int count = 0;
    ++count;
    if (m_lLimit && count >= m_lLimit)
        Stop();
}
```

Note the __stdcall calling convention and the dispinterface-style method signature required by
IDispEventImpl<>. The actual 'logging' code does nothing more than display a message box for
the message and keep track of the number of messages. When the number of logged messages passes
a threshold value, the code calls a Stop() method that we'll add to the class shortly. If m_lLimit is
0, the Stop() method is never called and logging continues indefinitely.

You'll need to add a long member to the class to hold the message logging limit and initialize it to
zero in the constructor. While you're there, add a CComPtr<> member to hold an IChatBuffer
interface pointer from the chat server as shown:

```
public:
    CComPtr<IChatBuffer> m_pServer;
    long m_lLimit;
    CChatterLogger() : m_lLimit(0)
    {
    }
```

Now add two methods to the IChatLogger interface using ClassView:

```
[id(1), helpstring("method Start")] HRESULT Start([in] long lLimit);
[id(2), helpstring("method Stop")] HRESULT Stop();
```

The first method will be used to create the chat server (or get a pointer to the running instance, since
it's a singleton) and advise it that we want to receive events on the _IChatBufferEvents interface.
The second method will break the connection with the server and release the reference that we have
to the server.

Implement Start() as shown below:

```
STDMETHODIMP CChatterLogger::Start(long lLimit)
{
    m_lLimit = lLimit;
    HRESULT hr = m_pServer.CoCreateInstance(CLSID_ChatBuffer);
    if (FAILED(hr))
        return hr;
    return DispEventAdvise(m_pServer);
}
```

Here we just set m_lLimit to the value passed to the method, create the ChatBuffer server, then
call IDispEventImpl<>::DispEventAdvise() to advise the server that we're interested in the
events. All the information and data members that the IConnectionPoint::Advise() method
needs are wrapped up in the IDispEventImpl<> base class and its template parameters, so we only
have to pass the IUnknown interface of the object that we want to advise. If we had more than one
IDispEventImpl<> as a base class, we'd need to specify which version of DispEventAdvise()
we were calling by scoping it with the name of the partciular base class. In this case, we only have
one base class, so that's not necessary.

`Stop()` does the reverse of `Start()`:

```
STDMETHODIMP CChatterLogger::Stop()
{
    HRESULT hr = S_OK;

    if (m_pServer)
    {
        hr = DispEventUnadvise(m_pServer);
        m_pServer.Release();
    }

    PostThreadMessage(_Module.dwThreadID, WM_QUIT, 0, 0);
    return hr;
}
```

This function unadvises the server using `IDispEventImpl<>::DispEventUnadvise()` then releases the server. Once again all the work of querying for the right interfaces, and passing the cookie back to the server is handled by the `IDispEventImpl<>` base class.

`Stop()` also calls `PostThreadMessage()` to shut down the EXE server completely. This isn't the sort of code that you'd want to put in a server with multiple clients, but it's convenient for our purposes, since `ChatterLogger` objects won't be createable externally.

> *If you want to shutdown a true COM server prematurely, you would normally make sure that all connections to clients are broken by calling* `CoDisconnectObject()`. *This only makes sense if the server method has a reference to all the outstanding objects (for example if you have an ATL singleton, or you have a custom class factory). When you call* `CoDisconnectObject()` *it makes sure that any new calls to the specified object will fail with* `CO_E_OBJECTNOTCONNECTED`, *but any outstanding calls will complete. In this example, we don't need to make this call because the logger object is not externally creatable and there is no way for any external clients to get a reference to this object.*

We'll just create a single logger object in `_tWinMain()` that will demonstrate that the code works. Add the code shown below just before the message loop:

```
    _ASSERTE(SUCCEEDED(hRes));

    CComPtr<IChatterLogger> pLogger;
    CStdCreator<CChatterLogger>::CreateInstance(&pLogger);
    pLogger->Start(5);    // Log 5 messages then quit

    MSG msg;
    while (GetMessage(&msg, 0, 0, 0))
        DispatchMessage(&msg);
```

Here I create a `CChatterLogger` object, get its `IChatterLogger` interface and start the logging process. By passing 5 as an argument to `Start()`, I've told the logger to log 5 messages then quit.

This code uses a template class, called `CStdCreator<>`, that simplifies the creation of internal COM objects. It wraps up all the mess in a simple, static, template function, removing the need for multiple parameters and ugly casts. You'll need to add this class definition to `ChatLogger.cpp` just below the `#includes`:

```
template <class YourATLClass>
class CStdCreator
{
public:
    template <class InterfaceClass>
        static HRESULT WINAPI CreateInstance(InterfaceClass** pp)
    {
        return CComCreator< CComObject < YourATLClass > >::CreateInstance(
            NULL,
            __uuidof(InterfaceClass),
            reinterpret_cast<void**>(pp));
    }
};
```

The only step remaining is to change the object map so that logger objects can't be created externally:

```
BEGIN_OBJECT_MAP(ObjectMap)
OBJECT_ENTRY_NON_CREATEABLE(CChatterLogger)
END_OBJECT_MAP()
```

That's all there is to it. You can build and execute the example. The logger will just sit there waiting for events, so you won't see much at first. However, if you use one of the chat clients created previously to send messages, you'll see a message box appear for each message sent. After the fifth message, the logger will have reached its limit and will unload itself.

# Connection Points over DCOM

I mentioned earlier that there was a problem with connection points over DCOM, and this is compounded if the connection point client is a control in Internet Explorer. The problem is that the server will need to call back to the client, and so the client should go to some lengths to ensure that the server account is allowed to do this. Earlier in the chapter, I suggested that you cheat by making the server account the same as the client account using DCOMCnfg. The problem with this method is that you may not be able to determine beforehand what account a client will be using.

It's true that you can use DCOMCnfg to set the server identity to **Launching User**, but this isn't really a solution to the problem. This option is designed for legacy applications, and instructs DCOM to use the security token used by the client rather than creating a new one. NT 4 does not support delegation, and so a security token can only be passed across one machine boundary (in this case, from the client to the server machine). It cannot be sent across *another* machine boundary, which it would need to do in this case – from the server to the client.

This token is being passed back and forth between machines because the client and server processes need to authenticate each other. To prevent spoofing (where a rogue application pretends to be another process), the security layer checks the DCOM client and server to ensure that they are who they say they are.

# Changing DCOM Security

There are two types of security settings: **declarative** and **programmatic**. The former uses entries in the registry that set security either for an individual server, or on a machine-wide basis. Note that the server *must* be an EXE – a DLL server will just take on the settings of the process that loads it. This is precisely the issue when a control is loaded into Internet Explorer: the control takes on the security settings applied to Internet Explorer, causing a problem that I'll address later in this chapter.

> *For more information about the interaction between DCOM security and NT security, you should consult* Professional DCOM Programming.

Assuming the server is packaged in an EXE, you can determine who can launch and access the server via named values in the server's AppID key in the registry. This key is for the *server* – it is not object-specific – and so using declarative security you cannot have different security settings for two different object types in the same EXE. To specify who can launch the server and access the objects in it, you should create the LaunchPermission and AccessPermission named values. These hold NT security access control lists (ACLs). Although you can do this with code, the easiest way to do it is to use DCOMCnfg.

Despite the statement above, DCOMCnfg lists coclasses for the servers whose AppIDs you can manipulate. Don't be confused by this: DCOMCnfg has just displayed the human-readable name of the first coclass served by the server, but the settings changed with DCOMCnfg will affect *all* coclasses in the server. Although DCOMCnfg can be used to set who can launch a server and access the objects created by the server, it does not allow you to set the authentication and impersonation levels for the server. With declarative security, the machine-wide settings for authentication and impersonation levels are used.

> *In Windows NT 5,* DCOMCnfg *will be fixed to list the server names, rather than the name of the first coclass.*

However, a server *can* set these security values programmatically by calling the CoInitializeSecurity() function:

```
HRESULT CoInitializeSecurity(
    PSECURITY_DESCRIPTOR pVoid,   // Points to security descriptor
    LONG cAuthSvc,                // Count of entries in asAuthSvc
    SOLE_AUTHENTICATION_SERVICE* asAuthSvc, // Array of names to register
    void* pReserved1,             // Reserved for future use
    DWORD dwAuthnLevel,           // Default authentication level for proxies
    DWORD dwImpLevel,             // Default impersonation level for proxies
    SOLE_AUTHENTICATION_LIST* pAuthList,    // Authentication info for each
                                  //   authentication service
    DWORD dwCapabilities,         // Additional client and/or server-side
                                  //   capabilities
    void* pReserved3              // Reserved for future use
);
```

The first parameter can be a pointer to an NT `SECURITY_DESCRIPTOR`, or to an object with the `IAccessControl` interface, or to an `AppID`. These three items can be used to give or deny access to objects in the server to certain groups or accounts. In the first two cases, the other parameters of the function allow a server to set authentication and impersonation levels; in the case of passing an `AppID` to the function, the authentication level is specified using the `AuthenticationLevel` named value in the specified `AppID` key.

> **Prior to Service Pack 4, NT 4 returns an error of `0x80070002` (which is the Win32 error `ERROR_FILE_NOT_FOUND`) if there is not an `AuthenticationLevel` named value under the specified `AppID` key. This error will also be returned if the `AccessPermission` is not present. In both cases, you can safely ignore the error because DCOM will just use the machine-wide permissions.**

If you pass an object with an `IAccessControl` interface, COM can call this object to determine whether an account has access to the objects served by the EXE server. If you have a special algorithm to make this determination, you can implement your own object. Alternatively, you can use the system-provided `CLSID_DCOMAccessControl` object that implements both `IAccessControl` and `IPersist`, initialized with the accounts that will have access.

If you pass an NT `SECURITY_DESCRIPTOR`, this will have an ACL (access control list) containing the accounts allowed or denied access to the server's objects; these will be the accounts that you know will try to access the server, and must include the built-in `SYSTEM` account because this is the account that will be used by the system's Server Control Manager to manage the server. A `SECURITY_DESCRIPTOR` also has members for the owner and group. You should ensure that these are set to the owner and group of the server process, because `CoInitializeSecurity()` will use the `AccessCheck()` API function to check the `SECURITY_DESCRIPTOR`, and it requires that the owner and group are set.

The one remaining issue is that NT ACLs specify that particular accounts or groups are allowed or denied a specific access right, but which right should this be? The answer is that the `COM_RIGHTS_EXECUTE` right should be used. Note that the authentication level (the fifth parameter to `CoInitializeSecurity()`) must be at least `RPC_C_AUTH_LEVEL_CONNECT`, since it makes no sense to provide a security descriptor if the users are anonymous. The function will fail if a lesser value is passed.

To prevent ACL checking, you can pass `NULL` for this first parameter, allowing access to all users. However, in this case you should also use the fifth parameter to turn off authentication. If you don't, COM will attempt to authenticate a client even though it will allow all accounts to have access, and there is a possibility that a call to access an object could fail if the server could not authenticate the client.

# CSecurityDescriptor

If you know who should be accessing a server, then you can build up an NT `SECURITY_DESCRIPTOR`, specifying accounts that are allowed or denied access. ATL helps here with a class called `CSecurityDescriptor`. This class has an embedded `SECURITY_DESCRIPTOR` data member that can be accessed externally through a conversion operator. Anywhere that a `PSECURITY_DESCRIPTOR` is required, you can pass an instance of `CSecurityDescriptor`.

That isn't a typo, by the way: the conversion operator will convert a CSecurityDescriptor to a PSECURITY_DESCRIPTOR, which is defined as LPVOID. If you want access to the underlying SECURITY_DESCRIPTOR structure, you will need a PISECURITY_DESCRIPTOR (notice that this starts with PIS and not PS). CoInitializeSecurity(), however, is happy with a PSECURITY_DESCRIPTOR.

A newly-created instance of CSecurityDescriptor has NULL as the pointer, so if you pass this to CoInitializeSecurity(), it is the same as using NULL. To make the object useful, you need to initialize it; doing so will create a new SECURITY_DESCRIPTOR, through which you can add users and groups to allow or deny access. There are three ways to do this:

| Method | Description |
|--------|-------------|
| Initialize() | Creates a SECURITY_DESCRIPTOR that gives access to everyone |
| InitializeFrom ProcessToken() | Creates a SECURITY_DESCRIPTOR that gives access to everyone and sets the owner and group SIDs to be those of the current process |
| InitializeFrom ThreadToken() | Creates a SECURITY_DESCRIPTOR that gives access to everyone and sets the owner and group SIDs to be those of the current thread |

The **owner SID** (Security ID) determines who owns the security descriptor, and hence who can alter it. For DCOM, this should be the SID of the account running the server process. Once a security descriptor is created, you can allow or deny access to particular accounts. To allow an account to have access, you can call Allow(), passing the name of the account and a mask of COM_RIGHTS_EXECUTE. Similarly, to deny an account access you can call Deny(), again passing the account name and a mask of COM_RIGHTS_EXECUTE. Finally, if the security descriptor has allow/deny information for an account and you want to remove this, call Revoke() with the account name.

The access control list must be ordered such that 'deny' entries are before 'allow' entries. The CSecurityDescriptor class ensures that this is done for you. Whenever a new call to Deny() or Allow() is made, the code will create a new ACL with 'deny' entries to the beginning and 'allow' entries at the end.

Remember that when you're creating a security descriptor for CoInitializeSecurity(), you must make sure that the SYSTEM account has access, and you should make the owner of the security descriptor and the group the same as the user that calls CoInitializeSecurity(). This second requirement is easy though, since you can just call InitializeFromProcessToken() or InitializeFromThreadToken().

# Turning off Security

If you decide to allow access to all users, there is another issue that you need to be aware of. When calls are made to an object, the installed security package will attempt to authenticate the user that made the call – that is, it will check to see if they are who they say they are. If authentication cannot be carried out, the call will fail, even if the account is allowed access. The default level is to authenticate users when the first method call is made on an object (RPC_C_AUTHN_LEVEL_CONNECT).

CoInitializeSecurity() can be used to make this check more often – on every method call that is made, for example, or when each packet of a multi-packet request is received. To allow *any* user (even those that the server's host machine cannot authenticate) to have access to an object, the authentication level can be set to RPC_C_AUTHN_LEVEL_NONE. This can be done either by using the fifth parameter or, if you pass an AppID, through the AuthenticationLevel named value.

Note that although the client and server both specify an authentication level, the value set by the server is the minimum allowed, and if the client calls in with a lower value, the call will fail. Assuming that the client level is OK, the value used specifies the default authentication that will be used when a proxy is created in the client. Sometimes, COM will promote certain default, client-set authentication to higher values. If the authentication level set for a particular proxy is not what you require, you can change it on a proxy-by-proxy basis with IClientSecurity::SetBlanket(), or the wrapper function CoSetProxyBlanket().

Before moving on, I must just mention **impersonation**. This is applied on the client side (which in the case of processes with connection points will also mean the server that implements the connection point objects), and is the level of trust that the client offers to the server. The impersonation level tells COM whether the server is allowed to discover who (what account) the client is, and whether it can impersonate the client when accessing some other securable object.

NT 4 allows two levels of impersonation: RPC_C_IMP_LEVEL_IDENTIFY and RPC_C_IMP_LEVEL_IMPERSONATE. The former means that the server can access the client's identity (and discover if the client is allowed access to a securable object), while the latter means that the server can actually impersonate the client when accessing securable objects (on the same machine). For servers that have connection points, this value should be RPC_C_IMP_LEVEL_IMPERSONATE, because the object will want to access the sink object in the client. When you call CoInitializeSecurity() with a security descriptor or an IAccessControl interface pointer, the sixth parameter specifies the impersonation level. If you pass an AppID, then the system default (which is usually RPC_C_IMP_LEVEL_IDENTIFY) is used.

Thus, to allow any user to access the objects in a server, you need to make the following call in both the client and the server before your server does any COM activity:

```
CoInitializeSecurity(NULL, -1, NULL, NULL, RPC_C_AUTHN_LEVEL_NONE,
                RPC_C_IMP_LEVEL_IMPERSONATE, NULL, EOAC_NONE, NULL);
```

The best place for this call is most likely after the call to CoInitializeEx() in _tWinMain().

Calling this in the server isn't usually a problem, but as I mentioned earlier, you won't have access to the process if the client is a COM object implemented in a DLL. By the time the DLL server has been loaded, the client process will have called CoInitializeSecurity() and will certainly have made some COM calls. You can't call CoInitializeSecurity() in a DLL.

The only option here is to allow the client object make calls to a middleman object that calls the remote object. This middleman will look like the remote object to the client (in other words, it will implement IConnectionPointContainer and the other interfaces that the remote object does), and it will look like the client to the remote object (so it will implement a sink object with the appropriate sink interface). The difference is that this object should be in an EXE server, and so you *can* call CoInitializeSecurity().

# Example: Using ChatBuffer Over DCOM

This example will create a middleman object called ChatBufferMM that looks like the ChatBuffer object to a client, and will forward all IChatBuffer method calls to the remote ChatBuffer. The middleman object creates a sink object, ChatBufferMMEvents, to handle the connection point mechanism between the client and the remote ChatBuffer, so that all events generated by ChatBuffer will be handled by this sink object and then forwarded to the connected clients.

When the middleman object is created, it will activate the remote object and then create an instance of ChatBufferMMEvents. The middleman can then pass this sink object the IUnknown pointer of the remote ChatBuffer object, so that it can set up the connection point. Clients create instances of the middleman object, so to allow them make their connection to the remote object via the ChatBufferMMEvents object, the middleman object implements a custom version of IConnectionPointContainer that delegates to the IConnectionPointContainer on ChatBufferMMEvents. Thus, when the client makes a connection to a connection point, it will actually be on the ChatBufferMMEvents object. This scheme is shown in the following diagram:

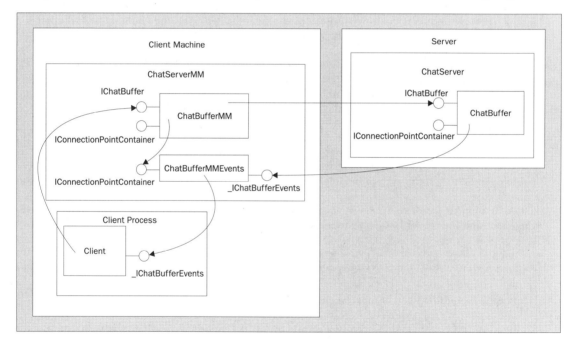

This example will use the middleman object to turn off authentication, and to give all users access to the remote server. Thus the, ChatServerMM and ChatServer servers will both call CoInitializeSecurity() with NULL as the first value, and RPC_C_AUTHN_LEVEL_NONE for the authentication level.

Start by creating an EXE project called ChatServerMM that has a **Simple Object** with a **Short Name** of ChatBufferMM. Note that you should use the **Attributes** tab to make the interface **Custom**. This is because you will need to delete this interface because the object will implement already defined interfaces, and making it custom will reduce the number of changes you will need to make to the ATL class. You *don't* have to give this object support for connection points.

Once the object has been created, you should use the ClassView context menu item Implement Interface... to add the IChatBuffer interface. This Wizard will complain that the type library has not been compiled, but since you don't want to use this project's type library, you can safely ignore this message and click on OK. The Wizard will list all the registered type libraries, and you should check **ChatServer 1.0 Type Library (1.0)**. In the next dialog, you should select the IChatBuffer dual interface.

The Wizard will add support for this interface to the ATL class. If the Object Wizard had created a dual interface when you first inserted the ATL object, then you would have found that when adding a new dual interface, the Wizard changed the interface map to get rid of the ambiguity in getting IDispatch. This is a change you would have had to undo when you deleted the IChatBufferMM interface. Since IChatBufferMM doesn't derive from IDispatch, this ambiguity does not exist.

Now you can edit the header for the ATL class and remove all reference to IChatBufferMM. These are the lines you need to get rid of:

```
public IChatBufferMM,
```

```
COM_INTERFACE_ENTRY(IChatBufferMM)
```

Unfortunately, the Implement Interface Wizard doesn't touch the IDL, so you will need to edit the coclass such that the object supports IChatBuffer, and uses the ChatServer type library to get the interface definitions:

```
importlib("..\ChatServer\ChatServer.tlb");

coclass ChatBufferMM
{
    [default] interface IChatBuffer;
};
```

You also need to remove the definition of IChatBufferMM.

> Note that when you add a new interface through ClassView like this, the Wizard will add definitions of the interface using #import in the object header file. This line will have an *absolute* path. This may be a problem if you share this code with others in a team using an archiving tool like Visual SourceSafe, because the other team members may not have the same directory structure as you. To solve this, you should edit the line to use a relative path.

Next, by hand, add support for IConnectionPointContainer. To begin, derive the class from the interface:

```
class ATL_NO_VTABLE CChatBufferMM :
    public CComObjectRootEx<CComSingleThreadModel>,
    public CComCoClass<CChatBufferMM, &CLSID_ChatBufferMM>,
    public IDispatchImpl<IChatBuffer, &IID_IChatBuffer, &LIBID_CHATSERVERLib>,
    public IConnectionPointContainer
```

Then, add it to the COM map:

```
BEGIN_COM_MAP(CChatBufferMM)
    COM_INTERFACE_ENTRY(IDispatch)
    COM_INTERFACE_ENTRY(IChatBuffer)
    COM_INTERFACE_ENTRY(IConnectionPointContainer)
END_COM_MAP()
```

Finally, add the method prototypes:

```
public:
// IChatBuffer
    STDMETHOD(Say)(BSTR bstrMsg);

// IConnectionPointContainer
    STDMETHOD(EnumConnectionPoints)(IEnumConnectionPoints** ppEnum);
    STDMETHOD(FindConnectionPoint)(REFIID riid, IConnectionPoint** ppCP);
};
```

In addition, I have moved the implementation of Say() to the CPP file. For now, add stubs for the IConnectionPointContainer methods, so that you can compile the code.

```
STDMETHODIMP CChatBufferMM::EnumConnectionPoints(IEnumConnectionPoints** ppEnum)
{
    return E_NOTIMPL;
}

STDMETHODIMP CChatBufferMM::FindConnectionPoint(
                                    REFIID riid, IConnectionPoint** ppCP)
{
    return E_NOTIMPL;
}
```

The Say() method just delegates to the remote object, so the CChatBufferMM class should have a reference to this object:

```
private:
    CComPtr<IChatBuffer> m_pServer;
};
```

This is initialized in FinalConstruct() and released when the class instance is destroyed (and the smart pointer is destroyed), so add the prototype to the class:

```
public:
    CChatBufferMM()
    {
    }

    HRESULT FinalConstruct();
```

The implementation looks like this:

```
HRESULT CChatBufferMM::FinalConstruct()
{
    USES_CONVERSION;
    HRESULT hr;
    CRegKey key;
    TCHAR strServer[MAX_COMPUTERNAME_LENGTH + 1];
    DWORD dwSize = MAX_COMPUTERNAME_LENGTH + 1;

    if(key.Open(HKEY_CURRENT_USER,
                        _T("Software\\Wrox\\ChatBuffer")) == ERROR_SUCCESS)
    {
        key.QueryValue(strServer, _T("Server"), &dwSize);
    }
    else
        strServer[0] = _T('\0');

    COSERVERINFO csi = {0, T2W(strServer), NULL, 0};
    MULTI_QI mqi = {&IID_IChatBuffer, 0, 0};

    TCHAR strThisComputer[MAX_COMPUTERNAME_LENGTH + 1];
    dwSize = MAX_COMPUTERNAME_LENGTH + 1;
    GetComputerName(strThisComputer, &dwSize);

    if(lstrcmpi(strThisComputer, strServer)==0 || lstrlen(strServer)==0)
        hr = CoCreateInstanceEx(
                        CLSID_ChatBuffer, NULL, CLSCTX_ALL, NULL, 1, &mqi);
    else
        hr = CoCreateInstanceEx(
                        CLSID_ChatBuffer, NULL, CLSCTX_ALL, &csi, 1, &mqi);

    if(FAILED(hr))
        return hr;

    m_pServer.Attach(reinterpret_cast<IChatBuffer*>(mqi.pItf));
    return S_OK;
}
```

The middleman object must determine where the ChatServer is located. In this example, the name of the remote host is held in the registry, and the first few lines of the method obtain this value. Next, the code gets the current machine name and compares the two names. If they are the same, the server is on the same machine and the COSERVERINFO structure is not needed. After creating the ChatBuffer object, the code attaches the interface pointer to the m_pServer.

Now you can implement Say():

```
STDMETHODIMP CChatBufferMM::Say(BSTR bstrMsg);
{
    return m_pServer->Say(bstrMsg);
}
```

Of course, the whole point of this exercise is to turn off authentication, so add this line to `_tWinMain()`:

```
CoInitializeSecurity(NULL, -1, NULL, NULL, RPC_C_AUTHN_LEVEL_NONE,
                     RPC_C_IMP_LEVEL_IMPERSONATE, NULL, EOAC_NONE, NULL);
_Module.Init(ObjectMap, hInstance, &LIBID_CHATSERVERMMLib);
_Module.dwThreadID = GetCurrentThreadId();
```

There is one extra change that needs to be made. Do you remember that tools like Visual Basic will examine an object's type library for an outgoing interface to see whether it supports connection points? Although this object has the `IConnectionPointContainer` interface, Visual Basic won't know that unless there is a declared outgoing interface, and so you should add this declaration to the object's `coclass` entry in the IDL file. This is quite safe, because when Visual Basic sees this, it will call `QueryInterface()` for `IConnectionPointContainer`. The middleman object will delegate all calls on this interface to the `ChatBufferMMEvents` object that does the actual work, as you'll see in a moment.

```
coclass ChatBufferMM
{
    [default] interface IChatBuffer;
    [default, source] dispinterface _IChatBufferEvents;
};
```

*Although this code is incomplete, it should compile, and it's worth doing that now to make sure that you have typed everything correctly.*

Next, you need to create the object to handle the events from the remote server. Use the Object Wizard to create a **Simple Object** called `ChatBufferMMEvents`, and use the **Attributes** tab to select **Support Connection** **P**oints.

The first thing you should do with your new object is to edit the IDL file and *delete* the declaration of the `_IChatBufferMMEventsEvents` dispinterface, because this object will implement the already defined `_IChatBufferEvents` interface. You must also delete the mention of this interface from the `coclass` declaration for `ChatBufferMMEvents`.

Since the `ChatBufferMMEvents` object will implement the `_IChatBufferEvents` sink dispinterface, you need to fake this with a `dual` interface, and you can do so with `IChatBufferMMEvents`. Visual Basic and other type library browsers should not have access to information about this, so you should add the `[hidden]` attribute:

```
[
    uuid(F8B29E60-DADE-11D1-9B4D-0060973044A8),
    hidden
]
coclass ChatBufferMMEvents
{
    [default] interface IChatBufferMMEvents;
};
```

This ensures that the Visual Basic IDE will not give a developer the option of creating a ChatBufferMMEvents object – indeed, this object should *only* be created by ChatBufferMM, so to prevent external clients from creating one you should edit the object map in ChatServerMM.cpp:

```
BEGIN_OBJECT_MAP(ObjectMap)
   OBJECT_ENTRY(CLSID_ChatBufferMM, CChatBufferMM)
   OBJECT_ENTRY_NON_CREATEABLE(CChatBufferMMEvents)
END_OBJECT_MAP()
```

This will prevent other clients from creating this object but you will still have code in the object that is used if the object is externally created. So, to go the whole hog, you can remove CComCoClass<> as a base class, since this class is needed for the object to be created externally. However, if you do this, you will need to add the following code to the class, because OBJECT_ENTRY_NON_CREATEABLE() references the GetCategoryMap() method:

```
static const struct _ATL_CATMAP_ENTRY* GetCategoryMap()
{
    return NULL;
};
```

You can use the interface added to the object by the Object Wizard to implement the sink dispinterface, as was done earlier in this chapter. To do this, use ClassView to add the OnNewMessage() event to IChatBufferMMEvents with a DISPID of 1, and then add the following to the COM map:

```
COM_INTERFACE_ENTRY_IID(DIID__IChatBufferEvents, IChatBufferMMEvents)
```

You will also need to add this outgoing interface to the connection point map, so use the ClassView context menu to add the connection point proxy class, as you did earlier with ChatServer. Right click on CChatBufferMMEvents, select **Implement Connection Point...**, and use **Add Typelib...** to get hold of the type library for ChatServer. Select the _IChatBufferEvents interface, and click OK. Again, check that the Wizard has put the correct entry into the connection point map. You may also decide to remove the excessive entry for IConnectionPointContainer from the COM map.

The implementation for OnNewMessage() is trivial:

```
STDMETHODIMP CChatBufferMMEvents::OnNewMessage(BSTR bstrMsg)
{
    Fire_OnNewMessage(bstrMsg);
    return S_OK;
}
```

Of course, this assumes that the server has generated the event, and to allow it to do this the ChatBufferMMEvents object must set up the connection. This needs two data items: an IUnknown interface pointer to the server, and a DWORD for the result of the call to AtlAdvise():

```
private:
    CComPtr<IUnknown> m_pServer;
    DWORD m_dwCookie;
};
```

To make the connection, the object must have an initialized interface pointer, and so the
ChatBufferMM object must call a method, say Init(), on the ChatBufferMMEvents object
when it is created (remember that COM objects don't have constructors – yet). Add Init() to the
IChatBufferMMEvents interface with this IDL:

```
[id(2)] HRESULT Init([in] IUnknown* pUnk);
```

It is implemented like this; the CComPtr<>::Advise() function just calls AtlAdvise():

```
STDMETHODIMP CChatBufferMMEvents::Init(IUnknown *pUnk)
{
    if (!m_pServer)
    {
        m_pServer.Attach(pUnk);
        return m_pServer.Advise(
                    GetUnknown(), DIID__IChatBufferEvents, &m_dwCookie);
    }
    return S_OK;
}
```

Similarly, the sink object must be told that it should break the connection, and this is done in a
method called Die():

```
[id(3)] HRESULT Die();
```

This is implemented like so:

```
STDMETHODIMP CChatBufferMMEvents::Die()
{
    return AtlUnadvise(m_pServer, DIID__IChatBufferEvents, m_dwCookie);
}
```

This breaks the connection, but m_pServer is still a valid interface pointer to the remote object.
This is not a problem, however, because it's a smart pointer, and so the interface will be released
when the smart pointer is destroyed. The ChatBufferMMEvents object will be destroyed as soon as
the smart pointer to it in the ChatBufferMM object is destroyed. I have not put the call to
AtlUnadvise() in the FinalRelease() method of CChatBufferMMEvents, because this
would prevent the method from ever being called.

Finally, you can make the last adjustments to the ChatBufferMM object. Add a data member for the
interface pointer to the object:

```
private:
    CComPtr<IChatBuffer> m_pServer;
    CComPtr<IConnectionPointContainer> m_pSinker;
};
```

This object is created in FinalConstruct(), so add this to ChatBufferMM.cpp:

```
#include "ChatBufferMMEvents.h"
```

Then, add this code to `FinalConstruct()`, in which the `ChatBufferMMEvents` object is first created and then initialized with the `ChatBuffer` remote object:

```
m_pServer.Attach(reinterpret_cast<IChatBuffer*>(mqi.pItf));

CComObject<CChatBufferMMEvents>* pObj;
hr = CComObject<CChatBufferMMEvents>::CreateInstance(&pObj);
if(FAILED(hr))
    return hr;

hr = pObj->QueryInterface(IID_IConnectionPointContainer, (void**)&m_pSinker);
if(FAILED(hr))
{
    delete pObj;
    return hr;
}
CComQIPtr<IChatBufferMMEvents> pInit;
pInit = m_pSinker;
return pInit->Init(m_pServer);
}
```

The sink object is told to die in the `FinalRelease()`, so add the prototype:

```
void FinalRelease();
```

And this implementation:

```
void CChatBufferMM::FinalRelease()
{
    CComQIPtr<IChatBufferMMEvents> pObj;
    pObj = m_pSinker;
    pObj->Die();
}
```

This effectively calls `QueryInterface()` for the `IChatBufferMMEvents` interface, through which it can call `Die()` to tell the object to break the bi-directional connection to the server.

This does not go against the warnings I gave earlier, because the reference counts on the `ChatBufferMM` object reflect the clients that are connected, so when the last client shuts down, `FinalRelease()` will be called. This will then tell the `ChatBufferMMEvents` object to die. It cannot do this by calling `Release()`, because the remote object will have a reference on the object, so instead the `Die()` method is called explicitly.

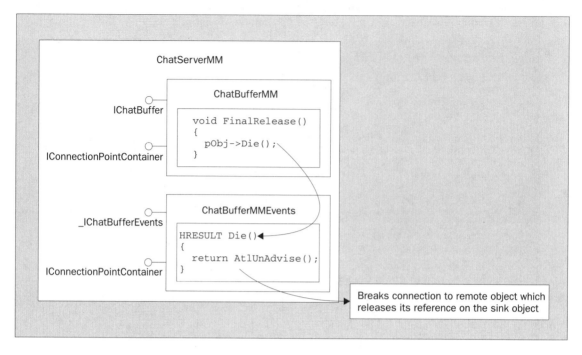

Finally, now that you have the sink object, you can implement the connection point container interface:

```
STDMETHODIMP CChatBufferMM::EnumConnectionPoints(IEnumConnectionPoints** ppEnum)
{
    return m_pSinker->EnumConnectionPoints(ppEnum);
}

STDMETHODIMP CChatBufferMM::FindConnectionPoint(
                                    REFIID riid, IConnectionPoint** ppCP)
{
    return m_pSinker->FindConnectionPoint(riid, ppCP);
}
```

The middleman will connect to the `ChatServer` object on a remote machine, but the `IChatBuffer` interface uses type library marshaling, so you need to make sure that the type library defining this interface is registered on the client machine. To do this, you need to add the type library to the `ChatServerMM` project as a resource, and change the registration code to register and unregister it.

The first thing to do is to add the type library as a resource, so from the <u>V</u>iew menu, click on Resource <u>I</u>ncludes.... In the <u>C</u>ompile-time directives, add:

```
2 TYPELIB "..\ChatServer\ChatServer.tlb"
```

Ignore any warnings that the IDE gives you. Next, you need to make sure that when the server is registered, it will register this type library. To do this you need to change _tWinMain().

```
while (lpszToken != NULL)
{
    if (lstrcmpi(lpszToken, _T("UnregServer"))==0)
    {
        _Module.UpdateRegistryFromResource(IDR_ChatServerMM, FALSE);
        nRet = _Module.UnregisterServer(TRUE);
        nRet = _Module.UnRegisterTypeLib(_T("\\2"));
        bRun = FALSE;
        break;
    }
    if (lstrcmpi(lpszToken, _T("RegServer"))==0)
    {
        _Module.UpdateRegistryFromResource(IDR_ChatServerMM, TRUE);
        nRet = _Module.RegisterServer(TRUE);
        nRet = _Module.RegisterTypeLib(_T("\\2"));
        bRun = FALSE;
        break;
    }
    lpszToken = FindOneOf(lpszToken, szTokens);
}
```

These two lines will make sure that the new type library resource is registered. Why the odd syntax? Well, RegisterTypeLib() ultimately ends up in a call to the API ::RegisterTypeLib(), and if this is passed a path to a module (EXE or DLL), it will register the type library in that module. In fact, it will register the *first* type library resource it finds. To get it to register another type library resource, you need to append the path with \n, where n is the ID of the resource. CComModule::RegisterTypeLib() takes a string, and hence '\2' is used as a parameter. Both objects are now complete, so you can compile the project.

The middleman server is complete, but there's one further change that needs to be made to the actual chat server project. The ChatServer EXE must *also* turn off authentication, so add the following line to _tWinMain():

```
CoInitializeSecurity(NULL, -1, NULL, NULL, RPC_C_AUTHN_LEVEL_NONE,
            RPC_C_IMP_LEVEL_IMPERSONATE, NULL, EOAC_NONE, NULL);
_Module.Init(ObjectMap, hInstance, &LIBID_CHATSERVERLib);
_Module.dwThreadID = GetCurrentThreadId();
```

## Clients

So that you can test the code, you need to change the two clients that you have developed so far to access the middleman object rather than the actual chat server object. First, load the Visual Basic project and through the References dialog uncheck ChatServer 1.0 Type Library and check ChatServerMM 1.0 Type Library.

Next, change the declaration at the top of the form code:

```
Private WithEvents ChatServer As ChatBufferMM
```

Also, change `Form_Load`:

```
Private Sub Form_Load()
    strUser = InputBox("Your Name?", "Chatter", "User")
    Caption = Caption + " - " + strUser
    Set ChatServer = New ChatBufferMM
End Sub
```

That's all you need to do here, but the client control needs some work too. Open the control header and add the following line:

```
#import "..\ChatServerMM\ChatServerMM.tlb" no_namespace, \
                      named_guids, raw_interfaces_only, raw_native_types
```

And finally, change `InPlaceActivate()`:

```
        hr = m_pServer.CoCreateInstance(CLSID_ChatBufferMM);
```

This can now be compiled.

# Testing the ChatServer

Copy `ChatServerMM.exe` to the client machines, and register it. Also copy the appropriate client. (Note that the Visual Basic client requires `MSVBVM60.dll` and the updated version of `OLEAut32.dll` that's installed with Visual Studio 6.0). If you intend to use the control, then you will need to register it. Use the RegEdit tool to add the following key:

```
HKEY_CURRENT_USER\Software\Wrox\ChatBuffer
```

Add a string value called `Server`, and edit it to have the name of the server machine.

Copy `ChatServer.exe` to the server machine, and register it. Run `DCOMCnfg` and change the launch permission for `ChatBuffer Class` to allow `Everyone` to launch the server; you do not need to change the access permissions because the call to `CoInitializeSecurity()` will allow anonymous access. However, you *will* need to use the **Identity** tab to change the identity from the default (**Launching User**) to **This User**, and add the name of a local or domain account (it does not matter which).

Now you're ready for the tests. On one of the client machines, start one of the client programs (either the Visual Basic client or the `Chatter.htm` file created by the Object Wizard) and give your user name when asked. Do the same on another client machine, but use a different user name so that you can verify that the messages are from different clients. Now you should be able to send messages using the **Send Message** button, and receive messages from other clients.

To convince yourself that the middleman object is being used, you should run Task Manager on the client and server machines. When the client (say, Chatter.exe) starts, you should find that the Processes list contains Chatter.exe and ChatServerMM.exe. Similarly, the server machine should have ChatServer.exe started. When the client process shuts down, you should notice that a few seconds later ChatServerMM.exe will close on the client machine and ChatServer.exe will shut down on the server machine.

Finally, to be absolutely sure that authentication is turned off, you should try connecting to the server using a client logged on with an account unknown to the server machine.

# Improvements to ChatServer

Of course, there are many ways that you can improve on this design, but here are a few suggestions. You could make the ChatServer object implement an interface called, perhaps, IUserDetails, something like this:

```
interface IUserDetails : IDispatch
{
    [id(1)] HRESULT RegisterName([in] BSTR bstrName);
    [id(2)] HRESULT UnregisterName([in] BSTR bstrName);
    [id(3)] HRESULT EnumNames([out] LPVARIANT pEnum);
};
```

The ChatServer object could hold a list of registered names, and RegisterName() will add a new name to this list. If it is called with an already registered name, the function can return a failure HRESULT, and the user will have to try another name. UnregisterName() can be called when a client shuts down, and removes the name from the list.

The ChatServer could also add an event to the _IChatBufferEvents dispinterface:

```
    [id(4)] HRESULT OnName([in] BSTR bstrName, [in] BOOL bAdd);
```

The clients could show a list box of connected users, and handle this event by either adding a name when bAdd is true, or removing a name when it is false. This, however, just deals with changes to the *connected* clients, so when a client first 'attaches', it should call EnumNames() to get an enumerator that will give access to all the names.

# Summary

Bi-directional communication doesn't *require* connection points, but you will find that in most situations it is better to use connection points rather than trying to implement your own. In particular, if you are using VBScript, you have no choice but to use connection points. Also, the IDE support in Visual Basic 6 makes using connection points much easier than using your own sink interfaces.

ATL 3.0 uses the same classes to implement connection points as its predecessor – that is, the connection point container implementation is in IConnectionPointContainerImpl<>, and the connection point implementation provided by IConnectionPointImpl<>. This class is added to your class as a proxy class created through ClassView. The connection point map maps an outgoing interface IID to the base class proxy class that implements the connection point.

The big change in ATL 3.0 is the sink map. This is has been added for the new composite control type, which allows you to host other add ActiveX controls within your own. These child controls can generate events, and so your control must be able to implement appropriate sink interfaces and handle the events. The sink map allows you to add these handler methods using the control's IDispatch interface. In fact, the sink map is more versatile than this implies. It can be used independently of composite controls, as you saw in the IDispEventImpl<> example.

The big changes in Visual C++ 6.0 Wizards are the fixing of the bugs in the connection point proxy generator (and the addition of a few new ones in the ClassView Wizard), and moving it so that it's a context menu item in ClassView. Object Wizard has also been improved, and it reasonably assumes that if an object has been specified to Support Connection Points, then it will need an outgoing interface, so it generates one for you.

In this chapter, I have shown you how to use these tools, and I have addressed that often-discussed and perennial problem of implementing connection points over DCOM. If the client is a control (and therefore in-process), the only way that you can ensure the server will get access to the sink interface of the client is by using a middleman object. The example in this chapter showed you how to configure the security context of the object using such a technique.

# 9

# ATL Window Classes

A great deal of your interaction with Windows is through controls. Dialogs are composed of controls, which may be Windows controls – window classes that are usually DLL-based – or, more often these days, ActiveX controls – visual, in-process COM objects.

Controls are very much dependent upon a windowing system, since they provide visual feedback to the user. This means that when you write a control, you have to think about not only the COM aspect of the development work, but also the Windows aspect.

One area where Windows and COM have complementary mechanisms is in the handling of events. A control can be called through one of its COM interfaces, or it can be sent a message from Windows. In some cases, COM methods are called as a direct result of Windows messages. ATL helps here by using a **message map** that allows you to associate a window message with a method in your class; to implement a message map, a class must be derived from CMessageMap. Also, Visual C++ provides a message map Wizard (available via ClassView) that allows you to add message handlers with a minimum of fuss.

ATL provides many classes to wrap windows. CWindow, for example, is a thin wrapper around the Win32 windowing functions. One of the uses of this class is to wrap Windows controls on a composite control. Another ATL class is CAxDialogImpl<>, which is used to implement dialogs. This can be used to create a modal or a modeless dialog, and it's also used as the basis for the view of a composite control. Further, if you decide that you want to 'superclass' an existing window class or 'subclass' an existing window, you can do this using CContainedWindow. This class handles all the code required for registering a new window class, and for accessing existing window classes. The Object Wizard will create a data member of this class when you specify that your control is to be based on a window class.

In this chapter, we'll look at message maps, the ATL window classes mentioned above, and several more besides.

# Window Terminology

There's a lot of terminology involved with windows, so before we get too deep into the technical details, here's a quick summary.

A **window class** *is not* a C++ class; it is a set of attributes that Windows uses as a template to create a window. Each window class has a **window procedure** that processes messages for windows of that class. Window classes are registered with Windows using the `RegisterClassEx()` API. This can be used to make a window class available to more than one process, and is how standard controls like edit boxes and list boxes have a standard window procedure.

An **ATL window class** *is* a C++ class used to encapsulate the functionality of a window. Examples include `CWindow`, `CContainedWindow`, `CWindowImpl<>`, and `CAxDialogImpl<>`.

**Subclassing** is the mechanism whereby you replace the window procedure used to handle messages with your own procedure. There are two forms: **instance subclassing**, which replaces the window procedure for a single existing window instance, and **global subclassing** that replaces the window procedure that will be used for all newly created instances of a particular window class.

**Superclassing** is a technique where you create a new window class based on another (already registered) window class. In essence, you supply your own window procedure, and the default window procedure is then supplied by the class that you're superclassing. When you base your ATL control on a Windows control, you are actually creating a **contained window** that superclasses that particular Windows control.

ATL lets you perform both subclassing and superclassing.

# Message Maps

A message map is used to map a window message to a handler function in your class. Typically, a message map looks something like this:

```
BEGIN_MSG_MAP(CMyCtrl)
    MESSAGE_HANDLER(WM_CREATE, OnCreate)
    CHAIN_MSG_MAP(CComControl<CMyCtrl>)
END_MSG_MAP()
```

Here, the `MESSAGE_HANDLER()` entry says that when the control is sent the `WM_CREATE` message, `OnCreate()` will be called:

```
LRESULT OnCreate(UINT, WPARAM, LPARAM, BOOL&);
```

The `CHAIN_MSG_MAP()` entry says that any other messages will be forwarded to the message map in the `CComControl<>` base class. If this does not handle the message, it will be passed to the default message handler, as is normal practice for Windows programs. As you can see, the message map is really quite straightforward.

# Adding Message Handlers

Adding handlers is also straightforward: right-click on your class in ClassView and then choose Add Windows Message Handler... from the context menu:

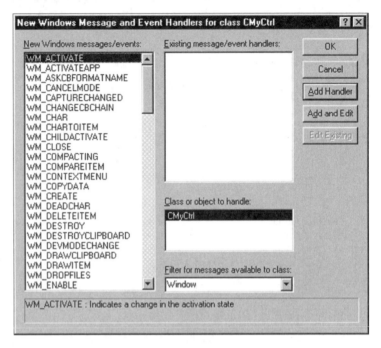

This dialog lists all the messages that are pertinent to the control selected in the Class or object to handle box. The Wizard will add your ATL class and the IDs of any child Windows or ActiveX controls to this box. You can use the Filter for messages available to class dropdown to filter the messages placed in the left hand list box so that only those pertinent to the type of window are shown. The possible filter types are:

- ❑ Child Window
- ❑ Dialog
- ❑ MDI Child Frame
- ❑ Topmost Frame
- ❑ Window
- ❑ Not a Window

The Window option is the most wide-ranging, allowing you to see all the messages that a window can receive. Not a Window is the most restrictive, displaying only non-Windows events.

To add a handler for a particular message, select it in the left-hand list box and then click on Add Handler to add the message to the list in the top right corner. When the dialog is closed, it will add the message to the message map and a suitable handler to your class. Alternatively, you can choose Add and Edit to add the message and close the dialog in one go.

*Note that once you have added a message handler, the only way to remove it is by hand – there is no button on the Wizard to do this.*

The Wizard does not attempt to interpret the parameters of the message. If you add a handler for, say, WM_KEYDOWN, it will *not* create a handler that interprets the WPARAM parameter as a virtual key code and the LPARAM as data about the key. In this way, it is deficient compared with MFC message maps, which do this message cracking for you.

# CMessageMap

All classes that maintain a window will use a message map, and so must derive from CMessageMap. The ATL class CWindowImpl<> does this, so CMessageMap is also a base class for the classes derived from CWindowImpl<>:

- ❑ CDialogImpl<>
- ❑ CAxDialogImpl<>
- ❑ CComControl<>
- ❑ CComCompositeControl<>

*Note that* CComControl<> *takes a window class as a template parameter. This parameter is used as a base class and* CWindowImpl<> *is the default.*

CMessageMap is an abstract class and looks like this:

```
class ATL_NO_VTABLE CMessageMap
{
public:
    virtual BOOL ProcessWindowMessage(HWND hWnd, UINT uMsg, WPARAM wParam,
                LPARAM lParam, LRESULT& lResult, DWORD dwMsgMapID) = 0;
};
```

This single method is called by the window procedure for the window. The implementation of ProcessWindowMessage() is added to your class by the message map macros. The BEGIN_MSG_MAP() macro looks like this:

```
#define BEGIN_MSG_MAP(theClass) \
public: \
    BOOL ProcessWindowMessage(HWND hWnd, UINT uMsg, WPARAM wParam, \
            LPARAM lParam, LRESULT& lResult, DWORD dwMsgMapID = 0) \
    { \
        BOOL bHandled = TRUE; \
        hWnd; \
        uMsg; \
        wParam; \
        lParam; \
        lResult; \
        bHandled; \
        switch(dwMsgMapID) \
        { \
        case 0:
```

BEGIN_MSG_MAP() *lists the parameters that are passed to the*
ProcessWindowMessage() *method to prevent the compiler from issuing a warning that a parameter has not been used. Curiously, the macro lists* bHandled, *despite having already given it a value.*

`END_MSG_MAP()` provides the end of the method, and looks like this:

```
#define END_MSG_MAP() \
        break; \
    default: \
        ATLTRACE2(atlTraceWindowing, 0, \
        _T("Invalid message map ID (%i)\n"), dwMsgMapID); \
        ATLASSERT(FALSE); \
        break; \
    } \
    return FALSE; \
}
```

As you can see, these macros set up a `switch` statement. This is used to select the required message map – a control may have alternate message maps within a single class, as you'll see later.

*Note that* `DECLARE_EMPTY_MSG_MAP()` *can be used to replace* `BEGIN_MSG_MAP()` *and* `END_MSG_MAP()` *to provide a stub implementation for* `ProcessWindowMessage()` *for classes that do not handle messages but derive indirectly from* `CMessageMap`.

# Message Handling Macros

Each message map is a series of `if` statements that are provided by the macros added to the map. `MESSAGE_HANDLER()`, for example, looks like this:

```
#define MESSAGE_HANDLER(msg, func) \
    if(uMsg == msg) \
    { \
        bHandled = TRUE; \
        lResult = func(uMsg, wParam, lParam, bHandled); \
        if(bHandled) \
            return TRUE; \
    }
```

Thus, multiple `MESSAGE_HANDLER()`s will result in a series of `if` statements, resembling the big `switch` statements that C programmers used to use in the old days of Windows development.

There are three main groups of message handling macros that you can use in a message map:

- ❑ Message handlers (for `WM_` messages)
- ❑ Command handlers (for `WM_COMMAND` messages)
- ❑ Notification handlers (for `WM_NOTIFY` messages)

Each of these groups requires a different prototype for the message handling function, but all three types take a reference to a `BOOL` as the final parameter (called `bHandled`). Your code should use this to specify whether it handled the message. The parameter is set to `TRUE` before the handler function is called, so if your handler *does* deal with the message, you need not change the value of this parameter. If it *does not* handle the message, you should change this parameter to `FALSE`, which will mean that the message is be passed to subsequent entries in the message map. In this case, it may be passed on to other message handlers in the same class, or to another message map through the chaining mechanism. If the message isn't handled by any of the entries in the map, it will be passed on to the default window procedure via the Win32 `DefWindowProc()` API function.

We'll examine each of these groups more closely in the next three sections.

## Message Handlers

Message handlers have the following prototype:

```
LRESULT MessageHandler(UINT uMsg, WPARAM wParam, LPARAM lParam, BOOL& bHandled);
```

The message map macros are:

| Macro | Description |
|---|---|
| MESSAGE_HANDLER (msg, func) | Gives the function that will handle a message |
| MESSAGE_RANGE_HANDLER (msgFirst, msgLast, func) | Gives the range of messages and the single function that will handle them |

These macros pass the window message and its parameters to the handler function as the first three parameters. As mentioned before, there is no message cracking carried out – you have to interpret the parameters in an appropriate manner yourself.

MESSAGE_HANDLER() specifies that a single message will be handled by a particular member function. In this situation, you can ignore the uMsg parameter passed to the handler function. MESSAGE_RANGE_HANDLER() specifies that a range of messages are handled by a single function, and you can use it to indicate the first and last message of the range. In this situation, you can tell which of the messages in the range is currently being handled by your function by checking the uMsg parameter. For example:

```
BEGIN_MSG_MAP(CMyCtrl)
    MESSAGE_RANGE_HANDLER(WM_MOUSEFIRST, WM_MOUSELAST, MouseHandler)
    CHAIN_MSG_MAP(CComControl<CMyCtrl>)
END_MSG_MAP()
```

This specifies that all mouse messages will be handled by the MouseHandler() function:

```
LRESULT MouseHandler(UINT uMsg, WPARAM wParam, LPARAM lParam, BOOL& bHandled)
{
    switch(uMsg)
    {
    case WM_MOUSEMOVE:
        break;
    case WM_LBUTTONDOWN:
        break;
    case WM_LBUTTONUP:
        break;
    case WM_LBUTTONDBLCLK:
        break;
    case WM_RBUTTONDOWN:
        break;
    case WM_RBUTTONUP:
        break;
```

```
        case WM_RBUTTONDBLCLK:
            break;
        default:
            break;
        }
        return 0;
    }
```

I haven't filled in the details, but you can see that by using the range handler macro, you can centralize related code.

## Command Handlers

Command messages are sent when a contained control sends a notification to its parent. The types of controls and the messages that can be handled are shown in the following table:

| Windows Control Type | Notification Codes |
| --- | --- |
| Animation Controls | ACN_ |
| Buttons | BN_ |
| Combo Boxes | CBN_ |
| Edit Controls | EN_ |
| List Boxes | LBN_ |
| Static Controls | STN_ |

There are two ways for a control to notify its parent about an event. Command messages are the older mechanism, so most of the controls you see in the table are basic Windows controls. The exception (there's always one) is the animation control, which is a common control.

The easiest way to add a message handler for a control is to use the message handler Wizard from the **Add Windows Message Handler...** context menu item. Since these are Windows controls, there is no way that the Wizard can ask the control what messages it can generate, so the messages that you see in the Wizard are those that the author of the Wizard has chosen for you as typical notifications. If you have a button, for example, the Wizard will give you the option of handling BN_CLICKED and BN_DOUBLECLICKED, but not the BN_KILLFOCUS or BN_SETFOCUS notifications. Although these last two notifications are less useful than the click notifications, you may still want to handle them. If you need to do this, you must edit the message map by hand to add the correct command macro and add an appropriate handler function.

Commands are sent from a control to its parent, and the WM_COMMAND message contains the ID of the control and the notification code. The COMMAND_ macros we'll discuss in a moment crack the message into the notification code, the control ID, and the window handle of the control. These are passed to the handler function, which has the following prototype:

```
LRESULT CommandHandler(
            WORD wNotifyCode, WORD wID, HWND hWndCtl, BOOL& bHandled);
```

The relevant message map entries are:

| Macro | Description |
|---|---|
| `COMMAND_HANDLER(id, code, func)` | Gives the function that will handle a `WM_COMMAND` message from a particular window |
| `COMMAND_CODE_HANDLER(code, func)` | Gives the function that will handle a message sent via `WM_COMMAND` |
| `COMMAND_ID_HANDLER(id, func)` | Gives the single function that will handle all the command messages for a window |
| `COMMAND_RANGE_HANDLER(idFirst, idLast, func)` | Gives the single function that will handle messages for a range of windows |

`COMMAND_HANDLER()` allows you to specify a function that will be used when a specific notification code comes in from a control with a particular ID; `COMMAND_CODE_HANDLER()` specifies a function that will be used when a specific notification code is received (irrespective of the source control). `COMMAND_ID_HANDLER()` gives the function that will handle all notifications from a specific control, and finally `COMMAND_RANGE_HANDLER()` specifies the function that handles notification messages from the specified range of control IDs.

### Example: Command Handlers

For example, imagine that you have a composite control with a list box (`IDC_MEMBERS`), two edit boxes (`IDC_FIRSTNAME` and `IDC_LASTNAME`), and a button (`IDC_ADDMEMBER`). The button is initially disabled and should only be enabled when either or both of the edit boxes contain text. When the button is clicked, the handler should read the text in the two edit boxes, construct a 'full name' string from the first name and the last name, and add it to the list box. The message map could look like this:

```
BEGIN_MSG_MAP(CMemberList)
    CHAIN_MSG_MAP(CComCompositeControl<CMemberList>)
    COMMAND_CODE_HANDLER(EN_CHANGE, OnCheckText)
    COMMAND_HANDLER(IDC_ADDMEMBER, BN_CLICKED, OnAddMember)
    COMMAND_ID_HANDLER(IDC_MEMBERS, OnMembersList)
END_MSG_MAP()
```

The `COMMAND_CODE_HANDLER()` is used to determine whether the button should be enabled. Remember, I have said that it does not matter which edit box has text, so long as one of them does. The handler will be called if the text changes in *either* edit box (or in any edit boxes subsequently added to the control). The function could look like this:

```
LRESULT OnCheckText(WORD wNotifyCode, WORD wID, HWND hWndCtl, BOOL& bHandled)
{
    CWindow wndName;
    bool bHasText = false;

    // Find out if either of the name boxes contains text
    wndName = GetDlgItem(IDC_FIRSTNAME);
    bHasText = (wndName.GetWindowTextLength() > 0);
```

```
        wndName = GetDlgItem(IDC_LASTNAME);
        bHasText |= (wndName.GetWindowTextLength() > 0);

        // Enable or disable the Add Member button
        CWindow(GetDlgItem(IDC_ADDMEMBER)).EnableWindow(bHasText);
        return 0;
    }
```

Notice that I am using the CWindow class to wrap the HWND returned from the GetDlgItem() method; I'll give more details of this class later on. Incidentally, the composite control class also derives from CWindow, which implements the GetDlgItem() function used here.

When the user clicks on the button, this is handled by the OnAddMember() method. This handles the specific situation of the user clicking on this particular control, which is the reason why COMMAND_HANDLER() is used. The function could look like this:

```
    LRESULT OnAddMember(WORD wNotifyCode, WORD wID, HWND hWndCtl, BOOL& bHandled)
    {
        USES_CONVERSION;
        CWindow wnd;

        CComBSTR bstr;
        wnd = GetDlgItem(IDC_FIRSTNAME);
        wnd.GetWindowText(&bstr);
        wnd.SetWindowText(_T(""));

        CComBSTR bstrName = bstr;
        wnd = GetDlgItem(IDC_LASTNAME);
        wnd.GetWindowText(&bstr);
        wnd.SetWindowText(_T(""));

        if(bstrName.Length() > 0 && bstr.Length() > 0)
            bstrName += L" ";

        bstrName += bstr;

        wnd = GetDlgItem(IDC_MEMBERS);
        wnd.SendMessage(LB_ADDSTRING, 0, reinterpret_cast<LPARAM>(W2CT(bstrName)));
        return 0;
    }
```

This gets the text from an edit box using CWindow::GetWindowText(); one of the overloaded versions of this method takes a pointer to a BSTR. Through the use of smart pointers, the function checks to see if the BSTR already has a value and if so, it will free it, get hold of the text in the window, and fill the BSTR with it. I use a CComBSTR here for two reasons: firstly, it will manage the BSTR for me and will call SysFreeString() as appropriate; and secondly, it has an operator+=() that I can use to append text to an existing BSTR.

Note that ATL has no support for specific Windows controls, so to add the full name to the list box I have to send it the LB_ADDSTRING message. After reading text from the edit boxes, the code clears them; since this changes the text in the edit boxes, OnCheckText() will be called. When both boxes are cleared, OnCheckText() will disable the button.

The final entry in the sample message map, COMMAND_ID_HANDLER(), specifies that all messages sent by the list box will be handled by OnMembersList(). Imagine that the names in the list box are members of a club, and that the composite control is used to trace the movements of particular members. The control could allow an operator to click on a name to see if the member is currently using the club, or double-click on it to get further details about the member.

Since both of these operations require that the control should get the full name of the member selected in the list box, we could centralize this code in OnMembersList():

```
LRESULT OnMembersList( WORD wNotifyCode, WORD wID, HWND hWndCtl, BOOL& bHandled)
{
    CWindow wnd;
    wnd = GetDlgItem(IDC_MEMBERS);

    int index = wnd.SendMessage(LB_GETCURSEL);
    int size = wnd.SendMessage(LB_GETTEXTLEN, index);

    LPTSTR strName = new TCHAR[size + 1];
    wnd.SendMessage(LB_GETTEXT, index, reinterpret_cast<LPARAM>(strName));

    if(wNotifyCode == LBN_SELCHANGE)
        CheckIfMemberIsOnSite(strName);

    if(wNotifyCode == LBN_DBLCLK)
        ShowMemberDetails(strName);

    delete [] strName;
    return 0;
}
```

*You'll find a fully implemented project that includes all the functions from this and the other examples in this section in the source code that you can download from the Wrox Press web site. The project in question is called* MessageHandling.

## Notification Handlers

The other type of message comes in the forms of the WM_NOTIFY message, which is typically sent by Windows common controls:

| Common Control Type | Notification Codes | Window Class |
|---|---|---|
| General Notifications | NM_ | - |
| Extended Combo Box | CBEN_ | ComboBoxEx32 |
| Date and Time Picker | DTN_ | SysDateTimePick32 |
| Header Control | HDN_ | SysHeader32 |
| IP Address Control | IPN_ | SysIPAddress32 |
| List View | LVN_ | SysListView32 |
| Month Calendar Controls | MCN_ | SysMonthCal32 |

| Common Control Type | Notification Codes | Window Class |
| --- | --- | --- |
| Pager Controls | PGN_ | SysPager |
| Rebar Control | RBN_ | ReBarWindow32 |
| Rich Edit | EN_ | RichEdit |
| Status Bar | SBN_ | msctls_statusbar32 |
| Tab Control | TCN_ | SysTabControl32 |
| Toolbar Control | TBN_ | ToolbarWindow32 |
| ToolTip Control | TTN_ | tooltips_class32 |
| TreeView Control | TVN_ | SysTreeView32 |
| Up-Down Control | UDN_ | msctls_updown32 |

You can handle these messages using one of the NOTIFY_ macros:

| Macro | Description |
| --- | --- |
| NOTIFY_HANDLER(id, code, func) | Gives the function that will handle the notification from a particular control |
| NOTIFY_CODE_HANDLER(code, func) | Gives the function that will handle a particular notification code |
| NOTIFY_ID_HANDLER(id, func) | Gives the single function that will handle all notifications from a particular control |
| NOTIFY_RANGE_HANDLER (idFirst, idLast, func) | Gives the single function that will handle all notification messages from the controls in a particular range |

As with the command handlers before them, these allow you to handle a single message from a single control (NOTIFY_HANDLER()), where you have to specify the control ID, the notification code and the handler function; a particular message from any control (NOTIFY_CODE_HANDLER()), where you have to give the message and the handler; any messages from a particular control (NOTIFY_ID_HANDLER()), where you have to specify the control ID and the handler; or any message from a range of controls (NOTIFY_RANGE_HANDLER()) where you have to specify the range of control IDs.

The handler functions should have this prototype:

```
LRESULT NotifyHandler(int idCtrl, LPNMHDR pnmh, BOOL& bHandled);
```

The WM_NOTIFY message is passed the control ID in the WPARAM and a pointer to a NMHDR structure in the LPARAM. This is in contrast to the WM_COMMAND message, which tries to get all the message data in the two parameters. NMHDR looks like this:

```
typedef struct tagNMHDR
{
    HWND hwndFrom;
    UINT idFrom;
    UINT code;
} NMHDR;
```

At first, it's not clear what's being gained here – after all, this is just the information that
WM_COMMAND packs into the LPARAM and WPARAM parameters. In fact, though, different common
controls will actually pass a pointer to a structure specific to the control. In effect, these structures are
'derived' from NMHDR, although of course because Windows is based on C, there is no concept of
structure derivation. Instead, the first member of the control-specific structure is an NMHDR whose
members can be accessed by using a simple C cast.

The tree view control, for example, will send a pointer to an NMTREEVIEW structure in LPARAM for
some of its notification messages (TVN_ITEMEXPANDED, for instance):

```
typedef struct tagNMTREEVIEW
{
    NMHDR hdr;
    UINT action;
    TVITEM itemOld;
    TVITEM itemNew;
    POINT ptDrag;
} NMTREEVIEW, FAR* LPNMTREEVIEW;
```

Thus, casting a LPNMTREEVIEW to a LPNMHDR gives access to the members of hdr. Conversely, the
pointer passed to the notification message handler is an LPNMHDR, so in your code you have to cast it
back to LPNMTREEVIEW to get access to the members specific to the tree view control.

For example, suppose you have a composite control with a tree view, and you want to handle the
case of a user clicking on an item. The message map would look like this:

```
BEGIN_MSG_MAP(CNotify)
    NOTIFY_HANDLER(IDC_TREE, TVN_SELCHANGED, OnSelChangedTree)
    CHAIN_MSG_MAP(CComCompositeControl<CNotify>)
END_MSG_MAP()
```

The OnSelChangedTree() method could look like this:

```
LRESULT OnSelChangedTree(int idCtrl, LPNMHDR pnmh, BOOL& bHandled)
{
    NMTREEVIEW* pnmtv = (NMTREEVIEW*)pnmh;
    MessageBox(pnmtv->itemNew->pszText, _T("You selected"));
    return 0;
}
```

NMTREEVIEW is just one of the structures that can be sent via a notification message from a tree view
control. The other structures, and the structures for the other common controls, are shown in the
table below:

| Common Control Type | Notification Structures |
| --- | --- |
| Extended Combo Box | NMCBEENDEDIT, NMCBEDRAGBEGIN, NMCOMBOBOXEX |
| Date and Time Picker | NMDATETIMECHANGE, NMDATETIMEFORMAT, NMDATETIMEFORMATQUERY, NMDATETIMESTRING, NMDATETIME |
| Header Control | NMHDDISPINFO, NMHEADER |
| IP Address Control | NMIPADDRESS |
| List View | NMITEMACTIVATE, NMLISTVIEW, NMLVCACHEHINT, NMLVCUSTOMDRAW, NMLVDISPINFO, NMLVFINDITEM, NMLVGETINFOTIP, NMLVKEYDOWN, NMLVODSTATECHANGE |
| Month Calendar Controls | NMDAYSTATE, NMSELCHANGE |
| Pager Controls | NMPGCALCSIZE, NMPGSCROLL |
| Rebar Control | NMRBAUTOSIZE, NMREBAR, NMRRBARCHILDSIZE |
| Rich Edit | ENCORRECTTEXT, ENDDROPFILES, ENLINK, ENOLEOPFAILED, ENPROTECTED, ENSAVECLIPBOARD, MSGFILTER, REQSIZE, SELCHANGE |
| Status Bar | NMHDR |
| Tab Control | NMTCKEYDOWN |
| Toolbar Control | NMTBCUSTOMDRAW, NMTBDISPINFO, NMTBHOTITEM, NMTOOLBAR |
| ToolTip Control | NMTTCUSTOMDRAW, NMTTDISPINFO |
| TreeView Control | NMTREEVIEW, NMTVCUSTOMDRAW, NMTVDISPINFO, NMTVGETINFOTIP, NMTVKEYDOWN |
| Up-Down Control | NMUPDOWN |

# Alternative Message Maps

So far, you've seen how an ATL window class can handle messages sent to its window by Windows (by adding message handlers to the default message map). You've also seen how it can handle messages sent to it by its child windows (by adding command and notification handlers to the default message map).

What you haven't yet seen is how to use the message map of a parent window to handle the messages that Windows will send to a child window.

For example, if you want to handle the WM_LBUTTONDOWN message of a child control, you have two choices:

- ❑ Create an ATL window class for the child window and handle the message in the child window's message map.
- ❑ Handle the message in the message map of the parent window

To support the second approach, ATL provides a generic class for windows that passes all its messages to the message map in another class. This generic class is called CContainedWindow. The CContainedWindow constructor takes a CMessageMap* as one of its parameters to indicate the message map class that should handle the messages.

> CContainedWindow *is actually a* typedef *for a specialization of* CContainedWindowT<>.

The potential downside of this approach is that you may not want to handle the same message from each child control in the same way, and this is where alternative message maps help. In the discussion of the BEGIN_MSG_MAP() macro earlier in the chapter, you saw that the ProcessWindowMessage() function has a dwMsgMapID parameter, and a switch statement to determine which message map to use based on this information. A message will be destined for the default message map (with an ID of 0) or an alternate message map (with some other ID).

The start of the default message map is part of the BEGIN_MSG_MAP() macro. The start of an alternate message map is declared in a message map using the following macro.

| Macro | Description |
|-------|-------------|
| ALT_MSG_MAP(dwMsgMapID) | Declares an alternative message map |

The macro is passed the ID of the alternate message map. All message handlers appearing after this macro will be for this map (until the next ALT_MSG_MAP() macro, or END_MSG_MAP()).

You can tell CContainedWindow which message map (default or alternative) to forward its messages to by passing the message map ID to its constructor. The following diagram shows a simplified view of the way that a message for a child window is sent to its handler in the parent:

```
class CContainedWindowT<...>
{
public:
    CMessageMap* m_pObject; // The message map object
    DWORD m_dwMsgMapID;              // The message map ID
    static LRESULT WindowProc(...)
    {
        CContainedWindowT<...>* pThis = ...;
        pThis->m_pObject->ProcessWindowMessage(..., pThis->m_dwMsgMapID);
    }
};
```

```
class CParentCtrl : public CMessageMap
{
public:
    // This function is hidden by the message map macros
    BOOL ProcessWindowMessage(..., DWORD dwMsgmapID)
    {
        switch (dwMsgmapID)
        {
        case 0: // Default message map
            ...
        case 1: // Alternative message map 1
            if (msg == MSG)
                MessageHandler(...);
        }
    }

    // You supply this function explicitly
    LRESULT MessageHandler(...)
    {
        // Handle the message here
    }
};
```

As an example, whenever you create an ATL control based on a Windows control, the Object Wizard will create an alternate message map for you:

```
BEGIN_MSG_MAP(CParentCtrl)
    MESSAGE_HANDLER(WM_CREATE, OnCreate)
    MESSAGE_HANDLER(WM_SETFOCUS, OnSetFocus)
    CHAIN_MSG_MAP(CComControl<CParentCtrl>)
ALT_MSG_MAP(1)
    // Replace this with message map entries for superclassed Edit
END_MSG_MAP()
```

Here, the ALT_MSG_MAP() entry defines the start of the message map with the ID of 1. This is the same ID used as the message map ID parameter of the CContainedWindow constructor.

# Chained Message Maps

Your ATL class is a C++ class, so you can use inheritance or containment to get functionality from another class, which may also have message maps. If there were a message map entry that allowed you to pass messages from one message map to another, you could utilize the message maps in other classes and control the flow of message handling. You could give the other class a chance to handle a message before, after, or instead of your own message handlers. This is the purpose of ATL's message map chaining macros.

These macros work by calling `ProcessWindowMessage()` on the specified class or object. The macros are:

| Macro | Description |
| --- | --- |
| CHAIN_MSG_MAP(theChainClass) | Routes messages to the default message map of a base class |
| CHAIN_MSG_MAP_ALT(theChainClass, msgMapID) | Routes messages to the alternative message map of a base class |
| CHAIN_MSG_MAP_MEMBER (theChainMember) | Routes messages to the default message map of data member derived from CMessageMap |
| CHAIN_MSG_MAP_ALT_MEMBER (theChainMember, msgMapID) | Routes messages to the alternative message map of data member derived from CMessageMap |
| CHAIN_MSG_MAP_DYNAMIC (dynaChainID) | Routes messages to the default message map determined at runtime |

## Base Class Chaining

`CHAIN_MSG_MAP()` is really just a special case of `CHAIN_MSG_MAP_ALT()` with `msgMapID` set to 0. This simple macro lets you route any message through the base class that is specified as the parameter. `CHAIN_MSG_MAP()` is added for you when you create a control class:

```
BEGIN_MSG_MAP(CMyCtrl)
    MESSAGE_HANDLER(WM_CREATE, OnCreate)
    MESSAGE_HANDLER(WM_SETFOCUS, OnSetFocus)
    CHAIN_MSG_MAP(CComControl< CMyCtrl >)
END_MSG_MAP()
```

This specifies that if a message other than `WM_CREATE` or `WM_SETFOCUS` is received, it will be routed to the message map in the `CComControl<>` base class. If `WM_CREATE` or `WM_SETFOCUS` is received, and the handler functions set `bHandled` to false, these messages will also be passed to the base class.

The base class message map looks like this:

```
typedef CComControl< T, WinBase > thisClass;
BEGIN_MSG_MAP(thisClass)
    MESSAGE_HANDLER(WM_PAINT, CComControlBase::OnPaint)
```

```
    MESSAGE_HANDLER(WM_SETFOCUS, CComControlBase::OnSetFocus)
    MESSAGE_HANDLER(WM_KILLFOCUS, CComControlBase::OnKillFocus)
    MESSAGE_HANDLER(WM_MOUSEACTIVATE, CComControlBase::OnMouseActivate)
END_MSG_MAP()
```

## Member Chaining

You can also route messages through the message map of a contained member. To do this, your ATL class must have a data member derived from CMessageMap and you must specify the data member in the message map using CHAIN_MSG_MAP_MEMBER() to use the default message map, or CHAIN_MSG_MAP_ALT_MEMBER() to use a specified alternative message map. Once again, CHAIN_MSG_MAP_MEMBER() is just a special case of CHAIN_MSG_MAP_ALT_MEMBER().

*The object that you supply to these macros doesn't have to be a member of your class (as long as you can be sure that it will exist when it's needed), and it doesn't have to derive from* CMessageMap *(as long as it supplies an appropriate* ProcessWindowMessage() *function). The macros just call* ProcessWindowMessage() *through the direct member selection operator.*

### Example: Member Chaining

If you have a control based on an edit control, the Object Wizard will add a member to the class for the CContainedWindow. The messages generated for the edit control will be routed through the alternative message map in the class. You can move the edit control message handling out of this class by deriving another class from CContainedWindow:

```
class CEditHandler : public CContainedWindow
{
public:
    CEditHandler(
        LPCTSTR lpszClassName, CMessageMap* pObject, DWORD dwMsgMapID = 0)
                    : CContainedWindow(const_cast<LPTSTR>(lpszClassName),
                                        pObject, dwMsgMapID)
    {}

BEGIN_MSG_MAP(CEditHandler)
    MESSAGE_HANDLER(WM_LBUTTONDOWN, OnLButtonDown)
END_MSG_MAP()

    LRESULT OnLButtonDown(
                UINT uMsg, WPARAM wParam, LPARAM lParam, BOOL& bHandled)
    {
        MessageBox(_T("You clicked on me!"));
        return 0;
    }
};
```

If the control class is called CRouterCtrl, then you can use the handler class like this:

```
// This line is added by Object Wizard:
// CContainedWindow m_ctlEdit;
// Change it to the following one:
CEditHandler m_ctlEdit;
```

```
        CRouterCtrl() : m_ctlEdit(_T("Edit"), this, 1)
        {
            m_bWindowOnly = TRUE;
        }

    BEGIN_MSG_MAP(CRouterCtrl)
        MESSAGE_HANDLER(WM_CREATE, OnCreate)
        MESSAGE_HANDLER(WM_SETFOCUS, OnSetFocus)
        CHAIN_MSG_MAP(CComControl<CRouterCtrl>)
    ALT_MSG_MAP(1)
        CHAIN_MSG_MAP_MEMBER(m_ctlEdit)
    END_MSG_MAP()
```

The WM_LBUTTONDOWN message will be routed to the message map with ID 1. I have added the CHAIN_MSG_MAP_MEMBER() macro to route all control messages to the m_ctlEdit member. As you can see, this macro is useful for creating generic classes for contained windows.

## Dynamic Chaining

The final macro in this group is CHAIN_MSG_MAP_DYNAMIC(), which allows you to determine the object that will handle messages at runtime. To use this macro, you should derive your ATL class from CDynamicChain and then use CHAIN_MSG_MAP_DYNAMIC() to add a new chain to the map. The parameter to this macro is just a numeric identifier that can be any value you choose, as long as multiple CHAIN_MSG_MAP_DYNAMIC() entries in a message map have different identifiers.

The actual chain is created at runtime by calling SetChainEntry() on an instance of the class derived from CDynamicChain. This method associates the chain ID with an instance of an object derived from CMessageMap. SetChainEntry() adds a pointer to the handler object into an array. You can call this function many times to add several different handler objects; you can also call RemoveChainEntry() to remove a handler object. This means that you can change the message handling of a control at runtime by associating different handler objects with an ID, or even removing the handling provided for a particular ID.

### Example: Dynamic Chaining

For example, if this is the handler class:

```
    class CHandler : public CMessageMap
    {
    public:
        CHandler(LPCTSTR str) : m_str(str) {}

    BEGIN_MSG_MAP(CHandler)
        MESSAGE_HANDLER(WM_LBUTTONDOWN, OnLButtonDown)
    END_MSG_MAP()

        LRESULT OnLButtonDown(
                        UINT uMsg, WPARAM wParam, LPARAM lParam, BOOL& bHandled)
        {
            ATLTRACE(_T("Handled by: %s\n"), m_str);
            return 0;
        }
    private:
        LPCTSTR m_str;
    };
```

As long as the class `CDynamicRouterCtrl` is derived from `CDynamicChain`, you can write code like this:

```
CHandler m_weekendHandler;
CHandler m_weekdayHandler;

CDynamicRouterCtrl() : m_weekendHandler(_T("Weekend handler")),
                       m_weekdayHandler(_T("Weekday handler"))
{
    SYSTEMTIME st;
    GetLocalTime(&st);
    bool bSuccess = false;
    if(st.wDayOfWeek == 0 || st.wDayOfWeek == 6)
        bSuccess = SetChainEntry(1, &m_weekendHandler);
    else
        bSuccess = SetChainEntry(1, &m_weekdayHandler);
    if(!bSuccess)
        ATLTRACE(_T("Failed to set the dynamic chain entry\n"));
}

BEGIN_MSG_MAP(CDynamicRouterCtrl)
    CHAIN_MSG_MAP(CComControl<CDynamicRouterCtrl>)
    CHAIN_MSG_MAP_DYNAMIC(1)
    DEFAULT_REFLECTION_HANDLER()
END_MSG_MAP()
```

This ensures that during the week, the `WM_LBUTTONDOWN` message is handled by the `m_weekdayHandler`, which in this implementation just prints "Weekday Handler" to the debug stream. At the weekend, the message is handled by `m_weekendHandler`. As you can see, this allows you to change the behavior of the control dynamically.

In this example, I have set the chain in the control's constructor, but you could set it, or change it, anywhere in the control code. Also, `SetChainEntry()` is a `public` member of `CDynamicChain`, so you can call it from outside the class.

# Reflected Messages

A container handles window messages sent to it by an ActiveX control by sending the message back as a **reflected message**, which amounts to the original message plus the constant `OCM_BASE`. When the control gets these messages, it can identify them as being reflected from the container and handle them by sending an event.

| Macro | Description |
|---|---|
| `DEFAULT_REFLECTION_HANDLER()` | Default handler for reflected messages |
| `REFLECT_NOTIFICATIONS()` | Will reflect the message to the child code specified in the message |

The first macro converts a reflected message back to the original message and passes it to the default message handler (the Win32 API function `DefWindowProc()`). The second macro is used by a container to reflect messages back to a control.

If you create a Full or Lite control, the Object Wizard will add the
DEFAULT_REFLECTION_HANDLER() macro to the message map. For other control types (including
Full and Lite controls based on Windows controls) it will not add this macro. If your control has child
controls that will handle messages then you should use REFLECT_NOTIFICATIONS() so that the
controls will be allowed to handle the message.

## Message Maps Summary

The following diagram summarizes message maps and how they relate to the classes that you will use
in your controls:

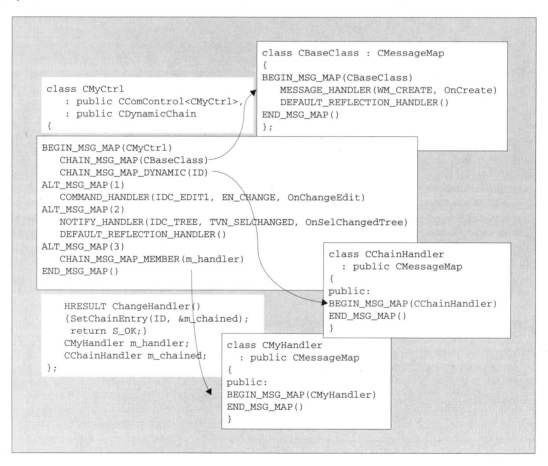

## The Window Procedure

Now that you understand how message maps work, you're probably wondering how the window
procedure works. After all, it must be a global or class static function because Windows defines its
signature that way, so how can it call non-static member functions (that is, the message handlers)?
Well, to see how it works, let's summarize the window creation process for a typical ATL window
class. The mechanics vary from class to class, but the principles remain the same.

Initially, you will create a C++ object based on one of ATL's window classes. The precise class you choose and the template parameters that you pass determine the window class represented by that object. When you need to create the window of the desired type, you can call the Create() member function, which will do three things:

- ❏ Register the window class if it hasn't already been registered
- ❏ Store information about the object in a module-wide linked list
- ❏ Create the window instance that you requested

When ATL registers the window class, it specifies a static member of the class called StartWindowProc() as the window procedure. It then stores the this pointer of the object along with the thread ID in a structure within a linked list maintained by the CComModule object representing your application. Finally, it creates the window.

When the window is created, Windows sends it a flurry of messages. The first message is sent to the registered window procedure for the window class, in other words, StartWindowProc(). The purpose of this method is to subclass the window instance to use the actual window procedure, another static member, usually called WindowProc(). More precisely, it sets up an instance-specific thunk that calls WindowProc().

To do this, StartWindowProc() first retrieves the window data previously stored in the linked list, removing the item as it does so. This gives it access to the this pointer for the object. Next, it sets the m_hWnd member of the object, so that any code within that class has access to the window handle. Once it knows the window handle is safe, it initializes the thunk with the this pointer and the address of the real window procedure. In this case, the thunk is a data member of the ATL window class, of type CWndProcThunk. This class contains an anonymous union in which the relevant element is a _WndProcThunk structure:

```
#pragma pack(push,1)
struct _WndProcThunk
{
    DWORD m_mov;
    DWORD m_this;
    BYTE m_jmp;
    DWORD m_relproc;
};
#pragma pack(pop)
```

*The #pragmas ensure that single-byte packing is used when initializing instances of this struct. By default, packing is carried out for Intel processors to make sure that members are aligned on DWORD boundaries (the compiler does this for efficiency). If that happened here, m_jmp would actually take up four bytes and not the single byte you wanted.*

This structure effectively sets up a small piece of machine code:

```
mov dword ptr [esp + 0x4], pThis
jmp WndProc
```

In this code, pThis is the this pointer of the current instance of the window, and WndProc is the static WindowProc() member. The code places the this pointer as the first parameter on the stack and then calls WindowProc().

To get this code to execute when Windows has a message to send, StartWindowProc() calls SetWindowLong() to replace the address of the window procedure with the start address of the thunk. Now, whenever it wants the window to handle a message, Windows will call into the thunk, which will replace the hWnd parameter with the this pointer and then call WindowProc():

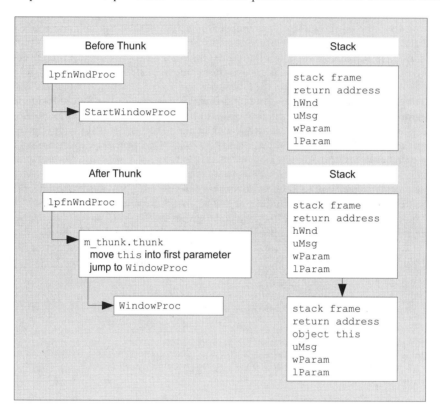

The hWnd parameter is unnecessary because it's also stored in the object's m_hWnd member, so replacing it with the this pointer doesn't result in a loss of information. WindowProc() can just cast the hWnd parameter back to a pointer of the appropriate type to obtain the this pointer of the ATL window object, and this allows it to call the ProcessWindowMessage() function (that is, the message map) to deal with the messages.

Messages that aren't handled by ProcessWindowMessage() are handled by calling a member function called DefWindowProc(). This member function is responsible for default message handling. In most of ATL's window classes, it does this by calling a function pointer contained in a member called m_pfnSuperWindowProc. This member is initialized to the address of the global Win32 function DefWindowProc() by default, but may be changed if superclassing or subclassing is involved. To enable users to call the DefWindowProc() member without any arguments, the window procedure has to keep track of the current message in a data member.

The only message that `WindowProc()` won't pass to `DefWindowProc()` is WM_NCDESTROY, which indicates that the window is being destroyed. `WindowProc()` will handle this by reversing any subclassing that has been carried out (other than through `StartWindowProc()`).

The implementation of `WindowProc()` in `CWindowImplBaseT<>` will also call a `virtual` function called `OnFinalMessage()` to give you a chance to perform some final cleanup before the window dies. Other ATL window classes don't allow you to do this.

## Thunks for the Memory

It is interesting to compare the window procedure thunking in ATL 3.0 with the version used in ATL 2.1. In the previous version, the thunk generated this code:

```
move ecx, pThis
jmp WndProc
```

In other words, the thunk put the `this` pointer into the ECX register. To get it out again, `WindowProc()` would use this code:

```
#ifdef _M_IX86
    _asm mov dword ptr[hWnd], ecx
#endif
    CWindowImplBase* pT = (CWindowImplBase*)hWnd;
```

This moves the `this` pointer from ECX and puts it into the hWnd parameter, then hWnd is cast to the object pointer. The new thunking mechanism in ATL 3.0 is an improvement because it moves some of the code out of the `WindowProc()` and puts it into the thunk.

# Window Classes

In the remainder of the chapter, we'll examine the following window classes:

- ❑ `CWindowImpl<>`
- ❑ `CWindow`
- ❑ `CContainedWindowT<>`
- ❑ `CSimpleDialog<>`
- ❑ `CDialogImpl<>`
- ❑ `CAxWindowT<>`
- ❑ `CAxDialogImpl<>`

## CWindowImpl<>

`CWindowImpl<>` is used to create a new window, or to subclass an existing window class. Its inheritance tree looks like this:

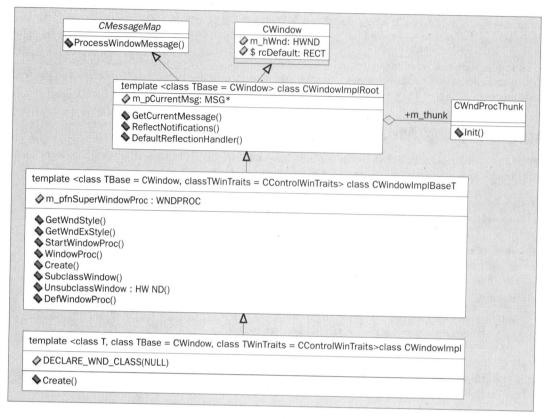

And the class itself looks like this:

```
template<class T, class TBase = CWindow, class TWinTraits = CControlWinTraits>
class ATL_NO_VTABLE CWindowImpl
    : public CWindowImplBaseT<TBase, TWinTraits>
{
public:
    DECLARE_WND_CLASS(NULL)

    HWND Create(HWND hWndParent, RECT& rcPos, LPCTSTR szWindowName = NULL,
                DWORD dwStyle = 0, DWORD dwExStyle = 0, UINT nID = 0,
                LPVOID lpCreateParam = NULL);
};
```

Most of the code is inherited from `CWindowImplBaseT<>`, but note the `DECLARE_WND_CLASS()` macro. This declares a method called `GetWndClassInfo()` that returns a reference to a `CWndClassInfo` object.

## CWndClassInfo

`CWndClassInfo` is a `typedef` for `_ATL_WNDCLASSINFOW` (or the ANSI version, `_ATL_WNDCLASSINFOA`):

```
struct _ATL_WNDCLASSINFOW
{
    WNDCLASSEXW m_wc;                       // Window class structure
    LPCWSTR     m_lpszOrigName;             // The class name
    WNDPROC     pWndProc;                   // Window procedure
    LPCWSTR     m_lpszCursorID;             // ID of the cursor in resources
    BOOL        m_bSystemCursor;            // Is the cursor a system cursor?
    ATOM        m_atom;                     // Identifies the registered class
    WCHAR       m_szAutoName[13];           // The class name
    ATOM Register(WNDPROC* p)
    {
        return AtlModuleRegisterWndClassInfoW(&_Module, this, p);
    }
};
```

In this structure, m_wc is the structure used to register the window class. This is done by calling the method Register() in this struct, which calls the global AtlModuleRegisterWndClassInfoW() function (or the ANSI version in the ANSI struct). The result of registering a window class is an ATOM, which is held in m_atom. This is used to make sure that the class is registered just once.

> ATOMs *are a remnant of 16-bit Windows that still have a place in Win32. The system implements a global* **atom table** *in which a process can store a string and get back an identifier called an* ATOM. *The process can then pass this* ATOM *to another process, which can use it to read the string. A process can also create a local atom table to maintain strings that it will use in its address space. When you register a window class, Windows will give you an* ATOM *to identify your class.*

The window can have its own cursor (that is, a mouse pointer). You can either use a cursor defined as a resource in the module, or a system cursor. If you want a system cursor, then m_bSystemCursor should be set to TRUE and m_lpszCursorID set to one of the system cursor constants, as specified in the documentation for the Win32 LoadCursor() function. If the cursor is declared in the module, then m_bSystemCursor is FALSE and m_lpszCursorID is the resource name of the cursor.

### DECLARE_WND_ Macros

DECLARE_WND_CLASS() is just one way to change the window class used for your control – there are some other macros that you can use. The complete list is shown below:

| Macro | Description |
| --- | --- |
| DECLARE_WND_CLASS(WndClassName) | Declares window class information |
| DECLARE_WND_CLASS_EX(WndClassName, style, bkgnd) | Declares window class information, and allows you to specify the background brush and style flags |
| DECLARE_WND_SUPERCLASS(WndClassName, OrigWndClassName) | Declares window class information for a superclass. You specify the original class name that you want to superclass, and the new class name |

Note that although there is space in CWndClassInfo for cursor info, there is no macro to allow you to specify it in your class. This is easy to fix with the following simple macro that I've called DECLARE_WND_CLASS_CUR():

```
#define DECLARE_WND_CLASS_CUR(WndClassName, style, bkgnd, Cursor, SysCur) \
static CWndClassInfo& GetWndClassInfo() \
{ \
   static CWndClassInfo wc = \
   { \
      { sizeof(WNDCLASSEX), style, StartWindowProc, \
        0, 0, NULL, NULL, NULL, (HBRUSH)(bkgnd + 1), NULL, \
        WndClassName, NULL \
      }, \
      NULL, NULL, Cursor, SysCur, 0, _T("") \
   }; \
   return wc; \
}
#define DECLARE_WND_CLASS_SYSCUR(WndClassName, style, bkgnd, Cursor) \
   DECLARE_WND_CLASS_CUR(WndClassName, style, bkgnd, Cursor, TRUE)
```

You will notice that the CWndClassInfo has two strings for the class name. The DECLARE_WND_ macros take the window class name that you intend to use. If this is NULL, then ATL will generate a name for you in m_szAutoName and the address of this will be put into the lpszClassName member of the WNDCLASSEXW structure. m_lpszOrigName is the name of the existing class if your class is superclassing another class.

The parameters in CWndClassInfo are used for the window class of the control, so if you create several controls in the same process, the registration need only be done once. Indeed, the CWndClassInfo::Register() method calls the global function AtlModuleRegisterWndClassInfoW(), which tests the m_atom member and only registers the class if it is zero.

When the Create() method is called, it first registers the window class that it will create. It does this by calling GetWndClassInfo() to get hold of the _ATL_WNDCLASSINFOW for the control, and then calling Register() to register the class. The ATOM returned from this method represents the window class name that has been registered, and it can be passed to CreateWindowEx() to create a window. Create() passes this ATOM and sizing and positional data to the base class implementation of Create() to make this API call.

## Window Traits

You can specify the style for a particular instance of a window. In Win32 programming, you specify these style bits in the call to CreateWindowEx(). In ATL, this call is buried deep in the code. These style bits, however, can be specified as **window traits**. If you look back at the declaration of CWindowImpl<>, you will find that the traits are passed as parameters to the template:

```
template <class T, class TBase = CWindow,
                          class TWinTraits = CControlWinTraits>
class ATL_NO_VTABLE CWindowImpl
   : public CWindowImplBaseT<TBase, TWinTraits>
```

The default parameter, CControlWinTraits is a typedef:

```
typedef CWinTraits<WS_CHILD | WS_VISIBLE | WS_CLIPCHILDREN |
                            WS_CLIPSIBLINGS, 0> CControlWinTraits;
```

The CWinTraits<> class looks like this:

```
template<DWORD t_dwStyle = 0, DWORD t_dwExStyle = 0>
class CWinTraits
{
public:
    static DWORD GetWndStyle(DWORD dwStyle)
    {
        return dwStyle == 0 ? t_dwStyle : dwStyle;
    }

    static DWORD GetWndExStyle(DWORD dwExStyle)
    {
        return dwExStyle == 0 ? t_dwExStyle : dwExStyle;
    }
};
```

The class is used to define two static methods, so you could use *any* class that has these two static members to describe your window traits. These methods are passed a style value; if it is non-zero then it is returned as the style, otherwise the default style in CWinTraits<> is returned. This behavior is used because the Create() methods inherited by CWindowImpl<> can take style bits and naturally you will want these to override any styles defined in the window traits.

ATL also defines another traits class called CWinTraitsOR<>:

```
template <DWORD t_dwStyle = 0, DWORD t_dwExStyle = 0,
                            class TWinTraits = CControlWinTraits>
class CWinTraitsOR
{
public:
    static DWORD GetWndStyle(DWORD dwStyle)
    {
        return dwStyle | t_dwStyle | TWinTraits::GetWndStyle(dwStyle);
    }

    static DWORD GetWndExStyle(DWORD dwExStyle)
    {
        return dwExStyle | t_dwExStyle | TWinTraits::GetWndExStyle(dwExStyle);
    }
};
```

The methods OR the style passed to them with the default style of the template and the style of an associated traits class. You can use this to combine styles.

## CWindowImplBaseT<>

CWindowImplBaseT<> is a base class of CWindowImpl<> and provides methods important for registering the window class and to subclass or superclass another class:

```
template <class TBase = CWindow, class TWinTraits = CControlWinTraits>
class ATL_NO_VTABLE CWindowImplBaseT
    : public CWindowImplRoot< TBase >
{
public:
    WNDPROC m_pfnSuperWindowProc;

    CWindowImplBaseT();
    static DWORD GetWndStyle(DWORD dwStyle);
    static DWORD GetWndExStyle(DWORD dwExStyle);
    virtual WNDPROC GetWindowProc();
    static LRESULT CALLBACK StartWindowProc(
                    HWND hWnd, UINT uMsg, WPARAM wParam, LPARAM lParam);
    static LRESULT CALLBACK WindowProc(
                    HWND hWnd, UINT uMsg, WPARAM wParam, LPARAM lParam);
    HWND Create(HWND hWndParent, RECT& rcPos, LPCTSTR szWindowName,
            DWORD dwStyle, DWORD dwExStyle, UINT nID, ATOM atom,
            LPVOID lpCreateParam = NULL);
    BOOL DestroyWindow();
    BOOL SubclassWindow(HWND hWnd);
    HWND UnsubclassWindow(BOOL bForce = FALSE);
    LRESULT DefWindowProc();
    LRESULT DefWindowProc(UINT uMsg, WPARAM wParam, LPARAM lParam);
    virtual void OnFinalMessage(HWND /*hWnd*/);
};
```

You can see that `CWindowImplBaseT<>` provides the `Create()`, `StartWindowProc()`,
`WindowProc()`, and `DefWindowProc()` members that we discussed earlier in the section on
window procedures. `DestroyWindow()` is called to destroy the window. In controls, this function is
called by the implementations for `IOleObject::Close()` and
`IOleInPlaceObject::InPlaceDeactivate()`.

## Example: Creating Windows with CWindowImpl<>

`CWindowImpl<>` is used to create windows. You can use this class to create windows from within a
control, or indeed any other sort of ATL project. As an example, create a new DLL server called
`MultiWin` and insert a Lite Control called `MultiWindow`. We'll use this control to create a new
window each time someone clicks on it.

You can start by creating the class for your new windows. These will be very simple popup windows
with a caption and the name of the window painted in the center. Add the following code to
`MultiWindow.h`, just above the code for `CMultiWindow`:

```
class MyWindow : public CWindowImpl<MyWindow, CWindow,
                CWinTraits<WS_CAPTION | WS_POPUPWINDOW | WS_VISIBLE, 0> >
{
public:
    MyWindow(LPCTSTR strName)
    {
        RECT rcPos;
        rcPos.left = 0;
        rcPos.top = 0;
        rcPos.right = 200;
        rcPos.bottom = 200;
```

```
        lstrcpy(m_strName, strName);
        Create(0, rcPos, strName);
    }

    ~MyWindow()
    {
        if(m_hWnd)
            DestroyWindow();
    }

BEGIN_MSG_MAP(MyWindow)
END_MSG_MAP()

private:
    TCHAR m_strName[80];
};
```

This class derives from CWindowImpl<>. The template parameter for the window traits specifies that the window is a popup window with a caption, and includes the WS_VISIBLE style so that you don't need to make a separate call to show the window after it has been created.

The constructor creates a window 200 by 200 pixels in size, and uses the parameter as its name. When the C++ object is destroyed, it calls DestroyWindow() to close the window (as long as the window handle is not NULL, which indicates that the window has already been destroyed).

MyWindow has an empty message map, which allows us to use the ClassView to add a message handler for the WM_PAINT message. Right-click on the class in ClassView, and select Add Windows Message Handler... from the context menu. Use this to add a handler for WM_PAINT; the Wizard will generate the following code:

```
BEGIN_MSG_MAP(MyWindow)
    MESSAGE_HANDLER(WM_PAINT, OnPaint)
END_MSG_MAP()

    LRESULT OnPaint(
                UINT uMsg, WPARAM wParam, LPARAM lParam, BOOL& bHandled)
    {
        // TODO : Add Code for message handler.
        // Call DefWindowProc if necessary.
        return 0;
    }
```

Drawing code can be a pain using the raw Win32 API, so we'll keep the implementation of this function simple. ATL helps you with the drawing code in controls (as you'll see in the next chapter), but MyWindow isn't a control, so we have to do the hard work – such as getting the device context and setting the mapping mode and origin – for ourselves. In fact, we'll avoid most of this difficulty by doing everything with relative units:

```
LRESULT OnPaint(UINT uMsg, WPARAM wParam, LPARAM lParam, BOOL& bHandled)
{
    PAINTSTRUCT ps;
    HDC hdc = (wParam != NULL) ?
                    reinterpret_cast<HDC>(wParam) : BeginPaint(&ps);
```

```
    if(hdc == NULL)
        return 0;

    RECT rc;
    GetClientRect(&rc);

    SIZE size;
    GetTextExtentPoint32(hdc, m_strName, lstrlen(m_strName), &size);

    TextOut(hdc, (rc.left + rc.right - size.cx) / 2,
        (rc.top + rc.bottom - size.cy) / 2, m_strName, lstrlen(m_strName));
    if(wParam == NULL)
        EndPaint(&ps);
    return 0;
}
```

This code is effectively copied from `CComControlBase::OnPaint()`.

The next task is to create the windows. This example should allow you to create several windows, so we'll need to create `MyWindow` objects dynamically and keep track of the pointers in an array. Since ATL provides a basic template array class called `CSimpleArray<>`, it makes sense to use this (and avoid the CRT overhead associated with the Standard Library). This class allows you to add items with the `Add()` method, and remove them with `Remove()`. The items in the array can be accessed with the `[]` operator.

Add a `CSimpleArray<>` data member to `CMultiWindow`:

```
private:
    CSimpleArray<MyWindow*> m_windows;
};
```

Now add a destructor to `CMultiWindow` to destroy the objects in the array when the control is destroyed:

```
~CMultiWindow()
{
    for(int i = 0 ; i < m_windows.GetSize() ; i++)
        delete m_windows[i];
}
```

Finally, use ClassView to add a handler for `WM_LBUTTONDOWN` to `CMultiWindow`. The mouse handler should create a new window and add it to the array:

```
LRESULT OnLButtonDown(
                UINT uMsg, WPARAM wParam, LPARAM lParam, BOOL& bHandled)
{
    TCHAR strName[80] = {0};
    wsprintf(strName, _T("Window %ld"), m_windows.GetSize());
    MyWindow* pWnd = new MyWindow(strName);
    m_windows.Add(pWnd);
    return 0;
}
```

Now you're ready to compile the project. Once it is built, load the Object Wizard generated HTML page into Internet Explorer, and click on the control to generate the windows. Each window will have its name in the center, and as its caption.

## Superclassing

To superclass a window, you use the DECLARE_WND_SUPERCLASS() macro. This takes the name of the base window class and the new class name (or NULL to let ATL create one for you). The base class name is used by AtlModuleRegisterWndClassInfoW() to get hold of the window class information for the base class, and then replace the class name with the new name, and replace the original window procedure with the new one (caching the original on the way). This information is then used to register the new class. The original window procedure of the base class is cached so that after your message map has had a chance to handle the message, it is passed to the original window procedure.

### Example: Superclassing a List Box

To see this in action, create a DLL project called Super and insert a Lite Control called SuperListBox. To base this control on a Win32 list box, add this line to the CSuperListBox class definition:

```
DECLARE_REGISTRY_RESOURCEID(IDR_SUPERLISTBOX)
DECLARE_WND_SUPERCLASS(NULL, _T("LISTBOX"))
DECLARE_PROTECT_FINAL_CONSTRUCT()
```

If you build this project, you will find that you will not see the list box – instead, you'll see the standard ATL 3.0 : SuperListBox message. The reason is that a full or lite control will be windowless if the container supports it. When windowless, the control is not responsible for creating a new window, so your superclassing will not occur. To get a new window created, you need to specify that the control has its own window:

```
public:
    CSuperListBox()
    {
        m_bWindowOnly = TRUE;
    }
```

This ensures that the control creates its own window, and messages will be redirected to it. However, you will still see the default message, because OnDraw() is drawing on top of the list box. To rectify this, you'll need to handle the WM_PAINT message in your class in a way that allows the list box to handle the drawing. It is not sufficient merely to delete OnDraw() from your class (and use the empty implementation inherited from CComControlBase) because CComControlBase::OnPaint() handles the WM_PAINT message, preventing the message being passed on to the list box window procedure.

Instead, you must handle the message yourself by explicitly passing the message on to the default message handler. So, add a handler for WM_PAINT as shown below. You can use the ClassView message handler Wizard or add the handler by hand, but make sure that the message map entry appears *before* the CHAIN_MSG_MAP() macro. The handler just calls DefWindowProc(), which passes the message on to the list box window procedure.

```
BEGIN_MSG_MAP(CSuperListBox)
    MESSAGE_HANDLER(WM_PAINT, OnPaint)
    CHAIN_MSG_MAP(CComControl<CSuperListBox>)
    DEFAULT_REFLECTION_HANDLER()
END_MSG_MAP()

LRESULT OnPaint(UINT uMsg, WPARAM wParam, LPARAM lParam, BOOL& bHandled)
{
    DefWindowProc();
    return 0;
}
```

If you do this, you can delete the OnDraw() method in the ATL class.

The code will now create and show the list box, but it will use the default styles defined in
CWinTraits<>. To change these styles, you can either pass different styles to the Create()
method that creates the control, or change the control's default traits. We'll take the second approach,
so add the following typedefs just above the definition for CSuperListBox:

```
// Forward declare
class CSuperListBox;

typedef CWinTraits<WS_CHILD | WS_VISIBLE | WS_BORDER | WS_VSCROLL, 0>
                                                          CMyListTraits;
typedef CComControl<CSuperListBox, CWindowImpl<CSuperListBox,
                        CWindow, CMyListTraits> > CMyListControlClass;
```

*Incidentally, you could use* CWinTraitsOR<> *here instead, using the following* typedef:

```
typedef CWinTraitsOR<WS_BORDER | WS_VSCROLL> CMyListTraits;
```

*This is slightly simpler code, but because it uses default values from* CControlWinTraits, *it
is not as clear as the previous code what styles the window will have. I will leave it to your
judgement to decide which version you prefer.*

Now derive the class from CMyListControlClass rather than CComControl<CSuperListBox>:

```
class ATL_NO_VTABLE CSuperListBox :
    public CComObjectRootEx<CComSingleThreadModel>,
    public IDispatchImpl<ISuperListBox, &IID_ISuperListBox, &LIBID_SUPERLib>,
// public CComControl<CSuperListBox>,
    public CMyListControlClass,
```

And change the message map to match:

```
BEGIN_MSG_MAP(CSuperListBox)
    MESSAGE_HANDLER(WM_PAINT, OnPaint)
    MESSAGE_HANDLER(LB_ADDSTRING, OnAddString)
// CHAIN_MSG_MAP(CComControl<CSuperListBox>)
    CHAIN_MSG_MAP(CMyListControlClass)
    DEFAULT_REFLECTION_HANDLER()
END_MSG_MAP()
```

Notice that I have also added a line to handle the LB_ADDSTRING message; this is so that you can verify that the list box is being superclassed with the following code:

```
LRESULT OnAddString(UINT uMsg, WPARAM wParam, LPARAM lParam, BOOL& bHandled)
{
    ATLTRACE("Adding %s\n", reinterpret_cast<LPCTSTR>(lParam));
    bHandled = FALSE;
    return 0;
}
```

Notice that bHandled is set to FALSE to ensure that the message is passed on to the list box window procedure. As a final touch, you can initialize the list box by overriding CreateControlWindow():

```
HWND CreateControlWindow(HWND hWndParent, RECT& rcPos)
{
    HWND hwnd = Create(hWndParent, rcPos);
    SendMessage(LB_ADDSTRING, 0, reinterpret_cast<LPARAM>(_T("One"))  );
    SendMessage(LB_ADDSTRING, 0, reinterpret_cast<LPARAM>(_T("Two"))  );
    SendMessage(LB_ADDSTRING, 0, reinterpret_cast<LPARAM>(_T("Three")));
    SendMessage(LB_ADDSTRING, 0, reinterpret_cast<LPARAM>(_T("Four")) );
    return hwnd;
}
```

When you run this code under the debugger (Using the test container, for example), you will see the following in the output window:

```
Adding One
Adding Two
Adding Three
Adding Four
```

This superclassing technique is handy, because you can use it to perform validation when a string is added.

### Subclassing

If you want to subclass an existing window, you should obtain a handle to that window and pass it to SubclassWindow(). This initializes the thunk, as explained before, and replaces the window procedure with the thunk. Before the window is destroyed, you should reverse the subclassing. You can do this either by calling UnsubclassWindow(), or allowing WindowProc() to handle WM_NCDESTROY, which unsubclasses the window for you.

It should be fairly obvious that you should not subclass and superclass at the same time — that is, on a single CWindowImpl<> instance, you should call either Create() or SubclassWindow(), never both.

# CWindow

CWindow wraps the Win32 functions used to manipulate windows, manages an HWND, and ensures that the window can only be used after it has been initialized. Usually, the CWindow wrapper functions are pretty thin, as you can see from the example of GetClientRect():

```
BOOL GetClientRect(LPRECT lpRect) const
{
    ATLASSERT(::IsWindow(m_hWnd));
    return ::GetClientRect(m_hWnd, lpRect);
}
```

Most of the functions just check the window handle for validity in debug builds, and remove the need to pass the window handle explicitly to the function. Although simple, these features are quite fundamental – it's all too easy to try to manipulate a window before it is actually created, or to use it after it has been destroyed. The assert helps to check for these cases during the debug cycle. The encapsulation of the window handle provides an object-oriented veneer to the Win32 API.

HWND maintenance is apparent in many of the methods of the class. There is a constructor, an assignment operator, and an Attach() method used to construct a CWindow object from an HWND. There's also an HWND conversion operator to return the wrapped HWND, and a Detach() method that's used to return and remove the wrapped HWND.

In addition, many of the CWindow wrappers supply sensible default parameters to the functions; others do some additional work for you. Let's take a look at these slightly 'thicker' wrapper methods:

| CWindow **Method** | **Description** |
|---|---|
| Create() | Creates a window |
| GetDlgControl() | Obtains the IUnknown for a child control on a dialog that is an ActiveX control |
| ResizeClient() | Resizes the window so that its client area is the specified size |
| GetDescendantWindow() | Gets a descendant window (a child window or one further down the tree) with the specified ID |
| SendMessageToDescendants() | Sends a message to a window's descendants |
| CenterWindow() | Centers a window with respect to another window |
| ModifyStyle() | Change the style of a window |
| ModifyStyleEx() | Change the extended style of a window |
| GetWindowText() | Fills a buffer with a window's text or caption |
| GetTopLevelParent() | Gets the topmost window in this window's family tree |
| GetTopLevelWindow() | Gets the topmost owner window |

`Create()` wraps the Win32 API function `CreateWindowEx()`. It makes a call to `_Module.GetModuleInstance()` to get the `HINSTANCE` necessary for the call, and places the returned `HWND` in the `m_hWnd` member of `CWindow`. Although you can use `CWindow` to create windows (and even subclass them), you'll usually want to use one of ATL's fuller-featured window classes, such as `CWindowImpl<>`, which handle the window procedure for you. Typically, you'll use `CWindow` directly by attaching an already existing window handle to it, or as a base class (just as `CWindowImpl<>` does by default).

If the wrapped `HWND` is a dialog, you can obtain the `HWND` of one of the child controls with a call to `GetDlgItem()`. If you know that the child control is an ActiveX control, then you can get its `IUnknown*` by calling `GetDlgControl()`. ATL wraps child controls with hosting code that handles the privately registered message `WM_ATLGETCONTROL`; when they receive this message, they reply by returning their `IUnknown*`. `GetDlgControl()` calls `AtlAxGetControl()`, which sends this message.

`GetDescendantWindow()` and `SendMessageToDescendants()` are recursive routines. The first moves through the family tree of a window and its children looking for a control with the specified ID, if it finds such a control, its `HWND` is returned. The second of the two will send a message to either a window's immediate children or, if `bDeep` is true, to all descendants.

The description of `CenterWindow()` is simple: it centers a window. However the code is a little more complicated than that. This method will center a window in relation to a specified window, or in relation to its parent or owner window (which could mean the desktop) if `NULL` is passed as the window handle.

`ModifyStyle()` and `ModifyStyleEx()` allow you to change the style of an existing window. These take three parameters: the first is a style to remove, the second is a style to add, and the third is a sizing or positioning flag that could be passed to `SetWindowPos()` (usually to show or hide a window).

`GetWindowText()` is overloaded with three versions. The first takes an `LPTSTR` and a size, and is a thin wrapper around the Win32 function. The other two take a pointer or a reference to a `BSTR`, and are much more useful. These two versions will allocate and fill a `BSTR` with the text in a window. Internally, of course, it calls `GetWindowTextLength()`, but it wraps all that gunk for you.

# CContainedWindowT<>

A contained window is a child window. The defining aspect of a contained window is that it does not have its own message map – instead, it uses the map of its parent, or containing class. The parent message map is passed as a parameter to the constructor or through the `Create()` method, along with the ID of the alternative message map in the parent.

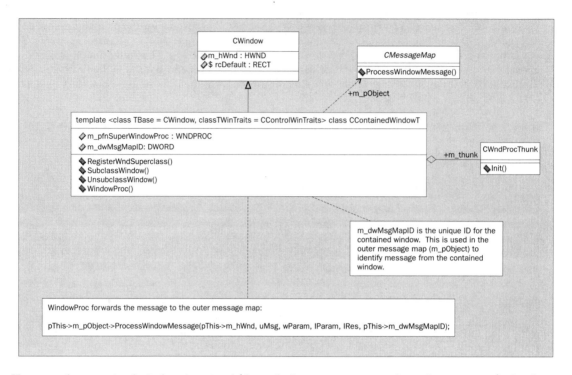

However the contained window is created (through the constructors or through `Create()`), the class needs a window class name. A contained window should *not* be initialized from an existing `HWND`, despite the fact that it derives from `CWindow` by default. This is because `CContainedWindowT<>` is used to sub- and superclass, and creating the object from an `HWND` bypasses the super- or subclassing mechanism.

This class provides `DefWindowProc()`, `StartWindowProc()` and `WindowProc()` just as `CWindowImpl<>` does, and the class superclasses the contained window with `RegisterWndSuperclass()`, passing `StartWindowProc()` as the superclass window procedure. As with `CWindowImpl<>`, this class uses a thunk to provide the `this` pointer through the window procedure's `hWnd` parameter.

## Superclassing

`CContainedWindowT<>` allows you to superclass existing window classes. Typically, you will pass the name of the class to be superclassed as an argument to the constructor.

The ATL Object Wizard will produce code that uses `CContainedWindowT<>` to superclass a window when you use the **Add control based on** option on the **Miscellaneous** page of the Object Wizard.

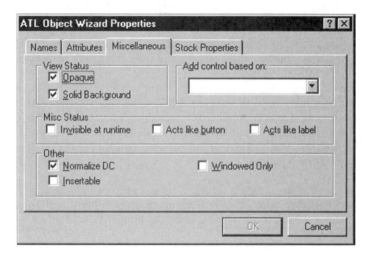

Object Wizard gives you the opportunity of basing your control on SysListView32, SysTreeView32, SysAnimate32, SysHeader32 and SysTabControl32, as well as the Rich Edit control and the standard controls (Edit, Button, Static, List Box, Combo Box and Scroll Bar). However, this is a combo box, so if you want to create a contained window based on any other window class, all you need to do is type the class name into the edit box.

For example, if you want to base a control on the Up-Down Control, you can type msctls_updown32 as the name for Add control based on. Object Wizard will create the following code:

```
CContainedWindow m_ctlmsctls_updown32;

CMyCtrl() : m_ctlmsctls_updown32(_T("msctls_updown32"), this, 1)
{
    m_bWindowOnly = TRUE;
}
```

*The constructor sets* m_bWindowOnly *to* TRUE. *This data member is inherited from* CComControlBase, *and is used to tell the ATL code never to allow windowless activation. The Wizard-generated code disallows this so that it can handle the* WM_CREATE *message for the control window, and create the contained control in response to that message.*

*If the control didn't have its own window, it would never receive the* WM_CREATE *message and the Up-Down control would not be created. The* WM_CREATE *message is used to create the superclassed control because you are guaranteed that the* WM_CREATE *handler will only ever be called once, when the ATL control is created.*

The Object Wizard will add code in the WM_CREATE handler for the control to create the specified common control, and it will also add code to handle the correct sizing of the contained control, based on the size of your ATL control.

### *Superclassing With and Without CContainedWindowT<>*

Earlier on in this chapter, you saw an example of superclassing using the
DECLARE_WND_SUPERCLASS() macro. This begs the question of when you should use
CContainedWindowT<>, and when you should use DECLARE_WND_SUPERCLASS().

Object Wizard provides support for superclassing using CContainedWindowT<>, which creates a
separate object within your control to handle the superclassing. This separate object has a
CMessageMap pointer as a data member that typically gets initialized with the this pointer of the
ATL control, but you could initialize it with any class derived from CMessageMap. In this situation,
there will be two windows created: the window for your control (which may not do much) and a
window for the superclassed window class.

In the case of DECLARE_WND_SUPERCLASS(), there is only one window, which is provided by the
control itself. This method is more efficient in terms of window handles than using
CContainedWindowT<>, but is not supported by the Object Wizard.

In either case, if your control needs the functionality of more than one existing window class, you can
add further CContainedWindowT<> members to your control and tie them into your control's
message map.

# CSimpleDialog<>

CSimpleDialog<>
allows you to create
simple dialogs based
on a dialog template.
Here's its inheritance
diagram:

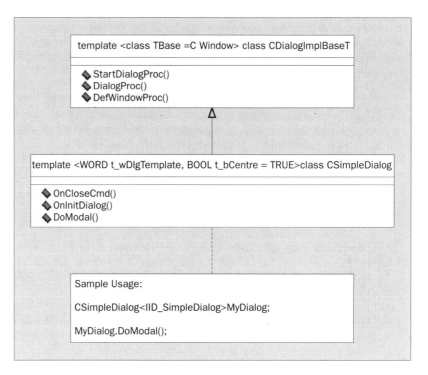

As it stands, the only controls that you can usefully place on the template are static controls, because there is no mechanism to get the values of the controls. So, if you have this template:

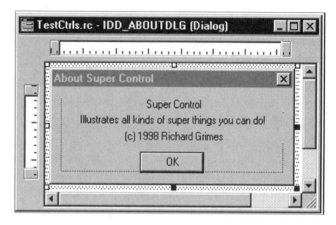

You could use CSimpleDialog<> in a right click handler like this:

```
LRESULT OnRButtonDown(
                 UINT uMsg, WPARAM wParam, LPARAM lParam, BOOL& bHandled)
{
    CSimpleDialog<IDD_ABOUTDLG> dlg;
    dlg.DoModal();
    return 0;
}
```

If you add controls to the dialog template, and you want to initialize them or get their values when the OK button is clicked, then you need to derive from this class and provide a handler for WM_INITDIALOG or the OK button click message. For example, you could have the following template, with a dropdown list box:

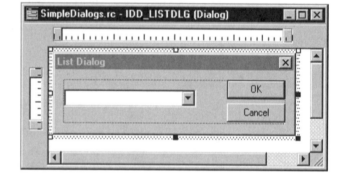

You could handle this using the following class:

```
class CListDialog : public CSimpleDialog<IDD_LISTDLG>
{
    typedef CSimpleDialog<IDD_LISTDLG> BaseClass;

public:
    BEGIN_MSG_MAP(CColorDialog)
        COMMAND_RANGE_HANDLER(IDOK, IDNO, OnOk)
        MESSAGE_HANDLER(WM_INITDIALOG, OnInitDialog)
        CHAIN_MSG_MAP(BaseClass)
    END_MSG_MAP()
```

```
LRESULT OnOk(WORD, WORD wID, HWND, BOOL&)
{
    GetDlgItemText(IDC_LIST, m_SelectedItem.m_str);
    ::EndDialog(m_hWnd, wID);
    return 0;
}

LRESULT OnInitDialog(
            UINT uMsg, WPARAM wParam, LPARAM lParam, BOOL& bHandled)
{
    USES_CONVERSION;
    CWindow combo(GetDlgItem(IDC_LIST));
    for(int i = 0 ; i < m_Items.GetSize() ; ++i)
        combo.SendMessage(CB_ADDSTRING, 0,
                    reinterpret_cast<LPARAM>(W2CT(m_Items[i].m_str)));

    SetWindowText(W2CT(m_Title));
    return BaseClass::OnInitDialog(uMsg, wParam, lParam, bHandled);
}

CComBSTR m_Title;
CComBSTR m_SelectedItem;
CSimpleArray<CComBSTR> m_Items;
};
```

The `WM_INITDIALOG` handler can be added with the message handler Wizard. This handler simply reads all the items in the `m_Items` member and adds them to the dropdown list box. Then, it sets the title of the dialog. The `IDOK` click handler merely obtains the selected item in the list box and copies it to the `m_SelectedItem` member. You could use this new class in code like this:

```
CListDialog dlg;
dlg.m_Title = L"Pick a color...";
dlg.m_Items.Add(CComBSTR("Red"));
dlg.m_Items.Add(CComBSTR("Green"));
dlg.m_Items.Add(CComBSTR("Blue"));

if(dlg.DoModal() == IDOK)
{
    USES_CONVERSION;
    ATLTRACE("clicked on OK\n");
    if(dlg.m_SelectedItem.Length() > 0)
        ATLTRACE("entered %s\n", W2CT(dlg.m_SelectedItem));
}
else
{
    ATLTRACE("clicked on Cancel\n");
}
```

The first few lines set the dialog title and put the items into the `CListDialog::m_Items` member. The code then calls `DoModal()` to show the dialog. If the user clicks on the OK button, then this method will return `IDOK`, so you can decide whether or not to get the value that the user selected.

*Once again, there's an example that incorporates this technique in the web site source code. The project is called* `SimpleDialogs`.

# CDialogImpl<>

If you want a bit more functionality – if you want to create a modeless dialog, for instance – you can use CDialogImpl<>. This derives from CDialogImplBase<> which, in turn, derives from CWindow and provides implementations for message reflection. CDialogImplBaseT<> provides DialogProc() to be used for the dialog's window procedure. It uses a thunk in StartDialogProc() to give access to the this pointer, as described before. DialogProc() handles messages through a message map. These functions are analogous to StartWindowProc() and WindowProc().

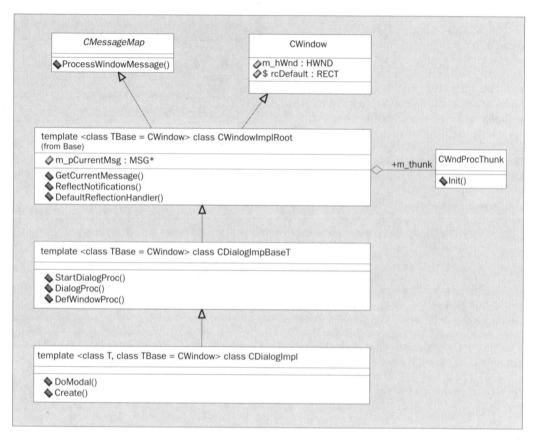

CDialogImpl<> does the work of creating and destroying a dialog. The dialog can be either modeless, in which case Create() should be used, or modal, in which case DoModal() should be used. In either case, the dialog is created from a dialog resource. You *must* supply the ID of this resource as a constant in your class, and it *must* be called IDD:

```
enum { IDD = IDD_MYDIALOG };
```

Note that CDialogImpl<> can only host Win32 controls. If you want to use ActiveX controls on the dialog resource, you should use CAxDialogImpl<>. In ATL 3.0, the dialogs created via Object Wizard derive from CAxDialogImpl<>.

## Example: Modeless Dialogs

As an example, let's create a control based on a list box that obtains its input through a modeless dialog. Since we already have a control based on a list box in the form of the SuperListBox that we created earlier in the chapter, we'll use that as the basis for the new project. Copy the Super project directory and rename it SuperII.

Now add a dialog resource to the new version of the project using the ResourceView context menu. (*Do not* use the Object Wizard.) Change the ID of the dialog to IDD_STRINGDLG, and set the title to Add/Remove Strings. To the dialog template, add a single edit box with the ID of IDC_STRING and two buttons (IDC_ADD and IDC_REMOVE). Finally, delete the OK and Cancel buttons. You should end up with a dialog looking something like this.

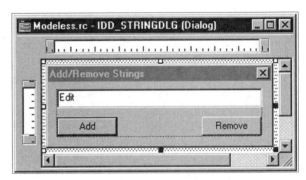

Now add the following code to SuperListBox.h before the typedefs and the CSuperListBox class definition:

```
class CStringDlg : public CDialogImpl<CStringDlg>
{
public:
    CStringDlg() { }

    enum { IDD = IDD_STRINGDLG };

BEGIN_MSG_MAP(CStringDlg)
END_MSG_MAP()
};
```

This just defines a simple dialog class based on CDialogImpl<>. You can see that the IDD enumeration constant has been set to the ID of the dialog resource that you just created.

Next, add an instance of the dialog class as a member of CSuperListBox:

```
public:
    CStringDlg m_dlg;
```

Although this will mean that an instance of the C++ dialog object will be created at the same time as the control, it does not mean that the dialog window will be created. To get the dialog window displayed, you'll need to add some code. Since we want the dialog to be displayed and hidden in response to the user right-clicking on the control, you'll need to add a handler for the WM_RBUTTONDOWN message to CSuperListBox. You can use ClassView to add the handler, but the Wizard will add the message handler to the end of the map, so you'll have to move it to the top:

```
    BEGIN_MSG_MAP(CSuperListBox)
        MESSAGE_HANDLER(WM_RBUTTONDOWN, OnRButtonDown)
        MESSAGE_HANDLER(WM_PAINT, OnPaint)
        MESSAGE_HANDLER(LB_ADDSTRING, OnAddString)
        CHAIN_MSG_MAP(CMyListControlClass)
        DEFAULT_REFLECTION_HANDLER()
    END_MSG_MAP()
```

Implement the handler like this:

```
    LRESULT OnRButtonDown(
                    UINT uMsg, WPARAM wParam, LPARAM lParam, BOOL& bHandled)
    {
        if(m_dlg.m_hWnd == NULL)
            m_dlg.Create(m_hWnd);
        if(m_dlg.IsWindowVisible())
            m_dlg.ShowWindow(SW_HIDE);
        else
            m_dlg.ShowWindow(SW_SHOW);
        return 0;
    }
```

This code creates the dialog window if it hasn't already been created, then it toggles the visibility of the window. If the dialog is visible, right-clicking the control will hide it. If the dialog is hidden, right-clicking the control will display it.

You also need to make sure that the dialog window is destroyed. The destructor for the m_dlg object does not destroy the window, so you need to do this manually. Implement the destructor of CSuperListBox like this:

```
    ~CSuperListBox()
    {
        if(m_dlg.m_hWnd)
            m_dlg.DestroyWindow();
    }
```

Compile this code, and run it in the test container. You should find that right-clicking on the control toggles the modeless dialog. Note that clicking the Close button in the corner of the dialog will neither dismiss nor destroy it.

At the moment, the Add and Remove buttons of the dialog do nothing, so let's do something about that. The dialog is used to add and remove strings from the list box, so let's pass the HWND of the list box to the dialog, so that it can add and remove the strings. Change the constructor of CStringDlg to take a reference to an HWND:

```
    CStringDlg(HWND& hWnd) : m_hParent(hWnd) { }
```

Add a private data member to hold it:

```
    private:
        HWND& m_hParent;
    };
```

I'll explain why a reference is used in a moment; in the meantime, add a single BN_CLICKED handler for both buttons:

```
BEGIN_MSG_MAP(CStringDlg)
    COMMAND_CODE_HANDLER(BN_CLICKED, OnAddRemoveString)
END_MSG_MAP()

    LRESULT OnAddRemoveString(
                WORD wNotifyCode, WORD wID, HWND hWndCtl, BOOL& bHandled)
    {
        USES_CONVERSION;
        CComBSTR bstr;
        GetDlgItemText(IDC_STRING, bstr.m_str);
        if(wID == IDC_ADD)
            SendMessage(m_hParent, LB_ADDSTRING, 0,
                                reinterpret_cast<LPARAM>(W2CT(bstr)));
        else if(wID == IDC_REMOVE)
        {
            CComBSTR bstr;
            GetDlgItemText(IDC_STRING, bstr.m_str);
            int iIndex = SendMessage(m_hParent, LB_FINDSTRING, 0,
                                reinterpret_cast<LPARAM>(W2CT(bstr)));
            if(iIndex != LB_ERR)
                SendMessage(m_hParent, LB_DELETESTRING, iIndex, 0);
        }
        return 0;
    }
```

The handler obtains the data from the edit box and then checks the control ID to determine whether it should add or remove the string. To do this, the code sends the appropriate message to the list box superclassed in the control.

Finally, you need to change CSuperListBox so that the CStringDlg is created using a reference to the HWND of the control. Change the constructor to look like this:

```
    CSuperListBox() : m_dlg(m_hWnd)
    {
        m_bWindowOnly = TRUE;
    }
```

The reason why it's important that the dialog constructor takes the window handle as a reference is that although the control is created before m_dlg is initialized, the list box window is not created until *after* the constructor is called. When the constructor is called, m_hWnd will not have a value. However, you know that it *will* have a valid value by the time Create() is called, so it will be accessible through the reference.

Finally, you can build the project and you'll be able to add and remove strings from the list box using the modeless dialog.

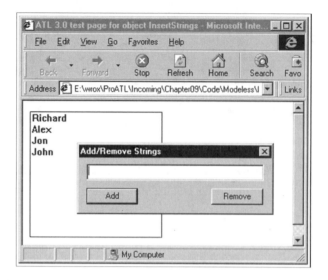

## CAxWindowT<>

CAxWindowT<> derives from CWindow. In addition to maintaining an HWND and providing wrappers for the Win32 window functions, this class provides methods to give access to an ActiveX control. Typically, you will use CAxWindow, which is a typedef:

```
template <class TBase = CWindow>
class CAxWindowT : public TBase
{
    // Other code
};

typedef CAxWindowT<CWindow> CAxWindow;
```

In other words, this derives from CWindow, and hence you get the benefits of HWND wrapping. This class is described more fully in the section on Internet Explorer classes in Chapter 10.

## CAxDialogImpl<>

This class derives from CDialogImplBaseT<> and its implementation is similar to CDialogImpl<>, except that rather than calling the Win32 API CreateDialogParam(), it calls AtlAxCreateDialog() (which can be found in atlhost.h).

This function loads two items from the project's resources. The first is a dialog template that has the types, IDs and positions of controls on the dialog, and is the same as the resources that you use to create a dialog with CDialogImpl<>. The second resource is a DLGINIT resource that has initialization data for the ActiveX controls in the dialog. AtlAxCreateDialog() merges both resources together using the inappropriately-named method SplitDialogTemplate(). This merged template is then passed to the Win32 CreateDialogIndirectParam() to create the dialog.

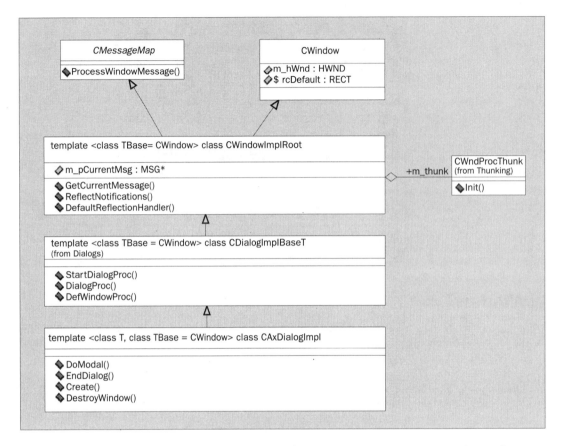

When you create a dialog using the Object Wizard (from the Miscellaneous section), it will create a class derived from CAxDialogImpl<>. The Wizard will also add a dialog resource to the project, on which you can place Win32 and ActiveX controls.

CAxDialogImpl<> is also used to provide the functionality for composite controls via the CComCompositeControl<> class, and there are further CAx classes used for hosting controls; we'll look at them in Chapter 11.

# Summary

Most ATL controls have a window, and they use this to present a user interface or to display results. If a control has a window, it means that it must handle window messages, and there are essentially two types of messages that it will be sent. System messages are sent by Windows to indicate when the user has interacted with the window (a mouse click, for example), or to tell the window that it has been created or is about to be destroyed. Notification messages are sent by child windows when things happen to them (when an item is selected in a list box, for example).

Every ATL Windows class that will manage messages must derive from the abstract class CMessageMap. This declares a single, pure virtual method that will be called to process messages as they are received. You do not have to implement this method directly because ATL has macros, arranged in a message map, that add this message processing method to your class. The macros provided by ATL allows you to manage both system and notification messages, and they also allow you to pass unhandled messages to other objects in your project. This 'chaining' can be determined at compile time, or dynamically at runtime.

Visual C++ now provides a message handler Wizard that will provide stub handler functions for the message that you want to handle. However, note that the ATL macros will not 'crack' the message parameters: it is up to you to interpret them correctly. You should also be careful with the order that message handlers appear in the map to make sure that messages are handled by the correct method. To help you to handle notification messages from child windows, ATL uses 'alternative' message maps within your control's message map that will only handle the notifications from a particular child.

ATL also provides a wrapper class called CWindow that maintains a window handle for a window, so that all calls that take an HWND will get a valid value. It also provides methods to perform most GDI tasks, but be aware that ATL does *not* provide a wrapper class for device contexts, so you have to manage these yourself. (The control classes do perform some device context manipulation for you, though, as you'll see in the next chapter.)

Finally, ATL provides CWindowImpl<> and some other classes to handle the registration, subclassing, superclassing, and creation of windows. When you create an ATL control, it will be derived from one of these Windows classes, but if you want to create a separate window you can use the classes directly. In this chapter, I have given examples of how create windows and modal and modeless dialogs using this technique.

# 10

# Controls

In Chapter 4, you saw that ATL 3.0 provides many new control types. In this chapter, we'll examine the ATL classes that provide support for properties, persistence, drawing and other control issues, and go deeper into how these control types are implemented.

A control can only be used when it's embedded as part of a container. A container communicates with a control using a gamut of COM interfaces. This communication is two-way, and is done through connection points, advise sinks and various 'site' interfaces. ATL provides your control with the correct interfaces and the necessary methods to perform the initial handshake that sets up these communications.

Controls can have **properties**, like the interface properties with which you are familiar. These properties can affect the behavior of a control, or they can be used to pass data to, or receive results from the control. A control can also support **stock properties**, which are standard properties like Font and BackColor.

Because stock properties are standard, there is a good chance that a container will know about them, and this means that they can be **bound**. Here, a control is allowed to inform the container that a stock property is about to change, and provides the container with an opportunity to veto that change. A control's properties can be made persistent, so that when a control is reactivated at a later stage, it can be initialized with the same state as before. ATL provides implementations of the COM persistence interfaces as well as the **property map** to specify which properties are to be made persistent.

Containers can also have properties, which are known as **ambient properties**. Ambient properties allow the container to provide information to the controls that it contains, so that it can offer a uniform look and feel across all its visible components. Controls can react when these ambient properties change to synchronize the appearance and behavior of all controls in the container.

With so many different properties, there's quite a lot of code needed, but ATL helps in all these areas. It provides code to manage ambient properties, it has a class to hold the stock properties and manage the notifications that should be sent to the container, and it provides classes to manage persistence to storage, streams, and property bags. The combination of the property map and ATL's classes means that there is actually very little work for you to do.

There are many different control types provided by the Object Wizard, but they can be split into three main groups. The first group (Full and Lite controls) are generic controls that comply with the OC96 standard. The second group (Composite and Lite Composite) comprises controls with dialog resources that can contain ActiveX controls. Using this control type, you can create controls built from other controls, much as you can with Visual Basic. The final group (HTML and Lite HTML controls) allows you to create a control based on a DHTML script. The difference between the standard and Lite controls in each of these groups is that while they are still complete controls, the Lite versions support fewer interfaces than the standard ones.

In this chapter, I will introduce you to classes that ATL provides for controls, and describe the general architecture used. The generic control classes and Composite controls will be covered here, leaving the HTML controls for the next and final chapter.

# CComControl<> and CComControlBase

The Object Wizard will generate enough code to create a fully working (if functionless) control. The class that Object Wizard generates derives from CComControl<> (which derives from CComControlBase) and a window class, which is CWindowImpl<> by default. These three classes implement much of the functionality for controls.

CComControlBase provides the implementation for some of the methods of the following interfaces:

- ❑   IQuickActivate
- ❑   IOleObject
- ❑   IOleInPlaceObject
- ❑   IViewObject
- ❑   IDataObject

It provides functions that can act as the implementations for IDataObject::GetData(), IViewObject::Draw(), and also provides a handler for WM_PAINT. These methods are used to draw the control, so it makes sense to centralize them in one place, allowing data members that affect drawing to be held by one class. CComControlBase also centralizes code related to managing the interaction between a control and its container.

However, `CComControlBase` does not implement interface methods directly – it only provides non-virtual, `inline` functions that can be *used* to implement these methods. In addition, it doesn't provide functions for *every* method in the interfaces mentioned. To get full implementations for these interfaces, the control needs to derive from the appropriate `Impl` class:

- ❑ `IQuickActivateImpl<>`
- ❑ `IOleObjectImpl<>`
- ❑ `IOleInPlaceActiveObjectImpl<>`
- ❑ `IViewObjectExImpl<>`
- ❑ `IDataObjectImpl<>`

In order to get access to the `public` data members and methods of your class (including those in `CComControlBase`), each of these takes your ATL class as a template parameter. Here is an example from the `IQuickActivateImpl<>` class, showing a call to a function (`IQuickActivate_QuickActivate()`) in `CComControlBase`:

```
template <class T>
class ATL_NO_VTABLE IQuickActivateImpl : public IQuickActivate
{
public:
    STDMETHOD(QuickActivate)(QACONTAINER* pQACont, QACONTROL* pQACtrl)
    {
        T* pT = static_cast<T*>(this);
        ATLTRACE2(atlTraceControls, 2, _T("IQuickActivateImpl::QuickActivate\n"));
        return pT->IQuickActivate_QuickActivate(pQACont, pQACtrl);
    }

    // Other stuff
};
```

`CComControlBase` has changed considerably since ATL 2.1. In particular, the previous version of this class held the implementations of the `IPersist` interfaces used by the control. This seemed like a good way to do things at the time, because these interfaces were designed to make the control's state persistent. However, many COM objects that *aren't* controls also use persistence, so ATL 3.0 has moved this persistence code out of `CComControlBase`. You'll see more about persistence later in the chapter.

> *To make things absolutely clear, my definition of 'control' here is anything that appears in the* Controls *section of the Object Wizard.*

# Message Handlers

Another difference between ATL 3.0 and its predecessor is how it manages some window messages. In ATL 2.1, `CComControlBase` implemented `OnGetFocus()` and `OnKillFocus()` to handle the window messages that occur when the control receives or loses focus. To use these handlers, your ATL class had to have entries in its message map. However, ATL 2.1 had the ability to chain messages through the message maps of base classes, so it was surprising that it didn't use this mechanism to provide default handlers. ATL 3.0 has remedied this; `CComControl<>` now has this message map:

```
typedef CComControl<T, WinBase> thisClass;
BEGIN_MSG_MAP(thisClass)
    MESSAGE_HANDLER(WM_PAINT, CComControlBase::OnPaint)
    MESSAGE_HANDLER(WM_SETFOCUS, CComControlBase::OnSetFocus)
    MESSAGE_HANDLER(WM_KILLFOCUS, CComControlBase::OnKillFocus)
    MESSAGE_HANDLER(WM_MOUSEACTIVATE, CComControlBase::OnMouseActivate)
END_MSG_MAP()
```

As you can see, these specify handlers in CComControlBase, the base class of CComControl<>. The handlers for these messages are slightly different to those in version 2.1, and they fix a couple of annoying problems. For example, the old version of OnSetFocus() meant that although the control got the focus, the user interface of the control was not activated. ATL 3.0 fixes this by telling the control that it should activate by calling IOleObject::DoVerb() to perform the OLEIVERB_UIACTIVATE verb (and hence run any activation code you may have provided). It then tells the container that it has got the focus by calling OnFocus() on the control's control site.

*In addition to this functionality, CComControlBase provides support for ambient and stock properties. We'll discuss this property support in the next section.*

# Properties

In this section, I will describe the three types of properties – stock, ambient, and your own custom properties – and how to implement them using ATL. Ambient properties are managed through methods and data items in CComControlBase, custom properties are added to your control's IDL and managed by get_ and put_ methods in your class, and stock properties come somewhere between the two – some code is provided by CComControlBase and CStockPropImpl<>, and other code is provided by your class.

# Ambient Properties

When Visual Basic 3.0 was first released, the market was flooded with applications that used horrendous color schemes and weird combinations of font typefaces, colors and sizes. Much of this lack of visual taste came from the Visual Basic form designers, but it was compounded by the fact that VBX controls could not ask the form for the colors and fonts that it used. Unless the form designer explicitly set these properties, the controls would use default values, which usually clashed with those of the form.

Ambient properties are properties implemented by the control container, and represent things like background color and font – in other words, the properties that will affect what most controls look like. Ambient properties are important because it gives your control the opportunity to use the same values as the container, and hence take on its 'look and feel'.

Ambient properties use a notification mechanism: if a property changes in the container, the control is notified and can change its own properties accordingly. Controls are not *required* to respond to ambient property changes, but they should. ATL doesn't provide any direct support for responding to these notifications, but it does supply easy access to the ambient properties via methods like GetAmbientBackColor() in CComControlBase.

When an ambient property changes, the container will call
`IOleControl::OnAmbientPropertyChange()` on your control, passing the DISPID of the
property that has changed. If you decide that your control will react to a change to a particular
ambient property, you should override this method, obtain the property value, and handle the
change. Note that COM defines ambient properties with standard, negative, DISPIDs.

## Example: Exercising Ambient Properties

As an example, create a DLL ATL project called `Properties` and insert a Lite Control called
AmbientProps. Add two `private` data members, and initialize them in the constructor:

```
private:
    OLE_COLOR m_clrBackColor;
    OLE_COLOR m_clrForeColor;

public:
    CAmbientProps() : m_clrBackColor(0xffffff),
                      m_clrForeColor(0)
    {}
```

Now change `OnDraw()` to use these colors:

```
HRESULT OnDraw(ATL_DRAWINFO& di)
{
    COLORREF clrFront, clrBack;
    OleTranslateColor(m_clrForeColor, NULL, &clrFront);
    OleTranslateColor(m_clrBackColor, NULL, &clrBack);

    HBRUSH hBrush = CreateSolidBrush(clrBack);
    HBRUSH hOldBrush = static_cast<HBRUSH>( SelectObject(di.hdcDraw, hBrush));

    HPEN hPen = CreatePen(PS_SOLID, 1, clrFront);
    HPEN hOldPen = static_cast<HPEN>(SelectObject(di.hdcDraw, hPen));

    const RECT& rc = *reinterpret_cast<const RECT*>(di.prcBounds);
    Rectangle(di.hdcDraw, rc.left, rc.top, rc.right, rc.bottom);

    SetTextColor(di.hdcDraw, clrFront);
    SetBkColor(di.hdcDraw, clrBack);

    SetTextAlign(di.hdcDraw, TA_CENTER|TA_BASELINE);
    LPCTSTR pszText = _T("ATL 3.0 : AmbientProps");
    TextOut(di.hdcDraw, (rc.left + rc.right) / 2,
                        (rc.top + rc.bottom) / 2, pszText, lstrlen(pszText));

    SelectObject(di.hdcDraw, hOldBrush);
    SelectObject(di.hdcDraw, hOldPen);
    return S_OK;
}
```

The ambient properties for the foreground and background color are held as OLECOLORs, whereas
GDI drawing functions use COLOREF, so the `OleTranslateColor()` function is called to convert
one to the other. The rest of the code changes the pen and brush objects of the device context so that
when the rectangle and text are drawn, they use the new colors.

To react to changes in these two ambient properties, you need to add the following to your class:

```
STDMETHOD(OnAmbientPropertyChange)(DISPID dispid)
{
    switch(dispid)
    {
    case DISPID_AMBIENT_BACKCOLOR :
        GetAmbientBackColor(m_clrBackColor);
        FireViewChange();
        break;

    case DISPID_AMBIENT_FORECOLOR :
        GetAmbientForeColor(m_clrForeColor);
        FireViewChange();
        break;
    }
    return S_OK;
}
```

This checks to see which property has changed, and if it is either the foreground or background color, then the appropriate method of `CComControlBase` is called to get the new value of the property. `FireViewChange()` is then called to get the control to repaint itself.

*Note that in the code on the Wrox web site, I have edited the IDB_AMBIENTPROPS resource to show a large 'A' on a gray background, so that you will be able to see this as the control toolbar button.*

To test this control, run the ActiveX Control Test Container. This application is an updated version of the test container provided with the previous version of Visual C++. You can run it from the Tools menu. Once running, select Insert New Control... from the Edit menu and select the AmbientProps Class item from the dialog. This will create a new control:

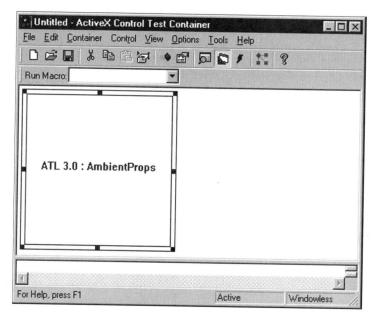

You can see that the default values set in the constructor are used: black for the foreground color, and white for the background color. To show that ambient properties are applicable to more than one control in a container, repeat the process and add another `AmbientProps` control. Select the border of the second control and drag it to the right so that the two controls are side by side.

Now from the Container menu, select the Ambient Properties... item to get the following dialog:

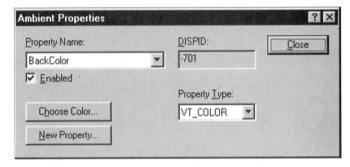

When you select a property from the Property Name box, the lower half of the dialog will change to show controls appropriate to the type of that property. These controls will allow you to supply the new property value. Use this dialog to change the `ForeColor` and `BackColor` properties. Make sure that when you have changed one property, you *close* the Ambient Properties dialog before attempting to change another property.

Here, I have changed the `ForeColor` to be white and the `BackColor` to be black.

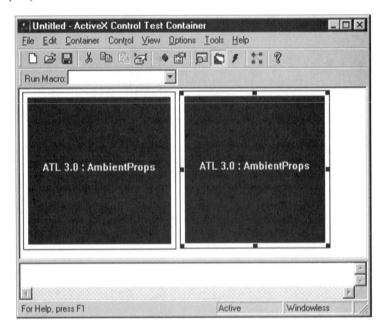

You'll see that when the ambient property changes, both control instances change: ambient properties affect *all* controls that choose to use them.

# Stock Properties

The mapping of DISPIDs to property names is carried out by `IDispatch::GetIDsOfNames()`. When a property is changed, `IDispatch::Invoke()` determines which one it is from the DISPID it receives. The properties that a control implements are listed in its type library, and ATL uses this to implement `IDispatch`.

If a container wants to change, say, the background color of a control, what DISPID should it use? When you add a property to an interface, you can use whatever DISPID you want – if you decide that the background color property has a DISPID of 84, then that is your choice. However, it does mean that only containers that know about it will be able to work out what changing this property means.

To get round this problem, Microsoft has defined 20 or so **stock properties** with specific DISPIDs, all of which have negative values. Thus, if a container wants to change the BackColor of a control, it uses the DISPID of -501 (DISPID_BACKCOLOR). If your control has a BackColor property, it should use this DISPID.

Recall that you add a property to an object using the ClassView **Add Property...** context menu item. However, this Wizard does not allow you to enter a symbol, nor does it allow you to enter a negative number. If you want to add a stock property, therefore, you must add a positive DISPID with the Wizard, and then edit the IDL by hand to make sure that the appropriate stock DISPID is used.

Object Wizard does make your life a little easier than this: the control types have a **Stock Properties** page:

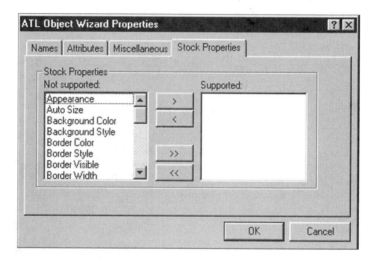

The list box on the left contains the stock properties that you *can* support, and the list box on the right shows those that you have decided your control *will* support.

When you add at least one stock property to your control, Object Wizard will derive your class from CStockPropImpl<>. This class implements the get_ and put_ methods for all stock properties. The Wizard will also add an appropriate data member for each stock property that you add. The get_ and put_ methods act upon this data member.

But wait – if CStockPropImpl<> has property code for *all* stock properties that acts on data members, and yet the Wizard only adds data members for the stock properties that you select, won't there be a problem compiling the code? There isn't. The reason is that CComControlBase has a large anonymous union with members for all stock properties. This means that for the properties you do not add to your class, the compiler will see a suitable member in the union and the code will compile. This member will never actually be accessed, of course, because the property is not part of your coclass.

In addition to adding a data member, the Object Wizard will adjust the IDL for the object to include the stock property, and it will add the property to the property map. For example, if you add the background and foreground color stock properties, you should find that the IDL looks like this:

```
interface IYourCtrl : IDispatch
{
    [propput, id(DISPID_BACKCOLOR)]
        HRESULT BackColor([in]OLE_COLOR clr);
    [propget, id(DISPID_BACKCOLOR)]
        HRESULT BackColor([out,retval]OLE_COLOR* pclr);
    [propput, id(DISPID_FORECOLOR)]
        HRESULT ForeColor([in]OLE_COLOR clr);
    [propget, id(DISPID_FORECOLOR)]
        HRESULT ForeColor([out,retval]OLE_COLOR* pclr);
};
```

The Wizard will derive your class from CStockPropImpl<> and add these two public data members:

```
OLE_COLOR m_clrBackColor;
OLE_COLOR m_clrForeColor;
```

They are public to allow CStockPropImpl<> to have access to them. Finally, the property map, which I'll cover in more detail in the next section, is adjusted to have these properties:

```
BEGIN_PROP_MAP(CYourCtrl)
    PROP_DATA_ENTRY("_cx", m_sizeExtent.cx, VT_UI4)
    PROP_DATA_ENTRY("_cy", m_sizeExtent.cy, VT_UI4)
    PROP_ENTRY("BackColor", DISPID_BACKCOLOR, CLSID_StockColorPage)
    PROP_ENTRY("ForeColor", DISPID_FORECOLOR, CLSID_StockColorPage)
END_PROP_MAP()
```

It is interesting to look at the code in CStockPropImpl<>. This class has two types of method: macro-generated and explicit. The macro-generated methods are all based on trivial types, and hence use generic code. There are separate macros for BSTR and BOOL properties, and there is a general macro that takes the property type as a parameter, as shown here:

```
#define IMPLEMENT_STOCKPROP(type, fname, pname, dispid) \
HRESULT STDMETHODCALLTYPE put_##fname(type pname) \
{ \
    ATLTRACE2(atlTraceControls,2, \
        _T("CStockPropImpl::put_%s\n"), #fname); \
    T* pT = (T*) this; \
    if (pT->FireOnRequestEdit(dispid) == S_FALSE) \
        return S_FALSE; \
    pT->m_##pname = pname; \
    pT->m_bRequiresSave = TRUE; \
    pT->FireOnChanged(dispid); \
    pT->FireViewChange(); \
    pT->SendOnDataChange(NULL); \
    return S_OK; \
} \
HRESULT STDMETHODCALLTYPE get_##fname(type* p##pname) \
{ \
```

```
        ATLTRACE2(atlTraceControls,2, \
            _T("CStockPropImpl::get_%s\n"), #fname); \
        T* pT = (T*) this; \
        *p##pname = pT->m_##pname; \
        return S_OK; \
    }
```

The `get_` method is straightforward: it returns the value of the property. The `put_` method is a little more involved. The first thing that it does is call `FireOnRequestEdit()` to tell the container that the control wants to change the stock property, and the container gets the option to allow or disallow this. If the container allows the change, then the method changes the property and sets `m_bRequiresSave` so that the persistence code knows that the internal state has changed. It then calls `FireOnChanged()` to tell the container that the property has actually changed (so the container can make a call to get hold of the new value if necessary). Next, `FireViewChange()` is called, which tells the control to repaint itself. Finally, the code calls `SendOnDataChange()` to notify the container via its advise sink (an object that implements `IAdviseSink`) that the control's data has changed.

So, what exactly are `FireOnRequestEdit()`, `FireOnChanged()`, `FireViewChange()`, and `SendOnDataChange()` and where do they come from? We'll examine that in the next section.

# Data Change Notifications

A container needs to be informed of a change in the state of a control in any of the following situations:

❑ If a property is marked `[requestedit]` in the IDL, the control must send a notification to the container when that property is about to be changed (but *before* it has been changed). This allows the container to specify that the property should be read-only at that time, or to allow the change.

❑ If a property is marked `[bindable]` in the IDL, the control must notify the container *after* the property has been changed. This allows the container to retrieve the latest value of the property.

❑ When the visual representation of the control changes, it should notify the container so that it can cache the latest visual representation of the control. This is particularly useful in OLE document containers that save a metafile representation of an object so that they have something to display without having to activate the control.

❑ When the data in a control changes, it should notify the container so that it can persist the latest state of the control.

The first two situations are handled by an interface called `IPropertyNotifySink`. The other two situations are handled by an interface called `IAdviseSink`. The container, not the control, implements both of these interfaces.

## *IPropertyNotifySink*

The `IPropertyNotifySink` interface looks like this:

```
interface IPropertyNotifySink : IUnknown
{
    HRESULT OnChanged([in] DISPID dispID);
    HRESULT OnRequestEdit([in] DISPID dispID);
}
```

Your control should call these methods when changes happen or are about to happen on [bindable] and [requestedit] properties.

A [bindable] property is one where the container is informed of changes in the property's value after it occurs. For these properties, the put_ method should call OnChanged() on all the connected sink objects. You should pass the DISPID of the property that's changed, or DISPID_UNKNOWN if more than one [bindable] property has changed.

A [requestedit] property is one where the container is informed of a potential change to a property before it occurs. For these properties, the put_ method should call OnRequestEdit() on all the connected sink objects. You should pass the DISPID of the property that's about to change, or DISPID_UNKNOWN if more than one [requestedit] property is about to change. OnRequestEdit() can return S_FALSE to indicate that the change should not occur.

### IPropertyNotifySink Connection Point

IPropertyNotifySink is handled by connection points. This means that for your ATL control to fire the events on the container's interface, it needs to:

❑  Derive from IConnectionPointContainerImpl<>
❑  Expose IConnectionPointContainer in the COM map
❑  Provide a connection point map with an entry for IID_IPropertyNotifySink
❑  Derive from a proxy class for the IPropertyNotifySink interface

You can add these items if you need to, and the Object Wizard will deal with the first two for you if you select **Support Connection** points when you generate your control. However, you always have to do the second two by hand.

ATL provides a proxy class called IPropertyNotifySinkCP<>:

```
template <class T, class CDV = CComDynamicUnkArray >
class ATL_NO_VTABLE IPropertyNotifySinkCP :
    public IConnectionPointImpl<T, &IID_IPropertyNotifySink, CDV>
{
public:
    typedef CFirePropNotifyEvent _ATL_PROP_NOTIFY_EVENT_CLASS;
};
```

At first sight, this doesn't appear to do very much: all it does is create a typedef called _ATL_PROP_NOTIFY_EVENT_CLASS. However, all controls that have properties have a property map, and the BEGIN_PROP_MAP() macro contains this typedef:

```
typedef _ATL_PROP_NOTIFY_EVENT_CLASS __ATL_PROP_NOTIFY_EVENT_CLASS;
```

This new typedef has *two* underscores at the beginning, and it is used by the FireOnRequestEdit() and FireOnChanged() methods in CComControl<>. You call these methods to fire the property events:

```
HRESULT FireOnRequestEdit(DISPID dispID)
{
   T* pT = static_cast<T*>(this);
   return T::__ATL_PROP_NOTIFY_EVENT_CLASS::FireOnRequestEdit(
      pT->GetUnknown(), dispID);
}

HRESULT FireOnChanged(DISPID dispID)
{
   T* pT = static_cast<T*>(this);
   return T::__ATL_PROP_NOTIFY_EVENT_CLASS::FireOnChanged(
      pT->GetUnknown(), dispID);
}
```

*The extra* typedef *is used because it ensures that if you call either of these methods, there must be a property map in your class. If there isn't, your control will not compile.*

So, when a control provides full IPropertyNotifySink support, you can call these methods in CComControl<> which then call methods with the same names in CFirePropNotifyEvent. The methods in CFirePropNotifyEvent ultimately call the methods on the container's IPropertyNotifySink interface.

*Note that* CFirePropNotifyEvent *doesn't use the ability to send* DISPID_UNKNOWN *to* IPropertyNotifySink. *If several* [bindable] *properties are changed at one time, for example, the container will get a slew of* OnChanged() *events.*

The question is, what happens when your control *doesn't* provide full IPropertyNotifySink support? You've already seen that the stock property code calls FireOnRequestEdit() and FireOnChanged(), so how does that code work when your control doesn't derive from IPropertyNotifySinkCP<>?

The answer is found in this global typedef that ATL provides in Atlcom.h:

```
typedef CFakeFirePropNotifyEvent _ATL_PROP_NOTIFY_EVENT_CLASS;
```

In the absence of the local typedef declared in IPropertyNotifySinkCP<> (which will only be present if you derive from this class), the global typedef will be used. In that situation, when (for example) FireOnRequestEdit() is called, the version in CFakeFirePropNotifyEvent will be used. This version merely returns S_OK without doing any work.

## IAdviseSink

The other notification mechanism uses an **advise sink**. IAdviseSink looks something like this:

```
interface IAdviseSink : IUnknown
{
   [local] void OnDataChange([in, unique] FORMATETC* pFormatetc,
                             [in, unique] STGMEDIUM* pStgmed);
   [local] void OnViewChange([in] DWORD dwAspect, [in] LONG lindex);
```

```
    [local] void OnRename([in] IMoniker* pmk);
    [local] void OnSave();
    [local] void OnClose();
}
```

I have just shown the [local] methods here because these are the ones that your control will call. The [call_as] methods (not shown here) are used to marshal the methods using code in ole32.dll.

As you can see, these notifications are pretty general: OnViewChange() indicates that the view of the control is about to change, OnRename() is called when the object is renamed, OnSave() and OnClose() are called when the object is saved or closed, and OnDataChange() is called when data in the object changes. The parameters of this last method are a storage medium that contains the data for the object, and the format of that data.

When the container creates a control, it goes through a series of handshakes that sets up all the connections between the container and the control, and one such connection is the advise sink. The control should implement IDataObject, which ATL provides through IDataObjectImpl<> on full controls.

The container passes its advise sink interface to the control by calling its IDataObject::DAdvise() method. The control should cache this interface pointer so that when it needs to notify the container, it can call the advise sink interface methods, in a similar way to calling event sink interface methods with connection points. The control should also return a cookie to the container to identify the connection.

The control should cache this interface in an **advise holder object**, which is similar to a connection point object. However, unlike the latter, an advise holder is implemented by COM and not your control. To create an advise holder, your control can call CreateDataAdviseHolder(), which creates an object with the IDataAdviseHolder interface. This object only knows about the OnDataChange() notification of the IAdviseSink interface.

Once the advise holder has been created, you can add a sink interface to it by calling the Advise() method on the holder interface. Just as a connection point object does, it returns a cookie. To generate the notification, the control calls the appropriate method on the IDataAdviseHolder and this calls the notification on all the sink interfaces that it holds. So, if your control calls IDataAdviseHolder::SendOnDataChange(), the advise holder will call IAdviseSink::OnDataChange() on all the interfaces it holds.

When the container wants to stop notifications, it calls IDataObject::DUnadvise(), passing the cookie it obtained earlier. Your control should call Unadvise() on the advise holder to remove the interface from the array it maintains.

As I mentioned above, the data advise holder will *only* send the OnDataChange() notification. However, COM also has a more general OLE advise holder that is created by calling CreateOleAdviseHolder(), and this implements the IOleAdviseHolder interface. This interface handles all the other notifications of the IAdviseSink interface, and a container asks to be notified of these by calling the control's IOleObject::Advise() method.

As you can see, advise notifications are very similar to connection points. ATL provides all the code to implement them: the advise holders are held as smart pointers in `CComControlBase` and initialized in the first calls to `IDataObjectImpl<>::DAdvise()` and `IOleObject_Advise()`.

The notification methods of these advise holders have similarly-named methods in `CComControlBase`. You can call these methods to fire notifications to the container via the advise holder. As you've already seen, the stock property implementations notify the container of data changes automatically with a call to `SendOnDataChange()`, but for custom properties you'll need to make these calls yourself. Here you can see the implementation of this function:

```
inline HRESULT CComControlBase::SendOnDataChange(DWORD advf)
{
   HRESULT hRes = S_OK;
   if(m_spDataAdviseHolder)
   {
      CComPtr<IDataObject> pdo;
      if(SUCCEEDED(ControlQueryInterface(IID_IDataObject, (void**)&pdo)))
         hRes = m_spDataAdviseHolder->SendOnDataChange(pdo, 0, advf);
   }
   return hRes;
}
```

# Custom Properties

Custom properties are added to your control using ClassView. The Wizard will add the property to the project's IDL and add stub `get_` and `put_` methods to your class. If the property is `[bindable]` or `[requestedit]`, you should use the **Attributes**... button to add this IDL attribute and you'll need to make sure that the control has a connection point map and derives from `IPropertyNotifySinkCP<>`. In addition, in the `put_` method you should inform all connected clients, as in the case of stock properties above. Generally, you will only make custom properties `[bindable]` or `[requestedit]` if you are also writing the container – containers that are written by other people won't know what to do with your property.

If your properties need to be made persistent, then you need to add an entry to the property map for the control. You may also consider calling `SendOnDataChange()` and `SetDirty()` in the `put_` method. These methods are important for controls that can be saved as part of a compound file; `SetDirty()` sets a flag that indicates that the data in the control has changed since it was last saved.

# Initializing Properties

Controls are COM objects, but COM objects are not like C++ objects as far as construction is concerned: COM objects do not have explicit constructors. When you create a COM object using a C++ class, you can use the C++ class's constructor to initialize the initial state of the object. However, if you use the ATL class factories, it means that your ATL class can only have a default constructor: the `CComObject<>::CreateInstance()` method, for example, only creates ATL objects using the default constructor. Furthermore, COM objects are created using `CoCreateInstance()` or by getting access to the class factory for the object and using that to create them (usually through `IClassFactory::CreateInstance()`). Neither of these mechanisms allows you to pass data to initialize the new object.

Instead, you have one of two choices: you can use a custom class factory, or you can initialize the object using an interface method. The former is only useful if you will write the client that will use the object, because only you will know about the custom class factory. This option is therefore inappropriate for controls, because they should be creatable by as wide a range of containers as possible. The second option is viable as long as the interface is well known, and that basically means the various IPersist interfaces.

Initializing objects with non-default values will be covered in the next section on persistence; this section is concerned with initialization using default values. When a new control is created, you can initialize the property values in the constructor of the ATL class, or in the FinalConstruct() method. However, if the control needs information from the container to initialize itself, you'll have to find another place to put your initialization code once the connection between the control and its container has been set up. There are three main possibilities here – you can override the implementation of one of the following methods, and do your initialization there:

- ❑ IOleObject::SetClientSite()
- ❑ CComControlBase::CreateControlWindow()
- ❑ IPersistStreamInit::InitNew() (or IPersistStorage::InitNew())

SetClientSite() is called by a control container when the control is created or initialized, and since all controls must be embedded in a client site, this method will always be called for controls. You could therefore consider this as a default constructor for controls. In ATL, you would usually override CComControlBase::IOleObject_SetClientSite() to achieve the same effect. If you do override the ATL implementation, you must make sure that you call the default implementation too.

CreateControlWindow() is actually called by CComControlBase::InPlaceActivate() when a control with a window *that has not already been created* is activated. CreateControlWindow() in CComControlBase is pure virtual, but there are implementations in CComControl<> and CComCompositeControl<>. The first just calls Create() to create the window, while the second calls Create() and initializes the connection points to the contained controls.

Since the control window is only created once, CreateControlWindow() will only be called when the control is created. Thus, you can override this method to initialize property values. However, note that the method is *not* called if the control is windowless, so this can only be regarded as a default constructor for windowed controls. Windowed and windowless controls are covered later in this chapter.

If an object implements IPersistStreamInit or IPersistStorage, then InitNew() will be called by the container when the control is first created to tell it to initialize itself to a default state. The version on IPersistStreamInit does not pass any parameters, but the version on IPersistStorage is passed a new storage into which the control will be persisted at a later stage. When you implement these IPersist interfaces, you specify that your object will have an explicit 'default' constructor method that a client can call and, unlike the other two methods I've mentioned, the object does not have to be a control.

ATL implements the InitNew() method in IPersistStreamInitImpl<> and
IPersistStorageImpl<>. In the first case, the implementation is empty and in the second case
ATL will call the implementation of InitNew() on IPersistStreamInit, thus centralizing the
code.

ATL Lite controls only implement IPersistStreamInit, but Full controls implement both
interfaces. However, you must be aware that if your control provides an implementation for
IPersistStreamInit::InitNew() it *must* also provide an implementation for
IPersistStreamInit::Load() to ensure that the container only calls *one* of these methods. Your
control must maintain a flag to indicate if one of these methods has been called, and return
E_UNEXPECTED if the other method is called subsequently. ATL does not do this work for you.

# Persistence

The IPersistxxx interfaces are used to ask an object to serialize its internal state to various media,
such as a stream, a storage, or a property bag. Generally, the IPersistxxx interfaces are used when
a control is used as part of a document (e.g. a Word or Excel document). They are also used in a
design environment like Visual Basic that needs to save the data that you apply during design time,
and then initialize the control with this data when the application is actually run.

However, serializing non-control objects is a useful technique too. For example, imagine an
application that uses business objects representing things like a customer, an order, a product and so
on. When an order is submitted, you will want to make a persistent copy of that order, and this is
likely to be in a relational database. However, if the order object and the objects it contains
(customer, products etc) implement IPersistxxx interfaces, then you have the opportunity to
persist the order to another storage type. You could persist it to a memory stream, and attach it to an
e-mail message to be sent to the dispatch office, where the dispatch clerk would have access to the
order without having access to the database. You could use these techniques to take a 'snapshot' of
current objects running in the application, so that at a later stage you could analyze the state of the
application, perhaps in response to an exception.

Persistence can also be useful if you want to pass an object by value, rather than by reference. For
example, if you want to put an object into a message queue (an MSMQ queue, perhaps) and then
forget about that object, it makes no sense to pass a reference, because the object may have been
released by the time the entry in the queue is accessed. A better idea is to place the *value* of the object
in the queue, so that the server reading the queue can create a clone of the original object from this
serialized state.

A final example of the use of persistence interfaces was shown in Chapter 7: the marshaling
optimization technique called marshal-by-value. By default, COM interfaces use marshal-by-reference
– that is, when you pass an interface pointer cross-process, information about the proxy is sent to the
*importing* process, but the actual data in the object remains in the *exporting* process. However, if the
object is immutable, then there are few reasons to have it implemented in another process, especially
if the client application will make many calls to the object. Marshaling by value allows you to pass
the entire state of the object to the client process, where a 'clone' of the object is created. While
marshal-by-value does not need the IPersistxxx interfaces, it clearly needs to serialize an object
state. The ATL property persistence mechanism provides code that you can reuse for this purpose.

OK: you're convinced that you want to have persistence interfaces on your object, but how do you do this in ATL? The standard mechanism is to derive from IPersistStreamInitImpl<> or IPersistStorageImpl<>, and mark the data members that will be made persistent by using a property map.

As I mentioned above, in ATL 2.1 these classes delegated to CComControlBase, and to use them you had to derive from CComControlBase and implement the control-specific ProcessWindowMessage() method, which looked odd because your class was *not* a control. In ATL 3.0, the implementation sof these interfaces delegate to global ATL methods, so your object can have a property map and derive from IPersistStreamInitImpl<> or IPersistStorageImpl<> without having to derive from CComControlBase.

However, these interface implementations *do* depend on the presence of a data member called m_bRequiresSave. Such a member is defined in CComControlBase, but if you don't derive from that class, you'll have to add this data member yourself.

There are three main persistence interfaces: IPersistStorage, IPersistStreamInit and IPersistPropertyBag. It's up to the container to decide which interfaces to use to persist your control. Some containers require the presence of one particular persistence interface, while others are more flexible.

> *There is an additional* IPersistxxx *interface that a control may implement:* IPersistStream. *This interface differs from* IPersistStreamInit *in that it does not contain* InitNew(), *but it has all of the other methods.*

The persistence interfaces are used to initialize the control to a known state – either to the default state using InitNew(), or to some other state via the Load() method. This state is most likely obtained by a previous call to Save() that tells the control to serialize its data. The three interfaces mentioned earlier all have these three methods, but the parameter passed to the methods are different in each case. A storage pointer is passed to the methods of IPersistStorage, a stream is passed to the methods of IPersistStreamInit, and an IPropertyBag pointer is passed to the IPersistPropertyBag methods.

In the first two interfaces, the control must read and write its state in one go. The serialized state is really only valid to this particular control's persistence interfaces; it's just a byte stream, and only this particular control will know how to interpret it. Data is read from and written to a stream using its Read() and Write() methods. These methods read and write from the current position in the stream, and are passed a caller-allocated buffer with the data to write (or for the data to be written to), and a count of the number of bytes to write (or read). To check that the call is successful, they are also passed a pointer to a caller count variable where the method will store the number of bytes actually written or read.

Since the stream methods read/write at the current stream position, there is no requirement to identify the data, but it does mean that access is serial and not random. The position in the stream can be changed with the Seek() method.

You cannot write data directly to a storage. Instead, an object must call `OpenStream()` to open an existing stream, or `CreateStream()` to create a new stream. The object can then use the stream's methods to read and write the data. The ATL implementation of `IPersistStorage` will use a stream called `Contents` by default, and implement the persistence code using the same code as in `IPersistStreamInitImpl<>`.

The `IPersistPropertyBag` interface is interesting because it allows data to be read or written item by item – in other words, using random access. The data is passed between the control and container using an object with the `IPropertyBag` interface and, like a stream, this has two methods: `Read()` and `Write()`. Unlike the stream methods, these give access to a data item by name rather than by position in a byte stream. The actual data is passed using a `VARIANT`, which describes the data type and hence the data size. If the `VARIANT` contains an object, then the container/control should call `QueryInterface()` on that object for either its `IPersistStream` or `IPersistPropertyBag` interface and then use the `Load()` or `Save()` methods on that.

`IPersistPropertyBag` is typically used by controls that have properties that are initialized by parameters on a web page, or that will be used in Visual Basic.

# Property Map

Most, but not necessarily all, of a control's internal state that should be made persistent is held in the control's properties. When a control is initialized through its `IPersistxxx` interfaces, the data passed to the control should be used to initialize these properties. Likewise, when the control is asked to serialize its state, it should serialize its properties.

Thoroughly generalized code to persist a control could work by reading the control's type library and then persisting all `[propget]` properties; likewise, the initialization code could read the type library and initialize all `[propput]` properties. However, you may decide that you do not want all of the control's properties to be saved in this way, or that you have state that is not held in properties. To provide a more flexible mechanism, ATL 3.0 uses **property maps** to allow you to specify those properties that can be initialized, or saved, through the `IPersistxxx` interfaces.

The property map is declared with the `BEGIN_PROP_MAP()` and `END_PROP_MAP()` macros like this:

```
BEGIN_PROP_MAP(CAmbientProps)
    PROP_DATA_ENTRY("_cx", m_sizeExtent.cx, VT_UI4)
    PROP_DATA_ENTRY("_cy", m_sizeExtent.cy, VT_UI4)
END_PROP_MAP()
```

*Note that ATL 3.0 uses* `BEGIN_PROP_MAP()` *where ATL 2.1 used* `BEGIN_PROPERTY_MAP()`. *This latter form is deprecated, but older code will still compile. The new version does not implicitly add the control size to the map (hence the presence of the entries for the* _cx *and* _cy *members). This allows the property map to be used by non-control ATL objects.*

The `BEGIN_PROP_MAP()` macro declares a `static` method called `GetPropertyMap()` that returns the property map to the caller. Behind the macros, the property map consists of an array of `ATL_PROPMAP_ENTRY` structures, which look like this:

```
struct ATL_PROPMAP_ENTRY
{
    LPCOLESTR szDesc;                       // Name of the property
    DISPID dispid;                          // Property DISPID
    const CLSID* pclsidPropPage;            // Property page
    const IID* piidDispatch;                // Interface for object properties
    DWORD dwOffsetData;                     // Offset of property in object
    DWORD dwSizeData;                       // Size of property
    VARTYPE vt;                             // Property type
};
```

There are two types of 'property' that can be put into a property map (and hence made persistent). First, there are the standard COM properties (those added to the IDL using [propput], [propputref] and [propget] attributes). Entries for these properties use the dispid member so that the persistence code can access them through IDispatch::Invoke(), and ultimately through their put_ and get_ methods.

Second, there are the simple data members of the ATL class. Since these are not COM properties, you cannot access them using a DISPID. Instead, the persistence code will access them through the this pointer. These members use the dwOffsetData, dwSizeData and vt members to identify where in the object the data is, how big it is, and its type.

An ATL class may have more than one IDispatch-based interface, and all these interfaces may have properties, so to identify the interface on which Invoke() is called, the property map can take the IID of the interface. You can specify this using the PROP_ENTRY_EX() macro. If the control has only one dual interface, then IID_IDispatch can be used, which is the default used by PROP_ENTRY().

The szDesc member of the structure is used to identify a property in a property bag, and this description should be a single word. Although the IPropertyBag interface doesn't place these limits on the description, most implementations will choke on descriptions that contain spaces. The other member in ATL_PROPMAP_ENTRY is pclsidPropPage, which identifies the property page that will be used to get a value for the property. This member is used by ISpecifyPropertyPagesImpl<> and IPerPropertyBrowsingImpl<>.

When you add a new property to a control interface using ClassView, the Wizard *will not* add the property to the property map – that is your responsibility. To add a property to the property map, use one of the following macros:

| Macro | Description |
| --- | --- |
| PROP_ENTRY() | Adds an interface property to the map |
| PROP_ENTRY_EX() | Adds an interface property for an interface other than the default |
| PROP_PAGE() | Adds a property page used to change property values |
| PROP_DATA_ENTRY() | Adds a non-interface data member to the map |

Here's an example of each:

```
BEGIN_PROP_MAP(CMyProps)
    PROP_DATA_ENTRY("_cx", m_sizeExtent.cx, VT_UI4)
    PROP_DATA_ENTRY("_cy", m_sizeExtent.cy, VT_UI4)
    PROP_ENTRY("Name", 1, CLSID_NULL)
    PROP_ENTRY_EX("Account", 2, CLSID_NULL, IID_MyOtherProps)
    PROP_PAGE(CLSID_MyProppage)
END_PROP_MAP()
```

As you can see, the property map is used to indicate the property pages that the control uses, as well as the properties that are made persistent.

The first two lines are added by the Object Wizard, and ensure that the control's size is saved. The data is saved with the descriptions _cx and _cy, and these are both unsigned int values (VT_UI4). The actual class data member is given as the second parameter, and from this the macro can calculate the offset from the this pointer of the data member, and its size.

The Name item is for an interface property that was added with ClassView; the second parameter to the macro is the DISPID of the property. The persistence code will obtain the property value in a VARIANT by using IDispatch::Invoke(). The VARIANT will have information about the property type, and hence its size.

The last parameter to PROP_ENTRY() is the CLSID of the property page that will be used with this property. In this case, a property page is not used, so CLSID_NULL is supplied. This property is part of the default dual interface (the interface that is used to supply the implementation of IDispatch), so we use PROP_ENTRY() to read and write the property through IDispatch.

However, this example has two dual interfaces, and on the second interface is a property called Account. The fourth entry in the gives the IID of this other interface so that the persistence code can call QueryInterface() for it before attempting to access the property.

Finally, the control has a general property page that's used to access the control's properties. This page could be used to change one or more properties. This item just indicates that the property page is used by this control, so that it can be returned by ISpecifyPropertyPagesImpl<>::GetPages().

*I won't develop a sample project that demonstrates how to access a control's properties through a property page here, but if you'd like to see one, you can download the source files for* Beginning ATL COM Programming *from the Wrox web site. The code for Chapter 8 contains a complete example.*

In the following sections, I will detail the persistence classes provided by ATL 3.0 and explain how they work.

# IPersistStreamInitImpl<>

All the controls generated by the Object Wizard implement IPersistStreamInit via the ATL implementation class IPersistStreamInitImpl<>. Since ATL doesn't add any code to InitNew(), this class can also be used to implement IPersistStream because this interface is vtable-compatible with IPersistStreamInit.

These are the methods of the IPersistStreamInit interface:

| Method | Description |
|---|---|
| GetClassID() | Returns the CLSID of the control. |
| IsDirty() | Tests the control to see if the state has changed |
| Load() | Initializes the control with previously serialized state |
| Save() | Asks the control to serialize its state |
| GetSizeMax() | Specifies how much space the control needs to serialize its state |
| InitNew() | Initializes the control to a default state |

When the container wants to get a control to serialize its state, it will create a stream object and pass this to the control via Save(). However, a container may not create a totally new stream; it may pass a stream that already has data in it, and give the control a *portion* of the stream by moving the stream pointer to a free position. Whether this stream is new or not, it must be large enough to fit the data from the control, or else it must be resizable.

Containers can find out how large the stream should be by calling GetSizeMax(). In most cases, it doesn't matter what GetSizeMax() returns (or even whether it's implemented at all), since the majority of streams are resizable. For this reason, the default implementation of GetSizeMax() returns E_NOTIMPL. In the cases where you do need to implement GetSizeMax(), you will need to read through the property map and calculate the total size required by Save(). The section called *Persisting Properties*, below, explains the amount of space required by the various property types, and the marshal by value example in Chapter 7 also illustrates how to do this.

One piece of information that a container may have already put in the stream is the control's CLSID, which can be obtained by calling GetClassID(). The reason for doing this is so that the container can recreate the serialized object. It can:

- ❑ Read the stream to access the CLSID
- ❑ Create an uninitialized control using CoCreateInstance()
- ❑ Get the IPersistStreamInit interface from the new control
- ❑ Pass the stream (with the stream pointer positioned after the CLSID) to IPersistStreamInit::Load() to get the control to initialize itself with the serialized state

When a container is about to save the document that contains the control, it will call IsDirty() to see if the state has changed since the last save. ATL maintains the 'dirty' state of the control in a member called m_bRequiresSave. The CComControlBase::SetDirty() method sets the flag, and calls to Save() clear it.

*Normally, an implementation of* IPersistStreamInit *should guard against* InitNew() *and* Load() *being called more than once (and against both being called). If one of these is called, and then either is called subsequently,* E_UNEXPECTED *should be returned. The ATL implementation does* not *perform this checking, so if you intend to use* InitNew(), *you should override these two methods to check whether the other has already been called and if not call the base class version.*

# IPersistStorageImpl<>

This class is added as a base class to standard controls, but not to Lite ones. In terms of persisting a control, IPersistStorage is regarded as a heavyweight version of IPersistStreamInit. Its methods are:

| Method | Description |
|---|---|
| GetClassID() | Returns the CLSID of the control |
| IsDirty() | Tests the control to see if the state has changed |
| Load() | Initializes the control with previously serialized state |
| Save() | Asks the control to serialize its state |
| InitNew() | Initializes the control to a default state |
| HandsOffStorage() | Indicates that the base storage is about to change, so the object must release any storage pointers |
| SaveCompleted() | Indicates that the change to the base storage has been completed |

The COM specification says objects that implement IPersistStorage can perform either full or incremental saves of the object. Incremental saves occur whenever the object decides it is necessary, and so it must cache the storage pointer that will be used to perform them. Full saves are done when Save() is called. Whichever is used, the specification says that the object must guarantee that it can do it *even if the system has no memory*. Because of this restriction, the object implementation should not create new streams in the storage during Save(). This may seem a rather odd requirement, because Save() is passed an IStorage pointer, and since you can only write data to a stream, some other code must already have created that stream.

The code that does this should be InitNew(); this method is passed the storage object that should be used by Save(), and the object can then cache this and create whatever streams it will require. Likewise, an object can support incremental loads through the storage passed through Load() and so must cache the pointer passed. As with IPersistStreamInit, only one of InitNew() or Load() will ever be called during the lifetime of an instance of a control. This is a bit like saying that a C++ object will be initialized with its default constructor or one of its constructors with parameters, but never both.

The other methods of this interface reflect its use. A container could create a separate compound file just for the control, and pass the root storage object of that file to the control. In this situation, the container may decide to change the name of the file, and to do this it must tell the control that it can no longer perform incremental saves by calling HandsOffStorage(). The control must then release the pointers that it may have cached, because they will become invalid. Once the container has finished messing around with the storage, it calls SaveCompleted(), passing the new storage pointer. The control can now obtain all the pointers it requires on this new storage.

As you can see, this is a bit complicated, but it does give the container flexibility in how it maintains object state. However, ATL does *not* implement this protocol in its implementation of `IPersistStorage`. Instead, it assumes that the control's data is saved in a stream called "Contents", which it creates in `Save()` (even though this could fail in low memory conditions, which the documentation says that the implementation should guard against). The implementations of `InitNew()`, `Load()` and `Save()` just call the `IPersistStreamInit` methods on the "Contents" stream.

Since `IPersistStorageImpl<>` just delegates all the hard work to `IPersistStreamInitImpl<>`, you may be wondering why ATL provides an implementation of the former interface at all. The simple reason is that some containers require that a control must support `IPersistStorage` before they can insert a control. An example of this is WordPad; if you try to insert a control that doesn't support `IPersistStorage`, you will get the following dialog:

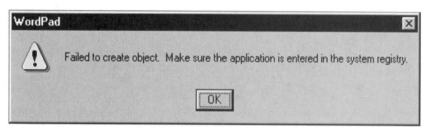

Despite the message, the reason for the dialog is that the control has been queried for `IPersistStorage`, and the control has returned `E_NOINTERFACE`.

# Persisting Properties

When `IPersistStreamInitImpl<>::Load()` is called (either directly, or through `IPersistStorageImpl<>::Load()`), it calls `IPersistStreamInit_Load()` through the control's `this` pointer (cast to the class passed as the parameter to `IPersistStreamInitImpl<>`).

> `IPersistStreamInit_Load()` *is implemented in* `IPersistStreamInitImpl<>`, *which may seem odd. The reason for the separate method is that ATL 2.1 implemented it on* `CComControlBase`, *and older ATL code could have overridden this method.*

In turn, this method calls the global `AtlIPersistStreamInit_Load()` function:

```
HRESULT IPersistStreamInit_Load(LPSTREAM pStm, ATL_PROPMAP_ENTRY* pMap)
{
    T* pT = static_cast<T*>(this);
    HRESULT hr = AtlIPersistStreamInit_Load(
                                pStm, pMap, pT, pT->GetUnknown());
    if(SUCCEEDED(hr))
        pT->m_bRequiresSave = FALSE;
    return hr;
}
```

pMap is a pointer to the property map obtained through a call to GetPropertyMap(). The purpose of AtlIPersistStreamInit_Load() is to loop through the property map and, for all items that represent properties, read their values from the stream.

The data that the method expects is shown in this figure:

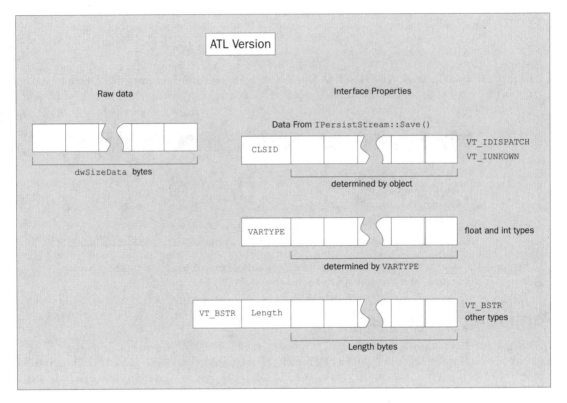

The ATL version for ATL 3.0 is 0x0300, and if the value in the stream is greater than this, the load operation will fail. Next, there are two choices: the property map will specify either that there is raw data, or that the data is an interface property. If the former is true, then the property map will specify how many bytes to read, and where to write it.

If the data is an interface property, then the code will check the property type from the property map to determine what to do next. If the data in the stream represents an object, then the object's CLSID and serialized state will follow. This serialized state will have been put into the stream at some stage by querying the object for IPersistStream and calling Save() (if that object was an ATL object, then the data would be in the same form as shown here). To read out this data, AtlIPersistStreamInit_Load() (via CComVariant::ReadFromStream()) creates an object instance and passes it the stream, so that the object can read out as many bytes as it needs. These two steps – creating the object and initializing it – are done with a call to OleLoadFromStream(). After this, the stream pointer should be at the next data item.

If the property is one of the integer or float types (which include the CY and DATE types, but not the DECIMAL type) then the stream will have the VARTYPE followed by the property bytes. For all other property types, the stream will have VT_BSTR, followed by the number of bytes in the BSTR it indicates, and then the bytes themselves. The method will use the length to allocate a BSTR and then read the bytes into it. If the type of the data is not BSTR, the COM API VariantChangeType() is called to convert the BSTR to the required type.

The Save() method carries out this process in reverse.

These IPersistStreamInit methods are suitable for most of the properties that you'll want to implement on your object. However, there are some omissions – for example, if you have an enumerator as a property to give access to an array or a collection of items, this persistence implementation will not be able to handle it. If this is the case, your object must override these methods to persist your property with custom code, but you must make sure that you call the base implementation, and you must implement both Save() and Load().

## Resources

If you create a composite control and add an ActiveX control to it, Visual C++ will create a DLGINIT binary resource that will be the stream passed to the control's IPersistStreamInit::Load() method when the composite dialog is initialized. For example:

```
IDD_MYCOMPOSITE DLGINIT
BEGIN
    IDC_SLIDER1, 0x376, 192, 0
0x0024, 0x0000, 0x0039, 0x0033, 0x0036, 0x0038, 0x0032, 0x0036, 0x0035,
0x0045, 0x002d, 0x0038, 0x0035, 0x0046, 0x0045, 0x002d, 0x0031, 0x0031,
0x0064, 0x0031, 0x002d, 0x0038, 0x0042, 0x0045, 0x0033, 0x002d, 0x0030,
0x0030, 0x0030, 0x0030, 0x0046, 0x0038, 0x0037, 0x0035, 0x0034, 0x0044,
0x0041, 0x0031, 0x4321, 0x1234, 0x0008, 0x0000, 0x1280, 0x0000, 0x0457,
0x0000, 0xae11, 0x0a2b, 0x0000, 0x0006, 0x001c, 0x0000, 0x0000, 0x0000,
0x0005, 0x0000, 0x0001, 0x0000, 0x0000, 0x0000, 0x000f, 0x0000, 0x0000,
0x006c, 0x0000, 0x0000, 0x0000, 0x0000, 0x0000, 0x0000, 0x0001, 0x0000,
0x0000, 0x0000, 0x0000, 0x0000, 0xef01, 0xabcd, 0x0000, 0x0005, 0x0e60,
0x0016, 0x0006, 0x0000, 0x0000, 0x0000, 0xc0c0, 0x00c0, 0xf1ec, 0x0012,
0xde1f, 0xbdec, 0x0001, 0x0005, 0xf1ec, 0x0012,
    0
END
```

Here, I have added a slider common control and changed one of the properties (I changed the Max value from 10 to 15). In response to this, the dialog editor changes the appropriate property and then calls IPersistStreamInit::Save() to get the state of the control, which it adds as the DLGINIT resource after converting the data to the hexadecimal string equivalent. When you add controls that you have written to a dialog template, the resource editor will do the same thing: if you add the control without changing any properties, the DLGINIT will not be created. Otherwise, the resource editor will call Save() on the control instance in the editor and create a DLGINIT from the persisted data.

# IPersistPropertyBagImpl<>

When a container serializes a control with `IPersistStreamInit`, it obtains a byte stream from the control. The container has no knowledge of what the byte stream actually means, and if you were to examine the byte stream, neither would you. Furthermore, the `IPersistStreamInit` methods are an all-or-nothing affair – all the control's properties are serialized in one go.

The `IPersistPropertyBag` interface has one main advantage over `IPersistStreamInit`: it simplifies the job of the client programmer by allowing the saving and loading of properties individually. Beneficial side effects are that this mechanism is more resistant to problems caused by version changes in a component, and it makes it easy for `IPropertyBag` implementers to persist the properties as human-readable text. This makes it useful for web pages and Visual Basic forms, where the `IPersistPropertyBag` interface is most frequently used.

For example, suppose you have a control that implements `IPersistPropertyBag` with this property map:

```
BEGIN_PROP_MAP(CMyCtrl)
    PROP_DATA_ENTRY("_cx", m_sizeExtent.cx, VT_UI4)
    PROP_DATA_ENTRY("_cy", m_sizeExtent.cy, VT_UI4)
    PROP_ENTRY("StringVal", 1, CLSID_NULL)
END_PROP_MAP()
```

When you insert it onto a Visual Basic 6.0 form and save it, you will get this code in the `.frm` file:

```
Begin MYCTRLSLib.MyCtrl MyCtrl1
    Height      =   2895
    Left        =   960
    TabIndex    =   0
    Top         =   120
    Width       =   2895
    _cx         =   5106
    _cy         =   5106
    StringVal   =   "String data"
End
```

The top five items are properties maintained by Visual Basic to position and size the control. The last three are properties of the control, and are obtained by Visual Basic calling `IPersistPropertyBag::Save()`. In response, the control iterates through the property map and writes each property to the property bag.

Note that `StringVal` doesn't have to be the name of a property; it's just the name used to identify some persisted information within the property bag. The control could have this in its IDL:

```
[propget, id(1)] HRESULT String([out, retval] BSTR* pVal);
[propput, id(1)] HRESULT String([in] BSTR newVal);
```

In other words, the property with DISPID 1 is called `String`, not `StringVal`. Remember that data members don't even correspond to COM properties, but they can still be identified by name in the property bag. Of course, it could get quite confusing if you used completely arbitrary names to identify data within a property bag, and it is usually good practice to use the actual property name in the `PROP_ENTRY()` macro, and the name of the data member in the `PROP_DATA_ENTRY()` macro.

The ATL implementation, `IPersistPropertyBagImpl<>`, uses the property map to determine the properties that it needs to load from, or save to, the property bag. The process is similar to the `IPersistStreamInitImpl<>` methods, but note that the data is written to a property bag as a `VARIANT`. If the property map item is raw data, then the data is converted to or from a `VARIANT` (depending on whether it is being read or written). However, only the integer types are supported (`signed` and `unsigned char`, `short`, `long`, `int` and `VARIANT_BOOL`). You'll see how to extend the range of types supported by your implementation of `IPersistPropertyBag` shortly.

Otherwise, if the entry is a property, it's accessed through the appropriate `IDispatch`-based interface using its `Invoke()` method. Because `Invoke()` is used, the data is accessed through a `VARIANT`. If the property is an object (that is, the `VARIANT` contains an `IUnknown*` or an `IDispatch*`) then the container that implements `IPropertyBag` will obtain the internal state of the object by getting access to one of the object's `IPersist` interfaces (either `IPersistPropertyBag` or `IPersistStream`).

For example, imagine you have a control called `Parent` that has a property called `Child` that itself supports `IPersistPropertyBag` and has two properties: `Name` and `Age`. Then, when you save the form, Visual Basic will get the values of the embedded object:

```
Begin EMBEDDEDOBJECTSLibCtl.Parent Parent1
    Height          =   2895
    Left            =   960
    TabIndex        =   0
    Top             =   120
    Width           =   2895
    _cx             =   5106
    _cy             =   5106
    BeginProperty Child
        {21B4E73E-EFB8-11D1-9B67-0060973044A8}
        Name            =   "Thomas"
        Age             =   3
    EndProperty
    MyName          =   "Richard"
End
```

As you can see, Visual Basic brackets the `Child`'s property values with `BeginProperty` and `EndProperty`, and also places the CLSID of that object so that when it activates the `Parent1` object at a later stage, it can create this embedded object and initialize the property.

# Example: Persistence

As I explained in the previous section, you can add raw data to the property map. However, if you want ATL to persist this data, you should only add integer members to the map – `AtlIPersistPropertyBag_Load()` and `AtlIPersistPropertyBag_Save()` only provide code for persisting raw integer data.

Fortunately, the ATL code doesn't prevent you from adding raw data members of other types to the property map and persisting them yourself. If you look in either of these functions, you will find an `if` statement and a `switch` like this:

```
if(pMap[i].dwSizeData != 0)
{
    ... // Code omitted for clarity
    switch(pMap[i].vt)
    {
        ... // Save or load the data here
```

The code knows that the map entry is for raw data because the `dwSizeData` member is non zero. If it *is* raw data, then the `switch` tests to see what type of data it is. The ATL code provides `cases` (and the corresponding code) for types `VT_UI1`, `VT_I1`, `VT_BOOL`, `VT_UI2`, `VT_UI4`, `VT_INT` and `VT_UINT`. If the `vt` member of the `ATL_PROPMAP_ENTRY` structure is for any other type, ATL just ignores that map entry.

This looks like it allows you to add any extra raw data types to the property map without upsetting existing ATL code, as long as you set the `vt` member to a type that ATL doesn't support. This would allow you to override `IPersistPropertyBag::Load()` and `IPersistPropertyBag::Save()` with your own code to persist data members not supported by ATL, and then to call ATL's implementation to load and save the standard data members that it *does* support.

However, before we get too carried away, let's think about some of the limitations of this approach. If we add custom data types to the property map, will we break ATL's other persistence code (provided by `IPersistStreamInitImpl<>`)? Well, it turns out that we won't. If you take a look at ATL's stream persistence code (in `AtlIPersistStreamInit_Save()` and `AtlIPersistStreamInit_Load()`), you'll see that it can cope with *any* fixed size data members already:

```
if(pMap[i].dwSizeData != 0)
{
    void* pData = (void*) (pMap[i].dwOffsetData + (DWORD)pThis);
    hr = pStm->Write(pData, pMap[i].dwSizeData, NULL);
    if(FAILED(hr))
        return hr;
    continue;
}
```

The `vt` member of the map entry is irrelevant to ATL's stream persistence code. All that's required is that the `dwSizeData` member is set correctly.

> Note that the ATL property macros only allow you to persist data members of your class, not global data. Both the PROP_DATA_ENTRY() macro and ATL's persistence code assume that you are using the property map for data members of your class. You can see that the code above calculates the address of a data member using an offset from the `this` pointer of your class. Note also that ATL's persistence code cannot persist pointer members, (or rather, it will persist the pointer rather than the data being pointed to).

*A further limitation on the type of data that can be put into a property map is imposed by the fact that the property map is a* `static` *array. That of course means that the property map is shared among all instances of the class. You can't use the property map for data that will vary in size between instances of a class. (It is theoretically possible to use the map for dynamically sized data that is the same size for all instances, but this isn't supported by ATL and it's easier to persist this data by hand anyway)*

## IPersistPropertyBagImpl_Ex<>

Now that we know a bit more about the limitations of ATL's `IPersistPropertyBagImpl<>` class in comparison with `IPersistStreamInitImpl<>`, let's create a new class to offer parity to property bag users. We'll call this class `IPersistPropertyBagImpl_Ex<>`. Let's examine what this class should look like in sections:

```
//  IPersistPropertyBagImpl_Ex.h
//
////////////////////////////////////////////////////////

#ifndef __IPERSISTPROPERTYBAGIMPL_EX_H_
#define __IPERSISTPROPERTYBAGIMPL_EX_H_

template <class T>
class IPersistPropertyBagImpl_Ex : public IPersistPropertyBagImpl<T>
{
private:
    typedef IPersistPropertyBagImpl<T> IPPBI;

public:
    enum { VTEX_FIXED_SIZE_BSTR_BLOB = 999 };
```

First, we define the new class as a template and derive it from ATL's existing implementation class. We need the template parameter to get access to the class that will derive from this template class, and so that we can pass that class on to `IPersistPropertyBagImpl<>`.

Beneath this, you can see a `private` typedef that we'll use to shorten any code that needs to deal with the ATL base class, and an anonymous `enum` that defines a constant `VTEX_FIXED_SIZE_BSTR_BLOB`. This constant will be used as the `vt` member of the property map entry, so it uses a value that we know won't clash with any existing `VT_` constants. This should help insulate us from future changes to ATL's implementation of `IPersistPropertyBagImpl<>`.

### Save()

```
STDMETHOD(Save)(
    LPPROPERTYBAG pPropBag, BOOL fClearDirty, BOOL fSaveAllProperties)
{
    T* pT = static_cast<T*>(this);
    ATL_PROPMAP_ENTRY* pMap = T::GetPropertyMap();
    ATLASSERT(pMap != NULL);

    for(int i = 0 ; pMap[i].pclsidPropPage != NULL ; ++i)
    {
        // We only handle raw data with a description
        if((pMap[i].dwSizeData == 0) || (pMap[i].szDesc == NULL))
            continue;
```

```
                        // Check the vt type
                        switch(pMap[i].vt)
                        {
                        case VTEX_FIXED_SIZE_BSTR_BLOB :
                            {
                                LPBYTE pData = reinterpret_cast<BYTE*>(
                                    pMap[i].dwOffsetData + reinterpret_cast<DWORD>(pT));
                                CComBSTR bstr;
                                Insert(&bstr, pData, pMap[i].dwSizeData);
                                CComVariant var(bstr);
                                HRESULT hr = pPropBag->Write(pMap[i].szDesc, &var);
                                if(FAILED(hr))
                                    return hr;
                            }
                        default :
                            continue;
                        }
                    }
                    return IPPBI::Save(pPropBag, fClearDirty, fSaveAllProperties);
        }
```

In the implementation of Save(), the code loops through the property map looking for raw data with a description. When it finds a raw data item, it checks to see if it is a type handled by this class (we only handle VTEX_FIXED_SIZE_BSTR_BLOB entries). For entries of the appropriate type, the code gets hold of a LPBYTE pointer to the data member, converts the data into a string by calling the Insert() helper, and saves this string to the property bag. All other property entries are handled (or not) by the code in the base class. The end of the property map is denoted by a NULL entry in the pclsidPropPage member.

*Note that the property map is traversed twice – once in our class, and once in the ATL base class. However, we know (by looking at the implementation of* IPersistPropertyBagImpl<>) *that the data will only be written or read once.*

## Load()

```
STDMETHOD(Load)(LPPROPERTYBAG pPropBag, LPERRORLOG pErrorLog)
{
    T* pT = static_cast<T*>(this);
    ATL_PROPMAP_ENTRY* pMap = T::GetPropertyMap();
    ATLASSERT(pMap != NULL);

    for(int i = 0 ; pMap[i].pclsidPropPage != NULL ; ++i)
    {
        // We only handle raw data with a description
        if((pMap[i].dwSizeData == 0) || (pMap[i].szDesc == NULL))
            continue;

        // Check the vt type
        switch(pMap[i].vt)
        {
        case VTEX_FIXED_SIZE_BSTR_BLOB :
            {
                CComVariant var;
                HRESULT hr = pPropBag->Read(
                                    pMap[i].szDesc, &var, pErrorLog);
```

```
            if(FAILED(hr))
                continue;

            LPBYTE pData = reinterpret_cast<BYTE*>(
                    pMap[i].dwOffsetData + reinterpret_cast<DWORD>(pT));
            int size = pMap[i].dwSizeData;
            LPCWSTR ptr = var.bstrVal;
            Extract(&ptr, pData, size);
        }
    default :
        continue;
        }
    }
    return IPPBI::Load(pPropBag, pErrorLog);
}
```

The implementation of Load() just does the reverse of Save(). It loops through the map until it finds an entry that we deal with, reads the corresponding value from the property bag, and writes the value to the data member using the Extract() helper. Once Load() has finished looping through the property map, it calls the base class version of Load() to load any entries not handled by our class.

### Insert() and Extract()

```
void Insert(BSTR* stream, void* pData, DWORD size)
{
    CComBSTR bstr;
    bstr.Attach(*stream);

    LPBYTE ptr = static_cast<LPBYTE>(pData);
    TCHAR strTemp[3] = {0};

    for(DWORD j = 0 ; j < size ; ++j)
    {
        BYTE ch = *ptr;
        strTemp[1] = (ch & 0xf) > 9 ? '7'+(ch & 0xf) : '0'+(ch & 0xf);
        ch = ch >> 4;
        strTemp[0] = (ch & 0xf) > 9 ? '7'+(ch & 0xf) : '0'+(ch & 0xf);
        ptr++;
        bstr += strTemp;
    }
    *stream = bstr.Detach();
}

void Extract(LPCWSTR* stream, void* pData, DWORD size)
{
    LPCWSTR str = *stream;
    LPBYTE ptr = static_cast<LPBYTE>(pData);

    for(DWORD j = 0 ; j < size ; ++j)
    {
        BYTE ch = (str[0] >= L'A') ? str[0] - L'7' : str[0] - L'0';
        ch *= 16;
        ch += (str[1] >= L'A') ? str[1] - L'7' : str[1] - L'0';
```

```
            *ptr = ch;
            ptr++;
            str += 2;
        }
        *stream = str;
    }
};

#endif // #ifndef __IPERSISTPROPERTYBAGIMPL_EX_H_
```

The idea of `Insert()` and `Extract()` is that they convert binary data to and from readable string data. Property bags are usually stored as text (such as Visual Basic's `.frm` files), so it's important to convert the data to human-readable strings without relying on non-printable characters.

`Insert()` is passed a BSTR, a pointer to a buffer, and the size of the buffer in bytes. It converts each byte in the buffer to a two-character readable hexadecimal string, and adds each onto the end of the BSTR. (The `CComBSTR` class reallocates as necessary).

`Extract()` does the opposite: it takes a LPWSTR pointer and extracts `size` two-byte hex strings, converting each to a byte and then placing them in the buffer pointed to by `pData`. The position in the input stream is updated to reflect how many characters have been read.

## Fixed length Data

Now we can test our new class out with an example. We'll create a control that represents the current, highest, and lowest values of some item – perhaps a temperature, or a stock value. The control will be based on data held in a `struct` that looks like this:

```
typedef struct HiLoData
{
    double dHigh;
    DATE dHighChanged;
    double dCurrent;
    DATE dCurrentChanged;
    double dLow;
    DATE dLowChanged;
} HiLoData;
```

The `struct` holds the expected values as `double`s, plus the times at which the high, low, or current values last changed.

Create a new ATL DLL project called `Controls`, and use Object Wizard to add a new Full Control called `HiLoValues`. At the top of `HiLoValues.h`, add the `HiLoData` struct described above, and add a `private` data member to the class:

```
private:
    HiLoData m_data;
};
```

Initialize the data member in the constructor:

```
CHiLoValues()
{
    memset(&m_data, 0, sizeof(HiLoData));
}
```

This data member is a good candidate to be persisted in the property bag because it has a fixed size, but we'll need our extended implementation of IPersistPropertyBag to do it. Make sure that you have the definition of IPersistPropertyBagImpl_Ex<> in a file called IPersistPropertyBagImpl_Ex.h, then add the #include to HiLoValues.h:

```
#include <atlctl.h>
#include "IPersistPropertyBagImpl_Ex.h"
```

Now derive the control from IPersistPropertyBagImpl_Ex<>:

```
    public IPersistPropertyBagImpl_Ex<CHiLoValues>,
    public CComCoClass<CHiLoValues, &CLSID_HiLoValues>
{
public:
```

Add the interface to the COM map:

```
    COM_INTERFACE_ENTRY(IPersistPropertyBag)
END_COM_MAP()
```

And add the data member to the property map:

```
    PROP_DATA_ENTRY("Values", m_data, VTEX_FIXED_SIZE_BSTR_BLOB)
END_PROP_MAP()
```

That's the persistence code dealt with; all we have to do now is implement the control so that we can tell whether it's worked. Add three read/write double properties, High, Current and Low, implementing them using the m_data member. When a value changes, record the time that it happened.

All the get_ functions will look like this:

```
STDMETHODIMP CHiLoValues::get_High(double *pVal)
{
    *pVal = m_data.dHigh;
    return S_OK;
}
```

`put_High()` and `put_Low()` will follow this implementation:

```
STDMETHODIMP CHiLoValues::put_High(double newVal)
{
    SYSTEMTIME st = {0};
    GetLocalTime(&st);

    m_data.dHigh = newVal;
    SystemTimeToVariantTime(&st, &m_data.dHighChanged);

    DataHasChanged();
    return S_OK;
}
```

`put_Current()` is slightly more complicated, since it needs to update the highest and lowest values as necessary.

```
STDMETHODIMP CHiLoValues::put_Current(double newVal)
{
    SYSTEMTIME st = {0};
    GetLocalTime(&st);

    m_data.dCurrent = newVal;
    SystemTimeToVariantTime(&st, &m_data.dCurrentChanged);

    if(m_data.dHigh < newVal)
    {
        m_data.dHigh = newVal;
        m_data.dHighChanged = m_data.dCurrentChanged;
    }

    if(m_data.dLow > newVal)
    {
        m_data.dLow = newVal;
        m_data.dLowChanged = m_data.dCurrentChanged;
    }

    DataHasChanged();
    return S_OK;
}
```

`DataHasChanged()` is a simple helper function that you can add to the class definition:

```
void DataHasChanged()
{
    SetDirty(true);
    FireViewChange();
    SendOnDataChange();
}
```

Now copy the body of `OnDraw()` to the source file and implement it like this:

```
HRESULT CHiLoValues::OnDraw(ATL_DRAWINFO& di)
{
    const RECT& rc = *reinterpret_cast<const RECT*>(di.prcBounds);
    Rectangle(di.hdcDraw, rc.left, rc.top, rc.right, rc.bottom);
    ShowValue(di, _T("High"), m_data.dHigh, m_data.dHighChanged, 0);
    ShowValue(di, _T("Current"), m_data.dCurrent, m_data.dCurrentChanged, 1);
    ShowValue(di, _T("Low"), m_data.dLow, m_data.dLowChanged, 2);
    return S_OK;
}
```

This uses a `private` method called `ShowValue()`, so add the prototype to the class

```
private:
    void ShowValue(ATL_DRAWINFO& di, LPCTSTR strName,
                                   double dVal, DATE dDate, int index);
    HiLoData m_data;
};
```

You can implement `ShowValue()` like this:

```
void CHiLoValues::ShowValue(ATL_DRAWINFO& di, LPCTSTR strName,
                                   double dVal, DATE dDate, int index)
{
    USES_CONVERSION;
    const RECT& rc = *reinterpret_cast<const RECT*>(di.prcBounds);
    SetTextAlign(di.hdcDraw, TA_LEFT | TA_BASELINE);

    TEXTMETRIC tm;
    GetTextMetrics(di.hdcDraw, &tm);
    int xPos = rc.left + tm.tmAveCharWidth;
    int yPos = rc.top + tm.tmHeight + (tm.tmHeight * index * 2);

    CComBSTR bstr(strName);
    bstr += L" = ";

    CComVariant var(dVal);
    var.ChangeType(VT_BSTR);
    bstr += var.bstrVal;

    TextOut(di.hdcDraw, xPos, yPos, W2CT(bstr), bstr.Length());
    yPos += tm.tmHeight;

    if(dDate == 0)
        bstr = L"Uninitialized";
    else
    {
        var.date = dDate;
        var.vt = VT_DATE;
        var.ChangeType(VT_BSTR);
        bstr = L"Last Changed: ";
        bstr += var.bstrVal;
    }
    TextOut(di.hdcDraw, xPos, yPos, W2CT(bstr), bstr.Length());
}
```

This is pretty standard stuff – the only thing worth pointing out is the use of `CComVariant` to convert from a `DATE` to a readable version of that date. You can't just assign a `DATE` to a `CComVariant` because `DATE` is actually a `double`, so the conversion would have just returned the string value of the `double`.

Now you can build the control and load it into Visual Basic:

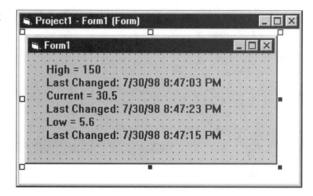

You should be able to save and reload the form file just as you would expect, and build and execute the Visual Basic executable. The `m_data` member is being successfully persisted via `IPersistPropertyBag` and `IPersistStreamInit`.

As an additional test, run the ActiveX Control Test Container and insert a new `HiLoValues` control. Then, change its property values using the **Invoke Methods** item on the **Control** menu item – to do this, select the appropriate **PropPut** method from the **Method Name** box and then type the new value in the **Parameter Value** box. Note that to set the value you must click on the **Set Value** button, and then on the **Invoke** button. Now you can select **Save to Property Bag** from the **Control** menu item to see how the properties are persisted:

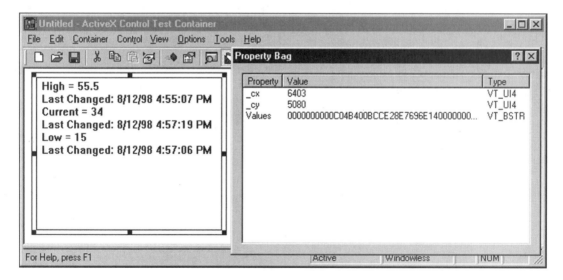

As you can see, there is a `BSTR` value that contains the hexadecimal string that represents the data in the `HiLoData` structure.

## *Variable Length Data*

The `IPersistPropertyBagImpl_Ex<>` class is great as far as it goes, but what about variable-sized data, like strings? How do you deal with a structure like this, for example?

```
typedef struct PersonData
{
    LPWSTR strName;
    short sAge;
    DWORD dwDetailsSize;
    LPBYTE pDetails;
} PersonData;
```

We've already seen that putting data like this into the property map isn't going to help, so we'll have to override the persistence methods. The trick, as usual, is to minimize the work that we have to do. We can do that by converting the data into a `CComVariant`. Once we've got a `CComVariant`, we can pass it to `IPropertyBag`, or use its `WriteToStream()` function to write the data to a stream. The great thing is that we've already got a couple of functions that make it relatively easy to turn arbitrary data into a `BSTR`, which we can use to create a `CComVariant`: the `Insert()` and `Extract()` functions provided by `IPersistPropertyBagImpl_Ex<>`.

Suppose you had a full control called `CPerson` with a `PersonData` data member called `m_data` that needed persisting. If this control derived from `IPersistPropertyBagImpl_Ex<>`, you could define a couple of functions to get and set the `m_data` based on a `CComVariant` like this:

```
void CPerson::SetPersonDataFromVariant(const CComVariant& var)
{
    int size = 0;
    LPCWSTR ptr = var.bstrVal;
    Extract(&ptr, &size, sizeof(size));

    if(m_data.strName)
    {
        delete [] m_data.strName;
        m_data.strName = 0;
    }

    if(size)
    {
        m_data.strName = new WCHAR[size + 1];
        Extract(&ptr, m_data.strName, size);
    }

    Extract(&ptr, &m_data.sAge, sizeof(m_data.sAge));
    Extract(&ptr, &m_data.dwDetailsSize, sizeof(m_data.dwDetailsSize));

    if(m_data.pDetails)
    {
        delete [] m_data.pDetails;
        m_data.pDetails = 0;
    }

    if(m_data.dwDetailsSize)
    {
```

```
      m_data.pDetails = new BYTE[m_data.dwDetailsSize];
      Extract(&ptr, m_data.pDetails, m_data.dwDetailsSize);
   }
}

CComVariant CPerson::GetPersonDataAsVariant()
{
   int size = 0;
   if(m_data.strName)
      size = (wcslen(m_data.strName) + 1) * sizeof(WCHAR);

   CComBSTR bstr;
   Insert(&bstr, &size, sizeof(int));

   if(m_data.strName != NULL)
      Insert(&bstr, m_data.strName, size);

   Insert(&bstr, &m_data.sAge, sizeof(m_data.sAge));
   Insert(&bstr, &m_data.dwDetailsSize, sizeof(m_data.dwDetailsSize));
   if(m_data.dwDetailsSize)
      Insert(&bstr, m_data.pDetails, m_data.dwDetailsSize);

   return bstr;
}
```

Now you can override the Save() and Load() implementations for IPersistPropertyBag and
IPersistStreamInit:

```
HRESULT CPerson::IPersistPropertyBag_Save(LPPROPERTYBAG pPropBag,
      BOOL fClearDirty, BOOL fSaveAllProperties, ATL_PROPMAP_ENTRY* pMap)
{
   HRESULT hr = pPropBag->Write(
                   CComBSTR(L"PersonData"), &GetPersonDataAsVariant());
   if(FAILED(hr))
      return hr;

   return IPPBI::IPersistPropertyBag_Save(
                   pPropBag, fClearDirty, fSaveAllProperties, pMap);
}

HRESULT CPerson::IPersistPropertyBag_Load(LPPROPERTYBAG pPropBag,
                   LPERRORLOG pErrorLog, ATL_PROPMAP_ENTRY* pMap)
{
   CComVariant var;
   HRESULT hr = pPropBag->Read(CComBSTR(L"PersonData"), &var, pErrorLog);
   if(FAILED(hr))
      return IPPBI::IPersistPropertyBag_Load(pPropBag, pErrorLog, pMap);

   SetPersonDataFromVariant(var);
   return IPPBI::IPersistPropertyBag_Load(pPropBag, pErrorLog, pMap);
}

HRESULT CPerson::IPersistStreamInit_Save(LPSTREAM pStm,
                      BOOL fClearDirty, ATL_PROPMAP_ENTRY* pMap)
{
```

```
    HRESULT hr = GetPersonDataAsVariant().WriteToStream(pStm);
    if(FAILED(hr))
       return hr;

    return IPSII::IPersistStreamInit_Save(pStm, fClearDirty, pMap);
}

HRESULT CPerson::IPersistStreamInit_Load(LPSTREAM pStm,
                                              ATL_PROPMAP_ENTRY* pMap)
{
    CComVariant var;
    HRESULT hr = var.ReadFromStream(pStm);
    if(FAILED(hr))
       return IPSII::IPersistStreamInit_Load(pStm, pMap);

    SetPersonDataFromVariant(var);
    return IPSII::IPersistStreamInit_Load(pStm, pMap);
}
```

These implementations use `typedefs` for the ATL implementation classes:

```
typedef IPersistPropertyBagImpl_Ex<CPerson> IPPBI;
typedef IPersistStreamInitImpl<CPerson> IPSII;
```

*I have added all the code developed in this section to the* `Controls` *sample project that's contained within the files you can download from the Wrox web site.*

As a footnote, you may be wondering if you really need to provide implementations of the `IPersistStreamInit` methods as well as the `IPersistPropertyBag` methods. Invariably, the answer is, "Yes." If your control is used by Visual Basic, then when a form is loaded into the IDE the control will be initialized using `IPersistPropertyBag::Load()`. When a form is saved, the values will be written to the FRM file using `IPersistPropertyBag::Save()`. However, when you create an executable from your project, the Visual Basic compiler will call `IPersistStreamInit::Save()` to get the control's state, which is added to the EXE. Correspondingly, when the Visual Basic application is run, this data is used to initialize the control with a call to `IPersistStreamInit::Load()`.

> **If you change the persistence methods of one persistence interface, you should check to see whether you should also make changes to the other interface.**

# Example: Property Browsing

In this example, I'll look at the techniques you can employ to make your controls easier to use from property browsers like Visual Basic's Properties window. I'll start by examining how you can use IDL to provide a limited range of input values by using an `enum` type for your property. Then, I'll move on to look at the `IPerPropertyBrowsing` interface, which can be used to enhance the features provided for your control by property browsers.

*In the example that follows, I'll talk about the Visual Basic* Properties *window. However, the discussion also applies to the Visual Basic for Applications* Properties *window that's supplied by the Microsoft Office products.*

## The Project

Create a new ATL DLL project called Browsing, and add a Full Control to it using the Object Wizard. The control should have a Short Name of Person, since you will use it to represent a person in the (admittedly rather contrived) example.

This control will need to work in Visual Basic or a web browser, so add IPersistPropertyBagImpl<> to the list of base classes, and include the appropriate entry in the COM map.

```
   public IProvideClassInfo2Impl<&CLSID_Person, NULL, &LIBID_BROWSINGLib>,
   public CComCoClass<CPerson, &CLSID_Person>, // Don't forget the comma!
   public IPersistPropertyBagImpl<CPerson>
{
public:
   CPerson()
   {
   }

DECLARE_REGISTRY_RESOURCEID(IDR_PERSON)

DECLARE_PROTECT_FINAL_CONSTRUCT()

BEGIN_COM_MAP(CPerson)
   COM_INTERFACE_ENTRY(IPerson)
   COM_INTERFACE_ENTRY(IDispatch)
   COM_INTERFACE_ENTRY(IPersistPropertyBag)
   COM_INTERFACE_ENTRY(IViewObjectEx)
```

## Enumerations in IDL

Now use ClassView to add two properties to the IPerson interface. The first should be a BSTR property called FullName, and the second should be a long property called Age. These properties will represent the name and age of the person. For simplicity's sake, we won't separate the name of the person into its component parts.

*The reason I use* FullName *for the property name is that Visual Basic always provides a 'property' called* Name *for every control that you add to the form. This* Name *'property' is not a COM property in terms of it being implemented by your control. Rather, it is used so that you can refer to the control in your Visual Basic code. However, since Visual Basic adds this 'property', it means that you must not use it as one of your property names.*

We'll want to refer to the DISPIDs of these properties in code – when we add their entries to the control's property map, for example – so let's define some constants for them to get rid of any magic numbers. We'll use a simple enumeration in the IDL file for this purpose, so that the constants can be used in the IDL file, and will also appear in the header file that MIDL generates.

Add the following code to the IDL file, and change the `[id()]` attributes of the properties to use the new DISPID constants:

```
cpp_quote("#ifdef __cplusplus")
cpp_quote("namespace IPersonDispIDs")
cpp_quote("{")
cpp_quote("#endif /* __cplusplus */")
enum EnumIPersonDispIDs
{
   dispid_FullName = DISPID_VALUE,
   dispid_Age      = 1
};
cpp_quote("#ifdef __cplusplus")
cpp_quote("};")
cpp_quote("#endif /* __cplusplus */")

   [
      ... // Attributes omitted for clarity
   ]
   interface IPerson : IDispatch
   {
      [propget, id(dispid_FullName), helpstring("property FullName")]
         HRESULT FullName([out, retval] BSTR *pVal);
      [propput, id(dispid_FullName), helpstring("property FullName")]
         HRESULT FullName([in] BSTR newVal);
      [propget, id(dispid_Age), helpstring("property Age")]
         HRESULT Age([out, retval] long *pVal);
      [propput, id(dispid_Age), helpstring("property Age")]
         HRESULT Age([in] long newVal);
   };
```

The code looks pretty complicated for a simple enumeration, because we're using `cpp_quote()` to output text in the header file that MIDL will generate. However, all the extra code does is check whether the header file is being used for C++ compilation; if it is, it outputs the enum in a namespace called `IPersonDispIDs`. The MIDL-generated header file code looks like this to a C++ compiler:

```
namespace IPersonDispIDs
{
   enum EnumIPersonDispIDs
   {
      dispid_FullName = DISPID_VALUE,
      dispid_Age      = 1
   };
};
```

A C compiler sees the enum, but doesn't get the namespace to go with it.

*Note that this enumeration will not show up in the type library. Only enums used as method parameters on interfaces defined or referenced within the library block will appear in the type library.*

Add data members for the `FullName` and `Age` properties to the `CPerson` class, and initialize them in the constructor as shown:

```
{
protected:
    CComBSTR m_bstrFullName;
    long m_lAge;

public:
    CPerson() : m_bstrFullName(L""), m_lAge(0)
    {
    }
```

Now add entries to the property map so that the properties can be persisted:

```
BEGIN_PROP_MAP(CPerson)
    PROP_DATA_ENTRY("_cx", m_sizeExtent.cx, VT_UI4)
    PROP_DATA_ENTRY("_cy", m_sizeExtent.cy, VT_UI4)
    PROP_ENTRY("FullName", dispid_FullName, CLSID_NULL)
    PROP_ENTRY("Age", dispid_Age, CLSID_NULL)
END_PROP_MAP()
```

Add the following code to the `Person.h` file, so that you don't have to specify the `namespace` to refer to the DISPID constants.

```
#include <atlctl.h>
using namespace IPersonDispIDs;
```

Finally, implement these properties in `Person.cpp` in the simplest way possible:

```
STDMETHODIMP CPerson::get_FullName(BSTR *pVal)
{
    return m_bstrFullName.CopyTo(pVal);
}

STDMETHODIMP CPerson::put_FullName(BSTR newVal)
{
    m_bstrFullName = newVal;
    SetDirty(true);
    return S_OK;
}

STDMETHODIMP CPerson::get_Age(long *pVal)
{
    *pVal = m_lAge;
    return S_OK;
}

STDMETHODIMP CPerson::put_Age(long newVal)
{
    m_lAge = newVal;
    SetDirty(true);
    return S_OK;
}
```

You can test the control in the container of your choice at this time. If you use Visual Basic, you'll see that you can just type freeform text into the Properties window for the `FullName` property, and you can enter any integer you like for the `Age` property.

## Enum Properties

Now that you've seen how to use `enum`s to provide constants to be used independently of COM methods, let's see how to use them to restrict the values that the user can enter for a property. Suppose that we want to categorize the people represented by our `Person` control by their hair color. We don't want to allow an infinite range of hair colors, so we'll narrow the list down to the following general categories using an enumeration:

```
enum HairColor
{
    hcWhite = 0xffffff,
    hcBlond = 0x00ffff,
    hcRed   = 0x0000ff,
    hcBlack = 0x000000,
    hcBrown = 0x404080
};
```

However, IDL is based on C, so with this definition, whenever you wanted to use a variable or parameter of this type, it would have to be declared as `enum HairColor` rather than just `HairColor`. To get round this, you could declare a `typedef` for an anonymous `enum` like this:

```
typedef enum
{
    hcWhite = 0xffffff,
    hcBlond = 0x00ffff,
    hcRed   = 0x0000ff,
    hcBlack = 0x000000,
    hcBrown = 0x404080
} HairColor;
```

The problem here is that MIDL doesn't let anonymous `enum`s stay anonymous for long – it will provide the `enum` with a name based on the name of the IDL file and a counter. This is what the `enum` looks like in the header file:

```
typedef /* [public] */
enum __MIDL___MIDL_itf_Browsing_0000_0001
{
    hcWhite = 0xffffff,
    hcBlond = 0x00ffff,
    hcRed   = 0x0000ff,
    hcBlack = 0x000000,
    hcBrown = 0x404080
} HairColor;
```

In this case, you can now refer to parameters of type `HairColor`, or `enum __MIDL___MIDL_itf_Browsing_0000_0001`. I think you'll agree that the former is preferable!

The best solution is to use the same tag name for the enum as for the typedef, so add the following code to Browsing.idl, just above the definition of the IPerson interface:

```
typedef enum HairColor
{
    hcWhite  = 0xffffff,
    hcBlond  = 0x00ffff,
    hcRed    = 0x0000ff,
    hcBlack  = 0x000000,
    hcBrown  = 0x404080
} HairColor;
```

Now you can use the type HairColor (or enum HairColor) as a parameter to interface methods.

### Adding the HairColor Property

Use ClassView to add a new property to the IPerson interface. This time, specify HairColor as its type, and call the property HairColor. Edit the IDL by hand to add a new DISPID constant called dispid_HairColor to the EnumIPersonDispIDs enumeration and change the [id()] for the property accordingly.

Now add a HairColor member to the class and initialize it in the constructor:

```
    long m_lAge;
    HairColor m_hcHairColor;

public:
    CPerson() : m_bstrFullName(L""), m_lAge(0), m_hcHairColor(hcBlond)
    {
```

Add the property to the map:

```
BEGIN_PROP_MAP(CPerson)
    ... // Entries omitted for clarity
    PROP_ENTRY("Age", dispid_Age, CLSID_NULL)
    PROP_ENTRY("HairColor", dispid_HairColor, CLSID_NULL)
END_PROP_MAP()
```

Finally, implement the methods:

```
STDMETHODIMP CPerson::get_HairColor(HairColor *pVal)
{
    *pVal = m_hcHairColor;
    return S_OK;
}

STDMETHODIMP CPerson::put_HairColor(HairColor newVal)
{
    m_hcHairColor = newVal;
    SetDirty(true);
    return S_OK;
}
```

Now you can build the project again and examine it with Visual Basic. If you look at the Object Browser, you'll see that the `HairColor` enumeration is shown, and the elements of the enumeration can be used as global constants. You'll also see that the Properties window displays the symbolic name along with the value of the `HairColor` property. The drop down list only allows you to change its value to another element of the `enum`.

enums also offer benefits to client programmers when they're writing code. Visual Basic will display the enumeration constants in a list as the user is typing code to set the `HairColor` property of the control:

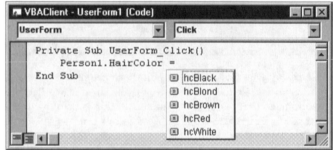

Now let's see what we can do for properties that *can't* be represented as enums. We'll use the `IPerPropertyBrowsing` interface to provide extra usability features to our control.

## IPerPropertyBrowsingImpl<>

The `IPerPropertyBrowsing` interface has three main roles:

- ❏ To provide display strings for property values via `GetDisplayString()`
- ❏ To provide a choice of predefined values (represented by strings) via `GetPredefinedStrings()` and `GetPredefinedValue()`
- ❏ To specify a property page for individual properties

ATL provides an implementation of `IPerPropertyBrowsing` in its `IPerPropertyBrowsingImpl<>` class, so let's see what happens when we add the ATL support to our control. To begin, add the implementation class to the list of base classes and expose the interface via the COM map:

```
        public CComCoClass<CPerson, &CLSID_Person>,
        public IPersistPropertyBagImpl<CPerson>,        // Don't forget the comma!
        public IPerPropertyBrowsingImpl<CPerson>
{
        // Code omitted for clarity
BEGIN_COM_MAP(CPerson)
        COM_INTERFACE_ENTRY(IPerson)
        COM_INTERFACE_ENTRY(IDispatch)
        COM_INTERFACE_ENTRY(IPersistPropertyBag)
        COM_INTERFACE_ENTRY(IPerPropertyBrowsing)
```

Now rebuild the project and go back to Visual Basic to examine the effects of this small change on the **Properties** window. When the focus enters the box for the Age or FullName properties that we've defined for our control, you'll see that a button with an ellipsis appears. If you're using VBA (from Word 97, for example), clicking on the button will do nothing. If you're using Visual Basic 6.0, clicking the button will display a dialog like this:

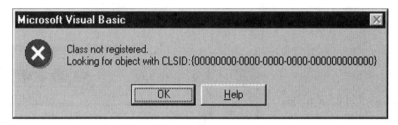

Either way, you can no longer edit these properties. You'll also notice that, although it's still possible to alter the HairColor property via the drop down list, the selected value no longer displays the symbolic constant – only the numeric value is displayed. It looks very much like applying IPerPropertyBrowsingImpl<> to our class was a step backwards. What's causing the problems, and how do we fix them?

### The Fix

First, we need to define a new template class, which we'll call IPerPropertyBrowsingImpl_Fix<>. This class will use the implementation of IPerPropertyBrowsingImpl<> as far as possible, but it will fix its limitations.

Create a new file called IPerPropertyBrowsingImpl_Fix.h and add the following code to it:

```
//    IPerPropertyBrowsingImpl_Fix.h
//
//////////////////////////////////////////////////////////////////////////////

#if !defined(__IPERPROPERTYBROWSINGIMPL_FIX_H__)
#define __IPERPROPERTYBROWSINGIMPL_FIX_H__

#if !defined(__cplusplus)
    #error This file requires C++ compilation (use a .cpp suffix)
#endif

#if _MSC_VER >= 1000
    #pragma once
```

```
    #endif

    template <class T>
    class IPerPropertyBrowsingImpl_Fix : public IPerPropertyBrowsingImpl<T>
    {
    public:
        STDMETHOD(MapPropertyToPage)(DISPID dispID, CLSID* pClsid)
        {
            typedef IPerPropertyBrowsingImpl<T> IPPBI;
            HRESULT hr = IPPBI::MapPropertyToPage(dispID, pClsid);
            if(SUCCEEDED(hr) && *pClsid == CLSID_NULL)
                hr = E_INVALIDARG;
            return hr;
        }

        STDMETHOD(GetDisplayString)(DISPID dispID, BSTR* pBstr)
        {
            return E_NOTIMPL;
        }
    };

    #endif // #ifndef __IPERPROPERTYBROWSINGIMPL_FIX_H__
```

Add `#include "IPerPropertyBrowsingImpl_Fix.h"` to `Person.h`, just below the `using` directive, and change the base class list to use `IPerPropertyBrowsingImpl_Fix<CPerson>`, rather than `IPerPropertyBrowsingImpl<CPerson>`.

Now build the control again and see how it behaves in Visual Basic. This time, you'll find that the control is behaving just as it did before we added support for `IPerPropertyBrowsing`. Let's see why this fix works, and in the process learn how to provide more useful code for this interface.

### MapPropertyToPage()

```
HRESULT MapPropertyToPage(
    /*[in]*/    DISPID dispID,    // Dispatch identifier for the property
    /*[out]*/   CLSID* pclsid     // Receives a pointer to CLSID for page
);
```

`MapPropertyToPage()` returns the CLSID of a property page that can be used to manipulate a given property (identified by its DISPID). ATL's implementation of `IPerPropertyBrowsing::MapPropertyToPage()` loops through the entries in the property map and returns the CLSID specified in the map. If there is no entry in the map for the specified DISPID, the implementation returns `E_INVALIDARG`.

Unfortunately, the ATL implementation doesn't discriminate between valid CLSIDs and the special value, `CLSID_NULL`, which is used to indicate that a property *doesn't have* an associated property page. This means that Visual Basic thinks that the property requires a property page to manipulate it, but can't display the page because the CLSID isn't valid.

Our fix simply lets the ATL implementation do its work, then checks the returned HRESULT and CLSID to see if we have a problem. If the HRESULT indicates success, but the CLSID is `CLSID_NULL`, we make sure that the client is sent a failure HRESULT. Otherwise, we just return the original value.

### GetDisplayString()

```
HRESULT GetDisplayString(
    /*[in]*/    DISPID dispID ,   // Dispatch identifier for the property
    /*[out]*/   BSTR* pbstr       // Receives a pointer to the string
                                  // describing the property
);
```

GetDisplayString() returns a text string describing the *value* of the property identified by the DISPID parameter, and you'll see an example of a useful implementation of this shortly. ATL provides an implementation of this method that just gets the property value and converts it to a string:

```
CComVariant var;
if(FAILED(CComDispatchDriver::GetProperty(pT, dispID, &var)))
    return S_FALSE;

BSTR bstrTemp = var.bstrVal;
if(var.vt != VT_BSTR)
{
    CComVariant varDest;
    if(FAILED(::VariantChangeType(&varDest, &var, VARIANT_NOVALUEPROP, VT_BSTR)))
        return S_FALSE;
    bstrTemp = varDest.bstrVal;
}
*pBstr = SysAllocString(bstrTemp);
```

In other words, all it does is get the actual value of the property and then convert it to a string. In the case of enums, this is actually worse than letting Visual Basic handle the display, since the ATL code doesn't display the corresponding symbolic value.

Worse still, Visual Basic assumes that if you return a success HRESULT for this method, you're going to provide either a list of predefined values for use with this property (in which case you have to implement GetPredefinedStrings() and GetPredefinedValue()) or a property page (in which case you have to provide a valid CLSID in the property map entry to be returned by MapPropertyToPage()). If you do neither of these things, your property will show up in Visual Basic's Properties window, but you won't be able to edit it.

By overriding this function to return E_NOTIMPL, we allow any existing properties to carry on working just as they did before.

## Extending the Example

Suppose the people represented by our control have three age categories: minors (up to age 18), adults (up to age 60), and seniors (60 and over). If we want to provide a drop down list for the Age property that lists these three categories and allows the user to pick one of them, we need to implement the IPerPropertyBrowsing methods GetPredefinedStrings() and GetPredefinedValue().

## GetPredefinedStrings()

```
HRESULT GetPredefinedStrings(
    /*[in]*/    DISPID dispID,     // Dispatch identifier for the property
    CALPOLESTR* pcaStringsOut,     // Receives a pointer to an array of strings
    CADWORD* pcaCookiesOut         // Receives a pointer to array of DWORDs
);
```

`GetPredefinedStrings()` returns an array of strings representing potential values for a property, along with an array of cookies that can be passed back to the control to get the corresponding value. We can implement this method so that it returns the strings `"Minor"`, `"Adult"`, and `"Senior"`. The corresponding cookie values can be anything you like; in this example it makes sense to use the lowest age in each group (that is, 0, 18, and 60 respectively) as a visual reminder, but as you'll see later, using these values helps reduce the code as well.

To implement this method, first add the declaration to the class definition in `Person.h`:

```
// IPerPropertyBrowsing
    STDMETHOD(GetPredefinedStrings)
            (DISPID dispID, CALPOLESTR* pCaStringsOut, CADWORD* pCaCookiesOut);
};
```

Now add the following code to the bottom of `Person.cpp`:

```
// This function can copy LPSTR, LPOLESTR, BSTR, and CComBSTR
void CopyStrToOLESTR(const CComBSTR& src, LPOLESTR* pDest)
{
    *pDest = static_cast<LPOLESTR>(CoTaskMemAlloc(
                                (src.Length() + 1) * sizeof(OLECHAR)));
    wcscpy(*pDest, src.m_str);
}

template <class ElementType>
ElementType* CoTaskMemAllocArray(unsigned int nElems)
{
    return static_cast<ElementType*>(CoTaskMemAlloc(
                                nElems * sizeof(ElementType)));
}

STDMETHODIMP CPerson::GetPredefinedStrings(DISPID dispID,
                    CALPOLESTR* pCaStringsOut, CADWORD* pCaCookiesOut)
{
    if(pCaStringsOut == NULL || pCaCookiesOut == NULL)
        return E_POINTER;

    switch(dispID)
    {
    case dispid_Age:
        {
            // Set the number of elements
            pCaStringsOut->cElems = pCaCookiesOut->cElems = 3;
```

```
                     // Allocate space for the arrays
                     pCaStringsOut->pElems = CoTaskMemAllocArray<LPOLESTR>(
                                                    pCaStringsOut->cElems);
                     pCaCookiesOut->pElems = CoTaskMemAllocArray<DWORD>(
                                                    pCaCookiesOut->cElems);

                     // Set the array elements
                     // The cookie value matches the lowest age of the group
                     CopyStrToOLESTR(L"Minor", &pCaStringsOut->pElems[0]);
                     pCaCookiesOut->pElems[0] = 0;

                     CopyStrToOLESTR(L"Adult", &pCaStringsOut->pElems[1]);
                     pCaCookiesOut->pElems[1] = 18;

                     CopyStrToOLESTR(L"Senior", &pCaStringsOut->pElems[2]);
                     pCaCookiesOut->pElems[2] = 60;
                     break;
                }
           default:
                pCaStringsOut->cElems = pCaCookiesOut->cElems = 0;
                pCaStringsOut->pElems = NULL;
                pCaCookiesOut->pElems = NULL;
           }
           return S_OK;
     }
```

We start by defining a couple of helper functions. The first of these, `CopyStrToOLESTR()`, simply copies a `CComBSTR` to a freshly allocated `LPOLESTR` and returns the result via the second parameter. The second function, `CoTaskMemAllocArray<>()`, is a template function that makes it easy to allocate space for an array of elements using `CoTaskMemAlloc()`.

The implementation of `GetPredefinedStrings()` consists of a `switch` statement based on the DISPID. In this case, there's only one `case` (apart from the `default`), and that corresponds to the `Age` property. When we know that the caller is interested in strings for the `Age` property, we:

❑ Set the number of elements in the string and cookie arrays
❑ Allocate memory for each array
❑ Set each element of the arrays to the values we discussed earlier.

*Note that the* `default` *case sets all the structure members to zero. This is important if you want to avoid crashing Visual Basic!*

### GetPredefinedValue()

When the user picks one of the predefined strings that we've just provided, Visual Basic will pass back the corresponding cookie to the `GetPredefinedValue()` method.

```
HRESULT GetPredefinedValue(
    /*[in]*/    DISPID dispID,      // Dispatch identifier for the property
    /*[in]*/    DWORD dwCookie,     // Token from GetPredefinedStrings()
    /*[out]*/   VARIANT* pVarOut    // The value corresponding to the token
);
```

This function has to recognize the DISPID and the token that it's passed, then pass back a VARIANT with a value that corresponds to the information that it's been given. In our case, the token *is* the value that we want to use, so our implementation is extremely simple. In more complicated cases, the token could be a key into a map.

Add the following code to the foot of `Person.cpp`:

```
STDMETHODIMP CPerson::GetPredefinedValue(
                            DISPID dispID, DWORD dwCookie, VARIANT* pVarOut)
{
    switch(dispID)
    {
    case dispid_Age:
        {
            CComVariant(dwCookie, VT_I4).Detach(pVarOut);
            break;
        }
    default:
        return E_INVALIDARG;
    }
    return S_OK;
}
```

Now add the method declaration to the header file:

```
// IPerPropertyBrowsing
    STDMETHOD(GetPredefinedStrings)
                (DISPID dispID, CALPOLESTR* pCaStringsOut, CADWORD* pCaCookiesOut);
    STDMETHOD(GetPredefinedValue)
                (DISPID dispID, DWORD dwCookie, VARIANT* pVarOut);
};
```

At this point, you can build and test the control once more. If you try to edit the Age property in Visual Basic's **Properties** window, you'll see that you can type directly into the box, as before, or you can pick one of the three categories from the drop down list. If you pick one of these categories, you'll see the Age property change to the lowest age in the selected group (0, 18, or 60).

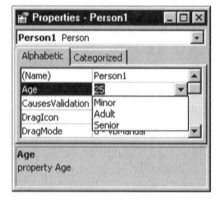

### GetDisplayString()

If you want the user to see the *name* of the value that they've selected, or you want to provide display names for any other values, you need to implement `GetDisplayString()`. A side effect of implementing this method is that Visual Basic will prevent the user from typing new values, only allowing them to select from the list of predefined strings.

Add one last function to the bottom of `Person.cpp`:

```
STDMETHODIMP CPerson::GetDisplayString(DISPID dispID, BSTR* pBstr)
{
    switch(dispID)
    {
    case dispid_Age:
        {
            if(m_lAge < 0)
                return IPerPropertyBrowsingImpl<CPerson>::
                                              GetDisplayString(dispID, pBstr);
            else if(m_lAge < 18)
                *pBstr = CComBSTR(L"Minor").Detach();
            else if(m_lAge < 60)
                *pBstr = CComBSTR(L"Adult").Detach();
            else
                *pBstr = CComBSTR(L"Senior").Detach();
            break;
        }
    default:
        return E_INVALIDARG;
    }
    return S_OK;
}
```

Once again, we've got a `switch` on the DISPID of the property. When the DISPID is `dispid_Age`, we check the latest value of the `Age` property and convert it into a string based on one of the categories that we defined earlier. If the age is less than zero (which shouldn't happen), we just let the ATL base class implementation turn that into a string for us.

> *Note that the strings returned by* `GetDisplayString()` *don't have to match the predefined strings at all. It's entirely up to you.*

Don't forget to add the method declaration to the header file:

```
    // IPerPropertyBrowsing
    STDMETHOD(GetPredefinedStrings)
              (DISPID dispID, CALPOLESTR* pCaStringsOut, CADWORD* pCaCookiesOut);
    STDMETHOD(GetPredefinedValue)
              (DISPID dispID, DWORD dwCookie, VARIANT* pVarOut);
    STDMETHOD(GetDisplayString)(DISPID dispID, BSTR* pBstr);
};
```

Now you can build and test the project once more. This time, you'll see that the **Properties** window only allows you to select items from the list. Once selected, the text stays in the box for the `Age` property.

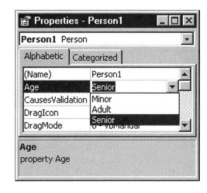

# Which Property Interfaces To Use?

In the previous sections, I have outlined the various persistence and property interfaces that can be used on a control, and I have also detailed how ATL implements them and how you use them. In this section, I will list some common applications that use controls and specify the persistence interfaces that you will need to implement in order that your controls work with them successfully. As a rule of thumb, if you want to use a control as part of a compound document, the control will have to be a Full control.

## Visual Basic 6.0

The only property interface actually *required* by Visual Basic 6.0 is IPersistStreamInit (or IPersistStream if the control doesn't implement IPersistStreamInit). The interface is used to initialize a control in the IDE, and when a Visual Basic application is started. When a new control is added to a form, Visual Basic calls IPersistStreamInit::InitNew() to initialize it to a default state. In the IDE, the developer will change the property values to reflect how the control should be used. When the developer creates an EXE from the project, Visual Basic calls IPersistStreamInit::Save() to get the control's state. It will save the stream in the project EXE, so that when it is run, the control can be initialized by calling IPersistStreamInit::Load().

If you have not made an EXE, but run the project in the IDE, Visual Basic will call IPersistStreamInit::Save() to get the control's state so that it can then call IPersistStreamInit::Load() to initialize the control as if it were being run as a compiled application.

When you save a form, Visual Basic will try to call IPersistPropertyBag::Save() to copy the property values to the .frm file. Correspondingly, when you load a form, IPersistPropertyBag::Load() will be called to initialize the control from the values in the .frm file. However, Visual Basic will use IPersistStreamInit to save and load the control's data in a .frx file if it finds that IPersistPropertyBag isn't supported.

If you want to use a property page to change one or more values, then the control will have to support ISpecifyPropertyPages. You may also decide that you'll want the facilities of IPerPropertyBrowsing, but both of these interfaces are optional.

## Internet Explorer 4.0

Internet Explorer will only use IPersistPropertyBag – in fact it will only ever call Load(), which it will do when the <PARAM> tag is used with the <OBJECT> tag. Tools like Visual InterDev will call IPersistPropertyBag::Save() to save the state of your control.

## Microsoft Office Applications

In general, controls that you intend to use with Office applications should be Full controls. The control's state will be initialized and saved using IPersistStorage, so when a control is first inserted into Word (for example), InitNew() is called. When the document is saved, Word will call Save(). Finally, when you open a document, Word will look into the storage that it holds for the control to get the CLSID of the control, and use this to instantiate it. It will then initialize the control with Load() by passing it the remainder of the storage.

# Drawing and Metafiles

Controls are visual objects – they show some result or provide a user interface with which to interact. A large proportion of the code in a control will involve drawing the control's visual representation.

The size of a control will not be fixed, so your control will need to take this size into account when drawing itself. Drawing and sizing is part of your control class's responsibility, but the ATL classes will do much of the work for you. In addition to preparing a device context for you to do your raw Win32 graphics work, these control classes will also negotiate with the container to determine the size of the control. Because the ATL classes do this work, your own work is relatively straightforward.

# Windowed and Windowless Controls

Windowless controls are an optimization – every windowed control uses a window, and each window takes up resources. To minimize the use of resources, a container can provide a single window that will be shared by all the windowless controls that it hosts. Windowless controls still have access to a window in which to draw their user interface; they just don't own it.

Since the container owns the window, it must forward window messages to the controls. For example, if the container gets a `WM_PAINT` message, it should determine which part of the window needs repainting and then determine which control this corresponds to. It must then inform the control that it should repaint itself, and the container should pass the control the device context of the window to use.

A windowless control implements the `IOleInPlaceObjectWindowless` interface in addition to the other OLE interfaces required for controls. The container implements the usual container interfaces, plus the `IOleInPlaceSiteWindowless` interface.

When the control is activated, it determines whether it should be created without a window. To do this, it queries its site (the container) for the `IOleInPlaceSiteWindowless` interface to see if the site supports windowless controls. If not, the control should revert to being a windowed control – that is, it should create and maintain its own window (in this case, ATL sets `CComControlBase::m_bWndLess` to `false`). The initial handshaking between control and site is a little more complicated than I've explained here, but this is the essence of it.

When the container gets a message that is appropriate for the control, the container calls `IOleInPlaceObjectWindowless::OnWindowMessage()` on the control to give it a chance to process the message. In ATL, this is implemented in `IOleInPlaceObjectWindowlessImpl<>::OnWindowMessage()`, which calls the control class's `ProcessWindowMessage()` method and hence uses its message map.

## User Interaction

Handling mouse messages and getting keyboard focus require special handling. Basically, because the control does not own its window, it cannot call `SetCapture()` to capture mouse messages, or `SetFocus()` to get the keyboard focus. Instead, it calls identically-named methods on the site's `IOleInPlaceSiteWindowless` interface. ATL does all the necessary work for you, using the value of `m_bWndLess` to determine whether it should behave as a windowed or a windowless control.

If a windowless control needs repainting, it is carried out by the container calling `IViewObject::Draw()`, rather than by passing on the `WM_PAINT` message to the control. This reduces the calls between container and control, because the container can pass the control the device context that it should use to draw itself, rather than requiring the control to call `GetDC()` and `ReleaseDC()` on the site's `IOleInPlaceSiteWindowless` interface. However, if you do want a device context (other than in `OnDraw()`), you can get one using the `CComControlBase::m_spInPlaceSite` member. Similarly, if a windowless control wants to invalidate its window, it should call `InvalidateRect()` on this member rather than using the Win32 API.

## Creating Windowless Controls

So, how do you make your control windowless? The easy way is to make sure that the **W**indowed Only check box is unchecked on the **M**iscellaneous page in Object Wizard:

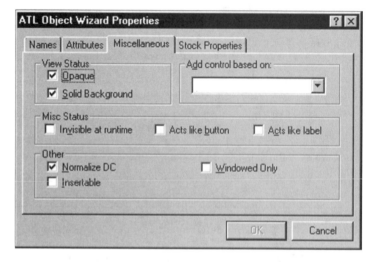

This will leave `CComControlBase::m_bWindowOnly` at its default value of `FALSE`. If you check this box, you are indicating that the control should always create its own window, and the Object Wizard indicates this by setting m_bWindowOnly in the control's constructor:

```
CMyWindowedCtrl()
{
    m_bWindowOnly = TRUE;
}
```

Whether the control has a window or is windowless, the ATL class will be derived from `IOleInPlaceObjectWindowlessImpl<>`, and will have `IOleInPlaceObjectWindowless` in the interface map. However, the container will only *use* this interface if the control tells the container that it is windowless by calling `IOleInPlaceSiteEx::OnInPlaceActivateEx()` using the `ACTIVATE_WINDOWLESS` flag.

The other options on this page are interesting, so it is worth examining what they do. When **N**ormalize DC is checked, which it is by default, the ATL implementation of `OnDrawAdvanced()` 'normalizes' the device context that you will use to draw the control. This means that the device units will be pixels, and that the origin of the drawing area will be (0,0) at the top left hand corner. Your drawing should be carried out in the `OnDraw()` method, which is called by `OnDrawAdvanced()`.

If this box is not checked, then Object Wizard will provide an override of OnDrawAdvanced() in your class that you should use to draw the control. The device context will not be normalized, and so you will have to determine the drawing units, the direction of the co-ordinate system, and the position of the origin. If you are happy to do this, you may gain a little in performance.

The other option in the Other section, Insertable, indicates that a control can be inserted into a container. This just adds the Insertable key to the control's CLSID. When a container uses the standard OLE Insert Object dialog, the dialog will only include objects that have this key. Note that to make a control insertable into *all* containers may require a little more work. I'll be covering the details in a later section, but basically not all containers use this standard dialog, and others may use component categories to determine whether a control is insertable.

The options in the Misc Status box affect the control's MiscStatus key in the registry. This is read by the control's implementation of IOleObject::GetMiscStatus(), which is called by a container to determine the status of the object. The options provided by Object Wizard are explained in the following table; the container uses these values to determine how it will manage the control:

| Option | Description |
|---|---|
| Invisible at Runtime | This indicates that the control does not have a runtime window, but should have one at design time |
| Acts like a button | The control acts like a button |
| Acts like a label | The control acts as a label, so that it activates the next control in the tab order when its mnemonic is pressed |

The View Status options determine the values returned by the control's IViewObjectEx::GetViewStatus() method. The options you specify will be added to your class using the DECLARE_VIEW_STATUS() macro, which declares a method called _GetViewStatus() that just returns these values. The container calls GetViewStatus() to ask the control about how the control will draw itself, and this helps the container to optimize its interaction with the control.

Note that the onus is on you as the developer to make sure that the control has the specified functionality. If you uncheck Solid Background, then the container will not optimize its calls by assuming that your control has a solid background, and it is up to you to make your control's background transparent.

# OnDraw()

OnDraw() is called in four situations:

- ❑ In response to a WM_PAINT message
- ❑ When the control is asked for a metafile representation
- ❑ When the control is being printed
- ❑ Any other time that the control itself decides that it needs to be redrawn

Note that **metafiles** are used to provide a view of the control that can be saved by a compound document container, so that when the document is loaded at a later stage, the control's view can be drawn without actually activating the control. Metafiles are also often used when a control is printed. You can test how your control renders itself into a metafile by using the ActiveX Control Test Container, through the Draw MetaFile item on the Control menu.

ATL prepares a normalized device context in any of these four situations, and channels it into a call to the virtual OnDraw() method:

```
virtual HRESULT OnDraw(ATL_DRAWINFO& di);
```

## ATL_DRAWINFO

Before looking at the four situations outlined above, let's look first at the general structure that's used to hold the information about the device context.

```
struct ATL_DRAWINFO
{
    UINT cbSize;
    DWORD dwDrawAspect;
    LONG lindex;
    DVTARGETDEVICE* ptd;
    HDC hicTargetDev;
    HDC hdcDraw;
    LPCRECTL prcBounds;
    LPCRECTL prcWBounds;
    BOOL bOptimize;
    BOOL bZoomed;
    BOOL bRectInHimetric;
    SIZEL ZoomNum;
    SIZEL ZoomDen;
};
```

The dwDrawAspect and lindex members are used to give information about the **aspect** of the drawing; typically, this will be content (that is, render the content of the control). hdcDraw will be the device context into which the control should be rendered. If the drawing is to be on a device other than the screen, then ptd and hicTargetDev will be used to pass more information about that device. In particular, ptd gives access to the DEVMODE of a printer (which can be used to get its capabilities), and hicTargetDev can be used to test out those capabilities.

prcBounds points to a RECTL that has the bounds of the area in which the drawing should be done; if the drawing will be into a metafile, then prcWBounds will be the bounds of the metafile that will contain the bounding rectangle.

The bOptimize flag indicates whther the device context has been normalized. If bZoomed is TRUE, then ZoomNum and ZoomDen give the ratio of the bounding rectangle to the natural size of the control. Finally, if bRectInHimetric is set, the units will be HIMETRIC; otherwise, they will be pixels.

## Redrawing the Control

Whenever the data in your control changes and you need to update its display, you should call `FireViewChange()`. It may seem odd to call an entirely new method when your control has a method to do the drawing, but remember that `OnDraw()` uses a specially prepared device context. If you want ATL to do this preparation for you, you can't call `OnDraw()` directly.

The other problem with calling `OnDraw()` directly is that the container will not be informed that the control's view has changed. This can be a problem because some containers cache a metafile of the control so that it can be saved in a compound document – when the document is displayed or printed, the metafile can be displayed rather than activating the control. If the container is not informed of changes, then its cached metafile will be out of date.

If the control is active, then calling `FireViewChange()` will invalidate the control's window using the Win32 `InvalidateRect()` function if the control has a window, or `IOleInPlaceSiteWindowless::InvalidateRect()` on the control's container if it is windowless. If the control is inactive, it calls `SendOnViewChange()` to inform the container that the view has changed through the `IAdviseSink` mechanism I explained earlier in the chapter.

If the control is windowless, the container will respond by calling `IViewObjectEx::Draw()` to tell the control to draw itself. This method's parameters have information about the device context and bounds into which the control should draw itself. If the control has a window, then Windows will send it the `WM_PAINT` message that the control handles with the `OnPaint()` handler.

## WM_PAINT Handler

If the control has its own window (that is, m_bWindowOnly is `true`) then a control will be told to draw itself by the system sending the `WM_PAINT` message to the control's window. Your control's message map will have a `CHAIN_MSG_MAP()` entry to route all unhandled messages to the `CComControl<>` base class, and `CComControl<>` has this message map:

```
typedef CComControl< T, WinBase > thisClass;
BEGIN_MSG_MAP(thisClass)
    MESSAGE_HANDLER(WM_PAINT, CComControlBase::OnPaint)
    MESSAGE_HANDLER(WM_SETFOCUS, CComControlBase::OnSetFocus)
    MESSAGE_HANDLER(WM_KILLFOCUS, CComControlBase::OnKillFocus)
    MESSAGE_HANDLER(WM_MOUSEACTIVATE, CComControlBase::OnMouseActivate)
END_MSG_MAP()
```

As you can see, the `WM_PAINT` message is delegated to the handler in `CComControl<>`'s base class, `CComControlBase`.

The control needs to get information from its window to send to `OnDraw()`. First, it obtains the window's device context by calling the Win32 `BeginPaint()` function, just as Windows applications do, and then it calls `GetClientRect()` to get the size of the drawing area. This information is packed into an `ATL_DRAWINFO` structure and passed to `OnDrawAdvanced()` to prepare the device context, ready for `OnDraw()`. After `OnDrawAdvanced()` returns, the Win32 `EndPaint()` function is called to release the device context.

## IViewObject::Draw()

If the control is windowless, then the container will handle any WM_PAINT messages. To get the visual representation of the control, the container calls IViewObject::Draw(). This method looks like this:

```
STDMETHOD(Draw)(DWORD dwDrawAspect, LONG lindex, void *pvAspect,
                DVTARGETDEVICE* ptd, HDC hicTargetDev, HDC hdcDraw,
                LPCRECTL prcBounds, LPCRECTL prcWBounds,
                BOOL(__stdcall * pfnContinue)(DWORD), DWORD dwContinue)
```

The aspect determines what the control should draw, and usually this will be the control's content. The aspect determines what the next parameter will be, and for content it will be -1. Some containers will support optimized drawing, and information about this will be passed in through the pointer in the third parameter. Typically though, this will be zero.

If the control is being asked to draw itself to the default device (the screen), then the device context is passed in hdcDraw. If another device is being used, information about this is passed in using ptd and hicTargetDev. The two parameters prcBounds and prcWBounds are used to pass bounding information; the former is sometimes used when the container wants to print the control, and the latter is used when metafile rendering is being performed. Typically, with a windowless control, these two parameters will be NULL and ATL will obtain the control bounding rectangle from information cached when the control is resized.

The final two parameters are used to pass a callback function and a parameter to pass to that callback; ATL ignores these parameters.

ATL handles IViewObject::Draw() by calling the IViewObject_Draw() method in CComControlBase. This method initializes ATL_DRAWINFO and calls OnDrawAdvanced().

## Metafile Rendering

IDataObject::GetData() is used when metafile rendering is required. A typical case of this occurs when you first insert a control into a Word document. Word will want to have a metafile of the control to save in the document, and so it will call IDataObject::GetData(). It will also request a new metafile rendering after the control calls SendOnDataChange().

*Note that* Lite *controls aren't generated with support for the* IDataObject *interface.*

GetData() has two parameters: the first indicates the target device and the format of the required rendering, while the second is an [out] parameter that returns the rendering. The mechanism is very flexible because this single method can be called for all kinds of rendering formats. The control can return the data to the container as a metafile, in a disk file, or using global memory, depending on the values given in the first parameter. Typically, containers will ask for a metafile rendering, which is the assumption that ATL makes. If a container asks for a different format, then the ATL implementation will return DATA_E_FORMATETC – that is, it cannot return the requested data.

This method is not passed a device context, and so the ATL implementation creates a metafile device context using `CreateMetaFile()`, which is then passed to `OnDrawAdvanced()` for normalizing. However, since `GetData()` is not given any information about the final size of the space in which the metafile will be displayed, it has to come up with suitable sizes to put into `ATL_DRAWINFO`. The control will have a natural size (for optimum drawing), as well as the size that the container has told the container it is. The code in `GetData()` determines which of these should be used, and then converts the units to pixels. `OnDrawAdvanced()` is then called and when it returns, the metafile will contain the rendering of the control. The method will then copy the metafile into global memory so that it can be returned back to the container.

> *One important aspect of metafile rendering is that not all GDI commands can be used. Since* `OnDraw()` *is used as a generic routine for drawing a control's view, you must be careful to make sure that it will not use commands that cannot be used in a metafile. Details of how to test for metafile rendering will be given in the later section on* Printing.

## OnDrawAdvanced()

The purpose of `OnDrawAdvanced()` is to prepare, or normalize, the device context that is passed to `OnDraw()`. Obviously, this takes processing time and if you are prepared to use `HIMETRIC` units then you can override this method and do your drawing here.

## Printing

I mentioned above that when you print a document with the control, it *may* ask the control for a metafile, and I chose my words advisedly. In fact, there are two ways for a container to ask the control for a rendering. The first is `IViewObject::Draw()`, and the second is `IDataObject::GetData()`.

If the container uses `Draw()`, then it will create a device context for the control to draw itself to. This device context may be a metafile, or more likely a device context of the printer device. If the container calls `GetData()`, then a metafile device context (created by the ATL code) will be passed to `OnDraw()`.

In a moment, I will outline how some popular containers handle printing, but first I want to explain why you should pay particular attention to printing.

When a container prints a document that contains your control, it is unlikely that it will just dump the pixels on the screen – this will always have a much lower resolution than your printer. Instead, it will either ask for a metafile rendering of the control – which is just the recorded GDI commands used to render the control, which it can replay in the printer device context – or it will give your control the printer device context and specify that the control must draw itself in a particular area.

Whichever device context is used, one thing is certain: it will not be the same as the device context that you draw into when showing the control on the screen. For example, if the container passes a metafile DC via `IViewObject::Draw()`, the ATL implementation passes this to `OnDrawAdvanced()`. However, this doesn't normalize metafile DCs, so you will have to be aware that the drawing units will not necessarily be pixels or normalized with (0,0) in the top left hand corner. Further, the default pen and brush could be different to the one that you will use on the screen, and the font may be a different size and typeface.

To maintain a consistent look between the image on the screen and the image on the paper, you must make sure that your version of OnDraw() prepares the device context carefully and doesn't use default drawing objects, and you must always size your drawing relative to the bounds that you have been passed – don't use absolute units.

> *In my tests, I have found that some containers clip the printing area. For example, using the default ATL code that draws a rectangle on the bounds of the control, I have found that Word clips the bottom and right edges, but Internet Explorer 4 clips the top and left edges. This inconsistent behavior is annoying, but you must take it into account when writing printing code. To remedy this problem you could make the rectangle one pixel smaller in all directions.*

How can you tell that the control is being printed? Well, since there are two ways that the container can get the control image, you really don't have any choice other than to test the device context passed to OnDraw(). You can call the Win32 GetDeviceCaps() and ask for the technology used by the device context:

```
int caps = GetDeviceCaps(di.hdcDraw, TECHNOLOGY);
```

You can then perform different drawing for the printer than for the screen. One thing you can be sure of is that if the drawing will be to the screen, then the return value will be DT_RASDISPLAY, otherwise you are likely to have DT_RASPRINTER or DT_METAFILE. If a printer device context is passed, you can get more information about the printer using the ptd member of the ATL_DRAWINFO structure.

One further thing to think about is that if you superclass a control, or if your control is a composite or an HTML control, then you will not necessarily be able to print child controls automatically. If they are ActiveX controls then you may be able to query for IViewObject or IDataObject and get hold of the image that way, but this will complicate the code, and may not work in all cases.

If the control is a Win32 control then you can pass a device context to it using the WM_PRINT or WM_PRINTCLIENT messages to get the control to draw itself, but there is no guarantee that the control author will have added support for these messages. If the control does not do this then you may have to resort to ugly actions like screen scraping.

Different containers handle printing in different ways, and here are the details of a few common containers. As you can see, the three containers I list here handle printing in three rather different ways.

### Visual Basic 6.0

When you print a form, either in the Visual Basic IDE (File | Print... menu), or using PrintForm in a Visual Basic application, then Visual Basic will call IViewObject::Draw(), passing a *metafile*. Because of this, ptd is NULL and additionally OnDrawAdvanced() does *not* normalize the device context.

### Internet Explorer 4.0

Internet Explorer 4 calls IViewObject::Draw(), and the device context passed to OnDraw() is the device context of the printer. The ptd member of the ATL_DRAWINFO points to DVTARGETDEVICE, which you can use to get the capabilities of the printer. OnDrawAdvanced() normalizes the device context.

Word calls `IDataObject::GetData()`, passing a value of `TYMED_MFPICT` in the `FORMATETC` parameter, so `OnDraw()` is passed a metafile. `OnDrawAdvanced()` normalizes the device context because the metafile is created by ATL.

# Sizing

The size of a control can be determined either by a control or its container. Usually, a container will want to size the control: the container knows how much space is available. However, some controls may only be able to draw themselves if they are a particular size, or their drawing may be the best quality when they are a particular size. If this is the situation, then the ATL control should set `m_bAutoSize` to `true` (by default, it is `false`). This member also supplies the value for the stock property `DISPID_AUTOSIZE`. When the control sets this value, it is saying that it will determine its own size, and the container will not be allowed to change it.

If the container is allowed to size the control, it can do it in one of two ways: **integral sizing** or **content sizing**. In integral sizing, the container tells the control the size it should use. The control has no option about this – it should create and draw itself in the area specified. In content sizing, the container *suggests* a size to the control. However, the control may decide that it can display itself better using a different size, its **natural size**.

The container calls `IViewObject::GetNaturalSize()` to pass the control the preferred size (if content sizing is used) *or* the actual size (if integral sizing is used). In the first case, the control can adjust the preferred size to match its natural size, or it can accept the preferred size. Whichever it uses, it will return the size to the container. If it accepts the preferred size, the control must resize itself to the specified size. ATL uses content sizing by default; to change this behavior you would have to override `IViewObjectExImpl<>::GetNaturalSize()`.

`CComControl<>` maintains two sizes for the control: `m_sizeNatural` and `m_sizeExtent`. The former is the natural size of the control, while the latter is returned if the container calls `IOleObject::GetExtent()`. If the control is best drawn using its natural size, then `m_bDrawFromNatural` should be set so that metafile rendering will use the natural size. The `CComControlBase` constructor sets both of these sizes to 2 inches in both *x* and *y* directions. If you want to change this size, you should do it in your constructor – an example is given in the `DiskFreeSpace` control given later.

When the container resizes the control, it will call `IOleObject::SetExtent()`, and `CComControl<>` will keep this new size in the `m_sizeExtent` member. Both of these sizes are in `HIMETRIC` units, but `OnDraw()` will expect the size of the drawing area to be in pixels, and so typically `AtlHiMetricToPixel()` will be called to do the conversion.

# Other Control Issues

I've now explained the most significant things you to consider when writing a control; in this section, I'll go through some other issues that you will need to bear in mind.

# Insertable Controls and Other Capabilities

Controls add entries to the registry to indicate their capabilities. The 'traditional' way to do this is to add a well-known key to the control's CLSID; other objects can then search for this key to determine whether the control can support the functionality. An example of this is the Insertable key, which indicates that the control can be inserted in a container.

The problem with this approach is that the control's CLSID key will get quite full of extra keys, and that's why the idea of **component categories** was developed. I talked about these in Chapter 3, and ATL simplifies adding a category by means of the category map. Newer containers will look for controls that have the CATID_Insertable component category, rather than looking for the Insertable key. However, if you want your control to be insertable in both older and newer containers, you should use both methods.

To indicate that the control has the 'insertable' category, you can use this code:

```
BEGIN_CATEGORY_MAP(CMyCtrl)
    IMPLEMENTED_CATEGORY(CATID_Insertable)
    IMPLEMENTED_CATEGORY(CATID_Control)
END_CATEGORY_MAP()
```

Note that the Object Wizard will not add a category map for you; you have to add the BEGIN_ and END_ macros by hand. You will also need to include comcat.h at the top of the header:

```
#include <comcat.h>
```

As a final word on insertable controls, you should know that even if you add the Insertable key and the insertable category, some containers will *still* refuse to show the control in their Insert Object dialog. Just such a container is Excel 97, which expects the Insertable key to be in the version-independent ProgID key, rather than the CLSID key. To add this, you will have to edit the control's RGS file by hand.

# Scripting

Internet Explorer uses the <OBJECT> tag to embed a control onto a web page. Once a control is on a web page, it can be initialized with the <PARAM> tag, its methods and properties can be invoked using scripting, and it can generate events to be caught by event handlers scripted on the page.

Of course, it is not *quite* that simple – a control could do nasty things to your machine, so you must be sure that you want to install it, but this is not usually a problem. If you install the control from the command line or a setup program, you have already consented to install the control. If the control is part of a web page, and is downloaded over the Internet, you will get a dialog asking you if you want to install the control – you will usually get a certificate to authenticate its source.

Often, though, a control is only *part* of the executable content of a page: the page will often have data to initialize the control, and scripting code to tell the control to do things. Even a benign control could be scripted to perform malicious acts. Because of this, when you attempt to initialize a control, or script it in Internet Explorer 4, you may be presented with the following dialog:

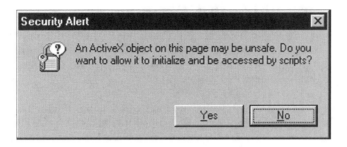

This is telling you that the web page is trying to script the control or initialize it with the <PARAM> tag, and that Internet Explorer does not know if this code and data will make the control do something nasty.

You can click on <u>Y</u>es and allow the control to do its stuff, or you can click on <u>N</u>o and forgo the use of this control. This check can be tiresome, and you can prevent Internet Explorer 4 from making it by turning off security checks in the **Security** tab of the **Options** dialog. However, this is only a good idea when you're developing and testing controls; it is unwise not to check controls you know nothing about. The preferred alternative is for the control itself to tell Internet Explorer that it will accept any initialization parameters or be scripted by any code. Such a control is called a **safe control**.

There are two ways to indicate that a control is safe. The first is for the control to have a component category saying that it is safe, and the second is to implement the IObjectSafety interface. The first method is trivial to implement – you just include the following two lines in your category map:

```
BEGIN_CATEGORY_MAP(CMyCtrl)
    IMPLEMENTED_CATEGORY(CATID_Insertable)
    IMPLEMENTED_CATEGORY(CATID_Control)
    IMPLEMENTED_CATEGORY(CATID_SafeForScripting)
    IMPLEMENTED_CATEGORY(CATID_SafeForInitializing)
END_CATEGORY_MAP()
```

These two categories are declared in objsafe.idl, which gets #included via the standard ATL header files. When Internet Explorer 4.0 is asked to load a control, it will check for these categories in the registry.

The other way to do the same thing is for the control to implement the IObjectSafety interface. This has a method called SetInterfaceSafetyOptions(), which Internet Explorer 4.0 will call to specify the options that it is expecting the control to support. This function is rather curiously named, because it also returns an indication of whether the control supports the safety level. The interface also supports a GetInterfaceSafetyOptions() method, which will return the safety options that are supported, and whether they are enabled.

ATL implements this interface with the `IObjectSafetyImpl<>` template, which provides suitable code for these methods. When Internet Explorer calls `SetInterfaceSafetyOptions()`, it will pass the IID of an interface that the page will use, or that Internet Explorer will use to initialize the control, and this class will check that the control supports the requested interface, and return `E_NOINTERFACE` if it doesn't. Internet Explorer will also pass the options that it wants to set and their values. This class will check the requested options against those that are appropriate for the control and will return `E_FAIL` if the options are not appropriate. Otherwise it will enable those options and return `S_OK`.

In effect, this method is used to check whether the control is safe for scripting and initialization, because the two options available are `INTERFACESAFE_FOR_UNTRUSTED_CALLER` and `INTERFACESAFE_FOR_UNTRUSTED_DATA`.

To specify that your control is safe for one or both of these, they should be included as the parameters to `IObjectSafetyImpl<>`, which can be used as a base class of your ATL class:

```
IObjectSafetyImpl<CMyCtrl,
          INTERFACESAFE_FOR_UNTRUSTED_CALLER | INTERFACESAFE_FOR_UNTRUSTED_DATA>
```

Of course, you must also add the `IObjectSafety` interface to the COM map.

## Example: Scripting

This example will illustrate how to make your object safe to be included on an Interface Explorer HTML page; it will also be used later in the chapter. The control looks like this:

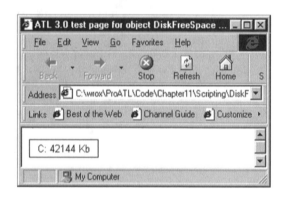

The control prints the number of kilobytes of free space on a drive on the local machine. The control has a property called `Drive` that holds the name of the drive, and has a method called `Update()` that's used by scripts to tell the control to re-read the free space on the drive. I could have implemented the control to create a worker thread that sets up a `FindFirstChangeNotification()` and then update the view of the control, but this manual method is better to illustrate scripting.

The first thing to do is create a DLL ATL project called `Scripting` and insert a Full Control called `DiskFreeSpace`. Although I will begin by using this in Internet Explorer 4.0 (for which purpose a Lite control would suffice), it has to be a full control because it will be used in a later example that requires one. In the Miscellaneous tab make the control Insertable, and in the Stock Properties tab select Fill Color, Font and Foreground Color. The first and last of these will be used to illustrate scripting, while the Font property will be used as an example of how to manipulate font properties. From the Attributes tab, select Support ISupportErrorInfo, so that the control can return rich error information.

Using ClassView, add a property called Drive of type BSTR and a read-only property called FreeSpace of type long. Finally, add a method called Update() that has no parameters:

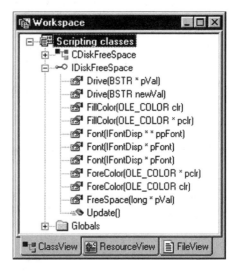

As usual, I have copied the body of OnDraw() to the source file because the drawing code is likely to change many times during development, and I want to reduce compile times.

Next, add a private data member for the drive name, and another to hold the free space:

```
public:
    STDMETHOD(Update)();
    STDMETHOD(get_FreeSpace)(/*[out, retval]*/ long *pVal);
    STDMETHOD(get_Drive)(/*[out, retval]*/ BSTR *pVal);
    STDMETHOD(put_Drive)(/*[in]*/ BSTR newVal);

    HRESULT OnDraw(ATL_DRAWINFO& di);

    OLE_COLOR m_clrFillColor;
    CComPtr<IFontDisp> m_spFont;
    OLE_COLOR m_clrForeColor;

private:
    CComBSTR m_bstrDrive;
    long m_lFreeSpaceKb;
};
```

A CComBSTR will initially hold a NULL string, so you don't need to initialize m_bstrDrive. m_lFreeSpaceKb will be initialized in the constructor, as you'll see later in this section. The accessor methods are fairly trivial, but the put_ method of Drive is a little more complicated – it uses the Win32 GetLogicalDrives() function to determine if the drive setting is valid:

```
STDMETHODIMP CDiskFreeSpace::get_Drive(BSTR* pVal)
{
    return m_bstrDrive.CopyTo(pVal);
}

STDMETHODIMP CDiskFreeSpace::put_Drive(BSTR newVal)
{
    USES_CONVERSION;
    CComBSTR bstr(newVal);

    // NULL string is OK
    if(bstr.Length() == 0)
        return S_OK;

    // Must be a single character
    if(bstr.Length() > 1)
        return Error(
                "Drive must be a single letter", IID_IDiskFreeSpace, E_INVALIDARG);

    // Must be a letter
    LPCTSTR strLetter = OLE2CT(bstr.m_str);
    if(strLetter[0] > _T('Z') || strLetter[0] < _T('A'))
        return Error(
            "Drive must be in the range A to Z", IID_IDiskFreeSpace, E_INVALIDARG);

    // Check that drive exists
    DWORD dwDrives = ::GetLogicalDrives();
    dwDrives &= (1 << (strLetter[0] - _T('A')));
    if(dwDrives == 0)
        return Error("Drive does not exist", IID_IDiskFreeSpace, E_INVALIDARG);

    m_bstrDrive = newVal;
    SetDirty(TRUE);
    Update();
    return S_OK;
}
```

The last section of code needs explaining: the Win32 `GetLogicalDrives()` function returns a
`DWORD` in which each bit represents the logical drives that are present: bit 1 for A, bit 2 for B, and so
on.

The `get_FreeSpace()` method is implemented like this:

```
STDMETHODIMP CDiskFreeSpace::get_FreeSpace(long *pVal)
{
    m_lFreeSpaceKb = _GetFreeSpace();
    *pVal = m_lFreeSpaceKb;
    FireViewChange();
    SendOnDataChange();
    return S_OK;
};
```

This calls `FireViewChange()` to redraw the control, and `SendOnDataChange()` to make a
container refresh its cached view of the control. However, it does not call `SetDirty()` because
`FreeSpace` is not one of the properties that gets persisted.

It's the `_GetFreeSpace()` function that actually calculates the free space, so add it as a `private` method:

```
private:
   long _GetFreeSpace();
   CComBSTR m_bstrDrive;
   long m_lFreeSpaceKb;
};
```

Implement `_GetFreeSpace()` like this:

```
long CDiskFreeSpace::_GetFreeSpace()
{
   USES_CONVERSION;
   DWORD dwSectorsPerCluster;
   DWORD dwBytesPerSector;
   DWORD dwNumberOfFreeClusters;
   DWORD dwTotalNumberOfClusters;

   // GetDiskFreeSpaceEx() is not available
   //   before Win95 OSR2, so we'll use GetDiskFreeSpace()
   if(m_bstrDrive.Length() == 0)
   {
      // If the drive name is NULL, the fn will use the current drive
      GetDiskFreeSpace(NULL, &dwSectorsPerCluster, &dwBytesPerSector,
                       &dwNumberOfFreeClusters, &dwTotalNumberOfClusters);
   }
   else
   {
      CComBSTR temp = m_bstrDrive;
      temp += L":\\";
      GetDiskFreeSpace(OLE2CT(temp), &dwSectorsPerCluster, &dwBytesPerSector,
                       &dwNumberOfFreeClusters, &dwTotalNumberOfClusters);
   }

   // The number of bytes per cluster should fit into a DWORD
   DWORD dwBytesPerCluster = dwSectorsPerCluster * dwBytesPerSector;

   // But the number of bytes on the disk needs careful handling
   hyper hypFreeBytes = UInt32x32To64(
                                    dwNumberOfFreeClusters, dwBytesPerCluster);

   // Now return the number of kilobytes, using 1Kb = 1024 bytes
   return static_cast<long>(hypFreeBytes >> 10);
}
```

If the drive letter is unset, then NULL is passed as the root drive to `GetDiskFreeSpace()` to tell it to use the 'current' drive. The number of bytes of free space on the drive is calculated, and then this value is shifted right by 10 bits (that is, divided by 1024) to get the number of kilobytes.

`Update()` simply calls `get_FreeSpace()` and updates the view of the control:

```
STDMETHODIMP CDiskFreeSpace::Update()
{
    m_lFreeSpaceKb = _GetFreeSpace();
    FireViewChange();
    SendOnDataChange();
    return S_OK;
}
```

The m_lFreeSpaceKb data member can be initialized in the constructor:

```
public:
    CDiskFreeSpace() : m_lFreeSpaceKb(_GetFreeSpace()),
                       m_clrFillColor(0xffffff),
                       m_clrForeColor(0)

    {
    }
```

When m_lFreeSpaceKb is initialized, m_bstrDrive should already have been initialized (as long as they are declared in the order given above), so calling _GetFreeSpace() is safe. The fill color is initialized to white and the foreground color is initialized to black. The font property must also be initialized, and this requires creating a COM object. Initialize the font like this in the constructor:

```
FONTDESC fd = {sizeof(FONTDESC), OLESTR("Arial"), FONTSIZE(10),
                        FW_NORMAL, ANSI_CHARSET, FALSE, FALSE, FALSE};
HRESULT hr = OleCreateFontIndirect(&fd, IID_IFontDisp,
                                    reinterpret_cast<void**>(&m_pFont));
```

The control should have a natural size of 1 inch wide by a quarter inch high, so add this to the constructor as well:

```
m_sizeExtent.cx = 2540; // one inch wide
m_sizeExtent.cy = 635;  // 1/4 inch high;
m_sizeNatural = m_sizeExtent; // set the natural extent
```

Of the properties that you have added with ClassView, only Drive needs to be made persistent, so add it to the property map with this entry:

```
PROP_ENTRY("Drive", 1, CLSID_NULL)
```

This control will be initialized in Internet Explorer 4.0, so it needs to implement IPersistPropertyBag, which means deriving the class from IPersistPropertyBagImpl<>:

```
public IPersistPropertyBagImpl<CDiskFreeSpace>,
```

And adding the interface to the property map:

```
COM_INTERFACE_ENTRY(IPersistPropertyBag)
```

The control will show the drive's size, so OnDraw() is implemented like this:

```
HRESULT CDiskFreeSpace::OnDraw(ATL_DRAWINFO& di)
{
    USES_CONVERSION;

    COLORREF clrFront, clrBack;
    OleTranslateColor(m_clrFillColor, NULL, &clrBack);
    OleTranslateColor(m_clrForeColor, NULL, &clrFront);

    HBRUSH hBrush = CreateSolidBrush(clrBack);
    HBRUSH hOldBrush = (HBRUSH)SelectObject(di.hdcDraw, hBrush);

    HPEN hPen = CreatePen(PS_SOLID, 1, clrFront);
    HPEN hOldPen = (HPEN)SelectObject(di.hdcDraw, hPen);

    HFONT hFont;
    CComQIPtr<IFont, &IID_IFont> pFont(m_pFont);
    pFont->get_hFont(&hFont);
    HFONT hOldFont = static_cast<HFONT>(SelectObject(di.hdcDraw, hFont));

    const RECT& rc = *reinterpret_cast<const RECT*>(di.prcBounds);
    Rectangle(di.hdcDraw, rc.left, rc.top, rc.right, rc.bottom);

    CComBSTR bstr = m_bstrDrive;
    if(bstr.Length() == 0)
    {
        DWORD dwSize = GetCurrentDirectory(0, NULL);
        LPTSTR strDrive = new TCHAR[dwSize];
        GetCurrentDirectory(dwSize, strDrive);
        strDrive[1] = 0;
        bstr = strDrive;
        delete [] strDrive;
    }

    TCHAR str[25] = {0};
    wsprintf(str, _T(": %lu Kb"), m_lFreeSpaceKb);
    bstr += str;

    TEXTMETRIC tm;
    GetTextMetrics(di.hdcDraw, &tm);

    SetTextColor(di.hdcDraw, clrFront);
    SetBkColor(di.hdcDraw, clrBack);
    SetTextAlign(di.hdcDraw, TA_CENTER | TA_TOP);

    TextOut(di.hdcDraw, (rc.left + rc.right) / 2,
        (rc.top + rc.bottom - tm.tmHeight) / 2, OLE2CT(bstr.m_str), bstr.Length());

    SelectObject(di.hdcDraw, hOldBrush);
    SelectObject(di.hdcDraw, hOldPen);
    SelectObject(di.hdcDraw, hOldFont);
    return S_OK;
}
```

If the drive is not set then the code calls GetCurrentDirectory() and then a string is constructed in the format "Drive: FreeSpace Kb". Notice that the format string in the call to wsprintf() uses lu; this is so that the size is interpreted as an unsigned value, making it better able to cope with large drives.

Now compile the example and then edit the Object Wizard generated web page:

```
<HTML>
<HEAD>
<TITLE>ATL 3.0 test page for object DiskFreeSpace</TITLE>
</HEAD>
<BODY>
<OBJECT ID="DiskFreeSpace" NAME="Obj"
   CLASSID="CLSID:962DDB1E-F259-11D1-9B6B-0060973044A8">
<PARAM NAME="Drive" VALUE="D">
<PARAM NAME="FillColor" VALUE="0">
<PARAM NAME="ForeColor" VALUE="16777215">
</OBJECT>
<P>
<INPUT TYPE="BUTTON" VALUE="Update" LANGUAGE="VBS" ONCLICK=bnClick>
<SCRIPT LANGUAGE="VBS">
Sub bnClick()
   Obj.UpDate
End Sub
</SCRIPT>
</BODY>
</HTML>
```

This sets the `Drive` to D, the `FillColor` to black, and the `ForeColor` to white. The HTML also puts a button on the page; when you click on this, the control is told to update itself. When you load the page in Internet Explorer 4.0, you'll probably see a security dialog. For now, click on Yes to let the control load. You should get something like this:

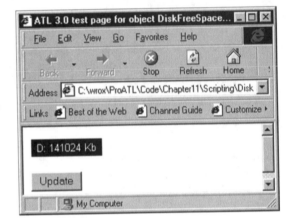

Now copy a largish file (greater than 1Kb) to the D drive and click on the Update button. This should show a decrease in the amount of free space.

This control doesn't do anything nasty with the host machine, so you can be assured that it can be initialized and scripted safely. So, to get rid of the annoying security dialog, derive the class from:

```
public IObjectSafetyImpl<CDiskFreeSpace,
         INTERFACESAFE_FOR_UNTRUSTED_CALLER | INTERFACESAFE_FOR_UNTRUSTED_DATA>
```

For good measure, also add the category map:

```
BEGIN_CATEGORY_MAP(CDiskFreeSpace)
    IMPLEMENTED_CATEGORY(CATID_Insertable)
    IMPLEMENTED_CATEGORY(CATID_Control)
    IMPLEMENTED_CATEGORY(CATID_SafeForScripting)
    IMPLEMENTED_CATEGORY(CATID_SafeForInitializing)
END_CATEGORY_MAP()
```

Now compile the project again. You will find that when you load the web page with Internet Explorer 4.0, you will no longer get the security dialog. To make absolutely sure, try changing the drive letter to a drive that your machine does not have (or is not mapped):

```
<PARAM NAME="Drive" VALUE="Z">
```

You will find that Internet Explorer does not complain – it just returns the free space on the current drive. This is because put_Drive() tests that the drive value is valid, and if it isn't the drive name is made NULL. Although put_Drive() returns an error (and an error object), Internet Explorer just ignores it.

Try changing the HTML to add this code:

```
<BR>
<INPUT TYPE="BUTTON" VALUE="Change Drive" LANGUAGE="VBS" ONCLICK=NewDrive>
<INPUT TYPE="TEXT" NAME="txtDrive">
<SCRIPT LANGUAGE="VBS">
Sub NewDrive()
    Obj.Drive = txtDrive.Value
End Sub
</SCRIPT>
```

When you click on the Change Drive button, you will be able to change the Drive property and hence update the view:

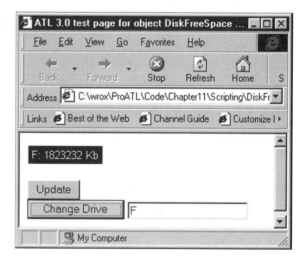

If you enter an invalid drive letter, you will get a dialog like this:

Here, Internet Explorer 4.0 is displaying the description in the error object thrown by `put_Drive()`. I have the script debugger installed, which is why the dialog asks me if I wish to debug the page.

# Object Wizard Control Types

Now that you have an understanding of the control classes, let's take a slightly deeper look at the control types that the Object Wizard supplies. Chapter 4 gave a brief overview of these control types, so bear that chapter in mind as you read on. I'm going to leave further coverage of the HTML controls until Chapter 11, so we'll just look at standard and composite controls in this section.

## Full and Lite Controls

As the name suggests, a full control has support for most of the interfaces that you'll need for compatibility with a wide range of containers (although, strangely, it doesn't include `IPersistPropertyBag`). As you have seen, some containers will require the interfaces that a full control supports, and if you want to support things like property pages, you will need to make your control full. A lite control keeps the number of interfaces that it supports to a minimum.

So, what exactly *do* you get? The Object Wizard will implement the required control interfaces on both full and lite controls: `IViewObjectEx`, `IOleInPlaceObjectWindowless`, `IOleInPlaceObject`, `IOleInPlaceActiveObject`, `IOleControl`, `IOleObject` and `IPersistStreamInit`. These allow your control to communicate with the container, initialize and save itself to a stream, and render itself on screen.

In addition to these, a full control has support for property pages (`ISpecifyPropertyPages`), rendering through data objects (`IDataObject`), providing information about the default source interface and the CLSID of the object (`IProvideClassInfo2`), initialization through storages (`IPersistStorage`) and quick activation (`IQuickActivate`).

This last interface is quite interesting. A control must communicate with its container, and to do so it must obtain interface pointers to various notification and client site objects in the container. Typically, this occurs through a series of exploratory method calls by the container on the control's `IOleObject` and `IOleControl` interfaces. The `IQuickActivate` interface provides methods to pass a structure with the necessary container interface and ambient properties in one call.

Lite controls have the bare minimum of support for a working control. In Visual C++ 5.0, these were called IE Controls, but the term Lite Control seems more apt. Full and lite controls have been used throughout this chapter to explain the ATL control classes, so I won't go into any more detail about them here.

# Composite Controls

Visual Basic 5.0 and Visual Basic CCE (Control Creation Edition) introduced the facility to take a Visual Basic form and repackage it as an ActiveX Control. This is a very useful feature, because a developer can take existing controls (native Windows controls and ActiveX controls) and, using scripting, add these together to create a new ActiveX control. The Visual Basic developer could 'add value' to existing controls.

ATL 2.1 didn't prevent you from doing this, but it didn't offer much in the way of support. If you wanted to use ActiveX controls, you had to write the required control site code yourself. In ATL 3.0, the composite control in Object Wizard allows you to do a similar thing without any of this pain.

Composite controls are based on the `CComCompositeControl<>` class, which derives from `CAxDialogImpl<>` class as we discussed in the last chapter. You just provide a dialog template, and the ATL classes will create a borderless dialog that initializes all contained ActiveX controls from the ATL control's resources.

## Example: Composite Control

As an example, let's use the `DiskFreeSpace` control we developed earlier. Open the `Scripting` project and insert a Composite Control called `Drives`. You will find that the Object Wizard creates a rather large dialog template, so your first task is to resize this to about 2 inches by 1 inch to make it more manageable (you can resize it more accurately as you add the controls).

Next, right-click on the dialog resource, select Insert ActiveX Control... and from the dialog that appears select the DiskFreeSpace Class. The dialog editor will create a new instance of the control and place it on the template. Resize and move this control to somewhere near the top, and then change its ID to `IDC_DFS`.

Now, from the Controls toolbar, add an edit control and a button to the dialog. Change the properties of the button control so that it has an ID of `IDC_CHANGEDRIVE` and a caption of Change Drive; you should also make it Disabled, and mark it as the Default button in the Styles tab. Give the edit box an ID of `IDC_DRIVE`. Depending on the order that you put the controls on the template, you may decide to set the tab order too. When you have finished, it will look something like this:

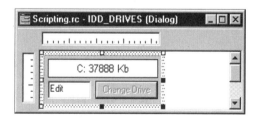

The top control is an ActiveX control that can respond to method calls, while the bottom two are Windows controls and will generate messages. The next thing to do is therefore to handle the messages from these controls.

Right click on the dialog resource and select Events... to bring up the message and event handler dialog. Select IDC_CHANGEDRIVE as the Class or object to handle, choose BN_CLICKED from the left hand box, click on Add Handler, and accept the default name. Do the same for the IDC_DRIVE control and the EN_CHANGE message. Then close the dialog.

You can now open the Drives.h header file and write the code that glues the controls together. The idea is that when the text in the edit box changes, the code should check to see if the edit box has some text — if it has, the button will be enabled. When the button is clicked, the handler should read the text in the edit box and use that to change the Drive property of the DiskFreeSpace control.

The handler for OnChangeDrive() looks like this:

```
LRESULT OnChangeDrive(WORD wNotifyCode, WORD wID, HWND hWndCtl, BOOL& bHandled)
{
    CWindow wndEdit(GetDlgItem(IDC_DRIVE));
    CWindow wndBn(GetDlgItem(IDC_CHANGEDRIVE));
    wndBn.EnableWindow((wndEdit.GetWindowTextLength() > 0) ? TRUE : FALSE);
    return 0;
}
```

And the handler for clicking on the button looks like this:

```
LRESULT OnClickedChangedrive(
                    WORD wNotifyCode, WORD wID, HWND hWndCtl, BOOL& bHandled)
{
    CComBSTR bstr;
    CWindow wndEdit(GetDlgItem(IDC_DRIVE));
    wndEdit.GetWindowText(bstr.m_str);

    CComPtr<IDiskFreeSpace> pDFS;
    HRESULT hr = GetDlgControl(
                    IDC_DFS, IID_IDiskFreeSpace, reinterpret_cast<void**>(&pDFS));
    if(FAILED(hr))
        return 0;                        // Unexpected failure

    hr = pDFS->put_Drive(bstr);
    if(SUCCEEDED(hr))
        return 0;                        // Success
    return 0;
}
```

Notice that to get access to the ActiveX control, this code calls GetDlgControl() passing the ID of the control and the IID of the interface that you are interested in. This method is implemented in CWindow, as explained in the last chapter. That's all you need to do, so compile the project.

*Since the Drives control uses a control in the same project, make sure that you have closed down the dialog template. If the template is open, then the DiskFreeSpace control will be loaded, and you won't be able to link Scripting.dll.*

You should be able to launch the `Drives.htm` web page in Internet Explorer 4.0 to see your new control:

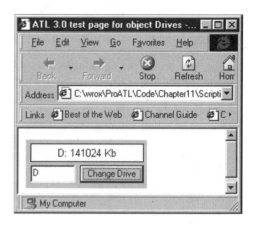

As this control loads, you may briefly see the default drawing code (with "ATL Composite Control"). This only appears when the control is first created, and if you find it annoying you can override `OnDraw()` in your code to do nothing.

The `DiskFreeSpace` control is hosted by the *dialog* and not by Internet Explorer, so if you enter an incorrect drive letter in the dialog box, there will be no warning. However, this is simple to remedy. Add the following code to `OnClickedChangedrive()`:

```
    if(SUCCEEDED(hr))
        return 0;                        // Success

    // If we failed, get error info and display a message box
    CComQIPtr<ISupportErrorInfo> pSEI(pDFS);
    if(!pSEI)
        return 0;                        // Object doesn't support error info

    if(pSEI->InterfaceSupportsErrorInfo(IID_IDiskFreeSpace) != S_OK)
        return 0;    // Object doesn't support error info on that interface

    CComPtr<IErrorInfo> pEI;
    GetErrorInfo(0, &pEI);
    if(!pEI)
        return 0;                        // Unexpected failure

    USES_CONVERSION;
    pEI->GetDescription(&bstr);
    MessageBox(OLE2CT(bstr), _T("DiskFreeSpace"));
    return 0;
}
```

As you can see, when you have existing ActiveX controls, this control type makes code reuse simple and effective.

# Summary

Controls are the visible manifestation of COM objects, and perhaps the most popular use of COM. The widespread use of controls belies the amount of work that is required to implement them. However, ATL has done most of this work for you in `CComControlBase` and the various `Impl` classes.

A control can hold its state, or change its behavior, using values in COM properties that are identified by DISPIDs. A control can have custom properties, but these will be known only to itself and to containers or scripts that were written especially for this control. To be more generic, a control can have stock properties, which have predefined DISPIDs and are known by all standard containers. Stock properties are usually bindable, which means that the container is informed when the property is about to change, or after it has changed. ATL has support for stock properties, and it will provide code to make properties bindable; you can specify which stock properties the control will support by using the Object Wizard.

Containers can have ambient properties, which they will use to suggest to controls how they should look and behave. If your control chooses to support ambient properties, it will respond when they change – the container carries out this notification by calling an interface method on the control. ATL has *some* support for ambient properties: it has methods to obtain the value of the ambient property from the container. However, you do have to write some code yourself – in particular, you must implement the interface method that recieves the notification and tests to see if it concerns of the properties that the control will respond to.

A control is typically initialized using some persisted data, and ATL provides default implementations of the various `IPersistxxx` interfaces. Although these interfaces persist the data in different ways, ATL centralizes much of the code and uses the property map to indicate which object properties are to be persisted. In the property map, you can specify interface properties or object data members; the latter are not accessible through COM, but they're still part of the state of the object. However, ATL only has support for a limited range of members' datatypes (basically, only integer members can be used), and in this chapter I have given code that will enable you to persist data members of other types, fixed and variable in size.

The most obvious aspect of a control is its visual representation, and ATL has plenty of code to help you in this regard. Although there are several ways that a container can tell a control to draw itself (depending on whether the control is windowed or windowless, and whether it is being drawn to the screen, or a metafile, or to some other device), ATL channels the drawing code into a single method: `OnDrawAdvanced()`. In fact, it goes further than that: the default implementation of this method will usually normalize the drawing device context so that the units will be pixels and the origin will be in the top left-hand corner. It then passes the normalized device context to `OnDraw()`, where you can put your drawing code if you do not want to draw to an un-normalized device context.

Finally, Object Wizard has support for generic control types and two other, more specific control types. I dealt with the composite control in this chapter, leaving the HTML control to be my subject for the next and final chapter.

# 11

# HTML Controls

One of the new control types introduced in Visual C++ 6.0 is the HTML control. This name is a little confusing because it will create an ATL control and much of the code you will write will be ATL code. The HTML control, in fact, *hosts* the Internet Explorer WebBrowser control and you can use this to access the rendering, script parsing, and internet browsing facilities of IE4.

To make full use of this control type you really need to have an understanding of the IE4 object model and DHTML. I will give some information about both of these, but if you need more information, I recommend *Professional IE4 Programming (Barta, et al)* for a detailed description of the IE4 object model, and *Instant IE4 Dynamic HTML Programmer's Reference (Homer and Ullman)* for complete coverage of DHTML. Both books are published by Wrox Press.

## The HTML ATL Control

Conceptually, your HTML control can be modeled like this:

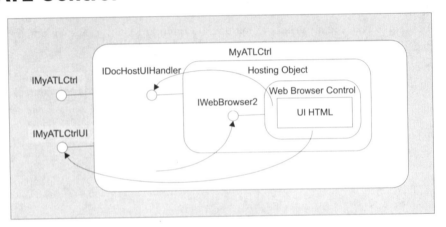

I will go into more details about these interfaces in later sections of this chapter. I present this picture here simply to point out to you that your ATL control (here, called `MyATLCtrl`) hosts an ATL supplied object that is used, in turn, to host the WebBrowser control. (The ATL 'hosting' object is not accessible outside your ATL control, and is not normally accessible by your ATL control). The `IWebBrowser2` interface on the WebBrowser control is cached as a data member of your ATL control so that you can manipulate it.

By default, the user interface of the control is provided by the WebBrowser control, which covers the entire area of your control. The WebBrowser control will render a user interface based on HTML stored as a resource in your control's project. You can use this resource to present text, HTML objects like text boxes and buttons, and even other ActiveX controls as part of your control's user interface.

When you create an HTML control, the Object Wizard will add *two* new interfaces to the generated class.

The first interface can be regarded as the 'external' interface of the control. This is the interface that your control's clients will use to access properties or methods of the control. It is equivalent to the main interface on any of the other control types generated by the Object Wizard.

The other interface, which is named with a `UI` suffix, is not intended to be accessed by external clients. Instead, this 'internal' interface is used to extend the object model exposed by Internet Explorer. This object model is accessible to script within the UI HTML used in the WebBrowser control. This interface provides a communication mechanism between scripting code that you add to your UI HTML and the control itself.

> *Note that the UI interface is added to the* `coclass` *block for the control in the IDL file. This is unnecessary since the interface will only be used by scripting code that you add to the UI HTML. You can remove this line if you like.*

Bear in mind this relationship between the IE4 control and your ATL control when you read the following sections. It will help you to understand the code that ATL provides.

# Internet Explorer

ATL 3.0 provides many classes to manipulate Internet Explorer, and an understanding of how Internet Explorer works will help you understand how these classes work.

When you start Internet Explorer, what you are actually seeing is a small container hosting the **WebBrowser control** (`SHDOCVW.dll`), which itself hosts the **MSHTML control** (`MSHTML.dll`). Conceptually Internet Explorer looks like this:

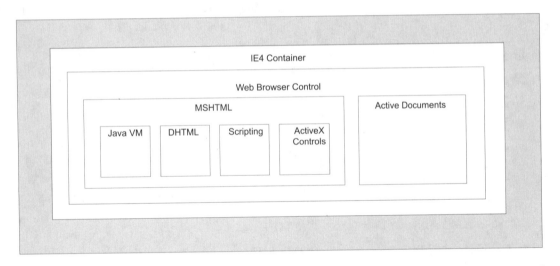

The WebBrowser control handles navigation, hyperlinking, favorites, and history management; it also has the interfaces to host Active Documents. The WebBrowser control hosts MSHTML to carry out HTML parsing and rendering. MSHTML, in turn, hosts the registered scripting engines, the Java VM and any other ActiveX controls that a web page contains.

Since these two DLLs are COM components, they can be used in your own applications. However, the process is not simple. In particular, if your application wants to host the WebBrowser, it needs to implement the IDocHostUIHandler interface in addition to all the standard container interfaces. This interface allows the host and the WebBrowser to communicate about the menus, context menus, and toolbars.

If you review the previous diagram showing the relationship between the WebBrowser control and the ATL control, you'll see that another object – the *hosting object* – is used to provide this interface, as well as the client site hosting code for the WebBrowser control.

# DHTML Interfaces

Access to the WebBrowser control is via the IWebBrowser2 interface. This interface allows you to specify a URL to load, go backward or forward in the history list, or refresh a loaded page, for example. In addition, it gives access to various properties that provide information about the application (such as the size and position of the main window). More importantly, IWebBrowser2 gives access to the DHTML object model.

The actual HTML on a web page is accessed through the document object, which implements the IHTMLDocument2 interface. This represents the loaded HTML page and provides access to the subobjects that make up the document. Each tag used on the web page is a COM object that has an interface and can generate events. The IHTMLDocument2 interface has properties for single instance objects (like the parentWindow object or the body object), and for collections which provide access to objects that may have more than one instance (like the links object that allows access to all the links on the web page).

The following table shows the interfaces that can be used to manipulate the various tags on an HTML page:

| Interface | HTML Element |
|---|---|
| IHTMLAnchorElement | A |
| IHTMLAreaElement | AREA |
| IHTMLBaseElement | BASE |
| IHTMLBaseFontElement | BASEFONT |
| IHTMLBodyElement | BODY |
| IHTMLBRElement | BR |
| IHTMLButtonElement | BUTTON |
| IHTMLCommentElement | COMMENT |
| IHTMLDDElement | DD |
| IHTMLDivElement | DIV |
| IHTMLDListElement | DL |
| IHTMLDTElement | DT |
| IHTMLElement | All element objects. |
| IHTMLFieldSetElement | FIELDSET |
| IHTMLFontElement | FONT |
| IHTMLFormElement | FORM |
| IHTMLFrameElement | FRAME |
| IHTMLFrameSetElement | FRAMESET |
| IHTMLHeaderElement | H1 through H6 |
| IHTMLHRElement | HR |
| IHTMLIFrameElement | IFRAME |
| IHTMLImgElement | IMG and INPUT of type image |
| IHTMLInputButtonElement | INPUT of type reset or submit |
| IHTMLInputFileElement | INPUT of type file |
| IHTMLInputHiddenElement | INPUT of type hidden |
| IHTMLInputTextElement | INPUT of type text |
| IHTMLIsIndexElement | ISINDEX |

| Interface | HTML Element |
|---|---|
| IHTMLLabelElement | LABEL |
| IHTMLLegendElement | LEGEND |
| IHTMLLIElement | LI |
| IHTMLLinkElement | LINK |
| IHTMLListElement | OL and UL |
| IHTMLMapElement | MAP |
| IHTMLMarqueeElement | MARQUEE |
| IHTMLMetaElement | META |
| IHTMLNextIdElement | NEXTID |
| IHTMLObjectElement | OBJECT |
| IHTMLOListElement | OL |
| IHTMLOptionButtonElement | INPUT of type radio |
| IHTMLOptionElement | OPTION |
| IHTMLParaElement | P |
| IHTMLPhraseElement | No matching object. |
| IHTMLScriptElement | SCRIPT |
| IHTMLSelectElement | SELECT |
| IHTMLSpanFlow | SPAN |
| IHTMLStyleElement | STYLE |
| IHTMLTable | TABLE |
| IHTMLTableCaption | CAPTION |
| IHTMLTableCell | TD and TH |
| IHTMLTableCol | COL and COLGROUP |
| IHTMLTableRow | TR |
| IHTMLTableSection | TBODY, THEAD, and TFOOT |
| IHTMLTextAreaElement | TEXTAREA |
| IHTMLTitleElement | TITLE |
| IHTMLUListElement | UL |

Note that the DHTML object model has not been designed for C++ programmers. It is really designed for script programmers using 'typeless' languages like VBScript or JScript. For this reason, many of the object properties that you obtain through these interfaces will return generic interface pointers (usually `IDispatch`), rather than the strongly typed equivalents shown in this table. Getting the typed interface pointer requires a call to `QueryInterface()`. This can get tedious, but you can use `CComQIPtr<>` to ease your burden.

Here's an example that shows how to iterate through the links in a document. Although, the `links` property is of type `IHTMLElementCollection` (not `IDispatch`), this collection interface returns `IDispatch` pointers to the elements in the collection, so you'll need to query for the dual interface that you are interested in.

```
CComPtr<IHTMLElementCollection> pColl;
pDoc2->get_links(&pColl);
long len;
pColl->get_length(&len);
for (long i= 0; i < len; ++i)
{
   CComVariant item, ind;
   item = i;                                // pass the item number in a VARIANT
   CComPtr<IDispatch> pDisp;
   pColl->item(item, ind, &pDisp);
   if (!pDisp)
      continue;

   CComQIPtr<IHTMLLinkElement> pLink(pDisp);
   // use the LINK object
}
```

## Accessing IE4 Hosted by your Control

When you generate an HTML control, the Object Wizard will add a member variable, `m_spBrowser`, that is initialized to the `IWebBrowser2` interface of the WebBrowser control hosted by your ATL control. Once the entire control has been fully initialized, you can call methods on this interface to get hold of the `document` object and through that the various subobjects on the page. You will see examples of doing this later in this chapter.

## Accessing IE4 Hosting your Control

It is also possible that you will want to access the Internet Explorer object model when your ATL control is being hosted by IE4 through the `<OBJECT>` tag on a web page. (Note that your control doesn't have to be an HTML control in this case – any control type will do).

In this case, there are two ways of getting into Internet Explorer:

The first way gets hold of the `IWebBrowser2` interface using a technique that you saw earlier in the book. If your control implements `IObjectWithSite` then IE4 will use the `SetSite()` method to pass to your control the `IUnknown` pointer to its site object. For ATL controls, this interface pointer is stored in the `IObjectWithSiteImpl<>::m_spUnkSite` member of your control. You can query this pointer for the `IServiceProvider` interface then use `IServiceProvider::QueryService()` to get a pointer to the `IWebBrowser2` interface. Here's the code that you need:

```
CComQIPtr<IServiceProvider> spSP(m_spUnkSite);
CComPtr<IWebBrowser2> pWebBrowser2;
spSP->QueryService(IID_IWebBrowserApp, IID_IWebBrowser2,
                                 reinterpret_cast<void**>(&pWebBrowser2));

if (pWebBrowser2)
{
    // use interface to get access to IE4 objects
}
```

The alternative method is to get hold of the container object for the web browser. Since the control will be embedded on a page, this container object will be the active document object, so you can query this object for the IHTMLDocument2 interface. As before, you need to start with the client site interface and use it to navigate to the interface that you're interested in:

For example, to change the background color to DARKORANGE you can use the following code:

```
HRESULT hr;
CComPtr<IOleContainer> spContainer;
m_spClientSite->GetContainer(&spContainer);

CComQIPtr<IHTMLDocument2> spDoc2(spContainer);
if (spDoc2)
{
    // Get body
    CComPtr<IHTMLElement> pElement;
    hr = spDoc2->get_body(&pElement);
    if (pElement)
    {
        CComQIPtr<IHTMLBodyElement> pBody(pElement);
        CComVariant var;
        var = _T("DARKORANGE");
        pBody->put_bgColor(var);
    }
}
else
{
    // not IE4
}
```

Note that this code attempts to access the IHTMLDocument2 interface on its container. This call will only be successful if the control is on a web page, so I've been careful to check that the interface pointer was returned successfully before using it in case the control is being hosted in another container.

# Host Interfaces

A host that contains the WebBrowser control can change the tool bars and context menus that the control implements. To do this the host must implement the following interfaces:

| Interface | Description |
|---|---|
| IDocHostUIHandler | Allows the menus, toolbars and context menus to be replaced by the host |
| IDocHostShowUIInterface | Allows the host to supply message boxes and help |

The host container creates the WebBrowser control and uses the standard mechanism for setting up the connections between itself and the control. This includes the host implementing IOleClientSite which it passes to the control in a call to IOleObject::SetClientSite(). The WebBrowser control can use this interface to call QueryInterface() for the IDocHost interfaces. It will call these when, for example, it wants to show help or show a context menu. This is how the WebBrowser control communicates with the frame window provided by Internet Explorer.

In addition, the host can extend the DHTML object model of the WebBrowser control (actually provided by the MSHTML control). The WebBrowser control will call IDocHostUIHandler::GetExternal() when it initializes, to obtain the IDispatch interface provided by the host. It will use this interface to resolve unknown names when these are called through the window.external object in scripts. This mechanism is the basis of how the HTML control works.

# Internet Explorer Resource URLs

The user interface of your HTML control is an HTML page. The WebBrowser control must be initialized with this page when it is created, so the control must always have access to this page. If it is accessed from a web server then your HTML control could fail to initialize properly – you cannot guarantee that the control will always be on a machine with access to the internet. If the web page is provided as a file on the local system, the user could inadvertently delete this file, or you could omit to copy the file when installing the control. It is far better to have the HTML bound as a resource into the control's module.

One of the lesser known features of Internet Explorer is that you *can* provide HTML as a resource in a DLL or EXE. Just as Internet Explorer can handle http:, ftp:, gopher: and mk: protocols, it can also handle the res: protocol. This protocol takes the name of a DLL (or EXE) name that contains the resource, plus the resource identifier (either its name or resource ID). If the resource has an ID rather than a name then you must give the number preceded by a #. In whichever way the resource is identified, you may also specify a resource type, although this is optional.

To see an example of the res: protocol, start Internet Explorer and bring up the About box:

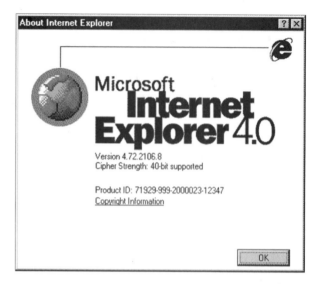

Click on the Copyright Information hyperlink and then click on the Next> button a few times until it becomes disabled:

Now click on the Take a Quick Tour link and you will find that Internet Explorer will attempt to load this URL:

```
res://ie4tour.dll/tour.htm#MinimalTour=1
```

This tells Internet Explorer to load the resource called
tour.htm from the ie4tour.dll file (which is typically
installed in your \System32 directory). ie4tour.dll
has many named resources, which you can view if you
load the DLL into Visual C++ as a resource:

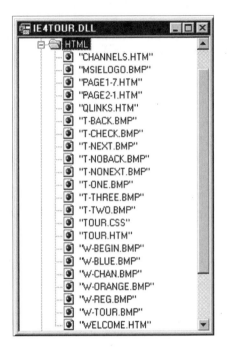

The res: protocol is important for the ATL HTML control type because it allows you to base your
control on HTML and bind that HTML directly into the control.

# Internet Explorer Host Classes

Earlier in this chapter, I explained what a host is, the responsibilities that it has, and the resources
that it can use. ATL allows your control to be a host for the WebBrowser control. Think about this:
all the functionality of the WebBrowser – hyperlinks, favorites, HTML rendering, scripting and more
– is available to your control.

> *Of course, this may seem a little odd if your control is being used on a web page because the
> container of the control will also be MSHTML. However, the control may be used in Visual Basic
> or any other control container and you will still have all this functionality.*

I mentioned that to be a host to the WebBrowser control, and extend the DHTML object model,
there are some interfaces that the host must implement. Further, since the host is a control container,
it must implement the control container interfaces. ATL has done all this work for you with the
CAxHostWindow class. This is one of several classes relevant to hosting the WebBrowser control,
and I will use the following sections to describe these classes. I'll describe the way that these classes
are used by the HTML control type more fully later on in the chapter.

# CAxHostWindow

An object that will host the WebBrowser control should implement the `IDocHostUIHandler` interface. The HTML control creates an instance of the `CAxHostWindow` class for the object that will host the WebBrowser control and this class provides stub implementations for the `IDocHostUIHandler` methods. These implementations are sufficient to keep the WebBrowser control happy.

In theory, you could provide your own implementation of this interface if you chose, and somehow pass a pointer to the hosting object which would then be able to call *your* methods when the WebBrowser calls the hosting object's methods. However, ATL takes a different approach. ATL defines a dispatch based interface called `IDocHostUIHandlerDispatch` (which you can find declared in `ATLIFace.idl`). If your ATL class wants to provide an implementation for `IDocHostUIHandler`, it should implement the dispatch version and pass a pointer to the `CAxHostWindow` instance with a call to `SetExternalUIHandler()`.

If you do not want to implement `IDocHostUIHandlerDispatch` in your ATL class, you can provide defaults for the information passed back to the control by the stub implementation of `IDocHostUIHandler` implemented by `CAxHostWindow`. For example `IDocHostUIHandler::GetHostInfo()` returns information to the control about the UI capabilities of the host. The ATL implementation looks like this:

```
STDMETHOD(GetHostInfo)(DOCHOSTUIINFO* pInfo)
{
    if (pInfo == NULL)
        return E_POINTER;

    if (m_spIDocHostUIHandlerDispatch != NULL)
        return m_spIDocHostUIHandlerDispatch->GetHostInfo(
            &pInfo->dwFlags, &pInfo->dwDoubleClick);

    pInfo->dwFlags = m_dwDocHostFlags;
    pInfo->dwDoubleClick = m_dwDocHostDoubleClickFlags;

    return S_OK;
}
```

The `m_spIDocHostUIHandlerDispatch` is set up in the call to `SetExternalUIHandler()`, if you do not call this, then the method uses the default value in `m_dwDocHostFlags` and `m_dwDocHostDoubleClickFlags`. These are initialized in the `CAxHostWindow` constructor, but you can change these defaults by changing these public data members when you create the object, or at a later stage by accessing its `IAxWinAmbientDispatch` interface. This interface provides properties for the following defaults:

| Property | Used by this `IDocHostUIHandler` method |
| --- | --- |
| DocHostFlags | GetHostInfo() |
| DocHostDoubleClickFlags | GetHostInfo() |

*Table Continued on Following Page*

| Property | Used by this `IDocHostUIHandler` method |
|----------|------------------------------------------|
| AllowContextMenu | ShowContextMenu() |
| AllowShowUI | ShowUI() |
| OptionKeyPath | GetOptionKeyPath() |

Since `CAxHostWindow` will act as a container for the WebBrowser control, it needs to provide the container interfaces. You can see these interfaces listed in the COM map for the class in `AtlHost.h`.

Control containers implement ambient properties, which are used to provide a consistent look and feel across all the controls hosted in the container. To implement these properties ATL defines ambient properties on the `IAxWinAmbientDispatch` interface. These properties are implemented to simply cache the property value and then tell the hosted control about the change.

The final, private interface that `CAxHostWindow` implements is `IAxWinHostWindow`. This allows a client to create new controls, get access to existing controls, or to change the host external `IDispatch` or external UI handler on the host.

# CAxWindowT<>

You do not create instances of `CAxHostWindow`, instead, your code creates instances of `CAxWindowT<>`. This class derives from its single template parameter, which is, by default, `CWindow`. ATL provides `CAxWindow` as a `typedef` for `CAxWindowT<CWindow>`. The main purpose of the class is to allow you to host an ActiveX control. These are the methods of the class:

| Method | Description |
|--------|-------------|
| Create() | Creates a window |
| CreateControl() | Creates a control and initializes it from a stream |
| CreateControlEx() | Creates a control, and passes it a sink interface |
| AttachControl() | Attaches an existing control to the class |
| QueryHost() | Obtains an interface on the control host |
| QueryControl() | Obtains an interface on the control |
| SetExternalDispatch() | Sets the external `IDispatch` interface |
| SetExternalUIHandler() | Sets the external implementation of `IDocHostUIHandler` |

*It is interesting to note that the various overloaded versions of* Create() *are implemented in terms of the methods in* CWindow *rather than the template parameter passed to* CAxWindowT<>. *This means that the class you supply as* TBase *must either derive from* CWindow *or provide a* typedef *for* CWindow, *so that this code will compile.*

In addition to these methods, CAxWindowT<> also implements a static method called GetWndClassName() that merely returns a string that gives the window class name of "AtlAxWin".

The methods given in this table are implementations of the IAxWinHostWindow interface mentioned earlier, but instances of CAxWindowT<> are not COM objects. CAxWindowT<> just creates and manages the host window. To see how it works let's look at a typical use of the class by examining the code generated by the Object Wizard for an HTML control.

## CreateControl()

CreateControl() is called in the OnCreate() handler when your ATL control's window is created:

```
LRESULT OnCreate(UINT, WPARAM, LPARAM, BOOL&)
{
   CAxWindow wnd(m_hWnd);
   HRESULT hr = wnd.CreateControl(IDH_MYCTRL);
   if (SUCCEEDED(hr))
      hr = wnd.SetExternalDispatch(static_cast<IMyCtrlUI*>(this));
   if (SUCCEEDED(hr))
      hr = wnd.QueryControl(IID_IWebBrowser2, (void**)&m_spBrowser);
   return SUCCEEDED(hr) ? 0 : -1;
}
```

Here you can see that the CAxWindow object, wnd, is a *stack* variable. When CreateControl() is called, it creates the *host object* on the *heap*. The lifetime of the host object is managed using IUnknown, so when the OnCreate() method returns, and wnd is destroyed, the host object still lives. The constructor of CAxWindow is passed the HWND of your ATL control and this is cached to be passed in the later call to AtlAxCreateControlEx() so that the host object gets access to this window.

CreateControl() is passed a resource ID that is used to indicate the control that the method should create. CreateControl() creates a host object with a WebBrowser control, as you'll see in a moment, and to get access to this control the code calls QueryControl(). In effect, this method sends a WM_ATLGETCONTROL message to the wrapper window that ATL puts round the control. The handler for this message returns the IUnknown of the control.

## Control Creation

Let's take a more detailed look at CreateControl().This function has several overloaded versions, so you can pass a resource ID, or a string to indicate the control that the method should create. In addition, you can pass a stream pointer that will be used to initialize the control (using the control's IPersistStreamInit interface) and an [out] parameter through which the method will return the IUnknown of the host object. This last parameter allows you to access the interfaces implemented on CAxHostWindow.

In OnCreate(), a resource ID is passed to CreateControl(). This is an HTML resource created by Object Wizard. CreateControl() uses this ID to construct a URL from the control's module file, for example:

```
res://c:\MyCtrls\debug\MyCtrls.dll/102
```

The number 102 is the value of IDH_MYCTRL, the resource ID passed to the method.

> *Instead of a resource ID, you can pass the stringified CLSID or ProgID of a control, or you can pass an* LPOLESTR *that contains HTML (this must be preceded with the string '*MSHTML: *').*

CreateControl() then calls AtlAxCreateControlEx() with this URL and the HWND that was passed to the constructor of the CAxWindow object (i.e. the HWND of the ATL control). This function first calls AtlAxWinInit() to register a window class for this control and some private window messages to communicate with it.

Next AtlAxCreateControlEx() creates a heap-based instance of CAxHostWindow, through the class factory typedef'd to _CreatorClass in CAxHostWindow:

```
hr = CAxHostWindow::_CreatorClass::CreateInstance(
                    NULL, IID_IUnknown, (void**)&spUnkContainer);
```

The CAxHostWindow class declares:

```
DECLARE_NO_REGISTRY()
DECLARE_POLY_AGGREGATABLE(CAxHostWindow)
```

So it is not externally creatable but it is aggregatable and creatable within the module.

At this point the CAxWindow object has created the host object, which is now ready to create the control that OnCreate() requested.

AtlAxCreateControlEx() queries for the IAxWinHostWindow interface and then calls IAxWinHostWindow::CreateControlEx() that actually does the work of creating and initializing the control. This method is passed the HWND of the ATL control which it passes to SubclassWindow() to subclass the CAxHostWindow on the control's window.

Next, CreateControlEx() calls CreateNormalizedObject() which creates the control based on the string that was passed from AtlAxCreateControlEx(). In the case of the code generated by Object Wizard, this is a URL, but it can be raw HTML prefixed with MSHTML:, a CLSID, or a ProgID. In the first case, the method creates an instance of the WebBrowser control. In the second case, it creates an instance of the MSHTML control and initializes it with the HTML. Otherwise, it creates an instance of the specified control. As you can see, this is quite flexible.

Once the control has been created, CreateControlEx() calls ActivateAx() to set up the client-site communications, the necessary advise sinks, and, if required, initialize the control using a stream.

Finally, the code tests the string once more to see if it is raw HTML or a URL to a resource. In the former case, the MSHTML control would have been created and so the code can get hold of the body element of the page and replace it with the raw HTML using IHTMLElement::put_innerHTML(). If the string is an actual URL then CreateControlEx() calls IWebBrowser2::Navigate2() to load the resource.

At this point, the control being hosted (the WebBrowser control, MSHTML control, or any other control) has been created.

### Host Object Lifetime Control

The host object *is* a COM object in that it has IUnknown methods to manage its lifetime and it lives as long as your ATL control does. When your control dies, it will destroy its window and this results in WM_NCDESTROY being sent to the host window. The host derives from CWindowImpl<> and so CWindowImpl<>::WindowProc() handles message by calling OnFinalMessage(). CAxHostWindow::OnFinalMessage() looks like this:

```
virtual void OnFinalMessage(HWND /*hWnd*/)
{
    GetControllingUnknown()->Release();
}
```

This should reduce the reference count to zero, allowing the host object to destroy itself.

## CAxFrameWindow and CAxUIWindow

A control container should implement the IOleInPlaceSite interface. A contained control uses this to communicate with the container and in particular, the control will call IOleInPlaceSite::GetWindowContext() to get access to the container's top level frame window (so that a control can add menu items and translate key strokes) and get information about the container's border space. This method should return the IOleInPlaceFrame and IOleInPlaceUIWindow interfaces of an object implemented by the container.

Since the host object may be used to host controls that will use the IOleInPlaceSite interface, it must have an implementation. This is the purpose of the ATL classes CAxFrameWindow and CAxUIWindow, the former implements IOleInPlaceFrame and the latter implements IOleInPlaceUIWindow. In fact, these classes just provide stub implementations for all the interface methods. These classes are designed simply to host the WebBrowser control without any menus and with the WebBrowser expanded to fill the entire window of the control.

## Creating an HTML Control

When you create an HTML control, Object Wizard will create *two* HTML files: one has the Short Name of the control and is the test page that you have seen before. The other is the scripting code for the control, and has the Short Name appended with UI (e.g. MyCtrlUI.htm). The default script that Object Wizard generates is this:

```
<HTML>
<BODY id=theBody>
<BUTTON onclick='window.external.OnClick(theBody, "red");'>Red</BUTTON>
<BR>
<BR>
<BUTTON onclick='window.external.OnClick(theBody, "green");'>Green</BUTTON>
<BR>
<BR>
<BUTTON onclick='window.external.OnClick(theBody, "blue");'>Blue</BUTTON>
</BODY>
</HTML>
```

In other words, there are three buttons, marked **Red**, **Green** and **Blue** and the `OnClick()` handler for each delegates to a handler that is part of the `window.external` object.

Of course, once you have decided what your control will do, you will replace most of this HTML. However, there are a few points to be made. The first is that the `<BODY>` tag has an ID that is passed to the UI interface of your ATL object. This actually passes the `IDispatch` pointer of the `BODY` object to the method. The `OnClick()` method can thus access the properties and methods of the `BODY` object through this pointer. This technique of identifying HTML tags is not limited to the `BODY` object, most other objects on a web page can have an ID. This means you can give your ATL code direct access to the object without having to negotiate the DHTML object model from the `IWebBrowser2` interface.

For example, you can pass a reference to the entire page if you add an ID to the HTML tag and pass `thePage` to `OnClick()`.

```
<HTML ID="thePage">
</HTML>
```

This would give your control access to the `IHTMLTextElement` interface (which is the same as the `IHTMLElement` interface) and through this you can call `get_all()` to get a collection of all the elements on the page. Another way of doing the same thing is to call `m_spBrowser->get_Document()` to get the `IHTMLDocument2` interface and then call `get_all()` on that interface. This second version is perhaps easier because its `get_all()` returns `IHTMLElementCollection` rather than `IDispatch` which is returned by `IHTMLElement::get_all()`.

The other important point is the call to the `window.external` object. This allows you to access any methods or properties on the interface that has been specified as the external dispatch interface.

# Extending the IE4 Object Model

The Object Wizard-generated HTML code calls the `OnClick()` method which has been decalred in the UI interface of your HTML control. The Object Wizard adds this code for the method:

```
STDMETHOD(OnClick)(IDispatch* pdispBody, VARIANT varColor)
{
   CComQIPtr<IHTMLBodyElement> spBody(pdispBody);
   if (spBody != NULL)
      spBody->put_bgColor(varColor);
   return S_OK;
}
```

The `bgColor` property is part of the `IHTMLBodyElement` interface, explained earlier in this chapter. This code changes this property to have the color passed as the second parameter. When you click on one of the buttons, a color and a pointer to the body element of the WebBrowser control is passed to your ATL class's `OnClick()` method, which then changes the back color of the web page.

If you like, you can regard the `window.external` as the DHTML's interface pointer to your ATL code, and the `m_spWebBrowser` as the reciprocal interface pointer to the DHTML code.

# Writing Your Own HTML Control

The Object Wizard will generate some test code for you when you first create your HTML control. Before you write your own HTML control, you should remove this code. Here are the steps:

1. In the IDL file, remove the OnClick() method added to your UI interface.

2. In the header file, remove the OnClick() method.

3. Add any methods and properties to the UI interface that you will want to access from the HTML as extensions to the DHTML object model.

4. Add any interface methods and properties to the other interface that you want to be used by clients of the control.

As mentioned previously, you can use the CAxHostWindow with the WebBrowser, MSHTML control, or a separate control. Let's take a quick look at how you can use these options. The three following examples can be found in a project called HTMLControls in the code for this book on the Wrox Press web site.

## WebBrowser

The default Object Wizard-generated code uses the WebBrowser control and caches a pointer to its IWebBrowser2 interface in the m_spBrowser member. You can use this interface to navigate to another page, allowing you to offer as much flexibility at run time as you need.

For example, you could define a method in the UI interface called OnNewPage() which lets the HTML code specify an integer that can be used to load a new UI page into the control. Here's an example of how you might implement such a method:

```
STDMETHODIMP CPageBrowser::OnNewPage(VARIANT varOption)
{
    CComVariant var(varOption);
    HRESULT hr = var.ChangeType(VT_I2);
    if (FAILED(hr))
        return hr;

    if (m_spBrowser)
    {
        CComVariant vEmpty;
        CComVariant vURL;
        switch (var.iVal)
        {
        case 0:
            vURL = "www.server.com/PageBrowserUI_00.htm";
            break;
        case 1:
            vURL = "www.server.com/PageBrowserUI_01.htm";
            break;
        case 2:
            vURL = "www.server.com/PageBrowserUI_02.htm";
            break;
        }
        m_spBrowser->Navigate2(&vURL, &vEmpty, &vEmpty, &vEmpty, &vEmpty);
    }
}
```

```
    return S_OK;
}
```

Here I convert the VARIANT to short (VT_I2) so that I can get the correct union member for the switch. In this code, I have hard coded the URLs that can be chosen, but you could use some more sophisticated code to generate the URL.

The UI HTML pages used in this example could be wizard-like pages like this:

```
<HTML>
<BODY id=theBody>
<H1>Page 0</H1>
<BUTTON onclick='window.external.OnNewPage(1);'>Next &gt;</BUTTON>
</BODY>
</HTML>
```

This code just has a single button labeled Next > that calls OnNewPage() to navigate to another page.

## MSHTML

When you create the WebBrowser control, you are also creating the MSHTML control. However, the WebBrowser has navigation functionality that you may not need. If you initialize the HTML control with raw HTML then you do not need navigation, so you can create the MSHTML control directly. When you do this, the raw HTML should be prefixed with MSHTML: so that the string is not mistaken for a URL or a CLSID. Note that in this case, it should not have the <HTML> tag and you will not be able to get access to the IDispatch interfaces of the page elements. For example:

```
LRESULT OnCreate(UINT, WPARAM, LPARAM, BOOL&)
{
    CAxWindow wnd(m_hWnd);
    CComBSTR strHTML = L"MSHTML:<BODY>";
    strHTML += L"<OBJECT ID=\"DiskFreeSpace\" NAME=\"Obj\"";
    strHTML += L"CLASSID=\"CLSID:962DDB1E-F259-11D1-9B6B-0060973044A8\">";
    strHTML += L"<PARAM NAME=\"Drive\" VALUE=\"C\">";
    strHTML += L"</OBJECT></BODY>";

    HRESULT hr = wnd.CreateControl(strHTML);
    if (SUCCEEDED(hr))
        hr = wnd.SetExternalDispatch(static_cast<IMSHTMLDirectUI*>(this));
    if (SUCCEEDED(hr))
        hr = wnd.QueryControl(IID_IHTMLDocument2,
                              reinterpret_cast<void**>(&m_spBrowser));
    return SUCCEEDED(hr) ? 0 : -1;
}
CComPtr<IHTMLDocument2> m_spBrowser;
```

Here, the code initializes a CComBSTR with some HTML that loads the DiskFreeSpace control developed in the last chapter. Note that I have changed m_spBrowser to be a smart pointer to IHTMLDocument2 so that the code can have access to the MSHTML control. However, note that since the HTML control is based on MSHTML rather than the WebBrowser control you have limited functionality. For example, if you right click on the control to look at the source HTML you will see this:

```
<p> </p>
```

In other words, there is *no* HTML. This means that you won't be able to manipulate it, nor access the objects on the page. It appears that if you add scripting code into this HTML, you cannot use it to refer to other objects on the page.

## Other Controls

Since `CAxHostWindow` will host any control, you can initialize it using a ProgID or a CLSID of a registered control, for example:

```
LRESULT OnCreate(UINT, WPARAM, LPARAM, BOOL&)
{
    CAxWindow wnd(m_hWnd);
    CComBSTR strHTML = L"Scripting.DiskFreeSpace.1";
    HRESULT hr = wnd.CreateControl(strHTML);
    return SUCCEEDED(hr) ? 0 : -1;
}
```

Of course, you would be better to use the HTML page generated by the Object Wizard than to use hard coded control names like this! However, there is nothing to stop you from dynamically checking a ProgID using some algorithm.

Also, note that the control that you create will be sized according to the HTML control. So in this example the `DiskFreeSpace` control, which is normally one inch by a quarter inch, will be resized (stretched) to the size of the HTML control, which has a default size of 2 by 2 inches.

# Example: Business Rules Object

Now that you've seen the fundamentals behind the HTML control, let's take a look at an example that addresses a real problem that is faced when you write objects that respond to particular business rules: how do you ensure that the object always has the most up to date rule?

For example, imagine that you have an object that calculates the retail price of a product based on the wholesale price. Head office could decide that initially the price should be set according to this formula:

```
Price = WholesalePrice * (Profit + SalesTax + 1)
```

Where `Profit` and `SalesTax` are expressed as proportion of the wholesale price (so for a 40% profit, `Profit` will be `0.4`).

You could hard code this formula into the object and obtain values for `WholesalePrice`, `Profit` and `SalesTax` from some persistent store that can be changed by an administrator, and this would work well out in the field.

However, after a couple of months Head Office decides that it would like to have a different profit during the weekend. This would allow them to charge less during the week and increase trade when customers are scarcer. This new rule could be specified in VBScript like this:

```
If Weekday(Now) = vbSaturday Or Weekday(Now) = vbSunday Then
    Price = WholesalePrice * (WeekendProfit + SalesTax + 1)
Else
    Price = WholesalePrice * (WeekdayProfit + SalesTax + 1)
End If
```

The reason that I'm using VBScript here will become apparent in a moment.

Your only option is to rewrite the object to use the new formula and distribute this to all of the retail outlets. Although the code change is small, the cost of distributing the object is high. There may not be a suitable 'technical' person at each site, and local management could insist on a site visit from the company IS support staff. Such a visit would be costly and time consuming. Although you may regard it as unnecessary for such a minor change, you must take into account that not everyone is able or happy to install and register an ActiveX control, particularly one that has such a large effect on profitability.

One solution to this problem could be to use an administration program that checks the Head Office web site once a day to see if a new control is available. Another option would be to use a web page as the client end of the application. This web page could use the <CODEBASE> tag to ensure that the control is always up to date. Both of these solutions would work, but an entire control would need to be downloaded despite a change to only a few lines of code.

A better solution would be to allow the local administrator to type the rule into the control. This approach would not involve installing any new software, nor would it require the local administrator to move away from the user interface with which they are familiar. You could automate this further by making the control download the rule from the Head Office web site. This rule, written in VBScript, would be extremely tiny and the download would be almost instantaneous.

Let's look at a simple example that implements this idea. Create a DLL project called `Prices` and then insert an HTML control called `Rules`. The first thing that you need to do is clean up the example code that Object Wizard added for you, so open the IDL file and remove the declaration of the `OnClick()` method and open the header and remove the method from the class.

The HTML used for the user interface will need to tell your ATL code to set the business rule. In addition, it will need to ask your code for the values of the sales tax and profit rate. The first will be carried out through a read/write property and the other two will be read-only properties. In this example, the `get_` methods for both sales tax and profit rate will return a hard coded value, but in a working control, these values would be returned from some persistent storage.

Add the following to `IRulesUI` using ClassView:

```
[propget] HRESULT Rule([out, retval] VARIANT *pVal);
[propput] HRESULT Rule([in] VARIANT newVal);
[propget] HRESULT SalesTax([out, retval] double *pVal);
[propget] HRESULT ProfitRate([out, retval] double *pVal);
```

Implement the properties like this:

```
STDMETHODIMP CRules::get_SalesTax(double *pVal)
{
    *pVal = 0.175; // UK sales tax rate
    return S_OK;
}

STDMETHODIMP CRules::get_ProfitRate(double *pVal)
{
    *pVal = 0.4;
    return S_OK;
}
```

Remember that `IRulesUI` is the interface that the HTML running in the contained WebBrowser control will use to communicate with your ATL control. The `IRules` interface is used to script the entire ATL control. In this example, `IRules` will need just one read/write `BSTR` property called `BusinessRule`, which can be used by a client to set the rule, so add this property using ClassView.

Note that you have two ways to set the business rule: the UI code can use `IRulesUI::put_Rule()` and clients can use `IRules::put_BusinessRule()`. It makes sense to implement the former in terms of the latter, so add the code shown below:

```
STDMETHODIMP CRules::get_Rule(VARIANT *pVal)
{
    pVal->vt = VT_BSTR;
    return get_BusinessRule(&pVal->bstrVal);
}

STDMETHODIMP CRules::put_Rule(VARIANT newVal)
{
    if (newVal.vt != VT_BSTR)
        return E_INVALIDARG;
    HRESULT hr = put_BusinessRule(newVal.bstrVal);
    FireViewChange();
    return hr;
}
```

Before you write the code for the `BusinessRule` property, edit the user interface HTML file as shown below. The `BusinessRule` property code will directly read and write this HTML, so you need to understand the structure of the HTML before you can write that code:

```
<HTML>
<BODY>
Rule:
<BR>
<TEXTAREA NAME="NewRule" ROWS=3 COLS=50></TEXTAREA>
<BR>
<BUTTON NAME="ChangeRule">New Rule</BUTTON>
<BR>
Wholesale Price <INPUT TYPE=TEXT NAME="Wholesale" VALUE="0">
<BUTTON NAME="DoRule">Calculate</BUTTON>
<BR>
<DIV ID="Result" STYLE="font-size:24"> 0
</DIV>
<BR>
</BODY>
</HTML>
```

This UI has two buttons, a multi-line text area, a text box and a 'static' area. The text area is used to display and enter the business rule, the text box is used to enter the wholesale price of the item and the 'static' area (between the <DIV> tags) will give the result of the calculation:

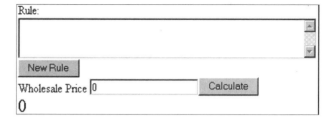

The purpose of this example is not to teach you HTML or good user interface design, so excuse the poor layout. The control will be 4.5 inches wide and 2 inches high, so change the natural extent in the constructor:

```
CRules()
{
    m_bWindowOnly = TRUE;
    m_sizeExtent.cx = 11430; // 4.5 inch wide
    m_sizeExtent.cy = 5080;  // 2 inch high;
    m_sizeNatural = m_sizeExtent;
}
```

When the page is loaded, you want to current rule to be displayed, so add a script block and the following code to do this:

```
<SCRIPT LANGUAGE="VBS">
Sub window_OnLoad()
    NewRule.Value = window.external.Rule
End Sub
</SCRIPT>
```

This code calls the ATL code to get hold of the business rule and then uses this to initialize the text area. The `window_OnLoad()` method is called when the window (the web page) is first loaded.

When the **New Rule** button is clicked, the text in the text area should be passed to the ATL code to set the business rule. This is done by assigning a value to the `Rule` property:

```
Sub ChangeRule_OnClick()
    window.external.Rule = NewRule.Value
End Sub
```

Finally, when the **Calculate** button is clicked, the rule must be invoked. This needs two methods:

```
Sub DoRule_OnClick()
    if Wholesale.Value = "" Then Wholesale.Value = "0"
    Result.innerText = Rule(Wholesale.Value)
End Sub

Function Rule(WholesalePrice)
    Rule = WholesalePrice
End Function
```

`DoRule_Click()` will be called when the Calculate button is clicked. This first checks that the wholesale price text box has a value and if not, it is initialized to zero. Next it passes the wholesale price to the `Rule()` function and puts the result into the 'static' area. This final function is the code that will be overwritten with the business rule that you type into the text area. In this code, I provide a default rule that simply returns the wholesale price as the retail price.

You should be able to compile the project at this point to check that you have no typing errors. The code will not be able to do anything other than to copy the wholesale price to the 'static' area.

The next step is to implement `IRules::get_BusinessRule()`. This will read the UI HTML and find the `Rule()` function and return the code inside this function. I will go through the code in sections:

```
STDMETHODIMP CRules::get_BusinessRule(BSTR *pVal)
{
    CComPtr<IDispatch> pDisp;
    CComQIPtr<IHTMLDocument2> pDoc2;
    m_spBrowser->get_Document(&pDisp);
    if (!pDisp)
        return E_UNEXPECTED;
    pDoc2 = pDisp;
    pDisp.Release();
    if (!pDoc2)
        return E_UNEXPECTED;
```

This first section obtains the document object of the control. Remember that in the `OnCreate()` method, the ATL code caches the interface pointer to the WebBrowser control. This is used to call the `get_Document()` method. Although this returns a pointer to the document, the actual pointer is to the `IDispatch` interface on that object, so I use `CComQIPtr<>` to a `QueryInterface()`.

```
    CComPtr<IHTMLElement> pElem;
    pDoc2->get_body(&pElem);
    if (pElem == NULL)
        return E_UNEXPECTED;
    CComBSTR bstrPage;
    pElem->get_outerHTML(&bstrPage);
```

Next, I need to obtain the body of the page so I use `get_body()` to return an `IHTMLElement` interface pointer, and then through this I call `get_outerHTML()` to get the HTML that represents the body.

At this point I have the HTML between (and including) the `<BODY>` and `</BODY>` tags and so I can then parse through this for the `Rule()` function:

```
    LPWSTR strRule;
    strRule = wcsstr(bstrPage, L"Function Rule(WholesalePrice)");
    if (strRule == NULL)
        return E_UNEXPECTED;
    strRule += wcslen(L"Function Rule(WholesalePrice)");
    while (*strRule == L' ' || *strRule == L'\n' || *strRule == L'\r'
                                                 || *strRule == L'\t')

        strRule++;
```

First, the code searches for the first line of the function. It then moves the string pointer to the next line by moving the length of the first line and then moving over any whitespace characters that appear afterwards.

```
    LPWSTR strEnd = strRule;
    strEnd++;
    strEnd = wcsstr(strEnd, L"End Function");
    if (strEnd == NULL)
        return E_UNEXPECTED;
    *strEnd = 0;

    *pVal = SysAllocString(strRule);
    return S_OK;
}
```

Finally, the code finds the end of the function and places a NULL character there so that just the code within the function is copied in the last few lines.

You should be able to compile the project at this point and load the control in the ActiveX Control Test Container or Internet Explorer to confirm that the business rule can be retrieved.

Before we go on, there may be a small doubt in your mind. In this code, I have obtained the function by reading the HTML of the body. I'm sure you are wondering why I did not use the IHTMLDocument2::get_scripts() method to obtain a collection of the scripts on the page. After all, this code will work:

```
    CComPtr<IHTMLElementCollection> pColl;
    pDoc2->get_scripts(&pColl);
    if (!pColl)
        return E_UNEXPECTED;
    long len;
    pColl->get_length(&len);
    for (long i= 0; i<len; i++)
    {
        CComVariant item, ind;
        item = i;
        pColl->item(item, ind, &pDisp);
        if (!pDisp)
            continue;

        CComQIPtr<IHTMLScriptElement> pScript(pDisp);
        CComBSTR bstrScript;
        pScript->get_text(&bstrScript);
        // do something with the script...
    }
```

However, there are two problems, the first is that to get the string of the scripts takes 16 lines of code rather than the 5 lines I have shown above. On the plus side, if there is more than one <SCRIPT> block, this code will allow you to parse through each block one at a time. If the body of each block is large, this will be quicker than the previous method. The other problem will become apparent in the put_ method described next: the pScript object returned is read-only, and I want to write the script code for the new Rule() function.

The put_ method is implemented like this:

```
STDMETHODIMP CRules::put_BusinessRule(BSTR newVal)
{
    CComBSTR bstrTemp = newVal;
    CComBSTR bstrRule;
    bstrTemp.ToUpper();

    LPWSTR ptr = wcsstr(bstrTemp.m_str, L"RULE");
    if (ptr != NULL)
    {
        if (ptr[4] != L'=' )
        {
            if (ptr[4] != L' ' || ptr[5] != L'=')
            {
                bstrRule = L"Rule = ";
                bstrRule += bstrTemp;
            }
            else bstrRule = newVal;
        }
        else bstrRule = newVal;
    }
    else bstrRule = newVal;
```

Rule() is a function, so the code passed from the UI code *must* have Rule= somewhere to return a value, if it doesn't, then I assume that the user has typed a single line for the function and hence I need to add Rule= to the front of that string. At the end of this section, bstrRule holds the body of the function.

Next, the code obtains the document and the text of the body as before:

```
CComPtr<IDispatch> pDisp;
CComQIPtr<IHTMLDocument2> pDoc2;
m_spBrowser->get_Document(&pDisp);
if (!pDisp)
    return E_UNEXPECTED;
pDoc2 = pDisp;
pDisp.Release();
if (!pDoc2)
    return E_UNEXPECTED;

CComPtr<IHTMLElement> pElem;
pDoc2->get_body(&pElem);
if (pElem == NULL)
    return E_UNEXPECTED;
CComBSTR bstrPage;
pElem->get_outerHTML(&bstrPage);
```

The next code needs to remove the function:

```
LPWSTR strEnd;
strEnd = wcsstr(bstrPage, L"Function Rule(WholesalePrice)");
if (strEnd == NULL)
    return E_UNEXPECTED;
*strEnd = 0;

strEnd++;
strEnd = wcsstr(strEnd, L"End Function");
```

```
  if (strEnd == NULL)
      return E_UNEXPECTED;
  strEnd += wcslen(L"End Function");
```

As you can see, it searches for the first line of the `Rule()` function and then places a `NULL` character so that I can copy the HTML before the function. Next, the code finds the end of the function and moves the string pointer past the end of that line. After this action, `bstrPage.m_str` points to the HTML *before* the `Rule()` function and `strEnd` points to the HTML *after* the function. Now the code can reconstruct the UI HTML using the new `Rule()` function:

```
  CComBSTR bstrScript;
  bstrScript = L"<HTML>\n";
  bstrScript += (LPWSTR)bstrPage;
  bstrScript += L"Function Rule(WholesalePrice)\n";
  bstrScript += bstrRule;                    // the new body of the function
  bstrScript += L"\n";
  bstrScript += L"End Function";
  bstrScript += strEnd;
  bstrScript += L"</HTML>\n";
```

This code has the `<HTML>` tags because it will be the *entire* page. The page contents are set by calling `IHTMLDocument2::write()`. This method will write a `SAFEARRAY` of `VARIANT`s to a stream opened with the `IHTMLDocument2::open()` method:

```
  CComBSTR bstrURL;
  CComVariant varDummy;
  pDoc2->open(bstrURL, varDummy, varDummy, varDummy, NULL);
```

An empty `BSTR` and empty `VARIANT`s indicate that the current page should be opened. The `SAFEARRAY` (with a single element) is created like this:

```
  SAFEARRAY* pSA;
  SAFEARRAYBOUND saBound = {1, 0};
  pSA = SafeArrayCreate(VT_VARIANT, 1, &saBound);
  VARIANT* pVar;
  SafeArrayAccessData(pSA, (void**)&pVar);
  varDummy = bstrScript;
  pVar[0] = varDummy;
  SafeArrayUnaccessData(pSA);
```

This is finally written to the page with the following code:

```
  pDoc2->write(pSA);
  SafeArrayDestroy(pSA);
  pDoc2->close();
  return S_OK;
}
```

The code is almost finished, but for now compile the project and test out changing the business rule. For example, change the rule to

```
Rule = WholesalePrice + 10
```

Remember to click on the New Rule button and then change the WholesalePrice to 56. When you click on the Calculate button, you should get a value of 66 printed at the bottom of the control:

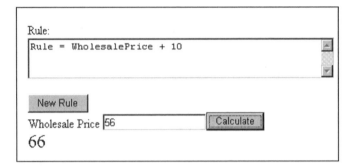

Now try another test. This time alter the rule so that 10 is added at the weeked, but 20 is added during the rest of the week:

```
If WeekDay(Now)= vbSaturday Or WeekDay(Now)= vbSunday Then
    Rule = WholesalePrice + 10
Else
    Rule = WholesalePrice + 20
End If
```

Experiment a bit with the code used to describe the rule to convince yourself that when New Rule is clicked the rule is copied to the control and this code is used when the Calculate button is clicked. If you're still not convinced, you can see that the code is being copied by right-clicking on the control and selecting the View Source context menu item:

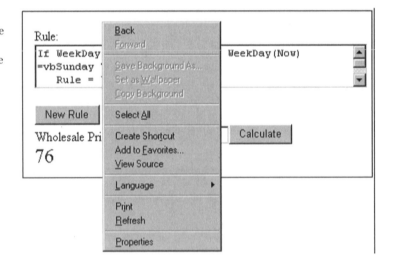

All that is left to do is tidy up the handling of the SalesTax and ProfitRate properties. These are exposed from the IRulesUI interface so you can access them from the script code. However, as it stands if you want to access the ProfitRate, for example, a user would have to type:

```
Rule = WholesalePrice * (1 + window.external.ProfitRate)
```

This goes against the design goal of isolating the user from technical details, so instead add the following VBScript functions to wrap these calls to the ATL object so that the rule can be entered in terms of SalesTax and ProfitRate:

```
Function SalesTax
   SalesTax = window.external.SalesTax
End Function

Function ProfitRate
   ProfitRate = window.external.ProfitRate
End Function
```

Now the user can write a rule like this:

```
Rule = WholesalePrice * (1 + ProfitRate + SalesTax)
```

Compile the project and try it out. Remember that you can use any VBScript that you like: you can have several lines of code, use temporary variables, even create COM objects to use from within your VBScript code. The current sales tax is in `SalesTax` and the current profit rate is in `ProfitRate`; the input to the `Rules()` function is via the `WholesalePrice` parameter, and you must return a value by assigning `Rules` to this value.

# Further Improvements

As it stands, the implementations of the `put_` and `get_` methods of the `BusinessRule` property access the VBScript on the UI HTML page to set and return the rule. This is fine for how the control has been used up to this point, since these methods have only been accessed when the window and the HTML have been loaded. However, there is a slight problem – the ATL implementations of the various `IPersist` interfaces will access the `BusinessRule` property through `IDispatch::Invoke()` to get the property type. By their nature, these interfaces will be used *before* the control has been fully initialized, so the WebBrowser control will not have been created at that point.

The solution is to change `get_BusinessRule()` and `put_BusinessRule()` to check `m_spBrowser` for validity before use. If the WebBrowser control hasn't been created, the methods should either cache the rule in a data member (for the `put_` method) or read the cached rule (for the `get_` method). The control also needs to make sure that the cached value is written to the `BusinessRule` property as soon as `m_spBrowser` has a valid value.

To do this add a `private` member called `m_Rule`:

```
private:
   CComBSTR m_Rule;
};
```

Add the following code to the top of `put_BusinessRule()`:

```
STDMETHODIMP CRules::put_BusinessRule(BSTR newVal)
{
   if (!m_spBrowser)
   {
      m_Rule = newVal;
      return S_OK;
   }
```

And add this code further on down:

```
CComPtr<IDispatch> pDisp;
CComQIPtr<IHTMLDocument2> pDoc2;
m_spBrowser->get_Document(&pDisp);
if (!pDisp)
{
   m_Rule = newVal;
   return S_OK;
}
pDoc2 = pDisp;
pDisp.Release();
if (!pDoc2)
   return E_UNEXPECTED;
```

The first new section of code checks to see if the WebBrowser control has been created. If it hasn't, it caches the value of the property. However, this does not completely solve the problem, because the WebBrowser control could be created, but the UI HTML may not be loaded, so the second new section of code handles this, again by caching the value.

This cached value needs to be read somewhere, and the best place to do this is in get_BusinessRule():

```
STDMETHODIMP CRules::get_BusinessRule(BSTR *pVal)
{
    if (!m_spBrowser)
    {
        return m_Rule.CopyTo(pval);
    }

    CComPtr<IDispatch> pDisp;
    CComQIPtr<IHTMLDocument2> pDoc2;
    m_spBrowser->get_Document(&pDisp);
    if (m_Rule.Length() > 0)
    {
        if (pDisp)
        {
            CComBSTR bstrTemp = m_Rule;
            m_Rule.Empty();
            put_BusinessRule(bstrTemp);
        }
    }
    if (!pDisp)
    {
        return m_Rule.CopyTo(pVal);
    }
    pDoc2 = pDisp;
    pDisp.Release();
    if (!pDoc2)
        return E_UNEXPECTED;
```

This code first checks to see if the WebBrowser control has been created, if it hasn't then the cached value is used. If the WebBrowser control has been created then the next section of code checks to see if there is a cached value and if so, it writes this to the property. Notice that I clear m_Rule *before* I call put_BusinessRule() the reason is that put_BusinessRule() will result in the window (that is, the new HTML code) being updated and so this will result in get_BusinessRule() being called. If I didn't clear m_Rule this would result in a recursive loop.

Now you can add the property to the property map:

```
BEGIN_PROP_MAP(CRules)
    PROP_DATA_ENTRY("_cx", m_sizeExtent.cx, VT_UI4)
    PROP_DATA_ENTRY("_cy", m_sizeExtent.cy, VT_UI4)
    PROP_ENTRY("BusinessRule", 1, CLSID_NULL)
END_PROP_MAP()
```

You should find that the control can be saved to a Visual Basic form and (if you add support for IPersistPropertyBag), you can initialize the control using the <PARAM> tag on a web page. However, be aware of two things: first Visual Basic does not allow you to add multiple lines in its **Properties** window, so this restricts you to providing a single line rule. This can be solved by using a property page for the control, which has a multi-line text box to enter the rule. I will leave this as an exercise for the reader.

The other problem is associated, if you can enter a value for BusinessRule that has newlines, you will find that Visual Basic will not like this too much – the frm file can only have single lines per property. Fortunately, Visual Basic will create an frx file and dump the property value as a binary value, but there's no help with the <PARAM> tags on a web page. To get round this you can use a solution presented in the previous chapter: use IPersistPropertyBagImpl_Ex<> to save the property as a hex encoded string.

This does not prevent you from setting the rule by accessing the BusinessRule from a script, for example using the following Visual Basic code:

```
Private Sub Form_Load()
  Dim rule As String
  'discount on a Monday
  rule = "If WeekDay(Now)=vbMonday Then"
  rule = rule + vbCrLf + vbTab + + "Rule = WholesalePrice * (0.9 + Profit)"
  rule = rule + vbCrLf + "Else"
  rule = rule + vbCrLf + vbTab + "Rule = WholesalePrice * (1 + Profit)"
  rule = rule + "End If"
  Rules1.BusinessRule = rule
End Sub
```

# Summary

The HTML control gives you the facilities of the Internet Explorer's WebBrowser control, you can use it to render HTML, bitmap images, load active documents, and use its navigation facilities. ATL does this by hosting the WebBrowser control within an object and then giving your ATL control an interface pointer to the WebBrowser control so that you can access the DHTML objects on the page. The WebBrowser control is initialized with a UI web page. ATL will bind this page to your control's DLL as a resource. This page can have any HTML code that Internet Explorer allows: DHTML objects, ActiveX controls, and scripts.

These scripts can call code in your ATL control through the `window.external` object, which represents the UI interface of your HTML control. The Object Wizard adds two new interfaces to your HTML control; one is the interface that scripting clients use to call your objects methods, and the other is passed to the WebBrowser control to provide access to your ATL control to the scripting code in the HTML resource.

# C++ Templates

The ANSI standard for C++ includes support for templates. If used unwisely, templates can be a problem, because they can bloat code and make the source unreadable. When used correctly, however, templates can shorten the development cycle by providing standard code that the developer does not need to rewrite. With careful use, they can even make your source code *more* readable.

## Why Templates?

C++ allows the programmer to define new types. Through its methods, a C++ class defines what this new type can do; through its operators, it describes how its objects interact with others of the same or different types. C++ allows **operator overloading**, which means that the same syntax can be used to perform operations on the same or different object types. If the programmer needs to define several similar object types, C++ inheritance can be used to ensure that common code can be written just once.

This adds great flexibility to the language, but there are occasions when the programmer will need to write a lot of similar code, and inheritance is *not* a solution. This soon becomes apparent when you're writing a class library to provide actions on several different types of object. A classic example of this is the use of **container classes**.

Much of the code in a linked list class is boilerplate. It must be possible to insert and remove nodes to and from the list, and there must be some method to iterate through the list. Conventionally, nodes contain objects or pointers to objects, and therefore a linked list class works with a specific object type. For example:

```
class CIntLinkedList
{
public:
    struct CNodeInt
    {
        CNodeInt(int cVal) : m_data(cVal), m_next(0) {}
        int        m_data;
        CNodeInt* m_next;
    };

    CIntLinkedList();
    ~CIntLinkedList();
    void AddTail(int);
    CNodeInt* GetHead() const;

protected:
    void AddNode(CNodeInt*);

private:
    CNodeInt* m_head;
    CNodeInt* m_last;
};
```

Using this simple class, a developer can create a linked list of `ints` by adding each item to the end of the list, and the class provides basic support to iterate though all the nodes. The nodes themselves are instances of the `CNodeInt` structure, which holds the data and hence is implicitly tied to the `int` type. The `AddTail()` method adds a new node to the list that contains the data passed as its parameter. This method uses the protected `AddNode()` method to add the new node to the list, but both of these can only be used with `ints`.

So, what happens if a developer needs a linked list of some other type – say, `float`? She will have to create a new class that defines a new node type to hold `floats`, as well as new methods to add items to the list. For two data types, this is tedious but bearable. If you wanted to provide a container for all possible data types, though, it would be impossible.

One way to get around the problem would be to make some of the code more generic by use of `void` pointers. For example, a generic base class could be defined as:

```
class CGenericLinkedList
{
public:
    struct CNode
    {
        CNode(void* pv) : m_data(pv), m_next(0) {}
        void*  m_data;
        CNode* m_next;
    }
    virtual ~CGenericLinkedList();
    CNode* GetHead() const;
```

```
protected:
    CGenericLinkedList();
    virtual void AddNode(CNode*);

private:
    CNode* m_head;
    CNode* m_current;
};
```

In this scheme, there is a 'generic' node that can hold data of any type by using a void pointer. The class has a protected constructor in order to prevent creation of any instances of *this* class, but to allow instances of *derived* classes to be created; this effectively makes the class abstract.

CGenericLinkedList has a generic AddNode() method that will add a pre-constructed CNode object into the list. To use this class, a developer must derive from it and then write methods specific to the types that will be added to the list:

```
class CLinkedListFloat : public CGenericLinkedList
{
public:
    CLinkedListListFloat() {}
    ~CLinkedListListFloat() {}
    void AddTail(float);
};

void CLinkedListFloat::AddTail(float val)
{
    float* pVal = new float(val);
    CNode* newNode = new CNode(reinterpret_cast<void*>(pVal));
    AddNode(newNode);
}
```

Now the programmer can define a series of classes – CLinkedListLong, CLinkedListShort, etc. – that have their own versions of AddTail() specific to the type that will be added to the list. All the developer needs to do is define the appropriate class and then implement the AddTail() method, which represents rather less code than having to implement the entire class.

The problem with this approach is that the items in the generic list are not type-safe, and to make them so you would need to write extra code. Also, in my example the code the developer has to write is repetitive; the version of AddTail() for CLinkedListLong could be written as:

```
void CLinkedListLong::AddTail(long val)
{
    long* pVal = new long(val);
    CNode* newNode = new CNode(reinterpret_cast<void*>(pVal));
    AddNode(newNode);
}
```

You can see here that I've changed the prototype of the function to take a long instead of a float, and that the first line of the function allocates a long* instead of a float*. So, rewriting this for a generic type T, we get:

```
void CLinkedListT::AddTail(T val)
{
    T* pVal = new T(val);
    CNode* newNode = new CNode(reinterpret_cast<void*>(pVal));
    AddNode(newNode);
}
```

T is a **placeholder** for a type, which can be a built-in primitive type, or a class (in this case, a class that has a copy constructor). If you want to create a list of shorts, for instance, you could write a tool that parses this source file and replaces each occurrence of the generic type T with short. In effect, this code provides a template with placeholders that will be replaced by the actual type that you want to use.

What you see before you are the bare bones of a template class, and in the parlance of C++ templates, the type T is the **parameter** of the template. Since you can create many types by using a different parameter, templates are often referred to as **parameterized types**. The tool that does the replacement is the C++ compiler, and you can regard a template class as a formula from which the compiler generates new classes.

Here's a template class for a simple linked list:

```
// CLinkedListT.h
template<class T>
class CLinkedListT
{
public:
    template<class T> struct CNode
    {
        CNode(const T& val, CNode<T>* pNext) : m_data(val), m_pNext(pNext) {}
        T m_data;
        CNode<T>* m_pNext;
    };

    CLinkedListT() : m_pHead(0), m_pTail(0) {}
    ~CLinkedListT();
    void AddTail(T n);

    CNode<T>* GetHead() const
    {
        return m_pHead;
    }

private:
    CNode<T>* m_pHead;
    CNode<T>* m_pTail;
};

template<class T>
CLinkedListT<T>::~CLinkedListT()
{
    while(m_pHead != 0)
    {
        CNode<T>* pNode = m_pHead;
        m_pHead = m_pHead->m_pNext;
```

```
          delete pNode;
      }
  }

  template<class T>
  void CLinkedListT<T>::AddTail(T n)
  {
      CNode<T>* pNewNode = new CNode<T>(n, 0);
      if(m_pHead == 0)
          m_pHead = m_pTail = pNewNode;
      else
      {
          m_pTail->m_pNext = pNewNode;
          m_pTail = pNewNode;
      }
  }
```

The definition of the class is qualified with the prefix `template<class T>`. This indicates that the class will use a type `T` that the compiler uses to generate a class from the template. Thus, the `AddTail(T n)` method adds an item of data type `T` to the list, and that type can be an `int`, a `float`, any other built-in type, or a class that you have defined. (Note that using the `typename` keyword instead of `class` is also valid here: `template<typename T>`.)

You will also notice that the name of the class when specified with the scope resolution operator is `CListListT<T>`; this indicates that it is a parameterized class. Another example of this can be seen with the nested class `CNode<T>`.

Another thing that you may have noticed is that the header file contains both the definition and the implementation of the template class. As a seasoned C++ programmer, you are used to creating classes with the definition in a header file and the implementation in a `.cpp` file, but this is not a good idea when you're using templates. You will find that the `.cpp` file will compile, but when you create a class from the template, you will get linker errors. This is not a problem with Visual C++, but is inherent in the behavior of templates. For example:

```
#include "CLinkedListT.h"

void SomeFunction()
{
    CLinkedListT<int> intList;
    CLinkedListT<char*> stringList;
    ...
}
```

In this snippet, you are declaring two lists: one will take `int`s and the other will take `char` pointers. If you have the templated code split into a header and a `.cpp` file, and then try to compile this, you'll find that the linker will complain that it cannot find the `CLinkedListT<int>` and `CLinkedListT<char*>` constructors and destructors. The reason for this is simply that the code will not have been generated. Putting *all* the templated code in a header allows the compiler to create the whole class, which will then be available to the linker.

I have chosen my words carefully here: the compiler *generates* code based on templates, so if you need lists of several different types, the compiler will generate classes for each type and this could compile to a large object file. If instead you use a generic list class based upon void pointers, like CGenericLinkedList, then much less code will be used. The moral is that templates are useful, but you must use them where they are appropriate.

You'll see this if you read through the ATL source code. Often, the CComPtr<> smart pointer template is not used, even though this smart pointer offers distinct advantages. The reason is that the extra code created by the compiler generating a smart pointer class may outweigh the advantages in using it.

Templates can be based on more than one parameter, and parameters can have default values. Furthermore, it's quite acceptable to use template classes as the parameters to a template. For example, the Standard Template Library (which I'll describe in a moment) has a sorted, associated container class called set<> that is defined as:

```
template<class Key, class Compare = less<Key> >
class set {...};
```

Here, the template is for a container that holds data of type Key, and these are sorted by using the function object of type Compare. If you declare a set<> and miss out this parameter, the default function object less<Key> will be used. This parameter to set<> is used to compare two keys, so that the container can order the items by key. The type of this parameter is itself parameterized with the Key type that is used in the comparison.

> **At the end of the first line above, there are two closing angled brackets next to each other with a space between them. If you miss out the space, the compiler will treat the symbol as the >> operator, and so the code will not compile.**

Templates can get quite complicated, and the code to declare objects from a template class can appear quite odd. Typically, C++ programmers use typedef on parameterized templates to make the code more readable. So, using the example code from above:

```
#include "CLinkedListT.h"

typedef CLinkedListT<int> CIntList;
typedef CLinkedListT<char*> CStrList;

void SomeFunction()
{
    CIntList intList;
    CStrList stringList;
    ...
}
```

For templates with several parameters, and for cases where you use parameterized parameters in the templates, this technique can make the code far more readable.

# Expression Arguments for Templates

All the examples I've shown you so far used types as template parameters, but this is not a requirement – template parameters can be constant expressions, for example:

```
template <DWORD t_dwStyle = 0, DWORD t_dwExStyle = 0>
class CWinTraits
{
public:
   static DWORD GetWndStyle(DWORD dwStyle)
   {
      return dwStyle == 0 ? t_dwStyle : dwStyle;
   }
   static DWORD GetWndExStyle(DWORD dwExStyle)
   {
      return dwExStyle == 0 ? t_dwExStyle : dwExStyle;
   }
};

typedef CWinTraits<WS_CHILD | WS_VISIBLE |
               WS_CLIPCHILDREN | WS_CLIPSIBLINGS, 0> CControlWinTraits;
```

Here, CWinTraits<> is used to hold the default style of a window, as you can see in the example typedef for CControlWinTraits. To a certain extent, you could use manifest symbols to similar effect, but using a template like this means that the value is held in the namespace of CWinTraits rather than being global. Another way to do this would be to pass a constant value as a constructor parameter, but this would mean that the constructor of the derived class having to call the base class constructor.

# The Standard Template Library

The C++ standard library includes the **Standard Template Library** (**STL**), which has templates for generic algorithms, iterators, containers, and function objects that act upon those containers. STL is a boon to C++ developers because it provides templates for the tasks that we commonly perform. So, rather than writing your own list class, you should use the STL list<> template, which is just one of many container types:

| Type | Description |
| --- | --- |
| vector<> | An ordered collection of elements that can be added or removed at its end |
| deque<> | An ordered collection of elements that can be added or removed from its beginning or its end |
| list<> | An ordered collection of elements that can be added or removed from any position in the collection |
| map<> | An associative container containing items sorted with a key; multimap<> allows duplicate keys |
| set<> | A container in which the items are held in a sorted order according to their value; multiset<> allows duplicate items |

In addition, STL provides **adapter templates** so that you can implement stack<>s, queue<>s and priority_queue<>s by using the other STL containers. STL is provided with Visual C++ 6, and you should always consider using the STL containers rather than the containers provided with MFC or writing your own.

ATL also has support for STL. It provides an adapter class (CAdapt<>) so that you can use CComBSTR and CComPtr<> items in STL containers, and it also provides IEnumOnSTLImpl<> and ICollectionOnSTLImpl<> for implementing enumerators and collections initialized with items held in an STL container.

Which container type you use depends on your application. If you intend to add and remove items from the end of the collection, it makes sense to use a vector<>; if items need to be added at positions within the collection, a list<> is a better choice. However, there are performance penalties associated with using a more generic class than you need for your problem, so try not to use a list<> when a vector<> would suffice.

STL has been designed such that inserting items into or accessing items from a collection uses the same method for the three collection types. This means that you can write code using a list<>, for example, and at a later stage change the collection to a deque<> or a vector<> to see if they provide better performance.

Finally, STL is written in generic, ANSI standard C++, and this means that code written with STL is portable across not only different platforms and C++ compilers, but also class libraries. Therefore, in most cases, it is possible to add STL containers and algorithms to your code without worrying about side effects caused by the implementation of that code. This is particularly useful if you are extending legacy code where redesigning the code is not possible.

# C++ Features used by ATL

This book is about ATL, not C++. However, you do need to be fully aware of some C++ features to be able to understand how ATL works.

## Templates for Parameterized Types

Parameterized types allow you to create generic code from which the compiler can create a specific class, based on one or more parameters. A classic example of this is a smart pointer template, and a suitable candidate for further investigation is ATL's CComPtr<> template class. Here is an edited version:

```
template<class T>
class CComPtr
{
public:
   CComPtr()
   {
      p = NULL;
   }

   CComPtr(T* lp)
   {
      if((p = lp) != NULL)
         p->AddRef();
   }
```

```
    ~CComPtr()
    {
        if(p)
            p->Release();
    }

    T* operator->() const
    {
        ATLASSERT(p != NULL);
        return p;
    }

    T* p;
};
```

The class wraps the interface pointer so that `AddRef()` is called when you copy an interface pointer, and `Release()` is called when you have finished with the pointer. To access the methods of the wrapped interface pointer, you use the `->` operator on the smart pointer class, which gives you access to the wrapped interface pointer. (In fact, in ATL 3 the `operator->()` does not return a `T*` pointer, but instead returns a pointer to a `_NoAddRefReleaseOnCComPtr<T>` to prevent you from calling `AddRef()` and `Release()` directly on the interface pointer, but we'll ignore those details here.)

You can use this smart pointer class like so:

```
void CallDoSomething(IMyInterface* pItf)
{
    CComPtr<IMyInterface> spItf(pItf);
    // Note: no explicit call to AddRef()

    spItf->DoSomething();                     // Calls spItf.operator->()
    // Note: no explicit call to Release()
}
```

Here, a copy of the interface pointer is made into the `spItf` variable, but there is no explicit call to `AddRef()` because the smart pointer does that in its constructor. Similarly, when the interface is no longer needed, there is no explicit call to `Release()` – instead, the call is made in the smart pointer destructor when `spItf` goes out of scope.

Using a template parameter to pass the interface type means that `CComPtr<>` can be used on *any* COM interface pointer. `CComPtr<>` is generic code that assumes only that its data member `p` has the `IUnknown` methods, but it enforces COM's reference counting rules.

# The Impl Trick

This section covers a slightly different way of using templates: adding code to a class. In this case, the template is designed not for creating instances, but to be added to another class through multiple inheritance. Here, for example, is a template I have designed to add reference counting to another class:

```
template<class Derived>
class CRefCountImpl
{
public:
    STDMETHOD_(ULONG, AddRef)()
    {
        Derived* pDerived = static_cast<Derived*>(this);
        return ++pDerived->m_ulRef;
    }

    STDMETHOD_(ULONG, Release)()
    {
        Derived* pDerived = static_cast<Derived*>(this);
        ULONG ul = --pDerived->m_ulRef;
        if(0 == ul)
            delete this;
        return ul;
    }
};

class CMyObject : public CRefCountImpl<CMyObject>
{
public:
    ULONG m_ulRef;
    CMyObject() : m_ulRef(0) {}

    // Other implementation
};
```

CRefCountImpl<> provides COM reference counting for the class passed as the parameter to the template. As you can see from the CMyObject class that's provided as a demonstration, CRefCountImpl<> relies on the parameter type having a public data member called m_ulRef. With these classes, you can write code like this:

```
CMyObject* pObj = new CMyObject;
ULONG ulRef;

ulRef = pObj->AddRef();
printf("ref count = %ld\n", ulRef);    // Prints 1
ulRef = pObj->Release();
printf("ref count = %ld\n", ulRef);    // Prints 0
```

Although pObj is created with new, you don't have to delete it because the CRefCountImpl<> reference counting mechanism has been added to the code, and this will delete an object when its reference count changes from 1 to 0.

Notice the strange way that CMyObject uses CRefCountImpl<>: it derives from the class and passes *its own class name* as the parameter. CRefCountImpl<> uses this class name to downcast the this pointer to a derived class pointer, and hence give it access to the m_ulRef member. In this example, CMyObject has just one base class, but if it had other base classes that also used the Impl trick, they would also have access to the m_ulRef member. For this trick to work, CRefCountImpl<> must be a base class (so that you can perform the cast) and the m_ulRef data member in the derived class must be public (so that the base class has access to it).

CRefCountImpl<> is just a small example that I've contrived to show you this trick, but you will find it used throughout ATL. In particular, it is used to provide default implementations of many of the standard COM interfaces. When you see a template with the suffix Impl, you know that to use it you must derive from it and (in most cases) pass your class name as the template parameter.

In the example above, the CRefCountImpl<> class requires that the derived class has a data member called m_ulRef. There is a similar requirement with most of the Impl classes in ATL, but thankfully you *don't* have to know what data members to add to your classes in order to use them. The reason for this is that the Impl classes work in conjunction with other ATL base classes. For example, the CStockPropImpl<> class allows a control to implement stock properties. To use this template, you need to derive from both CStockPropImpl<> and CComControlBase (which is the base class of CComControl<>):

```
class ATL_NO_VTABLE CMyControl :
    public CComObjectRootEx<CComSingleThreadModel>,
    public CComControl<CMyControl>,
    public CStockPropImpl<CMyControl, IMyControl, &IID_IMyControl, &LIBID_CTRLS>,
    // Other base classes
```

CComControlBase contains a union whose members are the items that are referenced by CStockPropImpl<>. The data members that you add to your class (to implement a particular stock property) will be used by CStockPropImpl<>, but if you miss them out, the union ensures that your ATL class will still compile.

This trick works for methods as well as data members. For example, the IOleObjectImpl<> class is largely implemented by calling methods in CComControlBase:

```
// From IOleObjectImpl<>
STDMETHOD(SetClientSite)(IOleClientSite* pClientSite)
{
    T* pT = static_cast<T*>(this);
    return pT->IOleObject_SetClientSite(pClientSite);
}
```

Here you can see that the code in IOleObjectImpl<> casts the this pointer to a pointer of the template parameter T. This gives the code access to all public members of T, including the public methods it inherits. In this case the code assumes that T is derived from CComControlBase (which it should be to use IOleObjectImpl<>) and calls the IOleObject_SetClientSite() member. This ensures that the method has access to the control's data, which is centralized in CComControlBase.

# Templates to Make Abstract Classes Concrete

A related case occurs with the ATL implementation of the IUnknown methods. These are provided by CComObject<> and its related classes, which are intended to be used like this:

```
CComObject<CMyObject>* pObj;
hr = CComObject<CMyObject>::CreateInstance(&pObj);
CComPtr<IMyInterface> pItf;
pObj->QueryInterface(IID_IMyInterface, reinterpret_cast<void**>(&pItf));
```

CComObject<> is declared as:

```
template<class Base>
class CComObject : public Base
{
    STDMETHOD_(ULONG, AddRef)();
    STDMETHOD_(ULONG, Release)();
    STDMETHOD(QueryInterface)(REFIID iid, void** ppvObject);

    // Other code
};
```

That is, when you apply your class as a parameter to CComObject<>, the compiler will generate a new class *derived from* your ATL class. This new class has access to the public and protected members of your class.

To see how this works, consider what happens when you derive your class from an interface, for example:

```
class ATL_NO_VTABLE CSimpleObject :
    public CComObjectRootEx<CComSingleThreadModel>,
    public CComCoClass<CSimpleObject, &CLSID_SimpleObject>,
    public ISimpleObject
{ /*Implementation*/ };
```

You have the abstract class, IUnknown, as a base inherited through an interface, in this case ISimpleObject. Neither of the other two base classes implements the IUnknown methods, so this makes your whole ATL class abstract. However, by using CComObject<> as shown above, you can provide an implementation of these methods and thus have a concrete class from which to create instances.

In fact, CComObject<> uses methods declared in your class to implement the IUnknown methods. The reason for this is that your class knows about its threading model and what interfaces it implements, and so an operation like incrementing a reference count is specific to your class. However, the choice of when or whether this operation is used is made by the appropriate CComObjectxxx<> class. So, CComObject<> manipulates your ATL class's m_dwRef in AddRef() and Release(), but CComObjectGlobal<>, on the other hand, manipulates the object server's lock count.

# ATL Collection and Enumerator Templates

Enumerators are useful when you want to return zero or more items of the same type to a client. An enumerator is a COM object that implements an **enumeration interface**, which a client can obtain simply by calling `QueryInterface()` on the object. Often, though, an object will provide a method to return a *separate* enumerator object, and this is what happens with a collection.

Collections are objects that have two properties at the very least: one is called `Count`, and the other is called `_NewEnum`. The `Count` property is used to return the number of items in the collection, while `_NewEnum` returns an enumerator object that contains these items. The main use for a collection is to allow access to the items it contains by scripting clients using the `For Each` syntax. Collections can also have properties that allow a client to get access to an individual item by index, and methods to add and remove items from the collection.

> On MSDN, there is a technical article on collections (*Implementing OLE Automation Collections*), and I recommend that you give it a read (mk:@MSITStore:H:\MSDN\techart.chm::/html/msdn_collect.htm). However, it states that `Item` property is compulsory, but I've found that `For Each` will still work even if a collection does not have this property.

The COM specification defines some enumeration interfaces, and if they do not fit the item that you want to enumerate, you can define your own. Enumeration interfaces should have the methods of the `IEnumXXXX` interface. This is not a real interface, and you will not find any marshaling code for it; it is used as an example of the methods that an enumeration interface should implement. `IEnumXXXX` is effectively a template, but because COM is language neutral, C++ templates cannot be used.

The most interesting of the enumeration interface's methods is Next(); here is the version from
IEnumString:

```
HRESULT Next(ULONG celt, LPOLESTR* rgelt, ULONG* pceltFetched);
```

You call this method to request that a number of items should be returned from the enumerator –
celt is the number requested, and rgelt is a caller-allocated array to hold the items that the
method will return. This array must have space for at least celt items. The actual number of items
returned is placed in the pceltFetched [out] parameter. The return value from this method is
S_OK if celt items are returned in the array, or S_FALSE if fewer than celt items are returned
(note that both are success codes). If for some reason the enumerator failed to get any items (because
of a memory error, for example) then a failure HRESULT will be returned.

Thus, you should use an enumerator by calling Next() repeatedly until the value returned in
pceltFetched is zero:

```
CComPtr<IEnumString> pEnum;
pEnum = GetEnumeratorFromSomewhere();
ULONG ulFetched = 0;
LPOLESTR pStr[5];
while(SUCCEEDED(pEnum->Next(5, pStr, &ulFetched)) && ulFetched > 0)
{
    for(ULONG ulIndex = 0 ; ulIndex < ulFetched ; ulIndex++)
    {
        wcout << pStr[ulIndex] << endl;
        CoTaskMemFree(lpStr[ulIndex]);
    }
}
```

Often, it's your responsibility to free the items returned to you, so if you use IEnumString you must
free the returned items using CoTaskMemFree(). If you use IEnumUnknown then you need to call
Release() on the items, and if you use IEnumVARIANT you must call VariantClear() on them.
Other interfaces pass data by value so, for example, you don't have to free the items returned from
IEnumGUID (these are UUIDs). Be wary, though, because allocated items can sometimes be hidden
from you: the IEnumSTATSTG interface will return STATSTG items, one member of which
(pwcsName) is allocated with CoTaskMemAlloc(), so you must make sure that you free it.

# Implementing Enumeration Interfaces

You have one of two options here. The enumerator could own the data that it is returning, or it could
return a reference to the data held by another object. What do I mean by this, and why does it
matter? Well, imagine that you have an enumerator that returns the names of the members of an
online chat room. This information is volatile: members can join and leave the chat room at any time,
so there is a question over exactly what information the enumerator returns.

The enumerator could copy the names into a new array and return items based on this copy. The
enumerator then 'owns' these items, and is responsible for releasing them when it gets released. This
enumerator is a 'snapshot' of the members at the particular time that the enumerator was requested.
Since the enumerator has its own copy of the membership list, it can return them in whatever order it
chooses, but obviously it must be consistent between calls to Next().

The other option is for the enumerator to access the *actual* member list, and return strings from that list. This means that the order names are returned in will be dictated by whatever order they had when they were returned from the member list. Since the enumerator returns names from the actual list, it also means that the names are dynamic – that is, if names are added or removed from the list *after* the current position that the enumerator is reading, this will be shown when later names are requested. An enumerator using this scheme is 'dynamic', and it does not own the items it enumerates. When the enumerator object dies, it should not free the data.

Of course, the type of the enumerator determines how you will use it. Enumeration interfaces have a `Reset()` method to start the enumeration from the start of the list that they enumerate. Although a client using a snapshot enumerator *can* call this method, it often will not: the idea of a snapshot is to get a once-only list of the items, and show them once. A dynamic enumerator is a different case: it is designed to be called repeatedly, and when a call to `Next()` returns a zero number of items, the client will call `Reset()` and start calling `Next()` again to get the (potentially) updated list.

The enumerator keeps an index to indicate the next item to read. When a client calls `Next()`, the enumerator changes this index accordingly; when it calls `Reset()` the index is reset. If the client wants to ignore a few items and rejoin the list a little later on, it can do so by calling `Skip()`, passing the number of items to ignore.

A client may decide to make a copy of an enumerator. Our chat room example could have a window that lists the members of the room at a particular time, and it might obtain a 'snapshot' enumerator in order to do this. If the user of the client then creates a new window to list the members, the client must make a copy of the enumerator – it can't create a *new* enumerator, because the members of the list may have changed. What is needed is a 'clone' of the enumerator, and for this purpose an enumerator must implement a `Clone()` method.

Note that the clone must have the same state as the enumerator that it copies, and this means that the index used to indicate the current item must be copied as well. This allows you to use a cloned enumerator as a 'cursor' – you can save the current position in an enumeration process by making a clone, and then return to this position at a later time even though you may have used the original enumerator to get further items.

# ATL Enumerators

ATL enumerators are not COM objects. Although they implement the appropriate enumerator methods, they do not implement the appropriate COM *lifetime* methods. This means that when you have an ATL enumerator, you must use it as a parameter to the ATL `CComObject<>` template to allow it to be used as a COM object.

There is a kind of a naming convention to the ATL enumeration template classes, although some of them could have more convenient names.

## Short Descriptions

`CComIEnum<>`
This is a template version of `IEnumXXXX`. This is not used by ATL, and is provided for your use.

CComEnum<>
A template class that has a COM map with the IID of the enumeration interface it exposes. It's used to create separate enumerator objects, but it has no lifetime methods.

CComEnumImpl<>
A template class to implement an enumeration that's initialized with Init() and 'kept alive' with m_spUnk. Derive your ATL class from this to add an enumeration interface to it.

IEnumOnSTLImpl<>
A template class that's iterated with an iterator (m_iter), initialized with Init() and m_pcollection, and 'kept alive' with m_spUnk. Derive your ATL class from this to add an enumeration interface to it.

CComEnumOnSTL<>
A template class that's just like CComEnum<>, except that it works with STL container classes rather than regular arrays.

# CComEnum<>

If you want to create a separate enumerator object, you will use CComEnum<> or CComEnumOnSTL<>. The difference between these two is where the data is held. In the former, it is in an array of items; in the latter, it's in an STL container. CComEnumImpl<> implements the appropriate enumerator interface methods, and you get this by using the derived class, CComEnum<>:

```
typedef CComEnum<IEnumVARIANT, &IID_IEnumVARIANT,
                        VARIANT, _Copy<VARIANT> > VarEnum;

CComObject<VarEnum>* pEnum;
pEnum = new CComObject<VarEnum>;
```

The first parameter is the name of the interface that the enumerator object will expose; CComEnum<> has a COM map with an entry for this interface. The next parameter is the IID of this interface (although the code could have used __uuidof() on the first parameter to get this). The type of the actual items that are enumerated is given in the third parameter. This is the type of the array passed in the second parameter of Next().

There are a few places where the enumerated data must be copied. For example, if the enumerator makes a copy of the entire data set (to get a 'snapshot') then this is done in the CComEnumImpl<>::Init() method. The Next() method will also copy items from the 'source' (either its copy or the original source of the data), and to do this it must know *how* these items are copied. In the fourth template parameter, you provide a class that has three static methods called init(), copy() and destroy(). init() and destroy() have parameters that are pointers to the data type you are enumerating, while copy() has two such parameters: the first is a pointer to the type you are enumerating (and hence the type returned through Next()), and the second one is a pointer to the type used in CComEnumImpl<>::Init() to initialize the enumerator. For CComEnum<>, these two will be the same.

ATL provides some copy classes for you (including specializations of _Copy<>), explained in the following table:

| Class | Notes |
| --- | --- |
| _Copy<> | Generic copy class; does a memcpy() |
| _Copy<VARIANT> | Copies, initializes and destroys VARIANTs using the VARIANT API |
| _Copy<LPOLESTR> | Allocates and frees memory using the task allocator |
| _Copy<OLEVERB> | Allocates and frees memory using the task allocator |
| _Copy<CONNECTDATA> | Copies the structure, ensuring that embedded interface pointers are correctly reference counted |
| _CopyInterface<> | Duplicates interface pointers, ensuring that they are correctly reference-counted |

The final template parameter to CComEnum<> is not shown in the example; it is called ThreadModel, and it's used because the template derives from CComObjectRootEx<> to implement a COM map. The default is the threading model defined by the project's XXX_THREADED symbol.

Once you have created the C++ enumerator object (don't think of it as a COM enumerator object yet), you have to initialize it. This is done by calling the Init() method:

```
template<class Base, const IID* piid, class T, class Copy>
HRESULT CComEnumImpl<Base, piid, T, Copy>::Init(
                   T* begin, T* end, IUnknown* pUnk, CComEnumFlags flags)
```

The data that is returned by the enumerator is described by the begin and end parameters. Init() assumes that the data is held in an array of contiguous memory, so the begin parameter points to the first member of this array, and end points to the memory location *after* the last item. These two values are cached in the enumerator object, and so it means that the enumerator will always return end - begin items.

> **You cannot change the total number of items returned through the enumerator after you have returned the enumerator to the client.**

If the source of your data is not an array (if it is held in an STL map<>, for example) then you will have to create an array, copy data into it, and pass this to Init(). Alternatively, if you have the data in an STL container, then you can use the IEnumOnSTLImpl<> template to implement the enumerator.

You can determine whether the enumerator is 'snapshot' or 'dynamic' by making use of the `flags` that are passed in the final parameter to `Init()`. This can be one of:

```
enum CComEnumFlags
{
    AtlFlagNoCopy = 0,
    AtlFlagTakeOwnership = 2,
    AtlFlagCopy = 3
};
```

If you want to take a 'snapshot', then you should use `AtlFlagCopy`. This creates an array big enough to hold all the items, and a copy is made of each item using the `copy()` method. When `AtlFlagCopy` is used, the enumerator object is independent of the object that created it.

The default value for `Init()` is `AtlFlagNoCopy`, which means that `Next()` will dynamically read the data indicated by `begin` and `end` from the original source of the data. If this is the case, then you must ensure that this data lives as long as the enumerator does. The following, for example, will not work:

```
VARIANT var[5];
long l;
for(l = 0 ; l < 5 ; l++) VariantInit(&var[l]);
for(l = 0 ; l < 5 ; l++) { var[l].vt = VT_I4; var[l].lVal = l;}
pEnum->Init(&var[0], &var[5], NULL, CComEnumFlags::AtlFlagNoCopy);
```

The problem is that the array is stack based, and the enumerator object will live longer than the method. Hence, when the client tries to access the data, it will no longer exist.

So how *do* you use `AtlFlagNoCopy`? The data could be in a global array, or it could be in another object (most likely the object that creates the enumerator). If this is the case, then the other object *must* be as long-lived as the enumerator – otherwise, if the parent object dies before `Next()` is called, `Next()` will reference invalid memory. To keep the parent object alive, you should pass its `IUnknown` pointer as the third parameter to `Init()`. This is then used to initialize a smart pointer, so that when the enumerator object dies, the parent reference is released, and so the latter can be allowed to die too.

Note that if you use `AtlFlagNoCopy`, you should be careful about changing the items. You should not change the *number* of items, but you may change the *value* of the items if you are careful. The need for this caution is that there's a potential thread synchronization problem: when `Next()` makes a copy of an item to return to the client, it does not bracket the call to `copy()` with locking calls (to allow only one thread to have access to the data). If your object is designed to run in an MTA, and you create a separate enumerator object using `CComEnum<>`, then you need to make sure that the enumerator cannot access the item at the same time that the object tries to change a value. To do this, you will have to implement your own version of `copy()` to perform the locking.

For example, if your object has a fixed-size array of numbers, `m_lNumbers[NUM_SIZE + 1]`, then the method to change these values should have locking:

```
CComAutoCriticalSection g_Lock;

HRESULT CMyObject::ChangeItem(short sIndex, long lVal)
{
    if(sIndex > NUM_SIZE)
      return E_INVALIDARG;
    g_Lock.Lock();
    m_lNumbers[sIndex] = lVal;
    g_Lock.Unlock();
    return S_OK;
}
```

And this locking object should also be used in the copy() method:

```
class _CopyLongThreadSafe
{
public:
    static HRESULT copy(long* p1, long* p2)
    {
        g_lock.Lock();
        *p1 = *p2;
        g_lock.Unlock();
        return S_OK;
    }
    static void init(long*) {}
    static void destroy(long*) {}
};
```

CComEnumImpl<> implements a Clone() method to create a clone of an enumerator object. By default, this will use the pointers cached during Init() to determine where the data is, and it will make a 'no copy' of this data using Init(). I say *no copy* because it will always pass a flag of AtlFlagNoCopy. Thus, the clone must live no longer than the object that created it, and because of this, Clone() will pass the IUnknown pointer to the clone's Init() method.

If the original object was created with AtlFlagCopy, then Clone() will still use AtlFlagNoCopy, and the pointers passed to Init() will be to the copy of the data that the original enumerator made. The clone must still live no longer than the object that created it, and so to indicate this *you* must set the public m_dwFlags member of the original object to a value of CComEnumImpl<>::BitCopy.

The clone will be the same as the object it was cloned from in all aspects except its identity (that is, the absolute value of its IUnknown pointer). The internal index that points to the next item to return through Next() has the same value in the clone and original, but once Reset(), Skip() or Next() is called on either object, the two will no longer be in sync.

Finally, note that even if you create your enumerator object using CComObject<>, you should *not* treat it as a COM object. The reason is that when it is created, the object will have a reference count of zero. This means that if it is passed to a client that calls Release() when it has finished its work, the reference count will change to -1, and the object will never die (ATL objects only die when the reference count changes from 1 to 0). Obviously, you should not write immortal objects like this one, and that's why I said you should not treat it as a COM object. To prevent this, you should call QueryInterface() on the enumerator for an appropriate interface, and this will have the side effect of bumping up the reference count to 1.

# CComEnumOnSTL<>

Often, you will use an STL container to hold collections of data, and so ATL provides an enumerator object to return data from this container. The majority of the code in `IEnumOnSTLImpl<>` and `CComEnumOnSTL<>` is used to provide an object that implements `QueryInterface()` and exposes the specified enumeration interface using a COM map. The template looks like this:

```
template <class Base, const IID* piid, class T, class Copy,
            class CollType, class ThreadModel = CComObjectThreadModel>
class ATL_NO_VTABLE CComEnumOnSTL :
```

The first four parameters and the final one have the same meanings as they had in `CComEnum<>`. The new parameter is `CollType`, which is used to specify the type of the container that holds the data that will be returned by the enumerator. The container itself is external to this class – that is, it will be a member of your ATL class, or a global variable.

The container that you use must have an `iterator` and support the `begin()` and `end()` methods. These criteria cover all the STL container types: `list<>`, `vector<>`, `deque<>`, `map<>` and `set<>`. However, note that if `map<>` is used, then you will have to write your own version of the Copy class, because the `copy()` method is called like this in `Next()`:

```
hr = Copy::copy(pelt, &*m_iter);
if(FAILED(hr))
{
    while(rgelt < pelt)
        Copy::destroy(rgelt++);
    nActual = 0;
}
else
{
    pelt++;
    m_iter++;
    nActual++;
}
```

The data items passed to `copy()` have the types `T*` (used in the template) and `std::pair<Key, T>*`, where `Key` and `T` are the parameters to the `map<>`. These two types are not the same (although the `T`s may be the same). Thus, you need to write a version of `copy()` that gets the required data out of the iterator. It may be as simple as this:

```
// Using std::map<CComBSTR, CComVariant> for CollType
class _CopyMap
{
public:
    static HRESULT copy(
                VARIANT* pCopy, std::pair<const CComBSTR, CComVariant>* pIt)
    {
        CComVariant v = pIt->second;
        v.Detach(pCopy);
        return S_OK;
    }
    static void init(VARIANT* p) {VariantInit(p);}
    static void destroy(VARIANT* p) {VariantClear(p);}
};
```

You initialize the enumerator with the `Init()` method:

```
// From IEnumOnSTLImpl<>
HRESULT Init(IUnknown* pUnkForRelease, CollType& collection)
{
    m_spUnk = pUnkForRelease;
    m_pcollection = &collection;
    m_iter = m_pcollection->begin();
    return S_OK;
}
CComPtr<IUnknown> m_spUnk;
CollType* m_pcollection;
CollType::iterator m_iter;
};
```

Notice that the address of the container is saved – *no copy is made of the items*. This is equivalent to initializing `CComEnum<>` with `AtlFlagNoCopy`. You have no choice about this, so you must make sure that the STL container lives as long as the enumerator, and the only way you can do this is to use a global instance or a container in another COM object. In the first case you can pass `NULL` for the first parameter of `Init()`, and in the second case you need to pass the `IUnknown` of the object that has the container.

> There is no equivalent of **AtlFlagCopy** with **CComEnumOnSTL<>**.

If your object is designed to run in an MTA, then you will need to ensure that there are no synchronization problems, as mentioned in the previous section.

# Implementing Objects with an Enumeration Interface

So, I hear you ask, why have the two classes `CComEnumImpl<>` and `CComEnum<>`? In the examples above, I've assumed that you will create a separate enumerator object using `CComObject<>`, and pass a pointer to an interface on this object as an `[out]` parameter of one of your object's methods. The thing is, you don't actually have to do all that. Your object could implement an enumeration interface itself. For example, imagine that you have a COM class called `WidgetCatalog` that implements the `IEnumString` interface, and uses this to return the names of the widgets that your company supplies. The object could read these names from a database, but in this simple example I'll hard code the names.

You can get support for this interface simply by deriving from `CComEnumImpl<>`:

```
class ATL_NO_VTABLE CWidgetCatalog :
    public CComObjectRootEx<CComSingleThreadModel>,
    public CComCoClass<CWidgetCatalog, &CLSID_WidgetCatalog>,
    public IDispatchImpl<IWidgetCatalog, &IID_IWidgetCatalog, &LIBID_WIDGETLib>,
    public CComEnumImpl<IEnumString, &IID_IEnumString,
                                      LPOLESTR, _Copy<LPOLESTR> >

{
public:
    CWidgetCatalog () {}
    HRESULT FinalConstruct()
    {
```

```
      m_Names[0] = L"Thingy";
      m_Names[1] = L"Whatsit";
      m_Names[2] = L"Grommet";
      m_Names[3] = L"Doobrey";
      Init(m_Names, &m_Names[4], NULL);
      return S_OK;
   }

DECLARE_REGISTRY_RESOURCEID(IDR_WIDGETCATALOG)
DECLARE_PROTECT_FINAL_CONSTRUCT()

BEGIN_COM_MAP(CWidgetCatalog)
   COM_INTERFACE_ENTRY(IWidgetCatalog)
   COM_INTERFACE_ENTRY(IDispatch)
   COM_INTERFACE_ENTRY(IEnumString)
END_COM_MAP()

// IWidgetCatalog
public:
private:
   LPOLESTR m_Names[4];
};
```

A client can now create an instance of `WidgetCatalog` and call `QueryInterface()` for
`IEnumString`, and this will get passed to the base class. Indeed, used like this, `CComEnumImpl<>`
could just as well be called `IEnumImpl<>`. Similarly, if you have an object that has data in an STL
container, then you can expose that through an enumerator interface using `IEnumOnSTLImpl<>`.

# Implementing an Enumerator of a Different Type from the Data

The templates lull you into thinking that the array that holds the data to be enumerated is the same
type as the item that is returned through the `Next()` method. The last section showed that this need
not be so, as long as you implement the `copy()` method to convert between the two types. So,
imagine that you have an array of LONGs and you want to return them as strings. You could use this
enumerator:

```
CComEnum<IEnumString, &IID_IEnumString, LPOLESTR, _CopyLongToLPOLESTR> >
```

Where _CopyLongToLPOLESTR is:

```
class _CopyLongToLPOLESTR
{
public:
   static HRESULT copy(LPOLESTR* p1, LONG* p2)
   {
      HRESULT hr = S_OK;

      // Assume that 12 chars will be used
      (*p1) = (LPOLESTR)CoTaskMemAlloc(sizeof(OLECHAR) * 13);
```

```
       if(*p1 == NULL)
           hr = E_OUTOFMEMORY;
       else
           swprintf(*p1, L"%ld", *p2);
       return hr;
   }
   static void init(LPOLESTR* p) {*p = NULL;}
   static void destroy(LPOLESTR* p) { CoTaskMemFree(*p);}
};
```

And if the data is held in `m_Numbers`, then you can initialize the enumerator with:

```
pEnum->Init(&m_Numbers[0], &m_Numbers[NUM_SIZE], this);
```

# ATL Collections

A collection is an object that exposes at least two properties: `_NewEnum` (with a DISPID of `DISPID_NEWENUM`) that returns an enumerator, and `Count` (any DISPID) that returns the number of items returned through the enumerator. Collections have the specific purpose of allowing scripting clients to use the `For Each` syntax:

```
Dim v as Variant
For Each v in MyCollection
    List1.AddItem v
Next
```

Collections should not allow copying of the enumerated data, because `Count` should always be calculated on the same collection of objects that was used to generate the enumerator. Collections can also have the `Item` property that returns a particular item using an index, and also the methods `Add()` and `Remove()` to change the contents of the collection. However, ATL has no support for these two methods.

# ICollectionOnSTLImpl<>

This template looks like this:

```
template <class T, class CollType, class ItemType,
                                   class CopyItem, class EnumType>
class ICollectionOnSTLImpl : public T
{
public:
    STDMETHOD(get_Count)(long* pcount);
    STDMETHOD(get_Item)(long Index, ItemType* pvar);
    STDMETHOD(get__NewEnum)(IUnknown** ppUnk);
    CollType m_coll;
};
```

As you can see, it supports the read-only properties Item, Count and _NewEnum. To use this, you must use the ClassView Wizard to add these properties, and then edit the IDL by hand to change the DISPID of _NewEnum to DISP_NEWENUM (you might also make this property [restricted]) and the DISPID of Item to DISPID_VALUE. Note that the only property that is typed is the Item property, which has *two* parameters: an index and an [out] parameter to the type of the items in the collection.

Unlike CComOnSTLImpl<>, where your class had to have an STL container as a data member, this class has the container as a public member called m_coll, so you do not need to add it to your class. The first parameter of the template is an interface on your object, and the reason why you do this is because the template code will be used with CComOnSTLImpl<>, and so you need the IUnknown to pass to Init() to make sure that the lifetime of the enumerator object is shorter than that of the parent object.

The second parameter is the collection type, the third is the type of the individual items that will be enumerated, and the fourth is the copy class to copy these items. Finally, the EnumType parameter is the enumerator you will use, and this will be a specialization of CComOnSTLImpl<>.

With so many templates within templates starting to get involved, it makes sense to produce some typedefs. Here I have a collection with the names of the colors of the rainbow returned through an IEnumVARIANT enumerator. The typedefs are

```
typedef std::vector<CComVariant> VarVec;
typedef CComEnumOnSTL<IEnumVARIANT, &IID_IEnumVARIANT, VARIANT,
   _Copy<VARIANT>, VarVec > VarEnum;
typedef ICollectionOnSTLImpl<IRainbow, VarVec, VARIANT,
   _Copy<VARIANT>, VarEnum > VarCol;
```

Note that For Each can return items that are Variant or Object, and hence the enumerator interface must be IEnumVARIANT. If you want to use collections from C++, then it does not matter what interface you use.

You need to derive from this class, but there is a problem: the first parameter of ICollectionOnSTLImpl<> is an interface on your object. If you derive from ICollectionOnSTLImpl<> *and* your object's interface (which the Object Wizard will do for you) then you will get the multiple base class problem. To solve this, you need to replace the references to this interface in the base classes of your object, and since in this example IRainbow is a dual interface, this means replacing the parameter of IDispatchImpl<>:

```
class ATL_NO_VTABLE CRainbow :
   public CComObjectRootEx<CComSingleThreadModel>,
   public CComCoClass<CRainbow, &CLSID_Rainbow>,
// public IDispatchImpl<IRainbow, &IID_IRainbow, &LIBID_COLORLib>
   public IDispatchImpl<VarCol, &IID_IRainbow, &LIBID_COLORLib>
```

Now your class has implementations of the Count, Item and _NewEnum properties, and so you need to delete the get_ functions that ClassView added to your class (make sure that you delete the methods from the CPP file too!).

Finally, you need to initialize your collection, and I have done this in `FinalConstruct()` (your class will most likely have interface methods to do this):

```
HRESULT FinalConstruct()
{
    m_coll.push_back(L"Red");
    m_coll.push_back(L"Orange");
    m_coll.push_back(L"Yellow");
    m_coll.push_back(L"Green");
    m_coll.push_back(L"Blue");
    m_coll.push_back(L"Indigo");
    m_coll.push_back(L"Violet");
    return S_OK;
}
```

Now you can write Visual Basic code like this:

```
Dim colors as New Rainbow
Dim v as Variant
For Each v in colors
    Debug.Print v
Next
```

Note that you should be careful about using this template. The template provides dynamic access to the `m_coll` container, so once one enumerator has been given out, you should not add or remove any items from the container. If you do, then clients will get inconsistent results – you can imagine the chaos that will ensue if a client reads `Count` to see that there are 6 items, and then before it has finished getting those items with the enumerator, you remove one of those items.

Finally, if the object will run in an MTA and you want to change individual items, then you will have to address synchronization problems using a locking mechanism.

# Index

## A

## Beginning ATL COM Programming

Authors: Various
ISBN: 1861000111
Price: $39.95 C$55.95 £36.99

This book is for fairly experienced C++ developers who want to get to grips with COM programming using the Active Template Library. The Beginning in the title of this book refers to COM and it refers to ATL. It does not refer to Programming.

We don't expect you to know anything about COM. The book explains the essentials of COM, how to use it, and how to get the most out of it. If you do already know something about COM, that's a bonus. You'll still learn a lot about the way that ATL works, and you'll be one step ahead of the COM neophytes.

Neither do we expect you to know anything about ATL. ATL is the focus of the book. If you've never touched ATL, or if you've been using it for a short while, but still have many unanswered questions, this is the book for you.

## Professional DCOM Application Development

Author: Jonathan Pinnock
ISBN: 1861001312
Price: $49.99 C$69.95 £45.99

Jonathan Pinnock writes:

"When you start building systems that stretch over an entire enterprise, things get complicated, and it gets more and more difficult to deliver flexible, reliable and timely solutions to your end users. Any tools that can simplify and standardize the process of developing enterprise-wide systems are therefore of immense significance. My view is that COM and DCOM and all the technologies that are based around them provide us with just that toolkit. I want to show you how to put them to use in building real solutions to real problems."

## Professional DCOM Programming

Author: Dr. Richard Grimes
ISBN: 186100060X
Price: $49.95  C$69.95  £46.99

This book is for Win32 programmers taking up the challenge of building applications using the distributed component object model. There is a strong emphasis on the practicalities of distributed object design and use, and the text is also a complete examination of COM programming. The code is described and developed using Visual C++ 5, MFC and ATL.

## Instant UML

Authors: Pierre-Alain Muller
ISBN: 1861000871
Price: $34.95  C$48.95  £32.49

UML is the Unified Modeling Language. Modeling languages have come into vogue with the rise of object-oriented development, as they provide a means of communicating and recording every stage of the project. The results of the analysis and design phases are captured using the formal syntax of the modeling language, producing a clear model of the system to be implemented.

Instant UML offers not only a complete description of the notation and proper use of UML, but also an introduction to the theory of object-oriented programming, and the way to approach object-oriented application development. This is UML in context, not a list of the syntax without rhyme or reason.

This book is relevant to programmers of C++, VB, Java and other OO-capable languages, users of Visual Modeler (which comes with the Enterprise Edition of Microsoft's Visual Studio) and novice users of Rational Rose and similar UML-compliant tools.

## Professional NT Services

Author: Kevin Miller
ISBN: 1861001304
Price: $59.99  C$83.95  £55.49

Professional NT Services teaches developers how to design and implement good NT services using all the features and tools supplied for the purpose by Microsoft Visual C++. The author develops a set of generic classes to facilitate service development, and introduces the concept of usage patterns — a way of categorizing the roles that services can fulfil in the overall architecture of a system. The book also gives developers a firm grounding in the security and configuration issues that must be taken into account when developing a service.

To date, the treatment of NT services has been sketchy and widely scattered. This book is aimed at bringing the range of relevant material together in an organized way. Its target readership is C/C++ Windows programmers with experience of programming under Win32 and basic knowledge of multithreaded and COM programming. At an architectural level, the book's development of usage patterns will be invaluable to client-server developers who want to include services as part of a multi-tiered system.

## Professional COM Applications with ATL

Authors: Sing Li and Panos Econompoulos
ISBN: 1861001703
Price: $49.99  C$69.95  £45.99

This book examines how and why you should use COM, ActiveX controls and DNA Business Objects, and how these components are linked together to form robust, flexible and scalable applications.

A key part of the book is the extended case study in which we produce a distributed events calendar that fits Microsoft's Distributed interNet Applications (DNA) model. This three-tier application uses flexible browser-based controls for the client user interface, business objects on both client and server to process the required information efficiently and Universal Data Access to perform the queries and updates. It depends on the support for component-based development now available for Windows NT server.

The additions and changes to this book make it both significant and relevant to readers of the first edition, Professional ActiveX/COM Control Programming.

## Professional MFC with Visual C++ 5

Author: Mike Blaszczak
ISBN: 1861000146
Price: $59.95  C$83.95  £56.49

Written by one of Microsoft's leading MFC developers, this is the book for professionals who want to get under the covers of the library. This is the 3rd revision of the best selling title formerly known as 'Revolutionary Guide to MFC 4' and covers the new Visual C++ 5.0 development environment.

This book will give a detailed discussion of the majority of classes present in Microsoft's application framework library. While it will point out what parameters are required for the member functions of those classes, it will concentrate more on describing what utility the classes really provide. You will learn how to write a few utilities, some DLLs, an ActiveX control and even an OLE document server, as well as examining Microsoft's Open Database Connectivity (ODBC) and Data Access Objects (DAO) strategies. At the very end of the book, you'll take a look at what the Microsoft Foundation Classes provide to make programming for the Internet easier.

There's a CD ROM included which has the complete book in HTML format - now you can use any browser to read your book on the road.

## Professional VB5.0 Business Objects

Author: Rockford Lhotka
ISBN: 186100043X
Price: $49.95  C$69.95  £45.99

In recent years, the concept of 'business objects' has taken hold in the developer community. Basically, these are the processes that deal with some input data and mediate the appropriate business response. Whether this be a stock-withdrawal from a warehouse supply system, an invoice-sender or whatever, writing the code in such a way that it can be used by an entire organization to maintain coherent information on the business is worthwhile.

Visual Basic 5 classes can be exposed as ActiveX objects. Such objects can use DCOM to communicate between machines, and can be both called and scripted by Active Server Pages and controlled by Microsoft Transaction Server. The book shows a variety of client-server designs, to illustrate how to design and deploy business objects.

· The only book dedicated to Business Objects with Visual Basic, the hottest topic for developers
· Covers component-based application development in Visual Basic 5
· Illustrates deployment of server-side Visual Basic 5 objects using DCOM
· Shows how to use Visual Basic 5, ASP and MTS to create an intranet application

## Clouds to Code

Author: Jesse Liberty  ISBN: 1861000952
Price: $40.00  C$55.95  £36.99

Clouds to Code is about the design and implementation of a real project, from start to finish, hiding nothing. Books on theory are all well and good, but there is nothing like living through the process. You'll watch as we struggle to understand the requirements, as we conceive a design, implement that design in C++, then ready it for testing and rollout. You'll see the complete iterative development process as it happens. This is not an example or a thought experiment, it's a real life case study written in real time.

Along the way you'll learn about object- oriented analysis and design with UML, as well as C++, design patterns, computer telephony, and COM. You'll also learn about professional software development and what it takes to ship a product on time and on budget. This is programming in the trenches.

# C⊕MDEVELOPER.COM

Microsoft's Component Object Model is the future of application development - a standard for creating software components in any language and using them on any platform. But with it comes the overhead of a whole new set of terms, types, interfaces and issues to confront and overcome. Whether you've been a COMHead for three years or three minutes, you'll find something of use here...

- · All the latest news on developments in the COM world
- · An up-to-date list of all the latest articles on COM around the web
- · Regular feature articles from noted COM authors and developers
- · Dedicated forum for COM and ATL queries and problems
- · Sample chapters from the complete series of WROX COM books
- · COM+ Watch - the first page of its kind which charts the progress of the next generation of the Component Object Model
- · Comprehensive listing of Other COM Websites

http://www.comdeveloper.com